GENDER BASICS

Feminist Perspectives on Women and Men

Anne Minas
University of Waterloo
Waterloo, Ontario

Wadsworth Publishing Company
Belmont, California
A Division of Wadsworth, Inc.

Philosophy Editor: Kenneth King
Editorial Assistant: Gay Meixel
Production: Ruth Cottrell
Print Buyer: Diana Spence
Permissions Editor: Robert Kauser
Designer: Polly Christensen, Christensen & Son Design
Copy Editor: Carol Talpers
Cover: Vargas/Williams/Design
Signing Representative: Donald Harris
Compositor: T·H Typecast
Printer: R. R. Donnelley

1 2 3 4 5 6 7 8 9 10 — 97 96 95 94 93

This book is printed on acid-free recycled paper.

Library of Congress Cataloging-in-Publication Data

Gender basics: feminist perspectives on women and men / [edited by]
Anne Minas.
    p. cm.
Includes bibliographical references.
ISBN 0-534-17814-6
   1. Sex role. 2. Feminist theory. I. Minas, Anne.
HQ1075.G462 1992
305.3 – dc20   92-35488
                                                 CIP

Contents

Part VII: *Sex and Sexuality* 301

Part VIII: *Rape and Sexual Harassment* 351

Preface

THIS COLLECTION GREW GRADUALLY out of my course "Philosophy of Women and Men" (originally "Philosophy of Women"), a first-year course in philosophy and women's studies that has run continuously at the University of Waterloo since 1976. My original intention had been to teach a course in feminism, which I saw as a cluster of positions focusing on the oppression of women. Student response, however, re-channeled the currents of the course around gender issues (these being issues in human life where gender is a factor). Theory seemed of interest to these students only as it served to clarify and sort out elements of an issue and illuminate a path toward its resolution. In addition, once feminism had brought gender into focus, many students wanted perspectives on the issues from both genders. This did not disturb my plan of restricting perspectives on these issues to feminist perspectives, since feminism is a moral position while male, like female, is a gender. Refusal to discuss an issue from a male perspective began to seem much like claiming that heterosexuality or some other mainstream perspective had a monopoly on good insights, good feminist insights in particular.

Because of the confusion and lack of settlement in this area, I have tried to include as many points of view as space allowed. Usually there are more facets to a gender issue than those where women's oppression is integral, and I have included writings that address some of these other facets as well. Instructors who use this as a text should find that it contains something to satisfy almost every student mentality. As final insurance on this matter, I have included bibliographies that are longer than usual in a text for a first course.

After seventeen years I now think my class deserves a text to meet its needs. This collection is thus dedicated to these students, past, present, and future, and their counterparts everywhere. They embody our hopes for a future of better gender relations.

Several people helped me take this project forward. James Horne and Rolf George, as chairs of the philosophy department, allowed me to mount and run my course during a time when many considered feminism too lightweight to be included in a scholarly curriculum. Jan Narveson also came forward rather quickly with the perception that feminism spoke to genuine moral and social issues, thus providing a sturdy backboard off which I could bounce my ideas. (More recently, he guided me through the rather bewildering maze of book production.)

Christopher Knapper introduced me to new teaching methods. Instead of filling class time with long, boring lectures, he suggested short introductions to the material, followed by study questions on overhead transparencies. Students may thus address the material on their own, or in small discussion groups, guided by the questions. My introductions and overhead transparencies quickly became, at the insistence of the students, bound materials distributed at the beginning of the term for students to use on their own time.

Because these introductions and questions have been cut in around the readings in this collection, an instructor who uses it as a text will probably have an experience something like mine, of finding her students less dependent upon her. I suggest a bright side to this situation. (1) Dependency in adults is an outmoded patriarchal idea, damaging to the human spirit; (2) as instructors, we have an obligation to send independent thinkers back into their communities; (3) when students miss class, it is a distinct advantage if they can get an understanding of the material on their own, instead of spending long, darkening afternoons in our offices doing so; and (4) when not all relevant material needs to be covered in class, a student has more options for assignment topics. As instructors, we are still useful as resource persons, as validation for students' ideas, and as restraints for keeping these ideas within acceptable limits.

One cold February night in 1991, a summary of my teaching materials fell into the hands of Ken King, Wadsworth's philosophy editor. This gave him a rather formidable option of bringing a new idea into a still turbulent area.

I thank and salute these men in feminism. I do not believe, however, that I could have accepted their help and support had they not been preceded by my father, Alexander P. Humphrey. He conveyed to me a generic sense of "man" that applied to me, him, and all others of our genders. He also warned against any hasty segmentation of the human world into "good" and "bad" (since everyone turns out to be a mixture of both).

Production editor Ruth Cottrell did a very nice job with the (rather badly needed) final polish. Susan Babbitt (Queen's University, Kingston, Ontario) inundated me with helpful last-minute suggestions, and Rosemarie Tong (Davidson College) and Christine Pierce (North Carolina State University) got the project off to a good start at the proposal stage. Other Wadsworth reviewers I should thank for their efforts are Gloria Cowan, California State University, San Bernadino; Alison Jaggar, University of Colorado, Boulder; Sharon M. Meagher, University of Scranton; Lani Roberts, Oregon State University; and Barbara E. Wall, Villanova University. Thanks are also due to the behind-the-scenes production team at Wadsworth (Peggy Mehan, Robert Kauser, and the many whose names I don't know). My mini-production team here (Debbie Dietrich, Anne Wagland, Derik Hawley, William Dolan, and Kelly Colucci) put marathon efforts into the many send-offs to Wadsworth.

Thanks, finally, to the writers who gave me permission to reprint their work, persons who in many cases have devoted not only their writing but also other parts of their lives to pushing back the frontiers in this important area.

Acknowledgments

Page 17. Woman Is Not Our Brother. From *The Second Sex* by Simone de Beauvoir, trans. H. M. Parshley. Copyright 1954 by Alfred A. Knopf, Inc. Reprinted by permission of the publisher.

Page 23. Why Men Resist. Abridged from "Why Men Resist" in *Rethinking the Family: Some Feminist Questions*. Barrie Thorne with Marilyn Yalom, ed., (New York, NY: Longman, Inc. 1982). Reprinted by permission of Institute for Research on Women and Gender.

Page 30. White Privilege and Male Privilege. © 1988 by Peggy McIntosh. Reprinted with permission of the author.

Page 39. "The Uses of Anger" in *Sister Outsider* by Audre Lorde (Trumansburg, NY: The Crossing Press, 1984). Reprinted by permission of the publisher and author.

Page 45. Growing Up Asian in America. From *Making Waves* by Asian Women United of California. Copyright © 1989 by Asian Women United of California. Reprinted by permission of Beacon Press and the author.

Page 50. Abridged from "Toward a Feminist Theory of Disability" in *Hypatia*, Volume 4, number 2 (Summer 1989), pp. 104–124. Also appeared in Helen Bequaert Holmes and Laura M. Purdy, Editors, *Feminist Perspectives in Medical Ethics*, Indiana University Press, 1992. Reprinted by permission.

Page 58. From *Outrageous Acts and Everyday Rebellions* by Gloria Steinem. Copyright © 1983 by Gloria Steinem. Copyright © 1984 by East Toledo Productions, Inc. Reprinted by permission of Henry Holt and Company, Inc. and the author.

Page 66. Abridged from "'Pricks and Chicks:' A Plea for 'Persons'," in *Philosophy and Sex*, Robert Baker and Frederick Elliston, eds. (Buffalo, NY: Prometheus Books). Copyright © 1975 by Prometheus Books. Reprinted by permission of the publisher and the author.

Page 68. Selected from "Who Is Man" in *Words and Women* by Casey Miller and Kate Swift. Copyright © 1976, 1991 by Casey Miller and Kate Swift. Reprinted by permission of Harper Collins Publishers Inc.

Page 75. Abridged from "Talking Back" in *Talking Back: Thinking Feminist, Thinking Black* (Boston, MA: South End Press, 116 Saint Botolph St., 1989). pp. 5–9. Reprinted by permission of the publisher.

Page 79. Gay Irony. From "Gay Jocks: A Phenomenology of Gay Men in Athletics" by B. Pronger. In *Sport, Men, and the Gender Order* (pp. 141–152) by M. A. Messner and D. F. Sabo (Eds.), 1990. Champaign, IL: Human Kinetics. Copyright 1990 by Dan Sabo, PhD and Michael Messner, PhD. Reprinted by permission.

Page 83. Abridgements of "Hair and Clothes" in *Femininity*. Copyright © 1984 by Susan Brownmiller. Reprinted by permission of Linden Press, a division of Simon & Schuster, Inc.

Page 90. From "The Unadorned Feminist" in *The Sceptical Feminist* by Janet Radcliffe-Richards (New York, NY: Penguin Books, 1980), pp. 225–251. Reprinted by permission of the author.

Page 98. © 1992 Anne Minas and Jake Minas.

Page 106. Abridged from "Women and Power in the Workplace" in *Women and Men: Interdisciplinary Readings on Gender*. Greta Hoffman Nemiroff, Ed. (Richmond Hill, Ontario: Fitzhenry and Whiteside Ltd., 1987) pp. 403–415. Reprinted by permission of the author and publisher.

Page 114. Is Marriage the Culprit? © 1992 Harriet Lyons. Originally appeared as part of the article "Affirmative Action: A Step in the Right Direction," *CAUT Bulletin*, April 1992. Reprinted by permission of the author.

Page 117. © 1992 Anne Minas.

Page 121. Abridged from "Introduction" and "Some Philosophical Considerations" in *Equity and Gender: The Comparable Worth Debate* (New Brunswick, NJ: Transaction Publishers, 1989), pp. 1–7, 109–130. Reprinted by permission of the publisher and author.

Page 128. Abridged from "Sharing the Shop Floor" by Stan Gray from *Canadian Dimension 18*, June 1984. Reprinted by permission of the author and publisher.

Page 137. From "Masculinities and Athletic Careers: Bonding and Status Differences" by M. A. Messner in *Sport, Men, and the Gender Order* (pp. 97–108) by M. A. Messner and D. F. Sabo (Eds.) 1990. Champaign, IL: Human Kinetics. Copyright 1990 by Dan Sabo, PhD and Michael Messner, PhD. Reprinted by permission.

Page 142. Abridged from "Doctors Have the First Word" and "Fit and Feminine" in *Out of Bounds: Women, Sport and Sexuality* by Helen Lenskyj, Toronto, Ontario: The Women's Press, 1986, pp. 17–33, 127–32. Reprinted by permission of the author and publisher.

Page 152. Abridged from "Love's Bond" in *The Examined Life: Philosophical Meditations*, (New York, NY, Simon & Schuster). Copyright © 1989 by Robert Nozick. Reprinted by permission of Simon & Schuster.

Page 160. Abridged from "Friends and Lovers" in *Person to Person*, George Graham and Hugh LaFollette, eds. (Philadelphia, PA: Temple University Press, 1989), pp. 182–198. Reprinted by permission of the author and publisher.

Page 168. Essay IX from Gorer, Geoffrey, *The Danger of Equality* (New York, NY: Weybright and Talley, 1966), pp. 126–132.

Page 172. Abridged from "Lovers Through the Looking Glass" in *Families We Choose: Lesbians, Gays, Kinship*: by Kath Weston (New York, NY: Columbia University Press, 1991), pp. 137–164. Reprinted by permission of the author.

Page 178. The Woman in Love. From *The Second Sex* by Simone de Beauvoir, trans. H. M. Parshley. Copyright 1954 by Alfred A. Knopf, Inc. Reprinted by permission of the publisher.

Page 192. Abridged from "Honesty and Intimacy" in *Person to Person*, George Graham and Hugh LaFollette, eds. (Philadelphia, PA: Temple University Press, 1989), pp. 167–181. Reprinted by permission of the publisher.

Page 196. Abridged from Chapter 4, "Transparency," in *What Sort of People Should There Be?* (New York, NY: Penguin Books, 1984). © 1984 Jonathan Glover. Reprinted by permission of Penguin Books, Ltd.

Page 220. The Civic Advocacy of Violence. © Wayne Ewing. Reprinted by permission of the author.

Page 205. Abridged from "Violence in Intimate Relationships: A Feminist Perspective" in *Talking Back: Thinking Feminist, Thinking Black* by bell hooks (Boston, MA: South End Press, 1989), pp. 84–91. Reprinted by permission of the publisher and the author.

Page 210. Altruism and Vulnerability. Abridgement of "The Feminine Virtues and Female Agency" in *Lesbian Ethics: Toward New Value* by Sarah Lucia Hoagland (Palo Alto, CA: Institute of Lesbian Studies: PO Box 60242, Palo Alto, CA 94306). Reprinted by permission of the author.

Page 223. Abridged from "Trusting Ex-Intimates" in *Person to Person*, George Graham and Hugh LaFollette, eds. (Philadelphia, PA: Temple University Press, 1989), pp. 269–281. Reprinted by permission of the publisher and author.

Page 236. Abridged from "Commitment and the Value of Marriage" in *Person to Person*, George Graham and Hugh LaFollette, eds. (Philadelphia, PA: Temple University Press, 1989), pp. 199–212. Reprinted by permission of the publisher and author.

Page 242. Abridged from "Marital Faithfulness" by Susan Mendus in *Philosophy* (59) 1984, pp. 243–52 (Cambridge University Press). Reprinted by permission of the publisher and author.

Page 248. The Princess. From the *Book of Sequels* by Christopher Cerf and Henry Beard. Copyright © 1991 by Christopher Cerf Associates. Reprinted by permission of Random House, Inc.

Page 252. Black Men/Black Women: Changing Roles and Relationships. From *Black Masculinity: The Black Male's Role in American Society* (Oakland, CA: The Black Scholar Press, 1982), Chapter 7. Reprinted by permission of the author.

Page 262. Abridged from "Implications of the Emerging Family," in *Shaping Tomorrow's Family: Theory and Policy for the 21st Century* by John Scanzoni, (Beverly Hills, CA: Sage Publications, Inc., 1983), pp. 155–194. Reprinted by permission of the author and publisher.

Page 270. Is "Straight" to "Gay" and "Family" Is to "No Family"? Abridged from "Exiles From Kinship," in *Families We Choose: Lesbians, Gays, Kinship* by Kath Weston (New York, NY: Columbia University Press, 1991), pp. 21–41. Reprinted by permission of the author.

Page 275. "Fighting for Same Sex Marriage" in *Partners*: Newsletter for Gay and Lesbian Couples, November/December 1991. Reprinted by permission of the author.

Page 277. The Married Woman. From *The Second Sex* by Simone de Beauvoir, trans. H. M. Parshley. Copyright 1954 by Alfred A. Knopf, Inc. Reprinted by permission of the publisher.

Page 285. The Case for Feminist Revolution. Text pp. 222–232 from *The Dialectic of Sex* by Shulamith Firestone. Copyright © 1970 by Shulamith Firestone. By permission of William Morrow & Company, Inc.

Page 291. Abridged from "Marriage as a Bad Business Deal: Distribution of Property on Divorce" in *Perspectives on the Family*, Robert C. L. Moffat, Joseph Grcic, Michael D. Bayles, eds. (Lewiston, NY: The Edwin Mellem Press, 1990), pp. 185–200. Reprinted by permission of the publisher.

Page 302. Abridged from "Sexuality" in *The Examined Life: Philosophical Meditation* (New York, NY: Simon & Schuster) Copyright © 1989 by Robert Nozick. Reprinted by permission of Simon & Schuster.

Page 306. The Heterosexual Questionnaire. From *Changing Men*, Spring 1982. Copyright © 1982 *Changing Men*. Reprinted by permission.

Page 307. The Language of Sex: Our Conception of Sexual Intercourse. Abridged from "'Pricks and Chicks:' A Plea for 'Persons',", in *Philosophy and Sex*, Robert Baker and Frederick Elliston, eds. (Buffalo, NY: Prometheus Books, 1975), pp. 57–64. Reprinted by permission of the author.

Page 312. Abridged from Buchbinder, Burstyn, Forbes, and Steedman: *Who's on Top? The Politics of Heterosexuality*, Garamond Press, Toronto, 1987. Reprinted with the permission of Garamond Press and the author.

Page 315. Abridged from "In Pursuit of the Perfect Penis: The Medicalization of Male Sexuality," in *Changing Men: New Directions in Research on Men and Masculinity*, Michael S. Kimmel, ed. (Beverly Hills, CA: Sage Publications, 1987), pp. 165–184. Reprinted by permission of the publisher.

Pages 320 and 324. "Gay Basics" and "Sex and Cultural Privacy." Abridged from 'Gay Basics: Some Questions, Facts and Values,' in *Gays/Justice : A Study of Ethics, Society and Law*, by Richard D. Mohr (New York, NY: Columbia University Press, 1988), pp. 21–45. Reprinted by permission of the author.

Page 334. Abridged from "Women and AIDS: Too Little, Too Late," in *Hypatia*, Volume 4, Number 3 (Fall 1989), pp. 3–22. Reprinted by permission of the author.

Page 341. Copyright © 1992 Brenda Timmins.

Page 352. Copyright © 1982 by Tim Beneke. From the book *Men on Rape* and reprinted with permission from St. Martin's Press Inc., New York, NY.

Page 358. Excerpt from *I Never Called It Rape* by Robin Warshaw. Copyright © 1988 by Ms. Foundation for Education and Communication, Inc. and Sarah Lazin Books. Reprinted by permission of HarperCollins Publishers Inc.

Page 364. Abridged from "Sexual Harassment" from "Black Perspectives on Women, Sex and the Law," *Women, Sex, and the Law* by Rosemarie Tong (Totowa NJ: Rowman and Littlefield, 1984). Reprinted by permission of the author and publisher.

Page 369. Abridged from *The Lecherous Professor: Sexual Harassment on Campus* by Billie Wright Dziech and Linda Weiner, eds.(Boston, MA: Beacon Press, 1984). Copyright © 1984 by Billie Wright Dziech and Linda Weiner. Reprinted by permission of Beacon Press and the author.

Page 380. Copyright © 1992 Terri-Lee d'Aaron. Used by permission.

Page 383. Abridged from "Charges Against Prostitution: An Attempt at a Philosophical Assessment," in *Ethics*, Volume 90 (April 1980), pp. 335–366. Reprinted by permission of The University of Chicago Press and the author.

Page 387. Abridged from "Defending Prostitution: Charges against Ericsson" in *Ethics*, Volume 93 (April 1983), pp. 561–565. Reprinted by permission of The University of Chicago Press and the author.

Page 389. Powerlessness. Abridged from "Pornography in Capitalism: Powerlessness," in *Pornography: Marxism, Feminism and the Future of Sexuality* by Alan Soble (New Haven, CT: Yale University Press, 1986), pp. 78–84. Reprinted by permission of the author and publisher.

Page 391. Abridged from "Francis Biddle's Sister: Pornography, Civil Rights, and Speech." For permission to photocopy this selection please contact Harvard University press. Reprinted by permission of the publishers from *Feminism Unmodified* by Catharine MacKinnon, Cambridge, Mass.: Harvard University Press, Copyright © 1987 by the President and Fellows of Harvard College.

Page 396. The Roots of Pornography. Copyright © 1987, 1989 by David Steinberg. All rights reserved. Used by permission of David Steinberg.

Page 400. Gays and the Pornography Movement: Having the Hots for Sex Discrimination. Copyright © 1985. John Stoltenberg is author of *Refusing to Be a Man* (Penguin US/Meridian).

Page 410. The Purpose of Sex. From *Summa Contra Gentiles Book Three* by St. Thomas Aquinas, Translated by Vernon J. Bourke. Translation copyright © 1956 by Doubleday, a division of Bantam Doubleday Dell Publishing Group, Inc. Used by permission of Doubleday, a division of Bantam Doubleday Dell Publishing Group, Inc.

Pages 412 and 416. Excerpts from "Society and the Fertile Woman" in *The Sceptical Feminist* by Janet Radcliffe-Richards (New York, NY: Penguin Books, 1980) pp. 252–289. Reprinted by permission of the author.

Page 424. The Mother. From *The Second Sex* by Simone de Beauvoir, trans. H. M. Parshley. Copyright 1954 by Alfred A. Knopf, Inc. Reprinted by permission of the publisher.

Page 429. Abridged from Don Marquis, "Why Abortion Is Immoral," in *The Journal of Philosophy*, 1989, pp. 183–201. Reprinted by permission of the author and publisher.

Page 432. © 1992 Brenda Timmins. Used by permission.

Page 436. © 1992 Alex Nalezinski. Used by permission.

Page 446. If Men Could Menstruate. From *Outrageous Acts and Everyday Rebellions* by Gloria Steinem. Copyright © 1983 by Gloria Steinem. Copyright © 1984 by East Toledo Productions, Inc. Reprinted by permission of Henry Holt and Company, Inc.

Page 448. Abridged from "Childbirth," in *Ethics and Human Reproduction: A Feminist Analysis* (Winchester, MA: Allen and Unwin, Inc., 1987), pp. 88-110. Reprinted by permission of the author.

Page 456. Francie Hornstein, "Children by Donor Insemination: A New Choice for Lesbians" from *Test Tube Women: What Future for Motherhood?* by Rita Arditti, Renate Duelli, and Shelley Minden, published by Pandora Press, an imprint of HarperCollins Publishers Limited. Reprinted by permission of the publisher.

Page 461. Abridged from "Selling Babies, Selling Bodies" in *Hypatia*, Volume 4, Number 3 (Fall, 1989). Reprinted by permission of the author.

Pages 468 and 473. "The Ethics of Surrogacy" and "Having Children and the Market Economy." Jonathan Glover, et al., *Ethics of New Reproductive Technologies: The Glover Report to the European Commission.* DeKalb: Northern Illinois University Press, 1989. Used with permission of the publisher.

Page 480. Abridgement of "Ambition" in *Femininity.* Copyright © 1984 by Susan Brownmiller. Reprinted by permission of Linden Press, a division of Simon & Schuster, Inc.

Page 483. Abridged and reprinted from "Marianismo: The Other Face of Machismo in Latin America," by Evelyn P. Stevens in *Female and Male in Latin America: Essays,* Ann Pescatello, Editor, by permission of the University of Pittsburgh Press. © 1973 by University of Pittsburgh Press.

Page 491. Abridged from "When Women and Men Mother" in *The Socialist Review* 49 (January–February 1980). Reprinted by permission of the publisher

Page 500. Abridged from M. Rivka Polatnick "Why Men Don't Rear Children: A Power Analysis," in *Berkeley Journal of Sociology* 18, (1973–4), pp. 35–86. Reprinted by permission of the publisher.

Page 508. Abridged from "Anna Karenina, Scarlett O'Hara and Gail Bezaire: Child Custody and Family Law Reform," in *In the Name of the Fathers* by Susan Crean (Toronto, Ontario: Amanita Enterprises, 1988), pp. 12-53. Reprinted by permission of the publisher and author.

Page 513. Abridged from "The Anti-Feminist Backlash: or Why Custody Is a Fatherhood Issue," pp. 99–140 in *In the Name of the Fathers* by Susan Crean (Toronto, Ontario: Amanita Enterprises, 1988). Reprinted by permission of the publisher.

Page 520. Why Young Women Are More Conservative. From *Outrageous Acts and Everyday Rebellions* by Gloria Steinem. Copyright © 1983 by Gloria Steinem. Copyright © 1984 by East Toledo Productions, Inc. Reprinted by permission of Henry Holt and Company, Inc.

Page 524. Abridged from "Age, Race, Class and Sex," in *Sister Outsider* by Audre Lorde (Trumansburg, NY: The Crossing Press, 1984). Reprinted by permission of the publisher.

Page 527. From Maturity to Old Age. From *The Second Sex* by Simone de Beauvoir, trans. H. M. Parshley. Copyright 1954 by Alfred A. Knopf, Inc. Reprinted by permission of the publisher.

Page 531. "It Hurts to Be Alive and Obsolete" by Zoe Moss from *Sisterhood Is Powerful: An Anthology of Writings from the Women's Liberation Movement,* edited by Robin Morgan. Copyright © 1970 by Robin Morgan. By permission.

Page 534. From *Look Me in the Eye: Old Women, Aging, and Ageism.* Copyright 1983, 1991, by Barbara Macdonald and Cynthia Rich. Reprinted with permission of the author and Spinsters Book Co.

Page 538. Abridged from "The View from Over the Hill" in *Over the Hill: Reflections on Ageism Between Women* by Baba Copper (Freedom, CA: The Crossing Press 1988), pp. 14–34. Reprinted by permission of the publisher.

Introduction

WE LIVE OUR LIVES as gendered human beings. As children, we are either boys or girls. As adults, we are either men or women. The fact that we are gendered means that we are called upon to think about certain issues and make decisions about them. Many of these issues are very important to us on a continuing basis.

A film is only a film. We see the film, it is over, we leave the theater and, if we read the reviews at all, we agree or disagree with them. The film may furnish material for interesting conversations with friends, but otherwise, once we have seen it, it is over for us.

Gender issues are not like films. As women and men we confront choices such as whether we should pair up with a particular person, whether we should marry or remain single, whether we should have children, whether we should be productive members of the work force in a particular type of position, and whether we will be happy doing the kind of work the position requires. Despite the fact that we reach and implement decisions about such matters, the issues involved often continue to linger afterwards. We married and had children, but was that really the best decision? We entered a certain line of work, but did we choose the one that was best for us? We decided to remain neutral about the issue of pornography, but should we have taken a position one way or another? Even irrevocable decisions have a tendency to come back and haunt us as issues, real or hypothetical dilemmas with no obvious solutions. Much as we are pleased with the three children we decided to have, they now seem to be at very difficult ages. This may lead us to wonder whether any two of them would have been more than enough.

Since such matters touch us directly, any reader must have already put thought into at least some them. Thus, the subjects addressed by the writers in this collection should not be totally new to anyone. These writers have only, perhaps, put more thought into the topics than has the average person. In addition, many of the writers have interesting or unusual perspectives on their chosen subjects.

Many issues involving gender arise in what is sometimes called one's "personal life." This is comprised of the activities a person decides upon taking no one into account except herself plus those where she also considers other people to whom she is related by personal ties. One's relation to a doctor is not usually personal because interest in her is limited to the quality of medical care she offers. Any other doctor offering care of similar quality would do just as well. A spouse, child, or friend, by contrast, is not so interchangeable with someone else. For this reason, we think of our ties to them as personal. In personal relations, gender can make a difference. Our choice of spouse depends on gender, and also on the qualities we think valuable (or productive of a valuable relationship with us) and we often see these qualities as gender related.

Gender issues are not, however, confined to private plots of life that can be cordoned off from the rest of human activity. We take our gender with us into the workplace and the rest of public life. Gender affects our perspectives on others and their perspectives on us, even when our relations with them cannot be classified as personal.

Very early in life we learn whether we are girls or boys and, accordingly, what we are expected to do or not do. Gender expectations for children (e.g., what types of clothing are appropriate for which gender) are relatively simple, however, compared to what is expected of adult women and men. Expectations for adults can be confining; also a particular sort of behavior can exact a much heavier price for one gender than for the other. For example, a certain posture that passes as "normal" for a man may precipitate unwelcome sexual attention if taken by a woman. Career paths in the work force are laid out according to gender; it is much easier for one gender than the other to enter particular careers and to remain and progress in them. All told, it is difficult to find any segment of human life where gender fails to make a difference.

Accordingly, the topics selected for this collection are drawn from both private and public life. I tried to select subjects where gender clearly plays a major role and where the writers locate and explain this role for the reader.

Most of the writers acknowledge, in one way or another, an important problem in gendered life, the oppression of women. Even though some writers note it only in passing as they focus their discussion on other matters, it is the one problem that infuses the collection as a whole. Society is, in a word, sexist. It systematically favors men over women, and it engineers and maintains structures to ensure that men receive better treatment and have more options available to them. These structures are robust and effective in both private and public life. Feminism, the movement that has brought this matter to our attention, is discussed after a brief discussion of the two title words of the collection, "basics" and "gender."

Basics

What are "basics"? Insofar as a subject is based on experience, its basics are those elements that are as close to experience as the subject allows. Despite their proximity to experience, these elements are always beliefs, or experience that has been structured by thought. Because we are thinking beings, we bring thought to all experience; thought serves to make sense of the experience and to incorporate it into the structure of beliefs we already have. Incorporation of a new experiential belief may strengthen this structure by giving us more confidence in it. Or it may require us to make changes in the existing structure because the new belief, which conflicts with some old ones in the structure, is more compelling.

As we know, people vary in important ways in what they believe. Since pre-existing beliefs always structure experience, it is not surprising that people who bring different beliefs to the same situation receive different experiential messages. People may disagree, perhaps argumentatively, about what actually happened. They have developed an issue at the most basic (experiential) level, having arrived at points of view at this level that are initially incompatible.

Not everything that matters in life is intellectually important. Whether the flower garden would look better if it included petunias may turn into a very emotional matter, but the subject has little theoretical interest to recommend it. Philosophy focuses on more interesting issues—ones that furnish material for thought—such as world hunger, punishment, and future generations. Moral philosophy focuses on what is right, wrong, allowable, mandatory, forbidden, etc. When moral philosophy is directed to social issues, such as those just mentioned, it becomes social philosophy as well. Social philosophy works out moral positions on social institutions—those structures in which human beings live as members of society.

This volume deals with issues in social philosophy because the writings concern institutions that have been shaped by social forces. For example, both prostitution and marriage assume their present form because of their social histories and their places in a wider social context. Even though we may feel that our choice of whom and whether to marry is more under our control than, say, whether and how to end world hunger, the alternatives we choose among in matters like marriage are socially formed entities. We may take steps to change these entities into something more suited and more valuable to us, but the socially formed structures we inherit are what we must begin with.

Gender issues are any controversies in which gender figures in a central way. Like other social and moral issues, gender issues can arise through conflict in our experiential beliefs about gendered human life. One perception of pornography is that it is simply one form of sexual material which can meet a particular sexual need or interest; it is relatively harmless unless it is misused, or contains depictions of persons being harmed as judged by standards external to sexuality. A quite different perception of pornography is that it portrays persons, women in particular, as sexual items that can be bought and sold. Thus, the same situation—marketing sexually explicit material—can generate different experiences because these experiences have been structured by different beliefs. The very contents of the experienced situation may thus become a matter of dispute.

The criterion for whether an issue is experientially basic is whether it can be described in terms that a lay thinker can comprehend. These terms would not be the property of any special theory that only particular groups of philosophers, sociologists, or scientists can understand. Instead they would belong to the large societywide vocabulary that we expect most educated persons to find intelligible. Persons acquainted with some subject matter, but lacking technical expertise in it, can then draw on this common vocabulary to think and converse with others about the subject. I have tried to select writings that can be understood without mastery of special theories. In these writings, thought, analysis and argumentation are usually confined to concepts and terminology that do not rise above the level of conceptualization which any thoughtful person can understand. This is as close to experience as well-developed perspectives on gender issues can get.

Gender

"Gender" is one pervasive idea that structures experiential basics. Much of the world, the human world in particular, is perceived as male or female. Webster's[1] so defines "gender": "1 a. (archaic); kind, sort. b. sex 2. linguistics . . . any subclasses within a grammatical class . . . of a language that are partly arbitrary, but also partly based on distinguishable characteristics, such as . . . sex." The latter linguistic meaning of "gender" became familiar to most of us as we struggled to memorize the gender of nouns and pronouns in other languages. However, when we speak of human beings, we are not addressing linguistic items. What we need instead is something like the meaning of "gender" that Webster's equates with "sex." The ancestry of "gender" (kind) does not mandate that we restrict the word to the masculine/feminine dichotomy in linguistic items; we are quite correct in using it to mark the differences between male and female humans, apes, and parts of flowers. The current puzzle seems instead to be this: Why do we have two words, "sex" and "gender," each marking the dichotomy between men and women?

Meanings of words are always a bit messy. Perfectly formed language would perhaps contain no two words with identical meaning. However, our problems with "sex" and "gender" run deeper than simple synonymy. In addition, language is in a state of flux; words gradually make their way from one meaning to another. W. V. Quine's term for this is "language drift."[2] One cause of language drift is social change, which gives us new matters to discuss. However, only our old vocabulary is already in use in the linguistic community. People understand this vocabulary, at least well enough for it to be useful. So why mint new words that will be difficult for others to understand?

Sometimes a better strategy is to take vocabulary already entrenched and, by transporting it to a new context, give it the meaning needed for purposes at hand. If an old word is used with new meaning in a new context often enough, the new meaning may gradually become attached to the old word. According to Quine, this is just what happened with the word "sex."[3] Recently there have been an increased number of occasions for discussing human copulation. Street language furnishes us with ample terminology for such discussions, as do medicine and science. However, we do need a term for polite conversation. The word "sex" is the obvious choice, being neither too technical nor too crude for simple talk about these encounters. However, the frequency with which the word "sex" is used to describe copulation puts spin on its meaning in that direction, thus making "sex" less appropriate for speaking of male/female differences, especially those differences which are not biological.

We have become increasingly aware of the possibility that some of the differences between men and women have social causes. We need some way of saying so, especially if we want to discuss how social structures may function in creating particular differences. Perhaps if we can change the structures, we may be able to change the differences they cause. (It hardly makes sense to direct social change at the genetic—the strictly biological—features.) Thus the word "sex" is coming to be restricted to biological, or genetic male/female differences, leaving its official synonym, "gender," free to drift toward meaning those differences that have social causes.

In fact, however, the matter is slightly more complicated; "gender" has drifted in two directions. Some use the word to talk about the differences between men and women (or boys and girls), that are caused by the social environment. [" . . . at the risk of oversimplification, sex . . . is a biological given, gender is a social acquisition."[4]] Others, however, prefer to use the word "gender" in a way that leaves the matter open as to the cause of the differences. I support this latter use, and I think it is important that others try to use "gender" in this way for the following reasons.

Many differences between men and women have mixed origins, and many have origins that are not well understood. Male and female hormones are biologically caused, whereas dress codes for men and women are the work of society. But how do we categorize differences such as the relative volume of male/female voices? Girl and boy babies both seem quite capable of crying their lungs out with enormous volume relative to their size; later, girls may be encouraged to speak quietly, boys to yell. However, not every boy and girl receives this type of "encouragement," and some simply defy it. For example, a girl considered to be a tomboy may be quite vocal on the playing field. Toward adolescence, men's vocal chords undergo a change that gives them more depth and more volume capacity. Men also develop greater lung capacity than women. Women's voices can be trained, sometimes to the point of creating a Wagnerian soprano who is quite capable of being heard, over a large orchestra, in the back row of an opera house. But the singer may still be perceived as having a soft speaking voice because people pay less attention to the voices of women and don't listen to what they say as carefully as they would to the same thing said by a man.

Now where are we in the social/genetic distinction in differential male/female voice development? Because we are not in a position to make such distinctions, we should simply label this "gender difference," meaning that the difference could be biological, social, or some combination of the two. Or we could mean that the cause, although known, is difficult to categorize as either exclusively social or exclusively nonsocial. (What if our soprano's voice were reduced to a mere whisper because of industrial pollution in the area of the opera house? Is this industrial pollution social, physical, or both?)

It is worth mentioning, finally, that humans, other animals, and plants are not the only sorts of gendered beings imaginable. In fact, our imaginations seem generous in endowing their creations with gender. When inanimate natural objects come to life in our thinking, they almost always appear with a gender. The sun, for example, is usually male when animated, whereas the moon is female. When extraterrestrials appear in films and on television screens, one of their most noticeable features is usually their gender. That even our most far-fetched imaginings include gender indicates the importance of this feature in human life.

Feminism

Feminism, as noted earlier, is the view that women have suffered oppression in virtually all areas of life. Christine Overall gives a fair definition of feminism.[5] The following is an amplification, with some modifications, of her definition.

Feminism is, first, a commitment to understanding women's own perceptions of their situations. These perceptions are what I have been calling gender basics, in this case the gender experiences from the perspective of women only. Feminists insist that because women as a group have been neglected in the past, we should make special efforts to pay attention to, understand, and respect women's reports of their experiences.

Since women have been oppressed, however, their experiences may have been altered by the instruments of oppression, and women may not possess the skills of communicating their experiences in ways that can be readily understood. Feminists, therefore, see part of their task as articulating women's reports or enabling women to articulate these reports themselves. Another task of the feminist is searching out and identifying the oppressive elements that have distorted women's experiences, including the experiences of feminists themselves.

Since these elements have threaded their way through all women's perceptions, a feminist must do her best to search out the oppressive elements and analyze women's experiences without expecting perfect results. One feminist's ideas may conflict with those of other feminists, even though all are earnestly striving for the correct answer, or answers.

The situation is further complicated by the fact that women's experiences, including those involving oppression, are not uniform. Race and class, as well as sexual orientation (heterosexual or homosexual), lend genuine diversity to human experience. Some commonalities can be expected, but as a feminist learns to listen to her inner voice and respect what she believes, she must, at least initially, take the same attitude toward those whose differences seem to produce different messages.

Women who are feminists must have an awareness of women's oppression; this is Overall's second defining feature of feminism. Feminists maintain that oppression of women is codified in legal, educational, and religious systems, and ingrained in our less formal relations to one another, as well as in our psychology and physiology. Women's oppression is also called "patriarchy" because feminists believe that this general organizational feature of society was initiated by men, continues to be maintained by men, and has men as its principal beneficiaries. A belief that patriarchy would be wrong *should* it happen to exist is insufficient for feminism. A feminist must believe in patriarchy's reality, beginning with her daily life as she experiences it.

Third, feminists are expected to have some explanation of patriarchy's origins and continuation. Male motivation to retain men's position as the advantaged gender is nearly always a large part of the explanation and may be the total one for many feminists. However, some feminists believe that other oppressive structures like capitalism or heterosexuality are essential buttresses of patriarchy. Some also maintain that the complicity of women is an important factor in explaining patriarchy's continuation.

Fourth, feminism is directed at social change. The objective is to end patriarchy either in particular areas or in its entirety. This is feminism's political aspect—political in that it is directed at influencing social policy. For many women, this is the most important part of feminism, because they believe that the elimination of patriarchal structures is the ultimate reason for searching them out and developing theories about them.

This fourth aspect of feminism—translating thought into action—may be one cause of the unpopularity of feminism, even among women who might benefit from feminist action. No matter what line of action is taken, some separation from patriarchal structures is required. This can be a frightening experience to someone who has always accepted patriarchy and lived her life within its constraints. In addition, acting against the current social mores, especially against the entrenched powers of society, can be costly. One must usually pay, either immediately or in the long run, for such defiance. Anyone who openly takes a stand as a feminist must be prepared for negative responses from others. Antifeminism is subtle and pervasive. Many women internalize their antifeminism and are conflicted about whether to take openly feminist action even when they believe in a cause clearly aligned with feminist belief. For example, a woman may support rape prevention but deny she is a feminist in doing so.

The principal theory in opposition to feminism is biological determinism. This view recognizes social differences between women and men, and it may even acknowledge the oppression of women; but it asserts that biology causes all gender differences which, in turn, totally explain women's relative social position. One popular view of biological determinism is that a woman's biology justifies her destiny as a wife in a heterosexual marriage, which is the role of bearing children and nurturing all family members, including her husband.

Writings that express this type of opposition to feminism are not included in this collection because of their speculative nature, even though biological determinism has a long history and has been associated with prominent thinkers, including philosophers from Aristotle to Hegel. A commitment to approaching gender issues through experience rules out any views based on speculation.

For a strikingly similar reason, no writings are included that address Overall's final feature of feminism: "a feminist perspective is characterized by the deliberate and self-conscious (in a positive sense) nature of its world view."[6] Feminists are developing theories of knowledge, ontologies, ethical systems, and theories of art, film, and even logic. However, these endeavors do leave the field of experiential basics and attempt to build theoretical structures. Such structures are quite often successful in illuminating women's experience or, more generally, the experience of both women and men as seen from the perspective of their respective genders. Since the more experiential writings use only the language, concepts, and theory of everyman/everywoman, as explained earlier, they furnish a more suitable place to begin any study of gender, including studies from a feminist perspective.

We Are Demiurges

Philosophers may have first heard of the demiurge as the lesser god of Plato's *Timeaus,* who fashioned (as best he could) the world as we know it. However, in its first origins (in Homer, for example) a *demiourgos* was simply a workman or craftsman. *Demi* has its Greek root in *demos* (man, person) and *ourgos* (worker). In Plato's philosophy, *demiourgos* acquired connotations of creative, spiritual power as well. The word retains this meaning today; "demiurgic" is: "pertaining to a demiurge or creative power."[7]

Feminists could well perceive themselves as demiurges. We have less power than the forces of patriarchy (as the demiurge of Plato was a lesser god). Nonetheless, we must coordinate our thoughts and powers to create a better world, as we try to rid institutions such as education, law, art, as well as our own bodies and spirits, of elements of patriarchal oppression.

However, we have at present two serious problems: factionalism and hubris. (Hubris is unjustified pride and overconfidence in oneself and one's own point of view.) In a fairly obvious way, hubris generates factionalism. If I get overconfident about my perspective and you develop a similar attitude about yours, we will have a difficult time listening to each other and identifying our commonalities and differences. We will also have a difficult time joining forces to do new things in feminism on the basis of both these commonalities and differences. For example, if I am indigenous and you are an immigrant, I may want to talk about *our* national experience as women as if only experiences of my kind are worth talking about and yours can be ignored. I could do the same with my race, ethnicity, sexual orientation, or class. In short, I could adopt the mentality of patriarchy toward you because you are different from me. I thus miss the point that we have a common cause in oppression as women and that, if we want to join forces, we must find some way of coming to terms with our differences. Ideally, these differences among us should function as a source of strength, furnishing us a variety of sources of thought and energy about how to approach our problems.

My own view, not shared by all feminists, is that we need to develop new relations with men as well, now that the patriarchal structures which kept us in separate spheres are showing the first signs of decay. We should be prepared to address differences of gender in much the same spirit as race or class difference. As long as different gender perspectives exist, neither gender has a monopoly on insight into gender issues, including the all-important matter of women's oppression, just as this is not the prerogative of any one race or class. Our best hope at present, then, is to pool perspectives from different races, classes, sexual orientations, and genders. Surely we can expect the results to be better than if we had limited our field of vision by eliminating one or more of these perspectives.

I compiled this collection of writings with as much variety as I could as a hopeful step in the direction of better understanding of gender matters and the more effective resolution of problems related to gender, especially the problem of women's oppression.

NOTES

1. *Webster's Third New International Dictionary of the English Language* (Unabridged).

2. W. V. Quine. *Quiddities: An Intermittently Philosophical Dictionary* (Cambridge, MA: The Belknap Press of Harvard University Press, 1987), pp. 111–114.

3. *Ibid.,* pp. 78–82.

4. Casey Miller and Kate Swift. *Words and Women* (New York: Anchor Books, 1976), p. 47.

5. Christine Overall. *Ethics and Human Reproduction: A Feminist Analysis* (Winchester, MA: Allen and Unwin, Inc., 1987), pp. 2–4.

6. *Ibid.,* p. 3f.

7. *Webster's New 20th Century Dictionary,* Unabridged, Second Edition.

Part I

Oppression

Introduction

THE CENTRAL THEME OF THIS COLLECTION is that patriarchy—male control—is a serious form of oppression that affects the lives of women (and men along with them, to some extent) in detrimental ways. Other forms of oppression compound patriarchal oppression. This section contains descriptions and explanations of oppressive structures. Frye, de Beauvoir, and Goode focus on the oppression of women by men; McIntosh, Lorde, and Noda speak to oppression that results from racism and social stratification; McIntosh also discusses the oppression of homosexuals by systems favoring heterosexuals; Wendell describes the oppression of the disabled.

I.1   Oppression

MARILYN FRYE

Marilyn Frye compares the oppression of women to the situation of a bird in a cage. A woman can become caught in a bind where, no matter what she chooses to think, say, or do, a bar puts difficulties in her path. These barriers are often difficult to recognize, because it is not easy to perceive them as parts of a configuration, and because of the attempts made to hide their more pernicious aspects. This configuration of bars restricts men, as well. But the system, as a whole, benefits men.

Frye teaches philosophy and feminist theory at Michigan State University. Her writings are based directly on her life as a woman and lesbian. (Selections by Marilyn Frye are also included in Parts IV and VII.)

Reading Questions

1. What is the difference between being miserable and being oppressed?
2. What is the difference between having limits set for you, having barriers put in your way, and being oppressed?
3. What is the difference between frustration and oppression?

IT IS A FUNDAMENTAL CLAIM of feminism that women are oppressed. The word 'oppression' is a strong word. It repels and attracts. It is dangerous and dangerously fashionable and endangered. It is much misused, and sometimes not innocently.

The statement that women are oppressed is frequently met with the claim that men are oppressed too. We hear that oppressing is oppressive to those who oppress as well as to those they oppress. Some men cite as evidence of their oppression their much-advertised inability to cry. It is tough, we are told, to be masculine. When the stresses and frustrations of being a man are cited as evidence that oppressors are oppressed by their oppressing, the word 'oppression' is being stretched to meaninglessness; it is treated as

though its scope includes any and all human experience of limitation or suffering, no matter the cause, degree or consequence. Once such usage has been put over on us, then if ever we deny that any person or group is oppressed, we seem to imply that we think they never suffer and have no feelings. We are accused of insensitivity; even of bigotry. For women, such accusation is particularly intimidating, since sensitivity is one of the few virtues that has been assigned to us. If we are found insensitive, we may fear we have no redeeming traits at all and perhaps are not real women. Thus are we silenced before we begin: the name of our situation drained of meaning and our guilt mechanisms tripped.

But this is nonsense. Human beings can be miserable without being oppressed, and it is per-

Abridged from "Oppression" in The Politics of Reality: Essays in Feminist Theory *(Trumansburg, NY: The Crossing Press, 1983) pp. 1–16.*

fectly consistent to deny that a person or group is oppressed without denying that they have feelings or that they suffer.

We need to think clearly about oppression, and there is much that mitigates against this. I do not want to undertake to prove that women are oppressed (or that men are not), but I want to make clear what is being said when we say it. We need this word, this concept, and we need it to be sharp and sure.

I

The root of the word 'oppression' is the element 'press'. *The press of the crowd; pressed into military service; to press a pair of pants; printing press; press the button*. Presses are used to mold things or flatten them or reduce them in bulk, sometimes to reduce them by squeezing out the gasses or liquids in them. Something pressed is something caught between or among forces and barriers which are so related to each other that jointly they restrain, restrict or prevent the thing's motion or mobility. Mold. Immobilize. Reduce.

The mundane experience of the oppressed provides another clue. One of the most characteristic and ubiquitous features of the world as experienced by oppressed people is the double bind—situations in which options are reduced to a very few and all of them expose one to penalty, censure or deprivation. For example, it is often a requirement upon oppressed people that we smile and be cheerful. If we comply, we signal our docility and our acquiescence in our situation. We need not, then, be taken note of. We acquiesce in being made invisible, in our occupying no space. We participate in our own erasure. On the other hand, anything but the sunniest countenance exposes us to being perceived as mean, bitter, angry or dangerous. This means, at the least, that we may be found "difficult" or unpleasant to work with, which is enough to cost one one's livelihood; at worst, being seen as mean, bitter, angry or dangerous has been known to result in rape, arrest, beating and mur-

der. One can only choose to risk one's preferred form and rate of annihilation.

Another example: It is common in the United States that women, especially younger women, are in a bind where neither sexual activity nor sexual inactivity is all right. If she is heterosexually active, a woman is open to censure and punishment for being loose, unprincipled or a whore. The "punishment" comes in the form of criticism, snide and embarrassing remarks, being treated as an easy lay by men, scorn from her more restrained female friends. She may have to lie and hide her behavior from her parents. She must juggle the risks of unwanted pregnancy and dangerous contraceptives. On the other hand, if she refrains from heterosexual activity, she is fairly constantly harassed by men who try to persuade her into it and pressure her to "relax" and "let her hair down"; she is threatened with labels like "frigid," "uptight," "manhater," "bitch" and "cocktease." The same parents who would be disapproving of her sexual activity may be worried by her inactivity because it suggests she is not or will not be popular, or is not sexually normal. She may be charged with lesbianism. If a woman is raped, then if she has been heterosexually active she is subject to the presumption that she liked it (since her activity is presumed to show that she likes sex), and if she has not been heterosexually active, she is subject to the presumption that she liked it (since she is supposedly "repressed and frustrated"). Both heterosexual activity and heterosexual nonactivity are likely to be taken as proof that you wanted to be raped, and hence, of course, weren't *really* raped at all. You can't win. You are caught in a bind, caught between systematically related pressures.

Women are caught like this, too, by networks of forces and barriers that expose one to penalty, loss or contempt whether one works outside the home or not, is on welfare or not, bears children or not, raises children or not, marries or not, stays married or not, is heterosexual, lesbian, both or neither. Economic necessity; confinement to racial and/or sexual job ghettos; sexual harassment; sex discrimination; pressures of competing expectations and judgments about *women, wives* and *mothers* (in the society at large, in racial and ethnic subcultures and in one's own mind); dependence (full or partial) on husbands, parents or the state; commitment to political ideas; loyalties to racial or ethnic or other "minority" groups; the demands of self-respect and responsibilities to others. Each of these factors exists in complex tension with every other, penalizing or prohibiting all of the apparently available options. And nipping at one's heels, always, is the endless pack of little things. If one dresses one way, one is subject to the assumption that one is advertising one's sexual availability; if one dresses another way, one appears to "not care about oneself" or to be "unfeminine." If one uses "strong language," one invites categorization as a whore or slut; if one does not, one invites categorization as a "lady"—one too delicately constituted to cope with robust speech or the realities to which it presumably refers.

The experience of oppressed people is that the living of one's life is confined and shaped by forces and barriers which are not accidental or occasional and hence avoidable, but are systematically related to each other in such a way as to catch one between and among them and restrict or penalize motion in any direction. It is the experience of being caged in: all avenues, in every direction, are blocked or booby trapped.

Cages. Consider a birdcage. If you look very closely at just one wire in the cage, you cannot see the other wires. If your conception of what is before you is determined by this myopic focus, you could look at that one wire, up and down the length of it, and be unable to see why a bird would not just fly around the wire any time it wanted to go somewhere. Furthermore, even if, one day at a time, you myopically inspected each wire, you still could not see why a bird would have trouble going past the wires to get anywhere. There is no physical property of any one wire, *nothing* that the closest scrutiny could discover, that will reveal how a bird could be inhibited or harmed by it except in the most

accidental way. It is only when you step back, stop looking at the wires one by one, microscopically, and take a macroscopic view of the whole cage, that you can see why the bird does not go anywhere; and then you will see it in a moment. It will require no great subtlety of mental powers. It is perfectly *obvious* that the bird is surrounded by a network of systematically related barriers, no one of which would be the least hindrance to its flight, but which, by their relations to each other, are as confining as the solid walls of a dungeon.

It is now possible to grasp one of the reasons why oppression can be hard to see and recognize: one can study the elements of an oppressive structure with great care and some good will without seeing the structure as a whole, and hence without seeing or being able to understand that one is looking at a cage and that there are people there who are caged, whose motion and mobility are restricted, whose lives are shaped and reduced.

The arresting of vision at a microscopic level yields such common confusion as that about the male door-opening ritual. This ritual, which is remarkably widespread across classes and races, puzzles many people, some of whom do and some of whom do not find it offensive. Look at the scene of the two people approaching a door. The male steps slightly ahead and opens the door. The male holds the door open while the female glides through. Then the male goes through. The door closes after them. "Now how," one innocently asks, "can those crazy womenslibbers say that is oppressive? The guy *removed* a barrier to the lady's smooth and unruffled progress." But each repetition of this ritual has a place in a pattern, in fact in several patterns. One has to shift the level of one's perception in order to see the whole picture.

The door-opening pretends to be a helpful service, but the helpfulness is false. This can be seen by noting that it will be done whether or not it makes any practical sense. Infirm men and men burdened with packages will open doors for able-bodied women who are free of physical burdens. Men will impose themselves awkwardly and jostle everyone in order to get to the door first. The act is not determined by convenience or grace. Furthermore, these very numerous acts of unneeded or even noisome "help" occur in counterpoint to a pattern of men not being helpful in many practical ways in which women might welcome help. What *women* experience is a world in which gallant princes charming commonly make a fuss about being helpful and providing small services when help and services are of little or no use, but in which there are rarely ingenious and adroit princes at hand when substantial assistance is really wanted either in mundane affairs or in situations of threat, assault or terror. There is no help with the (his) laundry; no help typing a report at 4:00 a.m.; no help in mediating disputes among relatives or children. There is nothing but advice that women should stay indoors after dark, be chaperoned by a man, or when it comes down to it, "lie back and enjoy it."

The gallant gestures have no practical meaning. Their meaning is symbolic. The door-opening and similar services provided are services which really are needed by people who are for one reason or another incapacitated—unwell, burdened with parcels, etc. So the message is that women are incapable. The detachment of the acts from the concrete realities of what women need and do not need is a vehicle for the message that women's actual needs and interests are unimportant or irrelevant. Finally, these gestures imitate the behavior of servants toward masters and thus mock women, who are in most respects the servants and caretakers of men. The message of the false helpfulness of male gallantry is female dependence, the invisibility or insignificance of women, and contempt for women.

One cannot see the meanings of these rituals if one's focus is riveted upon the individual event in all its particularity, including the particularity of the individual man's present conscious intentions and motives and the individual woman's conscious perception of the event in the moment. It seems sometimes that people take a deliberately myopic view and fill their eyes with things seen microscopically in order not to see macroscopi-

cally. At any rate, whether it is deliberate or not, people can and do fail to see the oppression of women because they fail to see macroscopically and hence fail to see the various elements of the situation as systematically related in larger schemes.

As the cageness of the bird cage is a macroscopic phenomenon, the oppressiveness of the situations in which women live our various and different lives is a macroscopic phenomenon. Neither can be *seen* from a microscopic perspective. But when you look macroscopically you can see it—a network of forces and barriers which are systematically related and which conspire to the immobilization, reduction and molding of women and the lives we live . . .

* * *

III

It seems to be the human condition that in one degree or another we all suffer frustration and limitation, all encounter unwelcome barriers, and all are damaged and hurt in various ways. Since we are a social species, almost all of our behavior and activities are structured by more than individual inclination and the conditions of the planet and its atmosphere. No human is free of social structures, nor (perhaps) would happiness consist in such freedom. Structure consists of boundaries, limits and barriers; in a structured whole, some motions and changes are possible, and others are not. If one is looking for an excuse to dilute the word 'oppression', one can use the fact of social structure as an excuse and say that everyone is oppressed. But if one would rather get clear about what oppression is and is not, one needs to sort out the sufferings, harms and limitations and figure out which are elements of oppression and which are not.

From what I have already said here, it is clear that if one wants to determine whether a particular suffering, harm or limitation is part of someone's being oppressed, one has to look at it *in context* in order to tell whether it is an element in an oppressive structure: one has to see if it is part of an enclosing structure of forces and barriers which tends to the immobilization and reduction of a group or category of people. One has to look at how the barrier or force fits with others and to whose benefit or detriment it works. As soon as one looks at examples, it becomes obvious that not everything which frustrates or limits a person is oppressive, and not every harm or damage is due to or contributes to oppression.

If a rich white playboy who lives off income from his investments in South African diamond mines should break a leg in a skiing accident at Aspen and wait in pain in a blizzard for hours before he is rescued, we may assume that in that period he suffers. But the suffering comes to an end; his leg is repaired by the best surgeon money can buy and he is soon recuperating in a lavish suite, sipping Chivas Regal. Nothing in this picture suggests a structure of barriers and forces. He is a member of several oppressor groups and does not suddenly become oppressed because he is injured and in pain. Even if the accident was caused by someone's malicious negligence, and hence someone can be blamed for it and morally faulted, that person still has not been an agent of oppression.

Consider also the restriction of having to drive one's vehicle on a certain side of the road. There is no doubt that this restriction is almost unbearably frustrating at times, when one's lane is not moving and the other lane is clear. There are surely times, even, when abiding by this regulation would have harmful consequences. But the restriction is obviously wholesome for most of us most of the time. The restraint is imposed for our benefit, and does benefit us; its operation tends to encourage our *continued* motion, not to immobilize us. The limits imposed by traffic regulations are limits most of us would cheerfully impose on ourselves given that we knew others would follow them too. They are part of a structure which shapes our behavior, not to our reduction and immobilization, but rather to the protection of our continued ability to move and act as we will.

Another example: The boundaries of a racial ghetto in an American city serve to some extent to keep white people from going in, as well as to keep ghetto dwellers from going out. A particular white citizen may be frustrated or feel deprived because s/he cannot stroll around there and enjoy the "exotic" aura of a "foreign" culture, or shop for bargains in the ghetto swap shops. In fact, the existence of the ghetto, of racial segregation, does deprive the white person of knowledge and harm her/his character by nurturing unwarranted feelings of superiority. But this does not make the white person in this situation a member of an oppressed race or a person oppressed because of her/his race. One must look at the barrier. It limits the activities and the access of those on both sides of it (though to different degrees). But it is a product of the intention, planning and action of whites for the benefit of whites, to secure and maintain privileges that are available to whites generally, as members of the dominant and privileged group. Though the existence of the barrier has some bad consequences for whites, the barrier does not exist in systematic relationship with other barriers and forces forming a structure oppressive to whites; quite the contrary. It is part of a structure which oppresses the ghetto dwellers and thereby (and by white intention) protects and furthers white interests as dominant white culture understands them. This barrier is not oppressive to whites, even though it is a barrier to whites.

Barriers have different meanings to those on opposite sides of them, even though they are barriers to both. The physical walls of a prison no more dissolve to let an outsider in than to let an insider out, but for the insider they are confining and limiting while to the outsider they may mean protection from what s/he takes to be threats posed by insiders—freedom from harm or anxiety. A set of social and economic barriers and forces separating two groups may be felt, even painfully, by members of both groups and yet may mean confinement to one and liberty and enlargement of opportunity to the other.

The service sector of the wives/mommas/assistants/girls is almost exclusively a woman-only sector; its boundaries not only enclose women but to a very great extent keep men out. Some men sometimes encounter this barrier and experience it as a restriction on their movements, their activities, their control or their choices of "lifestyle." Thinking they might like the simple nurturant life (which they may imagine to be quite free of stress, alienation, and hard work), and feeling deprived since it seems closed to them, they thereupon announce the discovery that they are oppressed, too, by "sex roles." But that barrier is erected and maintained by men, for the benefit of men. It consists of cultural and economic forces and pressures in a culture and economy controlled by men in which, at every economic level and in all racial and ethnic subcultures, economy, tradition—and even ideologies of liberation—work to keep at least local culture and economy in male control.*

The boundary that sets apart women's sphere is maintained and promoted by men generally for the benefit of men generally, and men generally do benefit from its existence, even the man who bumps into it and complains of the inconvenience. That barrier is protecting his classification and status as a male, as superior, as having a right to sexual access to a female or females. It protects a kind of citizenship which is superior to that of females of his class and race, his access to a wider range of better paying and higher status work, and his right to prefer unemployment to the degradation of doing lower status or "women's" work.

If a person's life or activity is affected by some force or barrier that person encounters, one may not conclude that the person is oppressed simply because the person encounters that barrier or

force; nor simply because the encounter is unpleasant, frustrating or painful to that person at that time; nor simply because the existence of the barrier or force, or the processes which maintain or apply it, serve to deprive that person of something of value. One must look at the barrier or force and answer certain questions about it. Who constructs and maintains it? Whose interests are served by its existence? Is it part of a structure which tends to confine, reduce and immobilize some group? Is the individual a member of the confined group? Various forces, barriers and limitations a person may encounter or live with may be part of an oppressive structure or not, and if they are, that person may be on either the oppressed or the oppressor side of it. One cannot tell which by how loudly or how little the person complains.

IV

Many of the restrictions and limitations we live with are more or less internalized and self-monitored, and are part of our adaptations to the requirements and expectations imposed by the needs and tastes and tyrannies of others. I have in mind such things as women's cramped postures and attenuated strides and men's restraint of emotional self-expression (except for anger). Who gets what out of the practice of those disciplines, and who imposes what penalties for improper relaxations of them? What are the rewards of this self-discipline?

Can men cry? Yes, in the company of women. If a man cannot cry, it is in the company of men that he cannot cry. It is men, not women, who require this restraint; and men not only require it, they reward it. The man who maintains a steely or tough or laid-back demeanor (all are forms which suggest invulnerability) marks himself as a member of the male community and is esteemed by other men. Consequently, the maintenance of that demeanor contributes to the man's self-esteem. It is felt as good, and he can

---

* Of course this is complicated by race and class. Machismo and "Black manhood" politics seem to help keep Latin or Black men in control of more cash than Latin or Black women control; but these politics seem to me also to ultimately help keep the larger economy in *white* male control.

feel good about himself. The way this restriction fits into the structures of men's lives is as one of the socially required behaviors which, if carried off, contribute to their acceptance and respect by significant others and to their own self-esteem. It is to their benefit to practice this discipline.

Consider, by comparison, the discipline of women's cramped physical postures and attenuated stride. This discipline can be relaxed in the company of women; it generally is at its most strenuous in the company of men.* Like men's emotional restraint, women's physical restraint is required by men. But unlike the case of men's emotional restraint, women's physical restraint is not rewarded. What do we get for it? Respect and esteem and acceptance? No. They mock us and parody our mincing steps. We look silly, incompetent, weak, and generally contemptible. Our exercise of this discipline tends to low esteem and low self-esteem. It does not benefit us. It fits in a network of behaviors through which we constantly announce to others our membership in a lower caste and our unwillingness and/or inability to defend our bodily or moral integrity. It is degrading and part of a pattern of degradation.

Acceptable behavior for both groups, men and women, involves a required restraint that seems in itself silly and perhaps damaging. But the social effect is drastically different. The woman's restraint is part of a structure oppressive to women; the man's restraint is part of a structure oppressive to women.

---

* Cf., *Let's Take Back Our Space: "Female" and "Male" Body Language as a Result of Patriarchal Structures*, by Marianne Wex (Frauenliteraturverlag Hermine Fees, West Germany, 1979), especially p. 173. This remarkable book presents literally thousands of candid photographs of women and men, in public, seated, standing and lying down. It vividly demonstrates the very systematic differences in women's and men's postures and gestures.

V

One is marked for application of oppressive pressures by one's membership in some group or category. Much of one's suffering and frustration befalls one partly or largely because one is a member of that category. In the case at hand, it is the category, *woman*. Being a woman is a major factor in my not having a better job than I do; being a woman selects me as a likely victim of sexual assault or harassment; it is my being a woman that reduces the power of my anger to a proof of my insanity. If a woman has little or no economic or political power, or achieves little of what she wants to achieve, a major causal factor in this is that she is a woman. For any woman of any race or economic class, being a woman is significantly attached to whatever disadvantages and deprivations she suffers, be they great or small.

None of this is the case with respect to a person's being a man. Simply being a man is not what stands between him and a better job; whatever assaults and harassments he is subject to, being male is not what selects him for victimization; being male is not a factor which would make his anger impotent—quite the opposite. If a man has little or no material or political power, or achieves little of what he wants to achieve, his being male is no part of the explanation. Being male is something he has going *for* him, even if race or class or age or disability is going against him.

Women are oppressed, *as women*. Members of certain racial and/or economic groups and classes, both the males and the females, are oppressed *as* members of those races and/or classes. But men are not oppressed *as men*.

. . . and isn't it strange that any of us should have been confused and mystified about such a simple thing?

Further Questions

1. Think of a situation that is an example of being caught in the type of birdcage Frye describes. Can a person's confinement in such a birdcage be seen only by viewing the larger situation, as Frye claims?

2. Frye says that the action of a man opening a door for a woman is part of an oppressive structure. Do you agree?

3. Frye believes that men's inability to cry is not a form of oppression. Does she make too little of this constraint on men's behavior?

Woman Is Not Our Brother   I.2

SIMONE DE BEAUVOIR

Referring to Laforgue, Simone de Beauvoir claims that "woman is not our brother." Men and women are always in a state of tension with respect to each other. These conflicts are due to their roles of oppressor and oppressed; each blames the other for their respective situations. De Beauvoir hopes for a future where social and economic equality of men and women will bring about a flourishing of new and better forms of relations among them.

Simone de Beauvoir (1908–1986) was one of the leaders of the existentialist movement and wrote many essays and books developing themes of existentialism. She is perhaps best remembered, however, for her two-volume study of women, *The Second Sex,* which became a new watershed for feminist thinking all over the world. (Selections from this work are also included in Parts IV, VI, X, and XIII.)

Reading Questions

1. Are many women intent on "trapping a man"? If so, what might be the cause of this motivation?

2. Do many men try to spare women burdens of responsibility and decision making? Is this doing women a real favor?

3. If a person finds herself in an underprivileged position with no evident means of escape, is cruelty to her oppressor an option that would naturally occur to her?

"No, WOMAN IS NOT OUR BROTHER; through indolence and depravity we have made of her a being apart, unknown, having no weapon other than her sex, which not only means constant strife but is moreover an unfair weapon of the eternal little slave's mistrust—adoring or hating, but never our frank companion, a being set apart as if in *esprit de corps* and freemasonry."

Many men would still subscribe to these words of Laforgue; many think that there will always be "strife and dispute," as Montaigne put it, and that fraternity will never be possible. The fact is that today neither men nor women are satisfied with each other. But the question is to know whether there is an original curse that condemns them to rend each other or whether the conflicts in which they are opposed merely mark a transitional moment in human history. . . .

. . . Society, being codified by man, decrees that woman is inferior: she can do away with this inferiority only by destroying the male's superiority. She sets about mutilating, dominating man, she contradicts him, she denies his truth and his values. But in doing this she is only defending herself; it was neither a changeless essence nor a mistaken choice that doomed her . . . to inferiority. They were imposed upon her. All oppression creates a state of war. And this is no exception. . . .

. . . The "feminine" woman in making herself prey tries to reduce man, also, to her carnal passivity; she occupies herself in catching him in her trap, in enchaining him by means of the desire she arouses in him in submissively making herself a thing. The emancipated woman, on the contrary, wants to be active, a taker, and refuses the passivity man means to impose on her. . . . But the "modern" woman accepts masculine values: she prides herself on thinking, taking action, working, creating, on the same terms as men; instead of seeking to disparage them, she declares herself their equal.

In so far as she expresses herself in definite action, this claim is legitimate, and male insolence must then bear the blame. But in men's defense it must be said that women are wont to confuse the issue. A Mabel Dodge Luhan intended to subjugate D. H. Lawrence by her feminine charms so as to dominate him spiritually thereafter; many women, in order to show by their successes their equivalence to men, try to secure male support by sexual means; they play on both sides, de-

manding old-fashioned respect and modern esteem, banking on their old magic and their new rights. It is understandable that a man becomes irritated and puts himself on the defensive; but he is also double-dealing when he requires woman to play the game fairly while he denies them the indispensable trump cards through distrust and hostility. Indeed, the struggle cannot be clearly drawn between them. . . . When she makes weapons at once of her weakness and of her strength, it is not a matter of designing calculation: she seeks salvation spontaneously in the way that has been imposed on her, that of passivity, at the same time when she is actively demanding her sovereignty; and no doubt this procedure is unfair tactics, but it is dictated to her by the ambiguous situation assigned her. Man, however, becomes indignant when he treats her as a free and independent being and then realizes that she is still a trap for him; if he gratifies and satisfies her in her posture as prey, he finds her claims to autonomy irritating; whatever he does, he feels tricked and she feels wronged. . . .

. . . It is vain to apportion praise and blame. The truth is that if the vicious circle is so hard to break, it is because the two sexes are each the victim at once of the other and of itself. Between two adversaries confronting each other in their pure liberty, an agreement could be easily reached: the more so as the war profits neither. But the complexity of the whole affair derives from the fact that each camp is giving aid and comfort to the enemy; woman is pursuing a dream of submission, man a dream of identification. . . . Man is concerned with the effort to appear male, important, superior; he pretends so as to get pretense in return; he, too, is aggressive, uneasy; he feels hostility for women because he is afraid of them, he is afraid of them because he is afraid of the personage, the image, with which he identifies himself. What time and strength he squanders in liquidating, sublimating, transferring complexes, in talking about women, in seducing them, in fearing them! He would be liberated himself in their liberation. But this is precisely what he dreads. And so he obstinately persists in the mystifications intended to keep woman in her chains. . . .

That she is being tricked, many men have realized. "What a misfortune to be a woman! And yet the misfortune, when one is a woman, is at bottom not to comprehend that it is one," says Kirkegaard. For a long time there have been efforts to disguise this misfortune. . . . To forbid her working, to keep her at home, is to defend her against herself and to assure her happiness. We have seen what poetic veils are thrown over her monotonous burdens of housekeeping and maternity: in exchange for her liberty she has received the false treasures of her "femininity." Balzac illustrates this maneuver very well in counseling man to treat her as a slave while persuading her that she is a queen. Less cynical, many men try to convince themselves that she is really privileged. There are American sociologists who seriously teach today the theory of "low-class gain." In France, also, it has often been proclaimed—although in a less scientific manner —that the workers are very fortunate in not being obliged to "keep up appearances" and still more so the bums who can dress in rags and sleep on the sidewalks, pleasures forbidden to the Count de Beaumont and the Wendels. Like the carefree wretches gaily scratching at their vermin, like the merry Negroes laughing under the lash and those joyous Tunisian Arabs burying their starved children with a smile, woman enjoys that incomparable privilege: irresponsibility. Free from troublesome burdens and cares, she obviously has "the better part." But it is disturbing that with an obstinate perversity—connected no doubt with original sin—down through the centuries and in all countries, the people who have the better part are always crying to their benefactors: "It is too much! I will be satisfied with yours!" But the munificent capitalists, the generous colonists, the superb males, stick to their guns: "Keep the better part, hold on to it!"

It must be admitted that the males find in woman more complicity than the oppressor usually finds in the oppressed. And in bad faith they take authorization from this to declare that she has *desired* the destiny they have imposed on her. . . . If a child is taught idleness by being amused all day long and never being led to study, or shown its usefulness, it will hardly be said, when he grows up, that he chose to be incapable and ignorant; yet this is how woman is brought up, without ever being impressed with the necessity of taking charge of her own existence. So she readily lets herself come to count on the protection, love, assistance, and supervision of others, she lets herself be fascinated with the hope of self-realization without *doing* anything. She does wrong in yielding to the temptation; but man is in no position to blame her, since he has led her into the temptation. When conflict arises between them, each will hold the other responsible for the situation; she will reproach him with having made her what she is: "No one taught me to reason or to earn my own living"; he will reproach her with having accepted the consequences: "You don't know anything, you are an incompetent," and so on. Each sex thinks it can justify itself by taking the offensive; but the wrongs done by one do not make the other innocent.

The innumerable conflicts that set men and women against one another come from the fact that neither is prepared to assume all the consequences of this situation which the one has offered and the other accepted. The doubtful concept of "equality in inequality," which the one uses to mask his despotism and the other to mask her cowardice, does not stand the test of experience: in their exchanges, woman appeals to the theoretical equality she has been guaranteed, and man the concrete inequality that exists. The result is that in every association an endless debate goes on concerning the ambiguous meaning of the words *give* and *take:* she complains of giving her all, he protests that she takes his all. Woman has to learn that exchanges—it is a fundamental law of political economy—are based on the value the merchandise offered has for the buyer, and not for the seller: she has been deceived in being persuaded that her worth is priceless. The truth is that for man she is an amusement, a pleasure, company, an inessential boon; he is for her the meaning, the justification of her existence. The exchange, therefore, is not of two items of equal value.

This inequality will be especially brought out in the fact that the time they spend together—which fallaciously seems to be the same time—does not have the same value for both partners. During the evening the lover spends with his mistress he could be doing something of advantage to his career, seeing friends, cultivating business relationships, seeking recreation; for a man normally integrated in society, time is a positive value: money, reputation, pleasure. For the idle, bored woman, on the contrary, it is a burden she wishes to get rid of; when she succeeds in killing time, it is a benefit to her: the man's presence is pure profit. In a liaison what most clearly interests the man, in many cases, is the sexual benefit he gets from it: if need be, he can be content to spend no more time with his mistress than is required for the sexual act; but—with exceptions—what she, on her part, wants is to kill all the excess time she has on her hands; and—like the storekeeper who will not sell potatoes unless the customer will take turnips also—she will not yield her body unless her lover will take hours of conversation and "going out" into the bargain. A balance is reached if, on the whole, the cost does not seem too high to the man, and this depends, of course, on the strength of his desire and the importance he gives to what is to be sacrificed. But if the woman demands—offers—too much time, she becomes wholly intrusive, like the river overflowing its banks, and the man will prefer to have nothing rather than too much. Then she reduces her demands; but very often the balance is reached at the cost of a double tension: she feels that the man has "had" her at a bargain, and he thinks her price is too high. This analysis, of course, is put in somewhat humorous terms; but—except for those affairs of jealous and exclu-

sive passion in which the man wants total possession of the woman—this conflict constantly appears in cases of affection, desire, and even love. He always has "other things to do" with his time; whereas she has time to burn; and he considers much of the time she gives him not as a gift but as a burden.

As a rule he consents to assume the burden because he knows very well that he is on the privileged side, he has a bad conscience; and if he is of reasonable good will he tries to compensate for the inequality by being generous. He prides himself on his compassion, however, and at the first clash he treats the woman as ungrateful and thinks, with some irritation: "I'm too good to her." She feels she is behaving like a beggar when she is convinced of the high value of her gifts, and that humiliates her.

Here we find the explanation of the cruelty that woman often shows she is capable of practicing; she has a good conscience because she is on the unprivileged side; she feels she is under no obligation to deal gently with the favored caste, and her only thought is to defend herself. She will even be very happy if she has occasion to show her resentment to a lover who has not been able to satisfy all her demands: since he does not give her enough, she takes savage delight in taking back everything from him. At this point the wounded lover suddenly discovers the value *in toto* of a liaison each moment of which he held more or less in contempt: he is ready to promise her everything, even though he will feel exploited again when he has to make good. He accuses his mistress of blackmailing him: she calls him stingy; both feel wronged.

Once again it is useless to apportion blame and excuses: justice can never be done in the midst of injustice. A colonial administrator has no possibility of acting rightly toward the natives, nor a general toward his soldiers; the only solution is to be neither colonist nor military chief; but a man could not prevent himself from being a man. So there he is, culpable in spite of himself and laboring under the effects of a fault he did not himself commit; and here she is, victim and shrew in spite of herself. Sometimes he rebels and becomes cruel, but then he makes himself an accomplice of the injustice, and the fault becomes really his. Sometimes he lets himself be annihilated, devoured, by his demanding victim; but in that case he feels duped. Often he stops at a compromise that at once belittles him and leaves him ill at ease. A well-disposed man will be more tortured by the situation than the woman herself: in a sense it is always better to be on the side of the vanquished; but if she is well-disposed also, incapable of self-sufficiency, reluctant to crush the man with the weight of her destiny, she struggles in hopeless confusion.

In daily life we meet with an abundance of these cases which are incapable of satisfactory solution because they are determined by unsatisfactory conditions. A man who is compelled to go on materially and morally supporting a woman whom he no longer loves feels he is victimized; but if he abandons without resources the woman who has pledged her whole life to him, she will be quite as unjustly victimized. The evil originates not in the perversity of individuals—and bad faith first appears when each blames the other—it originates rather in a situation against which all individual action is powerless. Women are "clinging," they are a dead weight, and they suffer for it; the point is that their situation is like that of a parasite sucking out the living strength of another organism. Let them be provided with living strength of their own, let them have the means to attack the world and wrest from it their own subsistence, and their dependence will be abolished—that of man also. There is no doubt that both men and women will profit greatly from the new situation. . . .

But is it enough to change laws, institutions, customs, public opinion, and the whole social context, for men and women to become truly equal? "Women will always be women," say the skeptics. Other seers prophesy that in casting off

their femininity they will not succeed in changing themselves into men and they will become monsters. This would be to admit that the woman of today is a creation of nature; it must be repeated once more that in human society nothing is natural and that woman, like much else, is a product elaborated by civilization. The intervention of others in her destiny is fundamental: if this action took a different direction, it would produce a quite different result. Woman is determined not by her hormones or by mysterious instincts, but by the manner in which her body and her relation to the world are modified through the action of others than herself. . . . It is not a question of abolishing in woman the contingencies and miseries of the human condition, but of giving her the means for transcending them.

Woman is the victim of no mysterious fatality; the peculiarities that identify her as specifically a woman get their importance from the significance placed upon them. They can be surmounted, in the future, when they are regarded in new perspectives. . . .

I shall be told that all this is utopian fancy, because woman cannot be "made over" unless society has first made her really the equal of man. Conservatives have never failed in such circumstances to refer to that vicious circle; history, however, does not revolve. If a caste is kept in a state of inferiority, no doubt it remains inferior; but liberty can break the circle. Let the Negroes vote and they become worthy of having the vote; let woman be given responsibilities and she is able to assume them. The fact is that oppressors cannot be expected to make a move of gratuitous generosity; but at one time the revolt of the oppressed, at another time even the very evolution of the privileged caste itself, creates new situations; thus men have been led, in their own interest, to give partial emancipation to women: it remains only for women to continue their ascent, and the successes they are obtaining are an encouragement for them to do so. It seems almost certain that sooner or later they will arrive at complete economic and social equality, which will bring about an inner metamorphosis. . . .

Let us not forget that our lack of imagination always depopulates the future; for us it is only an abstraction; each one of us secretly deplores the absence there of the one who was himself. But the humanity of tomorrow will be living in its flesh and in its conscious liberty; that time will be its present and it will in turn prefer it. New relations of flesh and sentiment of which we have no conception will arise between the sexes; already, indeed, there have appeared between men and women friendships, rivalries, complicities, comradeships—chaste or sensual—which past centuries could not have conceived. To mention one point, nothing could seem to me more debatable than the opinion that dooms the new world to uniformity and hence to boredom. I fail to see that this present world is free from boredom or that liberty ever creates uniformity.

To begin with, there will always be certain differences between man and woman; her eroticism, and therefore her sexual world, have a special form of their own and therefore cannot fail to engender a sensuality, a sensitivity, of a special nature. This means that her relations to her own body, to that of the male, to the child, will never be identical with those the male bears to his own body, to that of the female, and to the child; those who make much of "equality in difference" could not with good grace refuse to grant me the possible existence of differences in equality. Then again, it is institutions that create uniformity. Young and pretty, the slaves of the harem are always the same in the sultan's embrace; Christianity gave eroticism its savor of sin and legend when it endowed the human female with a soul; if society restores her sovereign individuality to woman, it will not thereby destroy the power of love's embrace to move the heart.

It is nonsense to assert that revelry, vice, ecstasy, passion, would become impossible if man and woman were equal in concrete matters; the contradictions that put the flesh in opposition to the spirit, the instant to time, the swoon of immanence to the challenge of transcendence, the absolute of pleasure to the nothingness of forgetting, will never be resolved; in sexuality will always be materialized the tension, the anguish, the joy, the frustration, and the triumph of existence. To emancipate woman is to refuse to confine her to the relations she bears to man, not to deny them to her; let her have her independent existence and she will continue none the less to exist for him *also:* mutually recognizing each other as subject, each will yet remain for the other an *other.* The reciprocity of their relations will not do away with the miracles—desire, possession, love, dream, adventure—worked by the division of human beings into two separate categories; and the words that move us—giving, conquering, uniting—will not lose their meaning. On the contrary, when we abolish the slavery of half of humanity, together with the whole system of hypocrisy that it implies, then the "division" of humanity will reveal its genuine significance and the human couple will find its true form. "The direct, natural, necessary relation of human creatures is the *relation of man to woman,*" Marx has said.[1] "The nature of this relation determines to what point man himself is to be considered as a *generic being,* as mankind; the relation of man to woman is the most natural relation of human being to human being. By it is shown, therefore, to what point the *natural* behavior of man has become *human* or to what point the *human* being has become his *natural* being, to what point his *human nature* has become his *nature.*"

The case could not be better stated. It is for man to establish the reign of liberty in the midst of the world of the given. To gain the supreme victory, it is necessary, for one thing, that by and through their natural differentiation men and women unequivocally affirm their brotherhood.

NOTE

1. *Philosophical Works,* Vol. VI (Marx's italics).

Further Questions

1. Do you believe that relations between men and women would acquire a more creative dimension under conditions of greater equality?

2. In particular, is companionship of equals an important goal in relations between women and men?

3. If a man and a woman spend time together, is the time taken out of the rest of his life more important to him than her time is to her? If so, what are possible solutions to this problem?

Why Men Resist   I.3

WILLIAM J. GOODE

William J. Goode tries to explain why men resist efforts toward more gender equality. It is obvious that men are reluctant to relinquish their powers and privileges. However, there are also less obvious reasons. Men feel hurt and betrayed, because they feel that, as breadwinners, they have given to women more than they have received in return. Men also feel keenly the decrease in perceived importance of being male, which results from women's achievement of increased equality.

Goode taught sociology for many years and is the author of much respected work on the family and related subjects.

Reading Questions

1. Are men prevented from taking full advantage of male privilege because they care about the women in their lives and share a common destiny with them?

2. Is the male or the female role more flexible? That is, which of these roles allows for greater latitude in behavior?

3. Have men, as family breadwinners, made many sacrifices for women? Or were their "gifts" completely deserved by the recipients?

ALTHOUGH FEW IF ANY MEN in the United States remain entirely untouched by the women's movement, to most men what is happening seems to be "out there" and has little direct effect on their own roles. To them, the movement is a dialogue mainly among women, conferences of women about women, a mixture of just or exaggerated complaints and shrill and foolish demands to which men need not even respond, except now and then. When men see that a woman resents a common male act of condescension, such as making fun of women in sports or management, most males are still as surprised as corporation heads are when told to stop polluting a river.

For the time being, men are correct in this perception if one focuses on the short run only. It is not often that social behavior deeply rooted in tradition alters rapidly. Over the longer run, they are not likely to be correct, and indeed I believe they are vaguely uneasy when they consider their present situation. As against numerous popular commentators, I do not think we are now witnessing a return to the old ways, a politically reactionary trend, and I do not think the contemporary attack on male privilege will ultimately fail.

The worldwide demand for equality is voiced not only by women; many groups have pressed for it, with more persistence, strength, and success over the past generation than in any prior epoch of world history. It has also been pressed by more kinds of people than ever before: ethnic and racial groups, castes, subnational groups such as the Scots or Basques, classes, colonies, and political regimes. An ideal so profoundly moving will ultimately prevail, in some measure, where the structural bases for traditional dominance are weakened. The ancient bases for male dominance are no longer as secure as they once were, and male resistance to these pressures will weaken.

Males will stubbornly resist, but reluctantly adjust, because women will continue to want more equality than they now enjoy and will be unhappy if they do not get it; because men on average will prefer that their women be happy; because a majority of either sex will not find an adequate substitute for the other sex; and because neither will be able to build an alternative social system alone. When dominant classes or groups cannot rig the system as much in their favor as they once did, they will work within it just the same; to revise an old adage, if that is the only roulette wheel in town, they will play it even if it is honest and fair.

To many women, the very title of my essay is an exercise in banality, for there is no puzzle. To analyze the peculiar thoughtways of men seems unnecessary, since ultimately their resistance is that of dominant groups throughout history: They enjoy an exploitive position that yields them an unearned profit in money, power, and prestige. Why should they give it up?

The answer contains of course some part of the truth, but we shall move more effectively toward equality only if we grasp much more of the truth that bitter view reveals. If it were completely true, then the greater power of men would have made all societies male-vanity cultures, in which women are kept behind blank walls and forced to work at productive tasks only with their sisters, while men laze away their hours in parasitic pleasure. In fact, one can observe that the position of women varies a good deal by class, by society, and over time, and no one has succeeded in proving that those variations are the simple result of men's exploitation.

Indeed there are inherent socioeconomic contradictions in any attempt by males to create a fully exploitative set of material advantages for all males. Moreover, there are inherent *emotional* contradictions in any effort to achieve full domination in that intimate sphere.

As to the first contradiction, women—and men in the same situation—who are powerless, slavish, and ignorant are most easily exploitable, and thus there are always some male pressures to place them in that position. Unfortunately, such women do not yield much surplus product. In fact, they do not produce much at all. Women who are freer and are more in command of productive skills, as in hunting and gathering societies and increasingly in modern industrial ones, produce far more, but they are also more resistant to exploitation or domination. Without understanding that powerful relationship, men have moved throughout history toward one or the other of these great choices, with their built-in disadvantages and advantages.

As to emotional ties, men would like to be lords of their castle and to be loved absolutely—if successful, this is the cheapest exploitative system—but in real life this is less likely to happen unless one loves in return. In that case what happens is what happens in real life: Men care about the joys and sorrows of their women. Mutual caring reduces the degree to which men are willing to exploit their wives, mothers, and sisters. More interesting, their caring also takes the form of wanting to prevent *other* men from exploiting these women when they are in the outside world. That is, men as individuals know that *they* are to be trusted, and so should have great power, but other men cannot be trusted, and so the laws should restrain such fellows.

These large sets of contrary tensions have some effect on even those contemporary men who do not believe that the present relations between men and women are unjust. Both sets, moreover, support the present trend toward greater equality. In short, men do resist, but these and other tensions prevent them from resisting as fully as they might otherwise, while not so much as a cynical interpretation of their private attitudes would expect. On the other hand, they do resist somewhat more strenuously than we should predict from their public assertion in favor of, for example, equal pay, or slogans like "liberty and justice for all.". . .

A first glance at descriptions of the male role, especially as described in the literature about mass media, social stereotypes, family roles, and personality attributes, suggests that the male role is definite, narrow, and agreed upon. Males, we are told, are pressed into a specific mold. For example, ". . . the male role prescribes that men be active, aggressive, competitive, . . . while the female role prescribes that women should be nurturant, warm, altruistic . . . and the like."[1] The male role requires the suppression of emotion, or "the male role, as personally and socially defined, requires men to appear tough, objective, striving, achieving, unsentimental. . . . If he weeps, if he shows weakness, he will likely be viewed as unmanly. . . . " Or: "Men are programmed to be strong and 'aggressive.'"[2]

We are so accustomed to reading such descriptions that we almost believe them, unless we stop to ask, first, how many men do we actually know who carry out these social prescriptions (i.e., how many are emotionally anesthetized, aggressive, physically tough and daring, unwilling or unable to give nurturance to a child)? Second, and this is the test of a social role, do they lose their membership cards in the male fraternity if they fail in these respects? If socialization and social pressures are so all-powerful, where are all the John Wayne types in our society? Or, to ask a more searching question, how seriously should we take such sex-role prescriptions if so few men live up to them?

The key fact is not that many men do not live up to such prescriptions; rather, it is that many other qualities and performances are also viewed as acceptable or admirable, and this is true even among boys, who are often thought to be strong supporters of sex stereotypes. The *macho* boy is admired, but so is the one who edits the school newspaper, who draws cartoons, or who is simply a warm friend. There are at least a handful of ways of being an admired professor. Indeed a common feminist complaint against the present system is that women are much more narrowly confined in the ways they are permitted to be professors, or members of any occupation.

But we can go further. A much more profound observation is that oppressed groups are *typically* given narrow ranges of social roles, while dominant groups afford their members a far wider set of behavior patterns, each qualitatively different but each still accepted or esteemed in varying degrees. One of the privileges granted, or simply assumed, by ruling groups, is that they can indulge in a variety of eccentricities while still demanding and getting a fair measure of authority or prestige. Consider in this connection, to cite only one spectacular example, the crotchets and quirks cultivated by the English upper classes over the centuries. . . .

We assert, then, that men manage to be in charge of things in all societies but that their very control permits them to create a wide range of ideal male roles, with the consequence that large numbers of men, not just a few, can locate rewarding positions in the social structure. Thereby, too, they considerably narrow the options left for feminine sex roles. Feminists especially resent the narrowness of the feminine role in informal inter-action, where they feel they are dealt with only as women, however this may be softened by per-sonal warmth or affection.

We can recognize that general relationship in a widespread male view, echoed over the centuries, that males are people, individuals, while women are lumped together as an aggregate. Or, in more modern language: Women have roles, a delimited number of parts to play, but men cannot be de-scribed so simply. . . .

The Sociology of Superordinates

That set of relationships is only part of the com-plex male view, and I want to continue with my sketch of the main elements in what may be called the "sociology of superordinates." That is, I believe there are some general principles or regularities to be found in the view held by superordinates—here, the sex-class called males—about relations with subordinates, in this in-stance women. These regularities do not justify, but they do explain in some degree, the modern resistance of men to their new social situation.[3] Here are some of them:

1. The observations made by either men or women about members of the other sex are limited and somewhat biased by what they are most interested in and by their lack of opportunity to observe behind the scenes of each others' lives.[4] However, far less of what men do is determined by women; what men do affects women much more. As a conse-quence, men are often simply less motivated to observe carefully many aspects of women's behavior and activity because women's behavior does not usually affect what men propose to do. By contrast, almost every-thing men do will affect what women *have* to do, and thus women are motivated to observe men's behavior as keenly as they can.

2. Since any given cohort of men know they did not create the system that gives them their advantages, they reject any charges that they conspired to dominate women.

3. Since men, like other dominants or super-ordinates, take for granted the system that gives them their status, they are not aware of how much the social structure, from attitude patterns to laws, pervasively yields small, cumulative, and eventually large advantages in most competitions. As a consequence, they assume that their greater accomplish-ments are actually the result of inborn superiority.

4. As a corollary to this male view, when men weigh their situation, they are more aware of the burdens and responsibilities they bear than of their unearned advantages.

5. Superiors, and thus men, do not easily notice the talents or accomplishments of subordinates, and men have not in the past seen much wisdom in giving women more opportunities for growth, for women are not capable of much anyway, especially in the areas of men's special skills. Thus, in the past, few women have embarrassed men by becoming superior in those areas. When they did, their superiority was seen, and is often still seen, as an odd exception. As a conse-quence, men see their superior position as a just one.

6. Men view even small losses of deference, advantages, or opportunities as large threats. Their own gains, or their maintenance of old advantages, are not noticed as much.[5]

Although the male view is similar to that of superordinates generally, as the foregoing princi-ples suggest, one cannot simply equate the two. The structural position of males is different from that of superordinate groups, classes, ethnic pop-ulations, or castes. Males are, first, not a group, but a social segment or a statistical aggregate within the society. They share much of a com-mon destiny, but they share few if any *group* or *collective* goals (within small groups they may be buddies, but not with all males). Second, males share with certain women whatever gain or loss they experience as members of high or low castes, ethnic groups, or classes. For example, women in a ruling stratum share with their men a high social rank, deference from the lower orders, and so on; men in a lowly Indian caste share that rank with their women, too. In modern societies, men and women in the same family are on a more or less equal basis with respect to "inheritance, educational opportunity (at least undergraduate), personal consumption of goods, most rights before the law, and the love and responsibility of their children."[6] They are not fully equal, to be sure, but much more equal than are members of very different castes or social classes.

Moreover, from the male view, women also enjoy certain exemptions:"freedom from military conscription, whole or partial exemption from certain kinds of heavy work, preferential courtesies of various kinds." Indeed, men believe, on the whole, that their own lot is the more difficult one.[7]

Most important as a structural fact that prevents the male view from being simply that of a superordinate is that these superordinates, like their women, do not live in set-apart communities, neighborhoods, or families. Of course, other such categories are not seqestered either, such as alcoholics, ex-mental patients, or the physically handicapped; but these are, as Goffman points out, "scattered somewhat haphazardly through the social structure." That is not so for men; like their women, they are allocated to households in a nonrandom way, for "law and custom allow only one to a household, but strongly encourage the presence of that one."[8]

A consequence of this important structural arrangement is that men and women are separated from their own sex by having a stake in the organization that gives each a set of different roles, or a different emphasis to similar roles; women especially come to have a vested interest in the social unit that at the same time imposes inequalities on them. This coalition between the two

individuals makes it difficult for members of the same sex to join with large numbers of persons of their own sex for purposes of defense or exploitation. This applies equally to men and women. . . .

Responses of Superordinates to Rebellion[9]

First, men are surprised at the outbreak. They simply had not known the depth of resentment that many women harbored, though of course many women had not known it either. Second, men are also hurt, for they feel betrayed. They discover, or begin to suspect, that the previously contented or pleasant facade their women presented to them was false, that they have been manipulated to believe in that presentation of self. Because males view themselves as giving protection against anyone exploiting or hurting their women, they respond with anger to the hostility they encounter, to the discovery that they were deceived, and to the charge that they have selfishly used the dominant position they feel they have rightfully earned.

A deeper, more complex source of male anger requires a few additional comments, for it relates to a central male role, that of jobholder and breadwinner. Most men, but especially most men outside the privileged stratum of professionals and managers, see their job as not yielding much intrinsic satisfaction, not being fun in itself, but they pride themselves on the hard work and personal sacrifice they make as breadwinners. In the male view, men make a gift of all this to their wives and children.[10]

Now they are told that it was not a gift, and they have not earned any special deference for it. In fact, their wives earned what they received, and indeed nothing is owing. If work was a sacrifice, they are told, so were all the services, comforts, and self-deprivations women provided. Whatever the justice of either claim, clearly if you think you are giving or sacrificing much to make gifts to someone over a period of time, and then you learn he or she feels the gifts were completely deserved, for the countergifts are asserted to have been as great and no gratitude or special debt was incurred, you are likely to be hurt or angry.[11]

I am reasonably certain about the processes I have just described. Let me go a step further and speculate that the male resentment is the greater because many fathers had already come to suspect that their children, especially in adolescence, were indifferent to those sacrifices, as well as to the values that justified them.[12] Thus, when women too begin to assert that men's gifts are not worth as much as men thought, the worth of the male is further denied.

Some Areas of Change and Nonchange

Although I have not heard specific complaints about it, I believe that the most important change in men's position, as they experience it, is a loss of centrality, a decline in the extent to which they are the center of attention. In our time, other superordinates have also suffered this loss: colonial rulers, monarchs and nobles, and U.S. whites both northern and southern, to name a few.

Boys and grown men have always taken for granted that what they were doing was more important than what the other sex was doing, that where they were, was where the action was. Their women accepted that definition. Men occupied the center of the stage, and women's attention was focused on them. Although that position is at times perilous, open to failure, it is also desirable.

Men are still there of course, and will be there throughout our lifetime. Nevertheless, some changes are perceptible. The center of attention shifts to women more now than in the past. I believe that this shift troubles men far more, and creates more of their resistance, than the women's demand for equal opportunity and pay in employment.

The change is especially observable in informal relations, and men who are involved with women in the liberation movement experience it most often. Women find each other more interesting than in the past, and focus more on what each other is doing, for they are in fact doing more interesting things. Even when they are not, their work occupies more of their attention, whether they are professionals or factory workers. Being without a man for a while does not seem to be so bereft a state as it once was. I also believe that this change affects men more now than at the time of the suffragist movement half a century ago, not only because more women now participate in it but also because men were then more solidary and could rely on more all-male organizations and clubs; now, they are more dependent on women for solace and intimacy.

As a side issue, let me note that the loss of centrality has its counterpart among feminist women too, and its subtlety should be noted. Such women now reject a certain type of traditional centrality they used to experience, because its costs are too great. Most women know the experience of being the center of attention: When they enter a male group, conversation changes in tone and subject. They are likely to be the focus of comments, many of them pleasurable: affectionate teasing, compliments, warmth. However, these comments put women into a special mold, the stereotyped female. Their serious comments are not welcomed or applauded, or their ideas are treated as merely amusing. Their sexuality is emphasized. Now, feminist women find that kind of centrality less pleasant—in fact, condescending—and they avoid it when they can. In turn, many men feel awkward in this new situation, for their repertory of social graces is now called boorish. . . .

Phrased in more theoretical terms, the underlying shift is toward the decreasing marginal utility of males, and this I suspect is the main source of men's resistance to women's liberation. That is, fewer people believe that what the male does is indispensable, nonsubstitutable, or adds such a special value to any endeavor that it justifies his extra "price" or reward. In past wars, for example, males enjoyed a very high value not only because it was felt that they could do the job better than women but also because they might well make the difference between being conquered and remaining free. In many societies, their marginal utility came from their contribution of animal protein through hunting. As revolutionary heroes, explorers, hunters, warriors, and daring capitalist entrepreneurs, men felt, and doubtless their women did too, that their contribution was beyond anything women could do. This earned men extra privileges of rank, authority, and creature services.

It is not then as individuals, as persons, that males will be deemed less worthy in the future or their contributions less needed. Rather, they will be seen as having no claim to *extra* rewards solely because they are members of the male sex-class. This is part of a still broader trend of our generation, which will also increasingly deny that being white, or an upper-caste or upper-class person, produces a marginally superior result and thus justifies extra privileges. . . .

NOTES

1. Joseph H. Pleck, "The Psychology of Sex Roles: Traditional and New Views," in *Women and Men: Changing Roles, Relationship and Perceptions,* ed. Libby A. Cater and Anne F. Scott (New York: Aspen Institute for Humanistic Studies, 1976), p. 182. Pleck has carried out the most extensive research on male roles, and I am indebted to him for special help in this inquiry.

2. For these two quotations, see Sidney M. Jourard, "Some Lethal Aspects of the Male Role," p. 22, and Irving London, "Frigidity, Sensitivity, and Sexual Roles," p. 42, in *Men and Masculinity,* ed. Joseph H. Pleck and Jack Sawyer (Englewood Cliffs, N.J.: Prentice-Hall, 1974). See also the summary of such traits in I. K. Braverman et al., "Sex-Role Stereotypes: A Current Appraisal," in *Women and Achievement,* ed. Martha T. S. Mednick, S. S. Tangri, and Lois W. Hoffman (New York: Wiley, 1975), pp. 32–47.

3. Robert Bierstedt's "The Sociology of the Majority," in his *Power and Progress* (New York: McGraw-Hill, 1974), pp. 199–220, does not state these principles, but I was led to them by thinking about his analysis.

4. Robert K. Merton, in "The Perspectives of Insiders and Outsiders," in his *The Sociology of Science* (Chicago: University of Chicago Press, 1973), pp. 99–136, has analyzed this view in some detail.

5. This general pattern is noted at various points in my monograph *The Celebration of Heroes: Prestige as a Social Control System* (Berkeley: University of California Press, 1979).

6. Erving Goffman, "The Arrangement Between the Sexes," *Theory and Society* 4 (1977): 307.

7. Hazel Erskine, "The Polls: Women's Roles," *Public Opinion Quarterly* 35 (Summer 1971).

8. Goffman, "Arrangement Between the Sexes," p. 308.

9. A simple analysis of these responses is presented in William J. Goode, *Principles of Sociology* (New York: McGraw-Hill, 1977), pp. 359 ff.

10. See Joseph H. Pleck, "The Power of Men," in *Women and Men: The Consequences of Power,* ed. Dana V. Hiller and R. Sheets (Cincinnati: Office of Women's Studies, University of Cincinnati, 1977), p. 20. See also Colin Bell and Howard Newby, "Husbands and Wives: The Dynamic of the Deferential Dialectic," in *Dependence and Exploitation in Work and Marriage,* ed. Diana L. Barker and Sheila Allen (London: Longman, 1976), pp. 162–63; as well as Richard Sennett and Jonathan Cobb, *The Hidden Injuries of Class* (New York: Vintage, 1973), p. 125. On the satisfactions of work, see Daniel Yankelovich, "The Meaning of Work," in *The Worker and the Job,* ed. Jerome Rosow (Englewood Cliffs, N.J.: Prentice-Hall, 1974), pp. 19–49.

11. Whatever other sacrifices women want from men, until recently a large majority did *not* believe men should do more housework. On this matter, see Joseph H. Pleck, "Men's New Roles in the Family: Housework and Child Care," to appear in *Family and Sex Roles,* ed. Constantina Safilios-Rothschild, forthcoming. In the mid-1970s, only about one-fourth to one-fifth of wives agreed to such a proposal.

12. Sennett and Cobb, *The Hidden Injuries of Class,* p. 125.

Further Questions

1. Do you believe being male adds something of special value to participants in enterprises outside the personal realm (for example, war, capitalistic ventures, sports, exploration)?

2. Can women acquire a vested interest in a structure, like the family, that creates inequalities for them?

3. Are men forgiven for their behavior in dominating women because, as individuals, men played little part in creating structures that allow them to reap the benefits of male domination?

I.4   White Privilege and Male Privilege: A Personal Account of Coming to See Correspondences Through Work in Women's Studies*

PEGGY MCINTOSH

Peggy McIntosh compares privileges of being white with male privilege. Both are protected by being denied. Those possessing such privileges, in particular, are taught not to recognize them as such. She lists 46 types of circumstances in which white skin is an unearned advantage. She also lists 8 areas in which being heterosexual is an (unearned) social asset, like white skin in being taken for granted by persons so advantaged.

McIntosh is Associate Director of the Center for Research on Women at Wellesley College, Wellesley, MA.

Reading Questions

1. Think of some everyday situations where you are advantaged/disadvantaged by race or class. Then compare your list with McIntosh's. What were the highlights of this comparison?

2. Think of some everyday situations in which you are advantaged/disadvantaged by sexual orientation (homosexual or heterosexual). How do your experiences in this area compare with those mentioned by McIntosh?

* I have appreciated commentary on this paper from the Working Papers Committee of the Wellesley College Center for Research on Women, from members of the Dodge seminar, and from many individuals, including Margaret Andersen, Sorel Berman, Joanne Braxton, Johnella Butler, Sandra Dickerson, Marnie Evans, Beverly Guy-Sheftall, Sandra Harding, Eleanor Hinton Hoyt, Pauline Houston, Paul Lauter, Joyce Miller, Mary Norris, Gloria Oden, Beverly Smith, and John Walter.

THROUGH WORK to bring materials and perspectives from Women's Studies into the rest of the curriculum, I have often noticed men's unwillingness to grant that they are overprivileged in the curriculum, even though they may grant that women are disadvantaged. Denials that amount to taboos surround the subject of advantages that men gain from women's disadvantages. These denials protect male privilege from being fully recognized, acknowledged, lessened, or ended.

Thinking through unacknowledged male privilege as a phenomenon with a life of its own, I realized that since hierarchies in our society are interlocking, there was most likely a phenomenon of white privilege that was similarly denied and protected, but alive and real in its effects. As a white person, I realized I had been taught about racism as something that puts others at a disadvantage, but had been taught not to see one of its corollary aspects, white privilege, which puts me at an advantage.

I think whites are carefully taught not to recognize white privilege, as males are taught not to recognize male privilege. So I have begun in an untutored way to ask what it is like to have white privilege. This paper is a partial record of my personal observations and not a scholarly analysis. It is based on my daily experiences within my particular circumstances.

I have come to see white privilege as an invisible package of unearned assets that I can count on cashing in each day, but about which I was "meant" to remain oblivious. White privilege is like an invisible weightless knapsack of special provisions, assurances, tools, maps, guides, codebooks, passports, visas, clothes, compass, emergency gear, and blank checks.

Since I have had trouble facing white privilege, and describing its results in my life, I saw parallels here with men's reluctance to acknowledge male privilege. Only rarely will a man go beyond acknowledging that women are disadvantaged to acknowledging that men have unearned advantage, or that unearned privilege has not been good for men's development as human beings, or for society's development, or that privilege systems might ever be challenged and *changed*.

I will review here several types or layers of denial that I see at work protecting, and preventing awareness about, entrenched male privilege. Then I will draw parallels, from my own experience, with the denials that veil the facts of white privilege. Finally, I will list forty-six ordinary and daily ways in which I experience having white privilege, by contrast with my African American colleagues in the same building. This list is not intended to be generalizable. Others can make their own lists from within their own life circumstances.

Writing this paper has been difficult, despite warm receptions for the talks on which it is based.[1] For describing white privilege makes one newly accountable. As we in Women's Studies work reveal male privilege and ask men to give up some of their power, so one who writes about having white privilege must ask, "Having described it, what will I do to lessen or end it?"

The denial of men's overprivileged state takes many forms in discussions of curriculum change work. Some claim that men must be central in the curriculum because they have done most of what is important or distinctive in life or in civilization. Some recognize sexism in the curriculum but deny that it makes male students seem unduly important in life. Others agree that certain *individual* thinkers are male oriented but deny that there is any *systemic* tendency in disciplinary frameworks or epistemology to overempower men as a group. Those men who do grant that male privilege takes institutionalized and embedded forms are still likely to deny that male hegemony has opened doors for them personally. Virtually all men deny that male overreward alone can explain men's centrality in all the inner sanctums of our most powerful institutions. Moreover, those few who will acknowledge that male privilege systems have overempowered them usually end up doubting that we could dismantle these privilege systems. They may say they will work to improve women's status, in the society or in the university, but they can't or won't support the idea of lessening men's. In curricular terms, this is the point at which they say that they regret they cannot use any of the interesting new scholarship on women because the syllabus is full. When the talk turns to giving men less cultural room, even the most thoughtful and fair-minded of the men I know will tend to reflect, or fall back on, conservative assumptions about the inevitability of present gender relations and distributions of power, calling on precedent or sociobiology and psychobiology to demonstrate that male domination is natural and follows inevitably from evolutionary pressures. Others resort to arguments from "experience" or religion or social responsibility or wishing and dreaming.

After I realized, through faculty development work in Women's Studies, the extent to which men work from a base of unacknowledged privilege, I understood that much of their oppressiveness was unconscious. Then I remembered the frequent charges from women of color that white women whom they encounter are oppressive. I began to understand why we are justly seen as oppressive, even when we don't see ourselves that way. At the very least, obliviousness of one's privileged state can make a person or group irritating to be with. I began to count the ways in which I enjoy unearned skin privilege and have been conditioned into oblivion about its existence, unable to see that it put me "ahead" in any way, or put my people ahead, overrewarding us and yet also paradoxically damaging us, or that it could or should be changed.

My schooling gave me no training in seeing myself as an oppressor, as an unfairly advantaged person, or as a participant in a damaged culture. I was taught to see myself as an individual whose moral state depended on her individual moral will. At school, we were not taught about slavery in any depth; we were not taught to see slaveholders as damaged people. Slaves were seen as

the only group at risk of being dehumanized. My schooling followed the pattern which Elizabeth Minnich has pointed out: whites are taught to think of their lives as morally neutral, normative, and average, and also ideal, so that when we work to benefit others, this is seen as work that will allow "them" to be more like "us." I think many of us know how obnoxious this attitude can be in men.

After frustration with men who would not recognize male privilege, I decided to try to work on myself at least by identifying some of the daily effects of white privilege in my life. It is crude work, at this stage, but I will give here a list of special circumstances and conditions I experience that I did not earn but that I have been made to feel are mine by birth, by citizenship, and by virtue of being a conscientious law-abiding "normal" person of goodwill. I have chosen those conditions that I think in my case *attach somewhat more to skin-color privilege* than to class, religion, ethnic status, or geographical location, though these other privileging factors are intricately intertwined. As far as I can see, my Afro-American co-workers, friends, and acquaintances with whom I come into daily or frequent contact in this particular time, place, and line of work cannot count on most of these conditions.

1. I can, if I wish, arrange to be in the company of people of my race most of the time.

2. I can avoid spending time with people whom I was trained to mistrust and who have learned to mistrust my kind or me.

3. If I should need to move, I can be pretty sure of renting or purchasing housing in an area which I can afford and in which I would want to live.

4. I can be reasonably sure that my neighbors in such a location will be neutral or pleasant to me.

5. I can go shopping alone most of the time, fairly well assured that I will not be followed or harassed by store detectives.

6. I can turn on the television or open to the front page of the paper and see people of my race widely and positively represented.

7. When I am told about our national heritage or about "civilization," I am shown that people of my color made it what it is.

8. I can be sure that my children will be given curricular materials that testify to the existence of their race.

9. If I want to, I can be pretty sure of finding a publisher for this piece on white privilege.

10. I can be fairly sure of having my voice heard in a group in which I am the only member of my race.

11. I can be casual about whether or not to listen to another woman's voice in a group in which she is the only member of her race.

12. I can go into a book shop and count on finding the writing of my race represented, into a supermarket and find the staple foods that fit with my cultural traditions, into a hairdresser's shop and find someone who can deal with my hair.

13. Whether I use checks, credit cards, or cash, I can count on my skin color not to work against the appearance that I am financially reliable.

14. I could arrange to protect our young children most of the time from people who might not like them.

15. I did not have to educate our children to be aware of systemic racism for their own daily physical protection.

16. I can be pretty sure that my children's teachers and employers will tolerate them if they fit school and workplace norms; my chief worries about them do not concern others' attitudes toward their race.

17. I can talk with my mouth full and not have people put this down to my color.

18. I can swear, or dress in secondhand clothes, or not answer letters, without having people attribute these choices to the bad morals, the poverty, or the illiteracy of my race.

19. I can speak in public to a powerful male group without putting my race on trial.

20. I can do well in a challenging situation without being called a credit to my race.

21. I am never asked to speak for all the people of my racial group.

22. I can remain oblivious to the language and customs of persons of color who constitute the world's majority without feeling in my culture any penalty for such oblivion.

23. I can criticize our government and talk about how much I fear its policies and behavior without being seen as a cultural outsider.

24. I can be reasonably sure that if I ask to talk to "the person in charge," I will be facing a person of my race.

25. If a traffic cop pulls me over or if the IRS audits my tax return, I can be sure I haven't been singled out because of my race.

26. I can easily buy posters, postcards, picture books, greeting cards, dolls, toys, and children's magazines featuring people of my race.

27. I can go home from most meetings of organizations I belong to feeling somewhat tied in, rather than isolated, out of place, outnumbered, unheard, held at a distance, or feared.

28. I can be pretty sure that an argument with a colleague of another race is more likely to jeopardize her chances for advancement than to jeopardize mine.

29. I can be fairly sure that if I argue for the promotion of a person of another race, or a program centering on race, this is not likely to cost me heavily within my present setting, even if my colleagues disagree with me.

30. If I declare there is a racial issue at hand, or there isn't a racial issue at hand, my race will lend me more credibility for either position than a person of color will have.

31. I can choose to ignore developments in minority writing and minority activist programs, or disparage them, or learn from them, but in any case, I can find ways to be more or

less protected from negative consequences of any of these choices.

32. My culture gives me little fear about ignoring the perspectives and powers of people of other races.

33. I am not made acutely aware that my shape, bearing, or body odor will be taken as a reflection on my race.

34. I can worry about racism without being seen as self-interested or self-seeking.

35. I can take a job with an affirmative action employer without having my co-workers on the job suspect that I got it because of my race.

36. If my day, week, or year is going badly, I need not ask of each negative episode or situation whether it has racial overtones.

37. I can be pretty sure of finding people who would be willing to talk with me and advise me about my next steps, professionally.

38. I can think over many options, social, political, imaginative, or professional, without asking whether a person of my race would be accepted or allowed to do what I want to do.

39. I can be late to a meeting without having the lateness reflect on my race.

40. I can choose public accommodation without fearing that people of my race cannot get in or will be mistreated in the places I have chosen.

41. I can be sure that if I need legal or medical help, my race will not work against me.

42. I can arrange my activities so that I will never have to experience feelings of rejection owing to my race.

43. If I have low credibility as a leader, I can be sure that my race is not the problem.

44. I can easily find academic courses and institutions that give attention only to people of my race.

45. I can expect figurative language and imagery in all of the arts to testify to experiences of my race.

46. I can choose blemish cover or bandages in "flesh" color and have them more or less match my skin.

I repeatedly forgot each of the realizations on this list until I wrote it down. For me, white privilege has turned out to be an elusive and fugitive subject. The pressure to avoid it is great, for in facing it I must give up the myth of meritocracy. If these things are true, this is not such a free country; one's life is not what one makes it; many doors open for certain people through no virtues of their own. These perceptions mean also that my moral condition is not what I had been led to believe. The appearance of being a good citizen rather than a troublemaker comes in large part from having all sorts of doors open automatically because of my color.

A further paralysis of nerve comes from literary silence protecting privilege. My clearest memories of finding such analysis are in Lillian Smith's unparalleled *Killers of the Dream* and Margaret Andersen's review of Karen and Mamie Fields' *Lemon Swamp*. Smith, for example, wrote about walking toward black children on the street and knowing they would step into the gutter; Andersen contrasted the pleasure that she, as a white child, took on summer driving trips to the south with Karen Fields' memories of driving in a closed car stocked with all necessities lest, in stopping, her black family should suffer "insult, or worse." Adrienne Rich also recognizes and writes about daily experiences of privilege, but in my observation, white women's writing in this area is far more often on systemic racism than on our daily lives as light-skinned women.[2]

In unpacking this invisible knapsack of white privilege, I have listed conditions of daily experience that I once took for granted, as neutral, normal, and universally available to everybody, just as I once thought of a male-focused curriculum as the neutral or accurate account that can speak for all. Nor did I think of any of these perquisites as bad for the holder. I now think that we need a more finely differentiated taxonomy of privilege, for some of these varieties are only what one would want for everyone in a just society, and others give license to be ignorant, oblivious, arrogant, and destructive. Before proposing some more finely tuned categorization, I will make some observations about the general effects of these conditions on my life and expectations.

In this potpourri of examples, some privileges make me feel at home in the world. Others allow me to escape penalties or dangers that others suffer. Through some, I escape fear, anxiety, insult, injury, or a sense of not being welcome, not being real. Some keep me from having to hide, to be in disguise, to feel sick or crazy, to negotiate each transaction from the position of being an outsider or, within my group, a person who is suspected of having too close links with a dominant culture. Most keep me from having to be angry.

I see a pattern running through the matrix of white privilege, a pattern of assumptions that were passed on to me as a white person. There was one main piece of cultural turf; it was my own turf, and I was among those who could control the turf. I could measure up to the cultural standards and take advantage of the many options I saw around me to make what the culture would call a success of my life. *My skin color was an asset for any move I was educated to want to make.* I could think of myself as "belonging" in major ways and of making social systems work for me. I could freely disparage, fear, neglect, or be oblivious to anything outside of the dominant cultural forms. Being of the main culture, I could also criticize it fairly freely. My life was reflected back to me frequently enough so that I felt, with regard to my race, if not to my sex, like one of the real people.

Whether through the curriculum or in the newspaper, the television, the economic system, or the general look of people in the streets, I received daily signals and indications that my people counted and that others *either didn't exist or must be trying, not very successfully, to be like people of my race.* I was given cultural permission not to hear voices of people of other races or a tepid cultural tolerance for hearing or acting on such voices. I was also raised not to suffer seriously from anything that darker-skinned people might

say about my group, "protected," though perhaps I should more accurately say *prohibited,* through the habits of my economic class and social group, from living in racially mixed groups or being reflective about interactions between people of differing races.

In proportion as my racial group was being made confident, comfortable, and oblivious, other groups were likely being made unconfident, uncomfortable, and alienated. Whiteness protected me from many kinds of hostility, distress, and violence, which I was being subtly trained to visit in turn upon people of color.

For this reason, the word "privilege" now seems to me misleading. Its connotations are too positive to fit the conditions and behaviors which "privilege systems" produce. We usually think of privilege as being a favored state, whether earned, or conferred by birth or luck. School graduates are reminded they are privileged and urged to use their (enviable) assets well. The word "privilege" carries the connotation of being something everyone must want. Yet some of the conditions I have described here work to systemically overempower certain groups. Such privilege simply *confers dominance,* gives permission to control, because of one's race or sex. The kind of privilege that gives license to some people to be, at best, thoughtless and, at worst, murderous should not continue to be referred to as a desirable attribute. Such "privilege" may be widely desired without being in any way beneficial to the whole society.

Moreover, though "privilege" may confer power, it does not confer moral strength. Those who do not depend on conferred dominance have traits and qualities that may never develop in those who do. Just as Women's Studies courses indicate that women survive their political circumstances to lead lives that hold the human race together, so "underprivileged" people of color who are the world's majority have survived their oppression and lived survivors' lives from which the white global minority can and must learn. In some groups, those dominated have actually become strong through *not* having all of these unearned advantages, and this gives them a great deal to teach the others. Members of so-called privileged groups can seem foolish, ridiculous, infantile, or dangerous by contrast.

I want, then, to distinguish between earned strength and unearned power conferred systemically. Power from unearned privilege can look like strength when it is, in fact, permission to escape or to dominate. But not all of the privileges on my list are inevitably damaging. Some, like the expectation that neighbors will be decent to you, or that your race will not count against you in court, should be the norm in a just society and should be considered as the entitlement of everyone. Others, like the privilege not to listen to less powerful people, distort the humanity of the holders as well as the ignored groups. Still others, like finding one's staple foods everywhere, may be a function of being a member of a numerical majority in the population. Others have to do with not having to labor under pervasive negative stereotyping and mythology.

We might at least start by distinguishing between positive advantages that we can work to spread, to the point where they are not advantages at all but simply part of the normal civic and social fabric, and negative types of advantage that unless rejected will always reinforce our present hierarchies. For example, the positive "privilege" of belonging, the feeling that one belongs within the human circle, as Native Americans say, fosters development and should not be seen as privilege for a few. It is, let us say, an entitlement that none of us should have to earn; ideally it is an *unearned entitlement*. At present, since only a few have it, it is an *unearned advantage* for them. The negative "privilege" that gave me cultural permission not to take darker-skinned Others seriously can be seen as arbitrarily conferred dominance and should not be desirable for anyone. This paper results from a process of coming to see that some of the power that I originally saw as attendant on being a human being in the United States consisted in *unearned advantage* and *con-*

ferred dominance, as well as other kinds of special circumstance not universally taken for granted.

In writing this paper I have also realized that white identity and status (as well as class identity and status) give me considerable power to choose whether to broach this subject and its trouble. I can pretty well decide whether to disappear and avoid and not listen and escape the dislike I may engender in other people through this essay, or interrupt, answer, interpret, preach, correct, criticize, and control to some extent what goes on in reaction to it. Being white, I am given considerable power to escape many kinds of danger or penalty as well as to choose which risks I want to take.

There is an analogy here, once again, with Women's Studies. Our male colleagues do not have a great deal to lose in supporting Women's Studies, but they do not have a great deal to lose if they oppose it either. They simply have the power to decide whether to commit themselves to more equitable distributions of power. They will probably feel few penalties whatever choice they make; they do not seem, in any obvious short-term sense, the ones at risk, though they and we are all at risk because of the behaviors that have been rewarded in them.

Through Women's Studies work I have met very few men who are truly distressed about systemic, unearned male advantage and conferred dominance. And so one question for me and others like me is whether we will be like them, or whether we will get truly distressed, even outraged, about unearned race advantage and conferred dominance and if so, what we will do to lessen them. In any case, we need to do more work in identifying how they actually affect our daily lives. We need more down-to-earth writing by people about these taboo subjects. We need more understanding of the ways in which white "privilege" damages white people, for these are not the same ways in which it damages the victimized. Skewed white psyches are an inseparable part of the picture, though I do not want to confuse the kinds of damage done to the holders of special assets and to those who suffer the deficits. Many, perhaps most, of our white students in the United States think that racism doesn't affect them because they are not people of color; they do not see "whiteness" as a racial identity. Many men likewise think that Women's Studies does not bear on their own existences because they are not female; they do not see themselves as having gendered identities. Insisting on the universal "effects" of "privilege" systems, then, becomes one of our chief tasks, and being more explicit about the *particular* effects in particular contexts in another. Men need to join us in this work.

In addition, since race and sex are not the only advantaging systems at work, we need to similarly examine the daily experience of having age advantage, or ethnic advantage, or physical ability, or advantage related to nationality, religion, or sexual orientation. Professor Marnie Evans suggested to me that in many ways the list I made also applies directly to heterosexual privilege. This is a still more taboo subject than race privilege: the daily ways in which heterosexual privilege makes some persons comfortable or powerful, providing supports, assets, approvals, and rewards to those who live or expect to live in heterosexual pairs. Unpacking that content is still more difficult, owing to the deeper imbeddedness of heterosexual advantage and dominance and stricter taboos surrounding these.

But to start such an analysis I would put this observation from my own experience: The fact that I live under the same roof with a man triggers all kinds of societal assumptions about my worth, politics, life, and values and triggers a host of unearned advantages and powers. After recasting many elements from the original list I would add further observations like these:

1. My children do not have to answer questions about why I live with my partner (my husband).
2. I have no difficulty finding neighborhoods where people approve of our household.

3. Our children are given texts and classes that implicitly support our kind of family unit and do not turn them against my choice of domestic partnership.
4. I can travel alone or with my husband without expecting embarrassment or hostility in those who deal with us.
5. Most people I meet will see my marital arrangements as an asset to my life or as a favorable comment on my likability, my competence, or my mental health.
6. I can talk about the social events of a weekend without fearing most listeners' reactions.
7. I will feel welcomed and "normal" in the usual walks of public life, institutional and social.
8. In many contexts, I am seen as "all right" in daily work on women because I do not live chiefly with women.

Difficulties and dangers surrounding the task of finding parallels are many. Since racism, sexism, and heterosexism are not the same, the advantages associated with them should not be seen as the same. In addition, it is hard to isolate aspects of unearned advantage that derive chiefly from social class, economic class, race, religion, region, sex, or ethnic identity. The oppressions are both distinct and interlocking, as the Combahee River Collective statement of 1977 continues to remind us eloquently.[3]

One factor seems clear about all of the interlocking oppressions. They take both active forms that we can see and embedded forms that members of the dominant group are taught not to see. In my class and place, I did not see myself as racist because I was taught to recognize racism only in individual acts of meanness by members of my group, never in invisible systems conferring racial dominance on my group from birth. Likewise, we are taught to think that sexism or heterosexism is carried on only through intentional, individual acts of discrimination, meanness, or cruelty, rather than in invisible systems conferring unsought dominance on certain groups. Disapproving of the systems won't be enough to change them. I was taught to think that racism could end if white individuals changed their attitudes; many men think sexism can be ended by individual changes in daily behavior toward women. But a man's sex provides advantage for him whether or not he approves of the way in which dominance has been conferred on his group. A "white" skin in the United States opens many doors for whites whether or not we approve of the way dominance has been conferred on us. Individual acts can palliate, but cannot end, these problems. To redesign social systems, we need first to acknowledge their colossal unseen dimensions. The silences and denials surrounding privilege are the key political tool here. They keep the thinking about equality or equity incomplete, protecting unearned advantage and conferred dominance by making these taboo subjects. Most talk by whites about equal opportunity seems to me now to be about equal opportunity to try to get into a position of dominance while denying that *systems* of dominance exist.

Obliviousness about white advantage, like obliviousness about male advantage, is kept strongly inculturated in the United States so as to maintain the myth of meritocracy, the myth that democratic choice is equally available to all. Keeping most people unaware that freedom of confident action is there for just a small number of people props up those in power and serves to keep power in the hands of the same groups that have most of it already. Though systemic change takes many decades, there are pressing questions for me and I imagine for some others like me if we raise our daily consciousness on the perquisites of being light-skinned. What will we do with such knowledge? As we know from watching men, it is an open question whether we will choose to use unearned advantage to weaken invisible privilege systems and whether we will use any of our arbitrarily awarded power to try to reconstruct power systems on a broader base.

NOTES

1. This paper was presented at the Virginia Women's Studies Association conference in Richmond in April, 1986, and the American Educational Research Association conference in Boston in October, 1986, and discussed with two groups of participants in the Dodge seminars for Secondary School Teachers in New York and Boston in the spring of 1987.

2. Andersen, Margaret, "Race and the Social Science Curriculum: A Teaching and Learning Discussion." *Radical Teacher,* November, 1984, pp. 17–20. Smith, Lillian, *Killers of the Dream,* New York: W. W. Norton, 1949.

3. "A Black Feminist Statement," The Combahee River Collective, pp. 13–22 in G. Hull, P. Scott, B. Smith, Eds., *All the Women Are White, All the Blacks Are Men, But Some of Us Are Brave: Black Women's Studies,* Old Westbury, NY: The Feminist Press, 1982.

Further Questions

1. If you are of the advantaged race or sexual orientation, do you easily forget the unearned advantages that come your way because of this?

2. Do you agree that unearned privileges confer only power and dominance, and do not necessarily make advantaged groups morally correct or morally strong?

3. How does recognition of white and heterosexual privileges enlighten you about the system of male privilege?

The Uses of Anger: Women Responding to Racism* I.5

AUDRE LORDE

Audre Lorde discusses anger as a response to racism; her comments, however, apply to oppression of any sort. She is angry that white women believe in the inevitability of systems that put whites at the center, women of color somewhere on the fringe. She sees no reason to refrain from expressing this anger out of fear of provoking guilt feelings either in herself or in the white women at which it is directed. Anger can be a positive force in bringing differences to the surface and making productive use of them.

Lorde teaches English at Hunter College in New York City. Many of her poems, essays, fiction, and speeches are articulate statements of her experience as a black lesbian feminist. (Another writing by Audre Lorde appears in Part XIII.)

Reading Questions

1. What is your idea of racism, and your response to it? Would your response be different if you were of a different race?

2. Is responding to racism among women too much of a distraction from the more important task of destroying patriarchy?

3. What productive response can you make to someone who is angry about your solidarity with a group that is oppressing her group?

RACISM. THE BELIEF in the inherent superiority of one race over all others and thereby the right to dominance, manifest and implied.

Women respond to racism. My response to racism is anger. I have lived with that anger, ignoring it, feeding upon it, learning to use it before it laid my visions to waste, for most of my life. Once I did it in silence, afraid of the weight. My fear of anger taught me nothing. Your fear of that anger will teach you nothing, also.

Women responding to racism means women responding to anger; the anger of exclusion, of unquestioned privilege, of racial distortions, of silence, ill-use, stereotyping, defensiveness, misnaming, betrayal, and co-optation.

My anger is a response to racist attitudes and to the actions and presumptions that arise out of those attitudes. If your dealings with other women reflect those attitudes, then my anger and your attendant fears are spotlights that can be used for growth in the same way I have used learning to express anger for my growth. But for corrective surgery, not guilt. Guilt and defensiveness are bricks in a wall against which we all flounder; they serve none of our futures.

Because I do not want this to become a theoretical discussion, I am going to give a few examples of interchanges between women that illustrate these points. In the interest of time, I am going

* Keynote presentation at the National Women's Studies Association Conference, Storrs, Connecticut, June *1981*.

to cut them short. I want you to know there were many more.

For example:

- I speak out of direct and particular anger at an academic conference, and a white woman says, "Tell me how you feel but don't say it too harshly or I cannot hear you." But is it my manner that keeps her from hearing, or the threat of a message that her life may change?
- The Women's Studies Program of a southern university invites a Black woman to read following a week-long forum on Black and white women. "What has this week given to you?" I ask. The most vocal white woman says, "I think I've gotten a lot. I feel Black women really understand me a lot better now; they have a better idea of where I'm coming from." As if understanding her lay at the core of the racist problem.
- After fifteen years of a women's movement which professes to address the life concerns and possible futures of all women, I still hear, on campus after campus, "How can we address the issues of racism? No women of Color attended." Or, the other side of that statement, "We have no one in our department equipped to teach their work." In other words, racism is a Black women's problem, a problem of women of Color, and only we can discuss it.
- After I read from my work entitled "Poems for Women in Rage,"* a white woman asks me: "Are you going to do anything with how we can deal directly with *our* anger? I feel it's so important." I ask, "How do you use *your* rage?" And then I have to turn away from the blank look in her eyes, before she can invite me to participate in her own annihilation. I do not exist to feel her anger for her.

- White women are beginning to examine their relationships to Black women, yet often I hear them wanting only to deal with little colored children across the roads of childhood, the beloved nursemaid, the occasional second-grade classmate—those tender memories of what was once mysterious and intriguing or neutral. You avoid the childhood assumptions formed by the raucous laughter at Rastus and Alfalfa, the acute message of your mommy's handkerchief spread upon the park bench because I had just been sitting there, the indelible and dehumanizing portraits of Amos 'n Andy and your daddy's humorous bedtime stories.
- I wheel my two-year-old daughter in a shopping cart through a supermarket in Eastchester in 1967, and a little white girl riding past in her mother's cart calls out excitedly, "Oh look, Mommy, a baby maid!" And your mother shushes you, but she does not correct you. And so fifteen years later, at a conference on racism, you can still find that story humorous. But I hear your laughter is full of terror and dis-ease.
- A white academic welcomes the appearance of a collection by non-Black women of Color.† "It allows me to deal with racism without dealing with the harshness of Black women," she says to me.
- At an international cultural gathering of women, a well-known white american woman poet interrupts the reading of the work of women of Color to read her own poem, and then dashes off to an "important panel."

If women in the academy truly want a dialogue about racism, it will require recognizing

---

* One poem from this series is included in *Chosen Poems: Old and New* (W. W. Norton and Company, New York, 1978), pp. 105–108.

† *This Bridge Called My Back: Writings by Radical Women of Color* edited by Cherríe Moraga and Gloria Anzaldua (Kitchen Table: Women of Color Press, New York, 1984), first published in 1981.

the needs and the living contexts of other women. When an academic woman says, "I can't afford it," she may mean she is making a choice about how to spend her available money. But when a woman on welfare says, "I can't afford it," she means that she is surviving on an amount of money that was barely subsistence in 1972, and she often does not have enough to eat. Yet the National Women's Studies Association here in 1981 holds a conference in which it commits itself to responding to racism, yet refuses to waive the registration fee for poor women and women of Color who wished to present and conduct workshops. This has made it impossible for many women of Color—for instance, Wilmette Brown, of Black Women for Wages for Housework—to participate in this conference. Is this to be merely another case of the academy discussing life within the closed circuits of the academy?

To the white women present who recognize these attitudes as familiar, but most of all, to all my sisters of Color who live and survive thousands of such encounters—to my sisters of Color who like me still tremble their rage under harness, or who sometimes question the expression of our rage as useless and disruptive (the two most popular accusations)—I want to speak about anger, my anger, and what I have learned from my travels through its dominions.

Everything can be used / except what is wasteful / (you will need/ to remember this when you are accused of destruction.) *

Every woman has a well-stocked arsenal of anger potentially useful against those oppressions, personal and institutional, which brought that anger into being. Focused with precision it can become a powerful source of energy serving progress and change. And when I speak of change, I do not mean a simple switch of positions or a temporary lessening of tensions, nor

the ability to smile or feel good. I am speaking of a basic and radical alteration in those assumptions underlining our lives.

I have seen situations where white women hear a racist remark, resent what has been said, become filled with fury, and remain silent because they are afraid. That unexpressed anger lies within them like an undetonated device, usually to be hurled at the first woman of Color who talks about racism.

But anger expressed and translated into action in the service of our vision and our future is a liberating and strengthening act of clarification, for it is in the painful process of this translation that we identify who are our allies with whom we have grave differences, and who are our genuine enemies.

Anger is loaded with information and energy. When I speak of women of Color, I do not only mean Black women. The woman of Color who is not Black and who charges me with rendering her invisible by assuming that her struggles with racism are identical with my own has something to tell me that I had better learn from, lest we both waste ourselves fighting the truths between us. If I participate, knowingly or otherwise, in my sister's oppression and she calls me on it, to answer her anger with my own only blankets the substance of our exchange with reaction. It wastes energy. And yes, it is very difficult to stand still and to listen to another woman's voice delineate an agony I do not share, or one to which I myself have contributed.

In this place we speak removed from the more blatant reminders of our embattlement as women. This need not blind us to the size and complexities of the forces mounting against us and all that is most human within our environment. We are not here as women examining racism in a political and social vacuum. We operate in the teeth of a system for which racism and sexism are primary, established, and necessary props of profit. Women responding to racism is a topic so dangerous that when the local media attempt to discredit this conference they choose to focus

* From "For Each of You," first published in *From a Land Where Other People Live* (Broadside Press, Detroit, 1973), and collected in *Chosen Poems: Old and New* (W. W. Norton and Company, New York, 1982), p. 42.

upon the provision of lesbian housing as a diversionary device—as if the Hartford *Courant* dare not mention the topic chosen for discussion here, racism, lest it become apparent that women are in fact attempting to examine and to alter all the repressive conditions of our lives.

Mainstream communication does not want women, particularly white women, responding to racism. It wants racism to be accepted as an immutable given in the fabric of your existence, like eveningtime or the common cold.

So we are working in a context of opposition and threat, the cause of which is certainly not the angers which lie between us, but rather that virulent hatred leveled against all women, people of Color, lesbians and gay men, poor people—against all of us who are seeking to examine the particulars of our lives as we resist our oppressions, moving toward coalition and effective action.

Any discussion among women about racism must include the recognition and the use of anger. This discussion must be direct and creative because it is crucial. We cannot allow our fear of anger to deflect us nor seduce us into settling for anything less than the hard work of excavating honesty; we must be quite serious about the choice of this topic and the angers entwined within it because, rest assured, our opponents are quite serious about their hatred of us and of what we are trying to do here.

And while we scrutinize the often painful face of each other's anger, please remember that it is not our anger which makes me caution you to lock your doors at night and not to wander the streets of Hartford alone. It is the hatred which lurks in those streets, that urge to destroy us all if we truly work for change rather than merely indulge in academic rhetoric.

This hatred and our anger are very different. Hatred is the fury of those who do not share our goals, and its object is death and destruction. Anger is a grief of distortions between peers, and its object is change. But our time is getting shorter. We have been raised to view any differ-ence other than sex as a reason for destruction, and for Black women and white women to face each other's angers without denial or immobility or silence or guilt is in itself a heretical and generative idea. It implies peers meeting upon a common basis to examine difference, and to alter those distortions which history has created around our difference. For it is those distortions which separate us. And we must ask ourselves: Who profits from all this?

Women of Color in america have grown up within a symphony of anger, at being silenced, at being unchosen, at knowing that when we survive, it is in spite of a world that takes for granted our lack of humanness, and which hates our very existence outside of its service. And I say *symphony* rather than *cacophony* because we have had to learn to orchestrate those furies so that they do not tear us apart. We have had to learn to move through them and use them for strength and force and insight within our daily lives. Those of us who did not learn this difficult lesson did not survive. And part of my anger is always libation for my fallen sisters.

Anger is an appropriate reaction to racist attitudes, as is fury when the actions arising from those attitudes do not change. To those women here who fear the anger of women of Color more than their own unscrutinized racist attitudes, I ask: Is the anger of women of Color more threatening than the woman-hatred that tinges all aspects of our lives?

It is not the anger of other women that will destroy us but our refusals to stand still, to listen to its rhythms, to learn within it, to move beyond the manner of presentation to the substance, to tap that anger as an important source of empowerment.

I cannot hide my anger to spare you guilt, nor hurt feelings, nor answering anger; for to do so insults and trivializes all our efforts. Guilt is not a response to anger; it is a response to one's own actions or lack of action. If it leads to change then it can be useful, since it is then no longer guilt but the beginning of knowledge. Yet all too often, guilt is just another name for impotence, for defensiveness destructive of communication; it becomes a device to protect ignorance and the continuation of things the way they are, the ultimate protection for changelessness.

Most women have not developed tools for facing anger constructively. CR groups in the past, largely white, dealt with how to express anger, usually at the world of men. And these groups were made up of white women who shared the terms of their oppressions. There was usually little attempt to articulate the genuine differences between women, such as those of race, color, age, class, and sexual identity. There was no apparent need at that time to examine the contradictions of self, woman as oppressor. There was work on expressing anger, but very little on anger directed against each other. No tools were developed to deal with other women's anger except to avoid it, deflect it, or flee from it under a blanket of guilt.

I have no creative use for guilt, yours or my own. Guilt is only another way of avoiding informed action, of buying time out of the pressing need to make clear choices, out of the approaching storm that can feed the earth as well as bend the trees. If I speak to you in anger, at least I have spoken to you: I have not put a gun to your head and shot you down in the street; I have not looked at your bleeding sister's body and asked, "What did she do to deserve it?" This was the reaction of two white women to Mary Church Terrell's telling of the lynching of a pregnant Black woman whose baby was then torn from her body. That was in 1921, and Alice Paul had just refused to publicly endorse the enforcement of the Nineteenth Amendment for all women—by refusing to endorse the inclusion of women of Color, although we had worked to help bring about that amendment.

The angers between women will not kill us if we can articulate them with precision, if we listen to the content of what is said with at least as much intensity as we defend ourselves against the manner of saying. When we turn from anger we turn from insight, saying we will accept only the designs already known, deadly and safely familiar. I have tried to learn my anger's usefulness to me, as well as its limitations.

For women raised to fear, too often anger threatens annihilation. In the male construct of brute force, we were taught that our lives depended upon the good will of patriarchal power. The anger of others was to be avoided at all costs because there was nothing to be learned from it but pain, a judgment that we had been bad girls, come up lacking, not done what we were supposed to do. And if we accept our powerlessness, then of course any anger can destroy us.

But the strength of women lies in recognizing differences between us as creative, and in standing to those distortions which we inherited without blame, but which are now ours to alter. The angers of women can transform difference through insight into power. For anger between peers births change, not destruction, and the discomfort and sense of loss it often causes is not fatal, but a sign of growth.

My response to racism is anger. That anger has eaten clefts into my living only when it remained unspoken, useless to anyone. It has also served me in classrooms without light or learning, where the work and history of Black women was less than a vapor. It has served me as fire in the ice zone of uncomprehending eyes of white women who see in my experience and the experience of my people only new reasons for fear or guilt. And my anger is no excuse for not dealing with your blindness, no reason to withdraw from the results of your own actions.

When women of Color speak out of the anger that laces so many of our contacts with white women, we are often told that we are "creating a mood of hopelessness," "preventing white women from getting past guilt," or "standing in the way of trusting communication and action." All these quotes come directly from letters to me from members of this organization within the last two years. One woman wrote, "Because you are Black and Lesbian, you seem to speak with the moral authority of suffering." Yes, I am Black and Lesbian, and what you hear in my voice is fury, not suffering. Anger, not moral authority. There is a difference.

To turn aside from the anger of Black women with excuses or the pretexts of intimidation is to award no one power—it is merely another way of preserving racial blindness, the power of unaddressed privilege, unbreached, intact. Guilt is only another form of objectification. Oppressed peoples are always being asked to stretch a little more, to bridge the gap between blindness and humanity. Black women are expected to use our anger only in the service of other people's salvation or learning. But that time is over. My anger has meant pain to me but it has also meant survival, and before I give it up I'm going to be sure that there is something at least as powerful to replace it on the road to clarity.

What woman here is so enamoured of her own oppression that she cannot see her heelprint upon another woman's face? What woman's terms of oppression have become precious and necessary to her as a ticket into the fold of the righteous, away from the cold winds of self-scrutiny?

I am a lesbian woman of Color whose children eat regularly because I work in a university. If their full bellies make me fail to recognize my commonality with a woman of Color whose children do not eat because she cannot find work, or who has no children because her insides are rotted from home abortions and sterilization; if I fail to recognize the lesbian who chooses not to have children, the woman who remains closeted because her homophobic community is her only life support, the woman who chooses silence instead of another death, the woman who is terrified lest my anger trigger the explosion of hers; if I fail to recognize them as other faces of myself, then I am contributing not only to each of their oppressions but also to my own, and the anger which stands between us then must be used for clarity and mutual empowerment, not for evasion by guilt or for further separation. I am not free while any woman is unfree, even when her shackles are very different from my own. And I am not free as long as one person of Color remains chained. Nor is any one of you.

I speak here as a woman of Color who is not bent upon destruction, but upon survival. No woman is responsible for altering the psyche of her oppressor, even when that psyche is embodied in another woman. I have suckled the wolf's lip of anger and I have used it for illumination, laughter, protection, fire in places where there was no light, no food, no sisters, no quarter. We are not goddesses or matriarchs or edifices of divine forgiveness; we are not fiery fingers of judgment or instruments of flagellation; we are women forced back always upon our woman's power. We have learned to use anger as we have learned to use the dead flesh of animals, and bruised, battered, and changing, we have survived and grown and, in Angela Wilson's words, we *are* moving on. With or without uncolored women. We use whatever strengths we have fought for, including anger, to help define and fashion a world where all our sisters can grow, where our children can love, and where the power of touching and meeting another woman's difference and wonder will eventually transcend the need for destruction.

For it is not the anger of Black women which is dripping down over this globe like a diseased liquid. It is not my anger that launches rockets, spends over sixty thousand dollars a second on missiles and other agents of war and death, slaughters children in cities, stockpiles nerve gas and chemical bombs, sodomizes our daughters and our earth. It is not the anger of Black women which corrodes into blind, dehumanizing power, bent upon the annihilation of us all unless we meet it with what we have, our power to examine and to redefine the terms upon which we will live and work; our power to envision and to reconstruct, anger by painful anger, stone upon heavy stone, a future of pollinating difference and the earth to support our choices.

We welcome all women who can meet us, face to face, beyond objectification and beyond guilt.

Further Questions

1. Should you refrain from becoming angry about oppression because you might create a situation where you or someone else feels guilty?

2. Is someone's guilt reaction to anger at bottom a response to her own attitudes and actions?

3. Can anger be a useful force in breaking down ignorance and developing alternatives to continuation of an undesirable status quo?

Growing Up Asian in America   I.6

KESAYA E. NODA

Kesaya E. Noda is a Japanese American woman. She has difficulty defining herself, however, because of tensions between her sense of self as developed within her community and culture and the often hostile and ignorant messages she receives from outside this culture. "Japanese," "American," and "woman" are discussed from both perspectives.

Born in California, Kesaya Noda is a sansei writer who now lives in the Boston area.

Reading Questions

1. Do you think of yourself as part of the mainstream in your country because of your ancestry? If not, how do you feel about people who do think this way? How do you think they feel about you?

2. What does being a citizen or permanent resident of your country mean to you? If you or your parents were born elsewhere, how have you developed loyalties to your country? Do you feel more a part of your community than of your country?

3. What does it mean to you to be a woman (or man)?

SOMETIMES WHEN I was growing up, my identity seemed to hurtle toward me and paste itself right to my face. I felt that way, encountering the stereotypes of my race perpetuated by non-Japanese people (primarily white) who may or may not have had contact with other Japanese in America. "You don't like cheese, do you?" someone would ask. "I know your people don't like cheese." Sometimes questions came making allu-sions to history. That was another aspect of the identity. Events that had happened quite apart from the me who stood silent in that moment connected my face with an incomprehensible past. "Your parents were in California? Were they in those camps during the war?" And sometimes there were phrases or nicknames: "Lotus Blossom." I was sometimes addressed or referred to as racially Japanese, sometimes as Japanese American, and sometimes as an Asian woman. Confusions and distortions abounded.

How is one to know and define oneself? From the inside—within a context that is self defined, from a grounding in community and a connection with culture and history that are comfortably accepted? Or from the outside—in terms of messages received from the media and people who are often ignorant? Even as an adult I can still see two sides of my face and past. I can see from the inside out, in freedom. And I can see from the outside in, driven by the old voices of childhood and lost in anger and fear.

I Am Racially Japanese

A voice from my childhood says: "You are other. You are less than. You are unalterably alien." This voice has its own history. We have indeed been seen as other and alien since the early years of our arrival in the United States. The very first immigrants were welcomed and sought as laborers to replace the dwindling numbers of Chinese, whose influx had been cut off by the Chinese Exclusion Act of 1882. The Japanese fell natural heir to the same anti-Asian prejudice that had arisen against the Chinese. As soon as they began striking for better wages, they were no longer welcomed.

I can see myself today as a person historically defined by law and custom as being forever alien. Being neither "free white," nor "African," our people in California were deemed "aliens, ineligible for citizenship," no matter how long they intended to stay here. Aliens ineligible for citizenship were prohibited from owning, buying, or leasing land. They did not and could not belong here. The voice in me remembers that I am always a *Japanese* American in the eyes of many. A third-generation German American is an American. A third-generation Japanese American is a Japanese American. Being Japanese means being a danger to the country during the war and knowing how to use chopsticks. I wear this history on my face.

I move to the other side. I see a different light and claim a different context. My race is a line that stretches across ocean and time to link me to the shrine where my grandmother was raised. Two high, white banners lift in the wind at the top of the stone steps leading to the shrine. It is time for the summer festival. Black characters are written against the sky as boldly as the clouds, as lightly as kites, as sharply as the big black crows I used to see above the fields in New Hampshire. At festival time there is liquor and food, ritual, discipline, and abandonment. There is music and drunkenness and invocation. There is hope. Another season has come. Another season has gone.

I am racially Japanese. I have a certain claim to this crazy place where the prayers intoned by a neighboring Shinto priest (standing in for my grandmother's nephew who is sick) are drowned out by the rehearsals for the pop singing contest in which most of the villagers will compete later that night. The village elders, the priest, and I stand respectfully upon the immaculate, shining wooden floor of the outer shrine, bowing our heads before the hidden powers. During the patchy intervals when I can hear him, I notice the priest has a stutter. His voice flutters up to my ears only occasionally because two men and a woman are singing gustily into a microphone in the compound, testing the sound system. A prerecorded tape of guitars, samisens, and drums accompanies them. Rock music and Shinto prayers. That night, to loud applause and cheers, a young man is given the award for the most *netsuretsu*—passionate, burning—rendition of a song. We roar our approval of the reward. Never mind that his voice had wandered and slid, now slightly above, now slightly below the given line of the melody. Netsuretsu. Netsuretsu.

In the morning, my grandmother's sister kneels at the foot of the stone stairs to offer her morning prayers. She is too crippled to climb the stairs, so each morning she kneels here upon the path. She shuts her eyes for a few seconds, her motions as matter of fact as when she washes rice. I linger longer than she does, so reluctant to leave, savoring the connection I feel with my grandmother in America, the past, and the power that lives and shines in the morning sun.

Our family has served this shrine for generations. The family's need to protect this claim to identity and place outweighs any individual claim to any individual hope. I am Japanese.

I Am a Japanese American

"Weak." I hear the voice from my childhood years. "Passive," I hear. Our parents and grandparents were the ones who were put into those camps. They went without resistance; they offered cooperation as proof of loyalty to America. "Victim," I hear. And, "Silent."

Our parents are painted as hard workers who were socially uncomfortable and had difficulty expressing even the smallest opinion. Clean, quiet, motivated, and determined to match the American way; that is us, and that is the story of our time here.

"Why did you go into those camps," I raged at my parents, frightened by my own inner silence and timidity. "Why didn't you do anything to resist? Why didn't you name it the injustice it was?" Couldn't our parents even think? Couldn't they? Why were we so passive?

I shift my vision and my stance. I am in California. My uncle is in the midst of the sweet potato harvest. He is pressed, trying to get the harvesting crews onto the field as quickly as possible, worried about the flow of equipment and people. His big pickup is pulled off to the side, motor running, door ajar. I see two tractors in the yard in front of an old shed; the flat bed harvesting platform on which the workers will stand has already been brought over from the other field. It's early morning. The workers stand loosely grouped and at ease, but my uncle looks as harried and tense as a police officer trying to unsnarl a New York City traffic jam. Driving toward the shed, I pull my car off the road to make way for an approaching tractor. The front wheels of the car sink luxuriously into the soft, white

sand by the roadside and the car slides to a dreamy halt, tail still on the road. I try to move forward. I try to move back. The front bites contentedly into the sand, the back lifts itself at a jaunty angle. My uncle sees me and storms down the road, running. He is shouting before he is even near me.

"What's the matter with you," he screams. "What the hell are you doing?" In his frenzy, he grabs his hat off his head and slashes it through the air across his knee. He is beside himself. "Don't you know how to drive in sand? What's the matter with you? You've blocked the whole roadway. How am I supposed to get my tractors out of here? Can't you use your head? You've cut off the whole roadway, and we've got to get out of here."

I stand on the road before him helplessly thinking, "No, I don't know how to drive in sand. I've never driven in sand."

"I'm sorry, uncle," I say, burying a smile beneath a look of sincere apology. I notice my deep amusement and my affection for him with great curiosity. I am usually devastated by anger. Not this time.

During the several years that follow I learn about the people and the place, and much more about what has happened in this California village where my parents grew up. The issei, our grandparents, made this settlement in the desert. Their first crops were eaten by rabbits and ravaged by insects. The land was so barren that men walking from house to house sometimes got lost. Women came here too. They bore children in 114 degree heat, then carried the babies with them into the fields to nurse when they reached the end of each row of grapes or other truck farm crops.

I had had no idea what it meant to buy this kind of land and make it grow green. Or how, when the war came, there was no space at all for the subtlety of being who we were—Japanese Americans. Either/or was the way. I hadn't understood that people were literally afraid for their lives then, that their money had been frozen in banks; that there was a five-mile travel limit; that when the early evening curfew came and they were inside their houses, some of them watched helplessly as people they knew went into their barns to steal their belongings. The police were patrolling the road, interested only in violators of curfew. There was no help for them in the face of thievery. I had not been able to imagine before what it must have felt like to be an American—to know absolutely that one is an American—and yet to have almost everyone else deny it. Not only deny it, but challenge that identity with machine guns and troops of white American soldiers. In those circumstances it was difficult to say, "I'm a Japanese American." "American" had to do.

But now I can say that I am a Japanese American. It means I have a place here in this country, too. I have a place here on the East Coast, where our neighbor is so much a part of our family that my mother never passes her house at night without glancing at the lights to see if she is home and safe; where my parents have hauled hundreds of pounds of rocks from fields and arduously planted Christmas trees and blueberries, lilacs, asparagus, and crab apples; where my father still dreams of angling a stream to a new bed so that he can dig a pond in the field and fill it with water and fish. "The neighbors already came for their Christmas tree?" he asks in December. "Did they like it? Did they like it?"

I have a place on the West Coast where my relatives still farm, where I heard the stories of feuds and backbiting, and where I saw that people survived and flourished because fundamentally they trusted and relied upon one another. A death in the family is not just a death in a family; it is a death in the community. I saw people help each other with money, materials, labor, attention, and time. I saw men gather once a year, without fail, to clean the grounds of a ninety-year-old woman who had helped the community before, during, and after the war. I saw her remembering them with birthday cards sent to each of their children.

I come from a people with a long memory and a distinctive grace. We live our thanks. And we are Americans. Japanese Americans.

I Am a Japanese American Woman

Woman. The last piece of my identity. It has been easier by far for me to know myself in Japan and to see my place in America than it has been to accept my line of connection with my own mother. She was my dark self, a figure in whom I thought I saw all that I feared most in myself. Growing into womanhood and looking for some model of strength, I turned away from her. Of course, I could not find what I sought. I was looking for a black feminist or a white feminist. My mother is neither white nor black.

My mother is a woman who speaks with her life as much as with her tongue. I think of her with her own mother. Grandmother had Parkinson's disease and it had frozen her gait and set her fingers, tongue, and feet jerking and trembling in a terrible dance. My aunts and uncles wanted her to be able to live in her own home. They fed her, bathed her, dressed her, awoke at midnight to take her for one last trip to the bathroom. My aunts (her daughters-in-law) did most of the care, but my mother went from New Hampshire to California each summer to spend a month living with grandmother, because she wanted to and because she wanted to give my aunts at least a small rest. During those hot summer days, mother lay on the couch watching the television or reading, cooking foods that grandmother liked, and speaking little. Grandmother thrived under her care.

The time finally came when it was too dangerous for grandmother to live alone. My relatives kept finding her on the floor beside her bed when they went to wake her in the mornings. My mother flew to California to help clean the house and make arrangements for grandmother to enter a local nursing home. On her last day at home, while grandmother was sitting in her big, over-stuffed armchair, hair combed and wearing a green summer dress, my mother went to her and knelt at her feet. "Here, Mamma," she said. "I've polished your shoes." She lifted grandmother's legs and helped her into the shiny black shoes. My grandmother looked down and smiled slightly. She left her house walking, supported by her children, carrying her pocket book, and wearing her polished black shoes. "Look, Mamma," my mom had said, kneeling. "I've polished your shoes."

Just the other day, my mother came to Boston to visit. She had recently lost a lot of weight and was pleased with her new shape and her feeling of good health. "Look at me, Kes," she exclaimed, turning toward me, front and back, as naked as the day she was born. I saw her small breasts and the wide, brown scar, belly button to pubic hair, that marked her because my brother and I were both born by Caesarean section. Her hips were small. I was not a large baby, but there was so little room for me in her that when she was carrying me she could not even begin to bend over toward the floor. She hated it, she said.

"Don't I look good? Don't you think I look good?"

I looked at my mother, smiling and as happy as she, thinking of all the times I have seen her naked. I have seen both my parents naked throughout my life, as they have seen me. From childhood through adulthood we've had our naked moments, sharing baths, idle conversations picked up as we moved between showers and closets, hurried moments at the beginning of days, quiet moments at the end of days.

I know this to be Japanese, this ease with the physical, and it makes me think of an old, Japanese folk song. A young nursemaid, a fifteen-year-old girl, is singing a lullaby to a baby who is strapped to her back. The nursemaid has been sent as a servant to a place far from her own home. "We're the beggars," she says, "and they are the nice people. Nice people wear fine sashes. Nice clothes."

If I should drop dead,
bury me by the roadside!

I'll give a flower
to everyone who passes.

What kind of flower?
The cam-cam-camellia [tsun-tsun-tsubaki]
watered by Heaven:
alms water.[1]

The nursemaid is the intersection of heaven and earth, the intersection of the human, the natural world, the body, and the soul. In this song, with clear eyes, she looks steadily at life, which is sometimes so very terrible and sad. I think of her while looking at my mother, who is standing on the red and purple carpet before me, laughing, without any clothes.

I am my mother's daughter. And I am myself.
I am a Japanese American woman.

Epilogue

I recently heard a man from West Africa share some memories of his childhood. He was raised Muslim, but when he was a young man, he found himself deeply drawn to Christianity. He struggled against this inner impulse for years, trying to avoid the church yet feeling pushed to return to it again and again. "I would have done *anything* to avoid the change," he said. At last, he became Christian. Afterwards he was afraid to go home, fearing that he would not be accepted. The fear was groundless, he discovered, when at last he returned—he had separated himself, but his family and friends (all Muslim) had not separated themselves from him.

The man, who is now a professor of religion, said that in the Africa he knew as a child and a young man, pluralism was embraced rather than feared. There was "a kind of tolerance that did not deny your particularity," he said. He alluded to zestful, spontaneous debates that would sometimes loudly erupt between Muslims and Christians in the village's public spaces. His memories of an atheist who harangued the villagers when he came to visit them once a week moved me deeply. Perhaps the man was an agricultural advisor or inspector. He harassed the women. He would say:

> Don't go to the fields! Don't even bother to go to the fields. Let God take care of you. He'll send you the food. If you believe in God, why do you need to work? You don't need to work! Let God put the seeds in the ground. Stay home.

The professor said, "The women laughed, you know? They just laughed. Their attitude was, 'Here is a child of God. When will he come home?'"

The storyteller, the professor of religion, smiled a most fantastic, tender smile as he told this story. "In my country, there is a deep affirmation of the oneness of God," he said. "The atheist and the women were having quite different experiences in their encounter, though the atheist did not know this. He saw himself as quite separate from the women. But the women did not see themselves as being separate from him. 'Here is a child of God,' they said. 'When will he come home?'"

NOTE

1. Patia R. Isaku, *Mountain Storm, Pine Breeze: Folk Song in Japan* (Tucson, Ariz.: University of Arizona Press, 1981), 41.

Further Questions

1. Does being an alien (with ancestors from another country or of a minority race) mean being less than? Less than *what* and *why*?

2. Are there certain features of your ancestry or race which you believe are stereotypes, ideas in people's minds, rather than commonalities of your group or features of you in particular?

3. As a woman (or a man), do you feel that you are less than members of the other gender, or that you are sometimes perceived and treated that way?

I.7   Toward a Feminist Theory of Disability

SUSAN WENDELL

Susan Wendell argues that the disabled are oppressed in an able-bodied society, despite the lack of a theory linking this form of oppression with sexism, racism, and other oppressions. We idealize the human body so much that none of us feel completely accepting of our bodies. This idealization is a major force in excluding the physically disabled from the mainstream. We see disabled people as "other" than us, meaning that they are not fellow experiencing human beings in their own right; instead, they are mere objects in our own experience, usually symbolizing something we reject as a possible aspect of ourselves and project onto them.

Wendell teaches philosophy and women's studies at Simon Fraser University in British Columbia.

Reading Questions

1. In what ways, or for what reasons, do you think of a disabled person as different from you?

2. Do you think of yourself as having a disability? If so, do you try to deny it in yourself and conceal it from others?

3. Suppose someone says he has an illness, but it has not been recognized as such, or diagnosed by the medical profession. Is there a tendency to think it is all in his head?

IN 1985, I FELL ILL overnight with what turned out to be a disabling chronic disease. In the long struggle to come to terms with it, I had to learn to live with a body that felt entirely different to me—weak, tired, painful, nauseated, dizzy, unpredictable. I learned at first by listening to other people with chronic illnesses or disabilities; suddenly able-bodied people seemed to me profoundly ignorant of everything I most needed to know. Although doctors told me there was a good chance I would eventually recover completely, I realized after a year that waiting to get well, hoping to recover my healthy body, was a dangerous strategy. I began slowly to identify with my new disabled body and to learn to work with it. As I moved back into the world, I also began to experience the world as structured for people who have no weaknesses.[1] The process of encountering the able-bodied world led me gradually to identify myself as a disabled person, and to reflect on the nature of disability. . . .

Disabled women struggle with both the oppressions of being women in male-dominated societies and the oppressions of being disabled in societies dominated by the able-bodied. They are bringing the knowledge and concerns of women with disabilities into feminism and feminist perspectives into the disability rights movement. To build a feminist theory of disability that takes adequate account of our differences, we will need to know how experiences of disability and the social oppression of the disabled interact with sexism, racism, and class oppression. . . .

The Social Construction of Disability

If we ask the questions: Why are so many disabled people unemployed or underemployed, impoverished, lonely, isolated; why do so many find it difficult or impossible to get an education (Davis and Marshall 1987; Fine and Asch 1988, 10–11); why are they victims of violence and coercion; why do able-bodied people ridicule, avoid, pity, stereotype and patronize them?, we may be tempted to see the disabled as victims of nature or accident. Feminists should be, and many are, profoundly suspicious of this answer. We are used to countering claims that insofar as women are oppressed they are oppressed by nature, which puts them at a disadvantage in the competition for power and resources. We know that if being biologically female is a disadvantage, it is because a social context makes it a disadvantage. From the standpoint of a disabled person, one can see how society could minimize the disadvantages of most disabilities, and, in some instances, turn them into advantages.

Consider an extreme case: the situation of physicist Stephen Hawking, who has had Amyotrophic Lateral Sclerosis (Lou Gehrig's Disease) for more than 27 years. Professor Hawking can no longer speak and is capable of only the smallest muscle movements. Yet, in his context of social and technological support, he is able to function as a professor of physics at Cambridge University; indeed he says his disability has given him the *advantage* of having more time to think, and he is one of the foremost theoretical physicists of our time. He is a courageous and talented man, but he is able to live the creative life he has only because of the help of his family, three nurses, a graduate student who travels with him to maintain his computer-communications systems, and the fact that his talent had been developed and recognized before he fell seriously ill (*Newsweek* 1988).

Many people consider providing resources for disabled people a form of charity, . . . in part because the disabled are perceived as unproductive members of society. Yet most disabled people are placed in a double-bind: they have access to inadequate resources because they are unemployed or underemployed, and they are unemployed or underemployed because they lack the resources that would enable them to make their full contribution to society (Matthews 1983; Hannaford 1985). Often governments and charity organizations will spend far more money to keep disabled people in institutions where they have no chance to be productive than they will spend to enable the same people to live independently and productively. In addition, many of the "special" resources the disabled need merely compensate for bad social planning that is based on the illusion that everyone is young, strong, healthy (and, often, male).

Disability is also frequently regarded as a personal or family problem rather than a matter for social responsibility. Disabled people are often expected to overcome obstacles to participation by their own extraordinary efforts, or their families are expected to provide what they need (sometimes at great personal sacrifice). . . .

In the split between the public and the private worlds, women (and children) have been relegated to the private, and so have the disabled, the sick and the old (and mostly women to take care of them). The public world is the world of strength, the positive (valued) body, performance and production, the able-bodied and youth. Weakness, illness, rest and recovery, pain, death and the negative (de-valued) body are private, generally hidden, and often neglected. Coming into the public world with illness, pain or a de-valued body, we encounter resistance to mixing the two worlds; the split is vividly revealed. Much of our experience goes underground, because there is no socially acceptable way of expressing it and having our physical and psychological experience acknowledged and shared. A few close friends may share it, but there is a strong impulse to protect them from it too, because it seems so private, so unacceptable. I found that, after a couple of years of illness, even answering the question, "How are you?" became a difficult, conflict-ridden business. I don't want to alienate my friends from my experience, but I don't want to risk their discomfort and rejection by telling them what they don't want to know. . . . [2]

If the able-bodied saw the disabled as potentially themselves or as their future selves, they would be more inclined to feel that society should be organized to provide the resources that would make disabled people fully integrated and contributing members. They would feel that "charity" is as inappropriate a way of thinking about resources for disabled people as it is about emergency medical care or education.

Careful study of the lives of disabled people will reveal how artificial the line is that we draw between the biological and the social. Feminists have already challenged this line in part by showing how processes such as childbirth, menstruation and menopause, which may be represented, treated, and therefore experienced as illnesses or disabilities, are socially-constructed from biological reality (Rich 1976; Ehrenreich and English

1979). Disabled people's relations to our bodies involve elements of struggle which perhaps cannot be eliminated, perhaps not even mitigated, by social arrangements. *But,* much of what is *disabling* about our physical conditions is also a consequence of social arrangements (Finger 1983; Browne, Connors and Stern 1985; Fine and Asch 1988) which could, but do not, either compensate for our physical conditions, or accommodate them so that we can participate fully, or support our struggles and integrate us into the community *and our struggles into the cultural concept of life as it is ordinarily lived.* . . .

The Oppression of Disabled People Is the Oppression of Everyone's Real Body

Our real human bodies are exceedingly diverse—in size, shape, colour, texture, structure, function, range and habits of movement, and development—and they are constantly changing. Yet we do not absorb or reflect this simple fact in our culture. Instead, we idealize the human body. Our physical ideals change from time to time, but we always have ideals. These ideals are not just about appearance; they are also ideals of strength and energy and proper control of the body. We are perpetually bombarded with images of these ideals, demands for them, and offers of consumer products and services to help us achieve them.[3] Idealizing the body prevents everyone, able-bodied and disabled, from identifying with and loving her/his real body. Some people can have the illusion of acceptance that comes from believing that their bodies are "close enough" to the ideal, but this illusion only draws them deeper into identifying with the ideal and into the endless task of reconciling the reality with it. Sooner or later they must fail.

Before I became disabled, I was one of those people who felt "close enough" to cultural ideals to be reasonably accepting of my body. Like most feminists I know, I was aware of some alienation from it, and I worked at liking my body better. Nevertheless, I knew in my heart that too much of my liking still depended on being "close enough." When I was disabled by illness, I experienced a much more profound alienation from my body. After a year spent mostly in bed, I could barely identify my body as my own. I felt that "it" was torturing "me," trapping me in exhaustion, pain and inability to do many of the simplest things I did when I was healthy. The shock of this experience and the effort to identify with a new, disabled body, made me realize I had been living a luxury of the able-bodied. The able-bodied can postpone the task of identifying with their *real* bodies. The disabled don't have the luxury of demanding that their bodies fit the physical ideals of their culture. As Barbara Hillyer Davis says: "For all of us the difficult work of finding (one's) self includes the body, but people who live with disability in a society that glorifies fitness and physical conformity are forced to understand more fully what bodily integrity means" (Davis 1984,3).

In a society which idealizes the body, the physically disabled are marginalized. People learn to identify with their own strengths (by cultural standards) and to hate, fear and neglect their own weaknesses. The disabled are not only de-valued for their de-valued bodies (Hannaford 1985); they are constant reminders to the able-bodied of the negative body—of what the able-bodied are trying to avoid, forget and ignore (Lessing 1981). For example, if someone tells me she is in pain, she reminds me of the existence of pain, the imperfection and fragility of the body, the possibility of my own pain, the *inevitability* of it. The less willing I am to accept all these, the less I want to know about her pain; if I cannot avoid it in her presence, I will avoid her. I may even blame her for it. I may tell myself that she *could have* avoided it, in order to go on believing that I *can* avoid it. I want to believe I am not like her; I cling to the differences. Gradually, I make her "other" because I don't want to confront my real body, which I fear and cannot accept.[4]

Disabled people can participate in marginalizing ourselves. We can wish for bodies we do not have, with frustration, shame, self-hatred. We can feel trapped in the negative body; it is our internalized oppression to feel this. Every (visibly or invisibly) disabled person I have talked to or read has felt this; some never stop feeling it. In addition, disabled women suffer more than disabled men from the demand that people have "ideal" bodies, because in patriarchal culture people judge women more by their bodies than they do men. Disabled women often do not feel seen (because they are often not seen) by others as whole people, especially not as sexual people (Campling 1981; Matthews 1983; Hannaford 1985; Fine and Asch 1988). . . .

. . . In a culture which loves the idea that the body can be controlled, those who cannot control their bodies are seen (and may see themselves) as failures.

When you listen to this culture in a disabled body, you hear how often health and physical vigour are talked about as if they were moral virtues. People constantly praise others for their "energy," their stamina, their ability to work long hours. Of course, acting on behalf of one's health can be a virtue, and undermining one's health can be a vice, but "success" at being healthy, like beauty, is always partly a matter of luck and therefore beyond our control. When health is spoken of as a virtue, people who lack it are made to feel inadequate. I am not suggesting that it is always wrong to praise people's physical strength or accomplishments, any more than it is always wrong to praise their physical beauty. But just as treating cultural standards of beauty as essential virtues for women harms most women, treating health and vigour as moral virtues for everyone harms people with disabilities and illnesses.

The myth that the body can be controlled is not easily dispelled, because it is not very vulnerable to evidence against it. When I became ill, several people wanted to discuss with me what I thought I had done to "make myself" ill or "allow myself" to become sick. At first I fell in with this, generating theories about what I had done wrong; even though I had always taken good care of my health, I was able to find some (rather far-fetched) accounts of my responsibility for my illness. When a few close friends offered hypotheses as to how *they* might be responsible for my being ill, I began to suspect that something was wrong. Gradually, I realized that we were all trying to believe that nothing this important is beyond our control. . . .

Disabled People as "Other"

When we make people "other," we group them together as the objects of *our* experience instead of regarding them as fellow *subjects* of experience with whom we might identify. If you are "other" to me, I see you primarily as symbolic of something else—usually, but not always, something I reject and fear and that I project onto you. We can all do this to each other, but very often the process is not symmetrical, because one group of people may have more power to call itself the paradigm of humanity and to make the world suit its own needs and validate its own experiences.[5] Disabled people are "other" to able-bodied people. . . .

One recent attempt to reduce the "otherness" of disabled people is the introduction of the term, "differently-abled." I assume the point of using this term is to suggest that there is nothing *wrong* with being the way we are, just different. Yet to call someone "differently-abled" is much like calling her "differently-coloured" or "differently-gendered." It says: "This person is not the norm or paradigm of humanity." If anything, it increases the "otherness" of disabled people, because it reinforces the paradigm of humanity as young, strong and healthy, with all body parts working "perfectly," from which this person is "different." Using the term "differently-abled" also suggests a (polite? patronizing? protective? self-protective?) disregard of the special difficulties, struggles and suffering disabled people face. We are *dis-abled*. We live with particular social and physical struggles that are partly consequences of the conditions of our bodies and partly consequences of the structures and expectations of our societies, but they are struggles which only people with bodies like ours experience.

The positive side of the term "differently-abled" is that it might remind the able-bodied that to be disabled in some respects is not to be disabled in all respects. It also suggests that a disabled person may have abilities that the able-bodied lack in virtue of being able-bodied. Nevertheless, on the whole, the term "differently-abled" should be abandoned, because it reinforces the able-bodied paradigm of humanity and fails to acknowledge the struggles disabled people face.

The problems of being "the other" to a dominant group are always politically complex. One solution is to emphasize similarities to the dominant group in the hope that they will identify with the oppressed, recognize their rights, gradually give them equal opportunities, and eventually assimilate them. Many disabled people are tired of being symbols to the able-bodied, visible only or primarily for their disabilities, and they want nothing more than to be seen as individuals rather than as members of the group, "the disabled." Emphasizing similarities to the able-bodied, making their disabilities unnoticeable in comparison to their other human qualities may bring about assimilation one-by-one. It does not directly challenge the able-bodied paradigm of humanity, just as women moving into traditionally male arenas of power does not directly challenge the male paradigm of humanity, although both may produce a gradual change in the paradigms. In addition, assimilation may be very difficult for the disabled to achieve. Although the able-bodied like disabled tokens who do not seem very different from themselves, they may *need* someone to carry the burden of the negative body as long as they continue to idealize and try to control the body. They may therefore resist the assimilation of most disabled people.

The reasons in favour of the alternative solution to "otherness"—*emphasizing difference* from the able-bodied—are also reasons for emphasizing similarities among the disabled, especially so-cial and political similarities. Disabled people share positions of social oppression that separate us from the able-bodied, and we share physical, psychological and social experiences of disability. Emphasizing differences from the able-bodied demands that those differences be acknowledged and respected and fosters solidarity among the disabled. It challenges the able-bodied paradigm of humanity and creates the possibility of a deeper challenge to the idealization of the body and the demand for its control. Invisibly disabled people tend to be drawn to solutions that emphasize difference, because our need to have our struggles acknowledged is great, and we have far less experience than those who are visibly disabled of being symbolic to the able-bodied.

Whether one wants to emphasize sameness or difference in dealing with the problem of being "the other" depends in part on how radically one wants to challenge the value-structure of the dominant group. A very important issue in this category for both women and disabled people is the value of independence from the help of others, so highly esteemed in our patriarchal culture and now being questioned in feminist ethics (see, for example, Sherwin 1984, 1987; Kittay and Meyers 1987) and discussed in the writings of disabled women (see, for example, Fisher and Galler 1981; Davis 1984; Frank 1988). Many disabled people who can see the possibility of living as independently as any able-bodied person, or who have achieved this goal after long struggle, value their independence above everything. Dependence on the help of others is humiliating in a society which prizes independence. In addition, this issue holds special complications for disabled women; reading the stories of women who became disabled as adults, I was struck by their struggle with shame and loss of self-esteem at being transformed from people who took physical care of others (husbands and children) to people who were physically dependent. All this suggests that disabled people need every bit of independence we can get. Yet there are disabled people who will always need a lot of help from other individuals just to survive (those who have very little control of movement, for example), and to the extent that everyone considers independence necessary to respect and self-esteem, those people will be condemned to be de-valued. In addition, some disabled people spend tremendous energy being independent in ways that might be considered trivial in a culture less insistent on self-reliance; if our culture valued *interdependence* more highly, they could use that energy for more satisfying activities. . . .

When you are very ill, you desperately need medical validation of your experience, not only for economic reasons (insurance claims, pensions, welfare and disability benefits all depend upon official diagnosis), but also for social and psychological reasons. People with unrecognized illnesses are often abandoned by their friends and families.[6] Because almost everyone accepts the cognitive authority of medicine, the person whose bodily experience is radically different from medical descriptions of her/his condition is invalidated as a knower. Either you decide to hide your experience, or you are socially isolated with it by being labelled mentally ill[7] or dishonest. In both cases you are silenced.

Even when your experience is recognized by medicine, it is often re-described in ways that are inaccurate from your standpoint. The objectively observable condition of your body may be used to determine the severity of your pain, for instance, regardless of your own reports of it. For example, until recently, relatively few doctors were willing to acknowledge that severe phantom limb pain can persist for months or even years after an amputation. The accumulated experience of doctors who were themselves amputees has begun to legitimize the other patients' reports (Madruga 1979).

When you are forced to realize that other people have more social authority than you do to describe your experience of your own body, your confidence in yourself and your relationship to reality is radically undermined. What can you know if you cannot know that you are experiencing suffering or joy; what can you communicate to people who don't believe you know even this?[8] Most people will censor what they tell or say nothing rather than expose themselves repeatedly to such deeply felt invalidation. They are silenced by fear and confusion. The process is familiar from our understanding of how women are silenced in and by patriarchal culture.

One final caution: As with women's "special knowledge," there is a danger of sentimentalizing disabled people's knowledge and abilities and keeping us "other" by doing so. We need to bring this knowledge into the culture and to transform the culture and society so that everyone can receive and make use of it, so that it can be fully integrated, along with disabled people, into a shared social life. . . .

NOTES

1. Itzhak Perlman, when asked in a recent CBC interview about the problems of the disabled, said disabled people have two problems: the fact that the world is not made for people with any weaknesses but for supermen and the attitudes of able-bodied people.

2. Some people save me that trouble by *telling me* I am fine and walking away. Of course, people also encounter difficulties with answering "How are you?" during and after crises, such as separation from a partner, death of a loved one, or a nervous breakdown. There is a temporary alienation from what is considered ordinary shared experience. In disability, the alienation lasts longer, often for a lifetime, and, in my experience, it is more profound.

3. The idealization of the body is clearly related in complex ways to the economic processes of a consumer society. Since it pre-dated capitalism, we know that capitalism did not cause it, but it is undeniable that idealization now generates tremendous profits and that the quest for profit demands the reinforcement of idealization and the constant development of new ideals.

4. Susan Griffin, in a characteristically honest and insightful passage, describes an encounter with the fear that makes it hard to identify with disabled people. See Griffin 1982, 648–649.

5. When Simone de Beauvoir uses this term to elucidate men's view of women (and women's view of ourselves), she emphasizes that Man is considered essential, Woman inessential; Man is the Subject, Woman the Other (de Beauvoir 1952, xvi). Susan Griffin expands upon this idea by showing how we project rejected aspects of ourselves onto groups of people who are designated the Other (Griffin 1981).

6. Accounts of the experience of relatively unknown, newly-discovered, or hard-to-diagnose diseases and conditions confirm this. See, for example, Jeffreys 1982, for the story of an experience of Chronic Fatigue Syndrome, which is more common in women than in men.

7. Frequently people with undiagnosed illnesses are sent by their doctors to psychiatrists, who cannot help and may send them back to their doctors saying they must be physically ill. This can leave patients in a dangerous medical and social limbo. Sometimes they commit suicide because of it (Ramsay 1986). Psychiatrists who know enough about living with physical illness or disability to help someone cope with it are rare.

8. For more discussion of this subject, see Zaner 1983 and Rawlinson 1983.

REFERENCES

Addelson, Kathryn P. 1983. The man of professional wisdom. In *Discovering reality*. Sandra Harding and Merrill B. Hintikka, eds. Boston: D. Reidel.

Alcoff, Linda. 1988. Cultural feminism versus post-structuralism: The identity crisis in feminist theory. *Signs: Journal of Women in Culture and Society* 13(3):405–436.

Browne, Susan E., Debra Connors and Nanci Stern, eds. 1985. *With the power of each breath—a disabled women's anthology*. Pittsburgh: Cleis Press.

Bullard, David G. and Susan E. Knight, eds. 1981. *Sexuality and physical disability*. St. Louis: C.V. Mosby.

Bury, M.R. 1979. Disablement in society: Towards an integrated perspective. *International Journal of Rehabilitation Research* 2(1):33–40.

Beauvoir, Simone de. 1952. *The second sex*. New York: Alfred A. Knopf.

Campling, Jo, ed. 1981. *Images of ourselves—women with disabilities talking*. London: Routledge and Kegan Paul.

Davis, Barbara Hillyer. 1984. Women, disability and feminism: Notes toward a new theory. *Frontiers: A Journal of Women Studies* VIII(1):1–5.

Davis, Melanie and Catherine Marshall. 1987. Female and disabled: Challenged women in education. *National Women's Studies Association Perspectives* 5:39–41.

Deegan, Mary Jo and Nancy A. Brooks, eds. 1985. *Women and disability—the double handicap*. New Brunswick: Transaction Books.

Dinnerstein, Dorothy. 1976. *The mermaid and the minotaur: Sexual arrangements and human malaise*. New York: Harper and Row.

Ehrenreich, Barbara and Dierdre English. 1979. *For her own good: 150 years of the experts' advice to women*. New York: Anchor.

Fine, Michelle and Adrienne Asch, eds. 1988. *Women with disabilities: Essays in psychology, culture and politics*. Philadelphia: Temple University Press.

Finger, Anne. 1983. Disability and reproductive rights. *off our backs* 13(9):18–19.

Fisher, Bernice and Roberta Galler. 1981. Conversation between two friends about feminism and disability. *off our backs* 11(5):14–15.

Frank, Gelya. 1988. On embodiment: A case study of congenital limb deficiency in American culture. In *Women with disabilities*. Michelle Fine and Adrienne Asch, eds. Philadelphia: Temple University Press.

Griffin, Susan. 1981. *Pornography and silence: Culture's revenge against nature*. New York: Harper and Row.

Griffin, Susan. 1982. The way of all ideology. *Signs: Journal of Women in Culture and Society* 8(3):641–660.

Halpern, Sue M. 1988. Portrait of the artist. Review of *Under the eye of the clock* by Christopher Nolan. *The New York Review of Books*, June 30:3–4.

Hannaford, Susan. 1985. *Living outside inside. A disabled woman's experience. Towards a social and political perspective*. Berkeley: Canterbury Press.

Jeffreys, Toni. 1982. *The mile-high staircase*. Sydney: Hodder and Stoughton Ltd.

Kittay, Eva Feder and Diana T. Meyers, eds. 1987. *Women and moral theory*. Totowa, NJ: Rowman and Littlefield.

Kleinman, Arthur. 1988. *The illness narratives: Suffering, healing, and the human condition*. New York: Basic Books.

Lessing, Jill. 1981. Denial and disability. *off our backs* 11(5):21.

Madruga, Lenor. 1979. *One step at a time*. Toronto: McGraw-Hill.

Matthews, Gwyneth Ferguson. 1983. *Voices from the shadows: Women with disabilities speak out.* Toronto: Women's Educational Press.

Moore, Maureen. 1985. Coping with pelvic inflammatory disease. In *Women and Disability.* Frances Rooney and Pat Israel, eds. *Resources for Feminist Research* 14(1).

Newsweek. 1988. Reading God's mind. June 13:56–59.

Ramsay, A. Melvin. 1986. *Postviral fatigue syndrome, the saga of Royal Free disease.* London: Gower Medical Publishing.

Rawlinson, Mary C. 1983. The facticity of illness and the appropriation of health. In *Phenomenology in a pluralistic context.* William L. McBride and Calvin O. Schrag, eds. Albany: SUNY Press.

Rich, Adrienne. 1976. *Of woman born: Motherhood as experience and institution.* New York: W.W. Norton.

Rooney, Frances and Pat Israel, eds. 1985. *Women and disability. Resources for Feminist Research* 14(1).

Sacks, Oliver. 1988. The revolution of the deaf. *The New York Review of Books,* June 2, 23–28.

Saxton, Marsha and Florence Howe, eds. 1987. *With wings: an anthology of literature by and about women with disabilities.* New York: The Feminist Press.

Shaul, Susan L. and Jane Elder Bogle. 1981. Body image and the woman with a disability. In *Sexuality and physical disability.* David G. Bullard and Susan E. Knight, eds. St. Louis: C.V. Mosby.

Sherwin, Susan. 1984–85. A feminist approach to ethics. *Dalhousie Review* 64(4):704–713.

Sherwin, Susan. 1987. Feminist ethics and in vitro fertilization. In *Science, morality and feminist theory.* Marsha Hanen and Kai Nielsen, eds. Calgary: The University of Calgary Press.

Sontag, Susan. 1977. *Illness as metaphor.* New York: Random House.

U.N. Decade of Disabled Persons 1983–1992. 1983. *World programme of action concerning disabled persons.* New York: United Nations.

Whitbeck, Caroline. 1983. Afterword to the maternal instinct. In *Mothering: Essays in feminist theory.* Joyce Trebilcot, ed. Totowa: Rowman and Allanheld.

Zaner, Richard M. 1983. Flirtations or engagement? Prolegomenon to a philosophy of medicine. In *Phenomenology in a pluralistic context.* William L. McBride and Calvin O. Schrag, eds. Albany: SUNY Press.

Further Questions

1. Are there instances in which better social planning would make disabled persons more productive members of society? If so, in what sense are they disabled?

2. Do the disabled have good reason to feel trapped, frustrated, shame, and self-hatred?

3. Are health, physical well-being, and strength virtues? Does this mean that people who lack these characteristics are inadequate? Have the disabled invariably done something wrong that explains their disabilities?

I.8   Outrageous Acts and Everyday Rebellions

GLORIA STEINEM

Gloria Steinem notes that women who act individually in ways frowned upon by patriarchy can make the world a little different in only one day. She has a long list of suggested actions for individuals and another list for groups.

Steinem has been active in feminism in speeches and writing for twenty-five years. Her activities include editorship of *Ms.*, the first feminist magazine in the United States with wide, popular readership. (Other writings by Gloria Steinem appear in Part XI and Part XIII.)

Reading Questions

1. Given what you now know about patriarchy, think of a few things that you could do tomorrow as an individual to combat it. Compare your list with Steinem's.

2. Think of the groups to which you belong. What can these groups do to promote equality or justice within each group? Compare your results with Steinem's results.

3. Have you ever made a bargain with someone that you will both do something outrageous to oppressors and their sympathizers?

As Individuals

IN THE EARLY 1970S when I was traveling and lecturing with feminist lawyer and black activist Florynce Kennedy, one of her many epigrams went like this: "Unity in a movement situation is overrated. If you were the Establishment, which would you rather see coming in the door, five hundred mice or one lion?"

Mindful of her teaching, I now often end lectures with an organizer's deal. If each person in the room promises that in the twenty-four hours beginning the very next day she or he will do at least *one outrageous thing* in the cause of simple justice, then I promise I will, too. It doesn't matter whether the act is as small as saying, "Pick it up yourself" (a major step for those of us who have been our family's servants) or as large as calling a strike. The point is that, if each of us does as promised, we can be pretty sure of two results. First, the world one day later won't be quite the same. Second, we will have such a good time that we will never again get up in the morning saying, "*Will* I do anything outrageous?" but only "*What* outrageous act will I do today?"

Here are some samples I've recorded from the outrageous acts of real life.

- Announced a permanent refusal to contribute more money to a church or syna-

gogue until women too can become priests, ministers, and rabbis.
- Asked for a long-deserved raise, or, in the case of men and/or white folks, refused an undeserved one that is being given over the heads of others because of their race or sex.
- Written a well-reasoned critique of a sexist or racist textbook and passed it out on campus.
- Challenged some bit of woman-hating humor or imagery with the seriousness more often reserved for slurs based on religion or race.
- Shared with colleagues the knowledge of each other's salaries so that unfairnesses can be calculated. (It's interesting that employers try to keep us from telling the one fact we know.)
- Cared for a child or children so that an overworked mother could have a day that is her own. (This is especially revolutionary when done by a man.)
- Returned to a birth name or, in the case of a man, gave his children both parents' names.
- Left home for a week so that the father of your young child could learn to be a parent. (As one woman later reported calmly, "When I came home, my husband and the

baby had bonded, just the way women and babies do.")

- Petitioned for a Women's Studies section in a local library or bookstore.
- Checked a corporate employer's giving programs, see if they are really inclusive by benefiting women with at least half of their dollars, and made suggestions if not.
- Personally talked to a politician who needed persuasion to support, or reward for helping, issues of equality.
- Redivided a conventional house so that each person has a space for which he or she is solely responsible, with turns taken caring for kitchen, bathroom, and other shared rooms.
- Got married to an equal, or divorced from an unequal.
- Left a violent lover or husband.
- Led a walkout from a movie that presents rape scenes or other violence as titillating and just fine.
- Made a formal complaint about working (or living) in a white ghetto. White people are also being culturally deprived.
- Told the truth to a child, or a parent.
- Said proudly, "I am a feminist." (Because this word means a believer in equality, it's especially helpful when said by a man.)
- Organized a block, apartment house, or dormitory to register and vote.
- Personally picketed and/or sued a bigoted employer/teacher/athletic coach/foreman/union boss.

In addition to one-time outrageous acts, these are also the regular ones that should be the bottom line for each of us: writing five letters a week to lobby, criticize, or praise anything from TV shows to a senator; giving 10 percent of our incomes to social justice; going to one demonstration a month or one consciousness-raising group a week just to keep support and energy up; and figuring out how to lead our daily lives in a way that reflects what we believe. People who actually incorporate such day-by-day changes into their lives report that it isn't difficult: five lobbying letters can be written while watching "The Late Show"; giving 10 percent of their incomes often turns out to be the best investment they ever made; meetings create a free space, friends, and an antidote to isolation; and trying to transform a job or a family or a life-style in order to reflect beliefs, instead of the other way around, gives a satisfying sense of affecting the world.

If each of us only reached out and changed *five other people in our lifetimes,* the spiral of revolution would widen enormously—and we can do much more than that.

In Groups

Some of the most effective group actions are the simplest:

- Dividing membership lists according to political district, from precinct level up, so we can inform and get out the pro-equality vote.
- Asking each organization we belong to, whether community or professional, union or religious, to support issues of equality in their formal agendas.
- Making sure that the nonfeminist groups we're supporting don't have mostly women doing the work and mostly men on their boards.
- Making feminist groups *feminist;* that is, relevant to women of the widest diversity of age, race, economics, life-styles, and political labels practical for the work at hand. (An inclusiveness that's best begun among the founders. It's much tougher to start any group and only later reach out to "others.")
- Offering support where it's needed without being asked—for instance, to the school librarian who's fighting right-wing censorship of feminist and other books; or to the new family feeling racially isolated

in the neighborhood. (Would you want to have to ask people to help you?)

- Identifying groups for coalitions and allies for issues.
- Streamlining communications. If there were an emergency next week—a victim of discrimination who needed defending, a piece of sinister legislation gliding through city council—could your membership be alerted?
- Putting the group's money where its heart is, and not where it isn't. That may mean contributing to the local battered women's shelter and protesting a community fund that gives far more to Boy Scouts than to Girl Scouts; or publishing a directory of women-owned businesses; or withholding student-activity fees from a campus program that invites mostly white male speakers. (Be sure and let the other side know how much money they're missing. To be more forceful, put your contributions in an escrow account, with payment contingent on a specific improvement.)
- Organizing speak-outs and press conferences. There's nothing like personal testimonies from the people who have experienced the problem first-hand.
- Giving public awards and dinners to women (and men) who've made a positive difference.
- Bringing in speakers or women's studies courses to inform your members; running speakers' bureaus so your group's message gets out to the community.

- Making sure new members feel invited and welcome once they arrive, with old members assigned to brief them and transfer group knowledge.
- Connecting with other groups like yours regionally or nationally for shared experience, actions, and some insurance against reinventing the wheel.

Obviously, we must be able to choose the appropriate action from a full vocabulary of tactics, from voting to civil disobedience, from supporting women in the trades to economic boycotts and tax revolts, from congressional hearings to zap actions with humor and an eye to the evening news. . . .

In my first days of activism, I thought I would do this ("this" being feminism) for a few years and then return to my real life (what my "real life" might be, I did not know). Partly, that was a naïve belief that injustice only had to be pointed out in order to be cured. Partly, it was a simple lack of courage.

But like so many others now and in movements past, I've learned that this is not just something we care about for a year or two or three. We are in it for life—and for our lives. Not even the spiral of history is needed to show the distance traveled. We have only to look back at the less complete people we ourselves used to be.

And that is the last Survival Lesson: *we look at how far we've come, and then we know—there can be no turning back.*

Further Questions

1. If you could do any of Gloria Steinem's "outrageous acts," which ones would you choose to do and why?

2. Which of Steinem's suggestions would you take issue with as not being actions that promote justice or equality?

3. Is it easier to let other people do the things Steinem suggests, then share the benefits with them later? Is this a fair approach?

Suggested Moral of Part I

While we are surveying the world with a feminist eye, trying to discern control of women by men, we should not overlook other forms of oppression. Writers in this section have shown the pervasiveness of oppression of homosexuals, non-whites, and the disabled. The expected result of the presence of these other oppressive structures is a certain amount of diversity in patriarchal oppression. Feminism must be prepared to confront this diversity with a pluralistic approach. It should not expect problems of, or solutions to, male control to be the same for all races, classes, sexual orientations, or levels of ability or disability.

Further Readings for Part I: Oppression

We live in a hierarchical society which contains many possibilities for oppression. Good, accessible works on the subject are too numerous to mention. Below is only a small, selected sample. Many cover a wide variety of topics within the general category of oppression and outside of it as well.

I. RACIAL OPPRESSION

Margaret L. Andersen and Patricia Hill Collins, eds., *Race, Class and Gender: An Anthology* (Belmont, CA: Wadsworth Publishing Co., 1992)

Asian Women United of California, eds., *Making Waves: An Anthology of Writings by and about Asian American Women* (Boston, MA: Beacon Press, 1989)

Patricia Hill Collins, *Black Feminist Thought: Knowledge, Consciousness and the Politics of Empowerment* (New York, NY: Routledge, 1991)

J. David, ed. *The American Indian: The First Victim* (New York, NY: William Morrow and Co., 1972)

Diana L. Fowlkes, *White Political Women: Paths from Privilege to Empowerment* (Knoxville, TN: University of Tennessee Press, 1992)

bell hooks, *Talking Back: Thinking Feminist, Thinking Black* (Boston, MA: South End Press, 1989)

bell hooks, *Yearning: Race, Gender and Cultural Politics* (Boston, MA: South End Press, 1990)

Audre Lorde, *Sister Outsider: Essays and Speeches* (Freedom, CA: The Crossing Press, 1984)

Joan Moore and Harry Pachon, *Hispanics in the U.S.* (Englewood Cliffs, NJ: Prentice Hall, 1985)

Cherríe Moraga and Gloria Anzaldúa, eds., *This Bridge Called My Back: Radical Writings by Women of Color* (New York, NY: Kitchen Table Press, 1983)

Michael Omi and Harold Winnat, *Racial Formations in the United States* (New York, NY: Routledge and Kegan Paul, 1986)

Paula S. Rothenberg, ed., *Race, Class, and Gender in the United States* (New York, NY: St. Martin's Press, 2nd Edition, 1992)

Robert Staples, *Black Masculinity: The Black Male's Role in American Society* (San Francisco, CA: The Black Scholar Press, 1982)

Robert Staples, *The Black Woman in America: Sex, Marriage and the Family* (Chicago, IL: Nelson-Hall Publishers, 1973)

John Stone, ed., *Race, Ethnicity and Social Change* (Belmont, CA: Wadsworth Publishing Co., 1977)

Winged Words: American Indian Writers Speak (Lincoln, NE: University of Nebraska Press, 1990)

2. CLASS OPPRESSION

Paul Blumberg, *Inequality in an Age of Decline* (New York, NY: Oxford University Press, 1980)

Daniel Moynihan, ed., *On Understanding Poverty* (New York, NY: Basic Books, 1969)

Kevin Phillips, *The Politics of the Rich and the Poor* (New York, NY: Random House, 1990)

Lillian B. Rubin, *Worlds of Pain: Life in the Working Class Family* (New York, NY: Basic Books, 1976)

Richard Sennet and Jonathan Cobb, *The Hidden Injuries of Class* (New York, NY: Vintage Books, 1973)

William J. Wilson, *The Truly Disadvantaged: The Inner City, the Underclass and Public Policy* (Chicago, IL: University of Chicago Press, 1987)

3. OPPRESSION OF THE DISABLED

Esther Boylan, ed. *Women and Disability* (Atlantic Highlands, NJ: Zed Books, 1990)

Jo Campling, ed., *Images of Ourselves—Women with Disabilities Talking* (London: Routledge and Kegan Paul, 1981)

Michelle Fine and Adrienne Asch, eds., *Women with Disabilities: Essays in Psychology, Culture and Politics* (Philadelphia, PA: Temple University Press, 1988)

Susan Hannaford, *Living Outside Inside. A Disabled Woman's Experience. Towards a Social and Political Perspective* (Berkeley, CA: Canterbury Press, 1985)

Gwyneth Ferguson Matthews, *Voices from the Shadows: Women with Disabilities Speak Out* (Toronto: Women's Educational Press, 1983)

Karen Thompson and Julie Andrzejewski, *Why Can't Sharon Kowalski Come Home?* (San Francisco, CA: Spinsters, Aunt Lute, 1988)

4. GENDER OPPRESSION

(a) Classics on women's oppression from the beginning of the Women's Liberation Movement, around 1970.

Simone de Beauvoir, *The Second Sex* (New York, NY: Alfred A. Knopf Co., 1953)

Shulamith Firestone, *The Dialectic of Sex: The Case for Feminist Revolution* (New York, NY: William Morrow, 1970)

Vivian Gornick and Barbara K. Moran, eds., *Women in Sexist Society* (New York, NY: Signet, 1972)

Kate Millett, *Sexual Politics* (New York, NY: Ballantine Books, 1969)

Juliet Mitchell, *Women's Estate* (New York, NY: Pantheon Books, 1971)

Robin Morgan, ed., *Sisterhood is Powerful: An Anthology of Writings from the Women's Liberation Movement* (New York, NY: Vintage Books, 1970)

(b) Early responses by men to women's oppression.

Marc Feigen Fasteau, *The Male Machine* (New York, NY: Dell Publishing Co., 1975)

Michael Korda, *Male Chauvinism! How It Works* (New York, NY: Ballantine Books, 1973)

John Stuart Mill, 'The Subjection of Women' in *Essays on Sex Equality* by John Stuart Mill and Harriet Taylor Mill, Allice S. Rossi, ed. (Chicago: University of Chicago Press, 1970)

5. FURTHER READINGS FOR HETEROSEXIST OPPRESSION (OPPRESSION OF GAYS AND LESBIANS)

These can be found in Further Readings for Part VII: Sexuality.

Part II

Messages on the Surface:
Looks and Language

Introduction

LOOKS (PERSONAL APPEARANCE) AND LANGUAGE have two important functions in patriarchy and other oppressive structures. First, they convey messages about which segments of society are in control. And second, they serve to maintain that control. Looks and language are phenomena on the surface (easy to see or hear), even though their messages are often not easy to decipher.

II.1   "Pricks" and "Chicks": A Plea for "Persons"

ROBERT BAKER

Robert Baker describes how women appear to men, discussing terms that are, for some men in some contexts, interchangeable with "woman." This is not, ordinarily, terminology that women use to refer to themselves or to other women. Men often describe women in terminology whose literal meaning is an animal, toy, or plaything. (Baker's views on referring to women by their sexual anatomy are presented in Part VII.) He also suggests some terms for women, "lady," "gal," and "girl," which he calls "neutral"; perhaps what he means is that these terms have no objectionable connotations but only designate a woman as an adult, female human being.

Baker teaches philosophy at Union College (Schenectady, New York) and has written on a wide variety of subjects in philosophy. (The last part of this writing appears in Part VII.)

Reading Questions

1. What do you call a woman (in an impersonal context) when you do not refer to her as a woman? Is this terminology degrading? Would it make a difference if you were of the other gender?

2. Now compare your answers with Baker's ideas.

. . . THE MAJOR QUESTION before us is, "How are women conceived of in our culture?". . .

. . . Methods of nonpronominal identification can be discovered by determining which terms can be substituted for "woman" in such sentences as "Who is that woman over there?" without changing the meaning of the sentence. Virtually no term is interchangeable with "woman" in that sentence for all speakers on all occasions. Even "lady," which most speakers would accept as synonymous with "woman" in that sentence, will not do for a speaker who applies the term "lady" only to those women who display manners, poise, and sensitivity. In most contexts, a large number of students in one or more of my classes will accept the following types of terms as more or less interchangeable with "woman." (An asterisk indicates interchanges ac-

ceptable to both males and females; a plus sign indicates terms restricted to black students only. Terms with neither an asterisk nor a plus sign are acceptable by all males but are not normally used by females.)

A. NEUTRAL TERMS: *lady, *gal, *girl (especially with regard to a co-worker in an office or factory), *+sister, *broad (originally in the animal category, but most people do not think of the term as now meaning pregnant cow)

B. ANIMAL: *chick, bird, fox, vixen, filly, bitch (Many do not know the literal meaning of the term. Some men and most women construe this use as pejorative; they think of "bitch" in the context of "bitchy," that is, snappy, nasty, and so forth. But a large group of men claim that it is a standard nonpejorative term of identification—

which may perhaps indicate that women have come to be thought of as shrews by a large sub-class of men.)

C. PLAYTHING: babe, doll, cuddly. . . .

Except for two of the animal terms, "chick" and "broad"—but note that "broad" is probably neutral today—women do not typically identify themselves . . . as playthings, or as animals; *only males use nonneutral terms to identify women.* Hence, it would seem that there is a male conception of women and a female conception. Only males identify women as "foxes," "babes," . . . (and since all the other nonneutral identifications are male, it is reasonable to assume that the identification of a woman as a "chick" is primarily a male conception that some women have adopted).

What kind of conception do men have of women? Clearly they think that women share certain properties with certain types of animals, toys, and playthings. . . .

The . . . two nonneutral male classifications, animal and plaything, are *prima facie* denigrating (and I mean this in the literal sense of making one like a "nigger"). Consider the animal classification. All of the terms listed, with the possible exception of "bird," refer to animals that are either domesticated for servitude (to *man*) or hunted for sport. First, let us consider the term "bird." When I asked my students what sort of birds might be indicated, they suggested chick, canary (one member, in his forties, had suggested "canary" as a term of identification), chicken, pigeon, dove, parakeet, and hummingbird (one member). With the exception of the hummingbird, which like all the birds suggested is generally thought to be diminutive and pretty, all of the birds are domesticated, usually as pets (which reminds one that "my pet" is an expression of endearment). None of the birds were predators or symbols of intelligence or nobility (as are the owl, eagle, hawk, and falcon); nor did large but beautiful birds seem appropriate (for example, pheasants, peacocks, and swans). If one construes

the bird terms (and for that matter, "filly") as applicable to women because they are thought of as beautiful, or at least pretty, *then there is nothing denigrating about them.* If, on the other hand, the common properties that underlie the metaphorical identification are domesticity and servitude, then they are indeed denigrating (as for myself, I think that both domesticity and prettiness underlie the identification). "Broad," of course, is, or at least was, clearly denigrating, since nothing renders more service to a farmer than does a pregnant cow, and cows are not commonly thought of as paradigms of beauty.

With one exception all of the animal terms reflect a male conception of women either as domesticated servants or as pets, or as both. Indeed, some of the terms reflect a conception of women first as pets and then as servants. Thus, when a pretty, cuddly little chick grows older, she becomes a very useful servant—the egg-laying hen.

"Vixen" and "fox," variants of the same term, are the one clear exception. None of the other animals with whom women are metaphorically identified are generally thought to be intelligent, aggressive, or independent—but the fox is. A chick is a soft, cuddly, entertaining, pretty, diminutive, domesticated, and dumb animal. A fox too is soft, cuddly, entertaining, pretty, and diminutive, but it is neither dependent nor dumb. It is aggressive, intelligent, and a minor predator—indeed, it preys on chicks—and frequently outsmarts ("outfoxes") men.

Thus the term "fox" or "vixen" is generally taken to be a compliment by both men and women, and compared to any of the animal or plaything terms it is indeed a compliment. Yet considered in and of itself, the conception of a woman as a fox is not really complimentary at all, for the major connection between *man* and fox is that of predator and prey. The fox is an animal that men chase, and hunt, and kill for sport. If women are conceived of as foxes, then they are conceived of as prey that it is fun to hunt.

In considering plaything identifications, only one sentence is necessary. *All the plaything identifications are clearly denigrating since they assimilate women to the status of mindless or dependent objects.*

. . . Since the way we talk of things, and especially the way we identify them, is the way in which we conceive of them, any movement dedicated to breaking the bonds of female servitude must destroy these ways of identifying and hence of conceiving of women. Only when both sexes find the terms "babe," "doll," "chick," "broad," and so forth, as objectionable as "boy" and "nigger" will women come to be conceived of as independent *human beings*. . . .

Further Questions

1. Are "lady," "gal," and "girl" really *neutral* ways of referring to women, or are there some contexts in which they have offensive implications?

2. Is it harmless in an impersonal context to call a woman a chick, bird, fox, filly, or bitch, or do those words imply that women share properties with animals that are inappropriate in a human adult?

3. Do you agree with Baker that the fact that these terms are used most of the time by men as designations for women means that men do not think of women as human beings equal to themselves?

II.2   Who Is Man?

CASEY MILLER AND KATE SWIFT

Casey Miller and Kate Swift address the question of whether *man* is a gender neutral term or has a gender neutral meaning. Not now, they argue. The very ambiguity of *man* meaning *human* or *adult male human* allows the latter meaning to overshadow the former. This, in turn, makes it possible to neglect women by making them nameless. Women are invisible when *man* is used to designate them because they are not being spoken of explicitly.

Miller and Swift have been freelance partners since 1970 and are contributers of writings and photographs to many magazines. They live in Connecticut.

Reading Questions

1. Can a word have two distinct meanings if the meaning of one includes the meaning of the other? Can you think of any word but *man* about which this can be said?

2. Do you ever feel awkward using *he* to designate a person who might be male or female? Would you feel more awkward using *she* in that context?

... THE USE OF *MAN* to include both women and men may be grammatically "correct," but it is constantly in conflict with the more common use of *man* as distinguished from *woman*. This ambiguity renders *man* virtually unusable in what was once its generic sense—a sense all-too-accurately illustrated in Tennyson's line, "Woman is the lesser man." When Dr. Bronowski said that for years he had been fascinated by "the way in which man's ideas express what is essentially human in his nature,"[1] it is anybody's guess whether his vision included all the anonymous women of the past whose ideas and contributions to science and the arts are no less real for never having been identified.

The newspaper headline THREE-CENT PILL LAST HOPE OF MAN suggests that the story to follow may be an announcement by zero-population-growth researchers of a major contraceptive breakthrough, but actually the news item under that particular headline concerned the personal plight of a fifty-one-year-old Wichita, Kansas, man whose only chance for survival was an inexpensive drug called guanidine.[2] Examples of such ambiguity are endless, and the confusion they cause increases as women come to be seen less as the second sex and more as beings who are fully and essentially human.

Most dictionaries give two standard definitions of *man*: a human being, a male human being. A high school student, thinking about these two meanings, may well ask the obvious question, "How can the same word include women in one definition and exclude them in another?" At which point the teacher may dredge up the hoary platitude, "Man embraces woman" —which gets a laugh but leaves the question unanswered. And the student, perhaps distracted now by continuing snickers, may feel the question is too trivial (and somehow, if she is a girl, too demeaning) to pursue ...

Whatever may be known of the contributions females made to early human culture, an effective linguistic barrier prevents the assimilation of that knowledge in our present culture. Studies like those conducted by Harrison, Nilsen, and Schneider and Hacker clearly indicate that *man* in the sense of male so overshadows *man* in the sense of human being as to make the latter use inaccurate and misleading for purposes both of conceptualizing and communicating.

The "generic man" trap, in which "The Ascent of Man" was also caught, operates through every kind of medium whenever the human species is being talked about. Writing in a national magazine, the psychoanalyst Erich Fromm described man's "vital interests" as "life, food, access to females, etc."[3] One may be saddened but not surprised at the statement "man is the only primate that commits rape." Although, as commonly understood, it can apply to only half the human population, it is nevertheless semantically acceptable. But "man, being a mammal, breast-feeds his young" is taken as a joke.

Sometimes the ambiguity of *man* is dismissed on the grounds that two different words are involved and that they are homonyms, like a *row* of cabbages and a *row* on the lake. Two words cannot be homonyms, however, if one includes the other as does *man* in the first definition given by the most recent Webster's Collegiate Dictionary: "A human being, *especially* an adult male human." Since the definers do not explain who their italicized "especially" omits, one is left to wonder. Women, children, and adolescent males, perhaps? The unabridged Merriam-Webster Third New International Dictionary is more precise: man is "a member of the human race: a human being . . . now usually used of males except in general or indefinite applications. . . ."

The meaning of a homonym, like *row* or *bow* or *pool,* is usually clear from its context, but the overlapping definitions of *man* often make its meaning anything but clear. Can we be sure, without consulting the board of directors of the General Electric Company, what the slogan "Men helping Man" was supposed to convey? Since GE employs a large number of women, it should be a safe bet that both female and male employees were in the slogan writer's mind. Yet an ad for the company seems to tip the scales in the other direction: "As long as man is on earth, he's likely to cause problems. But the men at General Electric will keep trying to find answers."[4] Maybe the article *the* is the limiting factor, but it is hard to picture any of "the men at General Electric" as female men. Once again the conscious intention to describe man the human being has been subverted by the more persistent image of man the male.

If it were not for its ambiguity, *man* would be the shortest and simplest English word to distinguish humankind from all other animal species. The Latin scientific label *Homo sapiens* is long, foreign, and the *sapiens* part of questionable accuracy. But at least *homo*—like the Hebrew *'adham*—has the clear advantage of including both sexes. Its inclusiveness is demonstrated by the presence in Latin of the words *mas* and *vir*, both of which signify a male person only and distinguish him unequivocally from *femina* or *mulier*, Latin words for woman. Nevertheless, *homo* is sometimes erroneously understood to mean "male person," and semantic confusion runs riot when it is mistakenly thought to occur in *homosexual*, thereby limiting that term to males. (The prefix *homo-*, as in *homosexual*, *homonym*, and *homogeneous*, comes from the Greek *homos* meaning "same," and its similarity to the Latin *homo* is coincidental.)

To get back to humankind, the Greek word is *anthropos*, from which come words like anthropology and philanthropy as well as misanthropy, a blanket dislike of everybody regardless of sex. Like Latin and Hebrew, Greek has separate words for the sexes—*aner* for a male person (its stem form is *andr-*), *gune* (or *gyne*) for a female person. So in English *misandry* is the little-known partner of *misogyny;* but when the two Greek roots come together in *androgyny*, they form a word that is beginning to be used to describe the rare and happy human wholeness that counteracts the destructive linguistic polarization of the sexes.

Although they serve many uses in English, the words for humankind borrowed from classical Greek and Latin have not been called on to re-

solve the ambiguity of *man*. Native English grew out of a Teutonic branch of the Indo-European family of languages that also produced German, Danish, Norwegian, and Swedish. In the ancestor of all these tongues the word man meant a human being irrespective of sex or age. That sense survives in the modern derivitives *mensch* in German, *menneske* in Danish and Norwegian, and *människa* in Swedish, all of which can refer to a woman or a man, a girl or a boy.

The language we speak has no counterpart for these words. However, when *man* was first used in English—as *mann* or sometimes *monn*—it too had the prevailing sense of a human being irrespective of sex and age. About the year 1000 the Anglo-Saxon scholar Aelfric wrote, "His mother was a Christian, named Elen, a very full-of-faith man, and extremely pious."[5] The Oxford English Dictionary cites numerous other examples, including a description written in 1325 of a husband and wife as "right rich men" and a statement from a sermon of 1597 that "The Lord had but one pair of men in Paradise."[6]

At one time English also had separate and unambiguous words to distinguish a person by sex: *wif* for a female, *wer* and *carl* for a male. *Mann*—a human being—dropped the second *n* in combined forms like *waepman* and *carlman*, both of which meant an adult male person, and *wifman*, an adult female person. *Wifman* eventually became *women* (the plural, *women*, retains the original vowel sound in the pronunciation of the first syllable), while *wif* was narrowed in meaning to become *wife*. But *wer* and *waepman*, *carl* and *carlman* simply became obsolete; they were no longer needed once *man* was used to signify a male—especially. One cannot help but wonder what would have happened to the word that originally meant a human being if females rather than males had dominated the society in which English evolved through its first thousand years. Would *man* still mean a human being, but especially an adult female?

The question underlines the essential absurdity of using the same linguistic symbols for the human race in one breath and for only half of it in the next. Alma Graham, a lexicographer, draws these contrasts: "If a woman is swept off a ship into the water, the cry is 'Man overboard!' If she is killed by a hit-and-run driver, the charge is 'manslaughter.' If she is injured on the job, the coverage is 'workmen's compensation.' But if she arrives at a threshold marked 'Men Only,' she knows the admonition is not intended to bar animals or plants or inanimate objects. It is meant for her."[7]

Alleen Pace Nilsen notes that adults transfer to children their own lack of agreement about when the many compound words like workman and salesman apply to both sexes and when such compounds are to be used of males only. She offers some examples to illustrate the different levels of acceptability we sense in such words: "My mother's a salesman for Encyclopædia Britannica" and "Susy wants to be chairman of the dance" are acceptable to many people, but not to all, as is evident from the existence of the terms saleswoman, chairwoman, and chairperson. "Carol Burnett did a one-man show last night" and "Patsy is quite a horseman, isn't she?" are also acceptable, but they draw attention to the discrepancy between the masculine gender term and the subject's sex. "Miss Jones is our mailman" and "Stella Starbuck is KWWL's new weatherman" seem questionable, perhaps because of the newness in relation to women of the activities they describe. "My brother married a spaceman who works for NASA" and "That newsman is in her seventh month of pregnancy" are generally unacceptable.[8]

If adults cannot agree on when a compound of *man* may be a woman, these terms must be doubly confusing to young children, whose understanding of words is limited by their immediate experience. The meaning a child assigns to a word may be quite different from the meaning an adult assumes the child understands. One youngster, for example, when asked to illustrate the incident in the Garden of Eden story where God drives Adam and Eve from the garden, produced

a picture of God at the wheel of a pickup truck, with Adam and Eve sitting in the back surrounded by an assortment of flowering plants for their new home. And there is the story of the children who were disappointed to discover that the "dog doctor" was not a dog at all, but an ordinary human being.

It is not really known at what point children begin to come to terms with the dual role the word man has acquired or with the generalized use of *he* to mean "either he or she." Certainly the experience is different for boys and girls—ego-enhancing for the former and ego-deflating for the latter. The four-year-old girl who hides her father's reading glasses and waits for a cue line from him to go find them is *not* expecting to hear "If somebody will find my reading glasses, I'll give him a big hug." Yet the same child will sooner or later be taught that in such a sentence *him* can also mean *her.*

At a meeting of the Modern Language Association the story was told of twin girls who came home from school in tears one day because the teacher had explained the grammatical rule mandating the use of *he* when the referent is indefinite or unknown.[9] What emotions had reduced them to tears? Anger? Humiliation? A sense of injustice? It is unlikely that any woman can recapture her feelings when the arbitrariness of that rule first struck her consciousness: it happened a long time ago, no doubt, and it was only one among many assignments to secondary status. . . .

Some writers and speakers who recognize the generic masculine pronoun as a perpetuator of the male-is-norm viewpoint have begun to avoid using it. Dr. Benjamin Spock, for example, says, "Like everyone else writing in the child-care field, I have always referred to the baby and child with the pronouns 'he' and 'him.' There is a grammatical excuse, since these pronouns can be used correctly to refer to a girl or woman . . . just as the word 'man' may cover women too in certain contexts. But I now agree with the liberators of women that this is not enough of an excuse. The fact remains that this use of the male pronoun is one of many examples of discrimination, each of which may seem of small consequence in itself but which, when added up, help to keep women at an enormous disadvantage—in employment, in the courts, in the universities, and in conventional social life." [10] A prominent child psychologist, Dr. Lee Salk, comments in the preface to his recent book for parents, "An author interested in eliminating sexism from his or her work is immediately confronted with the masculine tradition of the English language. I personally reject the practice of using masculine pronouns to refer to human beings. Accordingly I have freely alternated my references, sometimes using the female gender and sometimes using the male gender." [11]

If pediatricians and child psychologists tend to be especially sensitive to the harm done by exclusionary language, some linguists are sensitive to what they see as a dangerous precedent when the conventional generic use is replaced by wording like Dr. Salk's "his or her work." James D. McCawley, professor of linguistics at the University of Chicago, maintains that the phrase "he or she" is actually more sexist than *he* alone, which, he says "loses its supposed sexual bias if it is used consistently." [12] In other words, never, never, never qualify the generic pronoun and you will always be understood to include both sexes. "Why not give him or her a subscription to *XYZ* magazine?" asks a promotional letter. A sexist way to word the question, one imagines Professor McCawley advising the advertising agency: "*He or she* does as much to combat sexism as a sign saying 'Negroes admitted' would do to combat racism—it makes women a special category of beings that are left out of the picture unless extra words are added to bring them in explicitly." [13] McCawley's analogy would be relevant if the sign in question were posted by an organization calling itself "The White People." But nobody ever uses *white* to mean both white and black, the way *he* is sometimes used to mean both he and she. Alma Graham makes the problem clear by stating it as a mathematical proposition: "If you have a group half of whose members are A's and half of whose members are B's and if you call the group C, then A's and B's may be equal members of group C. But if you call the group A, there is no way that B's can be equal to A's within it. The A's will always be the rule and the B's will always be the exception—the subgroup, the subspecies, the outsiders." [14]

Admittedly "he or she" is clumsy, and the reasonable argument that it should be alternated with "she or he" makes it still clumsier. Also, by the time any consideration of the pronoun problem gets to this stage, there is usually a large body of opinion to the effect that the whole issue is trivial. Observing that men more often take this view than women, the syndicated columnist Gena Corea has come up with a possible solution. All right, she suggests, "if women think it's important and men don't . . . let's use a pronoun that pleases women. Men don't care what it is as long as it's not clumsy so, from now on, let's use 'she' to refer to the standard human being. The word 'she' includes 'he' so that would be fair. Anyway, we've used 'he' for the past several thousand years and we'll use 'she' for the next few thousand; we're just taking turns." [15]

Men who work in fields where women have traditionally predominated—as nurses, secretaries, and primary school teachers, for example—know exactly how Corea's proposed generic pronoun would affect them: they've tried it and they don't like it. Until a few years ago most publications, writers, and speakers on the subject of primary and secondary education used *she* in referring to teachers. As the proportion of men in the profession increased, so did their annoyance with the generic use of feminine pronouns. By the mid-1960s, according to the journal of the National Education Association, some of the angry young men in teaching were claiming that references to the teacher as "she" were responsible in part for their poor public image and, consequently, in part for their low salaries. One man, speaking on the floor of the National Education Association Representative Assembly, said, "The incorrect and improper use of the English language is a vestige of the nineteenth century image of the teacher, and conflicts sharply with the vital image we attempt to set forth today. The interests of neither the women nor of the men in our profession are served by grammatical usage which conjures up an anachronistic image of the nineteenth century schoolmarm."[16]

Here is the male-is-norm argument in a nutshell. Although the custom of referring to elementary and secondary schoolteachers as "she" arose because most of them were women, it becomes grammatically "incorrect and improper" as soon as men enter the field in more than token numbers. Because the use of *she* excludes men, it conflicts with the "vital image" teachers attempt to project today. Women teachers are still in the majority, but the speaker feels it is neither incorrect nor improper to exclude them linguistically. In fact, he argues, it is proper to do so because the image called up by the pronoun she is that of a schoolmarm. To be vital, it appears, a teacher's image must be male.

No "schoolmarm" was responsible for making *man* and *he* the subsuming terms they have become, though female schoolteachers—to their own disadvantage—dutifully taught the usages schoolmasters decreed to be correct. Theodore M. Bernstein and Peter Farb, contemporary arbiters of usage, also invoke "schoolmarms" when they want to blame someone for what they consider overconservatism. Bernstein calls his scapegoat "Miss Thistlebottom" and Farb calls his "Miss Fiditch." But on the matter of generic singular pronouns, both men defend the rule that says *he* is the only choice.[17] Ethel Strainchamps, who eschews the role of arbiter, calls that "a recent Mr. Fuddydud 'rule'" and cites examples of contrary usage from the Oxford English Dictionary to prove her point.[18]

By and large, however, the "correctness" of using *man* and *he* generically is so firmly established that many people, especially those who deal professionally with English, have difficulty recognizing either the exclusionary power of these words or their failure to communicate real-

ity. In fact the yearning to understand masculine terminology as including both sexes is sometimes so strong that it asserts itself in defiance of literary or historic evidence to the contrary. Of *course* Alexander Pope's admonition, "Know then thyself . . . the proper study of mankind is man," was intended to include women, we say. But the reader to whom these lines were addressed is made more specific by the author's later reference in the same work to "thy dog, thy bottle, and thy wife." . . .

"Man is the highest form of life on earth," the Britannica Junior Encyclopædia explains. "His superior intelligence, combined with certain physical characteristics, have enabled man to achieve things that are impossible for other animals."[19] The response of a male child to this information is likely to be "Wow!"—that of a female child, "Who? Do they mean me too?" Even if the female child understands that yes, she too is part of man, she must still leap the hurdles of all those other terms that she knows from her experience refer to males only. When she is told that we are all brothers, that the brotherhood of man includes sisters, and that the faith of our fathers is also the faith of our mothers, does she really believe it? How does she internalize these concepts? "We must understand that 'the brotherhood of man' does not exclude our beloved sisters," the eminent scholar Jacques Barzun says.[20] But how do we accomplish that feat? By an act of will? By writing it on the blackboard a hundred and fifty times? Cases are pending in a dozen courtrooms today questioning this very understanding.

The subtle power of linguistic exclusion does not stop in the schoolroom, and it is not limited to words like man, men, brothers, sons, fathers, or forefathers. It is constantly being extended to words for anyone who is not female by definition. Musing on the nature of politics, for example, a television commentator says, "People won't give up power. They'll give up anything else first—money, home, wife, children—but not power."[21] A sociologist, discussing the correlates of high status, reports that "Americans of higher status have more years of education, more children attending college, less divorce, lower mortality, better dental care, and less chance of having a fat wife."[22] Members of the women's movement in France were arrested for displaying the slogan "One Frenchman in Two Is a Woman"; it was taken by some outraged French males to mean that 50 per cent of their number were homosexuals.[23]

If these items appear to be molehills, it must be remembered that the socializing process, that step-by-step path we follow in adapting to the needs of society, is made up of many small experiences that often go unnoticed. Given the male norm, it becomes natural to think of women as an auxiliary and subordinate class, and from there it is an easy jump to see them as a minority or a special interest group. A few years ago an authority on constitutional law wrote in *Fortune* magazine: "Various kinds of claims are working their way through the judicial system, and the Supreme Court may ultimately have to face them—suits seeking judicial determination of abortion statutes, the death penalty, environmental issues, the rights of women, the Vietnam war."[24] If the Supreme Court is ever asked to make a judicial determination of "the rights of men," it will be a sign that the rights of women and the rights of men have finally become parallel and equal constituents of human rights.

Some authorities, including Professor Barzun, insist that *man* is still a universal term clearly understood to mean "person," but the mass of evidence is against that view. As early as 1752, when David Hume referred in his *Political Discourses* to "all men, male and female," the word had to be qualified if it was not to be misunderstood. Dr. Richard P. Goldwater, a psychotherapist, goes to the heart of the matter when he asks, "If we take on its merits [the] assertion that *man* in its deepest origin of meaning stands for both sexes of our race, then how did it come to mean *male*? Did we males appropriate *man* for ourselves at the expense of the self-esteem of our sisters? Did

what we now call 'sexism' alter the flow of language through us?"[25]

Those who have grown up with a language that tells them they are at the same time men and not men are faced with ambivalence—not about their sex, but about their status as human beings. For the question "Who is man?" it seems, is a political one, and the very ambiguity of the word is what makes it a useful tool for those who have a stake in maintaining the status quo.

NOTES

1. J. Bronowski, *The Ascent of Man,* Boston, Little, Brown and Company, 1973, p. 24.

2. The Middletown (Conn.) *Press,* November 27, 1972.

3. Erich Fromm, "The Erich Fromm Theory of Aggression," New York *Times Magazine,* February 27, 1972.

4. The ad appeared in *Time* magazine, October 4, 1971.

5. Quoted by Marjorie Anderson and Blanche Williams, *Old English Handbook,* Boston, Houghton Mifflin Company, 1935, p. 207.

6. Both examples are given under the entry *man* in the Oxford English Dictionary. For convenience we have modernized the spelling.

7. Alma Graham, "How to Make Trouble: The Making of a Nonsexist Dictionary," *Ms.,* December 1973, p. 16.

8. Alleen Pace Nilsen, "Grammatical Gender and Its Relationship to the Equal Treatment of Males and Females in Children's Books," a thesis submitted in partial fulfillment of the requirements for the degree of Doctor of Philosophy in the College of Education in the Graduate College of the University of Iowa, 1973, pp. 86–87.

9. Patricia C. Nichols, "The Uses of Gender in English," revision of a paper read before the Women's Forum of the Modern Language Association in December 1971 under the title "Gender in English: Syntactic and Semantic Functions"; photocopy, p. 11.

10. Benjamin Spock, M.D., *Redbook,* November 1973, as quoted in *Today's Education,* September–October 1974, p. 110.

11. Lee Salk, *Preparing for Parenthood,* New York, David McKay Company, 1974.

12. James D. McCawley, Letter to the Editor, New York *Times Magazine,* November 10, 1974.

13. Ibid.

14. Alma Graham, Letter to the Editor, *The Columbia Forum,* Fall 1974.

15. Gena Corea, "Frankly Feminist," syndicated column dated June 28, 1974, reprinted in *Media Report to Women,* Vol. 3, No. 1, January 1, 1975.

16. *Today's Education,* September–October 1974, p. 110.

17. Theodore M. Bernstein, *The Careful Writer: A Modern Guide to English Usage,* New York, Atheneum, 1965, and *Watch Your Language,* Great Neck, N.Y., Channel Press, 1958; Peter Farb, *Word Play: What Happens When People Talk,* New York, Alfred A. Knopf, 1974.

18. Ethel Strainchamps, review of Peter Farb, *Word Play,* in *The Village Voice, Voice Literary Supplement,* March 21, 1974. Examples are cited by the Oxford English Dictionary under entries for *they, their, them,* and *themselves.*

19. Volume 10, p. 48B, 1971 edition. The Britannica Junior Encyclopædia for Boys and Girls is compiled with the editorial advice of the Faculties of the University of Chicago and the University Laboratory Schools and published by Encyclopædia Britannica, Inc.

20. Jacques Barzun, "A Few Words on a Few Words," *The Columbia Forum,* Summer 1974, p. 19.

21. The late Frank McGee, on the "Today Show," NBC Television, June 16, 1972.

22. Theodore Caplow, *Elementary Sociology,* Englewood Cliffs, N.J., Prentice-Hall, 1971, p. 310, quoted by Schneider and Hacker, "Sex Role Imagery," fn. 9.

23. Justine DeLacy, "How French Women Got That Way—And How to Handle Them," New York *Times,* January 13, 1974, "Travel and Resorts" section.

24. Robert H. Bork, "We Suddenly Feel That Law Is Vulnerable," *Fortune* magazine, December 1971.

25. Richard P. Goldwater, M.D., Letter to the Editor, *The Columbia Forum,* Fall 1974, p. 46.

Further Questions

1. Did it surprise you to read of the 1597 sermon reminding us, "The Lord had but one pair of men in Paradise"? What is the big surprise?

2. You have just been appointed head of a committee. Would you like to be called the "chair," "chairperson," "chairwoman," or "chairman"? Would you feel the same way if you were of the other gender?

3. If men don't care about the gender of personal pronouns and women do, why don't we just use "she" to refer to a standard human being?

Talking Back   II.3

bell hooks

bell hooks talks of her experiences of breaking through the surface of male-dominated language by "talking back." This means disagreeing, as an equal, with an authority figure, being seen as well as heard. Her craving to be heard was awakened, as a child, by talk among the black women in her home. She found her own empowerment to talk back through adopting an ancestor, bell hooks, as a mentor and as her own identity as a writer.

hooks teaches English at Oberlin College (Ohio) and has written widely from the perspective of a black feminist. Another section by hooks appears in Part V.

Reading Questions

1. If you were silenced as a child, how did this make you feel? What effect did this have on your later life?
2. In your experience, can the voices of men usually drown out the voices of women?
3. Have you found it easier, on occasion, to express disagreement with a more powerful person if you think of yourself as being someone else?

IN THE WORLD of the southern black community I grew up in, "back talk" and "talking back" meant speaking as an equal to an authority figure. It meant daring to disagree and sometimes it just meant having an opinion. In the "old school," children were meant to be seen and not heard. My great-grandparents, grandparents, and parents were all from the old school. To make yourself heard if you were a child was to invite punishment, the back-hand lick, the slap across the face that would catch you unaware, or the feel of switches stinging your arms and legs.

To speak then when one was not spoken to was a courageous act—an act of risk and daring. And yet it was hard not to speak in warm rooms where heated discussions began at the crack of dawn, women's voices filling the air, giving orders, making threats, fussing. Black men may have excelled in the art of poetic preaching in the male-dominated church, but in the church of the home, where the everyday rules of how to live and how to act were established, it was black women who preached. There, black women spoke in a language so rich, so poetic, that it felt to me like being shut off from life, smothered to death if one were not allowed to participate.

It was in that world of woman talk (the men were often silent, often absent) that was born in me the craving to speak, to have a voice, and not just any voice but one that could be identified as belonging to me. To make my voice, I had to speak, to hear myself talk—and talk I did—darting in and out of grown folks' conversations and dialogues, answering questions that were not directed at me, endlessly asking questions, making speeches. Needless to say, the punishments for these acts of speech seemed endless. They were intended to silence me—the child—and more particularly the girl child. Had I been a boy, they might have encouraged me to speak believing that I might someday be called to preach. There was no "calling" for talking girls, no legitimized rewarded speech. The punishments I received for "talking back" were intended to suppress all possibility that I would create my own speech. That speech was to be suppressed so that the "right speech of womanhood" would emerge.

Within feminist circles, silence is often seen as the sexist "right speech of womanhood"—the sign of woman's submission to patriarchal authority. This emphasis on woman's silence may be an accurate remembering of what has taken place in the households of women from WASP backgrounds in the United States, but in black communities (and diverse ethnic communities), women have not been silent. Their voices can be heard. Certainly for black women, our struggle has not been to emerge from silence into speech but to change the nature and direction of our speech, to make a speech that compels listeners, one that is heard.

Our speech, "the right speech of womanhood," was often the soliloquy, the talking into thin air, the talking to ears that do not hear you—the talk that is simply not listened to. Unlike the black male preacher whose speech was to be heard, who was to be listened to, whose words were to be remembered, the voices of black women—giving orders, making threats, fussing—could be tuned out, could become a kind of background music, audible but not acknowledged as significant speech. Dialogue—the sharing of speech and recognition—took place not between mother and child or mother and male authority figure but among black women. I can remember watching fascinated as our mother talked with her mother, sisters, and women friends. The intimacy and intensity of their speech—the satisfaction they received from talking to one another, the pleasure, the joy. It was in this world of woman speech, loud talk, angry words, women with tongues quick and sharp, tender sweet tongues, touching our world with their words, that I made speech my birthright—and the right to voice, to authorship, a privilege I would not be denied. It was in that world and because of it that I came to dream of writing, to write.

Writing was a way to capture speech, to hold onto it, keep it close. And so I wrote down bits and pieces of conversations, confessing in cheap diaries that soon fell apart from too much handling, expressing the intensity of my sorrow, the anguish of speech—for I was always saying the wrong thing, asking the wrong questions. I could not confine my speech to the necessary corners and concerns of life. I hid these writings under my bed, in pillow stuffings, among faded underwear. When my sisters found and read them, they ridiculed and mocked me—poking fun. I felt violated, ashamed, as if the secret parts of my self had been exposed, brought into the open, and hung like newly clean laundry, out in the air for everyone to see. The fear of exposure, the fear that one's deepest emotions and innermost thoughts will be dismissed as mere nonsense, felt by so many young girls keeping diaries, holding and hiding speech, seems to me now one of the barriers that women have always needed and still need to destroy so that we are no longer pushed into secrecy or silence.

Despite my feelings of violation, of exposure, I continued to speak and write, choosing my hiding places well, learning to destroy work when no safe place could be found. I was never taught absolute silence, I was taught that it was important to speak but to talk a talk that was in itself a silence. Taught to speak and yet beware of the betrayal of too much heard speech, I experienced intense confusion and deep anxiety in my efforts to speak and write. Reciting poems at Sunday afternoon church service might be rewarded. Writing a poem (when one's time could be "better" spent sweeping, ironing, learning to cook) was luxurious activity, indulged in at the expense of others. Questioning authority, raising issues that were not deemed appropriate subjects brought pain, punishments—like telling mama I wanted to die before her because I could not live without her—that was crazy talk, crazy speech, the kind that would lead you to end up in a mental institution. "Little girl," I would be told, "if you don't stop all this crazy talk and crazy acting you are going to end up right out there at Western State."

Madness, not just physical abuse, was the punishment for too much talk if you were female. Yet even as this fear of madness haunted me, hanging over my writing like a monstrous shadow, I could not stop the words, making thought, writing speech. For this terrible madness which I feared, which I was sure was the destiny of daring women born to intense speech (after all, the authorities emphasized this point daily), was not as threatening as imposed silence, as suppressed speech.

Safety and sanity were to be sacrificed if I was to experience defiant speech. Though I risked them both, deep-seated fears and anxieties characterized my childhood days. I would speak but I would not ride a bike, play hardball, or hold the gray kitten. Writing about the ways we are traumatized in our growing-up years, psychoanalyst Alice Miller makes the point in *For Your Own Good* that it is not clear why childhood wounds become for some folk an opportunity to grow, to move forward rather than backward in the process of self-realization. Certainly, when I reflect on the trials of my growing-up years, the many punishments, I can see now that in resistance I learned to be vigilant in the nourishment of my spirit, to be tough, to courageously protect that spirit from forces that would break it.

While punishing me, my parents often spoke about the necessity of breaking my spirit. Now when I ponder the silences, the voices that are not heard, the voices of those wounded and/or oppressed individuals who do not speak or write, I contemplate the acts of persecution, torture—the terrorism that breaks spirits, that makes creativity impossible. I write these words to bear witness to the primacy of resistance struggle in any situation of domination (even within family life); to the strength and power that emerges from sustained resistance and the profound conviction that these forces can be healing, can protect us from dehumanization and despair. . . .

. . . For us, true speaking is not solely an expression of creative power; it is an act of resistance, a political gesture that challenges politics of domination that would render us nameless and voiceless. As such, it is a courageous act—as such, it represents a threat. To those who wield oppressive power, that which is threatening must necessarily be wiped out, annihilated, silenced.

Recently, efforts by black women writers to call attention to our work serve to highlight both our presence and absence. Whenever I peruse women's bookstores, I am struck not by the rapidly growing body of feminist writing by black women, but by the paucity of available published material. Those of us who write and are published remain few in number. The context of

silence is varied and multi-dimensional. Most obvious are the ways racism, sexism, and class exploitation act to suppress and silence. Less obvious are the inner struggles, the efforts made to gain the necessary confidence to write, to rewrite, to fully develop craft and skill—and the extent to which such efforts fail.

Although I have wanted writing to be my life-work since childhood, it has been difficult for me to claim "writer" as part of that which identifies and shapes my everyday reality. Even after publishing books, I would often speak of wanting to be a writer as though these works did not exist. And though I would be told, "you are a writer," I was not yet ready to fully affirm this truth. Part of myself was still held captive by domineering forces of history, of familial life that had charted a map of silence, of right speech. I had not completely let go of the fear of saying the wrong thing, of being punished. Somewhere in the deep recesses of my mind, I believed I could avoid both responsibility and punishment if I did not declare myself a writer.

One of the many reasons I chose to write using the pseudonym bell hooks, a family name (mother to Sarah Oldham, grandmother to Rosa Bell Oldham, great-grandmother to me), was to construct a writer-identity that would challenge and subdue all impulses leading me away from speech into silence. I was a young girl buying bubble gum at the corner store when I first really heard the full name bell hooks. I had just "talked back" to a grown person. Even now I can recall the surprised look, the mocking tones that informed me I must be kin to bell hooks—a sharp-tongued woman, a woman who spoke her mind, a woman who was not afraid to talk back. I claimed this legacy of defiance, of will, of courage, affirming my link to female ancestors who were bold and daring in their speech. Unlike my bold and daring mother and grandmother, who were not supportive of talking back, even though they were assertive and powerful in their speech, bell hooks as I discovered, claimed, and invented her was my ally, my support.

That initial act of talking back outside the home was empowering. It was the first of many acts of defiant speech that would make it possible for me to emerge as an independent thinker and writer. In retrospect, "talking back" became for me a rite of initiation, testing my courage, strengthening my commitment, preparing me for the days ahead—the days when writing, rejection notices, periods of silence, publication, ongoing development seem impossible but necessary.

Moving from silence into speech is for the oppressed, the colonized, the exploited, and those who stand and struggle side by side a gesture of defiance that heals, that makes new life and new growth possible. It is that act of speech, of "talking back," that is no mere gesture of empty words, that is the expression of our movement from object to subject—the liberated voice.

Further Questions

1. What was your most successful effort at challenging authority by "talking back"?
2. What was the most successful effort made against you, as an authority, by someone "talking back" to you?
3. Is abandoning silence and expressing disagreement important for ending oppressive structures like racism and patriarchy? Think of a good example where spoken or written disagreement (or defiance) has caused a major change in an oppressive structure.

Gay Irony   II.4

BRIAN PRONGER

Brian Pronger speaks of how gay men can pass as straight in a society that takes heterosexuality as the norm and presumes that everyone fits in. Sexual orientation can be placed beneath the surface of appearance, allowing gays to assume the status of an invisible minority on occasions in which they wish to pass. Pronger calls this dissimulation "gay irony" and writes that it is highlighted by "radical drag": a man with a masculine, muscled body dressed as a slinky, sensuous woman.

Pronger is an associate researcher at the School of Physical and Health Education, University of Toronto (Toronto, Ontario).

Reading Questions

1. You go into a (same sex) locker room. What, if anything, do you assume about the sexual orientation of the people using it?

2. Imagine yourself homosexual but not visible as such. Do you sometimes feel a tension between the way you appear and the way you are?

3. Are there occasions when you dress in a way clearly appropriate to your gender because this will make life easier for you, even though this results in a discrepancy between the way you look and the way you feel?

The Fluidity of Being Gay and Passing as Straight

. . . GAY MEN PASS IN AND OUT of gay contexts, moment to moment, day to day, and through different periods of their lives. Gay contexts are created not only by the presence of gay men but also by their decisions to interpret a situation as gay. Consequently, it is possible for a gay man to go to a gymnasium, be completely involved in the athleticism of his workout, and experience that time as being simply athletic, devoid of any gay significance as far as he is concerned. Another day, he may go to the same gymnasium and find the same men there doing much the same exercises as they were previously; this time, however, he sees the experience as a gay experience. That is, he may find the situation sexy; he may find it ironic (as I will explain shortly); he may decide that he is with only other gay men and experience a sense of gay fraternity. The gay context depends on the man's interpretation. Self-concept also depends upon personal interpretation. A man who is a runner may enter the Boston Marathon, an event that he considers to be very important to himself athletically. His concerns are whether he will finish, what his time might be, or how painful the experience will be. Here, his concept of himself is overwhelmingly that of a runner. The same man could enter the same marathon another year, and having decided to wear a singlet with a large pink triangle emblazoned with the word *gay*, he sees himself as a gay runner and his participation in this race as an expression of his pride in being gay.

The fluidity of homosexuality is enhanced by the fact that gay men can and often do pass as straight men. In a society that assumes that everyone is heterosexual, it is relatively easy for homosexual men to "pass." This ability is a distinguishing feature of the homosexual minority; people of colour cannot easily pass as white, and women have a difficult time passing as men. Passing is particularly important in mainstream athletic culture where heterosexuality is expected (Kidd, 1987; Kopay & Young, 1977). Certainly, it is usually necessary for gay men to pass as straight in the potentially sexual situations of men's locker rooms and showers.

Afraid of losing their positions on teams, as a result of the compulsory heterosexuality of sport, many gay athletes find it necessary to hide their homosexuality by passing as straight. I interviewed an international competitive rower who said it was essential to seem to be heterosexual:

> You did everything you could to hang on to your seat, to make the crew, that you would never jeopardize—you wouldn't even tell the coach you had a cold. You could be *crippled* and you'd hide it from the coach, because if there's any perceived weakness, they'll put somebody else in the boat. So to hint that I was gay was to kiss rowing goodbye.

The Ironic Gay Sensibility

. . . Gay irony is a unique way of knowing that has its origins in the social construction of heterosexist society. The ways that gay men think are very much the results of having to deal with homophobia. To avoid suffering in potentially homophobic settings like athletic teams and locker rooms, gay men learn to pass as straight. Passing predisposes gay men to a sense of irony.

From an early age, gay men are aware of this important irony—they seem to be heterosexual when in fact they are not. Most social relations are organized around heterosexuality. For boys, the social side of sports is heterosexual. One's teammates form a "boys-wanting-girls club." When a young male athlete socializes with his teammates, inside or outside the locker room, talk is often about sex with girls and the problems of dating. Bars, clubs, or athletic dances held to mark the end of a sporting season or a school victory are always heterosexual functions. In their early years, most young gay people follow this social pattern.

A gay man may follow these patterns, but because he is not really part of the heterosexual action, the budding gay man is aware of himself as an outsider, an observer. The position of the observer is an ironic stance (Muecke, 1982). A young homosexual person can be aware of himself as an outsider without having understood himself as homosexual. In fact, this sense of being an outsider may lead to one's self-identification as homosexual. During this time the foundation for a young gay person's sense of irony develops. In his position as an observer, the young gay man, probably unconsciously, masters some of the basic skills of the ironist. As he grows older he becomes increasingly aware of himself as the observer who seems to be part of the action. Although he may never define his world as ironic, the gay man may, nevertheless, employ irony unwittingly. (One need not analyze and define the formal structure of a way of thinking or being in order to use that structure in day-to-day-life.) Growing up in a world in which heterosexuality is taken for granted, then, gay people may be introduced to the rudiments of irony. By developing this sense and seeing his world as ironic, the gay man can manipulate the socially constructed incompatibility of the appearance and the reality of his sexuality.

Wayne Booth (1974) says that fundamental to irony is its invitation to reconstruct something deeper than what is apparent on the surface. While inviting one to see deeper than the superficial appearance and thereby understand what is actually meant, irony preserves the appearance. The total truth includes both appearance and reality. This technique for understanding reality while maintaining a cosmetic appearance is very useful to gay men while passing as straight. It is a technique that many of us learn to use at very young ages simply in order to survive. Because gay men feel at home with irony, even when "the closet" is not an issue, they continue to interpret their worlds ironically. Because irony brings with it a sense of superiority, a sense of looking at the world from a higher place (Muecke, 1982), each gay ironic experience is a sublime reaffirmation of a gay worldview.

Gay irony is a way of thinking, communicating, and being that emerges out of the experience of being gay in a society in which people tend to believe that everyone is straight. It is a sensibility that is essentially fluid both through the lives of individuals and throughout society. The phenomenon of being gay is a matter of context; so too is the invocation of gay irony. Not all homosexual people see themselves as "gay," and not all gay people use irony. Being gay and the use of irony are conceptual dispositions and techniques that people use to think about themselves and interpret their worlds. Irony is a form of interpretation, a way of understanding that develops out of the experience of individuals' interactions with sexual and gender categories. Gay irony, therefore, is best understood as a tendency to interpret experience ironically rather than a consistent standpoint shared by all gay men. . . .

ANAGNORISIS

Gay men subtly communicate their shared worldview by using irony. This subtlety has important implications for gay men; it allows them to remain undiscovered by the uninitiated, thereby affording them some protection from the expressions of homophobia that frequently accompany detection. Especially important in gay irony is *anagnorisis,* which is the observer's recognition of the ironist as an ironist with a deeper intent than that which is immediately apparent on the surface. Anagnorisis occurs when the interpreter of the irony realizes the irony in the situation. In anagnorisis, the gay ironist not only reveals meanings that have been concealed by appearances, he also reveals himself. Eye contact is the way gay men usually recognize each other in non-gay settings. One manifestation of this eye contact can be a subtle, knowing look, which can be the clue for mutual anagnorisis. One man told me about being in a university weight room and watching an athlete to whom he was attracted lifting a weight. To most observers, the scenario would appear to be quite straight. A man whom he didn't know was standing nearby and watching the same athlete. Moving from the athlete to each other, their admiring eyes met, and with no more obvious gesture than a slight pause in their gazes, they became aware of their secret fraternity. In their sententious exchange of glances, having as novelist John Fowles said, "the undeclared knowledge of a shared imagination," their worlds touched. They uttered not a word.

ACTING VERSUS BEING

As a result of coming out in some contexts, gay men become more consciously aware of passing in others; gay men can start to see others' uses of masculinity as a technique for passing. This insight can bring them to a heightened awareness of their uses of masculinity as an ironic form. Rather than thinking of themselves as being masculine, gay men can come to think of themselves as acting masculine. In the 1970s, the disco group "The Village People" epitomized this masculine (and I think intensely ironic) act. Their outfits were ironic caricatures of masculinity: construction worker, policeman, Indian, and a hypermasculine-looking man with a mustache (a style known as the "clone"). One of their hit songs had the lyrics, "Macho, macho, man; I wanna be a macho man." The clue to their irony lies in the fact that they don't say they are macho men; rather, they "wanna be" macho men. That is, they look like macho men when in fact they are not. The macho look, especially that of the clone, became very popular in gay ghettos across North America and parts of Europe. The deep and sometimes subliminal irony of the gay masculine clone style[1] may best be appreciated in the light of Wallace Stevens (1977): "The final belief is to believe in a fiction, which you know to be a fiction, there being nothing else. The exquisite truth is to know that it is a fiction and that you believe in it willingly" (p. 163). . . .

This gay ironic play with masculinity is highlighted in radical drag. A man with bulging biceps and thunderous thighs wearing a slinky dress and a tiara is, through the juxtaposition of a masculine body and feminine clothes, expressing the overt irony of seeming to be "masculine" when he is also "feminine". . . .

NOTE

1. The fluidity of being gay should be kept in mind here; that is, there are men who may practice homosexuality who see their masculine behaviours not in this gay context but in a traditional patriarchal one. Moreover, they may switch from a traditional context to a gay one from time to time, depending on the situation.

BIBLIOGRAPHY

Booth, W. (1974). *A rhetoric of irony*. Chicago: University of Chicago Press.

Kidd, B. (1987). Sports and masculinity. In M. Kaufman (Ed.), *Beyond patriarchy: Essays by men on pleasure, power, and change* (pp. 250–265). Toronto: Oxford University Press.

Kopay, D., & Young, P. (1977). *The David Kopay story: An extraordinary self revelation*. New York: Arbor House.

Muecke, D. (1982). *Irony and the ironic*. London: Methuen.

Stevens, W. (1977). *Opus posthumous*. New York: Knopf.

Further Questions

1. Do you ever wear clothing, cosmetics, hairstyles, etc. that are usually worn only by the other gender? If so, why do you do this?

2. Do you find a man in obviously feminine clothing upsetting? Why? Is a woman in masculine clothing equally upsetting?

3. Do you have days when you think most of what you do in the sight of others is pure "fiction," not an expression of what you are really thinking or feeling?

Hair and Clothes   II.5

SUSAN BROWNMILLER

Susan Brownmiller notes that hair has always been used "to make a visual statement." In particular, a woman's hair says something about her sexual nature; silky, long hair and blond hair make the most eloquent statements in this area. Feminine clothes "never shut up." Their central point is that "a male is a male because a female dresses and looks and acts like another sort of creature." Most female clothes are confining. Also, it is necessary to bare one's skin in the right places to keep up with the competition, even on the most solemn, businesslike occasions. Men do not need to adorn themselves to appear well dressed in the workplace, although gay men have had an interesting effect on men's fashions, giving some of them better lines which reveal more of the contours of the body.

Brownmiller is a writer in New York City, contributor to many publications, and author of *Against Our Will: Men, Women and Rape.* Another selection by Brownmiller appears in Part XII.

Reading Questions

1. As a woman, how do you feel about your hair? How do you feel about the hair of men you are involved with in relationships or as friends or family members?

2. As a man, how do you feel about the appearance of women you are seen with in public? Does it matter whether you are in a relationship with the woman, or whether she is instead a co-worker, friend, or relative? Do you have the same level of concern about your own appearance?

3. What kind of statement do your clothes make? How does this statement differ from that of people who are clad differently?

Hair

... FROM TIME IMMEMORIAL, hair has been used to make a visual statement, for the body's most versatile raw material can be cut, plucked, shaved, curled, straightened, braided, greased, bleached, tinted, dyed and decorated with precious ornaments and totemic fancies. A change in the way one wears one's hair can affect the look of the face and alter a mood. A uniform hair style can set a group of people apart from others and signify conformity or rebellion, devotion to God or indulgence in sensual pleasures. Hair worn in a polarized manner has served to indicate the masculine and the feminine, the slave and the ruler, the young, the old, the virgin, the married, the widowed, the mourning. ....

It was Paul who told the Corinthians that a woman's long hair is "a glory to her," but the saint did not mean his words as a compliment to feminine beauty. He was laying down the creed that Christian men should offer up prayer with their heads uncovered because they were created as the image and glory of God, but women should cover their heads in church because they were created as the glory of man. "Judge in yourselves," he wrote in his epistle, "Is it comely that a woman pray unto God uncovered? Does not even nature itself teach you that if a man have long hair it is a shame unto him? But if a woman have long hair it is a glory to her: for her hair is given her for a covering."

Paul's thoughts about hair come after his famous creed that "the head of every man is Christ; and the head of the woman is the man." "It follows," wrote Saint Chrysostom, "that being covered is a mark of subjection and authority. For it induces her to look down and be ashamed and preserve entire her proper virtue."

Puritan moralists in sixteenth- and seventeenth-century England hammered away at this theme. The feminine woman, the virtuous woman, the woman who knew her place, was the female who wore her hair long, neatly arranged, with a concealing cap on her head. A wife's long hair, railed the pamphleteer Philip Stubbes, was her God-given "signe of subjection" before her husband and master, "as the Apostle proveth." Pamphleteer William Prynne also called up the apostle's proof. Women's long hair, he echoed, was something that "God and nature have given them for a covering, a token of subjection, and a natural badge to distinguish them from men." Denouncing the worldly fashions of his day—"our shorn English viragoes"—Prynne blasted off, "A woman with cut hair is a filthy spectacle and much like a monster."

So the male moralists protested, but always with the understanding that although a woman's long hair might be sacred it was also profane. Since it was given her by God to cover her nakedness, it was also a distressing symbol of her sexual nature. Out of control—unpinned, disheveled or free of a concealing cap—it was invested with dangerous powers. In myth the beautiful Lorelei, who sang while she combed her long blonde hair, lured sailors to wreck their boats on treacherous rocks. Sight of Medusa's hair of living snakes turned men into stone. The long, loose tresses that covered the nakedness of Lady Godiva as she rode her horse through town to honor her husband's oath seem less a "signe of subjection" than a very sexy image, and although it was hardly Saint Luke's intention, the unnamed sinner of his Gospel (often confused with Mary Magdalene) who penitently wiped the feet of Jesus with her hair became a paradigm of sensuality to Renaissance artists who delighted in painting this Biblical scene. ....

It is hard not to be influenced by the popular judgment that blondes are to the manner born, that whatever their individual features, they are prettier and luckier than dark-haired women, blessed by the Gods with a halo of good fortune. To be sure, I make my obeisance only before natural blondes, but this is a stubborn quirk that does not seem to be shared by the legions of men who are unabashed adorers of blondes, who will date only blondes, or who throw up their hands charmingly and confess that they have "a thing" for blondes whether or not they are dark at the roots. . . .

America's cult of blondeness reached its zenith in the Forties and Fifties, ironically at the moment in history when Nazi Germany and the cult of Aryan supremacy went down to defeat. The differences between the two sets of values are important to examine. Aryan supremacy had equated pale hair in both sexes with strength, intelligence and superior racial stock, whereas blondeness American style is a glittering prize that men seek in women but don't give two hoots about for themselves, except for a small group within the homosexual community who trade on blond hair as a way of appealing to other men. In the American tradition, blondeness is not associated with strength or intelligence. On the contrary, "dumb blonde" is practically one word on the lips of some people, and her innocent vapidity and daffy humor is counterposed to the loud, emotional intensity of know-it-all dark-haired women. (Even if the blonde is obviously smart and knowledgeable, she is perceived as less threatening or overbearing, and therefore more acceptably feminine, than her brunette sisters. There is no other way to explain the disproportionate number of blondes who hold coveted jobs as correspondents and newscasters on network television.) . . .

The irony was not lost on black women when Bo Derek, the blonde and perfect "Ten," was widely copied for her beaded braids—a style she had copied in turn from Cicely Tyson and some sophisticated black models who found the initial inspiration in African motifs. In jazz, rock music and hairdos it has been the fate of American blacks to see their originality exploited by the dominant white culture, but Bo Derek's braids caused a special black feminine anguish, for black women have suffered over their hair more than anyone else.

"Good" hair and "bad" hair are subjective judgments that are based on esthetic preference. "Good" hair does not do a superior job of protecting the scalp or allowing it to breathe.

"Good" hair is silken and soft to the touch, it is full, pliant and yielding, the feminine ideal in matters of anatomy as well as in character and personality. And "bad" hair—do we need to define that? "Bad" hair is split and broken ends, hair that is limp and stringy, hair that is wiry and unmanageable or too thin to hold a set, hair that is coarse to the touch of the fingers, hair that is naturally wild and kinky. . . .

Wild, springy hair was grandly positive in the African male tradition, a testament to virility and strength. By contrast the prototypical feminine head was tightly cornrowed, covered or shaved. Forcibly exposed to the esthetic and moral values of their white Christian masters, it was inevitable that American blacks would accept the judgment that this evidence of genetic heritage was difficult, shameful or bad. The celebration of Black Is Beautiful in the 1960s made pride in natural hair an easier matter for black men than for black women. Free of hot combs and straighteners, the Afro looked properly militant as a symbol of Black Power, but militance and femininity do not coexist with ease. The feminine Afro often had to be painstakingly teased to frame the face softly with a symmetrical halo.

Silky, long hair automatically inspires a cluster of preoccupied gestures that are considered sublimely feminine because they are sensuously self-involved: an absent-minded twisting of a stray curl, the freeing of loose ends that get caught under a coat collar, a dramatic toss of the entire mane, a brushing aside of the tendrils that fall so fetchingly across the forehead and into the eyes. A mass of long, soft hair is something to play with, a reassuring source of tactile sensation and a demanding presence that insists on the wearer's attention. Ntozake Shange sharply reminds us of these narcissistic feminine traits and how they exclude black women in her dramatic poem "today i'ma be a white girl," in which a black maid sarcastically reveals that "the first thing a white girl does in the morning is fling her hair," and that she falls back on flinging or swinging her hair whenever she is at a loss for something to do. . . .

Women, of course, are not yet entitled to be free of the bother. The hairdresser's appointment is as permanent a fixture on the calendar of the female executive as the lunchtime squash date on the calendar of her male counterpart. A television anchorman ducks in and out of the makeup room before he faces the camera; his female co-host must allot time as well for the curling iron and the fluff-out before she is deemed fit to be seen by the judgmental public. An evening out on the town is ritualistically preceded by an afternoon at the beauty parlor for millions of American women, an event that would be of anthropological significance if it occurred in a distant, exotic culture. In fact, anything a woman might do that is at all public, from singing in a nightclub to attending a funeral, or simply "going to the city," may be preceded by an allotment of time to do her hair or have it "done". . . .

Clothes

Who would deny that dressing feminine can be quite creative? A woman with a closetful of clothes for different moods and occasions is an amateur actress and a wily practitioner of the visual arts. A grand sense of theater reposes on that rack of hangers, offering a choice of imaginative roles from sexy vixen to old-fashioned, romantic lady. Children of both sexes love to dress up in their mother's costumes, complete with lipstick, handbag and high heels, because they adore the game of "Let's pretend." Feminine clothing induces the body to strut about in small, restrained yet show-offy ways. Feminine clothing produces its special feminine sounds: the staccato clickety-click of the heels, the musical jangle of bracelets, the soft rustle of silk, or, in an earlier era, the whisper of petticoats, the snap of a fan. And the finishing touches, the makeup and perfume, create a distinctive, sweet feminine smell.

And then there are the compliments, the ultimate reward, for men are known to be highly appreciative when a woman has taken the trouble to create an entire human being who looks and acts and smells so different from them.

Every wave of feminism has foundered on the question of dress reform. I suppose it is asking too much of women to give up their chief outward expression of the feminine difference, their continuing reassurance to men and to themselves that a male is a male because a female dresses and looks and acts like another sort of creature. . . .

Who said that clothes make a statement? What an understatement that was. Clothes never shut up. They gabble on endlessly, making their intentional and unintentional points.

It is written in Deuteronomy that "The woman shall not wear that which pertaineth unto a man, neither shall a man put on a woman's garment," and the reason given refers to the strongest displeasure of the highest authority. Failure to abide by a sex-distinctive dress code is an "abomination unto the Lord thy God."

Why should the Lord have cared so intensely about clothes? Was it to keep the sexes firmly apart and discourage promiscuity? Was it to reinforce the homosexual taboo? Was it a way of saying that women were not to be soldiers and that warriors were not to sneak about in women's clothes as a ruse to fool the enemy? I've read these differing explanations and while they all may apply to some extent, they avoid the basic point. Naked as He created them, Adam and Eve could not be mistaken. Dressed in fig leaves and animal skins after they came to know shame, their gender differences were partially obscured. A sex-distinctive dress code (a loincloth for Adam, a sarong for Eve; a striped tie for Adam, a pair of high heels for Eve) created an emblematic polarity that satisfied a societal need for unambiguous division, neat categories and stable order.

When a child is asked by its parents whether the naked person in the picture is a man or a woman and the child replies, "I can't tell because they're not wearing clothes," the joke is really quite profound. In a clothed culture the eye depends on artificial externals for its visual cues. When the cues are absent or conflicting, the psychological disturbance in the observer can be enormous. A blurring of the sartorial signposts can inspire hostility and rage. To mistake a man for a woman, or vice versa, is dangerous. An entire range of responses may be inappropriately misdirected. One's own sexual identity may be thrown into confusion, for how can we know who we are unless we are fairly certain who is the other? . . .

A skirt, any skirt, has a feminizing mission that goes beyond the drawing of a polite, yet teasing, shade over the female crotch and its functions, and of flattering or draping the rear end and stomach with graceful folds. Expansive, casual body gestures are characterized as immodest and unfeminine when practiced by women, and skirts restrict those large, free movements. One does not stride. One is perpetually reminded to be circumspect when sitting or bending down. Whatever its length, and however wide, the open-endedness of a skirt cannot help but guide the body into a set of conservative poses and smaller gestures, and the traditional feminine accessories that went with a skirt in an earlier era (corset, fan, muff, parasol and shawl) and the shoes and pocketbooks of today have always reinforced those restrictions. But of course. Feminine clothing has never been designed to be functional, for that would be a contradiction in terms. Functional clothing is a masculine privilege and practicality is a masculine virtue. To be truly feminine is to accept the handicap of restraint and restriction, and to come to adore it. . . .

No woman was more stubborn in her refusal to bow to the conventions of feminine dress than Joan of Arc, and no woman in history paid a higher price. In the glorious days of her triumph the Maid had exchanged her peasant's red skirt for a page's costume of gray and black; her pride was a suit of shining white armor for leading her troops in battle. After her capture Joan was beseeched by her jailors to put on a gown, but she would not comply. Her Voices had not told her that her mission was over, and besides, it was safer to dress as a soldier in a prison administered by men. Joan's inquisitors pondered obsessively on her masculine attire. Receiving the sacrament while dressed like a man was one of the crimes with which she was charged. A woman's gown was brought to her cell after she broke down and made her sworn confession. Joan put it on, then took it off. God's soldier could not bear the humiliation. Her relapse into masculine clothing sealed her fate, for this was proof that her mind had not submitted. Joan was taken to the stake and burned in a skirt and bodice, an additional triumph for her captors. . . .

This much can be said: Some women have worn men's clothes to accomplish their work. Some women have worn men's clothes to indicate their temporary or permanent sexual attraction to other women. Some women have worn men's clothes to experience the power and freedom of being a man. Some women have worn men's clothes because they hated their female bodies. Some women have worn men's clothes because they looked so adorable in them. Some women have worn men's clothes because they sought an alternative to the confining clothes they were expected to wear, and expected to delight in, as women. . . .

Winter and summer, touches of nudity are another proof of feminine expression. It is chic to bare the skin, to play the tease, however unwittingly, between the concealed and the exposed. A reluctance to show a thigh or reveal a midriff is construed as prudish timidity, old-fashioned dullness and a lack of confidence, or else it is circumstantial evidence of flaw: thick legs, flabby skin, a hideous, deforming scar. I am sympathetic to the argument that a woman should be free to wear what she wants without moral judgment or accusations of inviting assault (no study has ever shown that rapists seek out those who are provocatively dressed), yet I am not unmindful that the argument usually comes from very young women in the happy phase of exploring fashion with a pioneer spirit, and who look ahead to new frontiers. Those who resent gratuitous nudity are usually older, at an age where the flesh is less firm and the attitude less liberal. Because older women are placed automatically on the losing side of the competition to look sexually appealing, they are in possession of knowledge that escapes the young and the physically blessed. Exposure of flesh is not a mere matter of style, insouciance and modernity; it is a contest by which women are judged.

Was it inevitable that the movement for dress reform should have passed so blithely from the battle against restrictive clothing to a glamorous rivalry over how much nudity could be revealed? Erotic attire has often served as a smoke screen to deflect female consciousness from a lasting understanding of the nature of oppression. The décolleté ball gowns of the rich and the peekaboo costumes of whores historically shocked the industrious, God-fearing poor with their prideful displays of pampered flesh. Mrs. Grundy may have been a stereotype of conservative bourgeois values, but she was created by men of the bourgeoisie who wished to escape their own background. Her opposite number, the "liberated woman," is assumed to be a *femme fatale* in scanty dress. It is not accidental that as soon as women were freed from tight corsets and heavy, hampering clothes they were heartily encouraged to express the feminine difference in terms of exposure, for exposure was always the issue as the moralists saw it. . . .

Many gay men, as straight women often observe, are very attractive. There's a lot to be said for tight pants on a good body in excellent condition. However, the effort is seldom made on our behalf, except by a handful of rock stars and movie actors who absorb themselves in this colorful, sensuous manner—the word is narcissistic—because appearance and audience play a crucial role in how they earn a living. Most straight men do not need to rely on sexual plum-

age, either to earn a living or to entice a woman, and musculine tradition of the last two centuries has taught that sexualized clothing on a man is undignified and foppish. Men of action and power are colorless by choice, it would seem, when their status is unchallenged and secure. Only those most likely to be ignored or discounted, or who possess a special need to be noticed (a broad category that might include women, blacks, gay men, short men, men on the make and entertainers) are demonstrably more colorful and fashion-conscious.

Gays nevertheless have had a marked effect on men's fashions, chiefly because the new emphasis on slim-line jackets and close-fitting pants has reopened the question of pocketbooks and pockets. Women's clothes are rarely designed with functional pockets (the nineteenth-century feminist Charlotte Perkins Gilman wrote passionately about this) because the necessary objects a real pocket might be expected to hold—money, keys, comb, eyeglasses, pen and all the feminine etceteras—would spoil the graceful, smooth line. Influenced in part by European designers, a pioneering number of American men have persuaded themselves that it might not be too great a blow to their masculinity if they carried a shoulderstrap bag. Not a clutch or a handbag—that would be too feminine and inconvenient—but a neat, tailored carryall that is flat and unobtrusive. Perhaps the day may arrive when the pocketbook ceases to be a feminine symbol (how will the Freudians cope with that?), or perhaps this brave new accessory will prove too encumbering for general masculine appeal. Realistically, it is harder to imagine legions of women without their pocketbooks than legions of men with them, for men have a definite biological advantage when it comes to stowing a pack of cigarettes and a wallet. An inside breast pocket, or an outside breast pocket for that matter, is no place for a woman to carry anything. . . .

Serious women have a difficult time with clothes, not necessarily because they lack a developed sense of style, but because feminine clothes are not designed to project a serious demeanor. Part of the reason many people find old photographs of parading "suffragettes" so funny is that their elaborate dresses seem at odds with marching in unison down the street. Team spirit has always relied on a uniform dress code for maximum effect, as generals and bohemians well know. Despite the proliferation of advice manuals on what the up-and-coming young female executive should wear to the office, dressing feminine remains incompatible with looking corporate, credible and competent, and no dress-for-success book has been able to resolve the inherent contradictions, or provide the extra time and money that maintaining a feminine wardrobe requires.

Men resigned themselves to a lack of individuality in clothes a long time ago, but women still hold out the hope for clothes that are comfortable, feminine and appropriate for work in one all-purpose outfit. Major airlines periodically commission top designers to perform this feat for their flight attendants with mixed, and often peculiar, results. The U.S. Army has yet to resolve the weighty matter of the right kind of shoe for its female recruits. In tradition-minded occupations where women are breaking employment bars, an appropriate dress code seems particularly elusive. How should a woman dress for her job in a symphony orchestra where the men perform in regulation black tuxedos? At one concert I attended, the flutist wore a floor-length black skirt, the violinist wore a knee-length black skirt, and the cellist opted for black trousers. They managed to play harmoniously, and that was important.

In corporate law and finance, two conservative fields where ambitious women have established a tenuous foothold, the conventional uniform for the new female executive is the dull-colored jacket and matching knee-length skirt, suggesting a gentlemanly aspect on top and a ladylike aspect down below. Pants are not worn, except by an occasional secretary, for they lack an established tradition, and bright colors do not signal efficiency, responsibility and steadiness on the job. Calling attention to the breasts by wearing a sweater or a silk shirt without a jacket is unprofessional on the executive level, especially since men persist in wearing regulation suit jackets to show their gentleman status. Few think it odd that the brave new careerist must obscure her breasts and display her legs in order to prove she can function in a masculine world and yet retain some familiar, comforting aspect of the feminine difference. Tradition in clothes may well outlast tradition in occupation. When Sandra Day O'Connor was sworn in as the first woman to serve on the United States Supreme Court, there was no mistaking which one she was in the formal group picture. Eight smiling justices wore trousers and long black judicial robes that came to the ankles and one smiling justice wore a specially hemmed robe that came to the knees. Justice O'Connor was the one in nylon stockings. . . .

Further Questions

1. In a situation where there is a distinct gender code for dress (e.g., a job interview) what do you think would happen to you if you appeared in the apparel of the other gender?

2. Do you believe that the amount of flesh bared (e.g., how far down you cover your legs) should not be mandated by social pressure? Are you being realistic?

3. Do you think you spend too much time on your hair or other aspects of your appearance?

II.6   The Unadorned Feminist

JANET RADCLIFFE-RICHARDS

Janet Radcliffe-Richards discusses beauty, dress, and the sex-object question. The discussion is not of traditional feminine dress as such, but the reasons often given for it.

Radcliffe-Richards teaches philosophy at the Open University and at Oxford University. She is presently working on a second book. This selection and the one in Part X are excerpts from her first book.

Reading Questions

1. Are appearance standards for women too stringent compared to standards for men?
2. Do you think of a feminist as someone who defies fashion standards?
3. Do men care too much about looks in women?

The Issue

SURPRISING AS IT IS, after all these years, the commonest public image of a feminist still seems to be of a woman who has disposed of her bra, preferably by burning it in public. This idea is so firmly entrenched in many minds as to be almost equated with feminism at times: a radio interviewer recently asked a woman whether she was going to become-liberated-and-burn-her-bra, and a friend of mine said somewhat coyly of his new daughter-in-law that she was 'rather liberated, and went around without underwear'. As a matter of fact bras were never burned, as far as I know. But the picketers of the Miss America Pageant in 1968 did provide 'a huge Freedom Trash Can'[1] into which women were invited to throw bras, girdles, curlers, false eyelashes, wigs, and any other such 'woman garbage' they happened to have around the house; and certainly the disappearance of all such fripperies among the ranks of the liberated has become one of the most conspicuous parts of feminism.

As a reaction against the past, and women's having had the importance of their personal beauty forced down their throats for as long as anyone can remember, this is all very easy to understand. Feminism, however, is not supposed to be concerned just with reactions. It is supposed to be providing a blueprint for a better state of things, and there is no doubt at all that many feminists regard the rejection of 'woman garbage' as a *substantial* issue, a thing which feminists ought to be committed to, rather than just a gesture. That actually presents far more problems than may at first appear, and it is important to settle them. Many feminists regard women who persist in clinging to their traditional trappings as traitors to the cause, while on the other hand to many non-feminists this austerity in the movement is one of its most unattractive aspects. Feelings run high on both sides. The purpose of this chapter is to try to sort the issues out.

Feminists have several very good reasons for resisting many of the traditional pressures on women to beautify themselves. Women face far more demands for variety, expense and effort in dress than men do, and suffer far more public disapproval if these standards are not met. The effort needed takes their attention away from more important things, the standards set are far beyond the reach of most women, and fashions often make movement difficult or present dangers to health. All these things are legitimate targets of feminist complaint.

. . . To the extent that this is the motivation behind the rejection of 'woman garbage', it is obviously an important part of feminism.

The problem is, however, that this simply does not account for all that goes on. It is true that there are many feminists who steadfastly refuse to put any effort at all into their appearance, which supports the view that they are determinedly following their own priorities and doing nothing more than that. But that in itself does not account entirely for the deliberately unfeminine style of dress gone in for by nearly all. People have, after all, to choose their clothes whatever they are, and a feminist whose main motivation was to put as little time and money into them as possible should presumably go around in the first and cheapest thing she could find in a jumble sale, even if it happened to be a shapeless turquoise Crimplene dress with a pink cardigan.[2] No feminist would be seen dead in any such thing. Obviously, therefore, the aim is not just to take what is cheapest and easiest, even though considerations of that sort must come into the matter to some extent. Style is important. . . .

Feminist practice cannot be entirely accounted for, either, by ideas of comfort and practicality. A good many traditional feminine clothes are quite acceptably comfortable, and what counts as practical depends on what you are trying to do. All feminists whose daily life calls for their being prepared to shift a ton of coal at a moment's notice may have to wear the regulation blue jeans all the time, but that does not apply to the ones who type or teach or work on production lines, and even the coal-shifters (who have to change their clothes occasionally) have no reason based on time-wasting for not sometimes changing into pretty clothes for a party. The priorities argument simply is not enough to account for all aspects of the adoption of the usual feminist style of dress.

Of course women who dress like this may simply prefer it. They may positively wish to minimize sexual difference in dress, or enjoy being as casual as possible, or find the sort of dress they choose specially comfortable. If they do, of course, there is nothing to be said against it. One legitimate reason for opposing the rigid demands of feminine dress is to allow women to establish their own priorities and do as they please, and if feminists in their dress were doing nothing but pleasing themselves there would be no more to be said. However, that is simply not the case. The fact is that women who dress in a conventionally feminine way, or give the impression of caring about their appearance however little effort it actually takes, are regarded by many feminists as enemies. This attitude has nothing to do with a question of freedom to choose. Anyone who has tried looking feminine in a gathering of extreme feminists knows that the pressures against that sort of appearance are every bit as strong as any pressures about dress in the wider world; in fact at the moment they are probably stronger.

There really is a world of difference between deciding you must reluctantly stop putting much effort into something which has been given too high a priority by tradition, and in treating that thing as something inherently *pernicious,* to be got rid of whether it is any trouble or not. There is obviously more to the feminist rejection of 'woman garbage' than individual decisions about priorities. And as a matter of fact the man in the street, who thinks he knows that feminists burn their bras, also thinks he knows why they do it. It has nothing to do with time or trouble (obviously bras are no trouble); it is, he thinks, all part of a deliberate effort to prevent women's being thought of as *sex objects*.

He does, actually, find this extremely puzzling, since he does not regard braless women as in the least unsexy, but that is what he has been led to believe. Furthermore, frequent comments of feminists seem to bear out his theory. 'It is degrading to make yourself attractive to men', 'Any woman who tries to make herself attractive to men is as good as a prostitute', 'You're a tart, throwing yourself at men . . . a slut', 'To make yourself attractive is to make yourself a male plaything . . . a sexual object', 'Women tart themselves up to get husbands'; and so on.[3] It does seem to be for reasons connected with these ideas that many feminists regard it as essential to look deliberately unconcerned about their appearance and deliberately unfeminine. It is not just a matter of priorities, or freedom for women to do as they like, even though these things undoubtedly come into the matter and perhaps are the only concern of some. There is unquestionably a strong element of resistance to being an 'object of pleasure' for the male. It is this part of the impulse to provide trash cans for feminine fripperies which is the main concern of this chapter.

Sensual Pleasure

It cannot possibly be wrong to want to be pleasing to a lover. Nobody could get much satisfaction from the thought of being loved in spite of being *un*pleasing, and only as a result of pure altruism and grim determination on the part of their lover. If, therefore, the rejection of feminine adornment is to be seen as a refusal to please men (which it certainly often is) *and* an integral part of feminism, it must be seen as directed more specifically against particular types of pleasure. It must be directed against men who want women for the wrong reasons. These men are usually said to be the ones who want women as sex objects; the ones who want them for sex and nothing else. . . . Perhaps the essence of the feminist position can be caught by saying that the protest is against the male's demand that the female should be sensually pleasing to him in all respects, and his (presumed) lack of interest in very much else about her.

Anyway, feminists do complain that men have for far too long wanted women only for these superficial characteristics, and it seems that the feminist refusal to please men sensually may be a way of trying to separate the men who want women for the right reasons from the ones who (as our grandmothers would have said) want only one thing. And certainly it is easy to see why this feeling among women should lead to their determination not to adorn themselves. It is beyond all question true that if you refuse to be sexually pleasing you are not much use as a sex object, and if you are not beautiful you are unlikely to be loved for your beauty. If the aim of the deliberately unadorned feminist is to make sure that men who have the wrong attitude to women have no interest in her, she is likely to succeed.

That, however, does not conclude the matter. Although the method may be a very effective one for getting rid of the tares, it has the rather serious disadvantage of being likely to eliminate most of the wheat in the process as well. Certainly, it will get rid of the men who are interested in women only from the point of view of sensual pleasing, but it is bound to affect at the same time not only them, but also the ones with excellent senses of priority; the ones who value character, intelligence, kindness, sympathy, and all the rest far above mere sensual pleasing, but nevertheless would like that too if they could get it *as well* as all these other things. Caring about such matters is not the same thing as caring exclusively, or even mainly, about them. The best-judging man alive, confronted with two women identical in all matters of the soul but not equal in beauty, could hardly help choosing the beautiful one. Whatever anyone's set of priorities, *the pleasing in all respects must be preferable to the pleasing in only some,* and this means that any feminist who makes herself unattractive must deter not only the men who would have valued her *only* for her less important aspects, but many of the others too. Or if they did still choose her, they would be less well pleased with her than they would have been if she had been physically attractive as well. A man who would not change his woman for any other in the world might still know that she would please him even more if she looked like the centre fold from the latest *Playboy*.

If feminists make themselves deliberately un-attractive, they are not only keeping off the men who would value their more important qualities too little, but are also lessening their chances of attracting men who care about such things *at all*. If they think that is a good thing to do, they must be prepared to argue that it is positively bad to care about whether people are sensually pleasing or not; that if you do not care at all about people's beauty you are morally superior to someone who does. Perhaps some people think that is true. If so, however, they must also think it morally bad to care about beauty at all, since beauty is the same sort of thing whether it is in paintings, sunsets or people, and *someone who does not care about beauty in people is someone who simply does not care about beauty.*

Now of course beauty is often of a low pri-ority, and it is morally good to care relatively little about it when people are hungry, or unjustly treated, or unhappy in other ways. Most of us, however, would like people to have beauty as well as other things, because for most of them it is one of the delights of life; we complain when the government does not subsidize the arts, and get angry when people live in ugly environments. Some people do not care about art and environ-mental beauty, it is true, but that just means that they are aesthetically insensitive. It is not actually wicked to be aesthetically insensitive, but neither is it a virtue, any more than being tone deaf, or not feeling the cold, or having no interest in phi-losophy or football. People who do care about it are good when they sacrifice their pleasure in beauty for something more important, but only then. There is nothing whatever to be said for the puritanical idea that self-denial is good in itself. It is good only as a means to an end.[4]

Much the same goes for the sensual enjoy-ment of sex. We may perhaps say that sex is a lower thing than the love of souls, but in order to blame men for caring about it at all in women it is necessary to argue that it is actually a *bad thing, positively* bad, rather than simply something which is less important than other things. But if sensual pleasing is a good thing, why not wear pretty clothes? Why not wear a provocative bra, especially if it is as comfortable as any other? To do so is simply to make yourself more pleasing, in more respects, and with very little effort. To re-fuse to do that may show that you are not in-terested in men who are interested in sex, but that is a personal preference, and nothing to do with feminist ideals. It can be no part of a serious feminism to argue that there is anything inher-ently wrong with the sensual enjoyment of sex.

Although it may be morally good to give up sensual pleasure to achieve some other end, there is nothing to be said for giving it up *unless* there is some other end to achieve. Women cannot reasonably regard it as morally reprehensible in men that they should care about what women look like, even though they may reasonably ex-pect them to care more about other things. It is, however, amazing how much general confusion there is about this subject, and how ready the careless sentimental of all types (not only femi-nist) are to assure everyone that it doesn't matter if you are plain or deformed, because a really nice person won't care. . . .

. . . All the muddled distributors of moral reflections and cold comfort, feminist or other-wise, succeed in doing is to invite bitterness when people realize that according to these impossible standards there are very few 'nice' people around.

It is useless to argue that to foster this kind of attitude discriminates against ugly women. There is no question of fostering, merely of recognizing the inevitable. Of course it is unfair in some sense that some people are born more beautiful than others, just as it is unfair that some are cleverer than others, or have parents who brought them up to be pleasant rather than unpleasant, or are stronger or more agile than other people. Of course we should see what can be done to make things less unjust. However, it is not the solution to cosmic unfairnesses in the distribution of things to try to prove that they do not matter, or that they only seem to matter because of the evils of society. It is not an evil in society that beauty matters: other things being equal, it is impossible that it should not matter. . . .

The simple fact is that for a woman to make herself physically or sexually unattractive is to deflect all sexual interest: it is to distance alike the good and bad among men; the ones who have sexual interests among others and the ones whose interest in women is all sexual. That, of course, may be what some of the women who do it want. If that is so, however, it must be regarded as a personal inclination of their own; it cannot be seen as a reasonable feminist policy. Most women want to attract men, and if they do they must (at the very least) not make themselves deliberately unattractive. It is no part of the moral corruption of men that they care about beauty in women, and it is no mark of the highest sexual relationship that it should have no sensual content. For the woman who wants to separate the sheep from the lecherous goats, there is, unfortunately, no alternative to the tedious process of hand-sorting. It may be fraught with attendant risks of mistake and calculated deception, but it has to be done; the feminist who tries to make a short cut by her refusal to be beautiful or feminine is left with nothing but the grim satisfaction of finding, after having measured men with an infinite yard-stick, that they are all wanting.

Packaging

Let us then take it that there is nothing at all to be said for being deliberately unattractive, unless you actually want to keep off everyone who might be interested at all in sensual pleasures, and move on to what is unquestionably another idea at the back of many minds: that it is bad that women should put any *effort* into making themselves attractive to men. As was mentioned before, this is clearly not the whole of the argument against 'woman garbage' because it does not account for deliberate efforts to look unattractive, and choosing one style of appearance rather than another within the constraints of a given amount of effort. Still it certainly is an issue in its own

right, and for some feminists perhaps the main one. To dress up, or beautify, or aim to titillate men, is said to amount to *packaging,* which turns women into commodities, and is degrading.

There are a good many aspects to this issue, and it is made very difficult to deal with by the fact that its parts get entangled together and with parts of other separate issues. Still, they must be separated for the purpose of making them clear. A good starting point is the comment of one feminist speaking bitterly during a television broadcast about the effort women were expected to put into their appearance: 'They can't love you as you are, they must love you for what you have become.'

Forgetting the specific issue of beauty for the moment (it will reappear shortly), what about the general idea of being wanted for what you are, rather than what you have become? There are difficulties even about what this means (if it means anything), since what you have become *is* now what you are. However, it sounds as though what is implied is that you ought not to have to make any efforts to change yourself; whatever you are like, people ought to want you that way.

But what is the great advantage in remaining as you are? You might be something quite undesirable. You might be selfish, or careless, or boring, or uneducated, or socially inept, or illiterate, and if you are there seems everything to be said for making a change. Why should anyone be expected to like the original unimproved version? To suppose in some vague way that it must be specially valuable is to allow muddles about the natural to sneak in again. They must be resisted. Whatever is meant by 'what you are' in this context, there is nothing *a priori* to be said in favour of it.

Of course in most matters, like education and manners and morals, people are all in favour of improvement, and this argument would be accepted. For some reason, however, there seems to be an idea that there is something very different about *natural beauty*, and this is a point at which feminists find themselves slipping into the company of surprising allies in the conservative world. Something needs to be said about that in particular, therefore, and the main thing which needs doing is to separate various questions. 'Natural beauty' hides a multitude of confusions, which tend to coalesce into a blur under the general heading.

First, perhaps relatively unimportant in feminism but still worth mentioning, there is the sentimental idea that people are all by nature equally beautiful 'in their own way', and what we should be doing is getting people to recognize that, rather than encouraging everyone to try to conform to current tastes. This one can be dismissed straight away. By any possible standard it is quite straightforwardly *false* that everyone is equally beautiful. It makes no difference to argue that standards change and that there is some standard which could make anyone beautiful: even if that were true (which it almost certainly is not) it is irrelevant. Even if you would have been beautiful according to the taste of five hundred years ago it is not much consolation for being thought ugly now. It is no good to say that we ought to change our standards of beauty to incorporate everyone. No doubt we should aim for greater flexibility, but we cannot alter our standards to the extent of making everyone beautiful without getting rid of ideas of beauty altogether; there can be no standard of beauty if nothing would count as ugly. We cannot recommend that women should do nothing to improve themselves on the grounds that what they should really be doing is trying to make people accept that they are all beautiful just as they are.

The second idea about natural beauty is, roughly, that you can't possibly improve on nature, and therefore should leave well alone. That seems to put an unwarranted amount of faith in nature. Of course people *can* make themselves hideous with too much powder and paint, but that is not the point. That some people fail does not suggest that success is impossible in the nature of things. Of *course* there are things which people can do to make themselves more beautiful and otherwise attractive. It does not matter if

beauty is in the eye of the beholder: you can always find out what the beholder likes. You can darken your lashes or pluck your brows or curl your hair, and if those things are thought beautiful, you can in doing them make yourself more beautiful.

And finally (for this purpose) there is the idea shared by feminists[5] and, as I recall, one elderly nonconformist minister, that to attract by artificial beauty is to use false pretences. The idea of this one, presumably, is that a man is cheated if he thinks he has acquired a beautiful woman, and finds too late that when she takes off her false hair and eyelashes and nails, and removes the paint and corsets and padded bra, she is not what she seemed. If that is the idea of false pretences, of course, it does not apply to various beautifying procedures like plastic surgery, careful hair cutting and perming, slimming and the like, since those all have lasting effects. Any objection to that sort of thing must be another confusion about the 'natural' person being the real thing, and the unreal thing being a deception. But what about the less permanent cosmetic devices? Are men entitled to feel cheated by such artificial beauty in women? These days, of course, it hardly applies, since they usually have plenty of time to find out before being inveigled by these illusions into marriage. But anyway, a man who gets a woman who knows how to make herself *look* well, even though nature has made little of her, is obviously better off than a man who gets one who is beautiful neither by nature nor by contrivance; beauty is not a matter of what you *are,* it is a matter of what you *look* like. The idea that beauty is truth, however deeply entrenched in the romantic mind, is just nonsense. And to consider the matter again from the point of view of cheating, it might plausibly be argued that the man who gets a woman with the artistic skill to improve herself is actually doing better than one whose partner is beautiful only by nature: skill in making oneself beautiful has the advantage over natural beauty that it does not turn grey, or wrinkle, or sag, or spread.

Ideas of natural beauty, however they are defined and defended, cannot show that women ought to be satisfied with their looks as they are. We come now, therefore, to another proposition held by many feminists who are opposed to putting effort into appearance; that time spent on looks is time wasted. As one feminist said, 'a woman who spends time on her appearance is one who hasn't anything better to do.'[6] That sounds more reasonable; the argument is that beautifying is bad because it is a waste of time.

However, once the matter has been recast in this form it radically changes its character and, most importantly, ceases to be a feminist question. *The question of how much effort is worth putting into beauty has nothing to do with feminism.* It tends to look like a feminist matter, of course, because it is generally accepted that women make themselves beautiful for men while men go to no such trouble for women, but the idea that this has anything to do with women's not *caring* about beauty in men is a most extraordinary myth. They have not, of course, generally been able to demand it. For one thing, women traditionally had to look for economic security in men (because they could not generally have it in their own right) and that meant that other things had to come before the luxury of choosing a beautiful partner, whereas a man could often indulge himself in this way. For another thing, the general superiority of power of men over women has meant that women have been more anxious to please men than men have been to please women: to capture and keep their men women do all they can in the cause of beauty, while 'Man demands in his arrogance to be loved as he is',[7] as Germaine Greer said. But it is precisely this asymmetry of power which is the feminist question. The *feminist* concern is to make sure that man is in no position to demand more of woman than he is willing to give; the question of how much each ought to demand in general has nothing to do with feminism.

The question of the value of effort put into sensual pleasing returns us to one of the main points of the last section; that beauty was the same sort of thing whether it was in people or anywhere else. If people care about making their rooms pleasant for people to be in, there is nothing at all odd about their caring about whether they themselves are worth looking at. If it is worthwhile to go to the trouble of putting up Christmas decorations, it is equally worthwhile to go to the trouble of making oneself pretty for a party. People disagree about how much effort these things are worth, of course, but that depends on their own personal priorities. In the same way, people differ about how much (purely personal) concern they have in being beautiful, and in how much beauty they want in a partner. Some want a great deal, others do not care so much and would rather have other things. But, once again, there is nothing morally good about being aesthetically insensitive or sensually insensitive in any other way, and women who do care about beauty in men, and men who care about it in women, are not reprehensible.

Feminism is concerned with sexual justice, and not with the ultimate worthwhileness of one kind of preference over another. The fact that some feminists seem to confuse feminism and puritanism, and convey that it is part of the women's movement to see sex and sensual pleasing as a frivolous waste of time, is probably one of the main things which puts people off feminism. Anyone who wants a puritanical movement should call it that, and not cause trouble for feminism by trying to suggest the two are the same. . . .

Confrontation, and Women's Culture

The main general conclusion so far is that it is a very serious mistake to confuse feminism with an opposition to beauty and sensuality. Even if there are good arguments against these things, or against giving a high priority to them, they are not feminist arguments. Feminism is concerned only with sexual injustice, and therefore not with these things themselves but only the imbalance of power which allows men to exploit women sexually. The feminist problem is to stop women from being unable to get a fair bargain, or demand from men as much as they give. Therefore it is no part of feminism to insist that women should not make themselves attractive to men; any woman who does that is doing it as a matter of personal preference, and not out of feminist principle.

I want now to return to this last group of women, women who choose for personal reasons not to look attractive to men, and consider its position from the point of view of feminism.

Women may have either of two personal reasons for reacting strongly against the traditional feminine appearance. The first of these stems from not caring at all about dress, or wanting to be comfortable in a particular sort of way, or something else like that. That is not my concern here. The second is more important for feminism. There is no doubt that there are many women who deliberately choose to be unattractive to men because it seems the only way to deflect men's sexual interest.

The reasons for this vary. Some women find it convenient, no doubt, to keep sexual interest to a minimum in their professional lives. Some, presumably, just hate men and want to keep them off. Many others are horrified when they discover the nature of male sexual fantasy and are revolted at the thought that they might ever be the object of it. Others want to escape the nuisance of the wolf-whistle, the leer, and the salacious remark, whose annoyance is infinitely compounded by men's insolent presumption that women are pleased by them. Others want to avoid the danger of rape, or the lesser problem of more honourable pursuers who reproach women with having led men on by their appearance. (It is not only judges in rape cases who say that attractively dressed women ask for all they get; far more reasonable men sometimes imply that if a woman makes herself attractive she is unfair to refuse men's advances.) There is no doubt that one as-

pect or another of this constant onslaught has driven many women to retreat from conspicuous femininity to avoid the problems of being female.

However, this is not the right way to attack the problem, because it leaves completely untouched the basic trouble, which is that *many men do not treat women properly*. We are probably not entitled to include the fantasies in the bad treatment, since they do not involve actually doing anything to women, but we can certainly object strongly to everything else. A woman should be able to walk along the street without the risk of insolent remarks, attempts to pick her up, or rape. Men should not presume, as many seem to, that now a woman is no longer the property of any individual man she must therefore be the property of all; that if she make herself attractive she has invited all comers, who are entitled to feel aggrieved if she does not fulfil her universal promise. A woman should be able to make herself attractive to men, so putting herself in a position to have a wide range of them to choose from and increase the chances of finding one who comes up to her requirements, without being open to insulting remarks in the street, and nasty comments about leading on men whose advances she will not accept. Even when she makes herself look not just attractive but actually sexy, thereby expressing an interest in sex, it should not be taken to imply that she is interested in sex with just anyone.

The problem is obviously a difficult one, but what is absolutely clear is that it cannot be solved by women's making themselves unattractive. To do that is to give up in despair. You cannot touch the cause of the leer and the wolf-whistle by making yourself unwhistlable-at, and if you make yourself unattractive because you do not want to lead men on you are conceding by implication all they imply about universal invitations. In fact it is positively bad to protest about the way some men behave to women by putting oneself beyond the reach of what is objectionable, because if some women conspicuously withdraw themselves it probably makes men think all the more that any woman who does not is indeed expressing a general interest in men. Certainly, if all the intelligent and thoughtful women subside into scruffy unfemininity it will confirm men all the more in what they think they know already, that women with intelligence are never worth looking at.

Easy as it is to retreat in a baffled fury from all these intractable problems, and tempting as it is to confront men's complacency with defiance, it does not help because the women who do it cease to be of interest to men. What feminism really needs is exactly the opposite: women who are very desirable to men, but who will have nothing to do with any man who does not treat them properly. If men's behaviour provokes women into trying the other ways, they have pushed them into engineering their own defeat, and have won again. . . .

NOTES

1. 'No More Miss America!' in *Sisterhood is Powerful,* Robin Morgan (ed.) (New York) 1970, p. 585.

2. I owe the essence of this illustration to Bernadette Hill.

3. These are all quotations from feminists, collected by Carol Lee.

4. Incidentally, the idea that self-denial is good in itself is probably as good an example as one could find of a *conditioned response.* People learn to give things up as a means to an end, but get so used to the idea that giving things up is virtuous that they begin to feel they ought to do it anyway, and have guilt feelings about enjoying themselves.

5. Another of the feminist comments collected by Carol Lee (see n. 3) was 'A woman who dresses up to get a man is using false pretences.'

6. This was also recorded by Carol Lee.

7. Germaine Greer, *The Female Eunuch* (St. Albans) 1971, p. 261.

Further Questions

1. How much of your interest in your appearance has to do with attracting members of the gender in which you have an erotic interest?

2. Do you think you ought to be satisfied with your looks right now? Are you?

3. Is there such a thing as a feminine appearance that is too erotic in a particular situation? Can a man also be done up in too erotic a manner?

II.7   Geeks

ANNE MINAS AND JAKE MINAS

We see geeks as violators of social norms, including those having to do with interpersonal action and with appearance. We explain how geeks find their own solutions to universal human problems. Finally, we argue that patriarchy is particularly oppressive for female geeks, especially if these geeks break cardinal patriarchal rules that govern feminine appearance.

Anne Minas is the editor of this collection. She teaches philosophy at the University of Waterloo, Waterloo, Ontario. Jake Minas, her son, attends the University of Pennsylvania.

Reading Questions

1. Why do some people deliberately look so weird that we call them "geeks"?
2. Why do we think of geeks as creative or resourceful, even though they use unconventional ways of going about things?
3. Why do we empathize with geeks, even though they don't go by the rules?

A GEEK WAS ORIGINALLY "a carnival performer often billed as a wild man whose act usually includes biting the head off a live chicken or snake," according to *Webster's*. More generally, dialect English used "geek" or "geck" to mean "fool."

It often shows lack of wisdom when one does not conform to the norms of society, whatever these may be. Thus we use "geek" to refer to anyone who, in some conspicuous way, does not accede to current standards and, as a result, looks foolish. There usually is no obvious gain to the geek's unconventionality. He seems to achieve nothing other than, perhaps, calling attention to himself as a convention-violator. However, geeks are not, we think, total losers in life, completely without skills. They succeed in biting heads off chickens don't they? The puzzle is why they devote themselves to such projects.

Perhaps the type of geek who comes most readily to mind is the one who does up her appearance in a strange way. Let's call her a geek-in-looks. Such a geek, for example, might leave the house only if she were wearing pink—unless her destination was a bar where green was (for her) the mandatory color.

Looking weird is, perhaps, an even more direct route to becoming a social misfit than saying strange things. We rely on an individual's appearance as a source of information about that person. Thus, if someone violates convention in this area, we are likely to assume that she is not worth listening to.

We think of geeks as antisocial, because it is so difficult for geeks to gain social acceptance. However, geek thinkers can be highly sociable. They are simply odd in the ways they relate to people. Shakespeare's Hamlet, for example, is full of new ideas about how to treat those around him that make up his society. His only real difficulty lies in carrying out his socially appointed task of avenging his father's murder. Instead, he fills his time with innovative and unconventional verbal interactions with principal members of the Elsinore court and manages to get his aspiring assassins executed in his place by an ingenious switching of notes. Hamlet is offensive and alienating in high style. (He bites off human heads with his verbal skills.)

Geek Motivation

The circus geek chose his profession. He did not have to become part of the circus freak show. Similarly, we should assume that geeks we meet in ordinary life had some choice—therefore, what we consider weird about them was chosen freely. Why do geeks take unconventional options?

Our suggested answers:

1. A geek, like the rest of us, must come to terms with falling short of his aspirations. We

choose a path that we think we are able to follow and hope for the best. But the geek specializes by doing something weird and off the beaten track. Why? Perhaps, if his project is weird enough, it will not be as readily recognized as not very important. Off the beaten path, standards are less clearly marked, so it is more difficult for anyone, including the geek himself, to judge the value of his project.

2. *Webster's* defines "anomie" as "social instability resulting from a breakdown of standards and values." Anomie is part of the human condition. We all wonder at times what the point of anything is; we feel disoriented and isolated from goals, projects, each other, and even from ourselves. The prosaic person tries to deal with this by getting back on track, somehow. The most conventional of us have a ready-made solution— we find the conventionally acceptable track, get on it, and stay on it. The geek, by contrast, creates his own solution. He develops an idea and makes it important, then tries to structure his life around it. It's weird, it's unusual, but it becomes a handy way to solve a common human problem.

Hamlet was thrown into this state by his inability to carry out his mission of avenging his father's death. He toyed, verbally, with every member of the court. This unimportant pastime was transformed into an important project to fill his intolerable void. Hamlet's verbal geek-behavior was his way of salvaging himself from complete collapse.

3. If you are doing something weird, you are not doing the same kind of thing as everyone else. You are not playing, and so you do not have to compete with others. Alone in your area, you cannot be beaten or bettered by someone else.

4. Rules are irksome. Conventions about what is and what is not done sometimes seem to be in place just to annoy us. We want to rebel but cannot think of a good

enough justification for doing so. The geek, however, can. His project, he says, is important. (*We* do not see this, but we are merely judging by our dull conventional standards.) In fact, the geek's project is so important that he does not have to abide by ordinary conventions. For example, the mystic poet William Blake used to take his wife out nude into the garden to reenact Eden, so that he could revise conventional biblical orthodoxy to a religion more to his liking.

Do these four suggestions apply to geeks-in-looks?

1. Suppose that you are a geek who will wear only one color. No one can fill a closet with clothing for every possible occasion. We must go from place to place done up in more or less conventional attire. Our choice of specializing as blue collar, academic, or executive in appearance depends on our vocation, and also on what we feel most comfortable wearing most of the time. These categories are fairly conventional, so no one surprises anyone else by showing up dressed as an academic or an executive. But purple? That *is* different. Someone who wears purple for everything from a business lunch to cleaning the garage soon becomes quite noticeable as odd. He fits into no socially accepted genre. Here the geek is often at an advantage. He cannot be judged as better or worse in appearance by genre standards, because standards in his genre have yet to be developed. The fact that he is wearing only purple can obscure the fact that his appearance is shabby. This approach to appearance also assures the geek that he will not be nondescript, for being continuously purple is description enough.

2. The geek who wore pink outside the house and green to bars did give structure and a dimension of meaning to her life. She centered her life around a pair of colors, much as someone else might dote on two

children to rescue herself from an otherwise meaningless existence.

3. Certainly if you are the only person in the bar done up in a certain way, you have no competition. This is a clear signal that you are not playing. So, for you, there is no appearance competition in which you might lose to someone else. As an added bonus, you could attract attention from the gender of your preference because you are one-of-a-kind in appearance.

4. Finally, you are clearly in revolt against all dress codes. Not only does this save you time and energy that your conventional counterpart has to put into his appearance. It also enables you to defy standards that all of us find more or less oppressive.

So, it seems, a geek-in-looks can have the same kind of motivation for her unconventionality as any other type of geek.

Geeks and Patriarchy

We live in a patriarchal system where men have better opportunities. So it should not be surprising to find that opportunities for acceptance as geeks are more readily extended to men than to women.

Men are more likely to succeed in verbal projects like Hamlet's, because patriarchal forces tend to discourage intellectualism in women. Women should be seen and not heard. Geek intellectualism in women is in special conflict with patriarchal standards, because it is so difficult to understand, categorize, and assess. Patriarchy makes more effort to understand difficult male mentalities and tends to ignore or ostracize females mentalities when understanding them becomes too difficult. The rebellious streak in geek intellectualism is also more difficult for patriarchy to tolerate in women because patriarchy *is* a system to keep women in their place, whether they like that place or not. The male geek with an unusual, somewhat rebellious approach to his sub-

ject will probably be classified as merely a bit eccentric and get tenure. His female counterpart, on the other hand, may well be labeled just plain crazy and not even make it to the interview.

Such has been the fate of many feminist thinkers who wanted to try new methodology that was not only different from, but in rebellion against, traditional approaches in academia. They try new approaches but fall short of completing their self-appointed tasks of meeting patriarchy head-on and defeating it. Whether this makes them real geeks depends on their motivation. If they pursue feminism as dropouts from patriarchy, wishing only to do something outlandish that will escape patriarchal judgment, then they are geeks. On the other hand, if they believe in the validity of what they are doing and think of their projects as making improvements in existing patriarchal structures, they are not geeks, even though they may be perceived as similar to circus showmen. There is also the possibility that a feminist geek, like any other geek intellectual, may inadvertently make a permanent contribution to mainstream intellectual culture. Just as effort in a particular direction is not always rewarded with success, so a person may achieve success as measured in conventionally accepted terms when all she is trying to do is to defy convention.

The pretensions that geeks sometimes use to disguise inadequacies are also less tolerated in women, who are expected to play down, not play up, the importance of what they are doing. Women are expected to admit that much of what they do is not important, while men are not. Patriarchy is sympathetic toward men who try to retain their sense of self-importance; this sympathy extends, albeit in a somewhat diluted form, into the world of male geeks.

According to one prominent tradition, a beautiful woman can be forgiven almost anything. James Bond heroines, for example, can become entangled in the forces of evil. But because they are beautiful, their sins are forgiven. (James Bond, of course, performs the rites of forgiveness.) Plain women, on the other hand, are almost certain to be burdened with the full consequences of whatever they have done.

A geek-in-looks woman is in a predicament. She has broken the cardinal rule for women: Be beautiful. Who will rescue her? Who will help her when she needs help? Who will be seen with her? Who will choose her as a mate? Who will even be her friend? We know we are judged by the company we keep, and so it will be very difficult for those in the mainstream to associate with this social outcast. Anyone seen with such a person might find themselves cast out.

Here patriarchy hits with full force. A man out of step with convention in his appearance can be appreciated for other reasons. He can be liked for his mind or his personality. But a woman who defies the conventions about appearance had better be pretty stunning in her originality. That is, deviations in appearance can be tolerated only as long as her appearance benefits, or at least does not suffer, from the deviations.

Now, suppose our geek-in-pink wore badly matched, outdated, ill-fitting clothes, was too thin or too fat, had acne or wrinkles, and had unwashed hair that had never seen professional scissors. Not only is she slovenly, her affinity for only one color alerts others to the fact that, should they try to change any aspect of her appearance, they will probably fail. Would anyone really care about her as a person, or as a potential recruit for a secretarial pool or for a faculty position? Her personality would be totally eclipsed by the way she looks, because she has no personality in the sense in which Mae West talked about hers.* The geek is not appealing to men in her looks and as a consequence has little social value. Patriarchy can disguise its oppression of women a bit when it makes much of the beautiful woman as a wife or executive. It is in its treatment of the female geek-in-looks that patriarchy tips its hand, bringing the full force of oppression to bear on her because she is a woman unredeemed by an appearance that is pleasing to men.

---

* West used "my personality" to talk about her sexuality that had a life of its own as a chatty, humorous, nonmalicious Bad Girl persona that appealed to everyone. (E.g., her "Is that a pistol in your pocket or are you just glad to see me?" was off-color, but undermined neither men nor women.) Unfortunately, her appealing "personality" required her stunning appearance, something she never understood as she grew older.

Further Questions

1. Should we feel sorry for geeks, or are they getting away with something we might like to get away with as well?

2. Are we rougher on offensive geeks of one gender than we are on those of the other?

3. In particular, are we too hard on women geeks who will not follow conventional rules about appearance?

Suggested Moral of Part II

We respond to the surface aspects of social life because this is what we first catch a glimpse of: what people look like and what they say. We can expect power structures to be in evidence in some way on the surface, even though we may need thought and some ideas of what is going on beneath the surface to decode the messages. Patriarchy evidences itself in words that demean or neglect women. Also, the rules about appearance are much more stringent for women than for men because it is men, past and present, who make and maintain the rules for both genders.

Further Reading for Part II: Messages on the Surface: Looks and Language

LOOKS

Boston Women's Health Book Collective. *The New Our Bodies, Ourselves: A Book by and for Women* (New York, NY: Simon & Schuster, 1984). Good advice for women on health, fertility, relationships, violence, and other topics.

Susan Brownmiller. *Femininity* (New York, NY: Linden Press, Simon & Schuster, 1984). Worth reading in its entirety.

Shulamith Firestone. *The Dialectic of Sex: A Case for Feminist Revolution* (New York, NY: William Morrow, 1970), Chapter 7. Brief, pointed account of women's confusing their appearance with their individuality.

Barry Glassner. *Bodies: Why We Look the Way We Do* (New York, NY: Putnam, 1988). Contains an especially interesting account of the importance of muscle to male appearance.

Germaine Greer. *The Female Eunuch* (New York, NY: McGraw Hill, 1971), especially Part 1, "Body." Depiction of women as tailored to male specifications, *inter alia*, in appearance.

Linda A. Jackson. *Physical Appearance and Gender: Sociobiological and Sociocultural Perspectives* (Albany, NY: State University of New York Press, 1992). How gender similarities and differences affect the impact our physical appearance has on other people.

Susie Orbach, *Fat Is a Feminist Issue* (New York, NY: Berkeley Books, 1978). Develops the thesis that fat is a response to social pressures; to lose weight, you must understand these pressures and learn to like yourself.

Roberta Pollack Seid. *Never Too Thin: Why Women Are at War with Their Bodies* (New York, NY: Prentice Hall, 1989). Thorough discussion of myth that thinner is healthier, sexier, happier, and more beautiful.

Andrew Wernick. "From Voyeur to Narcissist: Imaging Men in Contemporary Advertising" in *Beyond Patriarchy, Essays by Men on Pleasure, Power and Change,* Michael Kaufmann, ed. (New York, NY: Oxford University Press, 1987). Argument that men as well as women have their appearances shaped by advertising.

Naomi Wolf. *The Beauty Myth* (New York, NY: Vintage, Random House, 1991). Women are straitjacketed by beauty requirements. Germaine Greer says it's "The most important feminist publication since [Greer's own] *The Female Eunuch.*"

LANGUAGE*

Dennis Baron. *Grammar and Gender* (New Haven, CT: Yale University Press, 1986). Comprehensive but rewarding book. Chapter on pronouns is especially interesting.

Deborah Cameron, ed. *The Feminist Critique of Language* (New York, NY: Routledge, 1990). Anthology of feminist writings on language, Virginia Woolf to the present.

Philip M. Smith. *Language, the Sexes and Society* (New York, NY: Basil Blackwell, 1985). Discussion of language as used to subordinate or devalue women.

* Thanks to Maryann Ayim and Diane Goossens for suggestions for these readings.

Dale Spender. *Man Made Language* (London: Routledge & Kegan Paul, 1980). Radical and angry statement of how language, and research on language, oppresses women.

Mary Vetterling-Braggin, ed. *Sexist Language: A Modern Philosophical Analysis*. (Littlefield, Adams and Co., 1981). Philosophers address themselves to sexist problems in language.

Everyone should have a guide for using language in a non-sexist manner. Two recommendations are:

Rosalie Maggio. *The Non-Sexist Word Finder: A Dictionary of Gender-Free Usage* (Boston, MA: Beacon Press, 1988).

Casey Miller and Kate Swift. *The Handbook of Non-Sexist Writing* (New York, NY: Harper & Row, 1980).

Part III

The Workplace and Sports

Introduction

THE GENDER STRUCTURE of the workplace deserves close examination because, in today's industrialized world, opportunities for meaningful activity are increasingly becoming organized around job positions in the workplace. In addition, a person's place in the work force is often a major source of his worth, as measured by the income, prestige, and power he gains through his job performance.

III.1   Women and Power in the Workplace

HILARY M. LIPS

Hilary M. Lips maintains that women's personal features and circumstances have been overplayed in explaining the continuation of male dominance in the workplace. The reality is that men use a variety of techniques, including considerable mythology about male and female psychology, to maintain their relative position.

Lips has taught psychology of sex and gender at the University of Winnipeg (Winnipeg, Manitoba) and has contributed numerous chapters, articles, and books in her field.

Reading Questions

1. As a woman, do you think that the likeliest way to be successful in your chosen career is to follow the model of the successful man?
2. Do you think the world is a reasonably fair and just place and that there are explanations adequate to justify why people hold the positions they do in the work force?
3. Are women in a double bind in trying to exercise power, since power is held to be unfeminine?

DURING MOST OF OUR RECENT HISTORY, the major thrust of women's struggle for power has been toward increased access to the major institutions in society. The struggle simply not to be excluded—from voting rights, jobs, organisations, full legal status as persons—has taken up much of women's collective energy for decades. A strong emphasis in the struggle has been on access to and equality in the world of paid employment, for women have intuited rightly that the income, status, knowledge and social networks that come with employment are crucial resources on which power, both individual and collective, can be based.

Power, it should be noted at the outset, is the capacity to have an impact on one's environment, to be able to make a difference through one's actions. It is the opposite of helplessness. There is no use in debating whether or not women should really want power, or whether it is appropriately feminist to strive for power. Such debates are based on a long outdated, narrow notion of power as a static quality possessed only by tyrants. In talking about women increasing their power, I am referring to an increase in effectiveness of influence, in strength.

More power for women means two things: increasing women's access to resources and to the positions from which these resources are controlled; and increasing women's impact on the formation of policy about how our institutions function. Because women have a long history of exclusion, the initial focus in the struggle to increase women's power has been to gain access for women to a variety of institutions.

The universities are a good case in point. For years, women were excluded from higher education on the grounds that we were unsuited for it and might even be damaged by it. Some "experts" even went so far as to argue that too much use of a woman's brain would damage her reproductive organs and thus endanger her vital child-bearing function (see Shields, 1975). Universities in many countries accept female students as a matter of course now. In Canada, we have come a long way from the time when the principal of a Laval University-affiliated college for women had to placate critics of her institution by interspersing piano recitals and afternoon teas with normal academic pursuits. Such activities were supposedly necessary to keep her delicate female students from breaking under the strain of uninterrupted intellectual work (Danylewycz, 1981). However, arguments about damaging the reproductive system are still being used in some quarters to exclude women from various arenas of professional and amateur sports. . . .

. . . [T]he sense of power that comes with women's perception of an increased range of career choices may be short-lived. Statistics on women's employment indicate that they may often get in the door, but no further. Females in almost every professional field, for example, are underemployed and underpaid relative to their male counterparts (Abella, 1984) and women in trade occupations still have a great deal of difficulty finding employment (Braid, 1982). Moreover, the research bleakly suggests that, as women grow more numerous in a particular profession or occupation, its status declines (Touhey, 1974).

Thus, although women's problems with access to the workplace are far from over, there is an increasing recognition that simply being allowed in—to a profession, a business organisation, a trade union—is only half the battle. How can women avoid being marginal members of the workplace community—tokens whose presence supposedly illustrates that "women can make it," but who are not at the centre of decision making and who are powerless to rise to the top of, or change the shape of, the institutions in which they work?

Much advice has been aimed at women in an effort to answer this question. Most of it boils down to a prescription that women carefully observe and follow the models provided by successful men. Successful businesswomen profiled in the media are (like their male counterparts) often heard to comment that, in the service of success, they have given up their social life, hobbies, and recreation, and find it difficult to make time for family and friendship.

Such an ideal, based on the model of a small number of high-achieving, powerful, visible men in high-status jobs, creates discomfort among many women. For some, the discomfort may stem from a fear of being labelled tough, competitive or ambitious—qualities that are incongruent with our culture's definition of femininity. For others, the idea of subordinating all other priorities to one's paid work seems unrealistic and unpleasant. The first objection is easily dealt with, at least in theory. The attention paid to the concept of androgyny in recent years has, if nothing else, shown that the qualities associated with strength are not necessarily antithetical to the traditional "feminine" virtues of nurturence, sensitivity and care for others (Colwill and Lips, 1978). It is possible to be tough without losing sight of what is fair, to be ambitious without trampling on everyone else on one's way to the top—and if women are going to make an impact in the workplace or anywhere else they are simply going to have to figure out how to blend these qualities.

The second objection, however, is one to be taken more seriously. How realistic, how desirable is it for women to adopt wholesale the myth that gaining success and power requires the subordination of all other activities, values, and interests to one's career? This model, which is held out to men as an ideal, is unworkable and destructive even for most of *them,* even though they have been socialised toward it and are provided by society with many more supports for this life style than are women (Harrison, 1978).

In order to devote all of her energy to a career, a woman needs someone taking care of the other aspects of her life: feeding her, cleaning up after her, making sure she has clean clothes, making dental appointments for her, keeping her social life organised, looking after her children, and so on. She needs, in essence, a wife. Employed women do not have wives, and it is simply impractical to try to follow the male model for career success without one. Now that fewer career men have wives who fill the traditional role, perhaps the male career model itself will begin to change. At any rate, business and professional women will have to develop their own model for career success.

The male model, presented in such glowing terms, is largely a myth. It is an ideal that is used to keep men in line, and there is no reason why women should fall in line behind them. While popular writers are exhorting women to map out career strategy years in advance the way men supposedly do, research suggests that, despite the ideal, most men do not plan their careers any more carefully than women do (Harlan and Weiss, 1980). While the advice-mongers are saying knowingly that women have not got what it takes to wheel and deal in the business world because they have never learned not to take conflict personally, many business and professional women have found to their chagrin that their male counterparts grow silent, withdraw, or become bitter and vindictive in their relationships to colleagues after being opposed on some policy or economic issue. While popular writers are fond of saying that women lack the training necessary to be good "team players" because they never passed through the proving ground of football, basketball and hockey, many a male ex-athlete will admit that his main legacy from high school football was a recurring knee injury and a sense of failure.

The writers who say these things have taken our society's definition of the male role and life pattern and elevated it unquestioningly to an ideal. If the shoe were on the other foot, if women were in the majority in business and the professions, these same writers would be telling aspiring career men that they were at a disadvantage in knowing how to be part of a co-operative business partnership because they had never gone through the "proving ground" of rearing chil-dren. Instead of advising women to bone up on football and hockey so that they would not feel left out of casual conversations with the men in the office, the experts (presuming traditional gender roles in this mythical situation) would be advising men to read romance novels, keep up with the latest recipes, talk about their children, and follow the careers of the great women runners and tennis players. Since men hold the majority of powerful business and professional positions, it is assumed that there must be something right about men's upbringing and life style—something that leads them into powerful positions—and if women would only emulate that pattern they too could make it to "the top" in large numbers. Not only does this analysis overlook the fact that our society is arranged in a way that makes it horribly impractical for the majority of women to follow the male model (i.e., not only do most women *not* have partners who fulfill the role of the traditional wife, but also they *do* have children for whom they usually have primary responsibility), but also the whole approach is rooted in our all-too-human need to rationalise the status quo.

Psychologists have been finding for years that people in general like to believe that the world is a reasonably fair and just place, that there is an order to things, and that people basically get what they deserve (e.g., Lerner, 1974). Thus, people are very good at thinking up reasons why things are the way they are—at justifying and rationalising our social arrangements rather than questioning them. It is easier, for example, to think of women as "unassertive" or poorly trained for leadership in order to explain how few women reach visible leadership positions than to think that there may be something askew with a system or an organisation in which this is the case. Since men are on top and women are the bottom, such thinking goes, what women are doing must be wrong . . . and men are the ones doing it right. Teach the women how to act like men, and their problems will be solved.

Perhaps the clearest way to see how this type of rationalisation works is to imagine the changes in explanation for the status quo that would be required if the positions of the two groups were reversed. Gloria Steinem provides an amusing example of this process in her article "If Men Could Menstruate" (Steinem, 1983). She fantasises that if men and not women had menstrual cycles, menstruation would be regarded as a sign of superiority. The fact that men were "in tune" with nature and the cycles of the moon would be thought to give them an advantage in making important decisions, and women's non-cyclic nature would be used as a reason for excluding them from high positions. In fact, women's menstrual cycle has been cited repeatedly (on very flimsy evidence) as a handicap that makes them unfit for certain possible positions. Here too, though, the only logic in the argument is that relating it to the status quo. Nowhere is it argued that, since women supposedly become so unreliable and irrational at certain times of the month, they should be relieved of the delicate job of caring for small, helpless children during such times. Similar logic asserts that women's allegedly superior manual dexterity makes them uniquely fit to be typists, while ignoring the possibility that it might make them uniquely fit to be surgeons or television repairpersons.

It is reasonable to be suspicious of any approach that purports to explain women's failure to advance, or their lack of impact, solely on the basis of flaws in their own behaviour. Of course there are things most women can learn to make themselves more effective, but that is also true for most men. What *may* be more true for women than for men in many organisations, however, is that support and security from the organisation is lacking. Women, while inside an organisation, often find that they are still outsiders. As Rosabeth Kanter's (1977) work shows, the issue is not whether or not women know how to play on teams, but whether a token woman can play on a team that does not want her on it.

It is becoming clear, then, that having broken down many initial access barriers, women taking up their newly-won positions in mainstream organisations often find that they are still far from the centres of power. Having dealt with many of the formal barriers to career participation, they find themselves blocked by less tangible but equally frustrating obstacles. They feel invisible. They feel (and they are often right) that no one takes them seriously. Such feelings are not limited to women in business, engineering, or other male-dominated professions, or to women in "white-collar" jobs. Women in teaching, nursing, secretarial work, carpentry and other trades, and factory work all report similar frustrations in their struggles to make an impact in their work environment. Understanding of the dilemmas faced by women trying to be effective in the workplace can be enhanced by examining their problems within the framework provided by psychological research on power.

Psychologists argue that power—the ability to make an impact or to get others to do what one wants them to do—is based on a person's access to certain resources that can be used to "back up" her influence attempts (French and Raven, 1959). In other words, in order for a person (or a group) to exert power, there have to be reasons—fear, respect, admiration, greed, loyalty—for others in the environment to co-operate or comply. The resources that provide the reasons for compliance include control over rewards (for example, the capacity to reward a person who complies with one's wishes by promoting her, giving her a raise, giving her the day off, giving her a gift) and control over punishments (such as the capacity to discipline someone, fire her, take something away from her). The resources on which power is based also include legitimacy, expertise, personal attractiveness or likableness, and the sheer amount of knowledge or information one can muster to support one's arguments. The amount of power or influence a person can wield depends at least partly on how much access she has, and is seen to have, to these kinds of resources.

A person's ability to influence others depends not only on her actual access to resources, but also on the amount of control over these resources that others see her as having. If a woman is an expert in a given field, for instance, that expertise will not provide her with a source of power with respect to others who do not recognise her as an expert. While women are often blocked from control over certain kinds of resources in their work settings, it is just as often true that the resources they do have go unrecognised. In the case of expertise, the stereotype of feminine incompetence often works against the perception of women as experts, particularly in traditionally male fields. In the case of legitimacy, not only do women rarely find themselves in positions of authority, but, even when they do, their automatic low status as women acts to contradict and undermine their authority in the eyes of others.

A consequence of these difficulties is that women sometimes find themselves relying more than they should or would like to on the resources of personal attractiveness or likableness to exert influence in the workplace. They smile a lot, try to win the friendship and good will of the people they must influence, and may sometimes use their sexuality in overt or covert ways as a basis of power. This is a strategy that often does work, but it tends to be a trap if relied on exclusively. A person using it does not enhance anyone's view of her competence and must be rather too careful about staying on everyone's good side. . . .

Not the least of the problems a person can face in trying to wield power is a negative bias in her own view of the resources she controls. If a person who is an expert lacks confidence in her own expertise, she will have difficulty exerting influence based on that expertise. Since women are continually being given the message that they are not expected to be experts, that people are pleasantly surprised when they know anything about important issues, lack of confidence is a dangerously seductive trap for them. Men too feel inadequate when they compare themselves to their colleagues. Our culture's specialised, competitive workplaces tend to foster this feeling. Men, however, have developed more strategies than women have for hiding this feeling of inadequacy. What must be kept in mind is that the exercise of power depends not only on what kinds of resources one controls, but also on the way one thinks one's own resources compare to everyone else's. In other words, how powerful a person or group feels can make a difference in how powerful they are.

A person's exercise of power is also affected by what she and others see as appropriate behaviour. Since "feminine" behaviour is, almost by definition, powerless behaviour, the woman trying to act in a powerful way is placed in a double bind. There may be times when she has the resources and knows she has the resources to wield power, but holds back out of a fear of being labelled pushy, aggressive, tough, or just plain not nice.

The three factors just described (what resources a person controls, how powerful she feels, and what she and others see as appropriate behaviour) affect not only the amount of impact she can have in a particular situation, but also the style or strategy of influence she employs. Her style of influence may be more or less direct, for example (Johnson, 1976). Someone who uses a direct style of influence asks for or demands openly what she wants, making it clear that she is the one who wants it. Someone using a very indirect style of influence, on the other hand, tries to get what she wants to happen without acknowledging that she is the source of the influence. A common example of the latter is the strategy of talking to someone behind the scenes rather than personally bringing up an issue at a meeting.

Both styles carry some risks, especially at the extremes. The person using the direct approach to influence may be viewed as abrasive, may be disliked, and may often find herself involved in conflict. The payoff is that, when she gets something positive to happen, she gets credit for it—credit that adds to her competence and expertise in the eyes of others and thus adds to the store of resources she can draw on in future situations.

The person using the indirect approach to influence, on the other hand, avoids the risk of being openly associated with an idea that turns out to be unpopular or unworkable, while keeping the opportunity for private satisfaction when she is the source of an initiative that works. However, sometimes this satisfaction can be a little too private. No matter how many good ideas she generates, a person can never build up her credibility if she is never seen as the originator of these ideas, if her influence is always indirect.

Clearly, to increase one's competence in the eyes of others, it is necessary to use influence directly and openly, at least some of the time. However, this is not to say that women should always avoid using indirect strategies. There are times when it is simply more important to get something done than to make an issue of it or get credit for it. In some organizations, for instance, people have managed to advance the cause of women considerably without ever being so obvious about it that they generated a fight.

Since it seems to be important to use influence directly and openly at least some of the time, it would seem to be a simple matter for women to get the message and start using more direct power styles in order to enhance their personal effectiveness and increase their acceptance within institutions. This, in essence, is what assertiveness training is supposed to be about: teaching people, especially women, to exert influence directly. Men rarely sign up for assertiveness training. Does this mean men have no trouble exerting influence openly? Perhaps, but it could also mean that men are more reluctant than women to accept for themselves the label of "unassertive." Also, many of the programmes are geared to women, on the unproven assumption that women need the training more. In fact, some Canadian research suggests that women are actually more appropriately assertive than men in many situations (Wine, Smye and Moses, 1980).

But while basic skills in assertiveness can only be helpful, they provide no magic cure for the power problems that women face in their working lives. How direct a woman is able to be in her attempts to exert influence depends only in a limited way on these skills. More importantly, it depends on the degree of actual control over resources that she brings to an interaction, how powerful she feels, and what kinds of behaviour she and those around her see as appropriate.

Women are often accused of relying on indirect or hidden power styles—of being manipulative and sneaky rather than open when trying to exert influence. In cases where this accusation is true, there are probably a number of factors operating that favour an indirect strategy. For example, the more resources one can command to back up one's requests or demands, the easier it is to be direct. This is particularly true of such resources as legitimacy, status and support. The more authority a person has in her position, the higher her status, and the more backing she feels from her co-workers, the easier it is for her to make strong, clear demands on people. For this reason, a teacher may have no hesitation about making certain clear demands on her students, but may be wary about adopting the same strong, direct style with school administrators. When dealing with students, she is operating from a position of recognised authority and of higher status within the institution. Moreover, she usually knows she is working within guidelines that are accepted by and will be supported by her colleagues. If she had no recognised authority over the people she was trying to influence, if she were operating from a position of lower status, if she felt isolated from her colleagues on a particular issue (all of which are more likely to be the case when she is trying to exert influence over an administrator instead of a student), it would be more difficult for her to be direct and assertive.

For women (or men, for that matter) who find themselves at the bottom of the ladder in a workplace that operates on a very hierarchical basis, it is unrealistic to expect a lot of direct, open use of power. This is doubly true if a woman has no network of support among her co-workers—a problem that plagues women who are breaking ground in a traditionally male job. Finally, it must be noted that women tend to start with a strike against them when it comes to status. The status ascribed to females in many jobs is automatically lower than that ascribed to men in the same job. Simply trying to teach or convince women to be more assertive and direct under these conditions is not the answer. Most women know how to be assertive under the right circumstances, but they avoid behaviour that is going to get them into more trouble than they want to handle.

Intervention to increase women's capacity to exert power in a direct way should not focus mainly on the behaviour of individual women. Rather, a more useful focus is on finding ways to increase women's access to resources, and to change the culture's image of femininity so that it is no longer synonymous with weakness or incompetence.

How can such changes be accomplished? They have already begun to happen. A crucial aspect of increasing women's access to resources in the workplace is the formation of support groups. Such groups not only provide much needed support (a resource in itself) for women who are isolated or ignored in male-dominated workplaces, they also enable women to share information and expertise—thus potentially increasing the competence (another resource) of all members. In some situations, these groups can also provide the political clout to help attain certain kinds of change beneficial to women (yet another resource). Also, the existence of network groups may provide a significant source of encouragement for more women to enter certain fields, an eventuality that will make it less common for women to find themselves isolated as tokens in their jobs.

It does not take a psychologist to tell most women that another extremely important aspect of increasing women's access to the resources on which power is based involves eliminating women's "double shift." Time and energy are themselves precious resources on which all attempts to have influence or make an impact on the world are based. For years, women's time and energy have been stolen from them by economic and cultural systems that have allocated to women virtually all of the responsibility for child care and the daily maintenance functions of cooking, cleaning, shopping and errand-running. Even in countries where serious attempts have been made to "socialise" child care functions, women are the ones faced with the housework when they return from work each day. And in Sweden, where new fathers and mothers are equally entitled to parental leave at 90 per cent of salary, few fathers avail themselves of the opportunity to stay home with their infants. No modern economic system has yet solved this problem of women's double day.

On an individual level, a woman is seriously handicapped in her attempts to have an impact outside of her own family by this double burden of labour. On a group level, the double shift weakens and dilutes women's impact on the values that shape the political process, the educational process, the arts, our own culture, and the future of the world. In the power terms discussed in this chapter, the cultural requirement that women perform a disproportionately large share of home-related work interferes with their access to almost every type of resource on which power can be based. Household responsibilities may make a woman less available for the extra meetings or social events where information is exchanged and contacts that lead to promotions and better jobs are made. They slow down her education, keeping her at a lower level in the job market. Thus, her access to information and expertise is curtailed, as is her access to the reward and punishment power that accompanies control over economic resources, and to the legitimacy that comes with holding a position of recognised authority. The only power base that is not guaranteed to be adversely affected by this situation is that of personal attractiveness or likability—and there is many a bleary-eyed, irritable woman with no time for exercise or sleep who will say that even that traditional source of female power is compromised by the double shift. Clearly, for women as individuals or for women as a group to have a greater impact on our cultural institutions, the relegation to women of most child care and household responsibilities would have to be changed.

The "powerless/incompetent" image of femininity would also have to be changed. While that change is beginning to happen as strong, competent women become more visible, efforts in some specific areas are called for. Ripe for revision, for instance, is the notion that women are incompetent to handle all things mathematical and technical. The pernicious stereotype of women as beings who cannot deal with numbers and who are too muddleheaded to balance a chequebook is not only wrong, it is dangerous in an age that is increasingly dominated by the computer. It will be helpful to remember that when the typewriter was first invented, it was thought to be too complicated a machine for women to handle!

It would also be useful to work against the idea that women must be physically weak. Not only is this view of women an obstacle to their employment in a variety of jobs requiring strength and stamina, but it may also be related to the general perception of women's effectiveness and their sense of power. Being weak fosters a need for protection from men—and this generates an attitude of protectiveness on men's part that generalises far beyond the physical realm into other aspects of women's lives.

A third aspect of the femininity stereotype that would-be powerful women need to challenge is that women are quiet, soft-spoken and polite. A growing body of research in psychology shows that, in the first place, people who talk more in groups tend to be accorded more status in those groups; and, in the second place, men tend to discourage women from speaking up in group situations by interrupting them and by ignoring their input. These tactics used by men tend to subdue women's efforts at participation in the discussion, allowing the men conversational control. Then, in a vicious circle, women are discounted more and more as they become increasingly silent, and they try less and less often to enter the conversation as they feel increasingly ignored. One approach to this problem is for women to try to train their male colleagues to stop interrupting them, but such training may not come easily. It is a rare and lucky woman who, after bringing the problem to the attention of the men she works with, finds she is never interrupted again! More probably, she will have to work actively to invalidate the feminine stereotype of politeness by refusing to defer to male speakers who try to interrupt her and by protesting such interruptions again and again. Since old habits die hard, and since change is more in women's interest than men's, it is unrealistic to rely too heavily on men to relinquish their conversational control tactics without continuous pressure from women.

As women gain more access to the resources on which power is based, they will find it easier to challenge the "powerless" image of femininity. And, concurrently, as the powerless image fades, women will find it easier to be recognised as strong, as competent, as experts. Thus, in a reversal of a "vicious circle," the two processes will feed into each other, ultimately making it easier for women to use such resources as expertise, information, and legitimacy. These resources become springboards for acquiring access to other resources—tangible ones such as money and control over decision making—and for opening the doors to these resources to other women. This is an optimistic perspective to be sure, but one that is consistent with the way many advances for women have been achieved over the years. For women, as for any relatively powerless group, the key to starting the "nonvicious circle" rolling is to use their most available resource: their numbers, their collectivity, pooled energy, and shared support. The payoff may well be not only more access to and impact in the workplace for women, but a more humane workplace for everyone.

REFERENCES

Abella, R. S. *Equality in Employment: A Royal Commission Report*. Ottawa: Canadian Government Publishing Centre, 1984.

Astin, A. W., King, M. R., and Richardson, G. T. *The American Freshman: National Norms for Fall 1975*. Los Angeles: University of California Laboratory for Research in Higher Education, 1975.

Braid, K. "Women in Trades in British Columbia." In M. Fitzgerald, C. Guberman, and M. Wolfe (eds.), *Still Ain't Satisfied! Canadian Feminism Today.* Toronto: The Woman's Press, 1982.

Colwill, N. L., and Lips, H. M. "Masculinity, Femininity, and Androgyny: What Have You Done for Us Lately?" Chapter in H. M. Lips and N. L. Colwill, *The Psychology of Sex Differences.* Englewood Cliffs, N.J.: Prentice-Hall, 1978.

Danylewycz, M. "Changing Relationships: Nuns and Feminists in Montréal, 1890–1925." *Histoire Sociale—Social History,* 14:28 (1981), 413–434.

French, J. P. R., and Raven, B. "The Bases of Social Power." In D. Cartwright (ed.), *Studies in Social Power.* Ann Arbor: Institute for Social Research, University of Michigan, 1959.

Harlan, A., and Weiss, C. L. "Moving Up: Women in Managerial Careers." Third progress report. Wellesley, Mass.: Wellesley College Center for Research on Women, 1980.

Harrison, J. "Warning: The Male Sex Role May Be Dangerous to Your Health." *Journal of Social Issues,* 34:1 (1978), 65–86.

Johnson, P. "Women and Power: Toward a Theory of Effectiveness." *Journal of Social Issues,* 32:3 (1976), 99–110.

Kanter, R. M. *Men and Women of the Corporation.* New York: Basic Books, 1977.

Lerner, M. J. "Social Psychology of Justice and Interpersonal Attraction." In T. L. Huston (ed.), *Foundations of Interpersonal Attraction.* New York: Academic Press, 1974.

Shields, S. A. "Functionalism, Darwinism, and the Psychology of Women: A Study in Social Myth." *American Psychologist,* 30:7 (1975), 739–754.

Steinem, G. *Outrageous Acts and Everyday Rebellions.* New York: Holt, Rinehart and Winston, 1983.

Touhey, J. C. "Effects of Additional Women Professionals on Rating of Occupational Prestige and Desirability." *Journal of Personality and Social Psychology,* 29: (1974), 86–89.

Wine, J. D., Smye, M. D., and Moses, B. "Assertiveness: Sex Differences in Relationships between Self-report and Behavioural Measures." In C. Stark-Adamec (ed.), *Sex Roles: Origins, Influences, and Implications for Women.* Montreal: Eden Press, 1980.

Further Questions

1. Is it desirable for a person to put his or her career first, subordinating everything else to this one part of life?

2. Is there something valuable about the way in which men have been brought up, and about the arrangement of their lifestyles (and conversely, perhaps, something lacking in these areas for women) that explains why men get ahead of women in the workplace?

3. Is a woman's ability to be direct in particular circumstances partly dependent on the character of the circumstances?

III.2   Is Marriage the Culprit?

HARRIET LYONS

One obvious possible explanation for women's lesser place in the workforce is their affinity for marriage and family responsibilities, which take up too much of their time and energy. Concentrating on universities, Harriet Lyons notes some ways in which marriage has lowered opportunities for women until the very recent past. She also mentions some ways in which married women have provided free or low cost labor for the benefit of universities.

Lyons teaches anthropology and is director of Women's Studies at the University of Waterloo (Waterloo, Ontario).

Reading Questions

1. Most heterosexual men and women marry. If you are a woman who plans to marry, are you clear about how you will combine a position in the work force with home and family responsibilities?
2. Is it important that spouses have equal mobility in the work force?
3. Is it in any way the concern of an employer whether and how an employee farms out the work connected with his position?

I

ONE ARGUMENT THAT REPEATEDLY SUR-FACES in attacks on affirmative action, within and outside of universities, is that it is not sexual discrimination which restricts women's access to desirable jobs or causes women to earn less than men in comparable positions. Rather, the barriers lie in the handicaps that marriage imposes on women. The argument is that marriage is a freely chosen state, and therefore no business of universities. It is worth examining whether free choice is really the sole explanation for the disadvantages women suffer as a result of marriage and, more importantly, whether universities are really neutral sites in which a pattern determined elsewhere has worked itself out.

A fact sheet on employment equity circulated in Canada recently offers the following Canadian data in support of this position:

1. The wage gap between men and women (women's incomes are widely quoted at about 64 percent of male incomes) is much smaller than usually believed if one restricts comparisons to "never-married" persons (where there has been a wage gap of 20 percent or less since 1941).

2. Married women with university degrees earn only $264 per annum more than married male high school graduates. However, among the never-married, women with university degrees earn $8,148 more than men with only high school diplomas, according to a 1985 study.*
3. In 1971, never-married women university graduates actually earned more than never-married men university graduates.

Marriage (formal or informal) is a state which the overwhelming majority of human beings of both sexes go through at some time in their lives, in all cultures. Thus, it is not clear why women should be penalized for a condition which they share with men. The pervasiveness of the married state also makes it questionable whether participation in it, for either men or women, can be said to be entirely a matter of free choice. Celibacy as a requirement for men teaching in all but a few religious institutions was eliminated by the end of the nineteenth century. Is it fair to retain it as a major determinant in the careers of women professors?

* *Fact Sheet on Employment Equity,* undated, anonymous fax sent to members of the Canadian Association of University Teachers (CAUT) Status of Women Committee. It is not unusual for members of this committee to receive communications of this sort.

II

Security of tenure, relatively high wages, time for research, access to funds for travel and other research expenses, and a voice in university governance are among the benefits which have been enjoyed by university staff. But these benefits have not been distributed evenhandedly to all comers. Rather, they have been disproportionately granted to those who were free to move anywhere in the country and could devote the most time to work at establishing a career at precisely the time of life when family responsibilities are greatest. What this has meant is that married women, teaching in universities, have been more likely than married men to be employed in part-time positions at low salaries with few benefits.

This would not constitute discrimination on the part of universities if it were the inevitable result of either the free choices made by women, or of generic social norms, in which universities took no special part. But is it? Universities have, with little clear academic reason, imposed anti-nepotism rules which prevented husbands and wives from teaching in the same department; they have refused to hire their own PhDs; they have excluded the dependent spouses of faculty members from eligibility for fellowships, and sometimes from even pursuing graduate programs at the spouse's employing university. Since husbands normally have the opportunity of earning their credentials before their wives, the disadvantaged spouse in such rules is almost always the wife. In addition, frequently there is only one employer of PhDs within a wide geographical radius, and wives are further limited in their choice of residence by their spouses' places of employment. Although most universities have dropped these rules, at least formally, the makeup of university faculties will show their effects for a long time to come.

It is interesting to note that universities have begun to take limited steps to improve the conditions of limited-term contractual faculty members (though not the enormous pay gap) at the precise moment when there is an increased proportion of men among their ranks. Meanwhile non-tenure-track faculty are still excluded from full membership in departments, faculty associations, etc., and from many benefits as well, such as pension plans.

III

If marriage is an impediment for women academics, it is often a bonus for their male counterparts. Feminists have long pointed out that the services wives perform for their husbands free those men for greater productivity in the labour force and constitute an enormous unrecognized subsidy to employers. It is not simply the unpaid research and clerical assistance provided by wives; it is also men's relatively greater freedom from the strains of domestic maintenance and childcare responsibilities.

Meanwhile, university employers, like other industries and services, often benefit from having ready at hand a pool of cheap labour for either academic or support positions. These are the married women who will accept low wages because their bargaining power is weakened by the constraints marriage imposes upon their mobility and schedules. In her study, *Behind Every Successful Man: Wives of Medicine and Academe* (Columbia University Press: 1980), Martha Fowlkes has examined the benefits husbands receive from the unpaid labour of faculty wives. This typically includes, in addition to housekeeping and child-rearing, the typing and editing of papers, assistance in research, and the hosting of gatherings for faculty, students, and visiting speakers. Also, many faculty wives have assisted with university fund-raising.

Male PhD students also may make use of their wives' paycheques for a significant portion of their support. (Although female PhD students have also sometimes been supported by their husbands, the husbands in question are more likely to be in career jobs, serving their own as well as their spouses' professional interests.)

Since universities have benefited from these services, in greater productivity of faculty and lessened need for student assistance and reduced costs for support staff, the imbalance in the rewards of single and married employees and the bargains struck between married couples are not mere personal matters. They are also the concern of universities as institutions.

IV

There are many ways of redressing this balance which would benefit both women and single men: payment for some of the services wives have traditionally performed without compensation, either through professional allowances or by hiring staff, is an obvious starting point. Improving the conditions of part-time employment and establishing methods of facilitating the move from sessional to continuing employment are other measures universities could take in bettering the lot of the faculty wife. What is needed, however, is a comprehensive plan covering all aspects of university activity. We can expect that in some cases more active, interventionist remedies will be required, e.g., target hiring, reviews of departmental personnel decisions and salary anomaly reviews.

Further Questions

1. If your career demanded it, would you be willing to forgo marriage and children, even if those interested you as well?

2. If you have your spouse type and edit your writing, assist you in your research, etc., do you think you are exploiting her or him?

3. Does an employer have a right to ask the spouse of an employee to serve, without remuneration, at social functions and to assist in fund-raising efforts?

Target Hiring   III.3

ANNE MINAS

This writing supports gender targets—setting in place goals of hiring certain percentages of women over a specified time, with the aim of increasing the numbers of women in certain positions. It is argued that this gives both genders fair opportunities for these positions and, at universities, is indispensable to fulfilling the proper function of these institutions.

Reading Questions

1. If gender is a factor in a decision to hire a certain candidate, does this mean that this candidate is less qualified than someone else who was considered for the position but not hired?

2. If a person has spent considerable time qualifying himself for a position with the belief that his gender would be favored in hiring decisions, is it fair to him to put in place targets that make it more likely that members of the other gender will be hired?

3. Do colleges and universities have an obligation to society at large to provide thoughtful ideas about gender relations?

I

AN UNFORTUNATE LEGACY OF PATRI-ARCHY is the inflated perception of male qualification—the belief that being male adds to a person's qualifications. Gender targets in hiring are devices to remedy that misperception. When an employer has a target (sometimes called a "soft quota") to hire a certain proportion of women, he is forced to recruit women and to look closely at their credentials. If women and men in the same candidate pool appear equally qualified or have credentials that seem commensurate with each other, the employer must give women benefit of doubt; he must hire women in such situations until he has met his gender target. A gender target forces an employer to examine his thinking to make sure he is not favoring males.

These targets usually mandate that a certain proportion of women be hired or that explanations be given—in terms of recruitment efforts, credentials of candidates, and procedures for judging these credentials—as to why that proportion of qualified women could not be found. There is, then, no real conflict between target hiring and hiring according to qualification; in both, qualification is given its maximum weight in hiring decisions. Targets merely specify procedures that must be used in recruiting and judging candidates to ensure that these processes are not interfered with by external forces like patriarchy.

We assume all institutions have an interest in turning out a high quality product. The institution may be in a situation in which its product must be marketed in competition with like products of other institutions. Alternatively, an institution might have a particular clientele to whom it owes quality production, as universities owe high quality teaching and research to their communities, benefactors, students, and governments. In either case, unless interfered with by other forces, institutions will gravitate toward hiring personnel who are competent to turn out such products.

Far from interfering with such gravitation toward competence, targets give institutions additional incentive to exercise care in hiring those who are best qualified. Suppose a gender target provides pressure to hire a woman. Those who have doubts about the competence of women for the position will react by carefully scrutinizing the credentials of the women candidates. Such persons are also likely to try to find a qualified man and to prove that he has better credentials than any of the female candidates. We can anticipate that such a situation will result in a detailed, careful investigation and recording of the recruitment procedures and the judgments about the credentials of the leading candidates of both genders. The fact that a gender target is in place virtually precludes hasty judgments in which gender is a major factor.[1]

II

Gender targets thus help eliminate patriarchal bias in hiring practices and ensure that women will have better opportunities to attain positions. The expectation is that this will encourage more interested women to qualify themselves and apply. The only way to discover the level of interest that women have, for example, in philosophy, is to open the doors and see how many women walk in and apply for such positions. An institution that makes known its gender targets is taking active steps to recruit qualified women. It can be even more forceful in these recruitment efforts if it goes out and tries to find such women instead of simply waiting for the women to find it.

An institution may or may not have obligations to hire the best qualified candidates. However, as we have just seen, gender targets do give maximum weight to qualifications as a consideration in hiring. Their force is to ensure that the gender that was previously neglected in hiring practices receives adequate consideration of its credentials. The idea is that the only effective way to ensure this is to opt for the woman when there is no perceived difference between her qualifications and those of the man being considered. Men as a gender already have adequate attention drawn to their credentials (even though factors like color and class still make a difference within both genders between those whose credentials are adequately considered and those whose credentials are relatively neglected.) Men will continue to receive attention as long as targets require hiring specific numbers from each gender. Targets that mandate taking the woman in case she has perceived qualifications equal in weight to those of the man (until the gender target is met) serve only to offset the inflated perception of males' qualifications as mentioned earlier.

III

However, there is more at stake in gender target hiring than simply fairness to applicants of both genders. Studies of Jewish populations have shown that Jews, as individuals, can be assimilated into a society until their percentage of the population in that society reaches about 10 percent. In numbers above that percentage, Jews become visible enough to become subject to persecution. However, when their numbers reach 30 percent to 40 percent, Jews become strong enough to forestall or resist persecution efforts, provided the Jews have enough internal cohesiveness.[2]

The report to the Canadian Philosophical Association from the Committee to Study Hiring Policies Affecting Women, May 1991,[3] states,

strikingly, that 13 percent of tenured and tenure-track positions in Canadian philosophy departments are held by women. The report recommends that the percentage of women in permanent faculty positions should be raised to 27 percent by the year 2000 and to 40 percent by the year 2010. These numbers would presumably make women strong enough so that they would not be vulnerable to victimization by male coalitions. The report also recommends that gender targets should exceed the current proportion of women in the candidate pool of new PhD recipients, which presently stands at about 28 percent. The message of the report is fairly clear. It encourages women to pursue careers in philosophy by attaining doctorates and applying for positions, so that philosophy departments and universities can meet their teaching and research responsibilities.

Our heritage has committed us to a tradition of democracy, which usually means rule by the majority. Sometimes, however, a majority becomes a coalition, acting in unison in pursuit of its interest at the expense of some group. This is often called "oligarchy." Patriarchy is a form of self-interested oligarchy, rule by men to benefit men at the expense of women. When men acquire and retain most of the positions connected with prestige, opportunities, and power—especially the power to determine who is hired, retained, or promoted—men can exclude women and, at the extreme, treat them ruthlessly. As long as the number of women hired is kept small, men can hold on to this power. According to the study of Jewish populations cited earlier, such patriarchal activity can function well in an environment in which 13 percent of the positions are held by women.

In addition, academic freedom gives all faculty a right to express themselves and behave toward each other as they see fit, within certain obvious limits. This can subject minority groups, including women, to what has become known as "a ton of feathers." Continual bombardment by patriarchally minded individuals speaking and acting individually can make women feel that there is something not quite right about them and that they lack full legitimacy as faculty members. A multitude of actions (e.g., general or quite specific questions about women's competence, exclusion from discussions where decision-making takes place, failure to consider women for positions of power, continually interrupting women, subjecting women to higher standards than male counterparts in everything from personal appearance and personal life to quality of teaching and research) can, in their totality, be quite devastating. The energy of women faculty is often dissipated on these brush fires, and their teaching and research may suffer. Yet even in such an environment, women are deemed inadequate if they fall short in their responsibilities as faculty members. Paradoxically, we women are often required to perform extraordinary feats of *machismo,* as when Peter O'Toole, as Lawrence of Arabia, leaves his hand in the candle flame saying, "The trick, you see, is not to *care* that it hurts." For example, a woman is not supposed to care if her chairman (as mine did) cuts her pay increase to, as he put it, "teach you a lesson."

The original intention of democracy and academic freedom in universities was to ensure a favorable climate for scholarship and teaching. But like many institutions that can be used to promote good, these can be used to promote just the opposite. Academic freedom leaves people free to say and do quite harmful things to one another. Democracy allows a majority to oppress a minority. In particular, men can use these two institutions to keep women in a subordinate position according to the principle of "might makes right."

Universities also see the odd phenomenon of the converse of this principle—right also makes might: " . . . because one knows what is morally right, it is morally appropriate . . . to dominate others. One understands one's agency as that of the judge, teacher/preacher, director, administrator."[4] Too many men still think themselves possessed of a moral vision that is superior to that of women, which allows them to exercise their patriarchal power to full capacity. This includes structuring hiring practices for new positions.

For example, when my philosophy department set its gender hiring quotas in the fall of 1990, none of our three women faculty were consulted. The decision was made by a small coalition of "right-thinking" men, apparently so sure of their vision that they simply announced it to the department as a whole as a *fait accompli.* (The coalition left out some of the men in the department as well. However, because the decision was about the relative gender composition of the department in the future, it was a real anomaly that representatives of only one gender were consulted.) Thus patriarchy perpetuates itself by shutting out voices of women as long as it has power to do so.

A university does not properly serve its students or its community by promulgating a single way of thinking, that of the white, able-bodied, ethnically correct, financially secure, heterosexual male. Graduates should not leave a university with the idea that philosophy, leadership, moral correctness, or anything else is the prerogative of just one kind of person. Universities should be about diversity as well as about whatever content of the disciplines remains constant through diversity. In particular, universities should not teach students that patriarchy is a form of justice, or that there are no alternative ways of organizing society.

Many women who presently hold faculty positions have lived through quite brutal encounters with patriarchy. Many of us hope our experiences were not in vain—that somehow things will be better for our younger counterparts. Gender target hiring until we become strong enough in numbers to resist patriarchy by democratic procedures may not be the only solution, but it is one solution.

NOTES

1. This is something like Mary Ann Warren's argument regarding quota hiring. Each occasion on which an employer favored gender A over qualification would have to be compensated on a later occasion by his favoring gender B over qualification to make his quotas come out properly. (Mary Ann Warren, "Secondary

Sexism and Quota Hiring," reprinted in *Philosophy and Women,* Sharon Bishop and Marjorie Weinzweig, eds., (Belmont, CA: Wadsworth Publishing Company, Inc., 1979), 243. Warren's argument should assuage anyone's worries about targets hardening into quotas in cases where targets specify the same gender proportions as those in the candidate pool. The employer would have no incentive to favor gender over qualifications.

2. Stanislav Andreski, "An Economic Interpretation of Antisemitism" in *Race, Ethnicity and Social Change,* John Stone, ed. (Belmont, CA: Wadsworth Publishing Company, Inc., 1977), 126–27.

3. Report to the Canadian Philosophical Association from the Committee to Study Hiring Policies Affecting Women, May 1991, Brenda Baker, Josiane Boulad Ayoub, Lorraine Code, Michael McDonald, Kathleen Okruhlik, Susan Sherwin, Wayne Summer (unpublished; copies circulated to all members of the Canadian Philosophical Association).

4. Marilyn Frye, "A Response to *Lesbian Ethics*" in *Feminist Ethics,* Claudia Card, ed. (Lawrence, KS: University Press of Kansas, 1991), 54.

Further Questions

1. If there is genuine doubt about whether someone can perform satisfactorily in a certain type of position, should the employer (1) scrutinize that candidate's credentials with extra care or (2) not scrutinize them at all?

2. Do men possess better leadership qualities than women, so that they should take charge of all matters in the workplace, including hiring decisions?

3. If middle-aged men have been the beneficiaries of gender discrimination in past hiring decisions, ought they be forced to step down from their positions so that gender targets will not lower the chances of younger men's being hired?

The Comparable Worth Debate   III.4

ELLEN FRANKEL PAUL

Ellen Frankel Paul discusses the concept of comparable worth, comparing two types of occupations to determine whether they are different or equal in value. Advocates of making such comparisons argue that women are often clustered in occupations equal in value to those in which men predominate, and therefore deserve to be paid the same as men in these comparable positions. Paul disagrees with these advocates.

Paul is research director and professor of political science at the Social Philosophy and Policy Center at Bowling Green State University. She is author of numerous articles and books in political, economic, and moral theory.

Reading Questions

1. Do different types of work have objective qualities that can be used to set the value of the work of each type?

2. Is one line of work better in all respects than a second line of work if it is paid a better wage?

3. Is an unregulated market a "democratic" way of setting prices and wages, since we all participate in the market by buying and selling goods and services?

COMPARABLE WORTH, or pay equity in its newer guise, is an attractive concept: if only employers could be required to pay female employees in traditionally female occupations the same salaries as males in male-dominated jobs of comparable value to their employers, then the wage gap would largely disappear. Advocates for women's equality have become increasingly enthusiastic about this strategy for achieving their goals, as they have seen other legal remedies—the Equal Pay Act, Title VII of the Civil Rights Act—fail to secure to women this elusive equality.

Comparable worth in the 1980s has achieved remarkable strides, virtually sweeping the country. Despite comparable worth's seeming novelty —it is a concept that has caught fire only recently —the idea has been around for quite a while. In fact, the notion of "comparable work" was employed by the National War Labor Board during World War II. The board required equal pay for comparable work and made job evaluations within plants between dissimilar jobs to determine whether any pay inequities existed. Every Congress since 1945 has entertained a comparable work bill of various types.[1]

"Equal pay for equal work" is not the objective of the comparable worth advocates, for that standard has been the law of the land since 1963, when the Equal Pay Act was approved by Congress as an amendment to the Fair Labor Standards Act. Since then, it has been illegal to pay women less than men doing "substantially equal" work.[2] For many advocates of women's equality, however, this standard does not go nearly far enough. It leaves important gaps in the protection afforded to women workers; for example, women who labor in jobs with no equivalent male jobs available for purposes of comparison are left unprotected as

are women whose work is comparable to men's but not equal by the "substantially equal" standard. If over half the women in the United States work in jobs that are 75 percent dominated by women, then more must be done to alleviate their lot than simply securing them equal pay for equal work.[3]

However, comparable worth's advocates are not merely pointing to a lacunae in the law. They seek sweeping reforms that would question the very foundation of our market-based economic system. What they doubt is not the efficiency of the market but its justice. Why, they ask, should a female registered nurse whose skills require years of training and whose responsibility for the preservation of human life is so great be paid less than a garbage man? Why should a social worker, another female-dominated job classification, receive less pay than a truck driver, when the social worker requires years of schooling and must exercise considerable judgment in guiding the lives of others? Why do women working full-time earn a mere 64 cents to men's one dollar? Something must be radically amiss in a market system that produces such patent inequities, the advocates conclude. . . .

Despite Marx's abhorrence of this fact, labor power is as much a commodity as anything else. The price of any particular kind of labor is set by the same criteria as any other good. The market price equates supply and demand; each laborer is paid the equivalent of his marginal productivity, his contribution to the enterprise. Marginal utility theory, thus, overcame another problem inherent in a labor theory of value: that every factor of production—labor, land, entrepreneurship— required a different theory to explain how its price was set.

Now, what bearing does all of this have on comparable worth? Comparable worth shares with the labor theory of value a desire to discover some objective characteristics of worth or value apart from the valuations in the marketplace derived from the choices of actual buyers. For comparable worth, the hours of labor embodied in a thing no longer set its value, but rather, the value of labor itself can be determined by assessing its components: knowledge, skills, mental demands, accountability, working conditions.

What comparable worth's proponents are searching for is some identifiable, objective qualities that are transferable from job to job and that everyone could, at least theoretically, agree upon. But are they not searching in vain? The perpetual squabbles among evaluators performing studies in the states, the instructions of consultants to the evaluation committees that they should go with their gut instincts in assessing points, and the reevaluations that go on once the scores have been assembled are empirical evidence of a problem that really lies on the theoretical level.

If there is no intrinsic value to a job, then it cannot be measured. Let us look at the wage-setting process as it unfolds in the market to see what the price of labor means, if it does not mean a measurement of intrinsic value.

A job has value to someone who creates it and is willing to pay someone to do it. The price of that job is set in the labor market, which is nothing more than an arena for satisfying the demands for labor of various sorts by numerous employers. What an employer is willing to pay for the type of labor he needs depends on his assessment of what that labor can contribute to the ultimate product and what price he thinks those products will command in the market. The labor market is an impersonal process. In most cases, employers and potential employees do not know each other before the process is begun. It is impersonal in another way, also. No individual employer can exercise much influence over the price of labor of the kind he needs. Only in the rarest of cases, where no alternative employers are available to willing workers, will any one employer have much of an impact on the overall job market. Such influence characterizes centrally planned, government-owned economies much more than it does market economies. To the extent that markets are distorted by government-imposed monopolies or cartels, the actual market departs from the theoretical one.

The supporters of comparable worth consider this view of the market naive. Rather, they say, markets are dominated by monopolies that dictate wages to workers who by-and-large have no other options. The problem with this argument is that it is simply not true that the labor market in the United States is largely dominated by monopolies. What has characterized capitalist economies since the Industrial Revolution is precisely the options that workers have, the fluidity of labor markets, and the ever-changing possibilities the market creates. Unlike the Middle Ages, where workers' options were essentially limited to following the paternal occupation and where class status was very nearly immutable, capitalism presents workers with a plethora of options.

Another problem with this quest for objective value or worth is that it confuses moral language with economic language. Surely, economists talk about value: they mean by the value of a commodity what it will trade for at any particular time in the marketplace. There is nothing mysterious, no essence that lies buried beneath this market value (at least since the labor theory of value was abandoned).

What the comparable worth people mean by value is something essential to any particular type of labor. They are looking for some higher order moral principle that, irrespective of the market, can compare the work of the plumber to the tree-trimmer to the grocer to the secretary to the nurse. Within our society, there is no agreement about higher order moral principles: about what contributes to the good life; what activities are worthy of pursuit in their own right; what kinds of behavior contribute to the welfare of society. How can we expect individuals in society to agree about how particular jobs contribute to ends, when those ends themselves are in dispute?

Wouldn't it be an unpleasant world if people did agree about values, if those values could be objectively measured as they were exemplified in different jobs, and if they were paid accordingly? Then, if Michael Jackson earned a million dollars for each performance while an emergency room nurse received $20 for her work during the same two hours, we would know that he was really worth 50,000 times as much as she; that is, that society valued her contribution so very much less. We would know, simply by the salary paid to each person in such a society, exactly what his social contribution and, presumably, his social status was. But on a market we cannot even infer that a plumber making $10 an hour is worth more or less to his employer than a teacher who earns the same wage is worth to hers. Such comparisons are vacuous. One's worth, in the moral sense, is not measured in the marketplace by one's wage. Price and salary are economic terms, and they depend upon the available supply and the demand for particular kinds of labor. Value and worth are moral terms, as comparable worth's supporters intend them, and they do not equate well at all with price in the marketplace. Thus, even the market cannot equate the worth (in the moral sense) of one job with another; all it shows is that at any particular time secretaries are paid more or less than zoo keepers.

Any attempt to employ "objective" job assessment criteria must be inherently discretionary. That blanket statement stands unrefuted by the comparable worth camp. I believe it is logically impossible for them to surmount this difficulty: for they cannot find objectivity by appealing to the views of experts who, as human beings, bring their prejudices to any assessment; nor can they find it by abandoning the market and embracing central planning, which is nothing more than personal whims enshrined in decrees. Either way, the judgments of bureaucrats or judges would be forcibly substituted for the assessments of those who are the actual purchasers of labor services.

This is unavoidable, since there is no intrinsic value to any job. The impersonal forces of the market would have to be replaced by subjective judgments, by the opinions of "experts." Even if these "experts" were bereft of all tastes—which is, of course, inconceivable—they could not implement a system of objective measurement. Where is the metric? None is to be found. While each person can order his own preferences, these separate preference orders cannot be equated. Similarly, different jobs cannot be equated on any objective scale, at least not until everyone is in agreement about ultimate moral values. Even then, their particular application would be open to differences of opinion.

The comparable worth critics are correct: there is no intrinsic value to any job, and, hence, they can neither be measured or compared. . . .

. . . if an employer, through discriminatory motivation or any other reason, wishes to pay less than the prevailing wage for a certain kind of labor, one of three things will normally happen. He will get no takers. He will get fewer takers than he needs. Or the quality of the applicant pool will be lower than the job requires. Conversely, if he wishes to pay more, he will get many applicants and some of them will be of higher quality than normal in that job classification.

In the former case, the employer jeopardizes his business by presumably making his products less marketable and his operation less efficient; in the latter case, the employer may benefit his business if his more skilled employees produce more products or a better product that the consumers are willing to pay a higher price to acquire. The consumer, however, may not be willing, and then the business would be jeopardized.

Thus, employers are, in the normal case, pretty much tied to paying prevailing market wages. Those employers who discriminate for irrelevant reasons—like race, sex, religion—put themselves at a competitive disadvantage by restricting the pool of labor from which they can select workers. If discrimination against blacks or women, for example, were prevalent in the society, the price of such labor would be lower than for comparable labor provided by members of other groups. Those employers willing to hire the despised will benefit from lower prices for their labor and will enjoy a competitive edge. In the absence of laws enshrined by governments to perpetuate discrimination, the market should correct for it over time by penalizing discriminatory employers and rewarding the others. Eventually, the wages of the discriminated will rise.

If jobs have no intrinsic worth, then the comparable worth position has been severely wounded, for it bases its case on precisely such an assumption. What I have argued is that jobs have no intrinsic value within the context of a market economy. Now, that is an important caveat. A competing system, one that sets the prices for all goods, services, and labor by a central planning agency could provide an alternative framework to the market. But would the price of various types of labor be objectively set in such a system? All we could say is that the planners would tell everyone else what each job was worth. Via job evaluations, direct flashes of insight, or whatever methodology they chose, the wages of labor would be set and everyone would abide by those directives. One might call such a system objective in the sense that departures from the assigned wages might be punishable, but using the term in the way we normally do, it seems like rampant subjectivism. As John Stuart Mill wrote a century ago:

> A fixed rule, like that of equality, might be acquiesced in, and so might chance, or an external necessity; but that a handful of human beings should weight everybody in the balance, and give more to one and less to another at their *sole* pleasure and judgment, would not be borne unless from persons believed to be more than men, and backed by supernatural terrors . . . [4]

. . . there is something else fundamentally flawed about the proponents' line of argument. Comparable worth cannot eliminate discrimination from the labor market, and neither can any

other scheme, including the market. The purpose of any hiring process is precisely to discriminate. A personnel director does not only look for skills in hiring an applicant. Such intangibles as personality, looks, motivation, and so forth play a factor. Just as any employer discriminates in hiring, so the consulting firms or wage boards would impose their tastes and value judgments.

One kind of discrimination that is particularly invidious is government-imposed discrimination. Apartheid is one example; the policies toward Hungarians in Rumania and Turks in Bulgaria, are others. What makes this kind of discrimination so odious is that it is government-imposed, and hence nearly inescapable. Discrimination in the market is haphazard and usually escapable: one employer may not like women, another doesn't like blacks but doesn't mind women, while most look for the best person to do the job. If you don't like the wages or the conditions in one firm, you can join another or start your own. The comparable worth consulting firms, and what I see as the inevitable wage boards, court-appointed masters, or judicial "wage boards," denote more the apartheid and less the market kind of discrimination. The standards would be government mandated and inescapable, except by leaving the country. . . .

If discrimination—meaning tastes—is irremediable, why should we prefer comparable worth and the discrimination of "experts" to the market and the discrimination generated by the free choices of all of us? . . .

Markets Express Consumer Sovereignty

Employers are consumers of labor, but they are also intermediaries between the ultimate consumers of their products and their laborers. Employers produce goods by combining various factors of production, and they hope these goods will mesh with what consumers want. They do so as efficiently as their competitors, or else they are soon out of business. Thus, comparable worth is not simply an attempt to replace the decisions of employers with the decisions of "experts," bureaucrats, and judges: Comparable worth seeks ultimately to replace the decisions of consumers themselves about how they wish to spend their money.

To most comparable worth advocates, those who embrace comparable worth because they see it as a means for bettering women's earnings, the tendency of comparable worth to undermine consumer sovereignty ought to be disturbing. Women are consumers, and they ought to value the liberty that has created the abundance we all enjoy. The more radical supporters of comparable worth, however, understand that the concept is a wedge they can use to undermine our free market economy, and I expect that they are not at all disconcerted by the tendency of comparable worth to replace the choice of consumers with the opinions of "experts." These radicals constitute, however, only a small proportion of those who support comparable worth.

Markets Are Impersonal

If secretaries and nurses on average receive lower salaries than accountants and auto mechanics, it is not because any one group of "experts" has determined that the latter are more worthy than the former. It is simply a function of supply and demand. While individual employers may operate their businesses as idiosyncratically as they like (within, of course, the current labor and civil rights laws of the United States), they follow discriminatory wage policies at their peril. If fewer women choose to become nurses and secretaries, these occupations will receive higher remuneration in the future.

To condemn the marketplace because some employers discriminate, as comparable worth does, and to expect that a system that eliminates discrimination can be devised, is to search for the Holy Grail. Such utopian quests typically end in disaster, in inflicting on human beings infinitely worse suffering than they endured before the revolutionaries tried to remake mankind. Our collective experience as a species with attempts to better society by placing decisions in the hands of enlightened experts, those who know the truth, have all been colossal failures. The record of revolutionary societies in our century in the treatment of minorities is much worse than the record of free market societies, South Africa included. If one doubts this, examine the lot of the Chinese in Vietnam, the Crimean Tatars, Jews, Germans, and other non-Russian peoples in the Soviet Union, the Turks in Bulgaria, the Hungarians in Rumania, the Eritreans in Ethiopia . . .

My purpose in adverting to this list of human atrocities is not to equate support for comparable worth with support for the gulags. Rather, I would caution the supporters of comparable worth that the attempt to make society dramatically better by perfecting the results of the free choices of real people is more often than not—dare I say, always—calamitous. Those we place in power to perfect us are human, too, and whatever failings they have tend to be magnified by the possession of power over other people's lives. To the extent that comparable worth replaces impersonal market forces with the opinions of "experts," it flirts with the potential of doing great harm.

Markets Are Efficient

In contrast to centrally planned economies, which have proven notoriously inefficient, market systems produce bounties undreamt of in past centuries. Comparable worth seems to require courts or wage boards to intervene continuously in the operations of all firms. With all the disruptions and inefficiencies such intervention would cause, a movement to explicit central planning of the economy would be the logical next step. Something would have to provide a "cure" for the dislocations caused by perpetual comparable worth evaluations, and since the market is out, central planning would be the only logical alternative. . . .

Markets Allow Freedom of Exit and Entry

If a woman does not like the terms of employment offered to her, if she thinks the proffered wage is too low, she is perfectly free to seek another employer or strike out on her own. No one is perpetually tied to a job, as has been the practice off and on in some centrally planned economies. If one feels that as a secretary one is being discriminated against in relation to an office manager, one can acquire new skills and become an office manager or go into an entirely different line of work.

Comparable worth's advocates deride such a fluid vision of women's choices: "Aren't women stuck in the low-paying jobs they've trained for? Millions of women have invested their time in becoming nurses, secretaries, teachers, and social workers. Let's make sure they are paid more; let's not demand that they change their occupations."

Where this line of argument misfires is in assuming that millions of women would have to change jobs to increase their wages. This simply is not true. If enough women (at the margin, to use the economist's term) moved out of these jobs, or more realistically, if younger women did not replace their departing older sisters in sufficient numbers, the wages for those remaining would rise—without comparable worth and just as a result of natural market forces.

Women should not expect to eat their cake and have it too. If they want to flock to these traditionally female occupations—for some perfectly good reasons relating to family responsibilities—they should understand that one of the drawbacks to making the same choice as millions of others is that one contributes to the oversupply of labor in one's chosen field. Men know this. If there are too many middle managers and the economy takes a nose dive, then middle managers will be pounding the pavement. If there are too many lawyers, their salaries will decline.

As free individuals, women have choices. Older women, if they are dissatisfied with their salaries as teachers or nurses, can retrain for other more lucrative jobs or can start businesses of their own, as indeed, many of them have done. Younger women can train for traditionally male occupations, as indeed, millions of them have. To insist, as comparable worth activists do, that women are entitled to remain secretaries and nurses, but that their pay should be jury-rigged upward, is to appear childish, dependent, and unknowledgeable about how the world of work functions. . . .

Comparable worth is a detour—not to say, a dead end—that will not aid women in the long run, will not encourage them to pursue new paths, to explore new possibilities. Rather than condemning the market system, feminists ought to be glorying in it, for it has proved remarkably adaptable to women's evolving desire to work full-time, to work throughout their lives, and to work in new and challenging jobs. Why do comparable worth supporters view women as requiring special dispensations from government to advance in the marketplace, precisely at the time when women have made such great advances in the professions, in business, and in nontraditional vocations? Why emphasize women's disadvantages—their alleged victimization, their helplessness—when feminism rightly understood should glory in women's remarkable advances?

Indeed, it is the opponents of comparable worth, rather than its advocates, who have a positive attitude toward women's abilities, who see women as capable of determining what is in their own best interests and of competing and working for these goals in the marketplace alongside men, without any special privileges.

NOTES

1. *County of Washington v. Gunther,* 452 U.S. 161 (1981), Rehnquist dissent at 185 n. 1.

2. The Equal Pay Act is Section 6 of the Fair Labor Standards Act of 1938. The "substantially equal" definition of equal work is judicially defined language. See: *Shultz v. Wheaton Glass Co.,* 421 F. 2d 259, *cert. denied,* 398 U.S. 905 (1970); *Brennan v. Prince William Hospital Corp.,* 503 F. 2d 282, *cert. denied,* 420 U.S. 972 (1975).

3. *Who's Working for Working Women,* National Committee on Pay Equity and the National Women's Political Caucus, 1984.

4. John Stuart Mill, *Principles of Political Economy,* Book I, chap. ii, par. 4; as quoted in F. A. Hayek, *The Road to Serfdom* (Chicago: University of Chicago Press, 1944), p. 112.

Further Questions

1. If we are not in agreement about what constitutes the good life, is there any way we can assess the value of an occupation according to the contribution it makes to human life?

2. If a job, like nursing, fails to attract qualified applicants because of its low wages, can we expect that the resulting shortage of nurses will make wages rise, that qualified applicants will then apply, and that the shortage will vanish?

3. When women are making too little money because of the occupation they are in, is it a viable solution for them to move to another occupation that pays more? That is, are women always in a position where they can make such a move?

III.5   Sharing the Shop Floor

STAN GRAY

Stan Gray writes about his experience as shop steward in admitting women into an all-male factory floor. It was not an easy task, because the sexist attitudes of the men would not allow women to work alongside them.

Gray is currently making contribution to a better world by working for Greenpeace Canada.

Reading Questions

1. Can the ways men talk and act in a factory environment be so rough that women should not be allowed to work in such an environment?

2. Are factory workers and other blue-collar workers used as objects, dehumanized, and treated as faceless bodies in much the same way feminists claim that women are?

3. Is a woman who works normally robbing a male breadwinner of adequate income for his family?

My Education Begins

. . . MY EDUCATION IN THE PROBLEMS of the Westinghouse women began in November 1978, when I was recalled to work following a bitter and unsuccessful five-month strike. The union represented eighteen hundred workers in three plants that produced turbines, motors, transformers, and switchgear equipment. When I was recalled to work it wasn't to my old Beach Road plant—where I had been a union steward and safety rep—but to an all-female department in the Switchgear plant and to a drastic drop in my labor grade. The plant was mostly segregated; in other words, jobs (and many departments) were either male or female. There were separate seniority lists and job descriptions. The dual-wage, dual-seniority system was enshrined in the collective agreement signed and enforced by both company and union.

At Switchgear I heard the complaints of the women, who worked the worst jobs in terms of monotony, speed, and work discipline but received lower pay, were denied chances for promotion, and were frequently laid off. They complained too of the union, accusing the male leadership of sanctioning and policing their inferior treatment. In cahoots with management, it swept the women's complaints under the carpet. From the first day it was obvious to me that the company enforced harsher standards for the women. They worked harder and faster, got less break time, and were allowed less leeway than the men. When I was later transferred to the all-male machine shop, the change was from night to day.

Meanwhile the men's club that ran the union made its views known to me early and clearly. The staff rep told me that he himself would never work with women. He boasted that he and his friends in the leadership drank in the one remaining all-male bar in the city. The local president was upset when he heard that I was seriously listening to the complaints of the women workers. He told me that he always just listened to their unfounded bitching, said "yes, yes, yes," and then completely ignored what he had been told. I ought to do the same, was his advice. Although I had just been elected to the executive in a rank-and-file rebellion against the old guard, he assumed that a common male bond would override our differences. When I persisted in taking the women's complaints seriously, the leadership started to ridicule me, calling me "the Ambas-

sador" and saying they were now happy that I was saving them the distasteful task of listening to the women's bitching.

Then in 1979 the boom fell at Switchgear: the company announced it would close the plant. For the women, this was a serious threat. In the new contract the seniority and wage lists had been integrated, thanks to a new Ontario Human Rights Code. But would the women be able to exercise their seniority and bump or transfer to jobs in the other Hamilton plants, or would they find themselves out in the street after years at Switchgear?

Divide and Conquer

By this time I had been recalled to my old department at the Beach Road plant, thanks to shop-floor pressure by the guys. There was a lot of worry in the plants about the prospect of large-scale transfers of women from Switchgear. A few women who had already been transferred had met with harassment and open hostility from the men. Some of us tried to raise the matter in the stewards' council, but the leadership was in no mood to discuss and confront sexism openly. The union bully boys went after us, threatening, shouting, breast beating, and blaming the women for the problems.

Since the union structures weren't going to touch the problem, we were left to our own resources in the shop. I worked in the Transformer Division, which the management was determined to keep all male. As a steward I insisted that the Switchgear women had every right to jobs in our department, at least to training and a trial period as stipulated by seniority. Since this was a legal and contractual right, management developed a strategy of Divide and Rule: present the women as a threat to men's jobs; create splits and get the hourly men to do the bosses' dirty work for them. Management had a secondary objective here, which was to break our shop-floor union organization. Since the trauma of the strike and post-strike repression, a number of stewards and safety reps had patiently rebuilt the union in the plant, block by block—fighting every grievance, hazard, and injustice with a variety of tactics and constructing some shop-floor unity. We did so in the teeth of opposition from both company and union, whose officials were overly anxious to get along peacefully with each other. A war of the sexes would be a weapon in management's counteroffensive against us.

For months before the anticipated transfers, foremen and their assorted rumor mongers stirred up the pot with the specter of the Invasion of the Women. Two hundred Switchgear women would come and throw all Beach Road breadwinners out in the street; no one's job would be safe. Day after day, week after week, we were fed the tales: for example, that fourteen women with thirty years' seniority were coming to the department in eight days and no male would be protected. Better start thinking now about unemployment insurance. . . .

For weeks before their arrival, the department was hyper-alive, everyone keyed to the Invasion of the Women. I was approached by one of the guys, who said that a number of them had discussed the problem and wanted me, as their steward, to tell management the men didn't want the women in here and would fight to keep them out.

The moment was a personal watershed for me. As I listened to him, I knew that half measures would no longer do. I would now have to take the bull by the horns. . . .

I told this guy, "No. These women from Switchgear are our sisters, and we have fought for them to come into our department. They are our fellow workers with seniority rights, and we want them to work here rather than get laid off. If we deny them their seniority rights, it hurts us, for once that goes down the drain, none of us has any protection. It is our enemies, the bosses, who are trying to do them out of jobs here. There's enough work for everyone; even if there weren't, seniority has to rule. For us as well as for

them. The guys should train the women when they come and make them feel welcome.". . .

It was easy to tease guys with the contradictions that male double standards led them to. Although they were afraid the women would overproduce, at the same time they insisted that women wouldn't be physically strong enough to do our "man's work." Either they could or they couldn't was the answer to that one, and if they could, they deserved the jobs. It would be up to us to initiate them into the department norms. Many of the guys said that the women would never be able to do certain of the heavy and rotten jobs. As steward and safety rep I always jumped on that one: we shouldn't do those jobs either. Hadn't we been fighting to make them safer and easier for ourselves? Well, they answered, the women would still not be able to do all the jobs. Right, I would say, but how many guys here have we protected from doing certain jobs because of back or heart problems, or age, or simply personal distaste? If the women can't do certain jobs, we treat them the same way as men who can't. We don't victimize people who can't do everything the company wants them to. We protect them: as our brothers, and as our sisters.

By pointing out the irrationalities of the sexist double standards, we were pushing the guys to apply their class principles—universal standards of equal treatment. Treat the women just as we treat men regarding work tasks, seniority, illness, and so on.

Countering Sexism

Male sexist culture strives to degrade women to nothing but pieces of flesh, physical bodies, mindless animals . . . something less than fully human, which the men can then be superior to. Name-calling becomes a means of putting women in a different category from *us,* to justify different and inferior treatment.

Part of the fight to identify the women as co-workers was therefore the battle against calling them "cunts" or "bitches." It was important to set the public standard whereby the women were labeled as part of us, not *them*. I wouldn't be silent with anyone using these sexist labels and pushed the point very aggressively. Eventually everyone referred to "the women."

After a while most of the men in the department came to agree that having the women in and giving them a chance was the right thing to do by any standard of fairness, unionism, or solidarity, and was required by the basic human decency that separates *us* from *them*. But then the focus shifted to other areas. Many men came back with traditional arguments against women in the work force. They belong at home with the kids, they're robbing male breadwinners of family income and so forth. But others disagreed: most of the guys' wives worked outside the home or had done so in the past; after all a family needed at least two wages these days. Some men answered that in bad times a family should have only one breadwinner so all would have an income. Fine, we told them, let's be really fair and square: you go home and clean the house and leave your wife at work. Alright, they countered, they could tolerate women working who supported a family, but not single women. And so I picked out four single men in our department and proposed they be immediately sacked.

Fairness and equality seemed to triumph here too. The guys understood that everyone who had a job at Westinghouse deserved equal protection. But then, some men found another objection. As one, Peter, put it, "I have no respect for any women who could come in to work here in these rotten conditions." The comeback was sharp: "What the hell are *you* putting up with this shit for? Why didn't *you* refuse to do that dirty job last month? Don't *you* deserve to be treated with respect?"[1]

As the Invasion Date approached I got worried. Reason and appeals to class solidarity had had a certain impact. Most of the guys were agreeing, grudgingly, to give the women a chance. But the campaign had been too short; fear and hostility were surfacing more and more. I was worried that there would be some ugly incident the first day or two that would set a pattern.

Much of the male hostility had been kept in check because I, as the union steward, had fought so aggressively on the issue. I decided to take this one step further and use some intimidation to enforce the basics of public behavior. In a tactic I later realized was a double-edged sword, I puffed myself up, assumed a cocky posture, and went for the jugular. I loudly challenged the masculinity of any worker who was opposed to the women. What kind of man is afraid of women? I asked. Only sissies and wimps are threatened by equality. A *real man* has nothing to be afraid of; he wants strong women. Any man worth his salt doesn't need the crutch of superiority over his sisters; he fears no female. A real man lives like an equal, doesn't step on women, doesn't degrade his sisters, doesn't have to rule the roost at home in order to affirm his manhood. Real men fight the boss, stand up with self-respect and dignity, rather than scapegoat our sisters.

I was sarcastic and cutting with my buddies: "This anti-woman crap of yours is a symbol of weakness. Stand up like a real man and behave and work as equals. The liberation of the women is the best thing that ever came along. . . . It's in *our* interests." To someone who boasted of how he made his wife cook his meals and clean his floors, I'd ask if she wiped his ass too? To the porno addicts I'd say, "You like that pervert shit? What's wrong with the real thing? Can you only get it up with those fantasies and cartoon women? Afraid of a real woman?" I'd outdo some of the worst guys in verbal intimidation and physical feats. Then I'd lecture them on women's equality and on welcoming our sisters the next week. I zeroed in on one or two of the sick types and physically threatened them if they pulled off anything with the women.

All of this worked, as I had hoped. It established an atmosphere of intimidation; no one was going to get smart with the women. Everyone would stand back for a while, some would cooperate, some would be neutral, and those I saw as "psycho-sexists" would keep out.

The tactic was effective because it spoke directly to a basic issue. But it was also effective because it took a leaf from the book of the psycho-sexists themselves.

At Westinghouse as elsewhere, some of the men were less chauvinistic and more sensible than others, but they often kept quiet in a group. They allowed the group pattern to be set by the most sexist bullies, whose style of woman baiting everyone at least gave in to. The psycho-sexists achieved this result because they challenged, directly or by implication, the masculinity of any male who didn't act the same way. All the men, whatever their real inclinations, are intimidated into acting or talking in a manner degrading to women. I had done the same thing, but in reverse. I had challenged the masculinity of any worker who would oppose the women. I had scared them off.

The Day the Women Arrived

The department crackled with tension the morning The Women arrived. There were only two of them to start with. The company was evidently scared by the volatile situation it had worked so hard to create. They backed off a direct confrontation by assigning my helper George and me to work with the women.

The two women were on their guard: Betty and Laura, in their late thirties, were expecting trouble. They were pleasantly shocked when I said matter-of-factly that we would train them on the job. They were overjoyed when I explained that the men had wanted them in our department and had fought the bosses to bring them here.

It was an unforgettable day. Men from all corners of the plant crept near the iron-stacking area to spy on us. I explained the work and we set about our tasks. We outproduced the standard rate by just a hair so that the company couldn't say the women weren't able to meet the normal requirements of the job.

My strategy was to get over the hump of the first few days. I knew that once the guys got used to the women being there, they'd begin to treat them as people, not as "women" and their hysteria would go away. It was essential to avoid incidents. Thus I forced the guys to interact with them. Calling over one of the male opponents, I introduced him as Bruce the Slinger who knew all the jobs and was an expert in lifts and would be happy to help them if asked and could always be called on to give a hand. This put him on the spot. Finally he flashed a big smile, and said, "Sure, just ask and I'd be pleased to show you anything, and to begin with, here's what to watch out for. . . ."

The morning went by. There were no incidents. From then on it was easy. More guys began to talk to the two women. They started to see them as Betty with four kids who lived on the mountain and knew wiring and was always cheerful; or Laura, who was a friend of John's uncle and was cranky early in the morning, who could easily operate the crane but had trouble with the impact gun, and who liked to heat up meat pies for lunch. After all, these men lived and worked with women all of their lives outside the plant—mothers, sisters, wives, in-laws, friends, daughters, and girlfriends. Having women at work was no big deal once they got over the trauma of the invasion of this male preserve. Just like helping your sister-in-law hang some wallpaper.

As the news spread, more and more women applied to transfer to our department. They were integrated with minimum fuss. The same thing happened in several adjoining departments. Quickly, men and women began to see each other as people and co-workers, not as enemies. Rather than man vs. woman it was John, Mary, Sue, Peter, Alice, George, and Laura. That Christmas we had a big party at someone's home—men and women of the department, drinking and dancing. The photos and various raucous tales of that night provided the basis for department storytelling for the next three months.

Was this, then, peace between the sexes? The integration of men and women as co-workers in the plant? Class solidarity triumphing over sex antagonism? Not quite. Although they were now together, it was not peace. The result was more complicated, for now the war between the sexes was being extended from the community into the workplace.

Workplace Culture

As our struggle showed, sexism coexists and often is at war with class consciousness and with the trade union solidarity that develops among factory men. Our campaign was successful to the extent that it was able to sharply polarize and push the contradictions between these two tendencies in each individual. With most of the men, their sense of class solidarity triumphed over male chauvinism.

Many of the men had resisted the female invasion of the workplace because for them it was the last sanctum of male culture. It was somewhere they could get away from the world of women, away from responsibility and children and the civilized society's cultural restraints. In the plant they could revel in the rough and tumble of a masculine world of physical harshness, of constant swearing and rough behavior, of half-serious fighting and competition with each other and more serious fighting with the boss. It was eight hours full of filth and dirt and grease and grime and sweat—manual labor and a manly atmosphere. They could be vulgar and obscene, talk about football and car repairs, and let their hair down. Boys could be boys.

The male workplace culture functions as a form of rebellion against the discipline of their society. Outside the workplace, women are the guardians of the community. They raise the kids and enforce some degree of family and collective responsibility. They frequently have to force this upon men, who would rather go drinking or play baseball while the women mind the kids, wash the family's clothes, attend to problems with the neighbors and in-laws, and so on. Like rebellious teenage sons escaping mother's control, male wage earners enter the factory gates, where in their male culture they feel free of the restraints of these repressive standards.

Even if all factory men don't share these attitudes, a large proportion do, to a greater or lesser degree.

The manly factory culture becomes an outlet for accumulated anger and frustration. But this is a vicious circle because the tedious work and the subordination to the bosses is in large part the very cause of the male worker's dissatisfaction. He is bitter against a world that has kept him down, exploited his labor power, bent him to meet the needs of production and profit, cheated him of a better life, and made the daily grind so harsh. Working men are treated like dirt everywhere: at work they are at the bottom of the heap and under the thumb of the boss; outside they are scorned by polite society. But, the men can say, we are better than them all in certain ways; we're doing men's work; it's physically tough; women can't do it; neither can the bankers and politicians. Tough work gives a sense of masculine superiority that compensates for being stepped on and ridiculed. All that was threatened by the Women's Invasion.

However, this male workplace culture is not one-sided, for it contains a fundamentally positive sense of class value. The workingmen contrast themselves to other classes and take pride in having a concrete grasp of the physical world around them. The big shots can talk fancy and manipulate words, flout their elegance and manners. But we control the nuts and bolts of production, have our hands on the machines and gears and valves, the wires and lathes and pumps, the furnaces and spindles and batteries. We're the masters of the real and the concrete; we manipulate the steel and the lead, the wood, oil, and aluminum. What we know is genuine, the real and specific world of daily life. Workers are the wheels that make a society go round, the creators of social value and wealth. There would be no fancy society, no civilized conditions if it were not for our labor.

The male workers are contemptuous of the mild-mannered parasites and soft-spoken vultures who live off our daily sweat: the managers and directors, the judges and entertainers, the lawyers, the coupon clippers, the administrators, the insurance brokers, the legislators . . . all those who profit from the shop floor, who build careers for themselves with the wealth we create. All that social overhead depends upon our mechanical skills, our concrete knowledge, our calloused hands, our technical ingenuity, our strained muscles and backs.

The Dignity of Labor, but society treats us like a pack of dumb animals, mere bodies with no minds or culture. We're physical labor power; the intelligence belongs to the management class. Workers are sneeringly regarded as society's bodies, the middle class as society's mind. One is inferior; the other is superior and fully human. The workers are less than human, close to animals, society's beasts of burden.

The male workplace culture tends to worship this self-identity of vulgar physicalness. It is as if the men enjoy wallowing in a masculine filth. They brag of being the wild men of the factory. Say it loud: I'm a brute and I'm proud.

Sexism thus undermines and subverts the proud tradition of the dignity of labor. It turns a class consciousness upside down by accepting and then glorifying the middle-class view of manual labor and physical activity as inferior, animalistic, and crude. When workers identify with the savages that the bosses see them as, they develop contempt for themselves. It is self-contempt to accept the scornful labels, the negative definitions, the insulting dehumanized treatment, the cartoon stereotypes of class chauvinism: the supermasculine menials, the industrial sweathogs.

Remember Peter, who couldn't respect a woman who would come to work in this hellhole. It was obviously a place where he felt he had lost his own self-respect. My reply to him was that he shouldn't put up with that rotten treatment, *that the men also deserved better.* We should be treated with dignity. Respect yourself—fight back like a man, not a macho fool who glorifies that which degrades him.

Everything gets turned inside out. It is seen as manly to be treated as less than a man, as just a physical, instinctual creature. But this is precisely how sexist society treats women: as mindless bodies, pieces of flesh . . . "biology is destiny." You would think that male factory workers and the women's movement would be natural allies, that they'd speak the same language. They share a common experience of being used as objects, dehumanized by those on top. Men in the factory are treated not as persons, but as bodies, replaceable numbers, commodities, faceless factors of production. The struggles of workingmen and of women revolve around similar things. The right to choice on abortion, for example, revolves around the right for women to control their own bodies. Is this not what the fight for health and safety on the shop floor is all about? To have some control over our bodies, not to let the bastards do what they want with our lives and limbs, to wreck us in their search for higher profits.

But male chauvinism turns many workingmen away from their natural allies, away from a rational and collective solution to their problems, diverting them from class unity with their sisters into oppressors and degraders of their sisters. Robbed of their real manhood—their humanity as men—they get a false sense of manhood by lording over women.

Playing the Foreman at Home

Many men compensate for their wage-labor status in the workplace by becoming the boss at home. Treated terribly in the factory, he plays foreman after work and rules with authority over his wife and kids. He thus gains at home that independence he loses on the shop floor. He becomes a part-time boss himself with women as his servants. This becomes key to his identity and sense of self-esteem. Working-class patriarchs, rulers of the roost.

This sense of authority has an economic underpinning. The male worker's role as primary breadwinner gives him power over the family and status in society. It also makes him the beneficiary of the woman's unpaid labor in the household.

A wage laborer not only lacks independence, he also lacks property, having nothing but his labor power to sell. Sexism gives him the sense of property, as owner of the family. His wife or girlfriend is his sexual property. As Elvis sang, "You are my only possession, you are my everything." This domination and ownership of a woman are basic to how he sees himself.

These things are powerful pressures toward individualism, a trait of the business class: foreman of the family, man of property, possessiveness. They elevate the wage earner above the category of the downtrodden common laborer, and in doing so divert him from the collective struggle with his brothers and sisters to change their conditions. Capitalism is based on competitiveness and encourages everyone to be better than the next guy, to rise up on the backs of your neighbors. Similarly the male chauvinist seeks superiority over others, of both sexes. Men tend to be competitive, always putting one another down, constantly playing one-upmanship. Men even express appreciation and affection for each other through good-natured mutual insults.

Sexist culture thus undermines the working-class traditions of equality and solidarity and provides a recruiting ground for labor's adversaries. Over the years at Westinghouse I had noticed that a high proportion of workers who became foremen were extreme chauvinists—sexual braggarts, degraders of women, aggressive, individualistic, ambitious, ever willing to push other

workers around. Male competition is counterproductive in the shop or union, where we ought to cooperate as equals and seek common solutions. The masculine ego makes for bad comradeship, bad brotherhood. It also makes it difficult for chauvinistic men to look at and deal objectively with many situations because their fragile egos are always on the line. They have to keep up a facade of superiority and are unable to handle criticism, no matter how constructive. Their chauvinistic crutches make them subjective, irrational, unreliable, and often self-destructive, as with men who want to work or drive dangerously.

Workingmen pay a high price for the limited material benefits they get from sexist structures. It is the bosses who make the big bucks and enjoy the real power from the inferior treatment of women. . . .

. . . the fight against sexism is also a fight for men. Sexism is destructive of the labor movement and the workingman's struggle. It has led men to confuse our class interests, to side with the boss time after time, to seek false and illusory solutions to our situation as exploited wage earners, and to escape the injustices of class by lording it over the women.

Sexism instills the ideas and values of the enemy class in our ranks. It ingrains false ideas of manhood and strength. It cultivates individualistic attitudes and competitive behavior when what we need is collective struggle. It deludes men and pushes them into irrational actions. It channels men's anger and rebellion along destructive paths—destructive to themselves as well as to our sisters. This sexist madness is part of how capitalism keeps male workers in line. It's anti-labor and anti-working class. We should so label it and treat it. In doing so, we are fighting for our own liberation, as well as that of our sisters. . . .

Authoritarianism, intimidation, aggression—these are a basic part of sexism. You can't separate aggression from sexism. Aggressive ways of relating to people are part of what sexism is. To be a male chauvinist is to establish a competitive power relationship to your own people, to seek to dominate your brothers and sisters, to treat *us* as *them*.

You can't combat sexism by reinforcing the fear of authority or by intimidating the men, by becoming the loudest shouter at the male lunch table. The peaceful women's table was stronger because it was collective and noncompetitive. During some of the campaigns at the plant, I saw that management was a lot more frightened of the quiet women than they were of the mouthy men. Force and authority can outlaw discriminatory practices and structures, but sexist attitudes cannot be fought with the weapons of authority. Authoritarianism itself must be undermined.

Labor has to go beyond paper resolutions and do more than place women in top positions. We have to deepen the struggle against sexism where it really counts—on the shop floor and within the locals.

Militant men in the labor movement have to organize themselves and speak out publicly. We need to express an anti-sexist position that reflects men's experiences, speaks in a masculine voice, and develops a language of our own. Such a position would label sexism as antilabor and show how it is harmful to women *and* to male wage earners. This rank-and-file male voice would be distinct from the women's voice but allied to it in a common fight.

Men need to speak to men about sexism. Men need to learn from the women who have been playing a dynamic part in the labor movement, and we must confront on our own the issues the women's movement has raised: equal treatment, union democracy, non-competitive structures, a humanization of the use of power, the relation between community and workplace problems, the family, sexuality, repression, authoritarianism. Men need to debate these issues in our own way, developing our own non-sexist answers.

The experience of women is enriching and strengthening the world of labor in many ways. Men have to recognize and appreciate these contributions. This means recasting our conception of work and labor as something uniquely masculine and accepting and learning from the distinct methods, rhythms, and styles of women assemblers, machinists, miners.

Workingmen share basic common interests with our sisters. When more of us recognize this, define and speak about these interests in our own way, and act in common with women, then we will be able to start moving the mountains that stand in our way.

NOTE

1. The names of the plant workers in this article are not their real ones.

Further Questions

1. Is it in the best interest of a community for the women to stay at home to guard the community's standards, while the men go to the workplace where they are allowed to break these standards?

2. If a job is too dirty and nasty for a woman, isn't it too dirty and nasty for a man as well?

3. Do men get a false sense of manhood by maintaining themselves in positions where they can control or exclude women?

Masculinities and Athletic Careers: Bonding and Status Differences   III.6

MICHAEL A. MESSNER

Michael A. Messner discusses the importance of sport to men from higher-status backgrounds and to those from lower-status backgrounds. The latter tend to find sport more important because of relative lack of access to other sources of achievement and recognition.

Messner teaches sociology in the Program for the Study of Women and Men in Society at the University of Southern California. He has numerous writings on masculinity and sports and has edited several anthologies in his field.

Reading Questions

1. Are sports a convenient, accessible area in which a boy or man can develop a masculine status? What, exactly, is the connection between achievement in sports and masculine status?

2. Is this status, once it is established, easily transferrable to education and career? Are there similarities between achievement in sport and achievement in education and career that facilitate transfer of masculine status from one to the other?

3. Is there something special about achievement in sport, in that it doesn't require that one own anything or be educated? Does ability in a sport mean that there is something special about a person's body that can be used to promote masculine status?

. . . ALL OF THE MEN IN THIS STUDY described the emotional salience of their earliest experiences in sports in terms of relationships with other males. It was not winning and victories that seemed important at first; it was something "fun" to do with fathers, older brothers, or uncles, and eventually with same-aged peers. As a man from a white, middle-class family said, "The most important thing was just being out there with the rest of the guys—being friends." A 32-year-old man from a poor Chicano family, whose mother had died when he was 9 years old, put it more succinctly:

What I think sports did for me is it brought me into kind of an instant family. By being on a Little League team, or even just playing with kids in the neighborhood, it brought what I really wanted, which was some kind of closeness.

Though sports participation may have initially promised "some kind of closeness," by the ages of 9 or 10, the less skilled boys were already becoming alienated from—or weeded out of—the highly competitive and hierarchical system of organized sports. Those who did experience some early successes received recognition from adult males (especially fathers and older brothers) and held higher status among peers. As a result, they began to pour more and more of their energies into athletic participation. It was only after they learned that they would get recognition from other people for being a good athlete—indeed, that this attention was contingent upon *being a winner*—that performance and winning (the dominant values of organized sports) became extremely important. For some, this created pressures that served to lessen or eliminated the fun of athletic participation (Messner 1987a, 1987b). . . .

To examine the impact of the social contexts, I divided my sample into two comparison groups. In the first group were 10 men from higher-status backgrounds, primarily white, middle-class, and professional families. In the second group were 20 men from lower-status backgrounds, primarily minority, poor, and working-class families. While my data offered evidence for the similarity of experiences and motivations of men from poor backgrounds, independent of race, I also found anecdotal evidence of a racial dynamic that operates independently of social class. However, my sample was not large enough to separate race and class, and so I have combined them to make two status groups.

In discussing these two groups, I will focus mainly on the high school years. During this crucial period, the athletic role may become a master status for a young man, and he is beginning to make assessments and choices about his future. It is here that many young men make a major commitment to—or begin to back away from—athletic careers.

Men from Higher-Status Backgrounds

The boyhood dream of one day becoming a professional athlete—a dream shared by nearly all the men interviewed in this study—is rarely realized. The sports world is extremely hierarchical. The pyramid of sports careers narrows very rapidly as one climbs from high school, to college, to professional levels of competition (Edwards 1984; Harris and Eitzen 1978; Hill and Lowe 1978). In fact, the chances of attaining professional status in sports are approximately 4/100,000 for a white man, 2/100,000 for a black man, and 3/100,000 for a Hispanic man in the United States (Leonard and Reyman 1988). For many young athletes,

their dream ends early when coaches inform them that they are not big enough, strong enough, fast enough, or skilled enough to compete at the higher levels. . . .

How and why do so many successful male athletes from higher-status backgrounds come to view sports careers as "pissing in the wind," or as "small potatoes"? How and why do they make this early assessment and choice to shift from sports and toward educational and professional goals? The white, middle-class institutional context, with its emphasis on education and income, makes it clear to them that choices exist and that the pursuit of an athletic career is not a particularly good choice to make. Where the young male once found sports to be a convenient institution within which to construct masculine status, the postadolescent and young adult man from a higher-status background simply *transfers* these same strivings to other institutional contexts: education and careers.

For the higher-status men who had chosen to shift from athletic careers, sports remained important on two levels. First, having been a successful high school or college athlete enhances one's adult status among other men in the community—but only as a badge of masculinity that is *added* to his professional status. In fact, several men in professions chose to be interviewed in their offices, where they publicly displayed the trophies and plaques that attested to their earlier athletic accomplishments. Their high school and college athletic careers may have appeared to them as "small potatoes," but many successful men speak of their earlier status as athletes as having "opened doors" for them in their present professions and in community affairs. Similarly, Farr's (1988) research on "Good Old Boys Sociability Groups" shows how sports, as part of the glue of masculine culture, continues to facilitate "dominance bonding" among privileged men long after active sports careers end. The college-educated, career-successful men in Farr's study rarely express overtly sexist, racist, or classist attitudes; in fact, in their relationships with women, they "often engage in expressive intimacies" and "make fun of exaggerated 'machismo'" (p. 276). But though they outwardly conform more to what Pleck (1982) calls "the modern male role," their informal relationships within their sociability groups, in effect, affirm their own gender and class status by constructing and clarifying the boundaries between themselves and women and lower-status men. This dominance bonding is based largely upon ritual forms of sociability (camaraderie, competition), "the superiority of which was first affirmed in the exclusionary play activities of young boys in groups" (Farr 1988, p. 265).

In addition to contributing to dominance bonding among higher-status adult men, sports remains salient in terms of the ideology of gender relations. Most men continued to watch, talk about, and identify with sports long after their own disengagement from athletic careers. Sports as a mediated spectacle provides an important context in which traditional conceptions of masculine superiority—conceptions recently contested by women—are shored up. As a 32-year-old white professional-class man said of one of the most feared professional football players today:

> A woman can do the same job as I can do—maybe even be my boss. But I'll be *damned* if she can go out on the football field and take a hit from Ronnie Lott.

Violent sports as spectacle provide linkages among men in the project of the domination of women, while at the same time helping to construct and clarify differences among various masculinities. The statement above is a clear identification with Ronnie Lott *as a man*, and the basis of the identification is the violent male body. . . .

. . . For middle-class men, the "tough guys" of the culture industry—the Rambos, the Ronnie Lotts who are fearsome "hitters," who "play hurt"—are the heroes who "prove" that "we men" are superior to women. At the same time, they play the role of the "primitive other," against

whom higher-status men define themselves as "modern" and "civilized."

Sports, then, is important from boyhood through adulthood for men from higher-status backgrounds. But it is significant that by adolescence and early adulthood, most of these young men have concluded that sports *careers* are not for them. Their middle-class cultural environment encourages them to decide to shift their masculine strivings in more "rational" directions: education and nonsports careers. Yet their previous sports participation continues to be very important to them in terms of constructing and validating their status within privileged male peer groups and within their chosen professional careers. And organized sports, as a public spectacle, is a crucial locus around which ideologies of male superiority over women, as well as higher-status men's superiority over lower-status men, are constructed and naturalized.

Men from Lower-Status Backgrounds

For the lower-status young men in this study, success in sports was not an added proof of masculinity; it was often their only hope of achieving public masculine status. A 34-year-old black bus driver who had been a star athlete in three sports in high school had neither the grades nor the money to attend college, so he accepted an offer from the U.S. Marine Corps to play on their baseball team. He ended up in Vietnam, where a grenade blew four fingers off his pitching hand. In retrospect, he believed that his youthful focus on sports stardom and his concomitant lack of effort in academics made sense:

> You can go anywhere with athletics—you don't have to have brains. I mean, I didn't feel like I was gonna go out there and be a computer expert, or something that was gonna make a lot of money. The only thing I could do and live comfortably would be to play sports—just to get a contract—doesn't matter if you play second or third team in the pros, you're gonna make big bucks. That's all I wanted, a confirmed livelihood

at the end of my ventures, and the only way I could do it would be through sports. So I tried. It failed, but that's what I tried.

Similar, and even more tragic, is the story of a 34-year-old black man who is now serving a life term in prison. After a career-ending knee injury at the age of 20 abruptly ended what had appeared to be a certain road to professional football fame and fortune, he decided that he "could still be rich and famous" by robbing a bank. During his high school and college years, he said, he was nearly illiterate:

> I'd hardly ever go to classes and they'd give me Cs. My coaches taught some of the classes. And I felt, "So what? They *owe* me that! I'm an *athlete!* I thought that was what I was born to do—to play sports—and everybody understood that.

Are lower-status boys and young men simply duped into putting all their eggs into one basket? My research suggested that there was more than "hope for the future" operating here. There were also immediate psychological reasons that they chose to pursue athletic careers. By the high school years, class and ethnic inequalities had become glaringly obvious, especially for those who attended socioeconomically heterogeneous schools. Cars, nice clothes, and other signs of status were often unavailable to these young men, and this contributed to a situation in which sports took on an expanded importance for them in terms of constructing masculine identities and status. . . .

"Respect" was what I heard over and over when talking with the men from lower-status backgrounds, especially black men. I interpret this type of respect to be a crystallization of the masculine quest for recognition through public achievement, unfolding within a system of structured constraints due to class and race inequities. The institutional context of education (sometimes with the collusion of teachers and coaches) and the constricted structure of opportunity in the economy made the pursuit of athletic careers appear to be the most rational choice to these young men. . . .

The same is not true of young lower-status women. Dunkle (1985) points out that from junior high school through adulthood, young black men are far more likely to place high value on sports than are young black women, who are more likely to value academic achievement. There appears to be a gender dynamic operating in adolescent male peer groups that contributes toward their valuing sports more highly than education. Franklin (1986, p. 161) has argued that many of the normative values of the black male peer group (little respect for nonaggressive solutions to disputes, contempt for nonmaterial culture) contribute to the constriction of black men's views of desirable social positions, especially through education. . . .

. . . For these lower-status men, as Baca Zinn (1982) and Majors (1986) argued in their respective studies of chicano men and black men, when institutional resources that signify masculine status and control are absent, physical presence, personal style, and expressiveness take on increased importance. What Majors (1986, p. 6) calls "cool pose" is black men's expressive, often aggressive, assertion of masculinity. This self-assertion often takes place within a social context in which the young man is quite aware of existing social inequities. As the black bus driver, referred to above, said of his high school years:

> See, the rich people use their money to do what they want to do. I use my ability. If you wanted to be around me, if you wanted to learn something about sports, I'd teach you. But you're gonna take me to lunch. You're gonna let me use your car. See what I'm saying? In high school I'd go where I wanted to go. I didn't have to be educated. I was well-respected. I'd go somewhere, and they'd say, "Hey, that's Mitch Harris,[1] yeah, that's a bad son of a bitch!"

Majors (1986) argues that although "cool pose" represents a creative survival technique within a hostile environment, the most likely long-term effect of this masculine posturing is educational and occupational dead ends. As a result, we can conclude, lower-status men's personal and peer-group responses to a constricted structure of opportunity—responses that are rooted, in part, in the developmental insecurities and ambivalences of masculinity—serve to lock many of these young men into limiting activities such as sports. . . .

Feminist scholars have demonstrated that organized sports gives men from all backgrounds a means of status enhancement that is not available to young women. Sports thus serve the interests of all men in helping to construct and legitimize their control of public life and their domination of women (Bryson 1987; Hall 1987; Theberge 1987). Yet concrete studies are suggesting that men's experiences within sports are not all of a piece. Brian Pronger's (1990) research suggests that gay men approach sports differently than straight men do, with a sense of "irony." And my research suggests that although sports are important for men from both higher- and lower-status backgrounds, there are crucial differences. In fact, it appears that the meaning that most men give to their athletic strivings has more to do with competing for status among men than it has to do with proving superiority over women. How can we explain this seeming contradiction between the feminist claim that sports links all men in the domination of women and the research findings that different groups of men relate to sports in very different ways?

The answer to this question lies in developing a means of conceptualizing the interrelationships between varying forms of domination and subordination. Marxist scholars of sports often falsely collapse everything into a class analysis; radical feminists often see gender domination as universally fundamental. Concrete examinations of sports, however, reveal complex and multilayered systems of inequality: Racial, class, gender, sexual preference, and age dynamics are all salient features of the athletic context. In examining this reality, Connell's (1987) concept of the "gender order" is useful. The gender order is a dynamic process that is constantly in a state of play. Moving beyond static gender-role theory and reductionist concepts of patriarchy that view men as an undifferentiated group which oppresses women, Connell argues that at any given historical moment, there are competing masculinities—some hegemonic, some marginalized, some stigmatized. Hegemonic masculinity (that definition of masculinity which is culturally ascendant) is constructed in relation to various subordinated masculinities as well as in relation to femininities. The project of male domination of women may tie all men together, but men share very unequally in the fruits of this domination. . . .

NOTE

1. "Mitch Harris" is a pseudonym.

REFERENCES

Berghorn, F. J. et al. 1988. "Racial Participation in Men's and Women's Intercollegiate Basketball: Continuity and Change, 1958–1985." *Sociology of Sport Journal* 5:107–24.

Bryson, L. 1987. "Sport and the Maintenance of Masculine Hegemony." *Women's Studies International Forum* 10:349–60.

Dunkle, M. 1985. "Minority and Low-Income Girls and Young Women in Athletics." *Equal Play* 5(Spring-Summer):12–13.

———. 1984. "The Collegiate Athletic Arms Race: Origins and Implications of the 'Rule 48' Controversy." *Journal of Sport and Social Issues* 8:4–22.

Farr, K. A. 1988. "Dominance Bonding Through the Good Old Boys Sociability Group." *Sex Roles* 18:259–77.

Franklin, C. W. II. 1984. *The Changing Definition of Masculinity.* New York: Plenum.

Hall, M. A. (ed.). 1987. "The Gendering of Sport, Leisure, and Physical Education." *Women's Studies International Forum* 10:361–474.

Harris, D. S. and D. S. Eitzen. 1978. "The Consequences of Failure in Sport." *Urban Life* 7:177–88.

Hill, P. and B. Lowe. 1978. "The Inevitable Metathesis of the Retiring Athlete." *International Review of Sport Sociology* 9:5–29.

Leonard, W. M. II and J. M. Reyman. 1988. "The Odds of Attaining Professional Athlete Status: Refining the Computations." *Sociology of Sport Journal* 5:162–69.

Majors, R. 1986. "Cool Pose: The Proud Signature of Black Survival." *Changing Men: Issues in Gender, Sex, and Politics* 17:5–6.

Messner, M. 1985. "The Changing Meaning of Male Identity in the Lifecourse of the Athlete." *Arena Review* 9:31–60.

———. 1987a. "The Meaning of Success: The Athletic Experience and the Development of Male Identity." Pp. 193–209 in *The Making of Masculinities: The New Men's Studies,* edited by H. Brod. Winchester, MA: Allen & Unwin.

———. 1987b. "The Life of a Man's Seasons: Male Identity in the Lifecourse of the Athlete." Pp. 53–67 in *Changing Men: New Directions in Research on Men and Masculinity,* edited by M. S. Kimmel. Newbury Park, CA: Sage.

Pleck, J. H. 1982. *The Myth of Masculinity.* Cambridge: MIT Press.

Pronger, B. 1990. "Gay Jocks: A Phenomenology of Gay Men in Athletics." In *Sport, Men, and the Gender Order: Critical Feminist Perspectives,* edited by M. A. Messner and D. S. Sabo. Champaign, IL: Human Kinetics.

Theberge, N. 1987. "Sport and Women's Empowerment." *Women's Studies International Forum* 10:387–93.

Wilson, W. J. and K. M. Neckerman. 1986. "Poverty and Family Structure: The Widening Gap Between Evidence and Public Policy Issues." Pp. 232–59 in *Fighting Poverty,* edited by S. H. Danzinger and D. H. Weinberg. Cambridge, MA: Harvard University Press.

Zinn, M. Baca. 1982. "Chicano Men and Masculinity." Journal of Ethnic Studies 10:29–44.

Further Questions

1. Does the masculinity and male-bonding provided by sports, or at least by some sports, mean that women and girls must be excluded?

2. Is the competitiveness and exclusivity associated with male sports necessarily a good thing?

3. How should women respond to the suggestion that sports give men a status in public life and a means of control of women?

III.7 Women, Sport, and Sexuality

HELEN LENSKYJ

Helen Lenskyj discusses some problems of women in sports. "Doctors Have the First Word" picks out some highlights of the control the medical profession has had over women's sports in the past century. "Fit and Feminine" traces the recent connection formed between being fit and attainment of the ideal of femininity.

Lenskyj teaches at the Ontario Institute for Studies in Education. She has been an active member of the Canadian Association for the Advancement of Women and Sport since 1982.

Reading Questions

1. Is it true, in some way, that childbearing is women's destiny, and therefore she has a lifelong commitment to avoid forms of exercise that interfere with this destiny?

2. For what reasons, if any, should housework be promoted as a healthy form of exercise?

3. Are fit bodies in women more feminine? (What do "fit" and "feminine" mean in this question?)

Doctors Have the First Word

OVER THE PAST CENTURY, the medical profession has played a dominant role in dictating safe and appropriate sporting activities for women. This dominance may be understood as yet another instance of medical control over women's lives in general, and over reproduction in particular.[1]

By the late 1800s, doctors were expanding their professional influence and their moral leadership on questions of women's health and women's place in society. Public health movements, through school and community programs, were bringing mothers, infants, and school children under medical influence. Medical advice literature—books, pamphlets, magazine articles—was becoming increasingly accessible to women of all social classes. Health professionals were addressing female health issues at meetings and conferences on education, recreation, social service, and social reform. Male doctors were directing athletic programs in a significant number of colleges and universities throughout Canada and the U.S.

At the turn of the century, when female sporting participation had become sufficiently widespread to attract public and medical attention, gynecology was well established as a specialized and profitable field in North America. The revival of the modern Olympics in 1896 and the formalization of school and university athletic programs at this time sparked early medical inter-

est in the physiological aspects of sport. This resulted in the subsequent specialization of sports medicine, a field which had its official beginnings in the 1920s.

As women challenged traditional constraints on education, work, and leisure pursuits in the last half of the nineteenth century, doctors reacted with efforts to establish women's physical and intellectual inferiority. They cited sex differences ranging from smaller brains to lighter bones to support their claims. Doctors also adhered to the widely held Victorian principle that women were the morally superior gender, the natural models of sexual and moral virtue, and therefore all the more blameworthy when they fell from grace. To jeopardize their god-given capacity to bear children, by straining body or brain, defied both common sense and divine decree.

The two themes converged in doctors' consideration of female sporting participation. Both women's unique anatomy and physiology and their special moral obligations disqualified them from vigorous physical activity. Women had a moral duty to preserve their vital energy for childbearing and to cultivate personality traits suited to the wife-and-mother role. Sport wasted vital force, strained female bodies, and fostered traits unbecoming to "true womanhood."

The medical profession's power and influence in these matters extended to women of all backgrounds, although medical priorities reflected class and ethnic biases. Doctors viewed the reproductive capacity of Anglo-Saxon, middle-class women as a more valuable commodity than that of their working-class, immigrant counterparts. They monitored the reproductive health of young women in private schools and universities more carefully than that of women who left school early for factory work or domestic service. Nevertheless, the myths surrounding menstruation—particularly prohibitions against swimming, bathing and strenuous activity during the period—were widely held, even though many women defied these restrictions.

More leisure hours and a greater range of organized sport and physical activities were available to privileged women, while time, energy, and financial resources were scarce for most working-class women at the end of their long work days. Marriage and motherhood reduced recreational opportunities for women of all classes; those who could afford domestic help had some leisure time, but it was more acceptable for middle-class wives and mothers to do charity work than to play tennis.

The bicycle, introduced in the late 1800s, significantly increased the leisure options for all women. Even working-class women could afford the relatively cheap rental or purchase price of a bicycle. In the face of a cycling craze that involved mass female participation throughout North America, doctors and other custodians of female morality eventually abandoned their crusade against the attire and activities of the "lady cyclist." Thus, cycling played an important part in liberating nineteenth-century women from rigid Victorian standards of acceptable dress and appropriate public behavior. . . .

Some doctors attempted to popularize housework as exercise, or as therapy for "young ladies" with health problems. According to one male expert, "All that is needed to make the delicate creatures well is to require them to change places with their mothers for a few weeks or months." "For ladies," he stated, "housework is admirably adapted to bring into play all the different muscles of the body."[2] . . .

[She] could swing a six-pound dumb-bell,
She could fence, and she could box,
She could row upon the river,
She could clamber on the rocks.
She could do some heavy bowling,
And play tennis all day long,
But she couldn't help her mother,
As she wasn't very strong.

Dr. Elizabeth Mitchell,
"The Rise of Athleticism Among Women and Girls," *National Council of Women of Canada Yearbook, 1895*
(Montreal: John Lovell, 1896), p. 107.

THE MONTHLY INCAPACITY

Increased female participation in sport by the end of the nineteenth century gave new prominence to the issue of medical restrictions on women's physical activity during menstruation. It needs to be understood in the wider context of women's reproductive health because menstruation was both a symbolic and a concrete reminder of fertility and femaleness. Moreover, its regular appearance reinforced the existing power relations between men and women: women experienced this monthly "incapacity," men did not.

At the turn of the century, malestream gynecology termed women's normal life changes "The Diseases of Women," and treated any menstrual variation as a condition demanding heroic medical intervention. In cases of amenorrhea, for example, poultices, mustard baths, leeches and vaginal injections were recommended to induce the period.[3] Many male doctors based their recommendations primarily on clinical practice; obviously, they saw more women who experienced menstruation-related health problems than women whose menstrual cycles were problem-free. At stake was the principle of male medical control over female sexuality, a problem that continues today in doctors' unequivocal pronouncements on the nature of the "normal" menstrual cycle.

Not surprisingly, it was women in the medical profession who redefined menstruation as a normal function rather than a sickness, and encouraged women to maintain a normal lifestyle regardless of the menstrual cycle. They documented the menstrual histories of large numbers of women over spans of several years in order to show that menstruation was not experienced as disabling by the majority of women.[4]

However, women's trustworthiness on matters of health, exercise, and menstruation presented a problem to many male doctors. While advocating moderate exercise for improved functional health, one doctor condemned the young woman who is "loath to give up her *amusements* during menstruation." He also censured those who continue "*pleasurable* exercise, no matter how severe, and dance, wheel, and skate regardless of the period." The doctor noted that "even *sports,* basketball, tennis . . . are followed by some."[5] Another bluntly stated that menstrual incapacity was of "a fictional nature."[6]

Whatever the motive, the implications were serious. Either menstrual pain was imaginary, or women were so untrustworthy, so self-centered and frivolous that they continued pleasurable activities throughout the month but avoided unpleasant obligations on the excuse of menstruation. Yet, for a woman to fulfil her destiny as mother, she was expected to monitor all her activities in the light of possible danger to her reproductive function. Failure to do so constituted a failure to fulfil her religious, moral, and patriotic duty: motherhood is "the most sacred trust the Almighty can bestow upon any woman."[7] The woman who ignored medical warnings regarding sporting participation challenged the primacy of the uterus.

Maternal obligations were, of course, affected by race and class. Mass immigration, wartime manpower losses and high birthrates in certain racial and ethnic groups fueled racist fears of Anglo-Saxon race suicide. Therefore there was a premium on the fertility of middle-class Anglo-Saxon women. In addition, working-class women were not expected to find menstruation, pregnancy, or any other "diseases of women" as disabling as their more privileged counterparts. . . .

THE MOTHERS OF TOMORROW

With mounting medical interest in the nation's wombs, it is not surprising that the health of girls as well as women attracted doctors' attention. One of the first manuals of physical education intended for a general, nonmedical and nonteaching audience, written in the 1890s, was critical of parents who raised their daughters "like hothouse plants," forbidding them to join in the outdoor games that made their brothers healthy. It warned that, "when called upon to fulfil the functions of wives and mothers, their lives are made miserable by reason of suffering."[8]

Similarly, Tait McKenzie's textbook, *Exercise in Education and Medicine,* widely read from 1909 to the 1940s, advocated that girls follow a special physical training program designed to develop "those characteristics of growth, poise, speech, carriage, and dress peculiar to [females]." However, McKenzie did not consider boys' outdoor games appropriate for girls, partly because, after puberty, "their periods of temporary disability make them take less interest in active and competitive games."[9]

By the 1920s, it was not girls' and women's inactivity, but their overexertion, that provoked medical censure. Still, the underlying "anatomy is destiny" rationale remained virtually unchanged. A 1929 statement on the dangers of Olympic competition for women contended that the development of beauty and femininity among young women was necessary "to attract the most worthy fathers for their children, provide the most healthful physiques for childbearing, and build the most maternal emotional and social behavior patterns."[10] There was little, if any, evidence, however, that sport did *not* build "healthful physiques for childbearing," or that it interfered with the reproductive process.[11] . . .

NOTES

1. For a comprehensive history of gynecology in the U.S.A., see Barbara Ehrenreich and Deidre English, *For Her Own Good: 150 Years of the Experts'*

Advice to Women (Garden City, New York: Anchor Books, 1979). For historical developments in Canada, see Wendy Mitchinson, "Historical Attitudes Towards Women and Childbirth," *Atlantis*, 4,2 Part 2 (Spring 1979), pp. 13–34, and "Gynecological Operations upon Insane Women, London, Ontario, 1895–1901," *Journal of Social History* 15,3 (Spring 1982), pp. 467–84.

2. John Kellogg, *Plain Facts for Young and Old* (1888; New York: Arno Press, 1974), p. 597.

3. *The Family Physician, or Every Man His Own Doctor,* compiled by Leading Canadian Medical Men [sic] (Toronto: Hunter Rose, n.d.), p. 172. It is estimated that this book was published between 1890 and 1905. See also Arthur Edis, *The Diseases of Women* (Philadelphia: Henry Lea's Sons, 1882); Charles Penrose, *Diseases of Women and Gyneocology* (New York: W. B. Saunders, 1904).

4. See, for example, Mary Jacobi, *The Question of Rest for Women during Menstruation* (New York: Putnam's, 1877); Clelia Mosher, *Health and the Woman Movement,* cited in Willystine Goodsell, *Pioneers of Women's Education in the United States* (New York: McGraw-Hill, 1930), pp. 298–299; Mosher, "A Physiologic Treatment of Congestive Dysmenorrhea and Kindred Disorders Associated with the Menstrual Function," *JAMA* 62 (April 1914), pp. 1297–1301; Alice Clow, "Menstruation during School Life," *British Medical Journal* 2 (October 1920), pp. 511–513.

5. George Englemann, "The American Girl of Today," *American Journal of Obstetrics* 42 (December 1990), pp. 782–783.

6. E. H. Arnold, cited by Goodsell, p. 299. In a two-year experiment conducted at the New Haven Normal School, Dr. Arnold reduced the time lost to menstrual incapacity in all sports except swimming. . . .

7. John Hastings, "Are We Giving the Child a Square Deal?" *Woman's Century* (Special Number, 1918), p. 152.

8. William Anderson, *Anderson's Physical Education* (Toronto: Harold Wilson, n.d.), p. 20. It is estimated that this book was published around the turn of the century.

9. R. Tait McKenzie, *Exercise in Education and Medicine,* 3rd ed. (Philadelphia: W. B. Sanders, 1923), pp. 76, 286–287.

10. Frederick Rand Rogers, "Olympics for Girls," in Women's Division, National Amateur Athletic Federation, ed., *Women and Athletics* (New York: Barnes, 1930), p. 77 (excerpt from Rogers' 1929 article in *School and Society*).

11. A survey of 1,200 Smith College graduates found that the level of participation in college athletics bore no significant relationship to difficult pregnancies or labors. See Linda Gage Roth, "Are Sports Harmful to Women?" *The Forum* 81 (May 1929), pp. 313–318.

Fit and Feminine

. . . During the 1980s, women showed increasing interest in bodybuilding. This activity is quite distinct from weight training programs for a specific sport. Its function is primarily aesthetic: muscular development for its own sake. For women, the goal is to "sculpt" a thin, strong, muscular body that meets current standards of glamour. Although male bodybuilders are often criticized for their alleged narcissism, it is generally taken for granted that middle-class women devote time, money, and effort to their appearance. Therefore, women's bodybuilding is often justified by the old "enhancement of femininity" rationale. Many private clubs offer dance exercise classes, fitness fashion boutiques, and "esthetician" services, along with the weight training equipment, so their female clients may more fully pursue the new feminine ideal. . . .

Aerobic exercises provided, by "natural" means, the glow and grace formerly promised by cosmetic companies and fashion designers. Not surprisingly, the image of the physically active woman replaced the more sedentary and decorative 1960s ideal of heterosexual glamour. Women cycling, skiing, skating, swimming, snorkeling, horseback riding, playing tennis and volleyball appeared in advertisements for products as diverse as cigarettes, alcohol, convenience foods, diet products, life insurance, mattresses, cosmetics, clothing and feminine hygiene products.

Such ads firmly established the active woman's heterosexual identity by showing her more often in company of males than alone or with females. The men were usually assisting or admiring the perpetually smiling but frequently inept "sportswoman."[1] One perfume company even introduced "Le Sport" ("because life is a contact sport"). Ads showed women engaged in leisure activities with men: "Le Sport is more than a fragrance. It's a way of life. The look. The feeling. The vitality of the new sport life style. Day and night, you play with style." "Vitality," the ad announced, "is the new sex appeal."[2]

In feminine hygiene advertising, the new image of the active woman could have countered the myth that menstruation was an obstacle to strenuous physical activity; however, some ads served only to perpetuate the stereotype. Most showed a model, dressed appropriately but with the physique and style of an obvious nonathlete. Proclaiming "Stayfree Mini-Pads are so absorbent, I can get back to doing things I like sooner," one young woman was shown jumping the short distance from a rock to a river bank, apparently an activity she had to curtail during menstruation. Equally out of touch were the ads showing gymnasts in high-cut white leotards, supposedly demonstrating the invisibility of Stayfree Maxi-Pads. (This was, however, one of the few products promoted by a well-known female athlete, in this case American Olympic gymnast Kathy Rigby.)[3]

By 1984, aerobic dance or dance exercise had become one of the most popular physical activities of North American women. Also termed jazzercise, dancercise, or slimnastics, it combined the aerobic elements of dancing, running, and jumping with flexibility and strength exercises, all performed to contemporary music. While its popularity signified greater female participation in regular physical activity, its association with the cosmetic and fashion industries made it, in many instances, another arena for women to compete for male attention. Like makeup and clothing, dance exercise produced more prescriptions for heterosexual appeal. The new requirements included thinness, muscularity, and shapeliness, enhanced by fashionable and expensive sportswear.

Competitiveness is not unusual, of course, in a sporting endeavor, so some degree of competitiveness in dance exercise was probably not surprising. Women of varying physiques and fitness levels, together in the gymnasium, change rooms, and showers for the first time since their high school physical education days, undoubtedly made comparisons, both with one another and the fitness ideal—the instructor. But dance exercise was supposedly noncompetitive. It was developed for women, offered at convenient times and locales, in predominantly or exclusively female environments that promised to be supportive and nonthreatening, especially to women new to physical activity. But many women felt pressured to lose weight, to work on specific body parts (thighs, hips, breasts) that fitness experts had diagnosed as a "problem," and to keep up with the instructor and the class, both in appearance and performance, regardless of individual goals, body type, or fitness level.[4] By 1984, dance exercise had been fully transformed into a competitive female activity: "Aerobic Championships" were being staged across the country, conducted in shopping malls, and promoted as "traffic builders."[5]

In many instances the dance exercise instructor served as an example of both the fitness and the feminine ideal. She was probably white, slim, and attractive, wearing the mandatory leotard, tights, and legwarmers. Until organizations such as the American Aerobics Association and the Ontario Fitness Council began monitoring programs in 1982–1983, instructors in private clubs were probably hired as much for appearance and style as for competence.[6] Some men were probably drawn to the classes, as spectators or participants, by the same considerations. Reducing the instructors to sex objects (especially the women on television "workout" shows) distorted and devalued the activity; many televised "classes" resembled soft porn rather than exercise.

The association between dance exercise and heterosexual glamour was firmly established in 1982 when Jane Fonda headed a long line of celebrities who produced glossy, expensive fitness manuals. Sharing the Hollywood approach, some authors with more legitimate qualifications —prima ballerina Karen Kain and world-class marathoner Gayle Olinekova, for example— placed as much emphasis on becoming slim, trim and sexy as on staying fit.[7] If female athletes had the same commercial opportunities as males, either during or after their sporting careers, one would see books on exercise and training written by female athletes, rather than by actresses. Moreover, if a male counterpart to Jane Fonda or Raquel Welch—Robert Redford, for example—had written a book on running, it is unlikely that it would have had the credibility of the book by heart specialist and veteran marathoner George Sheehan, even though Redford is arguably a better example of "masculinity." This double standard reflects the assumption that men are serious about recreational sporting activities, while women are easily duped by passing fads and self-proclaimed experts, as long as the promise of heterosexual glamour is sufficiently seductive.

NOTES

1. See Ahmed Belkaoui and Janice Belkaoui, "A Comparative Analysis of the Roles Portrayed by Women in Print Advertisements: 1958, 1970, 1972," *Journal of Marketing Research* 13 (May 1976), p. 171; Alison Poe, "Active Women in Ads," *Journal of Communication* 26 (Autumn 1976), pp. 185–192.

2. Le Sport ads, *Harper's Bazaar* 112 (September 1979), p. 14; *Cosmopolitan* (June 1979), pp. 22–23.

3. See Stayfree ads in *Good Housekeeping, Glamour, Cosmo, Redbook,* 1977–1983.

4. See, for example, Dorothy Kidd, "Getting Physical: Compulsory Heterosexuality and Sport," *Canadian Woman Studies* 4, 3(1983):62–5, pp. 62–63; Jacqui Salmon, "Cutting Class," *Women's Sports* 5 (March 1983), p. 60.

5. "The National Leotard League," *Sports Illustrated* 59 (November 18, 1983), p. 30; advertising package distributed by Inwood & Associates, Toronto, August 14, 1984. See also Helen Lenskyj, "Sexercise Sells," *Mudpie* 5 (December 1984), p. 17.

6. See, for example, Laura Grengo-De Rosa, "Aerobic Awareness," *WomenSports* 4 (December 1982), p. 23; Leigh Fenly, "Dance Exercise Guidelines Planned," *Physician and Sportsmedicine* 12 (September 1984), pp. 31–32. For another perspective, see "Blood, Sweat and Beers," *Toronto Life* (March 1984), p. 45.

7. *Karen Kain's Fitness Book* as told to Marilyn Linton (Toronto: Doubleday, 1983); Gayle Olinekova, *Go For It* (New York: Simon and Schuster, 1982). For more of this genre, see, for example, *Jane Fonda's Workout Book* (New York: Simon and Schuster, 1982).

Further Questions

1. Have aerobics classes eliminated undesirable competitive aspects of sports?

2. Do fitness books and videos (like those mentioned in the writing) promote an unattainable or undesirable ideal for most women?

3. Does treating menstruation systematically as a monthly incapacity reinforce the lesser position of women in sports and physical activity?

Suggested Moral of Part III

Opportunities for women in the workplace are not yet equal to those for men. Since workplace positions are becoming, increasingly, the locus of opportunity to do anything worthwhile, the lives of women are, accordingly, impoverished. In addition, gender discrepancies in power, prestige, and money that originate in the workplace find their way into relations between men and women in other parts of their lives in a society that is still organized by gender.

Further Readings for Part III: The Workplace and Sports

Pat Armstrong and Hugh Armstrong. *The Double Ghetto: Canadian Women and Their Segregated Work* (Toronto: McClelland and Stewart, Revised Edition, 1989). Argument that gender segregation in the labor force mirrors and is influenced by the division of domestic work by gender.

Martha Blaxall and Barbara Regan, eds. *Women and the Workplace: The Implications of Occupational Segregation* (Chicago, IL: The University of Chicago Press, 1976). Workplace gender segregation, its roots and consequences and some strategies for combatting it.

Barbara R. Bergman. *The Economic Emergence of Women* (New York, NY: Basic Books, 1986). Knowledgeable tracing of the exodus of women from home into the workforce, only to be occupationally segregated and become major victims of discrimination. Multifaceted agenda for change.

Jessie Bernard. *Academic Women* (New York, NY: Meridian, 1964). Discussion of the forces in academic life which hold women back by affecting their motivation, creativity, and productivity.

David L. Collinson. "Engineering Humor: Masculinity and Conflict in Shop Floor Relations," in *Organizational Studies*, 1988 9/2, pp. 181–199. Reprinted in Michael S. Kimmel and Michael A. Messner, eds. *Men's Lives* (New York, NY: Macmillan, 2nd Edition, 1992) pp. 232–246. The role of joking among men on the shop floor.

D. S. David and R. Brannon, eds. *The Forty-nine Percent Majority: The Male Sex Role* (Reading, MA: Addison-Wesley, 1976). Some good discussions of the workplace functioning as a primary component of masculinity.

D. S. Eitzen. *Sport in Contemporary Society: An Anthology* (New York, NY: St. Martin's Press, 1984).

Jane English. "Sex Equality in Sports," in *Philosophy and Public Affairs*, 7, no. 3, 1978, pp. 269–277.

Gertrude Ezorsky. *Racism and Justice: The Case for Affirmative Action* (Ithaca, NY: Cornell University Press, 1991). Good, thoughtful arguments for affirmative action in a racist society. Some are applicable to a sexist society as well.

Robert K. Fullenwider. *The Reverse Discrimination Controversy: A Moral and Legal Analysis* (Totowa, NJ: Rowman and Littlefield, 1981). Well-organized discussion of aspects of affirmative action.

Charlene Gannage. *Double Day, Double Bind: Women Garment Workers* (Toronto: The Women's Press, 1986). Bad situations experienced by women garment workers, especially immigrant workers.

Alan H. Goldman. *Justice and Reverse Discrimination.* (Princeton, NJ: Princeton University Press, 1979). Affirmative action again. Drier discussion than Ezorsky and Fullenwider.

Rosanna Hertz. *More Equal Than Others: Women and Men in Dual-Career Marriages* (Berkeley, CA: University of California Press, 1986). Both husband and wife suffer in a dual-career situation (especially if there are children) if the marriage retains its traditional structure.

Arlie Hochschild with Anne Machung. *The Second Shift* (New York, NY: Avon Books, 1989). Same argument as Hertz. The husband must share in the housework if both husband and wife are in the workforce.

Bruce Kidd. "Sports and Masculinity," in Michael Kaufman, ed. *Beyond Patriarchy: Essays by Men of Pleasure, Power and Change* (New York, NY: Oxford University Press, 1987) pp. 250–265.

Helen Lenskyj. *Out of Bounds: Women, Sport and Sexuality* (Toronto: The Women's Press, 1986). Sustained exposé of sexism and heterosexism in sport.

Martin P. Levine. "The Status of Gay Men in the Workplace" in Michael S. Kimmel and Michael A. Messner, eds. *Men's Lives* (New York, NY: Macmillan, 2nd Edition, 1992) pp. 251–266.

Martin P. Levine and Robert Leonard. "Discrimination Against Lesbians in the Workforce," in *Signs* 9 (4) pp. 700–710.

Michael A. Messner and Donald Sabo, eds. *Sport, Men and the Gender Order: Critical Feminist Perspectives* (Champaign, IL: Human Kinetics Books, 1990). Excellent writings by men and women addressing the problems of the traditional link between sport and masculinity.

C. A. Oglesby, ed. *Women and Sport: From Myth to Reality* (Philadelphia, PA: Lea and Febiger, 1978).

Richard R. Peterson. *Women, Work and Divorce* (Albany, NY: State University of New York Press, 1989). Divorce is an economic hardship on women, but it generally improves the position of women in the workplace. Work now appears to be better than marriage for a woman's economic security.

J. H. Pleck and J. Sawyer, eds. *Men and Masculinity* (Englewood Cliffs, NJ: Prentice Hall, 1974). More on breadwinner problems in the male role. The collection features Robert E. Gould's "Measuring Masculinity by the Size of a Paycheck."

Judith Posner. *The Feminine Mistake: Women, Work and Identity* (New York, NY: Warner Books, 1992). The mistake is believing that as a woman you can have it all—work in the fast track, and also be a supermom and a perfect wife. Slow down and find your own solution.

Anne Statham, Eleanor M. Miller, Haus O. Mauksch, eds. *The Worth of Women's Work* (Albany, NY: State University of New York Press, 1988). Women's work experiences in thirteen professions, from domestic service to policewoman.

Christine Williams. *Gender Differences at Work: Women and Men in Non-Traditional Occupations* (Berkeley, CA: University of California Press, 1991). Lively descriptions of experiences of men working in traditionally women's fields and vice-versa and the impact of such work on gender identity.

S. J. Wilson. *Women, the Family and the Economy* (New York, NY: McGraw-Hill Ryerson, 1982). Clear, lively discussion of the gender division of labor in the family and workplace.

Mary Wollstonecraft. *A Vindication of the Rights of Women*, C. H. Poston, ed. (New York, NY: Norton, 1975; original work published in 1792). Early insight into women's needs for intellectual and physical exercise.

Virginia Woolf. *A Room of One's Own* (Harmondsworth, England: Penguin Books, Ltd., 1945). "A woman must have money and a room of her own if she is to write fiction." Woolf's thesis is that women's creativity can flourish only if women are allowed the requisite privacy and free time.

Part IV

Love

Introduction

LOVE IS A TOPIC of continuing curiosity because it has such an important place in human life. Romantic love, in particular, seems to be receiving as much attention as work in questions concerning what human existence is about. Romantic love is also an area where we must confront gender directly, because gender is an essential element of the beloved. Finally, a situation of romantic love makes us feel our own gender most keenly; here, if anywhere, we recognize the importance of gendered life.

IV.1   Love's Bond

ROBERT NOZICK

Robert Nozick claims that infatuation becomes love when one develops the desire to form a "we" with the other person. He has some interesting ideas on why the "we" aspect of love precludes ideas of "trading up" to a better embodiment of the qualities appreciated in the beloved.

   Nozick is Arthur Kingsley Porter Professor of Philosophy at Harvard University and author of *Anarchy, State and Utopia* and *Philosophical Explanations*. "Love's Bond," from *The Examined Life,* contains some of Nozick's thoughts about life and living. Another selection from *The Examined Life* appears in Part VII.

Reading Questions

   1. How would you be able to tell whether a feeling was the real thing (love) this time, rather than a simple infatuation?

   2. We think of romantic love as having a unique object. Only this particular person will do as the beloved; someone with identical qualities, or better versions of them, will not do. Why is this?

   3. When you are contemplating beginning a romantic relationship with someone, is it appropriate to ask, as Nozick suggests, "Will it be fun"?

THE GENERAL PHENOMENON of love encompasses romantic love, the love of a parent for a child, love of one's country, and more. What is common to all love is this: Your own well-being is tied up with that of someone (or something) you love. When a bad thing happens to a friend, it happens to her and you feel sad for her; when something good happens, you feel happy for her. When something bad happens to one you love, though, something bad also happens *to you.* . . .

   This extension of your own well-being (or ill-being) is what marks all the different kinds of love: the love of children, the love of parents, the love of one's people, of one's country. Love is not necessarily a matter of caring equally or more about someone else than about yourself. These loves are large, but love in some amount is present when your well-being is affected to whatever extent (but in the same direction) by another's. As the other fares, so (to some extent) do you. The people you love are included inside your boundaries, their well-being is your own.

   Being "in love," infatuation, is an intense state that displays familiar features: almost always thinking of the person; wanting constantly to touch and to be together; excitement in the other's presence; losing sleep; expressing one's feelings through poetry, gifts, or still other ways to delight the beloved; gazing deeply into each other's eyes; candlelit dinners; feeling that short separations are long; smiling foolishly when remembering actions and remarks of the other;

feeling that the other's minor foibles are delightful; experiencing joy at having found the other and at being found by the other; and (as Tolstoy depicts Levin in *Anna Karenina* as he learns Kitty loves him) finding *everyone* charming and nice, and thinking they all must sense one's happiness. Other concerns and responsibilities become minor background details in the story of the romance, which becomes the predominant foreground event of life. (When major public responsibilities such as commanding Rome's armies or being king of England are put aside, the tales engross.) The vividness of the relationship can carry artistic or mythic proportions—lying together like figures in a painting, jointly living a new tale from Ovid. Familiar, too, is what happens when the love is not equally reciprocated: melancholy, obsessive rumination on what went wrong, fantasies about its being set right, lingering in places to catch a glimpse of the person, making telephone calls to hear the other's voice, finding that all other activities seem flat, occasionally having suicidal thoughts.

However and whenever infatuation begins, if given the opportunity it transforms itself into continuing romantic love or else it disappears. With this continuing romantic love, it feels to the two people that they have united to form and constitute a new entity in the world, what might be called a *we*.* You can be in romantic love with someone, however, without actually forming a *we* with her or him—that other person might not be in love with you. Love, romantic love, is *wanting* to form a *we* with that particular person, feeling, or perhaps wanting, that particular person to be the right one for you to form a *we* with, and also wanting the other to feel the same way about you. (It would be kinder if the realization that the other person is not the right one with whom to form a *we* always and immediately terminated

the desire to form it.) The desire to form a *we* with that other person is not simply something that goes along with romantic love, something that contingently happens when love does. That desire is intrinsic to the nature of love, I think; it is an important part of what love intends.

In a *we,* the two people are not bound physically like Siamese twins; they can be in distant places, feel differently about things, carry on different occupations. In what sense, then, do these people together constitute a new entity, a *we*? That new entity is created by a new web of relationships between them which makes them no longer so separate. Let me describe some features of this web; I will begin with two that have a somewhat cold and political-science sound.

First, the defining feature we mentioned which applies to love in general: Your own well-being is tied up with that of someone you love romantically. Love, then, among other things, can place you at risk. Bad things that happen to your loved one happen to you. But so too do good things; moreover, someone who loves you helps you with care and comfort to meet vicissitudes—not out of selfishness although her doing so does, in part, help maintain her own well-being too. Thus, love places a floor under your well-being; it provides insurance in the face of fate's blows. . . .

People who form a *we* pool not only their well-being but also their autonomy. They limit or curtail their own decision-making power and rights; some decisions can no longer be made alone. Which decisions these are will be parceled differently by different couples: where to live, how to live, who friends are and how to see them, whether to have children and how many, where to travel, whether to go to the movies that night and what to see. Each transfers some previous rights to make certain decisions unilaterally into a joint pool; somehow, decisions will be made together about how to be together. If your well-being so closely affects and is affected by another's, it is not surprising that decisions that

---

* For a discussion of love as the formation of a *we,* see Robert Solomon, *Love* (Garden City, N.Y.: Anchor Books, 1981).

importantly affect well-being, even in the first instance primarily your own, will no longer be made alone.*

The term *couple* used in reference to people who have formed a *we* is not accidental. The two people also view themselves as a new and continuing unit, and they present that face to the world. They want to be perceived publicly as a couple, to express and assert their identity as a couple in public. Hence those homosexual couples unable to do this face a serious impediment.

To be part of a *we* involves having a new identity, an additional one. This does *not* mean that you no longer have any individual identity or that your sole identity is as part of the *we*. However, the individual identity you did have will become altered. To have this new identity is to enter a certain psychological stance; and each party in the *we* has this stance toward the other. Each becomes psychologically part of the other's identity. How can we say more exactly what this means? To say that something is part of your identity when, if that thing changes or is lost, you feel like a different person, seems only to reintroduce the very notion of identity that needs to be explained. Here is something more helpful: To love someone might be, in part, to devote alertness to their well-being and to your connection with them. (More generally, shall we say that something is part of your identity when you continually make it one of your few areas of special alertness?) There are empirical tests of alertness in the case of your own separate identity —for example, how you hear your name mentioned through the noise of a conversation you were not consciously attending to; how a word that resembles your name "jumps out" from the page. We might find similar tests to check for that alertness involved in loving someone. For example, a person in a *we* often is considerably more worried about the dangers of traveling—air crashes or whatever—when the other is traveling alone than when both travel together or when himself or she herself is traveling alone; it seems plausible that a person in a *we* is alert, in general, to dangers to the other that would necessitate having to go back to a single individual identity, while these are made especially salient by a significant physical separation. Other criteria for the formation of a joint identity also might be suggested, such as a certain kind of division of labor. A person in a *we* might find himself coming across something interesting to read yet leaving it for the other person, not because he himself would not be interested in it but because the other would be more interested, and one of them reading it is sufficient for it to be registered by the wider identity now shared, the *we*. If the couple breaks up, they then might notice themselves reading all those things directly; the other person no longer can do it *for them*. (The list of criteria for the *we* might continue on to include something we discuss later, not seeking to "trade up" to another partner.) Sometimes the existence of the *we* can be very palpable. Just as a reflective person can walk along the street in friendly internal dialogue with himself, keeping himself company, so can one be with a loved person who is not physically present, thinking what she would say, conversing with her, noticing things as she would, for her, because she is not there to notice, saying things to others that she would say, in her tone of voice, carrying the full *we* along.

If we picture the individual self as a closed figure whose boundaries are continuous and solid, dividing what is inside from what is outside, then we might diagram the *we* as two figures with the boundary line between them erased

---

* This curtailment of unilateral decision-making rights extends even to a decision to end the romantic love relationship. This decision, if any, you would think you could make by yourself. And so you can, but only in certain ways at a certain pace. Another kind of relation might be ended because you feel like it or because you find it no longer satisfactory, but in a love relationship the other party "has a vote." This does not mean a permanent veto; but the other party has a right to have his or her say, to try to repair, to be convinced. After some time, to be sure, one party may insist on ending the relationship even without the other's consent, but what they each have forgone, in love, is the right to act unilaterally and swiftly.

where they come together. (Is that the traditional heart shape?) The unitive aspects of sexual experience, two persons flowing together and intensely merging, mirror and aid the formation of the *we*. Meaningful work, creative activity, and development can change the shape of the self. Intimate bonds change the boundaries of the self and alter its *topology*—romantic love in one way and friendship (as we shall see) in another.

The individual self can be related to the *we* it identifies with in two different ways. It can see the *we* as a very important *aspect* of itself, or it can see itself as part of the *we*, as contained within it. It may be that men more often take the former view, women the latter. Although both see the *we* as extremely important for the self, most men might draw the circle of themselves containing the circle of the *we* as an aspect *within* it, while most women might draw the circle of themselves within the circle of the *we*. In either case, the *we* need not consume an individual self or leave it without any autonomy. . . .

The heart of the love relationship is how the lovers view it from the inside, how they feel about their partner and about themselves within it, and the particular ways in which they are good *to* each other. Each person in love delights in the other, and also in giving delight; this often expresses itself in being playful together. In receiving adult love, we are held worthy of being the primary object of the most intense love, something we were not given in the childhood oedipal triangle. Seeing the other happy with us and made happy through our love, we become happier with ourselves.

To be englowed by someone's love, it must be we ourselves who are loved, not a whitewashed version of ourselves, not just a portion. In the complete intimacy of love, a partner knows us as we are, fully. It is no reassurance to be loved by someone ignorant of those traits and features we feel might make us unlovable. Sometimes these are character traits or areas of incompetence, clumsiness, or ignorance; sometimes these are personal bodily features. Complex are the ways

parents make children uncomfortable about sites of pleasure or elimination, and these feelings can be soothed or transformed in the closest attentive and loving sexual intimacy. In the full intimacy of love, the full person is known and cleansed and accepted. And healed.

To be made happy with yourself by being loved, it must be you who is loved, not some feature such as your money. People want, as they say, to be loved "for themselves." You are loved for something else when what you are loved for is a peripheral part of your own self-image or identity. However, someone for whom money, or the ability to make it, was central to his identity, or for whom good looks or great kindness or intelligence was, might not be averse to love's being prompted by these characteristics. You can fall in love with someone because of certain characteristics and you can continue to delight in these; but eventually you must love the person himself, and not *for* the characteristics, not, at any rate, for any delimited list of them. But what does this mean, exactly?

We love the person when being together with that person is a salient part of our identity as we think of it: "being with Eve," "being with Adam," rather than "being with someone who is (or has) such-and-such. . . ." How does this come about? Characteristics must have played some important role, for otherwise why was not a different person loved just as well? Yet if we continue to be loved "for" the characteristics, then the love seems conditional, something that might change or disappear if the characteristics do. Perhaps we should think of love as like imprinting in ducks, where a duckling will attach itself to the first sizable moving object it sees in a certain time period and follow that as its mother. With people, perhaps characteristics set off the imprint of love, but then the person is loved in a way that is no longer based upon retaining those characteristics. This will be helped if the love is based at first upon a wide range of characteristics; it begins as conditional, contingent upon the loved person's having these desirable characteristics, yet given their range and tenacity, it is not insecure.

However, love between people, unlike imprinting with ducks, is not unalterable. Though no longer dependent upon the particular characteristics that set it off, it *can* be overcome over time by new and sufficiently negative other characteristics. Or perhaps by a new imprinting onto another person. Yet this alteration will not be sought by someone within a *we*. If someone were loved "for" certain desirable or valuable characteristics, on the other hand, then if someone else came along who had those characteristics to a greater extent, or other even more valuable characteristics, it seems you should love this new person more. And in that case, why merely wait for a "better" person to turn up; why not actively seek to "trade up" to someone with a "higher score" along valuable dimensions? (Plato's theory is especially vulnerable to these questions, for there it is the Form of Beauty that is the ultimate and appropriate object of love; any particular person serves merely as a bearer of characteristics that awaken in the lover a love of the Form, and hence any such person should be replaceable by a better awakener.*)

A readiness to trade up, looking for someone with "better" characteristics, does not fit with an attitude of love. An illuminating view should explain why not, yet why, nevertheless, the attitude of love is not irrational. One possible and boring explanation is economic in form. Once you have come to know a person well, it would take a large investment of time and energy to reach the comparable point with another person, so there is a barrier to switching. (But couldn't the other person promise a greater return, even taking into account the new costs of investment?) There is uncertainty about a new person; only after long time and experience together, through arguments and crises, can one come to know a person's trustworthiness, reliability, resiliency, and compassion in hardships. Investigating an-

other candidate for coupledom, even an apparently promising one, is likely eventually to reach a negative conclusion and it probably will necessitate curtailing or ending one's current coupled state. So it is unwise to seek to trade up from a reasonably satisfactory situation; the energy you'd expend in search might better be invested in improving your current *we*.

These counsels of economic prudence are not silly—far from it—but they are external. According to them, nothing about the nature of love itself focuses upon the particular individual loved or involves an unwillingness to substitute another; rather, the likelihood of losses from the substitution is what militates against it. We can see why, if the economic analysis were so, we would welcome someone's directing an attitude of love toward us that includes commitment to a particular person, and we can see why we might have to trade the offering or semblance of such an attitude in order to receive it. But why would we want actually to give such a commitment to a particular person, shunning all other partners? What special value is reached through such a love relationship committed to particularism but in no other way? To add that we care about our partners and so do not want to cause them hurt by replacing them is true, yet does not answer the question fully.

Economic analysis might even provide somewhat more understanding.† Repeated trading with a fixed partner with special resources might make it rational to develop in yourself specialized assets for trading with that partner (and similarly on the partner's part toward you); and this specialization gives some assurance that you will continue to trade *with that party* (since the invested resources would be worth much less in exchanges with any third party). Moreover, to shape yourself and specialize so as to better fit and trade with that partner, and therefore to do so

* See Gregory Vlastos, "The Individual as an Object of Love in Plato," in his *Platonic Studies* (Princeton: Princeton University Press, 1973), pp. 3–34.

† This paragraph was suggested by the mode of economic analysis found in Oliver Williamson, *The Economic Institutions of Capitalism* (New York: The Free Press, 1986).

less well with others, you will want some commitment and guarantee that the party will continue to trade with you, a guarantee that goes beyond the party's own specialization to fit you. Under some conditions it will be economically advantageous for two such trading firms to combine into *one* firm, with all allocations now becoming internal. Here at last we come to something like the notion of a joint identity.

The intention in love is to form a *we* and to identify with it as an extended self, to identify one's fortunes in large part with its fortunes. A willingness to trade up, to destroy the very *we* you largely identify with, would then be a willingness to destroy your self in the form of your own extended self. One could not, therefore, intend to link into another *we* unless one had ceased to identify with a current one—unless, that is, one had already ceased to love. Even in that case, the intention to form the new *we* would be an intention to *then* no longer be open to trading up. It is intrinsic to the notion of love, and to the *we* formed by it, that there is not that willingness to trade up. One is no more willing to find another partner, even one with a "higher score," than to destroy the personal self one identifies with in order to allow another, possibly better, but discontinuous self to replace it. (This is not to say one is unwilling to improve or transform oneself.) Perhaps here lies one function of infatuation, to pave and smooth the way to uniting in a *we*; it provides enthusiasm to take one over the hurdles of concern for one's own autonomy, and it provides an initiation into *we*-thinking too, by constantly occupying the mind with thoughts of the other and of the two of you together. A more cynical view than mine might see infatuation as the temporary glue that manages to hold people together until they are stuck.

Part of the process by which people soften their boundaries and move into a *we* involves repeated expression of the desire to do so, repeatedly telling each other that they love each other. Their statement often will be tentative, subject to withdrawal if the other does not respond with

similar avowals. Holding hands, they walk into the water together, step by step. Their caution may become as great as when two suspicious groups or nations—Israel and the Palestinians might be an example—need to recognize the legitimacy of one another. Neither wants to recognize if the other does not, and it also will not suffice for each to announce that it will recognize if the other one does also. For each then will have announced a conditional recognition, contingent upon the other's unconditional recognition. Since neither one has offered this last, they haven't yet gotten started. Neither will it help if each says it will recognize conditional upon the other's conditional recognition: "I'll recognize you if you'll recognize me if I'll recognize you." For here each has given the other a three-part conditional announcement, one which is contingent upon, and goes into operation only when there exists, a two-part conditional announcement from the other party; so neither one has given the other exactly what will trigger that other's recognition, namely a two-part announcement. So long as they both symmetrically announce conditionals of the same length and complexity, they will not be able to get started. Some asymmetry is needed, then, but it need not be that either one begins by offering unconditional recognition. It would be enough for the first to offer the three-part recognition (which is contingent upon the other's simple two-part conditional recognition), and for the second to offer the two-part conditional recognition. The latter triggers the first to recognize outright and this, in turn, triggers the second to do the same. Between lovers, it never becomes this complicated explicitly. Neither makes the nested announcement "I will love you if you will love me if I will love you," and if either one did, this would not (to put it mildly) facilitate the formation of a *we*. Yet the frequency of their saying to each other, "I love you," and their attention to the other's response, may indicate a nesting that is implicit and very deep, as deep as the repeated triggering necessary to overcome caution and produce the actual and unconditional formation of the *we*. . . .

The desire to have love in one's life, to be part of a *we* someday, is not the same as loving a particular person, wanting to form a *we* with that person in particular. In the choice of a particular partner, reasons can play a significant role, I think. Yet in addition to the merits of the other person and her or his qualities, there also is the question of whether the thought of forming a *we* with that person brings excitement and delight. Does that identity seem a wonderful one for you to have? Will it be *fun*? Here the answer is as complicated and mysterious as your relation to your own separate identity. Neither case is completely governed by reasons, but still we might hope that our choices do meet what reasoned standards there are. (The desire to continue to feel that the other is the right partner in your *we* also helps one surmount the inevitable moments in life together when that feeling itself becomes bruised.) The feeling that there is just "one right person" in the world for you, implausible beforehand—what lucky accident made that one unique person inhabit your century?—becomes true after the *we* is formed. Now your identity is wrapped up in that particular *we* with that particular person, so for the particular *you* you now are, there *is* just one other person who is right.

In the view of a person who loves someone romantically, there couldn't be anyone else who was better as a partner. He might think that person he is in love with could be better somehow—stop leaving toothpaste in the sink or whatever—but any description he could offer of a better mate would be a description of his mate changed, not one of somebody *else*. No one else would do, no matter what her qualities. Perhaps this is due to the particularity of the qualities you come to love, not just a sense of humor but that particular one, not just some way of looking mock-stern but that one. Plato got the matter reversed, then; as love grows you love not general aspects or traits but more and more particular ones, not intelligence in general but that particular mind, not kindness in general but those particular ways of being kind. In trying to imagine a "better" mate, a person in romantic love will require her or him to have a very particular constellation of very particular traits and—leaving aside various "science fiction" possibilities—no other person *could* have precisely those traits; therefore, any imagined person will be the same mate (perhaps) somewhat changed, not somebody else. (If that same mate actually alters, though, the romantic partner may well come to love and require that new constellation of particulars.) Hence, a person in romantic love *could not* seek to "trade up"—he would have to seek out the very same person. A person not in love might seek someone with certain traits, yet after finding someone, even (remarkably) a person who has the traits sought, if he loves that person she will show those traits in a particularity he did not initially seek but now has come to love—her particular versions of these traits. Since a romantic mate eventually comes to be loved, not for any general dimensions or "score" on such dimensions—that, if anything, gets taken for granted—but for his or her own particular and nonduplicable way of embodying such general traits, a person in love could not make any coherent sense of his "trading up" to *another*. . . .

This does not yet show that a person could not have many such different focused desires, just as she might desire to read this particular book and also that one. I believe that the romantic desire is to form a *we* with that particular person *and* with no other. In the strong sense of the notion of identity involved here, one can no more be part of many *we*s which constitute one's identity than one can simultaneously have many individual identities. (What persons with multiple personality have is not many identities but not quite one.) In a *we*, the people *share* an identity and do not simply each have identities that are enlarged. The desire to share not only our life but our very identity with another marks our fullest openness. What more central and intimate thing could we share? . . .

It is instructive here to consider friendship, which too alters and recontours an individual's boundaries, providing a distinct shape and character to the self. The salient feature of friendship is *sharing*. In sharing things—food, happy occasions, football games, a concern with problems, events to celebrate—friends especially want these to be had together; while it might constitute something good when each person has the thing separately, friends want that it be had or done by both (or all) of them *together*. To be sure, a good thing does get magnified for you when it is shared with others, and some things can be more fun when done together—indeed, fun, in part, is just the sharing and taking of delight in something together. Yet in friendship the sharing is not desired simply to enlarge our individual benefits.

A friendship does not exist *solely* for further purposes, whether a political movement's larger goals, an occupational endeavor, or simply the participant's separate and individual benefits. Of course, there can be many further benefits that flow within friendship and from it, benefits so familiar as not to need listing. Aristotle held one of these to be most central; a friend, he said, is a "second self" who is a means to your own self-awareness. (In his listing of the virtuous characteristics one should seek in a friend, Aristotle takes your parents' view of who your friends should be.) Nevertheless, a relationship is a friendship to the extent that it shares activities for no further purpose than the sharing of them.

People seek to engage in sharing beyond the domain of personal friendship also. One important reason we read newspapers, I think, is not the importance or intrinsic interest of the news; we rarely take action whose direction depends upon what we read there, and if somehow we were shipwrecked for ten years on an isolated island, when we returned we would want a summary of what had happened meanwhile, but we certainly would not choose to peruse the back newspapers of the previous ten years. Rather, we read newspapers because we want to *share* information with our fellows, we want to have a range of information in common with them, a common stock of mental contents. We already share with them a geography and a language, and also a common fate in the face of large-scale events. That we also desire to share the daily flow of information shows how very intense our desire to share is.

Nonromantic friends do not, in general, share an *identity*. In part, this may be because of the crisscrossing web of friendships. The friend of your friend may be your acquaintance, but he or she is not necessarily someone you are close to or would meet with separately. As in the case of multiple bilateral defense treaties among nations, conflicts of action and attachment can occur that make it difficult to delineate any larger entity to which one safely can cede powers and make the bearer of a larger identity. Such considerations also help explain why it is not feasible for a person simultaneously to be part of multiple romantic couples (or of a trio), even were the person to desire this. Friends want to share the things they do *as* a sharing, and they think, correctly, that friendship is valuable partly *because* of its sharing —perhaps specially valuable because, unlike the case of romantic love, this valued sharing occurs *without* any sharing of identity. . . .

Further Questions

1. Would you think of your beloved as being part of yourself (or vice versa)? What exactly does this mean to you?

2. Do you find that a love relationship changes you in some ways? If you are positive about this, what explanation can you give for your attitude?

3. Why is it important that the person you love, love you as well?

4. Why can one have many friends, although, normally, only one person with whom one is in love?

IV.2   Friends and Lovers

LAURENCE THOMAS

Laurence Thomas tries to distinguish romantic love from friendship by some features other than the sexual aspect of romantic love. Friends have concern for each other, trust in each other and are loyal to each other. Romantic love was traditionally courtly love, sexual passion between a man and a woman on unequal terms. Egalitarian romantic love, however, is friendship plus sexual involvement in a context of fidelity. Since friendship also requires fidelity, on terms understood by the partners in the friendship, his conclusion is that friendship is very close to romantic love.

Thomas has taught philosophy at Oberlin College (Ohio) and Syracuse University (New York). He has written about ethics and moral character.

Reading Questions

1. What is sexual involvement? What part does it play in romantic love?
2. What features do you believe necessary for a relationship to be properly called a friendship?
3. When a friendship turns into romantic love, what actually happens? Would this be the culmination of a friendship?

TIME WAS WHEN IT SEEMED rather easy to distinguish conceptually between romantic love and friendship. Supposedly, there were natural roles for women and natural roles for men; and it was natural for a person to fall in love with a person of the opposite gender: a woman with a man and a man with a woman. Sometimes members of the same gender fell in love with one another, but such romantic love, if it was called that, was considered perverted. In times past, romantic love was tied to the view that men and women complement one another in a deeper and more profound way than is possible for members of the same gender to complement one another, however close they might be as friends. The view has it that while ideally friends of the same gender flourish together, the extent to which persons of opposite genders flourish together far exceeds anything friendship might offer. A view of natural roles for women and men according to which

women and men so complement one another yields a conceptual difference between friendship and romantic love. The former turns out to be an important but lesser form of interpersonal interaction. Let us refer to the conception of love suggested here as courtly romantic love.

Times are changing. Nowadays a great many liberals who align themselves with feminists subscribe to what I call an egalitarian conception of romantic love. This conception holds that whatever differences there are between women and men—it need not deny that there are any—the differences do not justify an assignment of social roles according to gender. It is not natural for women to care for the home and men to be the breadwinners; it is not natural for women to be subordinate to men; and so on. Indeed, the egalitarian conception rejects both the idea that the natural object of romantic love is a person of the opposite gender as well as the concomitant idea that romantic love between members of the same gender is perverted in some sense.

Given this conception of romantic love, a question that naturally arises is: What is the conceptual difference between it and friendship? The difference that most quickly comes to mind is sexual involvement: Romantic lovers are involved as sexual partners; friends are not. Indeed, it is not clear that one can point to anything else to distinguish these two interpersonal relationships. But can this difference bear the enormous weight that is put upon it? I do not believe so, as I try to show in this essay. That is, as a way of capturing what conceptually distinguishes friendship from egalitarian romantic love, sexual involvement with respect to the latter simply will not do. . . .

Friendships

Friends love one another, and for that very reason they take delight in one another's flourishing. There is an enormous bond of trust between them—a bond that is cemented by mutual self-disclosure. And they have a commanding perspective of one another's lives—a perspective that comes in the wake of their mutual self-disclosure and their maximizing the amount of time that they spend together. Finally, friends are deeply loyal to one another. Obviously, not all who call themselves friends are friends in this way. There are, following Aristotle, lesser forms of friendship —friendships of convenience and utility. So let us refer to individuals who are friends in the way just delineated as companion friends.[1]

As one might gather, what I take to be special about companion friends is that they share enormous amounts of private information about themselves with one another. I regard this as the predominant way in which such friends can and do contribute to one another's flourishing, where the emphasis here is upon the improvement of character and personality. Of course, I hardly mean to suggest that companion friends do not help one another in the usual sorts of ways. They speak to one another's needs, as their

resources permit it. However, I assume that, by and large, companion friends are self-sufficient or, in any case, that the material help each provides the other is quite ancillary to the friendship. This assumption, far from revealing a Western bias, enables us to see more clearly how rich a friendship can be that does not turn upon material offerings.

There are a variety of ways in which the sharing of private and personal information enables friends to contribute to one another's flourishing. This can best be brought out by noting that as a matter of propriety what aspect of other people's private lives we are entitled to discuss with them is not so much a function of what we happen to know about their lives but what they invite us to discuss via the route of self-disclosure. For example, suppose a chief executive officer has received in the mail a résumé from Murray listing her employment record. Upon making some inquiries, in particular a call to an especially reliable business acquaintance, the CEO learns that Murray has been dismissed from her previous position for a number of improprieties. The CEO has the secretary note this information and file it with Murray's résumé, so the secretary's being in possession of this information is not itself an impropriety. And let us suppose further that the secretary and Murray happen to get invited to the same party where it becomes evident to the secretary, from a few of Murray's remarks, that the application the secretary filed this afternoon belongs to this Murray. Needless to say, it would be highly inappropriate for the secretary to broach the topic of Murray's dismissal, despite hearing Murray lying to everyone in claiming to have left the previous job because it did not provide much opportunity for growth. The secretary should not even take Murray aside and inform her that the truth is known. Things would be rather different were Murray to confide in the secretary. They would also be different if, contrary to the spirit of the example, everyone knew that Murray was lying and the secretary was merely informing her of this. But notice that if everyone knows, then the secretary's knowing is hardly a matter of having privileged and confidential information.

Or, to take a different example, suppose that a man discovers quite by accident that the couple next door had adopted their child. The couple has a wireless telephone whose signals can sometimes be picked up by a CB-radio scanner. In a casual phone conversation the parents are reminiscing over how fortunate they are to have adopted Susan. While on automatic scanning, the neighbor's CB-radio picks up this conversation; and by the time he realizes that he has been halfheartedly listening to the conversation of the couple next door, he knows that Susan was adopted. Now, since the couple has never given him any reason to think that they are other than Susan's biological parents, it is clear that it would be quite out of place for him to inquire about the couple's experience with adopting Susan, though he has recently been thinking about doing the same himself, and everyone is on the best of speaking terms. To be sure, in a way that does not arouse suspicion he might want to make them aware of the occasional drawback of wireless phones.

As I have said, what we are entitled to discuss with others regarding their private lives is not so much a function of what we know about them as it is of the extent to which we have been invited by their self-disclosure to raise an issue with them. We may think of private information as information about a person that the members-at-large of any given community are not entitled to have at their disposal. One can be very public about things that are most private, as is the couple who openly talk about their sex life or the man who tells everyone what he earns. And that which is private can be known by several people: The five people who know that Jones was raped last year are those to whom Jones turned for comfort; those who have access to a faculty member's salary are the dean, the department head, and the appropriate members in the personnel department; the bank teller and the customer know that the customer just deposited a check for $25,000. Yet in each case the relevant information is private. Of course, whether a piece of information is private is not always obvious; indeed, whether it is may even be indeterminate. But this simply reveals what we already know, which is that life is full of different cases.

Now, it is because companion friends disclose considerable private information to one another that they can, without impropriety, raise issues and offer commentary concerning one another's behavior (words and deeds) that others cannot do without impropriety. Suppose, for instance, that contrary to what anyone would have thought, Murray uses formality to hide sexual attraction and has revealed this to Bower. Then Bower's querying Murray about her very formal behavior with so-and-so has a reasonableness to it that it could not otherwise have in the absence of this information about the way in which Murray uses formal behavior. What is more, Murray knows this.

Because companion friends invite one another, through reciprocal self-disclosure, to raise probing questions and press issues about one another's private lives, they can masterfully contribute to one another's moral flourishing in that through their interaction, self-examination and in turn self-understanding are facilitated.

David Hume observed that "the minds of men are mirrors to one another, not only because they reflect each other's emotions, but also because those rays of passion, sentiments, and opinions may often be reverberated" (1978, 5). Because of the depth of their self-disclosure, companion friends make the best mirrors for one another. Although they delight in one another's affection, they are not solicitous of the esteem and approval of one for the other to the point where they are unwilling to be forthright with one another where criticism is called for or, worse yet, to the point where they are blind to one another's failings. Companion friends are not sycophants. This does not mean that they are prepared to criticize at every turn. The idea rather is that they are aware of each other's strengths and weaknesses and bring their awareness of both to bear upon each other's lives in constructive ways.

Mutual love, trust, and self-disclosure are among the factors that give rise to loyalty. Companion friends are quite loyal to one another. Now, loyalty is to be distinguished from altruism in the following way. Loyalty presupposes a pre-existing bond or tie; altruism does not. Perfect strangers can be quite altruistic toward one another, but they cannot be loyal to one another under such circumstances. Loyalty involves a commitment to the good of a specific individual, whereas altruism is simply a matter of bestowing benefits—benefits that can be distributed indiscriminately first to this one and then to that one, as the needs of individuals require. Altruistic people can move from one person to the next offering assistance. By contrast, loyal people stand by particular people (up to a point, at any rate) even when the evidence clearly suggests that the individuals will be defeated in their aims.

Given that companion friends are loyal to one another, a question that obviously arises is this: Should they remain loyal to one another in the face of immoral behavior? Well, yes and no. Cicero observed:

> When two men of sound character are friends they should unreservedly share all their concerns and aims with one another. Indeed, even if by some chance a friend of ours possessed ambitions which, while not entirely laudable, nevertheless needed our assistance since either his life or reputation were at stake, then we should have some justification in turning aside from the path of strict moral rectitude—short, that is to say, of doing something absolutely disgraceful, since there are limits beyond which friendship could not excusably go (sec. 16, para. 59).

Obviously, there is something rather unsavory about ending a deep friendship just because from time to time one's friend's behavior is morally unacceptable. No one is morally perfect. And it is clear that because companion friends so profoundly identify with one another's good they will inevitably be supportive of one another at

times when their aims obviously fall short of being morally laudable. But this is not the same thing as having and supporting friends who, in taking themselves to have seen the light, embark upon an immoral life. Such friendships should end. For in continuing to be loyal to individuals committed to leading an immoral life we are supporting evil at least indirectly, which is bound to have an adverse effect upon our own moral character. For we cannot be loyal to an immoral person without becoming somewhat inured to evil itself.

Naturally, I do not mean to suggest that a companion friend should not attempt to rescue the other friend from the grip of immorality. But when a person has gone far enough along this line can certainly be a matter of controversy. The many relevant factors will weigh differently with different people. A weak-willed individual may have to stop in the attempt much sooner than a person of extraordinary resolve. If the change was wrought by a deep personal loss—say the individual was the only member of an entire family to survive a fire—then a measure of understanding is called for. These things must be given their due. My only claim is that one must stop short of becoming inured to evil itself. . . .

Romantic Love

Shakespeare speaks eloquently about romantic love through the mouths of Romeo and Juliet (II, ii).

Juliet: 'Tis almost morning. I would have thee gone,
  And yet no farther than a wanton's bird,
  That lets it hop a little from her hand,
  Like a poor prisoner in her twisted gyves,
  And with a silk thread plucks it back again,
  So loving-jealous of its liberty.
Romeo: I would I were thy bird.
Juliet: Sweet, so would I.
  Yet I should kill thee with much cherishing.
  Good night, good night! Parting is such sweet sorrow.
  That I shall say good night till it be morrow.

In *Women in Love* D. H. Lawrence's brush strokes are broader.

> She stared into his face with that slow, full gaze which was so curious and so exciting to him. . . . And he was aware of her dark, hot-looking eyes, dark, full-opened, hot, naked in their looking at him. . . . Her appearance was simple and complete, really beautiful. . . . She appealed to Gerald strongly. . . . The electricity was voluptuously rich, in his limbs.

Sexual passion is the fuel of romantic love—or so tradition has it. One is electrified by the features, style, and manners of one's would-be lover. The idea, presumably, is that when such electrification is reciprocated between two people, they are compatible enough to spend an eternity together; and the yearning that each has for the other is spoken to—not extinguished—through their sexual union. In the context of marriage, this union even has the blessings of Christianity, which (as traditionally interpreted) eschews sexual expression in all other respects.

For all the beauty that is now associated with the idea of romantic love, it may very well be that its origins are less than morally palpable. The Greeks thought that only men were capable of discerning and therefore experiencing true beauty. It was held natural for men to have greater affection for one another than for women because of the supposedly superior discerning and, more generally, intellectual powers of men; though since men want beautiful children, it was held natural for them to be attracted to beautiful women. The Judeo-Christian tradition, which does considerably better than the Greeks did in allowing women to appreciate beauty, still leaves much to be desired in terms of its attitude toward the intellectual powers of women. Women are still subordinate to men. Moreover, the woman is looking for a good provider for herself and her children; and the man is looking for a beautiful and faithful woman to provide for and to bear his children. Thus, on this view, women and men bring to their romantic relationship quite differ-

ent gifts and natural talents, children aside. The woman is compassionate, caring, and understanding; the man is firm and decisive. He is the voice of reason and so the one who leads. Men and women find one another electrifying for rather different reasons quite apart from sexual attraction itself. This is romantic love traditionally construed—that is, what I call courtly romantic love.

. . . [E]galitarian romantic love does not have the asymmetry just sketched. What it does inherit from courtly romantic love, however, is the importance of sexual passion. Thus the refrains of *Romeo and Juliet* and the feelings that D. H. Lawrence imbues Gerald with remain ever so apropos in egalitarian romantic love. And to sexual passion it would seem that this conception of romantic love adds only friendship, as there are no natural roles for women and men to play. Nor, in particular, is it held that sexual passion is more deeply kindled, or that romantic love is somehow more complete, when between women and men. Nor, again, does this conception of romantic love hold that fulfillment is tied to having offspring. It cannot, since it allows that equally fulfilling romantic love can occur between members of the same gender. Egalitarian romantic love, then, would seem to be reducible to sexual passion plus companion friendship.

Now, of course, there can be no ignoring the significance and power of sexual passion. One must allow, and not just for the sake of argument, that sexual intercourse between two individuals can make a qualitative difference in their relationship. The issue, however, is whether the difference between friendship and romantic love can turn it on. I do not believe so.

Friends and Lovers

The most pressing concern that arises when sexual intercourse is an expression of romantic love is that of fidelity—so much so that the two would seem to be conceptually linked. By contrast, the issue of fidelity or, rather, something that mirrors it does not seem to arise in the context of companion friendship; and this, too, seems to be a conceptual truth. If so, then it would appear that the sexual component can, after all, bear the weight that the difference between romantic love and companion friendship puts upon it. Indeed, since fidelity is (or can be construed as) a moral issue, we have a moral difference between romantic love and companion friendship if, as a matter of conceptual truth, the issue of fidelity can arise in connection with the former only, and not the latter.

It is this supposed difference that I concentrate on, although there are other differences that might come to mind. For instance, it might be thought that romantic love is an all-or-nothing matter and that this sharply distinguishes it from friendship, even companion friendship, since presumably all forms of friendship admit of degrees. Or it might be thought that romantic love is underwritten by biological considerations, but friendship is not, since the former and not the latter contributes to the production of offspring, which in turn insures the survival of the species. And, finally, this second consideration might be thought, via some route of moral naturalism, to entail that romantic loves just are deeper than companion friendship, and rightly so.

I do not believe that any of these considerations are compelling. First, even if sexual intercourse is conceded to be an all-or-nothing matter —and one need not concede that—there certainly are degrees of romantic love. Some people are more in love with one another than others are. The second difference makes sense only if it is held, contrary to what we are assuming, that romantic love is not equal to sex plus companion friendship. If it is equal to that, then if romantic love is underwritten by biological considerations, so is companion friendship. The third difference falls to the same response as the second. Again, it may very well be that romantic love is not to be understood as sex plus companion friendship. Here, I am not concerned to argue that it is. My concern, rather, is to show that romantic love

thus understood does not yield a conceptual difference between it and companion friendship, the issue of fidelity notwithstanding.

At this juncture let me pause just to record my awareness of the fact that the expressions "sexual intercourse" and "having sex" need not be strictly synonymous, with the latter having a wider range than the former; for the latter more clearly includes intimate physical activities that do not have coitus (vaginal penetration) as their final aim. Many individuals regard themselves as having (had) sex without having (had) sexual intercourse. The question of fidelity, of course, can be raised in either case, although it is clear that I am doing so primarily with sexual intercourse in mind. This is due to the historical fact that marriage has served as the paradigm context in which the issue of fidelity has been raised. In taking this route, I do not mean to disparage life styles or sexual orientations where coitus is not the final aim of intimate physical activity.

So to continue, the issue before us is whether the conceptual landscape of romantic love and companion friendship is as it is generally thought to be with respect to fidelity, and not what the practice is at present. It is indisputable that, currently, sexual involvement between romantic lovers is taken as the behavioral sign of union between them. A couple who have done everything else save have sex are thought to have yet a step to go. Indeed, it is regarded as necessary to consummate a marriage. Fidelity is important precisely because of the significance that the sex act has between romantic lovers. But the issue is not whether there is a widely held convention according to which the sex act between romantic lovers has the significance it has; for it is obvious that there is such a convention. Rather, the issue is whether it is a conceptual truth that this act must be taken to have this significance. And one does not show the latter simply by pointing to the universality of a convention.

Now, one extraordinarily compelling reason for maintaining that sexual intercourse need not have the significance that we now take it to have with regard to fidelity is that it has not always had that significance in Western culture. Fidelity as we now conceive of it is tied to monogamy, which was ushered in by Christianity.[2] Monogamy just is the view that at any given time a person should be involved in a sexual relationship with only one other person. Thus it is not sexual intercourse as such that makes fidelity a pressing issue between romantic lovers; rather, a monogamous view of sexual intercourse does. A different issue altogether is whether a monogamous view of sexual intercourse is preferable to a nonmonogamous one. I have not dealt with this issue at all.

This is worth noting: A consideration that powerfully supports what has just been said is that even in the context of monogamous relationships, men have generally thought the requirement of fidelity did not hold as stringently for them as it did for their female lovers; and more than a few women have been understanding in this regard. It is no doubt true that sexism is operating rather explictly here. But what follows from this? Not that the point made is mistaken, but that in a sexist world there has been a double standard with respect to fidelity.

Let us now look at companion friendships. Does it hold conceptually that nothing mirroring the issue of fidelity can arise in this context? I do not believe so. Fidelity has what we may call a possessive structure to it: There is something x which belongs to A and something y which belongs to B; and as a sign of unity between them A and B share x and y between them in that A allows B access to x and B allows A access to y; and none other has access to x and y. Indeed, x and y cannot be shared with any other without running the risk of rupturing the unity between A and B; and each believes this, as well as believing that the other believes this.

Well, suppose the widespread practice was that when two individuals took themselves to become companion friends, they purchased two very fine glasses of crystal. It is worth nothing that the attitude of the friends toward the crystal would mirror the attitude of fidelity in romantic love. It would certainly be expected by both friends that neither would leave these crystal glasses out for anybody and everybody to use or give them over to day-to-day use. The expectation, surely, would be that they would use the crystal glasses on special occasions, and most preferably with one another.

Moreover, suppose that the companion friendship between, say, A and B dissolves and A goes on to form a new companion friendship with C, where A and C in turn purchase fine crystal. It is very unlikely that A will parade in front of C the crystal that belongs to A and B. And one reason for thinking this is that in general we are careful in how we exalt our past friendships in front of our present ones. In particular, we are careful not to speak so highly of past companion friendships as to suggest that the present ones are inferior to them. And this is rather like not making too much of a previous lover. It is one thing to have learned some invaluable lessons from previous lovers or companion friends and to have grown during the time spent with them; it is another thing entirely to suggest that a past relationship was superior to the present one. This is so, interestingly, even if it was the death of the previous friend or lover that ended the relationship. Of course, none of this is meant to deny that previous relationships can be better; the point, rather, is that normally we do not extol the virtues of previous ones to our present lover or companion friend—at least not to the point of making it clear that our present relationship is inferior to a previous one. These comparative remarks are meant to show that the crystal example is not nearly as far-fetched as it might have first seemed. And this in turn supports the idea that something mirroring fidelity can hold among companion friendships. . . .

Two friends purchasing fine crystal is hardly the same as lovers engaging in sexual intercourse. There can be no doubt about that. But then, the issue was not that at all, but whether as a matter of conceptual truth nothing mirroring fidelity could obtain between friendships.

Aristotle has claimed, and John Cooper in defense of him, that companion friendship is essential to the flourishing of adults—so much so that a person would yet want to have such a friend though he should have all other goods in the world. On this view, one might very well have thought that if friends are not lovers, then they ought to be. Perhaps Aristotle has an answer as to why we are so disposed to think otherwise, writing: "Most people understand by friends those who are useful" (1169b25). . . .

NOTES

1. It would seem that all work on friendship owes much to Aristotle's views on the subject. The account offered here is no different in that respect. I have also profited from John M. Cooper's "Aristotle on Friendship." The reference to Cooper in the last paragraph of this essay is to that article.

2. Lord Patrick Devlin (1979) makes much of this, writing: "Morals and religion are inextricably joined—the moral standards generally accepted in Western civilization being those belonging to Christianity" (p. 4). "In England we believe in the Christian idea of marriage and therefore adopt monogamy as a moral principle. Consequently the Christian institution of marriage has become the basis of family life and so part of the structure of our society. It is there not because it is Christian. It has got there because it is Christian, but it remains there because it is built into the house in which we live and could not be removed without bringing it down. . . . A non-Christian is bound by it, not because it is part of Christianity but because, rightly or wrongly, it has been adopted by the society in which he lives" (p. 9).

REFERENCES

Cicero. 1984. *On the Good Life.* Michael Grant, trans. New York: Penguin.

Cooper, John M. 1980. "Aristotle on Friendship." In Amelie Rorty, ed. *Essays on Aristotle's Ethics.* Berkeley: University of California Press.

Devlin, Lord Patrick. 1979. *The Enforcement of Morals.* Oxford: Oxford University Press.

Hume, David. 1978. *A Treatise of Human Nature,* 2d ed. L. A. Selby-Bigge and P. H. Nidditch, eds. Oxford: Clarendon Press.

Singer, Irving. 1984. *The Nature of Love: Plato to Luther,* vol. 1, 2d ed.; *The Nature of Love: Courtly and Romantic,* vol. 2. Chicago: University of Chicago Press.

Thomas, Laurence. 1987. "Friendship," *Synthese,* 72.

———. 1980. "Sexism and Racism: Some Conceptual Differences." *Ethics,* 90.

Further Questions

1. Is fidelity important in romantic love, as Laurence claims? Is it important in friendships as well?

2. Should romantic love be also a friendship?

3. How critical can you be of someone before it is not appropriate to say you are friends with this person?

IV.3   On Falling in Love*

GEOFFREY GORER

Geoffrey Gorer questions the whole idea of romantic love. The capacity to fall in love, he says, is a gift some people have and some don't (like the ability to fall into a trance, or perfect pitch in music). Social conditions largely determine the extent to which such capacities are actualized. At present, too much emphasis is placed on romantic love, especially as a prerequisite for marriage.

Reading Questions

1. Do you, or did you, expect to fall in love someday and make this a central part of your life? Has it occurred to you that maybe you were, or are, expecting too much?
2. Do you consider people who never seem to fall in love failures in some way?
3. Is romantic love too unstable to function as a reliable basis for marriage?

ON THE BASIS of anthropological evidence it would appear that the capacity to fall passionately in love—to feel convinced that one can only achieve bliss by the union with one unique individual—is one of those uncommon potentialities which develop spontaneously in a few individuals in all human societies that have been described.

In its distribution it seems to have the same arbitrary character as those innate potentialities which form the basis of artistic and religious creations and performances: a "true" ear or a "true" hand for drawing, the ability to go into deep trance and the like. It is probable that in any society which comprises more than a few hundred people there will be some man or woman with "absolute pitch," and another with the ability to go easily into trance. Whether the people with these innate gifts will ever exercise them publicly will depend on the development and the values

of their society. If there is no polyphonic music, the person endowed with absolute pitch may go to his grave without ever having been aware of, much less exercised, his gift. The person with the ability to go easily into trance will probably not escape that experience; but if the religious climate is unfavorable, he or she may well have to hide this capacity as something shameful; and, if it be discovered, he or she may well be punished or killed as a witch possessed by the devil.

The analogy between these gifts and the ability to fall deeply in love may be pushed further. The gifts in their overpowering form, so that they manifest themselves whatever the climate of opinion and the customs of the society, are statistically rare; but a large part of the population is able to develop an approximation to these abilities if the society considers them desirable and punishes their absence. Thus, there is no

* This essay, originally written in 1960, is Essay IX from Geoffrey Gorer's *The Danger of Equality* (New York, NY: Weybright and Talley, 1966), pp. 126–132. Geoffrey Gorer (1905–1985) studied with Margaret Mead and Ruth Benedict, and was the author of a number of anthropological treatises.

reason to suppose that the ability to reproduce a tune correctly, to sing in harmony, is innately more common among the Welsh than among the English or (at least in the time of Mozart) among the Czechs than among the Austrians. But because the Welsh (or the Czechs of the eighteenth century) expected every person to be able to hold a worthy part in choral singing and arranged many of their more enjoyable and respected social events around choirs, far more people developed their originally weak musical ability in these societies than they did in the neighboring ones which had neither such expectations nor such institutions.

In most modern societies trance is a generally devalued condition, may indeed be considered to demand medical or psychiatric attention, and so it only manifests itself rarely, except among spiritualists and in ecstatic religious cults. But many other societies have demanded that every person, or every person of one sex, should experience trance at least once in their lives. Among a number of American Plains Indian tribes, a male could not become a warrior or hunter until he had found his guardian spirit in a trance vision; and in some West African societies, such as Dahomey, or among the Balinese in Indonesia, a great part of the population—perhaps half—develops the ability to go into at least light trance in the appropriate religious setting.

All the anthropological evidence suggests that the ability to fall passionately in love is completely analogous in its distribution to these other gifts. Even though a society may completely devalue romantic love, it will still occur spasmodically from time to time; and if a society puts a high valuation on this behavior, the greater part of the population will be able to convince themselves that they have these feelings, in the same way as the American Indian youths could nearly all convince themselves that they had had visions of their guardian spirit.

Probably because the spontaneous ability to fall deeply in love is so rare a phenomenon statistically, very few human societies (apart from Western Europe and North America in the last two centuries) have incorporated the expectation of romantic love into their social institutions, or demanded that every young man and every young woman should manifest it, should feel it at some time in their lives. There are records of one or two small societies in the islands of Polynesia or among the American Indians who have considered romantic love a necessary prelude to marriage; but, these very rare exceptions apart, marriage has typically been considered a *social* union between two groups rather than a *private* union between two individuals. Many societies will pay some attention to the preferences of the man and woman most intimately concerned and will not force a marriage of mutual repugnance (other societies do not pay even that attention to the girl's sentiments); but what is looked for in these societies of social marriage is mutual compatibility, nothing stronger. Marriage is too important to too many people, and to society itself; it cannot be allowed, so it is argued, to depend on the whims of young people who do not know their own minds.

Consequently, in nearly all the societies of which we have record, romantic love is considered to be quite unconnected with marriage, and is usually envisaged as socially disruptive. This disruption may be tragic—probably the most common development in literate societies—it may be comic, it may be a social nuisance or an interesting topic of conversation; but in nearly every society and at nearly every period romantic love is a disruptive force outside of, and interfering with, marriage.

This is the case with the European tradition of romantic love. The ladies for whom the troubadours sung were never their own wives nor capable of becoming so; if the poets were not married to someone else, then the objects of their devotion were. Guinevere and Isolde and Petrarch's Laura were married women; Dante was a married man when he met Beatrice, and Paolo and Francesca were both married to other people. Moreover, never in romantic poetry was there a suggestion that marriage was the aim of these lovers. Love and marriage are treated as antithetical; if the two people who fall in love are by any chance unmarried, then it is a fixed convention that the families of the two lovers are completely opposed to the union, as in *Romeo and Juliet* and many lesser poems and plays. The tragic love of two young people thwarted by the wishes of their families, and culminating either in suicide or in holy resignation, is a constant theme of literature and drama throughout Asia and much of Europe. Romantic love was the disturber, the wrecker of cities, in Sophocles' phrase; and parents were to be commiserated with if their children developed such unfortunate propensities.

About the middle of the eighteenth century the situation changed rapidly in Western Europe and North America. Judging from the literary evidence—and there is little else to go on—being romantically in love changed from a potentially tragic to a potentially desirable condition; and when the loving couple were in a position to marry, public sympathy went to the young people and was withdrawn from the parents who tried to impose their more prudent plans. A number of social changes accompanied this change of attitude: American independence, the French revolution, the beginning of the "industrial revolution," and the rise in influence and the increase in numbers of the middle classes.

All these changes probably had some influence; but I should be inclined to give the most weight to the last factor, the rise of the middle classes. Both the aristocracy and the peasantry were, in their different ways, attached to specific pieces of land; and the choice of daughter-in-law (or occasionally son-in-law) was very much influenced by considerations of agriculture and of inheritance; and neither group could maintain their living standards without the ownership of land. The middle classes, on the other hand, were mobile in every sense of the word; a family's prosperity was much less dependent on marriage settlements, and children were far more easily able to earn a living without parental approval or

assistance. Marriages based on romantic love were at least feasible.

Furthermore, the middle classes were the major, indeed almost the only, audience for poets and novelists; and it was the poets and novelists, above all the romantic poets of England and Germany, who preached the ecstasy of romantic love and claimed the enormous superiority of a marriage founded on love to one founded on prudential parental arrangements; and their preaching made converts.

During the nineteenth century young middle-class men and women came to expect that they would fall in love romantically, and that such falling in love was the only proper prelude to, and a guarantor of, a happy marriage. This does not seem to have been the case with the other classes in Western Europe. For the aristocracies and royalty suitability seems to have remained a far more important criterion for marriage than romantic love; and the tragedies of unsuitable and disruptive love (such as *Mayerling*) continued to occur. The urban working classes during the nineteenth century were most of them so oppressed by fatigue and poverty that they lacked both leisure and energy to search for the romantically loved one. In the novels of Dickens, the middle-class characters fall in love and eventually marry; but the pictures of working-class married life are without any suggestion of romance. Some research has been done, particularly for cities in the North Eastern United States, on the places of residence of married people before their marriage; and overwhelmingly, the married couples come from either the same small urban neighborhood or from stops on the same trolley line.

In the present century the aristocrats, the urban workers and the peasants have to a great extent abandoned their distinctive modes of life. Middle-class patterns have become increasingly widely adopted—an increase much hastened by the development of mass communications such as films, radio, and television, which offered their middle-class patterns of life to an increasingly heterogenous audience. Among these middle-class patterns none was more insistent than a demand for marriage founded on romantic love, which was the culmination of the vast majority of stories and plays offered for entertainment and as an example of proper behavior. A marriage founded on romantic love was seen as the birthright of every man and woman from Royal Princesses to seamstresses and factory hands. As far as the records go, nothing like this has ever happened before in a complex society. We know of no other society which has expected that every young man and young woman should fall deeply in love with an unmarried member of the opposite sex and should marry their love-choice; and moreover to decree that this love should occur only once in a life-time, and should be strong enough to sustain the marriage for ever after.

This expectation that everybody should feel romantic love undoubtedly puts as much strain on some individuals as the demand that everybody should sing in tune or go into ecstatic trance does on some members of other societies. As with these other rare spontaneous talents, the majority of any population can produce a sufficient approximation to the spontaneous gift to satisfy themselves and their neighbors that they feel what they ought to feel, and so to approach marriage in what they have learned is the only appropriate frame of mind. But besides the people born with a true ear there are those who are born tone deaf; besides the people who can fall spontaneously into trance there are those whom it is impossible to hypnotize; besides the natural lovers there are people who are temperamentally incapable of romantic love.

People of such a temperament—and we have no idea how numerous they are—are put to a grave disadvantage by the present social expectations; they feel themselves, and are often looked upon by their families and friends, as inadequate, as failures. Men and women who, in earlier centuries or in other societies, would have made the most satisfactory of spouses in marriages of suitability, may well remain unmarried and unhappy in a society which considers romantic love the only proper basis for marriage.

When romantic love is considered the supreme individual value, it can still be nearly as socially disruptive as it was in earlier periods or other societies where it was not allowed for at all. Among the most ethical people of the United States and some Western European countries between the wars it was considered profoundly immoral to stay married to a spouse who had fallen in love with somebody else; and there developed the paradox of the ethical divorce, when the self-sacrificing spouse nobly broke up his or her family life rather than thwart the partner's romantic love.

As far as my information goes, the children of these ethical divorcees tend to pay much less attention to the ecstasies of romantic love and much more attention to the companionate aspects of marriage and the pleasure of parenthood. Tender, nurturing fatherhood, which is so marked a feature of the family life of the youngest adult educated men in the United States and Britain, represents a very great change in men's emotional lives, and one for which there is no precedent in history. It seems probable that it will be incompatible with the very high valuation of romantic love which distinguished their parents' and grandparents' generations.

Many signs suggest that the pleasures of parenthood are becoming the most valued aspect of marriage in prosperous Western society; and this would imply that romantic love is again being devalued, except for those few for whom it is a temperamental necessity. If this be so, it will make for a calmer and more stable society, valuing permanent domestic happiness above the temporary ecstasies of passion. And then the universal demand for romantic love of the last two centuries will pass into history as one of the strange developments of which human beings are capable, somewhat like the dancing mania of the Middle Ages, or the glossolalia, the speaking with tongues, which falls on whole congregations in some ecstatic religious cults. As with these and the other examples earlier mentioned, a rare human potentiality will have for a short period dominated whole societies.

Further Questions

1. Have you ever thought you were in love with someone and then changed your mind about ever having been in love with them?
2. Have you felt social pressure (parental pressure or peer pressure) to fall in love?
3. Can you think of possible situations (e.g., the person who is too old or the "wrong" sexual orientation) in which there is definite pressure *not* to fall in love?

IV.4   Lovers Through the Looking Glass

KATH WESTON

Kath Weston discusses same-sex relationships. She sees a potential problem of incompleteness, because the pair has no genital or gendered difference; thus, each appears to be seeking his or her own reflection, as in a looking glass. Sometimes this sameness turns out to be fictional, as in the myth that gay men (like men everywhere?) want sex, while lesbians (like women everywhere?) want love.

Weston teaches in the Department of Social and Behavioral Sciences at Arizona State University West. *Families We Choose: Lesbians, Gays, Kinship,* from which this selection was taken, is her first book. Another excerpt appears in Part VI.

Reading Questions

1. Has entering into a romantic relationship (e.g., "coming out" by entering into a same-sex relationship) ever relieved you of a sense of "being the only one"?
2. Do you accept the idea that men form romantic relationships primarily for sex, whereas women form them primarily for love?
3. Have you ever entered a relationship (romantic or friendship) with the surprising realization that you see yourself in the other person?

But the picture? What was he to say of that? It held the secret of his life, and told his story. It had taught him to love his own beauty. Would it teach him to loathe his own soul?
—OSCAR WILDE, *The Picture of Dorian Gray*

VIEWED AGAINST THE BACKDROP of accounts that ground erotic relations in the symbolism of genital and gendered difference, lesbian or gay lovers appear "the same" and therefore incomplete. Looking-glass imagery casts gay couples in the one-dimensional relations of a likeness defined by its opposition to the differences of anatomy and gender understood to configure heterosexual marriage, sexuality, and procreation. To the extent that heterosexuals view lesbian or gay lovers as two like halves that cannot be reconciled to make a whole, gay relationships seem to yield a cultural unit deficient in meaning (which, as any good structuralist knows, must be generated through contrast). Representations that draw on mirror imagery reduce this apparent similarity of gay or lesbian partners to mere replication of the self, a narcissistic relation that creates no greater totality and brings little new into the world.. . .

The Looking-Glass Other

. . . In coming-out narratives, seeking one's own reflection often symbolizes an effort to affirm a coherent self in a situation that promises (or threatens) to transform identity. After his first night at a gay bar, as Al Collins told the story, "The next day at work I remember I went into the restroom and I looked at myself in the mirror—it was so funny—and I told myself, 'Okay, you're gay, but you're not weird!'" In another anecdote, a man described a mirror window that dominated the outside door to a gay bar, preventing passers-by from seeing in but permitting the narrator to pass through and encounter revelations about "gay life" on the other side. By evoking the popular notion of traveling through the looking glass to other realms, the mirror can serve not only to establish coherence of identity but also to signify an escape from isolation on an extended journey to gayness. Coming out presents one context in which the paradox of seeing ourselves in the act of gazing upon another presents a welcome alternative to the conventionalized terror of remaining imprisoned in the belief of being "the only one." . . .

Given the widespread influence of imagery that emphasizes gendered continuities between gay partners, it should not be surprising to find that lesbians and gay men in the Bay Area tended to depict one another as approaching relationships from different directions—women from the side of love and men from the side of sex. When they spoke in generalities, most agreed on the terms of the cultural equation: love + sex = a

relationship. To call a relationship "committed" signaled for both men and women not only a mutual intention for it to endure, but often a claim to kinship as well. This ideal combination of emotional with physical unity made gay couples "about" love and friendship as well as sex, in a manner consistent with twentieth-century ideologies of companionate marriage. But in their coming-out stories, men frequently highlighted the shock of realizing that it could be possible for two men to love, dance, kiss erotically, become jealous, or have ongoing relationships rather than a string of sexual encounters. Women, in contrast, were more likely to report originally finding it easy to imagine love between women without recognizing the option of adding an erotic component (cf. Peplau et al. 1978:8). When I asked interview participants if they were currently involved in a relationship, a few were uncertain how to answer. Of those who hesitated, the women wondered whether they should count primary emotional bonds as relationships in the absence of sexual involvement, while the men wondered whether to include routinized sexual relationships that lacked emotional depth and commitment.

Identifying (gay) men with sex and (lesbian) women with love reinforces the appearance of an overwhelming continuity and similarity between partners who share a common gender identity. Significantly, interviews and everyday encounters also turned up plenty of exceptions to such gender-typed generalizations: men whose first same-sex involvement occurred with a best friend, women sexually active with multiple partners since childhood. In a humorous play on conventional understandings of gendered difference, Louise Romero portrayed herself being socialized into the proper way for a lesbian to go about meeting a partner. . . .

Coffee goes good. Usually coffee first date, and then they go to bed with you, but otherwise forget it. . . . My other friend, Stacey, that I lived with, she said, "Louise, you got to stop going to bed with somebody in one night. You can't just do that. You got to date for a few months, and *then* go to bed with them." I said, "Date?" She said, "That's the only way you get a steady girlfriend. You just can't rush into things." So I tried it once with this one woman. She came over for dinner. I fixed it real nice, I had the fireplace going and everything. And then I talked to her the next day and stuff. She goes, "Well, I didn't think you were interested." It was like she put it on *me*. She wanted to go to bed that night!

With the advent of AIDS, gay wit pointed out the ironic combination of a "new romanticism" and more cautious attitude toward sex among gay men with the "rediscovery" of sex by lesbians. During the 1980s the same gay publications that featured how-to articles on dating for gay men presented lesbians with tongue-in-cheek tips on cruising for a sexual partner. Strip shows, erotic magazines, more candid discussions of sexuality, and debates about controversial practices like s/m captured the attention of many lesbians in the Bay Area during this decade. Within the same time frame, according to a survey conducted by the San Francisco AIDS Foundation, gay men reported having less sex, safe or unsafe (Helquist 1985). Some concluded from such survey results that sex had become less important to gay men, yet what I observed was the development of new forms of camaraderie in the face of the epidemic, accompanied by a redefinition of what qualifies as sex. "Years ago," Harold Sanders maintained,

> the way men would treat each other in a sexual context, it would be very covert. Then there might be something like [gruff voice], "Do you want to suck my cock?" And you knew that what the other person wanted was the same kind of tenderness and sharing of affection that you wanted, but that you could not possibly exempt [yourself from] that definition of being a man.

In the early 1980s, gay men incorporated miniature teddy bears into the handkerchief color code developed to indicate preferences for various specialized sexual practices. Handkerchiefs of particular colors placed in particular pockets (right or left) coexisted with this novel symbol of the desire to hug or be hugged, to "share emotion." A similar move toward integrating love and caring with masculinity and toughness surfaced in the context of AIDS organizing. Pamphlets distributed by a major AIDS organization in San Francisco displayed the title "A Call to Arms" next to the graphic of a teddy bear, mixing metaphors of militarism (the battle with AIDS) and affection. In the 1986 Gay Pride Parade one man had handcuffed a teddy bear to the back of his motorcycle where a lover might ride, while another dressed in a full set of leathers carried a small bear attached to a picture of his lover and his lover's date of death.[1]

To a degree, then, the identification of sex and emotion with men and women, respectively, would seem to have blurred for gay men and lesbians during the 1980s. Yet this apparent integration of the two domains coincided with a sense of exploring unknown territories that members of the "opposite gender" would better understand. If a gay man wanted to know about dating and romance, the person to go to for information was a woman; if a lesbian wanted to try picking up someone in a bar, why not ask a gay male friend for advice? Ideologies of gendered contrast and continuity also persisted in the form of the common belief that gay men have difficulty maintaining relationships, whereas lesbian couples suffer from too much intimacy. Among interview participants, the longest same-sex relationships listed by lesbians had endured on average for more years than the longest same-sex relationships listed by gay men. However, based upon this limited sample, the gap appeared to narrow as the number of years together extended. Nearly equal numbers of men and women had partners at the time of the interview, while similar proportions of single women and men claimed they desired a committed relationship. . . .

For every instance of a gay man or lesbian following the cultural logic of the looking glass, another portrayal contradicted or inverted its terms. When comparing themselves to straight men, many gay men described themselves as more sensitive or nurturing; in certain contexts, lesbians tended to present self-sufficiency, strength, and independence as characteristically lesbian traits. In the specific context of discourse on lovers, however, notions of gay relationships as relationships of likeness in which partners reflect back to one another their common gender identity shaped the way both lesbians and gay men configured eroticism and commitment.

Another correlate of the mirror metaphor, with its stress on sameness and the intensification of gender within gay relationships, is the application to couples of normative expectations that have long since been discredited in association with community. Roberta Osabe, like many of her peers, reported an initial anticipation of perfect harmony with her lover based on a shared gender identity.

> When I realized that just because you were a lesbian doesn't mean your relationships with women are cut out—it doesn't mean you'll find happiness—that's when I *really* got depressed. 'Cause I thought it was gonna be just like la-la-la, you know—flowers (laughs). Happiness! I'd found the yellow brick road, and it was on the way to the Emerald City. [Then] I realized you still had a shitty job. You still had all your problems. People are still gonna leave you. You're still gonna be alone, basically. And that was a *big* disappointment.

To search for the man or woman in the mirror, the lover at the end of a journey to self-love and self-acceptance, is to fall under the spell of the oversimplified contrasts of likeness and difference implicit in the mirror metaphor. As Paulette Ducharme observed, "I do definitely think I have a preference for women's bodies over men's bodies. But also [a preference for] beings—there are beings in those bodies, and all women certainly aren't exactly the same." In addition to idiosyncratic differences such as squeezing toothpaste

from different parts of the tube, differences of class, age, race, ethnicity, and a host of other identities that crosscut gender are sufficient to put to rest the notion of a single unified woman's or man's standpoint. The assumption that gender identity will be the primary *subjective* identity for every lesbian or gay man, universally and without respect to context, remains just that: an assumption.

Consider the case of interracial couples. Far from presenting an inherently unproblematic situation of sameness and identification between partners, the interracial aspect of a relationship can become a point of saliency that overwhelms any sense of likeness. For Leroy Campbell, a particular sort of difference, rooted in racist interpretations of the meaning of skin color and leading to painful reversals of situational expectations, became the overriding issue when he talked about trying to meet other men through the bars.

> See, I don't know if you can imagine what it's like seeing somebody walking towards you, or being in a bar and looking at someone, and feeling attracted to them, when there's a possibility that if you walk up to them and talk to them, that they're gonna say, 'I don't like black people.' So you have this perception of being attracted to this person who might *hate* you.

When issues of race and racism came up in her three-year relationship with a white woman, explained Eriko Yoshikawa, who was Japanese, "it always makes us feel how different we are, and it creates a certain kind of distance." On another occasion, Eriko's lover cautioned, "We're careful not to attribute all differences between us to the most obvious difference between us."

Some lesbians and gay men have extended mirror imagery to race and ethnicity with the argument that getting involved with someone of another race means "not really facing yourself," or through their expectation that relationships with someone of the same ethnic identification would prove intrinsically easier to negotiate. Yet likeness no more automatically follows from a common racial identity than from a shared gender identity. The challenge is to understand how, why, and in what contexts individuals abstract gender from a range of potential identities, elevating gender identity into *the* axis for defining sameness.

Some of the same individuals who emphasized gendered continuity when discussing their current lovers highlighted divergent racial identities, class backgrounds, or ages to explain recent breakups and describe past relationships. Because people in the United States conventionally attribute separation and divorce to "irreconcilable differences," here context becomes significant in determining whether the language of the looking glass will come into play. That individuals enjoy considerable interpretive leeway in this regard, however, is evident from a comment made by Kenny Nash as a black gay man: "It became more a matter of being gay [than being black] if a man I was with was white. . . . It was like, 'If you react badly because I'm with this man, it's not because he's white, it's because he's a man.'". . .

Narcissism, Kinship, and Class Convictions

Because gay and lesbian identity is organized primarily in terms of gender and sexuality rather than production or work, the most visible gay institutions have occupied the "personal" (read: egocentered) sphere of leisure and consumption. Yet the heterogeneity of the interview sample for this study alone belies conjecture that gay people are predominantly white, male, wealthy, selfish, recreation-oriented, and above all single (cf. Goodman et al. 1983). The very differences among lesbians and gay men that led to the widespread disaffiliation from the concept of a unified "gay community" affirm the absence of any uniform "gay lifestyle." To claim a lesbian or gay identity is not necessarily to subscribe to a particular way of organizing one's time or interests. . . .

People in the United States often view selfishness as an outgrowth of narcissistic self-absorption, but in the case of homosexuality allegations of selfishness also relate to beliefs about how les-

bians and gay men are situated within class relations. Typical of the class stereotyping of gay people is this unsupported generalization from a *Boston Herald* editorial against passage of a gay rights bill: "Gays tend to be better off financially than the average American" (in Allen 1987). There is a certain inconsistency, however, in accusing gay people of being irresponsibly "promiscuous" and failing to sustain stable relationships (much less family), while simultaneously attacking them for an affluence predicated upon the combined power of two incomes. Such portraits of class allegiances are further complicated by the (often erroneous) perception of gay men as leaders in the gentrification of urban areas. In Terri Burnett's opinion, gentrification in the Bay Area had fueled "anger that the loss of [neighborhood and ethnic] community is based upon gay male community."

Attributions of wealth that ascribe class privilege to all gay people are linked not only to the reduction of sexual identity to sexuality, but also to presumptions that gay men and lesbians lack family ties. "Doubtless to many . . . people," Quentin Crisp (1968:130) observed of his native Britain, "an effeminate homosexual was simply someone who liked sex but could not face the burdens, responsibilities, and decisions that might crush him if he married a woman." In the United States the very notion of responsibility is closely tied to family and adulthood. Among the well-to-do in the nineteenth century, "gay" described the relatively carefree existence led by single white women (Cott 1977).

In the context of families, responsibility carries an implicitly social orientation: a person is responsible to someone or for someone. A few lesbians and gay men in the Bay Area subscribed to the ideology of family as a burden and responsibility that restricted "personal freedom." When Nils Norgaard talked about family, he used the word in a procreative sense:

> If you get married, you sacrifice the rest of your life to raise a family—or a lot, if you get kids. And that's a very big responsibility. And a family

is more than the wife and a kid. You usually have a couple of dogs, you have your own little life with your family. And I'm not sure if I want that, because if I don't get married, I will have all the time for myself. And I can go wherever I want. I can travel, and I can see the world. I can't do that with a family so much.

More common, however, were complaints about coworkers and acquaintances who assumed that a gay man or lesbian had no "immediate family" or financial dependents. If an individual was known to have a lover, acquaintances sometimes trivialized the relationship or dismissed it as an illegitimate derivative of the self. Even in the wake of national publicity about custody cases and the lesbian baby boom, many heterosexuals still do not recognize the potential for lesbians and gay men to become involved in childcare and co-parenting arrangements, much less view them as persons capable of producing biological offspring. In a time and a culture that links sexual activity to identity, the nonprocreative character of sex between women or men casts gay men and lesbians as essentially nonprocreative beings. Since most people in the United States see discretionary income as an indicator of class privilege and a prerequisite for social mobility, the presumption that gay people do not contribute to the economic survival of others, including kin, lends a dubious credence to representations that systematically assign lesbians and gay men to a position of class dominance.

Not surprisingly, many of the gay men and lesbians I met had become adept at refuting accusations of gay selfishness and irresponsibility. Speakers from gay organizations who addressed high school classes, church groups, and other predominantly heterosexual audiences drew attention to the number of lesbian and gay parents and highlighted the contributions of gay people active in social service professions such as teaching or social work. Some people integrated notions of racial or ethnic identity into their rebuttals. Danny Carlson, himself Native American, told me he identified other lesbian and gay

Indians by their selflessness. "Gay Indian people," he said, "are very creative. Very progressive. And when they do things, they think of the people, they don't think of themself." Placing the people's needs over one's own Danny considered part of "the Indian way."

Evidence abounds that lesbians and gay men, like others in this society, create, maintain, and fulfill responsibilities to social others. Yet depictions that locate gay and lesbian lovers within a relation of sameness reinforce popular perceptions that gay people enjoy class privilege because they lack dependents and kinship ties. At issue are the nuances of narcissism embedded in a mirror imagery that conflates the persons within lesbian and gay couples, turning relations symbolically constituted by love back in upon the self.

NOTE

1. See Lon G. Nungesser, 1986, *Epidemic of Courage: Facing AIDS in America.* New York: St. Martin's Press, for stories of gay men with AIDS who describe learning about intimacy and affection through coping with the disease.

REFERENCES

Allen, Ronnie. 1987. "Times Have Changed at the *Herald.*" *Gay Community News* (June 28–July 4).

Cott, Nancy F. 1977. *The Bonds of Womanhood: "Woman's Sphere" in New England, 1780–1835.* New Haven: Yale University Press.

Crisp, Quentin. 1968. *The Naked Civil Servant.* New York: Holt, Rinehart & Winston.

Goodman, Gerre, George Lakey, Judy Lashof, and Erika Thorne. 1983. *No Turning Back: Lesbian and Gay Liberation for the '80s.* Philadelphia: New Society Publishers.

Helquist, M. 1985. "New Behavior Survey Released by SF AIDS Foundation." *Coming Up!* (August).

Nestle, Joan. 1987. *A Restricted Country.* Ithaca, N.Y.: Firebrand Books.

Peplau, Letitia Anne, Susan Cochran, Karen Rook, and Christine Padesky. 1978. "Loving Women: Attachment and Autonomy in Lesbian Relationships." *Journal of Social Issues* 34(3):7–27.

Further Questions

1. Have you ever believed that gays and lesbians, despite their social problems, are better off romantically, because they do not acquire responsibilities for dependents? Is this belief realistic?

2. Is it realistic to think of a gay or lesbian as so preoccupied with his or her sexuality that matters like community service and general awareness of other people are relatively neglected?

IV.5   The Woman in Love

SIMONE DE BEAUVOIR

Simone de Beauvoir maintains that there are significant gender differences, in heterosexual romantic relationships, caused by differences in social situations. Love plays a bigger part in the life of women because men have more other important things they must do. We have already seen how men are advantaged in the workplace. Accordingly, success for men depends to a large extent on workplace achievement. Women's best course to success in life, on the other hand, is often through romantic attachments. As might be expected, this disparity skews romantic relationships in undesirable ways.

Other selections by de Beauvoir appear in Parts I, VI, X, and XIII.

Reading Questions

1. Should a woman expect to abandon her own personality, likes, dislikes, habits, and activities when she enters a romantic relationship, and replace them with those of her beloved? Should a man expect to abandon these things to the same extent?

2. Is serving the other person an appropriate approach to a romantic relationship?

3. Can the fact that you have an ongoing relationship justify your existence?

THE WORD *LOVE* has by no means the same sense for both sexes, and this is one cause of the serious misunderstandings that divide them. Byron well said: "Man's love is of man's life a thing apart; 'Tis woman's whole existence." Nietzsche expresses the same idea in *The Gay Science:*

The single word love in fact signifies two different things for man and woman. What woman understands by love is clear enough: it is not only devotion, it is a total gift of body and soul, without reservation, without regard for anything whatever. This unconditional nature of her love is what makes it a *faith*,[1] the only one she has. As for man, if he loves a woman, what he *wants* is that love from her; he is in consequence far from postulating the same sentiment for himself as for woman; if there should be men who also felt that desire for complete abandonment, upon my word, they would not be men.

Men have found it possible to be passionate lovers at certain times in their lives, but there is not one of them who could be called "a great lover";[2] in their most violent transports, they never abdicate completely; even on their knees before a mistress, what they still want is to take possession of her; at the very heart of their lives they remain sovereign subjects; the beloved woman is only one value among others; they wish to integrate her into their existence and not to squander it entirely on her. For woman, on the contrary, to love is to relinquish everything for the benefit of a master. As Cécile Sauvage puts it: "Woman must forget her own personality when she is in love. It is a law of nature. A woman is nonexistent without a master. Without a master, she is a scattered bouquet."

The fact is that we have nothing to do here with laws of nature. It is the difference in their situations that is reflected in the difference men and women show in their conceptions of love. The individual who is a subject, who is himself, if he has the courageous inclination toward transcendence, endeavors to extend his grasp on the world: he is ambitious, he acts. But an inessential creature is incapable of sensing the absolute at the heart of her subjectivity; a being doomed to immanence cannot find self-realization in acts. Shut up in the sphere of the relative, destined to the male from childhood, habituated to seeing in him a superb being whom she cannot possibly equal, the woman who has not repressed her claim to humanity will dream of transcending her being toward one of these superior beings, of amalgamating herself with the sovereign subject. There is no other way out for her than to lose herself, body and soul, in him who is represented to her as the absolute, as the essential. Since she is anyway doomed to dependence, she will prefer to serve a god rather than obey tyrants—parents, husband, or protector. She chooses to desire her enslavement so ardently that it will seem to her the expression of her liberty; she will try to rise above her situation as inessential object by fully accepting it; through her flesh, her feelings, her behavior, she will enthrone

him as supreme value and reality: she will humble herself to nothingness before him. Love becomes for her a religion. . . .

. . . [W]hat woman wants in the first place is to serve; for in responding to her lover's demands, a woman will feel that she is necessary; she will be integrated with his existence, she will share his worth, she will be justified. Even mystics like to believe, according to Angelus Silesius, that God needs man; otherwise they would be giving themselves in vain. The more demands the man makes, the more gratified the woman feels. Although the seclusion imposed by Victor Hugo on Juliette Drouet weighed heavily on the young woman, one feels that she is happy in obeying him: to stay by the fireside is to do something for the master's pleasure. She tries also to be useful to him in a positive way. She cooks choice dishes for him and arranges a little nest where he can be at home; she looks after his clothes. "I want you to tear your clothes as much as possible," she writes to him, "and I want to mend and clean them all myself." She reads the papers, clips out articles, classifies letters and notes, copies manuscripts, for him. She is grieved when the poet entrusts a part of the work to his daughter Léopoldine.

Such traits are found in every woman in love. If need be, she herself tyrannizes over herself in her lover's name; all she is, all she has, every moment of her life, must be devoted to him and thus gain their *raison d'être;* she wishes to possess nothing save in him; what makes her unhappy is for him to require nothing of her, so much so that a sensitive lover will invent demands. She at first sought in love a confirmation of what she was, of her past, of her personality; but she also involves her future in it, and to justify her future she puts it in the hands of one who possesses all values. . . .

The woman who finds pleasure in submitting to male caprices also admires the evident action of a sovereign-free being in the tyranny practiced on her. It must be noted that if for some reason the lover's prestige is destroyed, his blows and demands become odious; they are precious only if they manifest the divinity of the loved one. But if they do, it is intoxicating joy to feel herself the prey of another's free action. An existent finds it a most amazing adventure to be justified through the varying and imperious will of another; one wearies of living always in the same skin, and blind obedience is the only chance for radical transformation known to a human being. Woman is thus slave, queen, flower, hind, stained-glass window, wanton, servant, courtesan, muse, companion, mother, sister, child, according to the fugitive dreams, the imperious commands, of her lover. She lends herself to these metamorphoses with ravishment as long as she does not realize that all the time her lips have retained the unvarying savor of submission. On the level of love, as on that of eroticism, it seems evident that masochism is one of the bypaths taken by the unsatisfied woman, disappointed in both the other and herself; but it is not the natural tendency of a happy resignation. Masochism perpetuates the presence of the ego in a bruised and degraded condition; love brings forgetfulness of self in favor of the essential subject.

The supreme goal of human love, as of mystical love, is identification with the loved one.[3] The measure of values, the truth of the world, are in his consciousness; hence it is not enough to serve him. The woman in love tries to see with his eyes; she reads the books he reads, prefers the pictures and the music he prefers; she is interested only in the landscapes she sees with him, in the ideas that come from him; she adopts his friendships, his enmities, his opinions; when she questions herself, it is his reply she tries to hear; she wants to have in her lungs the air he has already breathed; the fruits and flowers that do not come from his hands have no taste and no fragrance. Her idea of location in space, even, is upset: the center of the world is no longer the place where she is, but that occupied by her lover; all roads lead to his home, and from it. She uses his words, mimics his gestures, acquires his eccentricities and his tics. "I am Heathcliffe," says Catherine in *Wuthering Heights;* that is the cry of every woman in love; she is another incarnation of her loved one, his reflection, his double: she is *he*. She lets her own world collapse in contingence, for she really lives in his.

The supreme happiness of the woman in love is to be recognized by the loved man as a part of himself; when he says "we," she is associated and identified with him, she shares his prestige and reigns with him over the rest of the world; she never tires of repeating—even to excess—this delectable "we." As one necessary to a being who is absolute necessity, who stands forth in the world seeking necessary goals and who gives her back the world in necessary form, the woman in love acquires in her submission that magnificent possession, the absolute. It is this certitude that gives her lofty joys; she feels exalted to a place at the right hand of God. Small matter to her to have only second place if she has *her* place, forever, in a most wonderfully ordered world. So long as she is in love and is loved by and necessary to her loved one, she feels herself wholly justified: she knows peace and happiness. . . .

But this glorious felicity rarely lasts. No man really is God. The relations sustained by the mystic with the divine Absence depend on her fervor alone; but the deified man, who is not God, is present. And from this fact are to come the torments of the woman in love. . . . [W]oman, in assuming her role as the inessential, accepting a total dependence, creates a hell for herself. Every woman in love recognizes herself in Hans Andersen's little mermaid who exchanged her fishtail for feminine legs through love and then found herself walking on needles and live coals. It is not true that the loved man is absolutely necessary, above chance and circumstance, and the woman is not necessary to him; he is not really in a position to justify the feminine being who is consecrated to his worship, and he does not permit himself to be possessed by her.

An authentic love should assume the contingence of the other; that is to say, his lacks, his limitations, and his basic gratuitousness. It would not pretend to be a mode of salvation, but a human inter-relation. Idolatrous love attributes an absolute value to the loved one, a first falsity that is brilliantly apparent to all outsiders. "*He isn't worth all that love*," is whispered around the woman in love, and posterity wears a pitying smile at the thought of certain pallid heroes, like Count Guibert. It is a searing disappointment to the woman to discover the faults, the mediocrity of her idol. Novelists, like Colette, have often depicted this bitter anguish. The disillusion is still more cruel than that of the child who sees the father's prestige crumble, because the woman has herself selected the one to whom she has given over her entire being.

Even if the chosen one is worthy of the profoundest affection, his truth is of the earth, earthy, and it is no longer this mere man whom the woman loves as she kneels before a supreme being; she is duped by that spirit of seriousness which declines to take values as incidental—that is to say, declines to recognize that they have their source in human existence. . . . She offers him incense, she bows down, but she is not a friend to him since she does not realize that he is in danger in the world, that his projects and his aims are as fragile as he is; regarding him as the Faith, the Truth, she misunderstands his freedom —his hesitancy and anguish of spirit. This refusal to apply a human measuring scale to the lover explains many feminine paradoxes. The woman asks a favor from her lover. Is it granted? Then he is generous, rich, magnificent; he is kingly, he is divine. Is it refused? Then he is avaricious, mean, cruel; he is a devilish or a bestial creature. One might be tempted to object: if a "yes" is such an astounding and superb extravagance, should one be surprised at a "no"? If the "no" discloses such abject selfishness, why wonder so much at the "yes"? Between the superhuman and the inhuman is there no place for the human?

A fallen god is not a man: he is a fraud; the lover has no other alternative than to prove that he really is this king accepting adulation—or to confess himself a usurper. If he is no longer adored, he must be trampled on. In virtue of that glory with which she has haloed the brow of her beloved, the woman in love forbids him any weakness; she is disappointed and vexed if he does not live up to

the image she has put in his place. If he gets tired or careless, if he gets hungry or thirsty at the wrong time, if he makes a mistake or contradicts himself, she asserts that he is "not himself" and she makes a grievance of it. In this indirect way she will go so far as to take him to task for any of his ventures that she disapproves; she judges her judge, and she denies him his liberty so that he may deserve to remain her master. . . .

It is one of the curses afflicting the passionate woman that her generosity is soon converted into exigence. Having become identified with another, she wants to make up for her loss; she must take possession of that other person who has captured her. She gives herself to him entirely; but he must be completely available to receive this gift. She dedicates every moment to him, but he must be present at all times; she wants to live only in him—but she wants to live, and he must therefore devote himself to making her live. . . .

And yet she is not willing for him to be nothing but her prisoner. This is one of the painful paradoxes of love: a captive, the god is shorn of his divinity. Woman preserves her transcendence by transferring it to him; but he must bring it to bear upon the whole world. If two lovers sink together in the absolute of passion, all their liberty is degraded into immanence; death is then the only solution. That is one of the meanings of the *Tristan and Isolde* myth. Two lovers destined solely for each other are already dead: they die of ennui, of the slow agony of a love that feeds on itself.

Woman is aware of this danger. Save in crises of jealous frenzy, she herself demands that man be all project, all action, for he is no more a hero if he engages in no exploits. The knight departing for new adventures offends his lady, yet she has nothing but contempt for him if he remains at her feet. This is the torture of the impossible love; the woman wants to possess the man wholly, but she demands that he transcend any gift that could possibly be possessed: a free being cannot be *had*. . . .

Even in mutual love there is fundamental difference in the feelings of the lovers, which the woman tries to hide. The man must certainly be capable of justifying himself without her, since she hopes to be justified through him. If he is necessary to her, it means that she is evading her liberty; but if he accepts his liberty, without which he would be neither a hero nor even a man, no person or thing can be necessary to him. The dependence accepted by woman comes from her weakness; how, therefore, could she find a reciprocal dependence in the man she loves in his strength?

A passionately demanding soul cannot find repose in love, because the end she has in view is inherently contradictory. Torn and tortured, she risks becoming a burden to the man instead of his slave, as she had dreamed; unable to feel indispensable, she becomes importunate, a nuisance. This is, indeed, a common tragedy. If she is wiser and less intransigent, the woman in love becomes resigned. She is not all, she is not necessary: it is enough to be useful; another might easily fill her place: she is content to be the one who is there. She accepts her servitude without demanding the same in return. Thus she can enjoy a modest happiness; but even within these limits it will not be unclouded. . . .

Genuine love ought to be founded on the mutual recognition of two liberties; the lovers would then experience themselves both as self and as other: neither would give up transcendence, neither would be mutilated; together they would manifest values and aims in the world. For the one and the other, love would be revelation of self by the gift of self and enrichment of the world. . . .

Men have vied with one another in proclaiming that love is woman's supreme accomplishment. "A woman who loves as a woman becomes only the more feminine," says Nietzsche; and Balzac: "Among the first-rate, man's life is fame, woman's life is love. Woman is man's equal only when she makes her life a perpetual offering, as that of man is perpetual action." But therein, again, is a cruel deception, since what she offers, men are in no wise anxious to accept. Man has no need of the unconditional devotion he claims, nor of the idolatrous love that flatters his vanity; he accepts them only on condition that he need not satisfy the reciprocal demands these attitudes imply. He preaches to woman that she should give—and her gifts bore him to distraction; she is left in embarrassment with her useless offerings, her empty life. On the day when it will be possible for woman to love not in her weakness but in her strength, not to escape herself but to find herself, not to abase herself but to assert herself—on that day love will become for her, as for man, a source of life and not of mortal danger. In the meantime, love represents in its most touching form the curse that lies heavily upon woman confined in the feminine universe, woman mutilated, insufficient unto herself. The innumerable martyrs to love bear witness against the injustice of a fate that offers a sterile hell as ultimate salvation. . . .

NOTES

1. Nietzsche's italics.

2. In the sense that a woman may sometimes be called *"une grande amoureuse."*—TR.

3. See T. Reik's *Psychology of Sex Relations* (Farrar, Straus & Co., 1945).—TR.

Further Questions

1. Is love one good way of escaping "living always in the same skin"?

2. Can someone who puts herself in your hands in the name of love eventually turn out to be more of a burden than a benefit?

3. Are we ready for a time in heterosexual romance when two people meet each other halfway, each allowing the other the same amount of liberty of thought, choice, and action as he takes for himself?

The Arrogant Eye, the Loving Eye, and the Beloved   IV.6

MARILYN FRYE

Marilyn Frye distinguishes between the arrogant eye, whose aim is to appropriate for itself, and the loving eye, which recognizes the independence of the other. Her hope is that women who love women will be a positive force in helping women to free themselves from the arrogant eye of men and to realize and appreciate the independence of women.

Other selections by Marilyn Frye appear in Parts I and VII.

Reading Questions

1. Can you think of a situation in which a person consistently behaved in a certain way largely because this was expected of her, and in which these expectations were organized largely around someone else's interests?

2. Should we unconditionally praise those who serve others, or should we look into the circumstances and assess the service accordingly?

3. Can a person love someone, but still recognize where her own interests leave off and the other person's interests begin?

The Arrogant Eye

. . . THE IDEA OF THERE BEING more than one body's worth of substance, will, and wit lined up behind one's projects has its appeal. As one woman said, after going through the reasons, "My God, who *wouldn't* want a wife?"[1] Ti-Grace Atkinson pointed out in her analysis of the roots of oppression that there is an enormous gap between what one can do and what one can imagine doing. Humans have what she referred to as a "constructive imagination" which, though obviously a blessing in some ways, also is a source of great frustration. For it provides a constant tease of imagined accomplishments and imagined threats—to neither of which are we physically equal.[2] The majority of people do not deal with this problem and temptation by enslaving others overtly and by force . . .

But many, many people, most of them male, are in a cultural and material position to accomplish, to a great degree, the same end by other means and under other descriptions, means and descriptions which obscure to them and to their victims the fact that their end is the same. The end: acquisition of the service of others. The means: variations on the theme of enslavement—dis-integrating an integrated human organism and grafting its substance to oneself. . . .

The Bible says that all of nature (including woman) exists for man. Man is invited to subdue the earth and have dominion over every living thing on it, all of which is said to exist "to you" "for meat."[3] Woman is created to be man's helper. This captures in myth Western Civilization's primary answer to the philosophical question of man's place in nature: everything that is is

Abridged from "In and Out of Harm's Way: Arrogance and Love," in The Politics of Reality: Essays in Feminist Theory *(Trumansburg, NY: The Crossing Press, 1983), pp. 52–83.*

resource for man's exploitation. With this world view, men see with arrogant eyes which organize everything seen with reference to themselves and their own interests. The arrogating perceiver is a teleologist, a believer that everything exists and happens for some purpose, and he tends to animate things, imagining attitudes toward himself as the animating motives. Everything is either "for me" or "against me." This is the kind of vision that interprets the rock one trips on as hostile, the bolt one cannot loosen as stubborn, the woman who made meatloaf when he wanted spaghetti as "bad" (though he didn't say what he wanted). The arrogant perceiver does not countenance the possibility that the Other is independent, indifferent. The feminist separatist can only be a man-hater; Nature is called "Mother."

The arrogant perceiver falsifies—the Nature who makes both green beans and *Bacillus botulinus* doesn't give a passing damn whether humans live or die[4]—but he also coerces the objects of his perception into satisfying the conditions his perception imposes. He tries to accomplish in a glance what the slave masters and batterers accomplish by extended use of physical force, and to a great extent he succeeds. He manipulates the environment, perception and judgment of her whom he perceives so that her recognized options are limited, and the course she chooses will be such as coheres with his purposes. The seer himself is an element of her environment. The structures of his perception are as solid a fact in her situation as are the structures of a chair which seats her too low or of gestures which threaten.

How one sees another and how one expects the other to behave are in tight interdependence, and how one expects another to behave is a large factor in determining how the other does behave. Naomi Weisstein, in "Psychology Constructs the Female," reviewed experiments which show dramatically that this is true.

For instance, in one experiment subjects were to assign numbers to pictures of men's faces, with high numbers representing the subject's judgment that the man in the picture was a success-

ful person, and low numbers representing the subject's judgment that the man in the picture was an unsuccessful person. One group of experimenters was told that the subjects tended to rate the faces high; another group of experimenters was told that the subjects tended to rate the faces low. Each group of experimenters was instructed to follow precisely the same procedure: they were required to read to subjects a set of instructions and to *say nothing else*. For the 375 subjects run, the results show clearly that those subjects who performed the task with experimenters who expected high ratings gave high ratings, and those subjects who performed the task with experimenters who expected low ratings gave low ratings.[5]

When experimenters think the rats they are working with were bred for high intelligence, the rats they are working with learn faster; when the experimenters think their rats were bred for low intelligence, the rats learn less well. And children believed by their teachers to have high IQs show dramatic increases in their IQs. Weisstein concludes: "The concreteness of the changed conditions produced by expectations is a fact, a reality. . . . In some extremely important ways, people are what you expect them to be, or at least they behave as you expect them to behave."[6]

The experiments only boldly outline something we all know from experience. Women experience the coerciveness of this kind of "influence" when men perversely impose sexual meanings on our every movement. We know the palpable pressure of a man's reduction of our objection to an occasion for our instruction. Women do not so often experience ourselves imposing expectations on situations and making them stick, but some of the most awesome stories of women's successful resistance to male violence involve a woman's expecting the male assailant into the position of a little boy in the power of his mother.*

* I refer here to some experience of my own, and to such stories as the Success Stories included in "Do It Yourself-Self-Defense," by Pat James, in *Fight Back: Feminist Resistance to Male Violence,* edited by Frederique Delacoste & Felice Newman (Cleis Press, 1981), p. 205.

The power of expectations is enormous; it should be engaged and responded to attentively and with care. The arrogant perceiver engages it with the same unconsciousness with which he engages his muscles when he writes his name.

The arrogant perceiver's expectation creates in the space about him a sort of vacuum mold into which the other is sucked and held. But the other is not sucked into his structure always, nor always without resistance. In the absence of his manipulation, the other *is* not organized primarily with reference to his interests. To the extent that she is not shaped to his will, does not fit the conformation he imposes, there is friction, anomaly, or incoherence in his world. To the extent that he notices this incongruity, he can experience it in no other way than as something wrong with her. His perception is arrogating; his senses tell him that the world and everything in it (with the occasional exception of other men) is in the nature of things there *for* him, that she is by her constitution and *telos* his servant. He believes his senses. If woman does not serve man, it can only be because he is not a sufficiently skilled master or because there is something wrong with the woman. He may try to manage things better, but when that fails he can only conclude that she is defective: unnatural, flawed, broken, abnormal, damaged, sick. His norms of virtue and health are set according to the degree of congruence of the object of perception with the seer's interests. This is exactly wrong.

Though anyone might wish, for any of many reasons, to contribute to another's pursuit of her or his interests, the health and integrity of an organism is a matter of its being organized largely toward its own interests and welfare. The arrogant perceiver knows this in his own case, but he *arrogates* everything to himself and thus perceives as healthy or "right" everything that relates to him as his own substance does when he is healthy. But what's sauce for the gander is sauce for the goose. *She* is healthy and "working right" when *her* substance is organized primarily on principles which align it to *her* interests and wel-

fare. Cooperation is essential, of course, but it will not do that I arrange everything so that you get enough exercise: for me to be healthy, *I* must get enough exercise. My being adequately exercised is logically independent of your being so. . . .

The procurer-enslaver, working with overt force, constructs a situation in which the victim's pursuit of her own survival or health and her attempt to be good always require, as a matter of practical fact in that situation, actions which serve him. In the world constructed by the arrogant eye, this same connection is established not by terror but by definition.*

The official story about men who batter women is that they do so in large part because they suffer "low self-esteem." What this suggests to me is that they suffer a lack of arrogance and cannot fully believe in themselves as centers about which all else (but some other men) revolves and to which all else refers. Because of this they cannot effectively exercise the power of that expectation. But as men they "know" they are supposed to be centers of universes, so they are reduced to trying to create by force what more successful men, men who can carry off masculinity better, create by arrogant perception. This is, perhaps, one reason why some of the men who do not batter have contempt for men who do.

---

* Neither the arrogant perceiver nor the procurer works in a vacuum, of course. They are supported by a culture which in many ways "softens up" their victims for them, an economy which systematically places women in positions of economic dependence on men, and a community of men which threatens women with rape at every turn. Also, the existence of the procurers supports the arrogant perceiver by making him seem benign by comparison. The arrogant perceiver, in addition, has the support of a community of arrogant perceivers, among whom are all or most of the most powerful members of the community at large. I do want to claim that the power of perception, even exercised without "community support," is great; but as we normally experience it, it is augmented enormously by its being an instance of the "normal" perceiving among those who control the material media of culture and most other economic resources.

The Loving Eye

The attachment of the well-broken slave to the master has been confused with love. Under the name of Love, a willing and unconditional servitude has been promoted as something ecstatic, noble, fulfilling, and even redemptive. All praise is sung for the devoted wife who loves the husband and children she is willing to live for, and of the brave man who loves the god he is willing to kill for, the country he is willing to die for.

We can be taken in by this equation of servitude with love because we make two mistakes at once: we think, of both servitude and love, that they are selfless or unselfish. We tend to think of them as attachments in which the person is not engaged because of self-interest and does not pursue self-interest. The wife who married for money did not marry for love, we think; the mercenary soldier is despised by the loyal patriot. And the slave, we think, is selfless because she *can* do nothing but serve the interests of another. But this is wrong. Neither is the slave selfless, nor is the lover.

It is one mark of a voluntary association that the one person can survive displeasing the other, defying the other, dissociating from the other. The slave, the battered wife, the not-so-battered wife, is constantly in jeopardy. She is in a situation where she cannot, or reasonably believes she cannot, survive without the other's provision and protection, and where experience has made it credible to her that the other may kill her or abandon her if and when she displeases him. . . .

One who loves is not selfless either. If the loving eye is in any sense disinterested, it is not that the seer has lost herself, has no interests, or ignores or denies her interests. Any of these would seriously incapacitate her as a perceiver. What *is* the case, surely, is that unlike the slave or the master, the loving perceiver can see without the presupposition that the other poses a constant threat or that the other exists for the seer's service; nor does she see with the other's eye instead of her own. Her interest does not blend the seer and the seen, either empirically by terror or *a pri-*

ori by conceptual links forged by the arrogant eye. One who sees with a loving eye is separate from the other whom she sees. There are boundaries between them; she and the other are two; their interests are not identical; they are not blended in vital parasitic or symbiotic relations, nor does she believe they are or try to pretend they are.

The loving eye is a contrary of the arrogant eye.

The loving eye knows the independence of the other. It is the eye of a seer who knows that nature is indifferent. It is the eye of one who knows that to know the seen, one must consult something other than one's own will and interests and fears and imagination. One must look at the thing. One must look and listen and check and question.

The loving eye is one that pays a certain sort of attention. This attention can require a discipline but *not* a self-denial. The discipline is one of self-knowledge, knowledge of the scope and boundary of the self. What is required is that one know what are one's interests, desires and loathings, one's projects, hungers, fears and wishes, and that one know what is and what is not determined by these. In particular, it is a matter of being able to tell one's own interests from those of others and of knowing where one's self leaves off and another begins. Perhaps in another world this would be easy and not a matter of discipline, but here we are brought up among metaphysical cannibals and their robots. Some of us are taught we can have everything, some are taught we can have nothing. Either way we will acquire a great wanting. The wanting doesn't care about truth: it simplifies, where the truth is complex; it invents, when it should be investigating; it expects, when it should be waiting to find out; it would turn everything to its satisfaction; and what it finally thinks it cannot thus maneuver it hates. But the necessary discipline is not a denial of the wanting. On the contrary, it is a discipline of knowing and owning the wanting: identifying it, claiming it, knowing its scope, and through all this, knowing its distance from the truth.

The loving eye does not make the object of perception into something edible, does not try to assimilate it, does not reduce it to the size of the seer's desire, fear and imagination, and hence does not have to simplify. It knows the complexity of the other as something which will forever present new things to be known. The science of the loving eye would favor The Complexity Theory of Truth and presuppose The Endless Interestingness of the Universe.

The loving eye seems generous to its object, though it means neither to give nor to take, for not-being-invaded, not-being-coerced, not-being-annexed must be felt in a world such as ours as a great gift.

The Beloved

We who would love women, and well, who would change ourselves and change the world so that it is possible to love women well, we need to imagine the possibilities for what women might be if we lived lives free of the material and perceptual forces which subordinate women to men. The point is not to imagine a female human animal unaffected by the other humans around it, uninfluenced by its own and others' perceptions of others' interests, unaffected by culture. The point is only to imagine women not enslaved, to imagine these intelligent, willful and female bodies not subordinated in service to males, individually or via institutions (or to anybody, in any way); not pressed into a shape that suits an arrogant eye.

The forces which we want to imagine ourselves free of are a guide to what we might be when free of them. They mark the shape they mold us to, but they also suggest by implication the shapes we might have been without that molding. One can guess something of the magnitude and direction of the tendencies the thing would exhibit when free by attending to the magnitudes and directions of the forces required to confine and shape it. For instance, much pressure

is applied at the point of our verbal behavior, enforcing silence or limiting our speech.[7] One can reason that without that force we might show ourselves to be loquacious and perhaps prone to oratory, not to mention prone to saying things unpleasant to male ears. The threat of rape is a force of great magnitude which is, among other things, applied against our movement about the cities, towns and countryside. The implication is that without it a great many women might prove to be very prone to nomadic lives of exploration and adventure—why else should so much force be required to keep us at home?

But to speak most generally: the forces of men's material and perceptual violence mold Woman to dependence upon Man, in every meaning of 'dependence': contingent upon; conditional upon; necessitated by; defined in terms of; incomplete or unreal without; requiring the support or assistance of; being a subordinate part of; being an appurtenance to.

Dependence is forced upon us. It is not rash to speculate that without this force, much, most or all of what most or all of us are and do would not be contingent upon, conditional upon, necessitated by, or subordinate to any man or what belongs to or pertains to a man, men or masculinity. What we are and how we are, or what we would be and how we would be if not molded by the arrogating eye, is: *not molded to man, not dependent*.

I do not speak here of a specious absolute independence that would mean never responding to another's need and never needing another's response. I conceive here simply of a being whose needs and responses are not *bound* by concepts or by terror in a dependence upon those of another. The loving eye makes the correct assumption: the object of the seeing is *another* being whose existence and character are logically independent of the seer and who may be practically or empirically independent in any particular respect at any particular time.

. . . [T]here is in the fabric of our lives, not always visible but always affecting its texture and strength, a mortal dread of being outside the field of vision of the arrogant eye. That eye gives all things meaning by connecting all things to each other by way of their references to one point—Man. We fear that if we are not in that web of meaning there will be no meaning: our work will be meaningless, our lives of no value, our accomplishments empty, our identities illusory. The reason for this dread, I suggest, is that for most of us, including the exceptional, a woman existing outside the field of vision of man's arrogant eye is really inconceivable.

This is a terrible disability. If we have no intuition of ourselves as independent, unmediated beings in the world, then we cannot conceive ourselves surviving our liberation; for what our liberation will do is dissolve the structures and dismantle the mechanisms by which Woman is mediated by Man. If we cannot imagine ourselves surviving this, we certainly will not make it happen.

There probably is really no distinction, in the end, between imagination and courage. We can't imagine what we can't face, and we can't face what we can't imagine. To break out of the structures of the arrogant eye we have to dare to rely on ourselves to make meaning and we have to imagine ourselves beings capable of that: capable of weaving the web of meaning which will hold us in some kind of intelligibility. We do manage this, to some extent; but we also wobble and threaten to fall, like a beginner on a bicycle who does not get up enough momentum, partly for lack of nerve. . . .

We need to know women as independent: subjectively in our own beings, and in our appreciations of others. If we are to know it in ourselves, I think we may have to be under the gaze of a loving eye, the eye which presupposes our independence. The loving eye does not prohibit a woman's experiencing the world directly, does not force her to experience it by way of the interested interpretations of the seer in whose visual field she moves. In this situation, she *can* experience directly in her bones the contingent character of her relations to all others and to Nature. If we are to know women's independence in the being of others, I think we may have to cast a loving eye toward them . . . and wait, and see.

NOTES

1. "Why I Want A Wife," by Judy Syfers, *Radical Feminism*, edited by Anne Koedt, Ellen Levine, and Anita Rapone (Quadrangle, New York, 1973), pp. 60–62.

2. *Amazon Odyssey*, by Ti-Grace Atkinson (Links Books, New York, 1974), "Metaphysical Cannibalism."

3. Genesis 1:29.

4. Due to Catherine Madsen, from her review of *Wanderground*, by Sally Gearhart (Persephone Press, Watertown, Massachusetts, 1979), in *Conditions No. 7*, p. 138.

5. "Psychology Constructs the Female," by Naomi Weisstein, in *Woman In Sexist Society*, edited by Vivian Gornick and Barbara K. Moran (Basic Books, Inc., New York, 1971), pp. 138–139.

6. Ibid.

7. Cf., *Man-Made Language*, by Dale Spender (Routledge & Kegan Paul, London, 1980), pp. 43–50.

Further Questions

1. Is someone who fails to be of service when this is expected of her flawed, abnormal, or sick for that reason alone?

2. Is it too much to ask someone to devote herself entirely to the service of another?

3. Do women have reason to fear relinquishing men's mediation between the world and themselves? Do they have reason to overcome such a fear?

Suggested Moral of Part IV

Because romantic love is an area where gender is especially important, we might expect to find more problems arising from women's oppression here than in other areas of human life. de Beauvoir and Frye note some problems with love in a context where women are oppressed; however, both writers believe that it is possible for love to flourish if such oppressive elements are removed. Moreover, the other writers pay relatively little attention to this hazard of romantic love, preferring to discuss other features of it instead. The moral of this part, then, might be that gendered life, especially one of its most valued possibilities—romantic love—could continue, and even be improved, in a society free of patriarchal elements. Some of the writings of Part V continue the discussion of how patriarchy allows problems to develop in personal relationships (romantic relationships and friendships) and how some of these problems can be circumvented.

Further Readings for Part IV: Love

Jessica Benjamin. *The Bonds of Love: Psychoanalysis, Feminism, and the Problem of Domination* (New York, NY: Pantheon, 1988). Freudian explanation of the appeal of domination and submission and the consequent difficulty men and women have treating each other as equals.

Martin S. Bergman. *The Anatomy of Loving: The Story of Man's Quest to Know What Love Is* (New York, NY: Columbia University Press, 1987). History of man's concept of love, ancient Egypt through the present.

Robert Brown. *Analyzing Love* (New York, NY: Cambridge University Press, 1987). Interesting analyses of concepts of falling in love, being in love, the object of one's love, etc.

Rosalind Coward. *Female Desire* (London: Paladin, 1984). Follows de Beauvoir in arguing that female love is structured by the female gender role and oppressive for that reason.

Ilham Dilman. *Love and Human Separateness* (New York, NY: Basil Blackwell, 1987). Discussion of theories of love according to which love divides or unites human beings.

Mark Fisher. *Personal Love* (London: Duckworth, 1990). Nice, basic level discussion of aspects of personal love.

Paul Gilbert. *Human Relationships* (Cambridge, MA: Basil Blackwell, 1991). Love, sex, loving friends, "close encounters," etc.

Vernon W. Grant. *Falling in Love: The Psychology of the Romantic Emotion* (New York, NY: Springer Publishing Co., 1976). Psychological theory brought to bear on falling in love. Non-Freudian approach.

J. F. M. Hunter. *Thinking About Sex and Love* (Toronto: Macmillan Canada, 1980). Musings that sometimes stop short of making a solid point.

Søren Kierkegaard. *Either/Or: A Kierkegaard Anthology,* Robert Bretall, ed. (Princeton, NJ: Princeton University Press, 1946). Romance is immediate, founded on nothing, untested, and thus inferior to committed, conjugal love.

Bonnie Kreps. *Authentic Passion: Loving Without Losing Yourself* (Toronto: McClelland and Stewart, 1990). Men who write on love seem positive about it and fairly sure of what they are talking about. Women tend to write paperbacks, not explaining what love is but warning the (presumably female) reader of love's dangers ("losing yourself") and giving advice on how to avoid them. This effort is more intellectual, more creative, and more positive about love than most of the other paperback guides on love by women.

David L. Norton and Mary F. Kille, eds. *Philosophies of Love* (Totowa, NJ: Rowman and Allanheld, 1971). Anthology of writings on romantic love, eros, agape, "Tristanism," friendship, fellow feeling, and other love topics.

Michael Paluk, ed. *Other Selves: Philosophers on Friendship* (Indianapolis, IN: Hackett, 1986). Historically oriented: Aristotle, Plato, Emerson, etc.

Ronald Sharp. *Friendship and Literature* (Durham, NC: Duke University Press, 1989). Analysis of friendship as gift exchange. Argues that friendship creates roles enabling us to relate to one another.

Irving Singer, ed. *The Nature of Love* (Chicago, IL: University of Chicago Press, 1987). Three volume set of renditions of love by major figures, ending with some of Singer's own ideas.

Guy Siriello. *Love and Beauty* (Princeton, NJ: Princeton University Press, 1989). Loosely described experience of love and of the beloved, relating these to morality, reproduction, and the rest of the world.

Alan Soble, ed. *Eros, Agape and Philia: Readings in the Philosophy of Love* (New York, NY: Paragon House, 1989). Nice, well-balanced collection of writings.

Alan Soble. *The Structure of Love* (New Haven, CT: Yale University Press, 1990). Elaborate tour through various facets of love, leaving the reader somewhat out of breath.

Richard Taylor. *Having Love Affairs* (Buffalo, NY: Prometheus Books, 1982). Defense of adultery and other forms of teacher-student liaisons.

Dwight Van de Vare, Jr. *Romantic Love: A Philosophical Inquiry* (University Park, PA: Pennsylvania State University Press, 1981). Love as a social institution; love as used by individuals, singly and collectively.

Part V

Relationships: What Is Worth Seeking or Avoiding

Introduction

Personal relationships, including the romantic relationships and friendships discussed in Part IV, are important in our lives. Hence, it is a good idea to get some sense of what to pursue or avoid in this area of life. Self interest is one principal barrier to the emergence of value in relationships. Quite often this intrusive element is complicated by unenlightened beliefs about the form self interest should take in personal relationships with others.

V.1   Honesty and Intimacy

GEORGE GRAHAM AND HUGH LAFOLLETTE

George Graham and Hugh LaFollette discuss the role of honesty in an intimate relationship, first in connection with a scarlet sweater, and then in connection with a one-night stand.

Graham teaches philosophy at the University of Alabama at Birmingham. Hugh LaFollette teaches philosophy at East Tennessee State University. Both write in the area of ethics and personal relations. They co-edited the volume from which this selection was taken.

Reading Questions

1. If you believed an article of clothing your partner bought was tacky, and if you were asked for your opinion, what should you say?

2. You have just had, on impulse, a one-night stand. What, if anything, should you tell your partner about it?

3. If you were asked to be "completely honest" with someone, would you know what to do?

* * *

Why Honesty Is the Best Policy: Two Cases

THE SCARLET SWEATER

YOUR INTIMATE COMES HOME wearing a red sweater, proud as punch. "Look honey, I got a great buy on this sweater and I'm crazy about it. Don't you just love it?" In fact, you don't. You even think it's a bit tacky. How should you respond? Presumably, "Yes, it's quite nice, dear."

The tendered justification for lying goes something like this: It is crucial that both partners in an intimate relationship be revealing—that they share those features, beliefs, emotions, and so on that are central to their personalities. We have other features, however, which are peripheral to our personalities. Therefore, (1) this trifle is not revealing; withholding it would not be detrimen-

tal to the relationship. In circumstances like those just recounted, a decision to be honest about the sweater would not help the relationship, since we would be sharing only peripheral information about ourselves. Moreover, (2) it could hurt our partner, and sensitivity demands that we not do that. Thus there is no reason to share and good reason to lie. It might even be that we *ought* to lie.

This argument is initially plausible, but it has concealed hooks on which intimacy will flounder. We want to expose those hooks, to show how dishonesty can diminish an intimate relationship. Each of our objections to this common argument not only indicates what is wrong with lying in this case, but also suggests why, in general, intimates should be honest with one another.

We suspect that the line of reasoning in the argument for lying is often an unconscious subterfuge to avoid conflict. For instance, why would a partner think the sweater tacky if apparel were, in fact, peripheral? Is not the mere presence of a negative judgment a prima facie reason for thinking it not peripheral? But suppose it weren't a subterfuge. Not liking our partner's sweater is likely to affect how we relate to her wearing it. We may be less affectionate or even curt, and the partner is left in the dark as to the reason for this standoffishness. Also, one lie is seldom sufficient. On future occasions we will be expected to say complimentary things about the sweater and must be careful not to criticize similar sweaters on others.

We should also be wary of the claim that an intimate will be hurt by the discovery that we don't like the new sweater. She might be momentarily bothered, even miffed. But would she be hurt? She would have to be incredibly thin-skinned to feel hurt whenever someone disagrees with or disapproves of her. But one can't sustain genuine intimacy with such an emotionally fragile person. Persistent fear of hurting the other's frail constitution would greatly limit discussion and create an uneasy atmosphere. More generally, since all people will be annoyed by several features of their intimates, similar reasoning will lead them to lie about other "trivial" aspects of their intimates— for example, their hair or shoes or mannerisms— on the ground that such sharing will hurt their feelings. Thus, they will have to advance and then protect a network of lies. There is no way, however, to be comfortable with another if we are constantly on guard about what we say and do. Under such circumstances we could not have an intimate relationship.

Finally, even if both conditions are satisfied, that would not establish that we should lie. Wearing certain sorts of clothes or not having our hair cut in a certain way may not be peripheral to our intimate even if it is to us, in which case the intimate needs to know that. Each party should know the relative interest placed by an intimate on various activities, beliefs, or goals. Otherwise, we will be relating only to a phantom.

This suggests a more general problem with lying to intimates. If, as in the aforementioned example, we know that apparel is important to our intimate, but purposely hide our disparagement of this interest, we are not showing respect for the other. We have withheld information that may be pertinent to that person's assessment of the relationship. By doing so, we have deprived our intimate of information relevant to determining the future, thereby effectively limiting that person's freedom. This is true whenever someone is dishonest. . . . Intentionally to limit our intimate's options is to violate the presumption of trust on which the relationship is built. It is to treat the other as an object to be manipulated, not as an equal with whom we are close.

. . . People do not know precisely who they are, nor do they have completely determinate selves to reveal. One does not know entirely what is central and may have to find it. There may not even be a fact of the matter about what is central; a person may yet have to mold the (temporary) core of the self. This view of the self as malleable, evolving, and opaque suggests that intimates should be honest, even about matters which are presumed peripheral. Regular and detailed sharing with an intimate is often a means for uncovering those indistinct though relatively fixed elements of the self, and to forge those as-yet-unforged elements. Moreover, the intimate can encourage us to enhance that portrait as we alternately crystallize and modify ourselves. In this way, intimates help each other to be revealing—to have something central to tell or share.

Thus the primary goal of honesty in an intimate relationship is not the uncovering of each person's predetermined transparent self. Rather, it is a commitment to engage in the evolving, refurbishing, and creating of a mutable, amorphous self.

THE SCARLET LETTER

The second case often cited as justifying lying to an intimate is one where the matter is admittedly central, though honesty will substantially harm the intimate and possibly destroy the relationship. The typical example: A woman has a one-night stand while away at a convention. There was, in her mind, no love for the partner; her hormones simply got the better of her. Should she tell her spouse? Absolutely not. Why? Because he will be devastated and the relationship will be forever damaged.

Clearly this is a tough case. It is not difficult to see the force of the argument for lying. But the argument proceeds much too quickly and embraces the use of lying prematurely. Many of the previously adduced arguments are potent in urging one to be honest. For example denying an intimate such information is not to treat that person with due respect. The woman in our example is effectively coercing her spouse, making a decision for him by withholding access to information that is presumably relevant to continued participation in the relationship. Such a lie will have to be regularly enforced by still other lies, as she maneuvers gingerly around her spouse. This guarded atmosphere will encompass the relationship and inevitably limit the closeness. Or if the network of lies does not bother the perpetrator—if she can blithely lie to her spouse about something that is ex-hypothesis so important—then the relationship is already on the skids.

Admittedly, the adulterer can view the behavior in two different ways: (1) as indicating disgruntlements with the marriage, even if they were recognized only in retrospect, or (2) as perfectly compatible with a strong and abiding love for the spouse. On both options, dishonesty is unwarranted. On the first option, honesty is required to rebuild an admittedly deteriorating relationship. How else could they regain intimacy with a squalid secret between them polluting the atmosphere of trust? On the other hand, the wife who holds that marriage partners can freely engage in extramarital sex without any detrimental effects on the marriage should so inform her husband. If he holds a similar belief,

fine. There would be no need for deception. If he disagrees, however, he has a right to know his wife's beliefs on important matters so as to have some control over the relationship.

Now, there are two variations on this case where at least temporary dishonesty might be justified. But, as we shall see, these do not undermine our general thesis.

In the first variation the adulterer realizes that the affair signals trouble in the marriage but wants to work things out. The adulterer realizes a present lack of intimacy with the spouse, but wants to reestablish it. According to best predictions, however, sharing details of the affair now would destroy any chance of rebuilding it. So the adulterer tries to discuss with the spouse the troubles in the marriage, assuming that as intimacy begins to grow it will be possible to share the truth about the affair, along with an explanation for the deception. Such a maneuver, the adulterer claims, would ultimately be honest, though it would momentarily suspend honesty to help refurbish the relationship. A refurbished relationship would then be strong enough to withstand the momentary trauma of learning about the affair.

We do not intend to consider this argument in detail; we do not need to. For even if the argument is cogent, it does not undercut our thesis. According to this variation, the intimate relationship will be maintained only if one is ultimately honest. Moreover, the time that honesty is suspended is the very time when the relationship is admittedly less intimate. The thesis stands.

In the second variation the adulterer recognizes that the relationship is destroyed and plans to leave without telling the (ex-)spouse. The justification? To tell would only hurt. It would not help. Again, we are not going to pass judgment on the rationale. But whatever its moral force, it too does not undercut our general thesis. For the relationship has already dissolved. Our thesis concerns only ongoing intimate relationships, not has-been ones.

Honesty

We have tried to suggest why honesty is an essential ingredient in an intimate relationship. Now we must momentarily retreat for a close look at the concept of honesty. For not only must intimates decide whether to be honest; they must also discern what they must share to be honest. Determining what is honest is no simple matter. As we shall see, this complexity gives intimates additional reasons for being honest.

Honesty, we contend, can be comprehended only contextually. There is no simple dictum (such as "Just speak the truth") that one should follow. Certainly honesty cannot demand knowing every thought that wanders through our tangled brains—intimates would spend all day giving instant replays from our cerebral tape decks, and that could preclude understanding our intimate. Selective sharing of relevant data is more likely to communicate and reveal.

Consequently, individuals necessarily edit their thoughts and feelings, sharing only some with their intimates—presumably those which provide the listener with an honest picture of us. Which ones will do that? We cannot decide without knowing the receiver's perspective, background information, predispositions, and so forth. As every introductory logic teacher tells the students: The context in which something is uttered affects its meaning. Why presume matters would be different in personal relationships? The listener's mind-set is an integral part of the context.

For instance, every teacher knows that there is some order in which the course material must be presented if it is to be comprehended. Explanation of basic terms and simple concepts must pre-cede presentation of more complex notions. Knowing that, what must the teacher do to be honest? Present the simpler material first. Intentionally to present the more complex material prematurely would be in a sense dishonest—it would communicate an incorrect picture of the subject matter. The listener's receptiveness and ability to understand are important constraints on determining what is honest.

Honesty may thus demand telling different people different things. But we should be careful. For, in the important sense, we are not telling different people different things. We are giving them the same honest portrait; it is just that we use different approaches to do so.

We can now see that the notion of being honest with intimates is not simple. That is because honesty is an achievement; more accurately, it is a paradigmatically intended achievement. It will not suffice simply to mouth statements that truthfully describe our views. They must be directed to someone who is capable of constructing an honest (correct) picture of us. Thus to be honest each of us as intimates must know what is important about ourselves and must know the background of our intimate sufficiently well to know how to provide an adequate picture. We should not only tell the truth to the intimate; we should communicate the truth. Admittedly, this makes honesty a sometimes difficult achievement, for we might have to assess the context of sharing to discover what would honestly communicate. On our account, however, that is not an unwanted, or at least not a mistaken, consequence. Since honesty is less difficult when each intimate knows a great deal about the other, intimates have more reason to reveal seemingly insignificant details. . . .

Further Questions

1. If apparel is important to your partner but not to you, is it a good idea to ignore this difference by not listening to or responding to her questions about her apparel?

2. If you and your partner have different ideas about the importance of sexual fidelity, should you withhold information about your infidelities, because they were nothing to you and the information would only hurt her?

3. Are you quite sure what is central to your relationship and what is not (or what is central or peripheral to your self or that of your partner), so that you can cordon off an area of issues that are "not important enough" to discuss?

V.2   Openness

JONATHAN GLOVER

We may be on the threshold of accessing what is running through other people's minds. Jonathan Glover believes the impact of such openness on relationships would be positive in many ways. The problem is that the openness envisaged could be achieved against a person's will, posing problems for personal identity, privacy, and freedom.

Glover teaches philosophy as a Fellow at New College, Oxford University, and has written widely in the areas of ethics and philosophy of mind.

Reading Questions

1. Would it be beneficial in a relationship to be able to read the other person's mind (and have that person able to read yours)?

2. Do we need a certain amount of privacy, even in the closest of relationships, if only to keep the other person from interfering with our ability to think through matters of importance?

A remote radio-communications system using belt transceivers is presently undergoing prototype testing. Systems of this type can monitor geographical location and psychophysiological variables, as well as permit two-way coded communication with people in their natural social environment. Probable subjects include individuals susceptible to emergency medical conditions that occasionally preclude calling for help (e.g. epilepsy, diabetes, myocardial infarctions, geriatric or psychiatric outpatients, and parolees). It is conceivable, for example, that convicts

might be given the option of incarceration or parole with mandatory electronic surveillance. (Robert L. Schwitzgebel: *Emotions and Machines: A Commentary on the Context and Strategy of Psychotechnology*)

During the last few years, methodology has been developed to stimulate and record the electrical activity of the brain in completely unrestrained monkeys and chimpanzees. This procedure should be of considerable clinical interest because it permits exploration of the brain for unlimited periods in patients without disturbing their rest or normal spontaneous activities. (José M. R. Delgado: *Journal of Nervous and Mental Disease* 1968)

THE DEVELOPMENT OF ELECTRONIC monitoring devices makes it possible for us to keep people under surveillance without locking them up in prison. We could largely replace prison by a system of keeping track of convicted criminals without restricting their movements. This thought can arouse both anxiety and optimism. The anxiety (when not about the effectiveness of such a system in restraining criminal activity) is about the invasion of privacy involved in such monitoring. The optimism comes from the thought that submitting to a monitoring system might be much less terrible than going to prison. . . .

Let us suppose that these devices are developed, and that they are produced in conveniently portable form. You come into the room holding what looks like a small portable television. The next thing I know is that I hear coming from it the words that are running through my mind, and see my accompanying visual images on the screen. This technology will make people's minds largely transparent. Despite the problems about interpreting words and images, we will often have a fairly good idea of what others are thinking. . . .

The effects of transparency on relations would be in several ways beneficial. Deception, with its resulting erosion of love and friendship, would be impossible. And relationships now are obscured, not only by deception, but also by our limited ability to express our thoughts and feelings, and by our lack of perception about other people. The thought-reading machine, because of . . . problems about interpretation, would not abolish these limitations, but it would greatly reduce their obscuring effects. As we understood more about each other's mental lives, we would form more realistic pictures of each other, and it seems plausible that this would make relationships better rather than worse. And a stronger sense of

community might result from the barriers of privacy coming down, together with the ending of a sense of loneliness and isolation which some people feel because of their inability to share their experiences.

Sometimes a society of transparent relationships is held up as an ideal. In a fine interview on his seventieth birthday,[1] Jean-Paul Sartre was asked, 'Does it bother you when I ask you about yourself?' He replied:

> No, why? I believe that everyone should be able to speak of his innermost being to an interviewer. I think that what spoils relations among people is that each keeps something hidden from the other, something secret, not necessarily from everyone, but from whomever he is speaking to at the moment. I think transparency should always be substituted for what is secret, and I can quite well imagine the day when two men will no longer have secrets from each other, because no one will have any more secrets from anyone, because subjective life, as well as objective life, will be completely offered up, given . . . There is an as-for-myself (*quant-à-soi*), born of distrust, ignorance, and fear, which keeps me from being confidential with another, or not confidential enough. Personally, moreover, I do not express myself on all points with the people I meet, but I try to be as translucent as possible, because I feel that this dark region that we have within ourselves, which is at once dark for us and dark for others, can only be illuminated for ourselves in trying to illuminate it for others . . . One can't say everything, you know that well. But I think that later, that is, after my death, and perhaps after yours, people will talk about themselves more and more and that this will produce a great change. Moreover, I think that this change is linked to a real revolution. A man's existence must be entirely visible to his neighbour, whose own existence must in turn be entirely visible to him, in order for true social harmony to be established.

There is obviously a big difference between Sartre's ideal and the world of the thought-reading machine. Sartre envisages people voluntarily abandoning their own secrecy of thought, rather than having the power to invade that of others. His transition period would involve no loss of autonomy, and might involve relatively little distress. The introduction of the thought-reading machine would not respect people's autonomy, but would strip them of secrecy against their will. It is hard to see how the process could fail to cause great unhappiness, both to those losing protective secrecy and to those who would be hurt by the thoughts of others. Resistance would be so strong that there might develop an arms race of offensive and defensive technology: devices to jam the thought-reading machines, devices to jam the jammers, and so on. But if, after the horrors of the transition period, the world of the thought-reading machine became established, the effect on relationships might be much the same as that of voluntarily lowering the barriers. And it is not obvious that transparent relationships would be worse than opaque ones.

Identity and Individuality

In our present world, the sort of people we are is to some extent the result of our own choices. (The question of the extent to which our choices could have been different raises the problems about determinism and free will, which will not be discussed here. But, whatever the solution to those problems, most of us prefer to have our identity modifiable by our decisions.) It may be that privacy contributes to this control. Charles Fried has said that we often have thoughts we do not express, and that only when we choose to express them do we adopt them as part of ourselves. If the end of privacy is the end of any distinction between thoughts being endorsed and merely being entertained, then we may lose some control over our identity. It may have been some view of this kind which led Justices Warren and Brandeis to argue that a legal right to privacy is independent of more general property rights:

'The principle which protects personal writings and all other personal productions, not against theft and physical appropriation, but against publication in any form, is in reality not the principle of private property, but that of an inviolate personality.'[2]

In suggestions of this kind, there is something obscure about the idea of personality or identity. For what a person is depends on all his features, including those concealed from others. A sufficiently subtle thought-reading machine would detect the difference between thoughts merely coming to mind and thoughts being endorsed. All that would be lost is concealment of thoughts only entertained. But it is part of me that I do entertain these thoughts, and my identity is not changed because this aspect of it comes to light. So when people say that transparency might threaten our freedom to choose our identity, they may not have in mind 'identity' in the sense of being a particular kind of person, but 'identity' in a sense closer to 'images of ourselves projected to other people.' It is obviously true that the abolition of privacy will reduce the control we have over the pictures other people have of us. But this seems more of a threat to our reputation than to our identity. Our freedom to define ourselves, when not just a matter of manipulation of image, is our freedom to choose between beliefs and attitudes, and to opt for some kinds of actions and ways of life rather than others. And this is not destroyed by others knowing what different ideas we have also considered.

Perhaps the threat posed by transparency is more oblique. It may be that public scrutiny of my mind does not in itself change my identity, but rather has effects which will inhibit the development of individuality. You will know when I am contemplating the ideas and actions you disapprove of, and I will know at once of your attitude. This may create very strong pressures to conform. John Stuart Mill wrote in 1859 of the social pressures towards respectability and conformity: 'In our times, from the highest class of society down to the lowest, everyone lives as under the eye of a hostile and dreaded censorship.'[3] One result of transparency might be to extend the social censorship inwards, so that there would be the same pressures for conformity of thought and feeling as there are for conformity of behaviour. We have only partial control over our thoughts and feelings, but the social censorship might persuade us to turn away from lines of thought which we knew might lead us into dangerous areas, as well as not to act on ideas arousing disapproval.

Privacy is necessary if we are not to be stifled by other people. Even in our present world, without the thought-reading machine, being permanently observed, as in some prisons, can destroy individuality. (Sartre, in an earlier phase, talked in *Being and Nothingness* with an almost neurotic horror of being observed by other people, and vividly presented the awfulness of permanent scrutiny in *Huis Clos,* where hell for three people is being locked forever in a room together.) To be observed by other people can build up a feeling of pressure to justify what we are doing and how we are doing it, or to justify doing nothing. For many people, happiness, and perhaps creativity and originality, flourish where there are long stretches free from critical appraisal.

Perhaps we have the potential to grow more robust, and in a world of transparent relationships we might grow stronger in our resistance to pressures to conform. But it is hard to see how the extra pressures could be avoided, with their obvious threat to individuality.

The Two Perspectives

I have suggested that transparency would not in itself threaten our identity, and that its effects on relationships might, after a transition period, be beneficial. But it is plausible that it would allow new and powerful social pressures for conformity. If this account is accepted, our view of any proposed steps towards the transparent world will depend on how we weigh these different gains and losses. Any appraisal is difficult because it is hard to imagine relationships so transformed. If the threat to individuality seems much more clear than the benefits to relationships, many of us will be very cautious in our attitude to the dismantling of the barriers of privacy.

Yet it may be that our horror at the thought of entering the transparent world is nothing to the horror with which people in the transparent world will look back at our lives. They may think of us as hiding behind barriers of mutual pretence, like the inhabitants of a suburban street hiding behind fences and hedges. They might be far more concerned to avoid the reinstatement of the barriers of privacy than we are to avoid them being dismantled. The conflict between their perspective and ours, which will reappear in other contexts, raises a deep theoretical difficulty in deciding what sort of world we should aim for.

NOTES

1. 'Sartre at Seventy: An Interview', *New York Review of Books,* August 1975.
2. 'The Right to Privacy', *Harvard Law Review* 1890.
3. *On Liberty,* chapter 3.

Further Questions

1. "Does it bother you when I ask you about yourself?" Would you give Sartre's reply to this question?

2. Do we, as Charles Fried claims, often have thoughts that become part of us only when we choose to express them? If so, could another person interfere with this process of choice?

3. If you know too much about me, does this give you too much opportunity to control me? What kinds of things known about me could give you such control?

V.3   The Civic Advocacy of Violence

WAYNE EWING

Wayne Ewing recommends that "the abusive male is every man" and recounts the items in the cycle of male batterers. He argues that society not only tolerates male abusiveness but actually encourages it.

Reading Questions

1. Do you think that some deficiency in the childhood or background of a batterer excuses his violence and abusiveness?

2. Do you think that more attention has been paid to victims of battering than to their batterers because victims tend to bring battering upon themselves?

3. Batterers are often contrite and remorseful afterwards about their battering. Why is this?

THE RULING PARADIGM for male supremacy remains, to this hour, physical violence. This paradigm remains unchecked and untouched by change. Critically, the permissive environment for male violence against women is supported by a civic advocacy of violence as socially acceptable, appropriate and necessary. Physically abusive men, particularly men who batter their spouses, continue for the most part to be a protected population. And the sources which provide us with what we know of the batterer—largely clinical and treatment models—have themselves remained too isolated from sexual politics and from a social analysis of male cultures. Until the code of male violence is read, translated and undone, male batterers will not be largely affected by what we are coming to know about them.

Profiling the Male Batterer

I sometimes think that none of the literature will ever move our knowledge dramatically further than Erin Pizzey's observation that all batterers are either alcoholics or psychotics or psychopaths or just plain bullies. That is good common sense applied to the all too ordinary affair of men beating up women. I also think that the following observation, more often than not made rhetorically and politically, has a measure of significance that we can draw on. When the question is raised, "Who is the male batterer?" the answer is sometimes given, "Every man!" Without pushing too quickly let me simply point out here that this observation is accurate. It is not simply an attention-getter. Attempts to profile the male batterer always wind up with a significant body of information which points to . . . every man.

I believe the most striking example of this is found in those studies which support the—in my estimation, accurate—view of male violence as a learned behavior. Depending on the study, 81% to 63% of the population of batterers researched have either experienced abuse as victims in the home of their childhood or have witnessed their fathers beat their mothers. While that is significant enough to support our forming knowledge that socialization into violence in the home perpetuates violence, and that individual men can be conditioned to domestic violence as normal, I do not believe we have spent enough time looking at the chilling fact that remains: from 19% to 37% of these populations have literally invented violence in an intimate relationship. It is clear that the experience as victim or observer of physical violence is not necessary to "produce" a violent, abusive man.

And so it is with any of the many categories of inquiry applied to populations of male batterers. I will tick some of these off here, and in each case refer to the batterers with whom I work in Denver. *Ethnic backgrounds,* for example, will closely parallel the ethnic makeup of the community in which the study is made. In intake interviews of men either volunteering or ordered by the Courts into the men's groups of our project in Denver, the statistics generated on ethnicity are the statistics available about our community in general. *Age* is not a major factor. While most physically abusive men are in their 20s or early 30s, batterers are also under 20 and over 50. The fact that slightly more than half the men we deal with in Denver are in their 20s is attributable to so many other possibilities, that the fact itself recedes in significance. *Education* is not a major determinant. While a majority of batterers may have a high school education, the ones we know are equally balanced on either side by men with undergraduate, graduate and professional degrees and men with less than a high school education. *Income* studies do not support the popular idea that battering men are low income earners. Over a third of the men studied in Denver have incomes of $15,000 and above; and regular employment is as much a feature of the batterer as is infrequent employment. The *onset and frequency of violence* within a relationship are not consistent indicators of the behavior profile of the male batterer. The only conclusion safely drawn from these inquiries is that the probability of maiming and permanently crippling injury for the victim rises with the increase of frequency, and that the period of contrition on the part of the batterer becomes briefer between episodes as frequency increases. *Substance abuse* may as easily accompany battering episodes as not. In Denver, it is in-

volved in a little over a third, while in other populations studied, substance abuse may figure in as much as 80% of battering episodes. And of course the self-reported "*causes*" of violence from both victims and abusers runs from sex to in-laws to money to housework to children to employment and around and around and around. There is no real clue to the profile of the abusive male in these reported occasions for battering episodes. With respect to the *psychological makeup* of the abusive male, there is considerable consensus that these men evidence low self-esteem, dependency needs, unfamiliarity with their emotions, fear of intimacy, poor communication skills and performance orientation. But what is intriguing about these observations is that they span all of these other indicators.

And so I end this brief review where I started. The abusive male—that is, the violent man of low self-esteem, high dependency need, slow on affect, fearful of intimacy, poor in communicating emotions, and oriented to performance—the abusive male is every man.

The Cycle of Violence

How is it we know so little, then, about the male batterer? In part this is due to the fact that the movement begun by the female victims of male violence has not spawned a fervent desire to look at the abuser. The simple fact is that as massive as male domestic violence is, we know more about the victims than we do about the abusers. There are some very obvious realities at work here. If we are to serve, counsel, protect, renurture and heal victims, we must come to know them, to understand the cycle of violence in which they are terrorized and victimized. We need to elicit from them the motivation to break the cycle of violence. But if we are to intervene in the cycle of violence in society at large—which is after all, the sustainer of violence from men toward women—the batterer must be known as well. For every female victim who is freed from the cycle of violence without intervening in the actual be-havior of the male abuser, we still have a battering male-at-large.

We do know that a particular characteristic of the cycle of male violence—the period of contri-tion—is critical to how the cycle repeats itself in relationships: the building up of tension and conflict; the episode of battering; the time of re-morse; the idyllic time of reconciliation. And then the cycle begins again. What is going on in the time of remorse? How is it that this apparent recognition of violent behavior is insufficient to provoke change and to begin a cycle of nonvio-lent behaviors? It seems to me that remorse is a time-honored device, within male-dominant, sexist cultures, for "making things right" again. I refer of course to the Judeo-Christian model of "making things right"—as it was always stated until very recently in the texts of theology and of devotion—between "God and man." This whole pattern of remorse, guilt, repentance, newly in-vigorated belief, and forgiveness has had one of the most profound symbolic impacts on Western male consciousness.

When a man physically abuses a woman, it is a matter of course for him to fall back on this model. Things can be "made right," not by actual change, but by feeling awful, by confessing it, and by be-lieving that the renewal of the relationship is then effected. That this is more hocus-pocus than authentically religious hardly matters. A crippling consequence of this major model for renewal and change—remorse followed by forgiveness-taken-for-granted—is an almost guaranteed start up of the previous behavior once again. The *non* resolu-tion which we violent men rehearse by remorse and "resolve" is vacuous. It is the exercise of a mere accompaniment to violence. And particularly where our dependency on the female victim of our abuse is so strong, the simple telling of the "re-solve" not to be violent again is seen as establish-ing how good we are in fact.

Actually, the interweaving of the violence and the remorse is so tight that the expression of re-morse to the victim establishes how good we have been, and how good we are. The remorse is not even a future-oriented "resolve"; it is more an internalized benediction we give to the immedi-ately preceding episode of battery. There is no shock of recognition here in the cycle of violence. It is not a matter of "Oh my god, did I do that?" It is a matter of *stating* "Oh my god, I couldn't have done that," implying that *I in fact did not do it*. The confession of remorse then only reinforces the self-perception that I did not do it. Remorse, in this model of "making things right" again, literally wipes the slate clean. Over and over again we violent men are puzzled as to how it is our victims come to a place where they will not toler-ate our violence and so report us or walk out on us. Can't they see that the violence no longer counts as real, because I said I was sorry?

Whatever clinical research reveals to us about the population of batterers, the fact of denial built into the cycle of violence itself veils from both us and the batterer the reality of the vio-lence. Over and over again, abusive men will ask what the fuss is all about. They hold as a right and privilege the behavior of assault and battery against "their" women. Our groups in Denver are filled with men from all walks and circumstances of life to whom it has never occurred that batter-ing is wrong. In other words, one reason we know so little about male batterers is that they only reluctantly come to *speak* of battering at all.

Another factor further veils this population from us. Male batterers continue to be deliber-ately protected in the careful construction of familial silence; in the denial of neighbors, friends, clergy, teachers and the like that batter-ing can be "true" for John and Mary; in the fail-ure of law enforcement to "preserve and protect" the victims of domestic violence; in the unwill-ingness of local and state governments to provide shelter for victims; or in the editorializing of the Eagle Forum that the safe house movement is an anti-male, lesbian conspiracy. Male violence has become the ordinary, the expected, the usual.

The Civic Advocacy of Violence

What remains is for us to deal with what very few of us want to confront: American life remains sexist and male supremacist in spite of the strides of the second wave of American Feminism. Whether it be snide—"You've come a long way, baby"—or whether it be sophisticated—George Gilder's *Sexual Suicide*—the put down of women's quest for equality, dignity and freedom from male oppression is damn near total in the America of the 1980s. I contend that the ultimate put down is the continuing advocacy of violence against women, and that until we confront that advocacy with integrity and resolve, the revolution in men's consciousness and behavior cannot get underway.

I used to think that we simply tolerated and permitted male abusiveness in our society. I have now come to understand rather, that we *advocate* physical violence. Violence is presented as effective. Violence is taught as the normal, appropriate and necessary behavior of power and control.

We apparently have no meaningful response to violence. I am convinced that until the voices that say "No!" to male violence are more numerous than those that say "Yes!," we will not see change. Nor will we men who want to change our violent behaviors find the support necessary to change. And silence in the face of violence is heard as "Yes!"

Under the governing paradigm of violence as effective and normal, every man can find a place. The individual male who has not beaten a woman is still surrounded by a civic environment which claims that it *would* and *could* be appropriate for him to beat a woman. He is immersed in a civic advocacy of violence which therefore contends that should he have committed battery, it is normal; and should he have not committed battery, it is only that he has not *yet* committed battery, given the ordinary course of affairs. In sexual political terms, we men can simply be divided into pre-battery and post-battery phases of life.

The teaching of violence is so pervasive, so totally a part of male experience, that I think it best to acknowledge this teaching as a *civic*, rather than as a cultural or as a social phenomenon. Certainly there are social institutions which form pieces of the total advocacy of violence: marriage and family; ecclesiastical institutions; schools; economic and corporate institutions; government and political institutions. And there are cultural and sub-cultural variations on the theme and reality of violence, of course. I believe, however, that if we are to crack the code of violent male behavior, we must begin where the environment of advocacy is total. Total civic advocacy is the setting for all the varieties of cultural adaptations from which violent men come.

For this total, pervasive advocacy of violence, I can find no better word than *civic*. The word has a noble ring to it, and calls up the manner in which the people of a nation, a society, a culture are schooled in basic citizenship. That's precisely what I want to call up. Civic responsibilities and civil affairs are what we come to expect as normal, proper and necessary. Violence, in male experience, *is* just such an expectation. Violence is *learned* within the environment of civic advocacy.

Demonstrating this is perhaps belaboring the obvious. But when we fail to belabor the obvious, the obvious continues to escape us and becomes even in its pervasiveness, part of an apparently innocent environment or backdrop. "Oh, say can you see. . . ." Our National Anthem can perhaps be thought of as simply romanticizing war, mayhem, bloodshed and violence. But more than that, reflection on the content of the song shows that we pride ourselves, civically, on the fortress mentality of siege, endurance and battle. The headier virtues of civic responsibility—freedom and justice—are come to only in the context of violence. "The rockets' red glare, the bombs bursting in air," are as ordinary to us as the school event, the sporting event, the civic sanction in which we conjure up hailing America "o'er the ramparts."

"I pledge allegiance. . . ." The flag of violence becomes the object of fidelity and devotion for American children even before they know the meaning of "allegiance." Yet feudal-like obeisance —the hand over the heart and devotional hush to the recitation—to the liege lords of violence is sanctioned as appropriate behavior quite calmly with this ritual.

We might assume of course that because this is ritual no one takes it seriously. That's precisely my point. We don't take it seriously at all. We just take it, live it, breathe it, feel awkward when we don't participate in the ritual, feel condemnatory when others around us don't participate in the ritual, and so on. The environment of civic advocacy of violence *is* ordinary, and not extraordinary.

The Everyday Language of Violence

Language is not innocent of meaning, intent and passion. Otherwise, there would be no communication between us at all. Yet words fall from our mouths—even in the civil illustrations above—as if there were no meaning, intent and passion involved. What I make of this is that the advocacy of violence is so pervasive, that the human spirit somehow, someway, mercifully inures itself to the environment. We are numbed and paralyzed by violence, and so continue to speak the language of violence as automatons.

I am not referring to the overt, up front renditions of violence we men use in describing battery and battering. "Giving it to the old woman" and "kicking the shit out of her" however, are phenomenologically on the same level of meaning, intention and passion as: assaulting a problem; conquering fear, nature, a woman; shooting down opinions; striking out at injustices; beating you to the punch; beating an idea to death; striking a blow for free enterprise, democracy; whomping up a meal; pounding home an idea; being under the gun to perform; "It strikes me that. . . ." You can make your own list of violent language. Listen to yourself. Listen to those

around you. The meaning, intent and passion of violence are everywhere to be found in the ordinary language of ordinary experience.

Analyses which interweave the advocacy of male violence with "Super Bowl Culture" have never been refuted. It is too obvious. Civic expectations—translated into professionalism, financial commitments, city planning for recreational space, the raising of male children for competitive sport, the corporate ethics of business ownership of athletic teams, profiteering on entertainment—all result in the monument of the National Football League, symbol and reality at once of the advocacy of violence. How piously the network television cameras turn away from out-and-out riots on the fields and in the stands. But how expertly the technologies of the television medium replay, stop action, and replay and replay and replay "a clean hit." Like the feelies of George Orwell's 1984, giant screens in bar and home can go over and over the bone-crunching tackle, the quarterback sack, the mid-air hit— compared in slow motion to dance and ballet, sophisticating violence in aesthetic terms. We love it. We want it. We pay for it. And I don't mean the black market price of a Bronco season ticket or the inflated prices of the beer, automobile accessories and tires, shaving equipment and the like which put the violence on the screen. I mean the human toll, the broken women and children of our land, and we frightened men who beat them. And even if I were to claim that neither you nor I is affected by the civic advocacy of violence in commercialism and free enterprise, we would still have to note that the powers and scions of industry *believe*—to the tune of billions of dollars a year—that we are so affected.

Pornography is no more a needed release for prurient sexual energies than would be the continuation of temple prostitutes. But it is sanctioned, and the civic advocacy of violence through pornography is real. It is not on the decrease. Soft porn is no longer *Charlie's Angels* or the double entendres of a Johnny Carson-starlet interview; that's simply a matter of course. Soft porn is now *Playboy, Penthouse,* and *Oui,* where every month, right next to the chewing gum and razor blades at the corner grocery, air-sprayed photographs play into male masturbatory fantasies. Hard porn itself is becoming more "ordinary" every day; child porn and snuff films lead the race in capturing the male market for sex and violence. We love it. We want it. And we pay for it. Violence works.

Insofar as violence works, the male batterer is finally, and somewhat definitively, hidden from us. I would not denigrate or halt for a moment our struggle to know the male batterer through clinical research models. But I would call all who are interested in knowing him and in intervening in and ending the cycle of the violence of men against women, to the larger context of the civic advocacy of violence. There, I believe, is the complement of the analysis generated by profiling the male batterer.

Until the code of male violence is undone, male dominance and sexism will prevail. Until the commerce in violence against women ceases, and we finally create an environment in which violence is no longer acceptable or conceivable, male supremacy will remain a fact of life for all of us.

Further Questions

1. Can someone have a right or privilege of abusing or assaulting another human being?
2. Is it in any way normal and only to be expected that someone batters someone else?
3. Is it true that men batter, in part, because they see all around them the fact that violence works? *Should* violence work?

Violence in Intimate Relationships: A Feminist Perspective   V.4

bell hooks

How much violence is tolerable in an intimate relationship? bell hooks claims that no violence is tolerable in this context. Such violence strips the victim of her dignity and signals lack of integrity in the relationship.

Another selection by hooks appears in Part II.

Reading Questions

1. Is "battered woman" a stigmatizing term, inhibiting women from breaking the silence about problems of family violence? What would be a better word to use?
2. Does even occasional hitting occasion a breach of trust?
3. Can sharing intimate details of our lives (e.g., how we were abused as children) open up areas of vulnerability that partners can then exploit by creating similar scenarios?

RECENTLY, I BEGAN a conversation with a group of black adults about hitting children. They all agreed that hitting was sometimes necessary. A professional black male in a southern family setting with two children commented on the way he punished his daughters. Sitting them down, he would first interrogate them about the situation or circumstance for which they were being punished. He said with great pride, "I want them to be able to understand fully why they are being punished." I responded by saying that "they will likely become women whom a lover will attack using the same procedure you who have loved them so well used and they will not know how to respond." He resisted the idea that his behavior would have any impact on their responses to violence as adult women. I pointed to case after case of women in intimate relationships with men (and sometimes women) who are subjected to the same form of interrogation and punishment they experienced as children, who accept their lover assuming an abusive, authoritarian role. Children who are the victims of physical abuse—whether one beating or repeated beatings, one violent push or several—whose wounds are inflicted by a loved one, experience an extreme sense of dislocation. The world one has most intimately known, in which one felt relatively safe and secure, has collapsed. Another world has come into being, one filled with terrors, where it is difficult to distinguish between a safe situation and a dangerous one, a gesture of love and a violent, uncaring gesture. There is a feeling of vulnerability, exposure, that never goes away, that lurks beneath the surface. I know. I was one of those children. Adults hit by loved ones usually experience similar sensations of dislocation, of loss, of new found terrors.

Many children who are hit have never known what it feels like to be cared for, loved without physical aggression or abusive pain. Hitting is such a widespread practice that any of us are lucky if we can go through life without having this experience. One undiscussed aspect of the reality of children who are hit finding themselves as adults in similar circumstances is that we often share with friends and lovers the framework of our childhood pains and this may determine how they respond to us in difficult situations. We share the ways we are wounded and expose vulnerable areas. Often, these revelations provide a detailed model for anyone who wishes to wound or hurt us. While the literature about physical abuse often points to the fact that children who are abused are likely to become abusers or be abused, there is no attention given to sharing woundedness in such a way that we let intimate others know exactly what can be done to hurt us, to make us feel as though we are caught in the destructive patterns we have struggled to break. When partners create scenarios of abuse similar, if not exactly the same, to those we have experienced in childhood, the wounded person is hurt not only by the physical pain but by the feeling of calculated betrayal. Betrayal. When we are physically hurt by loved ones, we feel betrayed. We can no longer trust that care can be sustained. We are wounded, damaged—hurt to our hearts.

Feminist work calling attention to male violence against women has helped create a climate where the issues of physical abuse by loved ones can be freely addressed, especially sexual abuse within families. Exploration of male violence against women by feminists and non-feminists shows a connection between childhood experience of being hit by loved ones and the later occurrence of violence in adult relationships. While there is much material available discussing physical abuse of women by men, usually extreme physical abuse, there is not much discussion of the impact that one incident of hitting may have on a person in an intimate relationship, or how the person who is hit recovers from that experience. Increasingly, in discussion with women about physical abuse in relationships, irrespective of sexual preference, I find that most of us have had the experience of being violently hit at least once. There is little discussion of how we are damaged by such experiences (especially if we have been hit as children), of the ways we cope and recover from this wounding. This is an important area for feminist research precisely because many cases of extreme physical abuse begin with an isolated incident of hitting. Attention must be given to understanding and stopping these isolated incidents if we are to eliminate the possibility that women will be at risk in intimate relationships.

Critically thinking about issues of physical abuse has led me to question the way our culture, the way we as feminist advocates focus on the issue of violence and physical abuse by loved ones. The focus has been on male violence against women and, in particular, male sexual abuse of children. Given the nature of patriarchy, it has been necessary for feminists to focus on extreme cases to make people confront the issue, and acknowledge it to be serious and relevant. Unfortunately, an exclusive focus on extreme cases can and does lead us to ignore the more frequent, more common, yet less extreme case of occasional hitting. Women are also less likely to acknowledge occasional hitting for fear that they will then be seen as someone who is in a bad relationship or someone whose life is out of control. Currently, the literature about male violence against women identifies the physically abused woman as a "battered woman." While it has been important to have an accessible terminology to draw attention to the issue of male violence against women, the terms used reflect biases because they call attention to only one type of violence in intimate relationships. The term "battered woman" is problematical. It is not a term that emerged from feminist work on male violence against women; it was already used by psychologists and sociologists in the literature on domestic violence. This label "battered woman" places primary emphasis on physical assaults that are continuous, repeated, and unrelenting. The focus is on extreme violence, with little effort to link these cases with the everyday acceptance within intimate relationships of physical abuse that is not extreme, that may not be repeated. Yet these lesser forms of physical abuse damage individuals psychologically and, if not properly addressed and recovered from, can set the stage for more extreme incidents.

Most importantly, the term "battered woman" is used as though it constitutes a separate and unique category of womanness, as though it is an identity, a mark that sets one apart rather than being simply a descriptive term. It is as though the experience of being repeatedly violently hit is the sole defining characteristic of a woman's identity and all other aspects of who she is and what her experience has been are submerged. When I was hit, I too used the popular phrases "batterer," "battered woman," "battering" even though I did not feel that these words adequately described being hit once. However, these were the terms that people would listen to, would see as important, significant (as if it is not really significant for an individual, and more importantly for a woman, to be hit once). My partner was angry to be labelled a batterer by me. He was reluctant to talk about the experience of hitting me precisely because he did not want to be labelled a batterer. I had hit him once (not as badly as he had hit me) and I did not think of myself as a batterer. For both of us, these terms were inadequate. Rather than enabling us to cope effectively and positively with a negative situation, they were part of all the mechanisms of denial; they made us want to avoid confronting what had happened. This is the case for many people who are hit and those who hit.

Women who are hit once by men in their lives, and women who are hit repeatedly do not want to be placed in the category of "battered woman" because it is a label that appears to strip us of dignity, to deny that there has been any integrity in the relationships we are in. A person physically assaulted by a stranger or a casual friend with whom they are not intimate may be hit once or repeatedly but they do not have to be placed into a category before doctors, lawyers, family, counselors, etc. take their problem seriously. Again, it must be stated that establishing categories and terminology has been part of the effort to draw public attention to the seriousness of male violence against women in intimate relationships. Even though the use of convenient labels and categories has made it easier to identify problems of physical abuse, it does not mean the terminology should not be critiqued from a feminist perspective and changed if necessary.

Recently, I had an experience assisting a woman who had been brutally attacked by her husband (she never commented on whether this was the first incident or not), which caused me to reflect anew on the use of the term "battered woman." This young woman was not engaged in feminist thinking or aware that "battered woman" was a category. Her husband had tried to choke her to death. She managed to escape from him with only the clothes she was wearing. After she recovered from the trauma, she considered going back to this relationship. As a church-going woman, she believed that her marriage vows were sacred and that she should try to make the relationship work. In an effort to share my feeling that this could place her at great risk, I brought her Lenore Walker's *The Battered Woman* because it seemed to me that there was much that she was not revealing, that she felt alone, and that the experiences she would read about in the book would give her a sense that other women had experienced what she was going through. I hoped reading the book would give her the courage to confront the reality of her situation. Yet I found it difficult to share because I could see that her self-esteem had already been greatly attacked, that she had lost a sense of her worth and value, and that possibly this categorizing of her identity would add to the feeling that she should just forget, be silent (and certainly returning to a situation where one is likely to be abused is one way to mask the severity of the problem). Still I had to try. When I first gave her the book, it disappeared. An unidentified family member had thrown it away. They felt that she would be making a serious mistake if she began to see herself as an absolute victim which they felt the label "battered woman" implied. I stressed that she should ignore the labels and read the content. I believed the experience shared in this book helped give her the courage to be critical of her situation, to take constructive action.

Her response to the label "battered woman," as well as the responses of other women who have been victims of violence in intimate relationships, compelled me to critically explore further the use of this term. In conversation with many women, I found that it was seen as a stigmatizing label, one which victimized women seeking help felt themselves in no condition to critique. As in, "who cares what anybody is calling it—I just want to stop this pain." Within patriarchal society, women who are victimized by male violence have had to pay a price for breaking the silence and naming the problem. They have had to be seen as fallen women, who have failed in their "feminine" role to sensitize and civilize the beast in the man. A category like "battered woman" risks reinforcing this notion that the hurt woman, not only the rape victim, becomes a social pariah, set apart, marked forever by this experience.

A distinction must be made between having a terminology that enables women, and all victims of violent acts, to name the problem and categories of labeling that may inhibit that naming. When individuals are wounded, we are indeed often scarred, often damaged in ways that do set us apart from those who have not experienced a similar wounding, but an essential aspect of the recovery process is the healing of the wound, the removal of the scar. This is an empowering process that should not be diminished by labels that imply this wounding experience is the most significant aspect of identity.

As I have already stated, overemphasis on extreme cases of violent abuse may lead us to ignore the problem of occasional hitting, and it may make it difficult for women to talk about this problem. A critical issue that is not fully examined and written about in great detail by researchers who study and work with victims is the recovery process. There is a dearth of material discussing the recovery process of individuals who have been physically abused. In those cases where an individual is hit only once in an intimate relationship, however violently, there may be no recognition at all of the negative impact of this experience. There may be no conscious attempt by the victimized person to work at restoring her or his well-being, even if the person seeks therapeutic help, because the one incident may not be seen as serious or damaging. Alone and in isolation, the person who has been hit must struggle to regain broken trust—to forge some strategy of recovery. Individuals are often able to process an experience of being hit mentally that may not be processed emotionally. Many women I talked with felt that even after the incident was long forgotten, their bodies remain troubled. Instinctively, the person who has been hit may respond fearfully to any body movement on the part of a loved one that is similar to the posture used when pain was inflicted.

Being hit once by a partner can forever diminish sexual relationships if there has been no recovery process. Again there is little written about ways folks recover physically in their sexualities as loved ones who continue to be sexual with those who have hurt them. In most cases, sexual relationships are dramatically altered when hitting has occurred. The sexual realm may be the one space where the person who has been hit experiences again the sense of vulnerability, which may also arouse fear. This can lead either to an attempt to avoid sex or to unacknowledged sexual withdrawal wherein the person participates but is passive. I talked with women who had been hit by lovers who described sex as an ordeal, the one space where they confront their inability to trust a partner who has broken trust. One woman emphasized that to her, being hit was a "violation of her body space" and that she felt from then on she had to protect that space. This response, though a survival strategy, does not lead to healthy recovery.

Often, women who are hit in intimate relationships with male or female lovers feel as though we have lost an innocence that cannot be regained. Yet this very notion of innocence is connected to passive acceptance of concepts of romantic love under patriarchy which have served to mask problematic realities in relationships. The process of recovery must include a critique of this notion of innocence which is often linked to an unrealistic and fantastic vision of love and romance. It is only in letting go of the perfect, no-work, happily-ever-after union idea, that we can rid our psyches of the sense that we have failed in some way by not having such relationships. Those of us who never focussed on the negative impact of being hit as children find it necessary to reexamine the past in a therapeutic manner as part of our recovery process. Strategies that helped us survive as children may be detrimental for us to use in adult relationships.

Talking about being hit by loved ones with other women, both as children and as adults, I found that many of us had never really thought very much about our own relationship to violence. Many of us took pride in never feeling violent, never hitting. We had not thought deeply about our relationship to inflicting physical pain. Some of us expressed terror and awe when confronted with physical strength on the part of others. For us, the healing process included the need to learn how to use physical force constructively, to remove the terror—the dread. Despite the research that suggests children who are hit may become adults who hit—women hitting children, men hitting women and children—most of the women I talked with not only did not hit but were compulsive about not using physical force.

Overall the process by which women recover from the experience of being hit by loved ones is a complicated and multi-faceted one, an area where there must be much more feminist study and research. To many of us, feminists calling attention to the reality of violence in intimate relationships has not in and of itself compelled most people to take the issue seriously, and such violence seems to be daily on the increase. In this essay, I have raised issues that are not commonly talked about, even among folks who are particularly concerned about violence against women. I hope it will serve as a catalyst for further thought, that it will strengthen our efforts as feminist activists to create a world where domination and coercive abuse are never aspects of intimate relationships.

Further Questions

1. Is it shocking to hear that (irrespective of sexual preference) most women have been hit at least once in a relationship? What does this say about present relationships?

2. Suppose a battered woman somehow escapes her battering situation. Will other people treat her as well as they would treat someone they believed had not been battered?

3. If a woman is being hit in a relationship, does she have reasons to remain in the relationship, e.g., loyalty to her partner or to the relationship?

V.5   Altruism and Vulnerability

SARAH LUCIA HOAGLAND

Sarah Lucia Hoagland addresses altruism, vulnerability, and self-sacrifice, qualities traditionally expected of women in heterosexual relationships. These are not really good for women or their relationships, she argues. Her idea is to develop a new ethic for lesbian communities, even though much of what she says applies more generally to any human relationship.

Hoagland teaches philosophy and women's studies at Northeastern Illinois University in Chicago and gives frequent talks to lesbian communities in North America.

Reading Questions

1. In situations where altruism seems to be called for, is it better to begin by trying a method of conflict resolution that does not require one party to drop her interests?

2. Is it possible to be in a situation where "self-sacrifice" is, in many ways, the most advantageous choice to make?

3. Can someone's "self-sacrifice" be a burden to the person for whom the sacrifice is supposedly being made?

4. Is exhibiting vulnerability a good way to appear nonthreatening?

5. Can vulnerability be used as a method of keeping someone else at a distance and establishing control of the situation?

. . . I WANT TO SUGGEST that when people begin to talk about the importance of altruism and self-sacrifice, it indicates they perceive an inherent conflict of interests among those involved. Such a focus represents a narrowing of ethical attention to only certain kinds of interactions. Further, to resolve the conflict of interests, those with lesser institutional power will be expected to be altruistic. In this respect, altruism and self-sacrifice are considered "feminine virtues." 'Femininity' is a concept which makes female submission to male domination seem natural and normal. As such, the "feminine virtues" function to preserve the relationship of dominance and subordination, facilitating the access of those with greater institutional power to the resources of those with lesser institutional power.

However, within a relationship of dominance and subordination, the power of control can be exercised both from a position of dominance and from a position of subordination. Within a limited range of activity, considerable manipulative power can be exercised from the feminine position. Because of male domination, over time women have developed the ascribed feminine virtues into survival skills and created of them tools for control. And this power of manipulation is the essence of female agency promoted under heterosexualism.

When lesbians use these virtues among each other, we wind up using our survival skills against each other; thus our survival skills go awry. I want to suggest that the feminine virtues are a means of exercising control in relationships— whether as lovers, friends, or collective members —and that as a result they function to interrupt rather than promote lesbian connection.

Egoism and Altruism

My suggestion is that concern with altruism and self-sacrifice actually signals an underlying belief that the interests in question are inherently or essentially in conflict. That is, when there is a strong focus on altruism and self-sacrifice, it is an indication that the interests of those involved are already perceived as being in conflict. And given this, we may suspect that whenever we find an appeal to self-sacrifice or altruism, we will uncover an attempt to resolve that conflict by getting one party to drop their interests in favor of the other for the purpose of achieving and maintaining a certain social order. At any rate, in paradigm cases involving concepts of altruism and self-sacrifice, we can expect to find an underlying, possibly inherent, conflict of interests; and it is worth examining just what these interests are, and how the conflict is resolved . . .

In the case of the conflict of interests between women and men, altruism is expected of women but not essentially of men. While those in the subordinate position may hope for altruism from those in the dominant position, those in the dominant position extract it from their subordinates. That is to say, 'altruism' becomes a relevant concept when conflicts of interest are a central part of a social order. Further, altruism mediates conflicts of interest in that it accrues to the one in the subordinate position: those with lesser power are expected to drop their interests and concerns in favor of those with greater power. This is one reason altruism and self-sacrifice are considered feminine virtues. . . .

We need a moral revolution.

Instead of appealing to altruism, we can begin to seriously evaluate our individual and collective interests, particularly the differences among us. And given that we live in a capitalist as well as a patriarchal, racist society, we can explore ways to keep our economic exchanges out of the capitalist value framework. I want to suggest we begin weaving a new concept of lesbian economics.[1] As long as we subscribe to existing values, perceiving them as essential to our survival and well-being, altruism will appear to be an ideal. And, concomitantly, the marketplace will continue to render it the choice of fools or subordinates. . . .

The Feminine Principle

Men have designed the feminine virtues and the resulting sense of female agency, to promote their own interests. I include here 'vulnerability'. While vulnerability is not usually called a virtue, still a virtuous woman must make herself vulnerable by being nonreciprocally open, loyal, and dependent. For if self-seeking is a central concern that thwarts ethical possibility, then one who is open and vulnerable and not watching after her own interests and needs is virtuous. Altruism, self-sacrifice, and vulnerability—as virtues of subordination—function to channel women's energy and attention away from their selves and their own projects. . . .

. . . [W]hile men have designed 'the feminine' for their own purposes, women have refined these virtues in defense and resistance, developing them as a means of obtaining some control (individual and limited) in situations which *presume* female self-sacrifice. Women have developed the "giving" expected of them into survival skills, strategies for gaining some control in situations where their energy and attention are focused on others.

That is, the power of control can be exercised from the subordinate position, and under heterosexualism women have refined and developed the feminine virtues for just that purpose. Under heterosexualism, female agency involves manipulation and cunning—for example, a woman getting what she needs for herself and her children by manipulating a man in such a way that he thinks it was all his idea.

I will add here that manipulation, cunning, and deceit are not peculiar to women. Men are also extremely manipulative and deceitful, and can exhibit considerable cunning, for example, in keeping their dominance over their peers or subordinates from appearing overt, or in enlisting women to support them. The difference, finally, between men and women under heterosexualism may lie in who maintains dominance —though not, in every instance, in who maintains control.

Dominance is maintained by violence or the threat of violence—which, in the long run, means by destruction or the threat of destruction. If nothing else works, men will disrupt or destroy what is going on. Thus, to be different from men, women stress nonviolence. Under heterosexualism, manipulation and control are not challenged; what is challenged is only the threat of disruption or destruction. Women want men to "play fair" in the game of manipulation and control by not resorting to the one-upmanship of destruction.

While many claim that there is a feminine principle which must exert itself to counterbalance masculinism pervading world cultures, what they seem to ignore is that the feminine has its origin in masculinist ideology and does not represent a break from it.[a] Further, the counterbalancing works both ways. Because of the non-discriminatory nature of feminine receptivity, that is, a lack of evaluating or judging what the feminine responds to, the feminine requires the masculine to protect it from foreign invasion.

Within lesbian community, many lesbians embrace a feminine principle and suggest that self-sacrifice and vulnerability, as well as a romantic ideal of mothering and all-embracing nurturing, are desirable ethical norms in our relationships. I want to challenge this.

'Selfishness' and 'Self-Sacrifice'

Consider, first, the use of the label 'selfish'. Those who are judged to be selfish are often those who do not respond to demands from others: the question of selfishness is a question of whether a person thinks only of herself. This consideration often develops into a complaint that the person deemed selfish does not act in ways that contribute to a social structure such as the nation, the family, the synagogue or church, the corporation, the sewing circle, or the collective. Significantly, when a person goes along with the group, even if she is only thinking of herself—being "selfish"—she may well be considered ethical for doing the "right" thing. Further, someone who is perceived as selflessly opposing the group nevertheless often is judged immoral and unethical. Thus someone can be "selfish" and yet "good"—as well as "unselfish" and yet "bad."

Apparently, the relevant factor in judging a person to be selfish is, not whether she considers herself first, but whether or not she goes along with the group (or conforms to a higher order) in one of a number of prescribed ways.[b] It seems that selfishness is not of prime concern; rather, the label is used as an excuse to manipulate our participation toward someone else's end.

Secondly, masculinist ideology suggests that true female nature affirms itself through self-sacrifice. Mary Daly defines 'self-sacrifice' as the handing over of our identity and energy to individuals or institutions.[4] This ethical value encourages a woman to give up pursuit of her needs and interests in order to dedicate her efforts to pursuing others' needs and interests, usually those of her husband and children.

Self-sacrifice appears to be a sacrifice of self-interest. Yet women face limited options: men limit women's options through conceptual, physical, and economic coercion. As a result, when a woman engages in self-denial, acquiesces to male authority, and apparently sacrifices her own interests to those of a man in conformity with the dictates of the feminine stereotype, she may actually be acting from self-interest, doing what she deems necessary to her own survival.

Drawing upon Kathleen Barry's analysis of the strategy men use in female sexual slavery, Marilyn Frye suggests that when women who are trapped in actual conditions of female sexual slavery, or who are caught up in masculinist arrogant perception, apparently sacrifice their own needs and interests by aligning their resources in support of a man, they nevertheless are not acting selflessly or unselfishly. She argues, rather, that women facing such conditions are intently involved in acting in their own self-interest:

The slave, the battered wife, the not-so-battered wife, is constantly in jeopardy. She is in a situation where she cannot, or reasonably believes she cannot, survive without the other's provision and protection, and where experience has made it credible to her that the other may kill her or abandon her if and when she displeases him. . . . [W]hat she does "for the other" is ultimately done "for herself" more consistently and more profoundly than could ever be the case in voluntary association.[5]

The point is that because of coercion under patriarchy, the woman realigns her choices to focus on the man. While she is not working on her own projects, nevertheless she is intensely involved in acting in her own self-interest.

One consequence is that, except perhaps in extreme cases of female sexual slavery, when a woman is in a situation in which she is expected to shift her identity to that of a man or a child, the stage is set for her to work to control the arena wherein her identity is located. She has not sacrificed her self: by altruistically adopting another's interests, she has transferred that self, or rather it has been arrogated by the man.[6] And while she may have given up pursuit of her own unique interests and needs in favor of those of her husband (and to a lesser extent those of her children), she will pursue their interests and needs as her own.

This, in turn, gives rise to a double bind of heterosexualism: While she is expected to attend to everyone else's projects, she has no final say in how they are realized. She thus becomes the nagging wife or the fairy-tale stepmother. For example, mothers may "live vicariously" through their children and some wives may be "domineering." And those mothers who pursue their children's needs and interests too enthusiastically are criticized for not being passive enough. The stereotype of the jewish mother attests to the trap self-sacrifice sets up for women.

Thirdly, the concepts of 'self-sacrifice', 'altruism', 'selfishness', and 'self-interest' may appear to be factual descriptions, but the implications we can draw from sentences containing these words depend significantly on how we use them. For example, independently of male coercion, 'self-interest' could be used in such a way that any act, even an act of altruism or self-sacrifice, is actually a matter of self-interest. Someone who "self-sacrifices" may feel better about herself when she focuses on what she can do for others rather than having to assess her own needs; thus she might choose to engage in such behavior out of self-interest.

We could even argue that 'self-sacrifice'—acting with regard for another's interests to the exclusion of our own interests—is a matter of refusing to take risks or, even, is selfish. For if I disregard my own interests, I can live through someone else's choices, enjoying the fruits of their power if they are successful, for example, while if they fail, not being responsible for failure but only for bad choice. So I'm being selfish in not taking my own risks.

Further, if I actually self-sacrifice, I leave the task of caring for myself to someone else. I may become a burden to others (and thus selfishly inconsiderate of them); or if no one accepts the burden, I will become of no use to the one for whom I was self-sacrificing and hence, again, selfish. We can play around with these concepts and come up with all sorts of interesting results; and through all this, acting in consideration of our own needs and limits becomes lost in the shuffle.

Fourthly, the selfish/selfless (or egoism/altruism) dichotomy does not accurately categorize our interactions. Often we do not consider our interests and the interests of others as being in conflict.[7] Concern for ourselves does not imply disregarding the needs of others. For example, if we go to a healer when we are ill, work hard at our projects, take showers and baths, we are acting in our own self-interest. But this is hardly a matter of selfish conduct.[8] In addition, doing good for others need not involve disregarding ourselves. If I decide to help you build a frame for your futon, I may be taking a break from my work. But sharing this with you does not mean I thereby disregard my own needs or interests. It might be that sharing your project is just what I need at this time.

Now, fifthly, in challenging the concept of 'self-sacrifice', I do not mean to suggest that the sort of "selfish" behavior which self-sacrifice is supposed to counter does not exist among lesbians. For example, a lesbian may consistently act as if her feelings are the only ones, that she is warranted in interrupting anything else going on to demand attention (the strategies for this are many and varied). However, while the problem is real, the solution does not lie in advocating self-sacrifice. When a lesbian is acting this way, often it is because she hasn't a firm sense of herself in relation to others and is threatened; advocating self-sacrifice will only compound the problem.

Egocentrism is the perception that the world revolves around oneself. Now, it is important to have a healthy sense of oneself, centered and in relation to others. But egocentrism is our judgment that those around us have no other relationships, needs, commitments, or identity than that which they have with us. Egocentrism is perceiving and judging others only in relation to ourselves. Hence it is a confusion of our needs, reactions, and choices with those of others. Egocentrism is a form of "selfishness," for it entails a lack of consideration for others—it involves a lack of awareness that others are different and separate from us, and have needs distinct from our own. (Marilyn Frye has explored the phenomenon in terms of "the arrogant eye" of masculinist perception.[9])

Actually, there are at least two versions of egocentrism we engage in. In one type, we use attention from others to bolster our self-esteem: we connect our egos to others' responses; and when others do not always act as we planned, we regard this as a reflection on ourselves, confirming our own lack of worth. For example, we may tell another we'll be at a certain place, presuming she will show up but not directly asking her, thus relying on a commitment that was never made. If she doesn't show up, we consider this a betrayal —without any regard for her choices, which may have nothing to do with us. Actually, the fact that her choices may have had nothing to do with us is part of the problem—it proves we weren't important. In this case we use others to determine our value when we have been unable to do so for ourselves.

In another type of situation, we construct the basis for our self-esteem by creating a story about the world, particularly our immediate environment. Then we interpret everyone's actions in terms of how they fit into that construct. For example, we may plan an event and decide we are doing this for others. We then expect them to interact and contribute in ways we specify. If the others don't go along, they will have betrayed our gesture. In this case, rather than allow their behavior to reflect back on us as in the first case, we determine their value only as they fit into our framework.

In general, when others don't play by the rules we've used to construct our reality, we reinterpret what they are doing to fit our game plan. As a result, we do not allow others their own responses and reasons. Rather than talking out our differences of judgment and attending what each other has to say, we simply avoid such engagement and construct our own reasons for the other's reactions. This involves a distortion because, while we create value by interacting, nevertheless we are not the only ones contributing to the situation; we are not the only ones involved.

In the community we tend to promote self-sacrifice as a virtue and a proper antidote for behavior resulting from egocentrism. However, self-sacrifice cannot solve the problem because egocentrism involves a confusion of needs similar in form to the confusion that occurs with self-sacrifice: my perception of my needs and concerns becomes so entwined with my perception of others that anything relating to the other must relate to me and vice versa.

The difference is that in the case of self-sacrifice we cease to have a distinct sense of ourselves. In the case of egocentrism we cease to have a distinct sense of the other. Thus, advocating self-sacrifice as a corrective measure to selfishness really feeds an underlying problem of ego boundary: the solution actually nurtures the problem.

Sixthly, another's "self-sacrifice" is not particularly helpful when we are pursuing our goals. Some of us joke about wanting a wife. Yet in considering what most contributes to the development of my work, I find that it is *not* those around me giving up their goals to pursue mine. What helps me is others vitally and intently pursuing *their* goals—their music, their writing, their photography, their pottery, their editing, their collective and organizational work, work through which they weave their own meaning as lesbians—work, thus, which contributes to our lesbian ground of be-ing. Certainly I want encouragement and criticism—an exchange of ideas which feeds us both. I need and want attention; but this comes from those who are actively pursuing their own goals, who have ideas which rub against mine, and who spark and are sparked by an exchange. This pursuit of goals is neither a matter of self-sacrifice nor of selfishness. It is a matter of weaving tapestries of lesbian value, it is a matter of creating meaning in this living.

Someone might argue that self-sacrifice is important in certain political situations; that under certain conditions, sacrificing ourselves to the feminist or lesbian struggle is feasible and acceptable. Yet lesbian burn-out results from self-sacrifice in political projects, especially when the project does not develop in the direction or as quickly as the lesbian imagined—burnout which in turn results in virtual or even complete withdrawal from the lesbian community. If a lesbian devotes herself to a project in such a way that her identity merges with it while her life goes on hold, and she does not gauge her own needs and limits, she may become unable to pull back at times and so become devastated if things don't go exactly and immediately as she believes they ought to. She may work frantically, as if responsible for the whole situation . . . until something snaps and she ceases to care, ceases to be able to respond. Self-sacrifice is not a means of engaging.

When we engage in political work, or projects and relationships, we need not regard this as taking us away from our everyday concerns, as being in conflict with our personal goals, and hence as a sacrifice. Nor is it useful to believe we must sacrifice in order to feel we are truly struggling. Rather, we can regard our work as a matter of pursuing our needs and interests, as part of our means of living in heteropatriarchy, as our means of creating meaning in our living. Ours is a choice of where to engage our energy, and as a result we can understand why we find the project valuable, gauge our abilities and needs, understand our limits, consider at what point the work would cease to be meaningful for us. In this way we make choices, take risks, make mistakes, revalue our commitment as things progress, but we do not so easily lose our self in self-sacrifice and burn-out. (And the prerequisite for this is self-understanding.)

And this brings me to my seventh point. We tend to regard choosing to do something as a sacrifice. I want to suggest, instead, that we regard choosing to do something as a creation. From heterosexualism we tend to believe that any time we help another, we are sacrificing something. Thus, we might regard helping a friend fix a carburetor, spending an evening listening to her when she's upset rather than going to a party, or helping her move, as a matter of self-sacrifice. But these acts do not necessarily involve self-sacrifice. Rather, they involve a choice between two or more things to do, and we will have reasons for any choice we make. Often we have choices to make. But that we have to make choices is not itself a matter of sacrifice.

Certainly, at times a lesbian might set herself against another's project, forcing the other to choose between herself and the project in order to gain "proof" of the other's love. Further, it is certainly possible that a lesbian may become so dependent on one friend that, in attempting to meet the lesbian's needs, the friend ultimately

will have to set aside her own goals. (And at that point the friend will likely begin to demand authority over the lesbian's choices.) But, in general, helping others is not a matter of self-sacrifice.

There is another way of approaching this: we can regard our choosing to interact as part of how we engage in this living. Such choices are a matter of focus, not sacrifice. That I attend certain things and not others, that I focus here and not there, is part of how I create value. Far from sacrificing myself, or part of myself, I am creating; I am weaving lesbian value.

As I engage in lesbian living, I make choices—to start this relationship, to work on this project, to withdraw now, to dream now. I make daily choices; and at one time I may choose to help another, at another time not. But in choosing to help another, I am not thereby sacrificing myself. Instead, this is part of what I involve myself in. When we regard interacting with others as a sacrifice and not as an engagement, it is time to reassess the relationship.

Nor, when we make a choice to engage here rather than there, do we need to regard ourselves as sacrificing or compromising parts of ourselves. When we interact, we pursue certain interests. We may have other interests, and we can choose which we want to develop, involving ourselves elsewhere for some. In any given engagement, what is possible exists only as a result of how those involved connect—as a result of what each brings to the engagement and of how it all works out. So when we decide to interact, we do not need to regard ourselves as compromising or losing anything, but rather as embarking on an adventure.

For example, a lesbian develops a friendship with another lesbian. They may have a common interest in the martial arts and work out together. In the process, they create possibilities that were not there, maybe eventually deciding over time to open a lesbian martial arts school. They may develop strategies specific to women and lesbians. And in the process they have created a connection between them, one that changes over the years. During this time, they are not opening a bookstore, writing a book, building a house—actually, they may take on another project, but there will be things they do not do. And they may create other possibilities with other lesbians, their lovers, for example. My point is that in making their choices, they have not sacrificed themselves or other projects. They have created something that did not exist.

What we choose is what we've decided to try to create. And we may change our minds, find that what we thought we were working for isn't what emerges, find it has emerged but that we don't really like it, find it is what we want but later find ourselves wanting to go on to something else, find that over time it changes significantly and so leave it. But even this is not a sacrifice. For as we change, what once existed also changes; if we leave it, we are not leaving what we originally created but rather something different. Thus, our choice to go on to something else is also not a sacrifice.

There is an idea floating about to the effect that if we cannot do everything, if we have to choose some and let other things go, then we are sacrificing something. Given traditional anglo-european philosophy and u.s. imperialist ideology, u.s. lesbians, in particular, tend to think the whole world exists for us, that everything is potentially ours (or should be), so that when we have to choose between two or more options, we feel we are sacrificing something or that we have lost something. But everything is not ours; everything is not even potentially ours. In fact, nothing out there that exists is ours. Thus in acting, engaging, making choices—in choosing one thing rather than another—we are not losing anything. In acting, engaging, making choices, we are creating something. We create a relationship, we create value; as we focus on lesbian community and bring our backgrounds, interests, abilities, and desires to it, we create lesbian meaning.

What exists here as lesbian community is not some predetermined phenomenon which we

opted for but rather a result of what we've created. And the same is true of all our relationships. Thus, the choice to engage here rather than there is not a sacrifice of what's "out there"; to engage is to create something which did not exist before. I want to suggest that revaluing choice is central to Lesbian Ethics.

Now, if we decide to regard choice as a creation, not a sacrifice, situations requiring difficult decisions will still arise between us. However, we can regard our ability to make choices as a source of power, an enabling power, rather than a source of sacrifice or compromise. Thus by revaluing choice we begin to revalue female agency: female agency begins to be, not essentially a matter of sacrifice and manipulation, but rather a process of engagement and creation. (And the prerequisite for this is self-understanding.)

Understanding choice as creation, not sacrifice, helps us better understand choices we make typically considered "altruistic." We often are drawn to helping others. That's one reason so many are drawn to healing, to teaching, to volunteering to work at shelters, to practicing therapy, to working at community centers or in political campaigns, to going to nicaragua—to all kinds of political work. In doing such work, we feel we are creating something, that we are participating in something; we engage and we make a difference. . . .

Vulnerability

There is a belief among lesbians, not only that engaging and making choices is a matter of sacrifice, but also that the way to engage and establish trust among ourselves is to make ourselves vulnerable to each other. Many lesbian-feminists plan for a world in which we can be "safely vulnerable" to each other. I myself once had this idea and argued that so long as a society exercises power as control, vulnerability will be confused with impotency. Thus, one who is vulnerable is a target of attack, a victim. However, I went on, in a womyn-identified space—a space in which power can develop as ability, not control, can emanate from the dark core, and is a power of processes and changes—vulnerability may come from strength, not weakness. Then when we choose to make ourselves vulnerable, I thought, it will be because we are strong and flexible enough to absorb what may come.

That was my argument, and while superficially the idea sounded plausible, I soon began to wonder about it. I imagine a time when we can be open to each other with less caution and greater flexibility because we allow greater honesty to inform our exchanges. But I no longer believe this connects in any way with 'vulnerability'.

When playing with the dictionary one day, I discovered that 'vulnerable' comes from the latin *vulnerābilis,* meaning "to wound." An allegedly obsolete meaning is "having the power to wound." Current usage connects 'vulnerable' with either being wounded or being open to wounding or attack. I do not believe a concept tied this way to attack and wounding can involve any form of agency but the power of control and its resulting presumption of access—the resulting relationship of dominance and subordination.

The context of making ourselves vulnerable in order to establish trust emerges from the dynamics of all forms of oppression. Those who have been captured, conquered, colonized, enslaved, and exploited in any form are expected to show themselves to be non-threatening to their masters once the overt violence of conquest is over. At this point, covert forms of violence begin, and the oppressed are expected to make themselves vulnerable through the concept of 'cooperativeness' in order to gain their masters' trust in return for a few privileges the master might bestow such as freedom from overt forms of violence.

Thus, for example, "blue" and "pink" collar workers in the u.s. are expected to be open and completely honest with their employers about anything related to their job such as pregnancy, health, drug use, etc. And such honesty is supposed to indicate the willingness of the worker to work. Workers who conceal such non-reciprocal

information are considered sullen, uncooperative. Employers then use this information, not to determine their employee's best interests, but rather to determine who will be promoted, demoted, or fired—in order to determine their own ability to gain profit. The protestant work ethic encourages vulnerability in workers and maintains the power imbalance between employer and employee.

At this point in time, vulnerability is perhaps most intricately embedded in our lives through the concept of 'love' that emerges from heterosexualism. Women have been forced to make themselves vulnerable to men, to open themselves to wounding by extending themselves appeasingly and displaying their weakness or their alleged helplessness, during initial contact and ever after at regular intervals in order to prove they're not like Eve, Cleopatra, or Delilah. Women thereby reassure men that they would never be able to threaten men, that they understand the necessity of remaining loyal to men, and that men are beings who warrant such reassurances. Vulnerability and granting undue access to men—so matter of course that men often do not even need to solicit it—have evolved under the rule of the fathers, forcing women to establish that they are exceptional (that is, not like other, dangerous, women) and hence worthy of a man's attention and trust. Thus, the idea of making ourselves vulnerable in order to establish trust emerges from a context in which women have been forced to deny their common connections in order to survive, that is, in order to attain male acceptance and approval under the rule of the fathers. Such a sense of female agency does not promote lesbian connection.

Aside from constant appeasing postures, the primary way for a woman to prove to a given male that she is exceptional is to derogate the women around her. While waiting in new york's la guardia airport, I watched a young woman arrive and greet her boyfriend, who was there to meet her. She had been to a family gathering, and for the next twenty minutes of conversation she derogated each female member of her family, beginning with her grandmother. In the process, she was making herself vulnerable in two ways: In the first place, she was dissociating herself from her female bloodline and from women in general in order to prove, indirectly, that she, at least, could be trusted by him. This is the result of male-identification; she exposed herself to wounding by cutting herself off, and she will be wounded by the isolation—has been wounded already. And she was doing so in an attempt to survive by aligning herself with a male.

More interestingly, she was using vulnerability as a tool. She was exposing herself by exposing the weakness of the women of her bloodline to show that she could recognize their qualities as weaknesses and that she abhorred them as much as any man would. The case is interesting because she was using vulnerability in an attempt to gain security and avoid risk. She was exposing herself by exposing the weaknesses of her bloodline in order to ward off an attack on herself and in order to gain male approval—trust. If her boyfriend later hurls a charge at her that she, too, has these weaknesses, he will have betrayed her—she will affirm his male supremacy as long as he affirms her exceptionality. By giving him information that could be used to hurt her, in order to establish exceptionality and gain his trust, she was using vulnerability to gain some security and even a bit of control from a position of subordination.

There is a related pattern among heterosexual women who deny connections with feminism or with lesbians. There is also a related pattern among liberal or socialist feminists who take pains to deny connections with radical and separatist lesbians in order to make the men of their politics feel more comfortable. And there is a related pattern among women and lesbians who attack lesbians or women more vehemently than they would attack men in order to gain credit with whichever exceptional men they have chosen to engage.

After a heterosexual liaison has been established, vulnerability can be used in another way; it can become a means whereby a woman controls a man's access to her life in certain respects and forces him to keep his distance emotionally, if not physically. This way he can't consume her. One woman described her parents' relationship this way: The wife is submissive, vulnerable, and needs protection. As the husband is the dominant member of the pair and she has no separate means of self-realization, he is supposed to guess what she needs and, on occasion, wants. (Since he's supposed to be superior, let's see just how much he really knows.) She makes herself vulnerable by depending on him to guess and provide for her needs; if he fails, he wounds her. As inevitably he does fail at second-guessing her needs—while she is a whiz at guessing his since she has had to learn to observe him—she feels hurt and eventually angry owing to his fatuousness. In the process she makes him feel guilty. He is thus distanced and must attend to her even more closely (or have a nagging feeling of guilt), trying to guess her innermost needs while she goes competently about her business. Then at crucial moments she can call in her due; she can call certain shots in their relationship while keeping him at a distance.

This is but one heterosexual scenario. Given the power imbalance of the social mechanisms accompanying heterosexualism, vulnerability can be a way of gaining token, minor, individual control. And while the control may be minor relative to masculine autonomy, the *conceptual* difference between regarding the vulnerable woman as submissive, on the one hand, and regarding her as *resisting* total dissolution within the dominance/subordination scenario of heterosexualism, on the other hand, is significant for us; for this manipulation is the sense of female agency promoted under heterosexualism.[10]

One revealing television perfume commercial, aired around the turn of the decade for the december holidays, exhibits a seductively dressed white woman with a french accent who states, "I crave vulnerability; I think too much intimacy is dangerous." This is a significant contrast. The message is that she craves control and thinks too much openness dangerous. She makes herself vulnerable but does not permit the sort of understanding of herself which one who is intimate would have.

Yes, openness is dangerous for a woman trying to gain some control over her circumstances in a context denying all remnants of female independence. And out of this context emerges the idea of wrapping a man around the little finger—right or left, as the case may be. She keeps him at a distance, maintaining the mystery. If the mystery is dispelled through intimacy (knowledge a man often begins to gain when a woman continues to let down her defenses after first engaging in sexual intercourse with him), she becomes ordinary and hence no longer exceptional. (Then she may resort to other means to maintain her exceptionality.) Yes, in this context intimacy is dangerous, and vulnerability is a strategy for gaining control.

Again, under the rule of the fathers, women have fashioned the giving and vulnerability expected of them into various strategies for survival. And it is important to herald these strategies for what they are. However, because women as well as lesbians have so refined and perfected them, they may have become for many of us a matter of reaction and defense rather than a carefully planned course of action. Or, at least, very often we can resort to them without fully considering other options. Making ourselves vulnerable to gain control can be a matter of habit, and as a result we are in danger of using vulnerability unthinkingly against those who have no real power (control) over us.

Among lesbians, if I make myself vulnerable in order to establish trust, if I open to a lesbian in ways that invite her to wound me, if I open up before we have found a common ground of respect and hence a basis for trust, my opening is most likely an attempt to gain control in the relationship without acknowledging either the attempt or any control I might succeed in gaining. Further, even if this isn't my intention, it will likely be a consequence of my choice.

For example, if I share doubts about myself with a lesbian before we have grounds for trust, I am revealing to her what I am defensive about. If she then criticizes me for the very thing I am defensive about, she has declared open war because I "trusted" her with this information which I am sensitive about; she has betrayed my trust. This then acts as a constraint on her: so long as we remain friends she cannot openly criticize me in these areas; she must support me (i.e., not challenge me).[c] From the other direction, we often respond to others who share their doubts with us by feeling bound not to criticize them, even when protection from criticism was not their intent. Our engaging has thus become a binding; and our friendship has become, not an open, honest exchange of ideas, empathetic critiques, sympathetic suggestions, and perceptive support, but rather a means whereby we have enlisted someone to insulate (protect) us from our fears and pain (as opposed to holding us through them).[d]

For example, a white lesbian might come to a gathering to connect with lesbians of color. And she might choose to interact by making herself vulnerable in an attempt to undermine the dominance/subordination relationship of racism. She may confess past racist ideas she's had or acts she's committed, which she only just now has come to understand, in order to expose herself and thus disavow the power of her skin privilege. In the process, by admitting her racism she may expect a lesbian of color to feel grateful, surprised, relieved, even hopeful, and to regard her, thus, as trustworthy for having exposed herself, admitted her sins, and thereby somehow ensured that with this new found knowledge and understanding, such acts and ideas will never occur again on her part or in her presence without interruption. In the process, the white lesbian is nevertheless exercising control. She has put a constraint on the relationship which she is attempting to establish with the lesbian of color by "trusting" her with this information. If the lesbian of color chooses to pursue the relationship and later wants to explore her feelings in connection with racism or even calls her friend's actions racist, she will have "betrayed" the "trust" that was established by re-opening the white lesbian's exposed wounds.

In a related fashion, we might use vulnerability as a means of constructing barriers and setting up protection. For example, a lesbian of color may use vulnerability in an attempt to gain control in the racial dominance/subordination relationship. She may tell of her experiences of racial oppression in order to ensure that a white lesbian doesn't get too close or in order to protect herself from a white lesbian's questioning of certain political choices she's made or to block (rather than elucidate) critiques of aspects of her culture. Her use of vulnerability in the latter case invites partial examination of her culture, but suggests that full examination would wound her, and hence betray the trust she exhibited in opening up. While it is crucial that we continue to dismantle the dominance/subordination relationship of racism between us, this project will not succeed by means of vulnerability, particularly not through confession and absolution.

Vulnerability can also become a way of gaining undue access to another lesbian's life. In exchange for becoming vulnerable to you, I may expect automatic time priorities and constant explanations about what you are doing.[12] Or I may make assumptions about your willingness to do certain things which I would not make about other close friends. This is the taking for granted, the presumption, of lovers.

Further, if I attempt to establish closeness by using my vulnerability, then later on if I find your interests or needs changing, I will be more likely to perceive such a change as a betrayal of my "trust." But then my "trust" amounted to trusting that you would not change.

Finally, vulnerability can be connected to egocentrism. For example, I make myself vulnerable by telling you that something you do hurts me, that since we have begun our relationship, you continue to play poker with your friends every other friday. You may consider this, be con-cerned that I am upset, and yet decide to continue. It may have other meaning for you, it may involve part of the way you want to act in the world. I may then decide that the reason you do this is to hurt me, perceiving your actions only in relation to me, ignoring the fact that other factors may be involved. The one who makes herself vulnerable expects this to override all other considerations.[13]

Now, I do not mean to encourage using another lesbian's vulnerability as an excuse to avoid attending her in her pain or anger. There must be spaces where we can explore our wounds and the injustices done to us. And we must be able to ask for help. However, the other must also be able to refuse. What I am concerned with is our use of vulnerability as a means of engineering closeness or as a means of gaining access or (paradoxically) as a shield. And what we might watch for is the power play, the coercion.

In general, when we open to wounding for a purpose, we are in a sense holding ourselves up for ransom (the redemption of a political prisoner). And the price another must pay to redeem us is to refrain from criticizing us in certain areas. We *trust* the other will not hurt us; and if she does, even by just withdrawing because of her own wounds, then she can become a scapegoat for all that goes wrong in the relationship, thereby enabling us to avoid examining ourselves. More importantly, we can use vulnerability to avoid examining the values we affirm through the choices we make. . . .

Hailing vulnerability—the specific opening of ourselves to wounding—as a desirable virtue effectively obscures the fact that we live under the rule of the fathers, a rule of dominance and subordination, and that our survival is itself profoundly political because it means survival as lesbians, on our own terms. And, as Audre Lorde reminds us, we were never meant to survive.[14]

The appeal to vulnerability also buries the fact that turning the other cheek is an act of violence.[15] In turning the other cheek, we are inviting the other person to do us violence. (We may also be egging on an attacker, encouraging him.[c])

The belief that this action does not merit the name of violence stems from the same mode of thought exhibited by a wisconsin police officer who refused to alert the community to a rash of rapes, refused to warn women that a rapist was striking often and obviously, because he didn't want anyone to get hurt. It stems from the belief that violence done to women doesn't hurt anyone, or that breaches of women's integrity or health are not violations. . . .

NOTES

a. This dualism is related to the manichean good/evil dualism and the taoist yin/yang dualism. The manichean approach holds the two opposites in constant conflict, each attempting to dominate and vanquish the other. The taoist approach embraces the conflict but strives for harmony and balance of the two opposites. And while the taoist ideal involves harmony and balance, the nature of the opposites is significant: yin/yang, female/male, dark/light, black/white, cold/heat, weakness/strength. The one is the opposite of the other because it is the absence of it. Thus, strength is the absence of weakness as weakness is the absence of strength. Further, one of the pair is the absence of the other because it is a void. While there are two opposites, in the long run, there is only one essence. The dualism is actually a monism.[2]

In discussing the new spiritualism, Susan Leigh Star argues that the new mystics have managed to mask male identity beneath the guise of androgyny. Further, she points out, "Amidst the escalation, it is vital for us to understand that the new mysticism has to do with the control of women; that it may be seen as a sexual as well as a spiritual phenomenon; that it represents a subtler form of oppression, not a form of liberation."[3]

b. As a result, we find that there is really no room for anyone who finds the group, the social structure, or the higher order unacceptable and does not wish to go along in any of the prescribed ways. If she separates from the group or the structure or the order, she is judged unethical and ostracized by those caught up in the structure. Such judgment can come from those who would bring change through reform as well as from those who would retain the status quo.

c. In making these remarks, I am not suggesting that a lesbian who grew up learning to always hide her emotions should never open up.[11] What I am talking about here is a means of exercising control, not a means of growing.

d. While I am suggesting these ways of interacting emerge from survival skills developed from a position of subordination within heterosexuality, they are neither peculiarly "fem" nor peculiarly "butch." Both those who claim the label 'butch' and those who claim the label 'fem' can use vulnerability to erect barriers and gain control in a relationship.

e. Of course, such a strategy may work to stop an attack, as can happen for example in street fighting. Nevertheless, when such tactics are necessary, they are not a matter of opening or connecting but, rather, of avoiding violence.

1. For a beginning, note Jeffner Allen, "Lesbian Economics," *Trivia* 8 (Winter 1986): 37–53; Nett Hart, "Lesbians Feed Lesbians: A Lesbian Food Coop," *The Lesbian Insider/Insighter/Inciter* 11 (July 1983): 10; Nett Hart, "Appropriate Distribution: Toward a Lesbian Economy," *Maize: A Lesbian Country Magazine* 3 (Winter 1984/85): 4–7; Lee Lanning, "A Vision of Interdependence." *Maize* 3, p. 13.

2. Conversation, Marilyn Frye.

3. [Susan] Leigh Star, "The Politics of Wholeness: Feminism and the New Spirituality."

4. Mary Daly, *Gyn/Ecology*, pp. 374–5.

5. Marilyn Frye, "In and Out of Harm's Way: Arrogance and Love," in *The Politics of Reality: Essays in Feminist Theory* (Trumansburg, N.Y.: The Crossing Press, 1983, now in Freedom, Calif.), p. 73.

6. Ibid., pp. 66–72.

7. For further discussion, note Judith Tourmey, "Exploitation, Oppression, and Self-Sacrifice," in *Women and Philosophy*, ed. Carol C. Gould and Marx W. Wartofsky (New York: G. P. Putnam's Sons, 1976), pp. 206–21; and Larry Blum, Marcia Homiak, Judy Housman, and Naomi Scheman, "Altruism and Women's Oppression," in *Women and Philosophy*, pp. 222–47.

8. For further discussion, note James Rachels, "Morality and Self-Interest," in *Philosophical Issues: A Contemporary Introduction*, ed. James Rachels and Frank A. Tillman (New York: Harper & Row, 1972), pp. 120–1.

9. Marilyn Frye, "In and Out of Harm's Way."

10. Note for example, *The Emile of J. J. Rousseau*, trans. and ed. William Boyd (New York: Teachers College Press, 1971), book 5: "Marriage," pp. 129–69; also, Sarah Lucia Hoagland, "On the Reeducation of

Sophie," *Women's Studies: An Interdisciplinary Collection* (Westport, Conn.: Greenwood Press, 1978), pp. 13–4.

11. For a portrait of this, note Lee Lynch, *Toothpick House* (Tallahassee, Fla: The Naiad Press, 1983), especially 122, 124.

12. Conversation, Deidre D. McCalla and Sally Yeo.

13. Conversation, Anne Throop Leighton.

14. Audre Lorde, "The Transformation of Silence into Language and Action," *Sinister Wisdom* 6 (Summer 1978): 11–5; reprinted in *The Cancer Journals* (Argyle, N.Y.: Spinsters Ink, 1980, now Spinsters/Aunt Lute), pp. 18–23; and in *Sister Outsider* (Trumansburg, N.Y.: The Crossing Press, 1984, now in Freedom, Calif.), pp. 40–4.

15. Conversation, Deborah Snow.

Further Questions

1. Suppose you are in a situation where one of your alternatives is helping someone else. If you choose this alternative, are you more creative and less arrogant if you think of your choice, not as self-sacrifice, but as what you most wanted to do under the circumstances?

2. Should trust be established before a person makes herself vulnerable so that she will not use this vulnerability as a means of controlling the other person?

3. If you make yourself vulnerable to someone else, does this person owe you something in exchange?

4. Is turning the other cheek an act of violence because it may invite the person who hit the first cheek to do further violence?

Trusting Ex-Intimates   V.6

ANNETTE BAIER

Annette Baier maintains that the trust that accompanies love must outlast the love if we have entrusted to the loved person something we cannot recover when intimacy ceases. This raises a host of questions about the relations between intimacy and trust.

Baier teaches philosophy at the University of Pittsburgh and has published many writings on feminist subjects as well as in more traditional areas of philosophy.

Reading Questions

1. Is being let down by someone you once loved a cost you must pay (later) for the benefits enjoyed in the love relationship?

2. Is it then foolish to love anyone, since we thereby make ourselves lastingly vulnerable?

3. Are there limits on what we can expect from someone in the way of not betraying a trust, once the relationship is over?

Three Stories

FIRST STORY: GROWING APART

FLORENCE AND ENID were bosom friends while growing up together. Enid had a talent for drawing and painting and, when they were sixteen, made Florence a gift of one of her paintings, a large canvas depicting a picnic place by a river where they had spent many happy hours together. Florence treasured this painting for many years and took it with her when she moved away to another land. The two friends wrote to one another, but with decreasing frequency. Ten years and several residences after the gift of the painting, Florence faced another move and found the packing of the painting a bit of a nuisance. She had also come to like it less than she once did and reflected that she and Enid, as well as being separated by physical distance, had perhaps now grown apart in aesthetic taste. She decided to leave the large painting with the new tenant of the house she was vacating, technically on loan, to be reclaimed at an unspecified later date. Years passed. Enid and Florence exchanged letters at Christmas, met briefly on a few occasions. Florence forgot the painting. Then Enid one day wrote to announce that her painting was slowly gaining recognition and that a gallery wanted to exhibit her work, displaying its development over the years. Would Florence let her have the painting of the picnic place by the river, for this exhibition of her work? Florence realizes she has lost track of the painting, feels terrible, and has to confess the state of things to Enid, who is understandably hurt at what she is told.

SECOND STORY: THE SAD FATE OF THE ONCE-FAT CAT, METTERNICH

Roberta and Joe and their two young children, Tilly and Florian, all loved and spoiled their cat, Metternich, a very large and corpulent tabby. He in turn loved them and, although a clumsy and heavy animal, had always exhibited great gentleness with the children when they were small and

prone to be less gentle with him. But alas, Roberta and Joe fell out of love and into estrangement, then decided to separate. By mutual agreement, Joe, the more devoted parent, took the children with him when he left town for a new job, home, and wife, and Roberta was left in the old home with Metternich. The children had wanted to take him with them but were persuaded by their parents that Metternich had originally been their mother's cat, that she would now be lonely, so needed Metternich most, and that in any case a move might upset him. After the family broke up, Metternich clearly missed the children, but was a comfort to Roberta. Her life, however, did not go smoothly, and as time passed she became very unhappy and a little deranged. She began to neglect herself and Metternich too, leaving him alone and unfed on her increasingly frequent absences from the house. From having been a spoiled-rotten confident fat cat, Metternich became a somewhat bedraggled, puzzled, and thinner cat. Eventually he wandered off—perhaps searching for the children, or who knows for what. A week later Roberta, while driving home, sees with horror his run-over remains by the highway some distance from the house. Of course when Tilly and Florian next visit, they are heartbroken at the news. Joe hears from a neighbor a bit of what led up to Metternich's death, and reproaches Roberta. "We could have taken him, but you wanted him. We thought we could trust you to look after him."

THIRD STORY: A CONFIDENCE BREACHED

Meg and Stella were friends and colleagues in a large philosophy department. Meg was directing the dissertation of a graduate student, Duane, who was generally regarded as a clever but obnoxious young man, self-assertive and arrogant. Meg seems noticeably cooler in her relations to him than to other graduate students she works with, but no one is surprised at this, given Duane's character. To Stella, however, Meg on one occasion confides that while she shares the general disapproval of Duane's character, she also finds him physically very attractive. Since he is married and she does not want entanglements with married students, she is careful, she tells Stella, to keep her relations with him distanced and safe. That, not his objectionable character, is why she treats him differently from other students. Indeed, she muses to Stella, she has noted that her sexual tastes do seem deplorably out of line with her more reflective judgments, and she suspects that the very character traits she disapproves of in Duane are part of what she is also attracted by. Stella is a good listener, but makes few such self-disclosures in return. Time passes. Duane moves away. Meg and Stella both apply for a better position at another school, and Meg gets the job and moves away. They do not write or in other ways keep up the friendship. One evening Stella is at a departmental party where the conversation turns to Meg's impressive career. Someone says, "She is a bit too perfect," and Stella, a little under the influence, adds "except for her weakness for male bullies." She is instantly asked what on earth she means, and she makes an entertaining story out of the Meg–Duane relationship. Next morning she reflects ruefully that, given the proven course of friendship in a competitive and bibulous world, perhaps she had chosen the better course to remain buttoned up, not confiding in Meg the sorts of things Meg had confided in her. Confidences invite entertaining breaches of confidence (adaptation of a story Laurence Thomas tells in "Friendship").

Commentary on the Stories

Each story tells of a failure of a woman to do something that someone she once loved had trusted her to do. For trust must last longer than love, if, when we love, we then entrust to the loved person some valued thing which we have to leave indefinitely within the loved one's power to harm. We entrust all sorts of things to those we love—the well-being of more dependent loved ones, our secrets, the work of our heart and hands. The intimacy may end, but when it ends there are some entrusted things we cannot retrieve, such as the knowledge Stella has of Meg. Some things, like the well-being of pets or the affection of one's children once one's spouse has custody of them, we may have little choice but to trust to the ex-intimate. Other things we would try to retrieve only if the intimacy ends with great bitterness, and each returns all the other's gifts. Trusting continues once intimacy has faded or ended, sometimes because it must, sometimes because there seems no reason why it should not. Joe had no reason to expect Roberta to cease to care enough about Metternich, nor did it occur to Enid that Florence might just abandon her painting. But once these letdowns happen, even the victims will realize that they are victims of very frequent sorts of disappointment of trust. How can we be disappointed by such common failings? Can we really think that our friends, just because they are *our* friends or ex-friends, will be free from common human failings? Are we wrong to feel wronged when let down in these ways? Are these hurts just the normal costs of the benefits of intimacy, a sort of delayed payment for the vanished pleasures of old intimacies? What are reasonable ethical standards by which to judge one another for our behavior toward those who have been important in our lives, close to us, and loved by us?

Before trying to answer these questions let me first make some comments about the variety of disappointing behavior in an ex-intimate illustrated in my three stories. Roberta's bad behavior and Stella's can be characterized without referring to the fact that another person trusted them.[1] Roberta was cruel to Metternich, and Stella was a malicious gossip. That they may also be charged with letting down those they had loved compounds their crimes. Do those who let others down always display some other fault, in displaying the fault of untrustworthiness? Did Florence display any fault except the fault of not being true to the old friendship, not continuing to care enough about the painting her friend had made for her? Of the person victims in the three stories, Enid is in a way the one who suffered the worst hurt, and what seems to make it worse is that there is nothing wrong with what Florence did *except* that it failed Enid or insulted their friendship. After all, was not the painting hers, to do with as she saw fit? It is as if Roberta's unhappy insensitivity to Metternich's misery is almost an excuse for her disappointment of a trust; and Stella's wish to be popular with her colleagues by purveying gossip, or even her resentment of her ex-friend's greater success, is almost an excuse for her breach of confidence. But Florence has no such other vice or fault to excuse her failure to sustain Enid's trust. Is it a worse thing for decent people than for less decent people to let down those who trust them? There is a sense in which both Joe and Meg discover that they should never have trusted Roberta and Stella in the ways they did, but Enid does not discover that she should not have given Florence the painting. Nor need she regret the friendship. She will just be very hurt.

The degree of hurt here seems connected with *what* it is that Florence has neglected, or rather with the closeness of its connection with the trusting friend. To abandon a picture surely is not in itself as serious a thing as to abandon or neglect a living thing, like Metternich; but Metternich, however much he mattered to Joe, Tilly, and Florian, was not part of them in the way artists' works are part of their very selves.[2] And when the subject matter of the painting is a place of shared memory to the giver and the friend to whom it is given, the gift becomes even more meaningful, less properly seen as simply a piece of property which has been transferred by a free gift. Such a gift is not free, but richly entailed. To accept it is to accept a sort of indefinite trusteeship, which Florence in her own mind terminated when she let the painting out of her safekeeping, or at least out of her ability to keep track of. To make such a heavily freighted gift is to involve the recipient in one's life, and one can properly do

that only to those one has reason to think will want such involvement. It is a mark of real intimacy that it normally does involve the exchange of such unfree gifts. And it is a mark of a hostile ending to such an intimate relation to have the impulse to throw back all such gifts in the giver's face. Think how much worse it would have been for Enid if Florence had simply shipped the painting back when she tired of it. Losing track of it shows a cooling of friendship, but returning it would have shown a deliberate intention to declare the friendship over. Once we have given part of ourselves away, we cannot welcome it back again. It cannot go home again.

As for the sort of knowledge that Stella had of Meg, that Meg entrusted to Stella, and that Stella did not take proper care of, is it as close to the trusting person herself as Enid's painting is to Enid? This case of letting a trusting friend down is the most distasteful of the three, not because of the seriousness of the wrong done to Meg (she may suffer only insignificant ridicule, which may never come to her knowledge) or because hurting her reputation is tantamount to hurting her, but rather because of the shabbiness of Stella's motives for such abuse of trust. She uses her past intimacy for an unimportant end she occasionally adopts—wanting to have something interesting to say. Had she blackmailed Meg—written a letter saying, "I will spread what I know of your sexual tastes around the profession if you do not recommend my paper to Journal J for publication"—then her abuse of trust would be more serious, but no shabbier. Again, here it looks as if a graver wrong eclipses other wrongs. The very moral barbarism it would take to be an overt blackmailer is tantamount to disqualification from more delicate moral evaluation. Blackmail would remove one from the group of those purporting to be morally decent. Stella has not so removed herself—she fails at something she wants to succeed at, being the sort of person another could want as a friend. In this story what makes Stella look so bad is not that reputation is so important or that in harming it, Stella is harming

Meg herself. Stella is despicable rather than dangerous. This case is different from the other two in that Stella can be said to have abused not merely trust, but what was entrusted. Florence abandoned but did not misuse or abuse Enid's painting. (Had she sold it, for a high price, that might have been misuse of a meaningful gift.) Roberta neglected but did not abuse Metternich. Stella, however, did abuse Meg's self-disclosure. The proper use of such intimate knowledge as is gained in friendship is to enable better reciprocal aid and comfort, and more satisfying shared enjoyments. To pervert that knowledge for other ends, for petty or less petty personal profit, is to abuse it. One way to abuse trust is to abuse what is entrusted, for one particularly nasty way not to care for what is entrusted to one's care is to abuse it.

Whenever we come to trust another we make ourselves vulnerable in ways we earlier were not. Should the trusted one choose to hurt us, or be negligent or incompetent in the way they act toward us, we will suffer. In the three stories there not only is a trusting and a trusted person, but there is something that is entrusted, but is not properly looked after. In an earlier attempt to say what trust between persons is, I analyzed it as entrusting the care of something one cares about to the trusted, and in the foregoing discussion I have used that analysis. Metternich's well-being, the painting, special knowledge, were entrusted to persons who failed to look after these things properly. But in the third case, where secrets were not looked after, this analysis is a little strained. What matters most here, and possibly also in the painting case, is not the fate of the entrusted but what that revealed about the attitude of the trusted. What Florence and Stella do is insult or dishonor the past—Enid's past act of creating the painting and giving it, Meg's past act of self-disclosure. The continuing things, the painting and the special knowledge, are important mainly as carriers of the meaning of those past acts, and so it may seem artificial to insist on seeing their care as what the trusted one failed at. It is typical of trust between intimates, as distinct from, say,

trust of plane passengers in their pilot, that the things that are entrusted have this sort of symbolic or even memorial character. Destroying them or abusing them, as Stella did, is like desecration, like despoiling graves. Neglecting them is like letting a grave become overgrown. Losing them, as Florence did, is like forgetting the location of a loved one's grave. In such cases, the symbolic function or meaning of what our action or inaction literally affects is what gives a special type of gravity to any failings we are guilty of there. This dimension is lacking in Roberta's story, since Metternich is not a symbol but a living victim. He was important in his own right, not just for what he meant to others.

It is typical of intimacy not merely that it sets up these symbol-systems, and involves the exchange of what become sacred objects, gifts with emotional strings attached, but also that the increased vulnerability we thereby incur is not something we dwell on. The trust that intimacy involves brings greater vulnerability along with less *sense* of vulnerability than other trust relationships. For to have the thought, How she could wound me, if she chose! would be to impair the trusting intimacy. To the extent that the thought occurs, the intimacy is imperfect. But the unthought thought is nevertheless true, and to understand intimacy and the sorts of untrustworthiness it and its aftermath make possible we must recognize both the fact of the vulnerability, and the inappropriateness of even mentally alluding to it, as long as one wants intimacy to last.

The Morals of the Stories

What conclusions should we draw about the ethics of intimate friendship and of trust between intimate and ex-intimate friends? Is it foolish of us to make ourselves lastingly vulnerable, as we do when we become intimate with others? Or is it only that we are foolish to become intimate with those people who actually wound us during or after intimate friendships? Should we always in prudence consider how this person will behave once the intimacy is over before letting intimacy develop? Do those who choose intimacy with the untrustworthy get what they deserve, when they suffer what Meg, Enid, Roberta, Tilly, and Florian suffered, as their loved or once-loved ones let them down? Or should we criticize only the untrustworthy ones, not the trusting ones, in these cases? Is it a serious wrong to let down one's ex-intimates in the ways these stories illustrate?

The firm truth to keep fixed in our attempts to answer these questions is that, as Aristotle said, "without friends no one would choose to live." Bad friends may be better than no friends. Whatever moral judgments we endorse should be ones that protect, enhance, and encourage friendship, including intimate friendship, not ones that threaten it. So the last thing we should encourage is the form of caution that at the beginning or during the course of intimacy would have us consider the question, How well will my friend behave when we split up? For that would be a question too many. However it got answered, by arising at all it would deter or damage intimacy. Nevertheless we do sometimes want to deplore the character of trusting little drummer girls who are regular fair game for treacherous schemers.

If we do not want to encourage everyone on the brink of intimacy to envisage the possible endings and aftermaths of that intimacy, then what exactly would we seasoned ones advise during the beginning stages, as a preventive against deserved letdown later? My suggestion here picks up from a point noted earlier, that what shows untrustworthiness also usually shows some other fault in the untrustworthy person—insensitivity or cruelty, or a tendency to malicious gossip. And we should remember, when we select some character traits as virtues, others as faults, that "our situation . . . is in continued fluctuation." As Hume goes on, is it the case not merely that "a man who lies at a distance from us may, in a little time, become a familiar acquaintance" (1978, 581), but also that those who were familiar acquaintances may come in time to be distanced from us?

We can surely encourage people to be selective in their intimacies, to cultivate what Aristotle called character friendships, without thereby endangering intimacy and friendship themselves. Thoughts about most of the character traits of those with whom we are becoming, or already are, intimate do not seem thoughts too many. Even thoughts about trustworthiness may be perfectly appropriate—it is precise thoughts about how the others could wound us, if they chose, that seem the thoughts unsuitable to the continuation or enhancement of the intimacy. In order to safeguard ourselves against such possible wounds, we should try to have friends whose general character is such that the chances of their inflicting such wounds are slight enough not to be worth adverting to. This need not be the same as trying to assess each possible friend for long-term trustworthiness in specific respects.

Did Enid, in letting Florence become her bosom friend, act foolishly, choose as a friend a person of bad or shallow character, come to love someone whose love for her was not deep? This seems too tough a judgment, too tough on both the young friends. There is, in the story told, no sign that Florence ceased to care about Enid any more than Enid did for Florence—Enid's will to preserve mementos was not tested. It was Florence's bad moral luck to have a large and hard-to-transport memento on her hands, to have her aesthetic taste develop and diverge from Enid's in the way it did, and to be found out in her failure. It was more a failure of piety to the old days of the bosom friendship than a failure to continue to care about Enid. She may have cared very much—her distress at having to tell Enid, her feeling that she must nevertheless tell her the truth, not concoct some excusing story about fire or theft to get herself off the hook, show her regard and concern for her old friend. My verdict on this story is that good friends should be hurt by, and also should understand and forgive, the sort of failure Florence was guilty of. It shows neither a bad character, one that should have ruled her out as a character friend in the first place, nor a character that worsened as the close friendship was attenuated by time and distance. It would have been splendid had she made the effort to transport and live with the large painting, with its richness of sentimental value and (in her eyes) lack of aesthetic value, but we should not demand that our friends be so splendid. We can, however, *hope* that they may be splendid, and can expect that sentimental value will count for *something*.

Usually we will also hope that our friends find aesthetic and other value where we find it. The hurt to Enid would be as much in the realization that Florence must have come to like her painting less and less, as in the realization that its sentimental value was not enough to make her treasure it despite its perceived absence of other value. We want our friends to admire what we produce. This is natural, perhaps inevitable, but it is no duty of friendship to keep on admiring what we once, with the proper bias of a close friend, perhaps did sincerely admire. Friends know this, and so put up with the hurt of *not* having their old friends admire their old works. It is harder to put up with it in a new friend. There it could be taken as an indicator either of lukewarmness in the new friend, or of the fact that the friendship is not a character friendship. If the relationship is purely sexual, then the mutual attraction may be unaffected by the fact that each despises the work achievement of the other, unaffected even by the fact that each disapproves of the other's character. But in the intimate friendship, we expect that there will be shared standards of excellence, so that if you find your own work relatively good, not just in the enthusiasm of producing it, but on cooler reflection, then usually your friend will be expected to agree. Such agreement, however, depends upon mutual influence, on a shared life, and cannot be expected to continue when the only contact is exchange of yearly letters. So although of course the nonadmiration of one's work by an old friend hurts more than a stranger's indifference, it is certainly not treachery or betrayal. Nor is it treachery or inconstancy to come to dislike what one once admired, even when it might have been a sort of betrayal, or some failure of the heart, to have disliked it from the start. The only possible betrayal that Florence is guilty of is that of not bothering to keep, for sentimental reasons (in her attic perhaps), the painting that she no longer has aesthetic reasons to hang on her walls.

But would Enid have wanted her to have stored it in the attic? Do we really want our old friends to clutter their attics with works or gifts of ours that they can no longer bear to have closer at hand? We may of course hope for the impossible, that tastes not change, and that the judgments made at the height of friendship prove lasting and unbiased. But we do not reflectively endorse such hopes, so we are merely hurt, not morally indignant, when, like Enid, we find that sentimental and other values came to diverge, and that sentiment was outweighed. We would be almost as hurt, were we in Enid's place, to find out that the painting's only remaining value to Florence was sentimental, so that it was dusty but safe in her attic. Hurts of this sort are inevitable, and we accept them as part and parcel of what intimacy and the fading of intimacy involve.

Interestingly, it seems that where intimacy continues, such coming to dislike one's friend's early, and earlier liked, works is much less hurtful, in part because one's judgment will still be influencing and influenced by the friend's judgment, so that the painting may then get moved to the attic, or given to the jumble sale, by common agreement (if always with some lingering regret on its maker's part). It is because all that Florence has of Enid, besides yearly letters and an occasional brief meeting, is the painting, and its fellow-souvenirs, that it seems of more importance. It is a lesser matter to junk the early works of current intimates than of ex-intimates, and doing so is less likely to hurt them when they know of it. We value mementos and expect them to be valued when they are all, or almost all, that we have left of a relationship. Live intimacies do not yet need memorials.

Friends care about each other's well-being, and good friends continue to care when the intimacy is over. The ethics of friendship is much closer to being simply a matter of avoiding hurting the other than is the ethics of our relationships to nonfriends, even when those who are not friends trust us. For they trust us only on specific matters, make themselves vulnerable to our neglect or incompetence in a specific way, as for example I trust my mailman not to throw away my mail on the days when he feels too tired to deliver it. But even when, as a mailman, he is perfectly trustworthy, he may well hurt me in other ways—he may make unkind remarks to me about the upkeep of my lawn, or he may leave my gate open so that my visitor's dog strays. He need have done no wrong, certainly not disappointed a trust, by these thoughtless or less than optimally considerate actions. Usually, when we trust, we trust in a restricted respect—we do not simply trust the other not to hurt us in any way. With friends we are closer to having unrestricted trust. But although we may trust our intimate friends not to hurt or wound us in any avoidable intentional way, we need not trust their ability to avoid certain sorts of harming if they are put in a position to inflict them. However much Hippolyte de Saujon, Comtesse de Boufflers, trusted David Hume at the height of their intimacy, it is unlikely that she trusted him to hold or carry her favorite vases for her in her chateau, L'Isle Adam, given his well-known and obvious clumsiness. So even while we are intimate, there will be some matters on which we do not trust the others, because of what we know of their specific incompetencies. And once the intimacy is over, we should not trust their ability or their will to let sentimental value always outweigh other values, as time goes on. This will be partly because we do and should trust their estimate of our own willingness to put up with some small hurts incurred through the friendship. We trust each other to do some things, accept some sacrifices, for the sake of the past intimacy. For the sake of that bosom friendship, Enid puts up with the hurt of finding out that Florence did not keep the painting, and tries not to see anything to forgive. Were the old friendship to end in bitterness at this point, broken off when Florence asks for and fails to get forgiveness from Enid, or gets it, but in such a fashion that she does not want to risk that sort of scene again, who would be responsible for the ending of the friendship?

If we are wise, then, we will not become intimate with the cruel, or with those who care more about the brief glory of purveying some juicy bit of gossip than about the good of those they have loved; and if we are good friends we will not become insensitive, vindictive, or malicious when friendships fade, or when we find ourselves competitors of our old friends. But equally, if we are wise we will know that we cannot tell who will and who will not, when unhappy enough, become cruel or insensitive, or who will prove a malicious competitor, any more than we can tell how sentimental value will, over the years, weigh against other values, in our own scales or those of our intimates or possible intimates. We simply have to develop our taste in people, then trust it. If it fails us, then our friends may let us down. But if we do not trust it, we will have no friends. The ethics of trust in friends, then, throws us back on the ethics, or prudence, of trust in ourselves. Like all trust, it can be misplaced. Like trust in our friends, it is an indispensable condition of a bearable life. Unlike many forms of trust, it is unavoidable. We may, if we are distrustful enough of others, try to minimize our reliance on them, barricading ourselves against all possible attackers. In doing so, we will be trusting (and foolishly trusting) our distrust of others. Whatever we do, however vulnerable or invulnerable to others we choose to be (or try to be), we will have to trust some capacity of our own. Generalized distrust, of ourselves as much as others, is impossible—we must trust something or someone at least more than we trust the rest. Our trust in ourselves, however, will be better based, more appropriate, when we are in a position to say, I am not alone in trusting myself; some others also trust me. . . .

NOTES

Acknowledgments: I received help from Alisa Carse, Tamara Horowitz, Hugh LaFollette, and Lynne Tirrell; from all those who earlier provided the prereflective material for these reflections; from those who did not let me down; from those who let me down in instructive ways; from those who forgave my letting them down or refused to do so in instructive ways; from those who confided their similar experiences to me; and from all those who wrote great novels exploring these themes.

1. Lynne Tirrell and Alisa Carse made this point in a discussion of an earlier version of this paper at the University of Pittsburgh Philosophy Department's "Ethicists for Lunch" series, March 1986.

2. Tamara Horowitz emphasized this in the discussion of an earlier draft of this paper.

REFERENCES

Baier, Annette. 1986. "Trust and Antitrust." *Ethics,* 96, January.

Gibbard, Allan. 1986. "Risk and Value." In D. McLean, ed. *Values at Risk.* Totowa, N.J.: Rowman and Allanheld.

Nagel, Thomas. 1986. *The View from Nowhere.* Oxford: Oxford University Press.

Thomas, Laurence. 1987. "Friendship." *Synthese,* 72.

Further Questions

1. Can having bad (unreliable) friends be better than having no friends at all?

2. Even when we are on intimate terms with someone, is it a good idea not to trust them on matters where they are known to be unreliable?

3. Do good friends continue to care about each other, even when the intimacy is over?

4. Is our trust in ourselves strengthened when we know someone else trusts us as well?

Suggested Moral of Part V

Pursuit of virtue in relationships always carries potential costs to the individuals in the relationships. Patriarchal tradition tells us that the woman should bear these costs, the paradigm of a relationship being a heterosexual romantic intimacy. Therefore, we should look closely at what we are told are virtues in relationships to see what we can salvage (e.g., trust and honesty) that will be free of hidden mechanisms that trigger off power and control on the part of one of the participants.

Further Readings for Part V: Relationships: What Is Worth Seeking or Avoiding

Lawrence A. Blum. *Friendship, Altruism and Morality* (New York, NY: Routledge & Kegan Paul, 1980). Develops a morality built on concern for others, focusing on friendship.

Jeffrey Blustein. *Care and Commitment* (New York, NY: Oxford University Press, 1991). Scholarly discussion of issues in caring, integrity, and intimacy.

Jacqueline B. Carr. *Crisis in Intimacy: When Expectations Don't Meet Reality* (Pacific Grove, CA: Brooks/Cole, 1988). A self-help book, but one especially high in intellectual content.

Richard Christie and Florence L. Geis. *Studies in Machiavellianism* (New York, NY: Academic Press, 1970). The "mach" is the unit that measures how well manipulators fare in personal encounters. Well-written, scholarly, entertaining.

Valerian J. Derlega and Alan L. Chaikin. *Sharing Intimacy: What We Reveal to Others and Why* (Englewood Cliffs, NJ: Prentice-Hall, 1975). A discussion of self-disclosure, its costs and benefits.

Martin Fisher and George Stricker, eds. *Intimacy* (New York, NY: Plenum Press, 1982). Multi-faceted approach to intimacy.

Marilyn Frye. *The Politics of Reality: Essays in Feminist Theory* (Trumansburg, NY: The Crossing Press, 1983). Many of these essays offer sound, well-developed insights into problems women have in their relationships with men.

Carol Gilligan. *In a Different Voice* (Cambridge, MA: Harvard University Press, 1982). Controversial book claiming women's experience gives them a distinct basis for morality and personal relationships, which has been neglected by male-dominated psychology.

George Graham and Hugh LaFollette, eds. *Person to Person* (Philadelphia, PA: Temple University Press, 1989). Good, readable collection of essays on the nature of personal relationships and the features of good relationships.

C. Hendrick and S. Hendrick. *Liking, Loving and Relating* (Belmont, CA: Wadsworth, 1982).

Sarah Lucia Hoagland. *Lesbian Ethics: Toward New Value* (Palo Alto, CA: Institute of Lesbian Studies, 1988).

bell hooks. *Ain't I a Woman? Black Women and Feminism* (Boston, MA: South End Press, 1984).

———*From Margin to Center* (Boston, MA: South End Press, 1984). All of bell hooks' books (the other two are listed in Further Readings for Part I) contain excellent insights into sexism in personal relationships as well as good thinking on racism.

Harriet Goldhor Lerner. *The Dance of Intimacy: A Woman's Guide to Courageous Acts of Change in Key Relationships* (New York, NY: Harper & Row, 1989). Best-seller by the author of *The Dance of Anger*. A little on the practical, non-intellectual side.

Gilbert Meilander. *Friendship: A Study in Theological Ethics* (Notre Dame, IN: University of Notre Dame Press, 1981). A development of the virtues of friendship in the tradition of Aristotle and Aquinas.

Nel Noddings. *Caring: A Feminine Approach to Ethics and Moral Education* (Berkeley, CA: University of California Press, 1984). Controversial claim that women's moral awareness centers around caring.

Janice Raymond. *A Passion for Friends* (Boston, MA: Beacon Press, 1986). Aristotelian friendship forms a model for relationships, especially lesbian relationships.

Adrienne Rich. *On Lies, Secrets and Silence: Selected Prose, 1966–1978* (New York, NY: W. W. Norton and Co., Virago Press, 1979). Features "Women and Honor: Some Notes on Lying," an argument that patriarchy forces women to take refuge in dishonorable behavior.

Lillian B. Rubin. *Intimate Strangers: Men and Women Together* (New York, NY: Harper & Row, 1983). Much-read book on difficulties with intimacy in heterosexual relationships.

———*Just Friends: The Role of Friendship in Our Lives* (New York, NY: Harper & Row, 1985). A sequel to *Intimate Strangers;* much of it again focused on heterosexual relationships.

Laurence Thomas. *Living Morally: A Psychology of Moral Character* (Philadelphia, PA: Temple University Press, 1989). Careful development of a morality based partially on altruism and friendship, with the claim that moral flourishing is essential to human flourishing.

Paul J. Wadell. *Friendship and the Moral Life* (Notre Dame, IN: University of Notre Dame Press, 1989). Expansive view of friendship and morality to the point of the possibility of being friends with God.

R. Winch. *Mate Selection: A Study of Complementary Needs* (New York, NY: Harper & Row, 1958). Development of the old idea of genders as being different and complementary and thus male gender fitting neatly onto female to make a good relationship.

VIOLENCE IN PERSONAL RELATIONSHIPS

Douglas J. Besharov, ed. *Family Violence: Research and Public Policy Issues* (Washington, DC: The AEI Press, 1990).

David Finkelhor, Richard S. Gelles, Gerald T. Hotaling, and Murray A. Straus, eds. *The Dark Side of Families: Current Family Violence Research* (Beverly Hills, CA: Sage Publications, 1983).

Robert L. Hampton, ed. *Black Family Violence: Current Research and Theory* (Lexington, MA: Lexington Books, 1991).

Gerald T. Hotaling, David Finkelhor, John R. Kirkpatrick, and Murray A. Straus, eds. *Coping with Family Violence: Research and Policy Perspectives* (Newbury Park, CA: Sage Publications, 1988).

Barry Levy, ed. *Dating Violence: Young Women in Danger* (Seattle, WA: The Seal Press, 1991).

Mary Lystad, ed. *Violence in the Home: Interdisciplinary Perspectives* (New York, NY: Brunner/Mazel Publishers, 1986).

Gordon W. Russell, ed. *Violence in Intimate Relationships* (New York, NY: PMA Publishing Corporation, 1988).

Anson Shupe, William A. Stacey, and Lonnie R. Hazelwood. *Violent Men, Violent Couples: The Dynamics of Domestic Violence* (Lexington, MA: Lexington Books, 1987).

Daniel Jay Sonkin, Del Martin, and Lenore E. Auerbach, eds. *The Male Batterer: A Treatment Approach* (New York, NY: Springer Publishing Company, 1985).

William A. Stacey and Anson Shupe. *The Family Secret: Domestic Violence in America* (Boston, MA: Beacon Press, 1983).

Murray A. Straus, Richard Gelles, et al. *Physical Violence in American Families: Risk Factors and Adaptations to Violence in 8,145 Families* (New Brunswick, NJ: Transaction Publishers, 1990).

Ron Thorne-Finch. *Ending the Silence: The Origins and Treatment of Male Violence Against Women* (Toronto: University of Toronto Press, 1992).

Gillian A. Walker. *Family Violence and the Women's Movement: The Conceptual Politics of Struggle* (Toronto: University of Toronto Press, 1990).

Leonore E. Walker. *The Battered Woman* (New York, NY: Harper & Row, 1979).

———*Terrifying Love: Why Battered Women Kill and How Society Responds* (New York, NY: HarperCollins, 1989).

Part VI

Bonds

Introduction

A ROMANTIC RELATIONSHIP can eventuate in a commitment. Our present paradigm for this bond is heterosexual marriage as it has evolved in Judeo-Christian religion and in law. The first seven writers in this part endorse that idea as an option for all couples. The remaining three writers find flaws in the traditional idea.

VI.1   Commitment and the Value of Marriage

GORDON GRAHAM

Gordon Graham outlines two kinds of marriage that have developed within Christianity. One is based upon legitimate sex. The other is a spiritual union resulting from mutual commitment. He contrasts these ideas with the more modern view of personal marriage.

Graham is Lecturer in Moral Philosophy at the University of St. Andrews, Scotland. He is writing a book that includes material on feminism.

Reading Questions

1. Do you believe that sex is good only in marriage?
2. Do you think marriage, ideally, should be a union of two people, as distinguished from a relationship between two people?
3. Would you feel comfortable marrying someone you were not in love with?

... THE QUESTION "What is commitment to another person?" seems much too direct to be approachable. There is, however, a less direct approach whereby we inquire into commitment through what is perhaps its only unmistakable institutional form: marriage. Many aspects of this very ancient institution warrant attention in their own right, but examination of them, I believe, will also throw light on the modern notion of commitment.

Making Relationships Work

I

We rarely stop to ask whether marriage is valuable and, if it is, what makes it so. Most of us just assume that it is and that some positive account of its value can be given. This assumption shows itself, very often, in our attitude to statistics relating to divorce, which are often presented in a manner suggesting that a rise in the divorce rate is a social problem. But it is a problem only if there is something lamentable about the collapse of a marriage. If there is not, an increasing number of divorces is no more a problem than an increasing number of tennis matches.

Of course when we speak of divorce as a problem we usually make at least one of two hidden assumptions. We assume that divorce brings with it unhappiness. If so, what worries us, strictly, is not increasing divorce but a rise in the amount of unhappiness. The end of a marriage, on this view, is not lamentable *in itself.* Alternatively, we assume that lifelong marriage is some sort of ideal, so that the more divorces there are, the less this ideal is being realized. This is the more interesting assumption because it raises the question whether marriage *is* an ideal.

To answer it, we obviously need to say something about what marriage is, and here another interesting feature of modern thinking comes to the fore. As a human institution marriage has taken many different forms, and some of them are quite alien to our ways of thinking—marriage by arrangement and capture, marriages of the dead, marriages to inanimate objects, all of which are recorded in human history. These are not, however, the institutions modern Western supporters of marriage have in mind. What they mean to endorse is not marriage itself, but one form of it, roughly a relationship of sexual fidelity to one member of the opposite sex entered into voluntarily, unconditionally, and for good, regardless of how the future, including the future of the relationship, may go. It is the last part that is specially important because it is this that makes marriage a relationship entered into "for better, for worse, for richer, for poorer, in sickness and in health, till death do us part," and because it is here that we can see why some people have thought marriage to be a kind of institutionalized commitment between people. . . .

II

. . . Broadly, there are two common Christian understandings of marriage as revealed in the New Testament and in the liturgy of the church. The first is what we might call the low theology of marriage. According to this view all sexual activities and relations are prima facie evil. The reasons for this low view of sex have varied, but in general this view is connected with the belief that all fleshly desires have a tendency to pull the individual away from the true joys of heaven, and by thus coming between man and God they take on the distinguishing character of sin. But though sex does have this sinful aspect, it is as plain as anything can be that human beings need sex, both for the procreation of children and for the satisfaction of natural (God-given) desires. For this reason God has *ordained* a special relationship—matrimony—in the context of which sex becomes good, in fact *holy*, because it now stands apart from any other sexual activity. Matrimony, then, is a set of conditions ordained by God

under which alone sexual activity ceases to be sinful, and one of these conditions is lifelong fidelity to one partner.

To ask why lifelong fidelity should be one of the conditions of matrimony is to question the ordination of God, and though Christian theology has generally held that lifelong marriage is *good* for human beings and that this is the reason for its ordination, the final answer, as far as human beings are concerned, must be that lifelong fidelity is simply *ordained*. Its ultimate value for us must lie not in the fact that it makes us happy, which, as we know, it may or may not do, but in the fact that it provides for the satisfaction of our natural desires in a way that rescues us from sin.

This low theology might appear to make the institution of marriage of purely instrumental value rather than intrinsic value, but this is not strictly so. It is not that sex is made good *by* marriage, but that only *in* marriage is sex good. Marriage, on this view, we might say, is a constituent of the good life, not a means to it.

It is fairly clear on this low view what adultery is and why it is a ground for divorce. If only sex with one other person on the part of both parties throughout life can be good, sex with someone else on the part of either puts an end to that possibility. What is not so clear is whether remarriage is permissible, but however this may be, we can see easily enough why lifelong marriage is an ideal. It is that relationship alone under which a certain sort of purity is possible. And the desirability of that purity arises from its place in the Christian scheme of salvation, according to which, this life must be used as a preparation for the beatific vision of God. Of course, for those who have no understanding of salvation, this explanation will hardly be satisfactory, and in a more straightforward sense it will generally fail with those who knowingly prefer pleasure to purity. But to acknowledge this limitation is only to acknowledge that *all* explanations must stop somewhere and will not persuade those who are unwilling or unable to stop at that point.

The second Christian understanding of marriage, one more in keeping with the somewhat fleeting references to this subject in the Gospels perhaps, we might call the high view, because it appears to focus on metaphysical rather than moral features of marriage. (I do not mean to suggest that the two views are incompatible in any way.) On this view marriage is a sacrament and the resulting relationship, consummated in sexual relations, a wholly new entity, which is to say that the two parties to a marriage, by vowing fidelity to each other in the sight of God, bring something into existence, namely a unity of two persons in one. This may sound odd, but it does reflect ways of speaking with which we are quite familiar, as for instance the expression "united in matrimony." If, as has traditionally been said, such a sacrament can be performed only once within the lifetimes of the partners, under normal circumstances, divorce and remarriage are impossible; just as the chemicals that go to make up a compound (in contrast to a mixture) cannot be separated again, so the persons who make up a marriage are thereafter in some way inseparable.

It is plain that even the strictest interpretation of this sacramental character of marriage does not exclude *annulment,* which is quite different from *divorce.* When a marriage is annulled it is declared never to have been. When a divorce is granted the marriage is declared to be at an end, and on the high Christian view this is in reality impossible. It is not so much that those who have availed themselves of God's power to make of themselves a holy unity *ought* not to part company, but that in some deep sense they *cannot.*

The point may best be illustrated by comparing marriage with other relationships. If I have a brother, though I can of course ignore my responsibilities to him, I nonetheless stand in a relationship to him which only death can put to an end. I cannot decide to be a brother no longer. The parallel itself, however, suggests an alternative interpretation of the high view. The only sense of brother in which I cannot cease to be a brother is a biological one, and though "brother" generally has moral overtones, these overtones cannot be attributed to the biology alone. In the moral sense, therefore, it may in extreme circumstances be possible for me to cease to be a father, mother, son, brother, or any other family relationship, a possibility that the legal institution of adoption formalizes. The biological relation, on this view, is normally a sufficient condition of the moral one, but not always. Similarly, those who subscribe to the sacramental theory may in fact admit the permissibility of divorce, on the ground that certain activities—adultery and cruelty are the commonest causes—can rupture the relationship, a rupture that may properly be reflected in law.

But whatever its attitude to divorce, it is clear that the high view also has its account of the value of marriage, namely that through it individuals may participate in a sacramental union of two persons in one, which, like every other sacrament, makes marriage an outward sign of inner grace.

Both these understandings of marriage have attendant problems, not least of which is their employment of language that many people find hard to grasp or sympathize with. It is not my business here, however, to urge the merits of either understanding, but only to point out that both go some way toward explaining why, on the Christian view, marriage based upon self-conscious vows of lifelong sexual fidelity is to be thought of as an ideal, and why its collapse, even if in some cases it is to be regarded as the only sensible course, is still a cause for regret. On the first view, it makes possible a certain sort of purity, and with the demise of a marriage that purity is lost. On the second, it is a new creation that is lost, and even if we allow the permissibility of divorce and remarriage, this remains a loss, just as the death of one child cannot be compensated for by the birth of another, on any but the crudest of utilitarian views.

It might be thought that the Christian account of marriage as elaborated here does *not* explain its value, partly because the theology remains obscure and partly because it gives us no account of the place of love in the relationship.

Such a criticism misses the essential claim that the theology *goes some way* toward providing an explanation. To the question "What is valuable about marriage?" the answer may be given that it supplies the individual with a uniquely personal relationship to one other person. As a step in a process of explanation this answer may be of some value. But if, in response to the further question "What is that relationship?" we are obliged, for want of anything better, to answer, "The relationship of being married to them," then quite clearly we have learned nothing. We need something more at this point. And this is what Christian theology gives us, for on the first view it says "The relation of lawful sex" and in the second "Spiritual union." No one could claim that either answer settles all further queries, only that each provides *some* answer and suggests a direction for further inquiry.

That this further inquiry does not push us in the direction of love is not necessarily a weakness, because it may be that what is distinctively valuable in the relation between man and wife is *not* usefully thought of as love. Of course, on the Christian view, man and wife should love each other, but not more so than they should their children and indeed their neighbors and enemies. This is, of course, love in the sense of agape rather than eros. Whether in marriage there is some special role for romantic love is a question to which I shall return. At this point, however, I think enough has been said to throw some light on the uncertainty that so often surrounds secular views of marriage. For while they inherit the belief that in every divorce there is *some* cause for lamentation, at the same time they lack the background that enables them to explain why this is so. And this, or so I argue, reflects a further deficiency: their inability to explain the peculiar value of marriage in the first place. . . .

III

. . . Our modern view of marriage has been heavily influenced by romanticism, the belief that *feelings* are what make for authenticity. Under the influence of romanticism we find it difficult, as most other cultures have not, to see any value in arranged marriages of convenience, since true marriage, it is thought, must rest upon love. And the highest form of love is the undying love of a Romeo and a Juliet. Marriage is an ideal, therefore, precisely because it expresses in institutional form the value of such love.

There are many objectionable features to this sort of romanticism, not least its unreality for most ordinary human beings, and its relegating the idea of love to the realm of romantic feeling. . . . But to see its limitations in the present context no detailed exploration of romanticism as a whole is required. We need only agree that on this conception, either true marriage consists just in the right state of feeling, in which case *vows* are irrelevant, or the appropriate loving relationship must exist independently of the vows expressed in formal marriage. If the former, the romantic conception has no place at all for self-conscious marriage as we have been considering it; and if the latter, since the loving relationship that the marriage vows exist to express may cease almost as soon as the vows are made, there may quickly be nothing for the marriage to express and hence no reason to persist with it. On the other hand, such a relationship may well exist outside solemnized marriages.

In fact this possibility suggests, curiously enough, that the romantic conception is better suited to *common* marriage, an institution around which most of Europe's marriage laws have grown up. In a common-law marriage no vows are made: The relationship is not even begun with the intention of permanence. It is its continuation that eventually results in its being given a certain legal status; and this being so, it seems natural to say that common marriage expresses or recognizes a pre-existing relationship. But of course the relationship it expresses *lacks* just the feature that marriage proper is supposed to have: the vow to lifelong fidelity.

The romantic conception of love and marriage, then, seems unable to supply the sort of background that would explain the value of marriage proper. This in itself, of course, is not a reason to reject romanticism, as many romantics saw, for it may be that to the true romantic, marriage as we commonly understand it is *not* something to which we should aspire. This is not a conclusion which many are as yet willing to accept, and for this reason, perhaps, equally familiar is an alternative response to the demand, one which rejects the romantic idea of love independent of marriage and focuses instead upon the idea of commitment. True love, we are sometimes told, is not so much the state of feeling that precedes marriage as the relationship that is itself formed by the initiation and persistence of marriage. On this account marriage expresses commitment to another person. Before we can see the limitations of this response we must explore a little further the notion of commitment.

When we speak of commitment to other people, we often have in mind a relationship that is *essentially* personal. This is to say, to be committed to others is thought to go beyond being related to them under some general category—such as clients, patients, customers, penitents—and to constitute a relationship with them as the individuals they are, which is personal in a way that all others are impersonal and is special precisely because of its personal character. This is one way in which commitment might be thought a reasonable substitute for the theological conceptions we have left behind. On the low theology outlined earlier, to be committed to someone in marriage is to be related to that person such that good sex is possible with that one and with no other. On the high view it is to be joined in a mystic unity. Either way, there is some other person to whom an individual stands in a unique relation that is itself constitutive of a life supremely valuable for human beings. In place of such an understanding, it is commitment that is to be seen as providing this unique personal relation to one other.

There is need for some greater clarification here, but we can usefully proceed on the assumption that the idea of commitment to another person does indeed mark an aspiration to a relationship that could hold only with that one person. This way of talking can be misunderstood. No doubt all relationships can be brought under the head of *some* general category which will determine certain duties between the related parties. The talk of commitment, it seems to me, does not need to deny this. It claims only that if *all* relationships are understood *solely* in this way then an important aspect of human relationships, and what is as a matter of fact valued about them, is left out of the picture.

For example, we are related to our doctors in certain institutional ways according to which they owe certain duties to us and we to them. The exercise of these duties is generally valuable, such that were they to die or leave town, we should certainly miss them, regret being without a doctor, and take steps to find another. But it may also be the case that we miss our own particular doctor, and whereas, in a sense, *anyone* may replace this one as a doctor, *no one* can replace this one as the person in my life.

Such a personal element may suffuse almost any relationship. This is not to say, however, that all such relationships contain an element of commitment. Commitment implies an active resolution which, though not incompatible with the ties of mutual pleasure, affection, admiration, and the like—we generally love and like those we are committed to—is nonetheless to be contrasted with them. Though we may commit ourselves to others *because* we love or admire them, we cannot sensibly speak of a resolve to regard with affection. . . . People can resolve to take care of others in a context of intimacy; and this we may, if we wish, call a resolve to love. There is nothing in the English language that prevents it. But it remains true that there are always spontaneous elements in personal relationships that in part determine the value of the relationship—I cannot delight in your company unless I am sometimes amused by you and I cannot *resolve* to be amused. And so it is with those relationships of which it is common to speak of commitment.

Now, the idea we are concerned with considers marriage a relationship in which this personal element takes the form of the highest possible degree of commitment, a commitment that is legally or socially formalized, without, however, losing anything of its intensely personal character.

But this suggests a problem. How can commitment in the form of a marriage vow, which is a sort of promising or resolving, contrive to secure a relationship distinctive for its highly personal, and hence in part spontaneous, nature? It seems, on the present analysis, that it cannot. The best that can be said is that this sort of resolution, together with the legal relationship and the social recognition that result, can provide the means whereby the personal may be made more likely to flourish. To put it another way, commitment, and hence marriage, is in some sense an *instrument* in the development of a personal relationship. Thus we are brought to the second of the two justifications outlined earlier, that it promotes something of value.

It is a common view that the value of marriage lies chiefly in its being a means of promoting the interests of the two parties, where "interests" is widely understood, and to think of it in this way is to regard it as a contract. . . . Marriage, understood as an unconditional contract, is by its nature a relationship entered into regardless of the future benefits to either party or to both. This means that, at the point of marrying, though the expectation that neither party will benefit from the marriage would be a reason not to enter into it, the acknowledged *possibility* of shared disbenefit cannot be understood to supply a condition under which the marriage will be terminated. It is precisely all such possibilities that are excluded by the unconditional nature of the marriage vows. But further, there seems no reason to suppose that contracts cannot properly, and without remainder, be dissolved upon the simple agreement of both parties *on any grounds whatever,* and this in itself suggests that marriage is not to be understood simply as a contract between two people voluntarily entered into. For to conceive of it thus, we might say, is to make it *too* instrumental.

It is here that the idea of commitment may be expected to do its most useful work, because we may plausibly suppose that, though it is correct to locate marriage in the general area of promising and to emphasize its formal character, it cannot adequately be treated as a contract, with the instrumental and impersonal overtones that this idea brings. And this gives us reason to think of marriage as an act of commitment. The question then is whether commitment fares better than contract.

A commitment, it might be said, *has* to be more than a fair-weather agreement. Otherwise there is nothing in it that may be tested; there is, in fact, no real element of commitment. This does not mean, however, that all commitments are quite without conditions, and it may in principle be both possible and prudent to explore and to detail the terms of all our commitments, even those we have to our nearest and dearest. But it is not always wise to do so. For example, if asked for a meal at a restaurant by a comparative stranger, I have no very good reason to suppose that I will not be left to foot the bill. But if what I hope for is the development of a firm friendship, I would be wise not to ask for assurances before accepting the invitation. Similarly, or so it may be said, what we want in marrying is a long-term relationship of trust and intimacy with one other person; and in most cases, to spell out the precise conditions under which each party would be entitled to abandon the commitment would be a sure way to jeopardize the possibility of such a relationship from the outset. In other words, trust can only grow from trust, commitment from commitment.

This resulting view of marriage has much to commend it. It relies on no strange metaphysics and seems well adapted to the facts of modern marriage. And I am inclined to say that, so far as it goes, this appeal to commitment provides us with an intelligible view of it. But it does not make an ideal of the institution we have inherited. It does not do so because the permanence and exclusivity of the commitment matter only because the alternatives are, as a rule, best not thought of. Should it be the case, in any particular instance, that they *can* be thought of without detriment to the personal character of the relationship, they have no place at all in the account.

This is a matter of some importance because we can easily imagine couples making the sort of commitment that marriage requires, but allowing each other a measure of sexual freedom. And we can also imagine, more easily if anything, a commitment which, though it has no express time limit, is not generally expected to last past childrearing. In such circumstances, the idea of commitment would still have an important part to play in the explanation of these marriages and what was valuable about them, but it would secure nothing of the character of marriage as Christianity conceives it. . . .

Further Questions

1. Would a bad sexual experience have been any better if you had been married to the person with whom you had it? Would a good one have been improved?

2. Do you agree that it is all right to dissolve a (childless) marriage whenever both parties agree to the dissolution? Could such dissolution be on any grounds they chose?

3. Is it appropriate to dissolve a (childless) marriage when neither party is getting anything out of it at the personal level? Would this mean that there had been some defect in the original commitment?

VI.2   Marital Faithfulness

SUSAN MENDUS

Susan Mendus tries to disentangle confusions about marriage vows. The central problem is that these vows seem to promise feelings in the distant future, over which the person has no effective control. How can you promise to love someone fifty years hence?

Mendus is Lecturer in Philosophy and Morrell Fellow in Toleration at the University of York.

Reading Questions

1. Do you think that your love for someone is conditional upon him or her not changing any drastic way?

2. People do change, sometimes in drastic ways. If your feelings toward a person change as a result, do you plead that that individual has become a different person, hence not the person who was the original object of your feelings?

3. When you make commitments to people, do you usually couple them with "escape clauses" ("unless . . .")?

And so the two swore that at every time of their lives, until death took them, they would assuredly believe, feel and desire exactly as they had believed, felt and desired during the preceding weeks. What was as remarkable as the undertaking itself was the fact that nobody seemed at all surprised at what they swore.[1]

CYNICISM ABOUT THE PROPRIETY of the marriage promise has been widespread amongst philosophers and laymen alike for many years. Traditionally, the ground for suspicion has been the belief that the marriage promise is a promise about feelings where these are not directly under the control of the will. . . .

[For example, Bertrand Russell] tells of how his love for his wife 'evaporated' during the course of a bicycle ride. He simply 'realized,' he says, that he no longer loved her and was subsequently unable to show any affection for her.[2] This, anyway, is the most familiar objection to the marriage promise: that it is a promise about feelings, where these are not directly under the control of the will.

A second objection to the marriage promise is that it involves a commitment which extends over too long a period: promising to do something next Wednesday is one thing, promising to do something fifty years hence is quite another, and it is thought to be improper either to give or to extract promises extending over such a long period of time. . . .

Claiming that long-term promises do not carry any moral weight seems to be another way of claiming that unconditional promises do not carry any moral weight. Such an unconditional promise is the promise made in marriage, for when I promise to love and to honor I do not mutter under my breath, 'So long as you never become a member of the Conservative Party,' or 'Only if your principles do not change radically.' . . .

[In 'Later Selves and Moral Principles,' Derek Parfit[3] seems to suggest] that all promises (all promises which carry any moral weight, that is) are, and can be, made only on condition that there is no substantial change in the character either of promisor or promisee: if my husband's character changes radically, then I may think of the man before me not as my husband, but as some other person, some 'later self.' Similarly, it would seem that I cannot now promise to love another 'till death us do part,' since that would be like promising that another person will do something (in circumstances in which my character changes fundamentally over a period of time) and I cannot promise that another person will do something, but only that *I* will do something. Thus all promises must be conditional; all promises must be short-term. For what it is worth, I am not the least tempted to think that only short-term promises carry any moral weight and it is therefore a positive *disadvantage* for me that Parfit's theory has this consequence. But even if it were intuitively plausible that short-term promises alone carry moral weight, there are better arguments than intuitive ones and I hope I can mention some here.

The force of Parfit's argument is brought out by his 'Russian nobleman' example, described in 'Later Selves and Moral Principles':

> Imagine a Russian nobleman who, in several years will inherit vast estates. Because he has socialist ideals, he intends now to give the land to the peasants, but he knows that in time his ideals may fade. To guard against this possibility he does two things. He first signs a legal document, which will automatically give away the land and which can only be revoked with his wife's consent. He then says to his wife 'If I ever change my mind and ask you to revoke the document, promise me that you will not consent.' He might add 'I regard my ideals as essential to me. If I lose these ideals I want you to think that I cease to exist. I want you to think of your husband then, not as me, but only as his later self. Promise me that you would not do as he asks.'[4]

Parfit now comments:

> This plea seems understandable and if his wife made this promise and he later asked her to revoke the document *she* might well regard herself as in no way released from her commitment. It might seem to her as if she had obligations to two different people. She might think that to do

what her husband now asks would be to betray the young man whom she loved and married. And she might regard what her husband now says as unable to acquit her of disloyalty to this young man—to her husband's earlier self. [Suppose] the man's ideals fade and he asks his wife to revoke the document. Though she promised him to refuse, he now says that he releases her from this commitment . . . we can suppose she shares our view of commitment. If so, she will only believe that her husband is unable to release her from the commitment if she thinks that it is in some sense not *he* to whom she is committed . . . she may regard the young man's loss of ideals as involving replacement by a later self.[5]

Now, strictly speaking, and on Parfit's own account, the wife should not make such a promise: to do so would be like promising that another person will do something, since she has no guarantee that *she* will not change in character and ideals between now and the time of the inheritance. Further, there is a real question as to why anyone outside of a philosophical example should first draw up a document which can only be revoked with his wife's consent and then insist that his wife not consent whatever may happen. But we can let these points pass. What is important here, and what I wish to concentrate on, is the suggestion that my love for my husband is conditional upon his not changing in any substantial way: for this is what the example amounts to when stripped of its special story about later selves. (In his less extravagant moods Parfit himself allows that talk of later selves is, in any case, a mere '*façon de parler*.')[6]

The claim then is that all promises must be conditional upon there being no change in the character of the promisee: that if my husband's character and ideals change it is proper for me to look upon him as someone other than the person I loved and married. This view gains plausibility from reflection on the fact that people can, and often do, give up their commitments. There is, it will be said, such an institution as divorce, and

people do sometimes avail themselves of it. But although I might give up my commitment to my husband, and give as my reason a change in his character and principles, this goes no way towards showing that only short-term promises carry any moral weight, for there is a vital distinction here: the distinction between, on the one hand, the person who promises to love and to honor but who finds that, after a time, she has lost her commitment (perhaps on account of change in her husband's character), and, on the other hand, the person who promises to love and to honor only on condition that there be no such change in character. The former person may properly be said, under certain circumstances, to have given up a commitment; the latter person was never committed in the appropriate way at all. The wife of the Russian nobleman, by allowing in advance that she will love her husband only so long as he doesn't change in any of the aforementioned ways, fails properly to commit herself to him: for now her attitude to him seems to be one of respect or admiration, not commitment at all. Now she *does* mutter under her breath 'So long as you don't become a member of the Conservative Party.' But the marriage promise contains no such 'escape clause.' When Mrs. Micawber staunchly declares that she will never desert Mr. Micawber, she means just that. There are no conditions, nor could there be any, for otherwise we would fail to distinguish between respect or admiration *for the principles* of another and the sort of unconditional commitment to *him* which the marriage vow involves. There are many people whose ideals and principles I respect, and that respect would disappear were the ideals and principles to disappear, but my commitment to my husband is distinct from mere respect or admiration in just this sense, that it is not conditional on there being no change in his ideals and principles. I am now prepared to admit that my respect for another person would disappear were he revealed to be a cheat and a liar. I am not now prepared to admit that my love for my husband, my commitment to him, would disappear were he revealed to be a cheat and a liar. . . . Such is the case with commitment of the sort involved in the marriage vow. I promise to love and to honor and in so doing I cannot now envisage anything happening such as would make me give up that commitment. But, it might be asked, how can I be clairvoyant? How can I recognize that there is such a thing as divorce and at the same time declare that nothing will result in my giving up my commitment? The explanation lies in the denial that my claim . . . has the status of a prediction. My commitment to another should not be construed as a prediction that I will never desert that other. . . . But if my statement is not a prediction, then what is it? It is perhaps more like a statement of intention, where my claims about a man's intentions do not relate to his future actions in as simple a way as do my predictions about his future actions.

If I predict that A will do x and A does not do x, then my prediction is simply false. If, on the other hand, I claim that A intends to do x and he does not, it is not necessarily the case that my statement was false: for he may have had that intention and later withdrawn it. Similarly with commitment: if I claim that A is unconditionally committed to B, that is not a prediction that A will never desert B; it is a claim that there is in A a present intention to do something permanently, where that is distinct from A's having a permanent intention. Thus Mrs. Micawber's claim that she will never desert Mr. Micawber, if construed as a commitment to him, is to that extent different from a prediction that she will never desert him, for her commitment need not be thought never to have existed if she does desert him. Thus an unconditional commitment to another person today, a denial today that anything could happen such as would result in desertion of Mr. Micawber, is not incompatible with that commitment being given up at a later date.

In brief, then, what is wrong in Parfit's example is that the wife *now* allows that her commitment will endure only so long as there is no substantial change in character. She should not

behave thus, because her doing so indicates that she has only respect for her husband, or admiration for his principles, not a commitment to him: she need not behave thus, as there can be such a thing as unconditional commitment, analogous to intention and distinct from prediction in the way described.

All this points to the inherent oddity of the 'trial marriage.' It is bizarre to respond to 'wilt thou love her, comfort her, honor her and keep her?' with 'Well, I'll try.' Again, the response 'I will' must be seen as the expression of an intention to do something permanently, not a prediction that the speaker will permanently have that intention.

A further problem with the Russian nobleman example and the claim that only short-term promises carry any moral weight is this: when the wife of the Russian nobleman allows in advance that her commitment to her husband will cease should his principles change in any substantial way, she implies that a list of his present principles and ideals will give an exhaustive explanation of her loving him. But this is not good enough. If I now claim to be committed to my husband I precisely cannot give an exhaustive account of the characteristics he possesses in virtue of which I have that commitment to him: if I could do so, there would be a real question as to why I am not prepared to show the same commitment to another person who shares those characteristics (his twin brother, for example). Does this then mean that nothing fully explains my love for another and that commitment of this sort is irrationally based? I think we need not go so far as to say that: certainly, when asked to justify or explain my love I may point to certain qualities which the other person has, or which I believe him to have, but in the first place such an enumeration of qualities will not provide a complete account of why I love him, rather it will serve to explain, as it were, his 'lovableness.' It will make more intelligible my loving him, but will not itself amount to a complete and exhaustive explanation of my loving him. Further, it may well be that in giving my list of characteristics I cite some which the other person does not, in fact, have. If this is so, then the explanation may proceed in reverse order: the characteristics I cite will not explain or make intelligible my love, rather my love will explain my ascribing these characteristics. A case in point here is Dorothea's love for Casaubon, which is irrationally based in that Casaubon does not have the characteristics and qualities which Dorothea thinks him to have. Similarly, in the case of infatuation the lover's error lies in wrongly evaluating the qualities of the beloved. In this way Titania 'madly dotes' on the unfortunate Bottom who is trapped in an ass's head, and addresses him thus:

> Come sit thee down upon this flowery bed
> While I thy amiable cheeks do coy
> And stick musk roses in thy sleek, smooth
>   head
> And kiss thy fair, large ears my gentle joy.

and again

> I pray thee, gentle mortal, sing again.
> Mine ear is much enamoured of thy note;
> So is mine eye enthralled to thy shape,
> And thy fair virtue's force perforce doth move
>   me
> On the first view, to say, to swear, I love thee.[7]

Both cases involve some error on the part of the lover: in one case the error is false belief about the qualities the beloved possesses; in the other it is an error about the evaluation of the qualities the beloved possesses. These two combine to show that there can be such a thing as a 'proper object' of love. This will be the case where there is neither false belief nor faulty evaluation. They do not, however, show that in ascribing qualities and characteristics to the beloved the lover exhaustively explains and accounts for his love. The distinction between 'proper' love and irrationally based love, or between 'proper' love and infatuation, is to be drawn in terms of the correctness of beliefs and belief-based evaluations. By contrast, the distinction between love and respect or admiration is to be drawn in terms of the explanatory

power of the beliefs involved. In the case of respect or admiration the explanatory power of belief will be much greater than it is in the case of love. For this reason my respect for John's command of modal logic will disappear, and I am now prepared to admit that it will disappear, should I discover that my belief that he has a command of modal logic is false. Whereas I am not now prepared to admit that my commitment to and love for my husband will disappear if I discover that my beliefs about his qualities and characteristics are, to some extent, false. . . .

I turn now to a somewhat bizarre element in Parfit's talk of ideals. Parfit portrays the Russian nobleman as one who 'finds' that his ideals have faded, as one who 'loses' his ideals when circumstances and fortune change. What is bizarre in this talk is emphasized by the following extract from Alison Lurie's novel *Love and Friendship*:

> 'But, Will, promise me something.'
> 'Sure.'
> 'Promise me you'll never be unfaithful to me.'
> Silence.
> Emily raised her head, 'You won't promise?' she said incredulously.
> 'I can't, Emily. How can I promise how I'll feel for the next ten years? You want me to lie to you? You could change. I could change. I could meet somebody.'
> Emily pulled away. 'Don't you have any principles?' she asked.[8]

The trouble with the inappropriately named Will and the Russian nobleman in Parfit's example is that it is doubtful whether either man has any genuine principles at all. Each is portrayed as almost infinitely malleable, as one whose principles will alter in accordance with changing circumstances. The point about a moral principle however is that it must serve in some sense to rule out certain options as options at all. In his article 'Actions and Consequences,' John Casey refers us to the example of Addison's Cato who, when offered life, liberty, and the friendship of Caesar if he will surrender, and is asked to name his terms, replies:

Bid him disband his legions,
Restore the Commonwealth to liberty,
Submit his actions to the public censure
And stand the judgement of a Roman Senate.
Bid him do this and Cato is his friend.[9]

The genuine principles which Cato has determine that certain options will not ultimately be options at all for him. To say this, of course, is not to deny that life and liberty are attractive and desirable to him. Obviously he is, in large part, admirable precisely because they are attractive to him and yet he manages to resist their allure. The point is rather that not *any* sort of life is desirable. The sort of life he would, of necessity, lead after surrender—a life without honor—is not ultimately attractive to him and that it is not attractive is something which springs from his having the principles he does have. What Cato values above all else is honor and his refusal to surrender to Caesar is a refusal to lead a life without honor. By contrast, when the Russian nobleman draws up a legal document giving away his inheritance, we may suspect that he is concerned not with an honorable life or with a life which he now conceives of as honorable, but rather with his present principle. Where Cato values a certain sort of life, the Russian nobleman values a certain principle. It is this which is problematic and which generates, I believe, the bizarre talk of ideals fading. For Cato's adherence to his principles is strengthened, if not guaranteed, by the fact that he treats a certain sort of life as an end in itself and adopts the principles he does adopt because they lead to that end. The Russian nobleman, however, is portrayed more as a man who finds the principle important than as a man who finds the life to which the principle leads important. Obviously, in either case there may be temptation and inner struggle, but the temptation is less likely to be resisted by the Russian nobleman than by Cato, for the nobleman will find his principle undermined and threatened by the prospect of affluence, which is attractive to him. His ideals will fade. For Cato, on the other hand, things are not

so simple. He is not faced by a choice between two things, each of which he finds attractive. The fact that he treats a life of honor as an end in itself precludes his finding life attractive under *any* circumstances. For him, life will ultimately be attractive and desirable only where it can be conducted honorably. Nevertheless, he finds life attractive and desirable, but this means only that if he surrenders he will have *sacrificed* his ideals, not that his ideals will have faded. Thus, the nobleman is a victim, waiting for and guarding against attack upon his principles; Cato is an agent who may sacrifice his principles after a struggle, but not one who would find that they had altered.

In conclusion, then, the claim that the marriage vow is either impossible or improper is false. It is possible to commit oneself unconditionally because commitment is analogous to a statement of intention, not to a prediction or a piece of clairvoyance. It is proper, since if we refuse to allow such unconditional commitment, we run the risk, of failing to distinguish between, on the one hand, sentimentality and commitment and, on the other hand, respect or admiration and commitment. Further, it is simply not true that I am helpless in circumstances in which I find my commitment wavering: this is because my principles will initially serve to modify my view of the opportunities which present themselves, so that I simply will not see certain things as constituting success because my principles are such as to exclude such things being constitutive of success. In this way, my principles determine what is to count as a benefit and what is to count as an opportunity. As Shakespeare has it:

Some glory in their birth, some in their skill,
Some in their wealth, some in their body's
    force,
Some in their garments though new fangled
    ill:
Some in their hawks and hounds, some in
    their horse.
And every humour has his adjunct pleasure,
Wherein it finds a joy above the rest,

But these particulars are not my measure,
All these I better in one general best.
Thy love is better than high birth to me,
Richer than wealth, prouder than garments
    cost,
Of more delight than hawks and horses be:
And having these of all men's pride I boast.
Wretched in this alone, that thou may'st take
All this away, and me most wretched make.[10, 11]

NOTES

1. Thomas Hardy, *Jude the Obscure.*
2. Bertrand Russell, *Autobiography* (London: George Allen and Unwin, 1967–1969).
3. Derek Parfit, 'Later Selves and Moral Principles' in *Philosophy and Personal Relations,* A. Montefiore (ed.) (London: Routledge and Kegan Paul, 1973), 144.
4. *Ibid.,* 145.
5. *Ibid.,* 145–146.
6. *Ibid.,* 14, 161–162.
7. W. Shakespeare, *A Midsummer Night's Dream,* Acts III and I.
8. Alison Lurie, *Love and Friendship* (Harmondsworth: Penguin, 1962), 329–330.
9. As quoted in J. Casey, 'Actions and Consequences,' from *Morality and Moral Reasoning,* J. Casey (ed.) (London: Methuen, 1971), 201.
10. W. Shakespeare, Sonnet 91.
11. I wish to thank my colleague, Dr. Roger Woolhouse, for many helpful discussions on the topic of this paper.

Further Questions

1. Do you think that there is such a thing as discovering that you no longer have a commitment to a person to whom you once made the commitment?
2. Is a trial marriage, in which you *try* to love, honor, etc. someone else, a bizarre idea?
3. Is a person who cannot promise to be faithful to another too malleable?
4. Are marriage vows statements of intention, rather than predictions, as Mendus suggests?

VI.3   The Princess

"NICCOLA MACHIAVELLI"

"Niccola Machiavelli" (Niccolò Machiavelli's supposed wife) has her own reasons for preferring marriage to a romance without a commitment. These reasons have to do with the material possessions traditional marriage can bring a woman, whether or not that marriage turns out to be permanent.

Niccolò Machiavelli wrote *The Prince,* instructions to rulers about how to manipulate their subjects through duplicity, craftiness, etc. He also wrote a treatise on how to win at tennis doubles. Well, why can't there be a "Niccola Machiavelli" who gives similar instructions to women on how to win at marriage?

Reading Questions

1. Should a person who is contemplating marriage, or any committed relationship, be thinking about money and possessions?

2. Are prenuptial agreements, specifying distribution of property in case of divorce, a good idea?

3. When a marriage is dissolved, is it appropriate to take the other person "by the most direct route to where the cleaners dwell"?

The Various Kinds of Relationships Which the Princess May Enter Into and the Ways in Which They May Be Instituted

ALL RELATIONSHIPS through which women may hold sway over men are either informal liaisons or formal marriages. I will not here speak of informal liaisons, except insofar as they are a necessary and temporary prelude to the forging of more permanent and lasting bonds, for the Princess who uses her head for any other purpose than as a place to store her crown knows that a form of cohabitation that can be terminated without her consent, that does not require the intervention of a sympathetic court, and that leaves the determination of the amount of a cash settlement to the largesse of a lover whose ardor has cooled, is something to be avoided as if it were the very Plague itself.

I will therefore deal only with formal marriages, which may have as their object either a man who, previous to his wedding, lived according to his own desires, or one who has through a prior marriage become accustomed to the rule of another Princess. In either instance, the husband chosen by the Princess may be acquired by her through the exercise of craft and subterfuge, or else he may fall in love with her of his own accord, in which case the Princess, after a suitable delay calculated to disguise the preexistence of her nuptial intentions, allows herself to be conquered by the very object of her plans of conquest. In both instances, when the marriage is terminated, which may be by mutual consent or as the result of a complaint brought by one or the other based upon a real or an imagined grievance, the Princess, by virtue of her clear legal status, will be in a position to perform one last wifely duty, namely, to take the Prince by the most direct route possible to the place where the cleaners dwell.

Of the Art of Conversation, and Why the Princess Who Wishes to Impress a Man with Her Eloquence Ought to Remain Silent

When the Princess seeks to demonstrate to a man that she is well-spoken, she should on no account attempt to do so through the faculty of speech, for if there is one thing that men prefer to hear above all else, excepting only the plaudits of an approving crowd, it is the sound of their own voices. Thus, the Princess who is disposed to permit any man to talk at length without interruption on whatever subject he may choose will be adjudged a good conversationalist even if she has the intellect of a garden shrub, whereas if she interjects observations of her own, other than simple affirmations or expressions of awe and amusement, even if they be examples of great feats of learning or of rhetorical skill, she will be regarded as a nuisance and a vixen. And while it cannot be denied that the Princess may find it difficult to hold her tongue over long periods of time, she has only to content herself with the certain knowledge that once the marriage vows are irrevocably sealed, her husband is going to have need of a mason's tools to insert so much as a single word into the solid, unbroken wall of her discourse.

Of Pre-Nuptial Agreements

Although the Princess should always assure the Prince that it is his charms and not his wealth or situation that attract her to him, she should never consent to a practical demonstration of this assertion in the form of a contract limiting her claims upon his estate in the event of a divorce, for no matter how generous the prospective settlement may be, it will always amount to much less than can be obtained from a jury trial or extorted through threats of litigation. If the object of her matrimonial interest should press her upon this matter, the Princess should immediately protest with great sorrow and indignation that she is being treated as little better than a prostitute. It is a rare man who, when confronted with this accusation, will perceive that a business-like compact with a professional consort would, in fact, be a far more prudent course of action than the one he is about to embark upon, or that he is poised to enter into precisely such an arrangement with a gifted amateur without having first agreed upon the price.

Why the Princess, Once Wed, Should Contrive Without Delay to Become Pregnant

Regardless of any agreements she may have made with the Prince on the subject of when or whether to have children, the Princess, beginning on her wedding night, must apply her undivided attention and the totality of her womanly skills to the task of conceiving a child, taking advantage of the Prince's inevitable bafflement on matters regarding the inner workings of her anatomy to effect the process of impregnation without his active cooperation or knowledge if necessary. The imperative urgency of the matter is based upon a simple if melancholy fact: In the eyes of every juror who will ever sit to consider a bill of divorcement, there are but two images of a woman: The Harlot and The Madonna, the first being any childless woman who is not yet completely a crone, the second being any woman who has a child, even if she possesses the alluring beauty of Aphrodite. A married woman without progeny may well win the jury's admiring glances, but rarely their sympathy, and in awarding her a sum of alimony, they will invariably think in terms of the amounts appropriate to the payment of a prostitute, the value of whose time is set by convention. But were this same jury to regard the identical woman in the company of her children, they would not see a courtesan whose embraces they might think of sharing, but rather the image of their own mothers whom they would die to protect from any who might harbor those very thoughts and to whom they would gladly give all the gold in the world, or, so generous an award not being within their power, at the very least all the gold in the possession of the Prince.

The Way to Dominate a Man Who, Previous to Being Married, Lived According to His Own Desires

If the Princess marries a man who has been married before, she will find him accustomed to the subjugation of a wife and need only substitute her usages and commands for those of her divorced or deceased predecessor. But if the Prince has heretofore lived in a state of bachelorhood, and is used to liberty, the Princess must begin on the very day following the wedding the work of destroying his former way of life and imposing her rule.

To accomplish this end, she should declare at once that whatever lodgings he may occupy, no matter how sumptuous or well-appointed, are of insufficient grandeur for their joint habitation and she should select the accommodations that will replace them. She should then take in hand the decoration of their new apartments, ensuring that while their overall aspect is pleasing, there is nonetheless no single chamber among them in which the Prince feels wholly comfortable. She should further see to it that there are no rooms in which masculine pursuits, such as card-playing, billiards, or the like, can be carried on without considerable discomfort, owing to the absence of light, the awkwardness of the space, the inappropriateness of the furnishings, or the general inhospitality of the surroundings.

The Princess should next convince the Prince to change whatever style of clothing he has been accustomed to wear to another less suitable to him, and persuade him as well to take up new hobbies, interests, and pursuits and to forsake those which had formerly engaged his attention. And when the friends of his former unwed life make gentle fun at these transformations, she should take every opportunity to remind the Prince of these harmless remarks, converting them through repetition and exaggeration into cruel and unjustified insults to his person, and thereby gradually secure the banishment of these long-time comrades from his side on the grounds of rude behavior. Once she has arranged their removal from his affections, she may replace them with trustworthy companions from her own circle, who may be relied upon to report to her in confidence on all the Prince's activities and to take her part in any disputes that may occur. Only when she has accomplished all these things may the Princess be truly said to have gained ascendancy in her own household.

Why Tears Are a More Effective Response to an Affront Than the Aerial Dispatch of Crockery

If the Princess takes offense at some action or remark of the Prince, she should not seek an immediate redress of the insult by throwing dishware at him, for if she misses, she will look ridiculous, and if she succeeds in doing him an injury, no matter how satisfying this may be to her, it will cause him but slight pain for a brief period; and further it will permit the Prince to judge himself to be the aggrieved party and to present himself in that role to others, displaying his bruise as proof of the Princess' wayward nature. If, on the other hand, the Princess contains her anger and responds with copious tears, then once the Prince's temper has abated, he will blame himself for his meanness and will wound himself many times over with the memory of his incivility and thereby suffer a far greater hurt over a much longer time than any that could be in-

flicted by the impact of a dish, even if it were hurled by Athena herself. And the Princess will be able, on countless future occasions, to remind him of his discourtesy and thereby obtain for herself costly gifts to assuage the great distress she will claim to feel at her recollection of the indignity she endured at his hands.

Why the Princess Should Encourage the Prince to Confess to Her His Past Misdeeds, and Then Once He Does So, in Spite of Having Pledged to Be of a Forgiving Nature, Instead Come Down Upon His Head Like an Hundredweight of Roofing-tiles

As soon following the marriage ceremony as the opportunity presents itself, the Princess should, by means of sweet words and assurances of understanding and forgiveness, prevail upon the Prince to reveal to her his past amorous history in the name of furthering the trust between them by making all of their secrets as open to each other as their hearts themselves. When at last the Prince, moved by her professions of love and his own male pride, consents to divulge the details of his youthful escapades, the Princess should attend to his recital in stony silence, and then, when he has finished, fly into an inconsolable fury at the proof, offered from his very lips, of his wanton conduct. She should accuse him of every vice she can think of, from vile carnality to the venal sin of lust, not failing in her tirade to reprove herself for her singular lack of judgment in having formed a holy union with a lecher and a reprobate.

If the Prince should remind her of her promise to pardon all, she should say that she will indeed endeavor to forgive his abominable debauchery and turpitude, but that it is not in her power ever to forget them. At this, the Prince will feel not only mortifying shame at his conduct, but also bitter frustration at his own idiocy in having provided evidence against himself, and upon these twin pillars of his sense of disgrace and his feeling of foolishness, the Princess will begin to lay the firm foundations of a secure and prosperous marriage.

Further Questions

1. When you become involved with someone, how do you know they do not have "Niccola Machiavellian" designs on you?

2. Sometimes a man without money has difficulty finding a woman who agrees to be a friend, lover, or wife. Does this show anything significant about the mentality of women?

3. Henry Kissinger once said that "power is the ultimate aphrodisiac." Was he right?

VI.4   Black Men/Black Women: Changing Roles and Relationships

ROBERT STAPLES

Robert Staples mentions some economic and social forces that preclude marriage as an option between black men and black women. Sometimes black couples "date," but these same forces preclude even "dating" among many blacks. In addition, black men may misuse their power over black women in any coupling arrangement.

Staples is Professor of Sociology at the University of California, San Francisco, and author of numerous books and articles focusing on black society and culture in the United States.

Reading Questions

1. Would you avoid a legal marriage with someone who had no skills, education, or steady income? Would you consider having some other sort of relationship with him or her instead?

2. According to your understanding of "dating," is this activity possible only if the two people on the "date" have a certain amount of money? Must the person with the money be the man?

3. In order to secure a "date," does someone need to spend a lot of money and time on clothes, cosmetics, hairstyling, etc.? Is this cost greater for one gender than it is for the other?

THE DECADE OF THE SEVENTIES was witness to a number of changes in marriage and the family. Considering the sanctity of the nuclear family as an American institution, the changes that transpired were only short of revolutionary. In 1979 almost half of the women in the 20 to 24 year-old age bracket were still single, compared with only 28 percent in 1960. Even in the later years, 25 to 29, 20 percent of them remained un-married in 1979. During the period 1970 to 1979, the ratio of divorced persons per 1,000 husbands and wives in intact marriages increased by 96 per-cent from 47 per 1,000 to 92 per 1,000.[1] As star-tling as these figures may be, they do not begin to mirror the changes in single and marital status and fertility behavior among the Afro-American population. The majority of Afro-Americans, over the age of 18, are no longer in intact mar-riages. About 47 percent of black men and 56 per-cent of black women are not married and living with a spouse. Almost half (48.7 percent) of all black families are headed by a single parent. The majority of black children are born out-of-wedlock and only a minority of black children live in a two-parent household.[2] Thus, at the end of the seventies, the black family had under-gone a radical transformation. The nuclear family is no longer the assumed structure. This fact raises the question of why and how the transfor-mation occurred.

It is clear that the white American family is changing in the same direction but the magni-tude of these changes have been much greater for black Americans. Seemingly, blacks have come almost full circle to the period of slavery when marriage was denied them. However, after the demise of "the peculiar institution," they married in record numbers. By the beginning of the twen-tieth century three out of four adult blacks were members of a nuclear family. About 90 percent of all black children were born in wedlock during that same period.[3] Even in the more recent era, black women over 65 years of age had a higher rate of marriage (96.5) than comparable white women (93.1).[4] Historically, a legal marriage was em-ployed as a device by which status was deter-mined. Blacks were considered respectable or non-respectable based on whether they were le-gally married or cohabitating. My guess is that the black American's desire to be in a nuclear family has not changed but the conditions which permit fulfillment of that desire have been altered significantly.

Black Singles

The increase in black singles is consistent with the constraints on the supply of eligible mates available for and interested in a monogamous marriage. Not only is there an excess of one mil-lion adult black women (over age 18) in the black population but the institutional decimation of black men leaves working class black women with an extremely low supply of desirable men (i.e. employed and mentally stable) from which to choose. This is particularly true of men who reach the age of thirty and are single or divorced. Paradoxically, there is a larger number of never-married black men at lower class levels than there are similar black women.[5] In the lower classes, these men are without skills, education and a steady income. Thus, it makes sense in terms of daily economic security for black women to avoid a legal marriage with such men. They may live with these men and have children by them; but, as one black woman asserted: "Without marriage I know I've got security. My welfare check keeps coming as long as I am not married. Otherwise I don't know if he's going to keep his job or if he's going to start "acting up" and staying out drinking and fooling around with other women. This way I might not have the respecta-bility of marriage, but at least I know how much I got."

Many of the stable black marriages are among couples in the black working class. These are the blacks who finished high school but have less than four years of college. The men in this group tend to be dependent on the wife's income to maintain a decent standard of living. Because they avoid the harsh economic repression of black males in the underclass, it seems easier for them to maintain a stable marriage and average standard of living. Often, they are the "silent ma-jority," the men who are unrepresented in the literature and general stereotypes about black males.

When we ascend the socio-economic scale, the men between the ages 35 to 54 years[6] in the middle class are more likely to remain single than their female counterparts, at least those with five years of college or more. Many of those men are exclusive homosexuals, for whom a legal marriage is not possible.

Among the black middle class (i.e. 4 years of college or more), the shortage of black males is complicated by a number of factors. Assuming a woman wants to marry a male of comparable education, there were only 339,000 black male college graduates for 417,000 black female college graduates in 1977. Moreover, the eligible pool of college educated black men is further reduced by homosexuality, interracial marriages and the fact that many of them marry women with less than a college education. As a result, among blacks (ages 35–54) with 5 years or more of college, there are 52,000 eligible women for only 15,000 men. To illustrate the seriousness of the problem, the census bureau lists 15,000 divorced black women in that same category and *no* black males (actually less than 500).[7] Small wonder, then, that competition among black women is keen for that low supply of college educated black males. And, it is the competition for those men that largely explains their high divorce rate. The marriages of these black males often are disrupted by "the other woman." We see it in the statistics which show that black women are more likely than white women to marry men who are four and more years their senior and who have been married before.[8]

The Cost of Being Male and Single

It is commonplace to hear of families cutting back on expenses to cope with the increasing cost of goods and services. Reducing their expenditures is easily accomplished among married couples since they perceive themselves as an inseparable unit with the same goals. But, there is another group whose expenses continue to rise. This group consists of individuals whom we typically refer to as the swinging single men. Among blacks, they are more than a crowd—they are al-

most the majority of adult black men. As of 1979, almost half of the black men, ages 18 and above, had never been married, or are separated, divorced or widowed. Approximately 47 percent of adult black men and 56 percent of comparable black women are eligible for the "take-out, make-out" game known as dating.[9] Yet due to age, poverty, children, or lack of opportunity, the majority of black singles do not go out on dates—at least not very often.

Dating, in fact, is a relatively new concept to most blacks. Prior to the desegregation of public facilities, there were few places to go. Most blacks met in the church, school or neighborhood, and spent leisurely evenings sitting on their front porches. Marriage followed soon afterwards. Presently, blacks are more likely to remain unmarried for a longer period of time, especially those who are considered middle class. Almost a third of the black women who go to college remain unmarried past the age of thirty. Men with the same educational background tend to marry at an earlier age but a high divorce rate throws many of them back into the singles world.[10] And, the purpose of dating has changed. No longer is it solely a form of courtship, especially for men, where each person's intent is to explore the potential for marriage or a stable relationship. Some still use it to serve that function. However, a large number of men and women view it as recreation, a free night's entertainment, a time for sexual seduction and status enhancement.

While the purpose of dating has changed considerably the roles have not altered that much. Men are still expected to bear the costs of dating. Why this tradition continues to exist is somewhat of a mystery. Few college educated black women live at home with their parents, bereft of any visible means of support and in fact, college educated black women earn 90 percent of the income of their male peers. One answer is that it is a self-serving interpretation of a custom designed for an earlier era and it is one that has been largely unaffected by the women's liberation movement. It is a sacrosanct tradition with a great deal of force behind it. Men who violate that tradition are labelled as cheap. The ability to escort a woman in style is often the measure of the man, especially in this inflationary period. Dr. Joyce Brothers once commented that when economic times are hard, women look for signs of a man's socioeconomic status. When we were in a period of economic prosperity, women were attracted to men with sex appeal as exhibited in snappy apparel such as tight-fitting pants and open chested shirts. Now, it is the three piece suit, signaling arrival, which turns women on.

For middle class black men, appealing to women can be an expensive proposition. The higher status clothes and car can be very expensive outlays. Most good quality suits cost at least $500. The "right" kind of car (e.g. Porsche, BMW, Mercedes) sells for twenty thousand dollars and above. Since the initial attraction of the sexes to each other is based on external, visible factors, those accoutrements are necessary. A man's possession of money is important but not as important as his willingness to spend it. One black woman, a 33 year old college professor, once called a man she dated "cheap." When asked why, she cited the case of their initial meeting at a bar where she sat with three female companions. After ordering a drink and talking to them for a period of time, the bill for $34 arrived. To their surprise, he insisted on paying only for his own drink and not picking up the entire tab.

The more formal dating situations can be quite expensive. An investment counselor, Ray Devoe has constructed a "cost of loving index." Using 1954 as his base year, he calculated that the cost of dating has increased twice as much as the advance in the consumer price index—340 percent vs. 172 percent. And, the cost of an average date is now about $43.[11] Of course, it can be higher or lower, depending on the choice of activity and location. Since women may judge men on their willingness to spend, a "cheap date" may be costly. There is a cadre of women who do not know any cheap forms of entertainment and an equal number who do not appreciate them. As

one woman, a 34 year old nurse, told me: "the one time you don't worry about being on a diet is when a man is picking up the tab." And, how many men look first at the prices on a restaurant menu and multiply by two before they consider a choice of food? Going out to eat is often necessary since many younger black women (southern women being an exception) do not know how to cook. A man living in the expensive urban centers such as New York, Boston, Washington, and San Francisco, and planning on going to the theatre, having dinner and drinks, must also figure on paying $100 for the night. As the investment counselor has noted, "the dating game doesn't come cheap. And, carried to an excess, it can quickly bankrupt you."[12]

There are several anticipated consequences of the cost of dating. As many women reported to me, they do not get many invitations for dates. Some men go out with other men and split expenses down the middle. It is not uncommon to go to concerts, plays, restaurants and see men grouped with men, women with women and some men alone. Another common complaint of the women was that men simply dropped by their homes and wanted to watch television, get high or otherwise hang out. As one woman reported to me, "the only place men ever took me was from the living room into the bedroom."* And that is yet another consequence of the rising cost of dating. Men become sexually aggressive faster because they cannot afford to prolong dating for an extended period of time. One man, a 37 year old lawyer, told me: "I can't see taking a woman out and spending $50 for the night's entertainment. There was this one woman whose taste ran to French restaurants. Not only did she order the most expensive dish on the menu and a bottle of expensive wine but I even had to pay for the Perrier she ordered. After getting the bill for $89, I was determined to

---

* Unless otherwise identified or footnoted, quotes are taken from the black singles data. See chapter six [of *Black Masculinity*] for a description of the study.

get some reward for my money." Such an attitude led one woman, a 32 year old social worker to ask the question: "Are women expected to screw for their supper? All a man gets for taking me out is the 'pleasure of my company.'"

Considering the cost of dating, only a certain category of men can and will engage in it for long periods of time. A noticeable trend is toward women in their twenties and thirties dating men in their late forties and early fifties. When I asked one woman, a 32 year old specialist in multicultural education, why she dated so many men in their forties, she replied: "because you don't have to pick up the tab for your own dinner. They come from the old school and know how to treat a woman. Besides, they know if they want to date a woman 15 years their junior, they have to spend money on her." These older men, of course, are often at the peak of their earning power, some are recently divorced and new to the dating game. Also, some men are in positions where they can write off the costs of dating on expense accounts or as tax deductions.

Women, however, are not spared the expense of dating or finding a man. Since a man's willingness to spend money on her is often based on how attractive she is, she must lay out fairly large sums of money for cosmetics, hairstyling and fashionable clothes. Since fashions in clothes and hairstyles fluctuate almost yearly, they are a considerable expense for her.[13] Moreover, many women incur the costs of going to places in order to meet men. Even if a woman goes with a girlfriend to a bar or club, she generally pays her own way. Then, there is the conference circuit. Some women save their pennies all year in order to attend the annual meetings of the National Medical or Bar Association, and as a result, many predominantly black conferences have a disproportionate number of women in attendance, in relationship to their numbers in the profession. Most of the men, however, are married and, therefore, "single for the conference only."

Hence, dating is not just a case of men paying and women receiving. Furthermore, as men and

women enter into stable relationships, they often stay home together or she invites him over to dinner. And, there are increasing instances of women sharing the cost of the evening's entertainment. Ann Arbor, Michigan, a college town, was the only city where this seemed to be the norm. After having coffee with a young woman there, I picked up the bill for $1.10 and she asked if I wanted her to pay for her cup of coffee. When I said no, she replied that you had to do that in Ann Arbor since the men were quick to pick out the cost of their meal and pay only that amount. Possibly Ann Arbor's practice may be the harbinger of the future. If not, the cost of dating in the future will have outpriced most black men. Based on my own calculations, a man who remains single and "dates" steadily for twenty years can expect to spend almost $75,000 for dating alone.

There are a few other costs that blacks must pay for all the singles in their midst. In the past, many black families maintained a decent or middle class standard of living through the double wages of both husband and wife. Since there are no longer as many black husband/wife couples, the standard of living has decreased for blacks. According to the Bureau of the Census report, between 1976 and 1978, the proportion of black families with two or more earners declined from 48 to 46 percent. The proportion of white families with two or more earners remained at 55 percent. While that may be attributed to a decline in the employment status of black women, only 48 percent of the adult black women were reported as married and living with a spouse in 1976. That was a considerable decline from the 66 percent who were married, with spouse present, in 1950. The difference that marriage makes is illustrated in the figures that show black husband/wife families (husband under 35 years old), in the North and West, in which both spouses were earners and achieved incomes equal to those of their white peers in 1976. On the other hand, the median income of the black family (which includes single parent households) declined from 60 percent of white family income in 1974 to 57 percent in 1977.[14]

Unmarried blacks who share the American dream of owning their own home may have to forget it. Presently, the average home seems to be available only to two wage families. According to recent surveys, over 54 percent of home buyers relied on two incomes to buy a house in 1979. And, among first time buyers, those families in which the wife was employed accounted for 64 percent of the total.[15] Few single blacks have the income required to meet the monthly mortgage payments for most new homes. Ironically, it is, in part, the dramatic increase in the number of singles that accounts for the rapid rise in housing prices.[16] In the last decade the number of households increased more than twice as fast as the number of people in them. In 1978, more than half of all households consisted of only one or two individuals. In other words, the housing that used to accommodate a husband/wife couple must now be doubled to house the unmarried individual.

Interestingly enough, it may also be economic factors that will stem the tide of increasing singleness. More and more blacks seem to be gravitating toward marriage this year. Certainly inflationary trends combined with an economic recession have forced many of them to seek the security of a stable relationship as opposed to a casual dating lifestyle. Women used to seek security in marriages, then began to seek it in jobs. As the job picture, especially for blacks, became more bleak *and* uncertain, they are again looking to marriage for security. Another factor is that the high cost of dating insures only the most attractive women (and sometimes not them) a steady pool of men willing to bear those expenses. Perforce, many black women are remaining at home alone or going out primarily with other women. Dating may be an idea whose time has come and gone.

Many blacks will continue to remain unmarried due to demographic factors. There remains in the black community an imbalance in the sex ratio, resulting from the institutional decimation of black men, who cannot get jobs and who wind up on drugs, in the military or prison or dead at a young age. The black singles world is characterized by a large proportion of men who are uneducated, with low incomes, and an equally disproportionate number of women with college degrees and high incomes. Until some of our values change, it is evident that few of the former will be dating the latter. As has often been the case, economics is a strong determinant of one's marital status.

Unfaithful Women and Jealous Men

After hunger and sex, sexual jealousy is one of the strongest passions experienced by homo sapiens. Jealousy does not exist in every culture and emerged in Western culture as a result of the development of private property.[17] Certainly it is a common emotion among Americans. Jealousy of one's mate is a major cause of marital disruption and interpersonal violence. It is such a destructive emotion that therapists generally attempt to label it as a pathological state of mind. Various theories attribute jealousy to low self-esteem, misanthropy, personal unhappiness, etc. While it seems obvious that much jealousy is irrational, we rarely hear about rational jealousy and the social forces that promote jealousy. If absolute fidelity is required from a mate, what are the chances that it will be given? In today's society, the chances are fairly low. This fact will give rise to jealous suspicions that are unfounded in particular but true in general. Hence, it is incumbent upon us to examine infidelity as well as sexual jealousy in order to understand their relationship to one another.

Although little has been written about it, sexual jealousy is not unknown in the black community. Indeed, one study found that 40 percent of blacks, whose marriages had terminated, gave as at least one of the reasons, often as the only reason, jealousy and infidelity.[18] One pronounced difference in black jealousy is that these suspicious attitudes are not that uncommon to men.

In the same study previously cited, black men felt that a wife would search for sexual gratification elsewhere if relations did not go well.[19] And, that belief is confirmed in the findings of Bell that almost half of his black female subjects believed that a married woman would be justified in running around.[20] The Rainwater study found that 31 percent of the divorced women in the survey admitted to at least one extramarital affair.[21] In another study of college-educated black divorcees, 54 percent believed that their ex-husbands had engaged in extramarital sexual activity.[22]

It must be emphasized that infidelity per se is seldom the cause of divorce, especially when women terminate the marriage. Lower income women may divorce a man who is unfaithful *and* also fails to support his family. Both violations of societal norms may be too much for her to bear. Among middle class blacks, male infidelity may be tolerated if he is taking care of home (i.e. sexual and financial needs are satisfied). Lower income black males may be more tolerant of extramarital sexual activity by their wives. Often, they are more dependent upon their wives for certain services and do not have the economic wherewithal to insure a wife's fidelity. On the other hand, college educated black males are more likely to terminate a marriage if the wife is known to be unfaithful. The norms of his class require him to save face by the rejection of the wandering wife. A lesser educated male may resort to physical abuse to bring the unfaithful wife in line.

However, it is often jealousy, not the act of infidelity, that is a disruptive force in male/female relationships. An act of infidelity is a *fait accompli* and known to both parties. Jealousy is the nagging suspicion that one's partner is unfaithful. It may be based on reality or be a reflection of other psychological forces. At best, it can be an emotionally draining experience for both partners. He may experience anxiety and anger over the feeling that she is consorting with other men. If his suspicions are untrue, she may be pained by his lack of trust in her, the constant accusations and even constraints on her movements and emotions. There are numerous cases of women who eventually were unfaithful in retaliation for the male partner's unfounded suspicions about their fidelity.

While jealousy can be a destructive force in a relationship, there are social forces that have given rise to its increase among married *and* unmarried couples. One of them is the permanent availability of many individuals in American society.[23] Even marriage is no longer seen as a permanent alliance as people constantly exit from relationships in the search for somebody better, the perfect mate. It is common, for instance, for married men who get a divorce to remarry another woman within a year. Often, that woman was a sexual partner during the course of his marriage. While her presence may not have been the dominant factor in the marital disruption, her availability (and pressure) certainly contributed to his willingness to dissolve the marriage. Thus, jealousy that is rooted in the fear of losing one's partner is not totally unfounded.

Another social force impinging on attitudes of jealousy are the changes in the female role. Infidelity was once considered a male practice, with female infidelity subject to all the scorn a society could muster. Various studies indicate that 50–60 percent of wives will engage in extramarital sexual activity during the course of their marriages.[24] In general, women have not engaged in extramarital sex for the same reasons as men—sexual variety and recreation. Often, they were "forced" to do so because of the husband's neglect, sexual incompetency or blatant infidelity. These remain the dominant reasons for infidelity but the sexual revolution and its concomitants have produced a new kind of woman.

We should be clear on what the sexual revolution was all about. It eroded the double sexual standard but did not eliminate all its aspects. Women had been totally denied the pleasures of sex except within the context of marriage. And even today, they still are subject to a different set of standards than men. Men do not expect women to have the same number of sexual partners or variety of sexual experiences as males. And, they are expected to be discrete in the sexual liaisons they do have. At the same time, the legacy of the double standard has provided women with more opportunities for sexual outlets than most men. It is still men who are the buyers and women who are the sellers in the sexual marketplace. For women whose values allow permissive sexual activity, there is no shortage of partners in a sellers' market. Male sexual jealousy may be shaped by this knowledge of a woman's greater chances for sexual adventures. She neither has to wine and dine in order to obtain a sexual consort nor do many men require a commitment from her before indulging in coitus. As one woman remarked: "it's easier to get a man in bed than a drink of water."

Many women have asserted their sexual rights and opportunities. According to one survey, (1) 54 percent of the married women had had extramarital affairs, (2) 55 percent had engaged in sex on their lunch hours, (3) 48 percent had made love with more than one man in the same day, (4) 82 percent had seduced a man at least once.[25] Again, we can see the visible evidence of sexual liberalization among women and the natural concomitant is increased male jealousy. For example, the increase of women in the labor force has brought men and women into contact with each other in heretofore unprecedented ways. A major problem of integrating police cars with male and female officers has been the jealousy of the spouse over such an arrangement. This is especially a problem among white collar workers, where there is ample time for socializing on the job and discretionary time for having sexual affairs.

Another social arrangement that promotes sexual jealousy is the increase in opposite sex friendships. Many of these friendships are platonic and provide an enriching experience in heterosexual communication and interaction. Others are a mask for cheating on one's partner—married or otherwise. Women are more likely to have such friendships since men tend to keep

their affairs underground. A woman's male friends are often former lovers who may turn out to be future lovers as well. Some are current lovers masquerading as platonic friends. When one relationship is ended, the woman's next mate is frequently a man who was formerly a "friend." A woman may use a man who is a platonic friend as a reserve lover for the future in case her present relationship does not work out. It is the contact with these men and former lovers that generates much male jealousy.

Women may define boundaries for their male friends that prohibit sexual contact but give the appearance of infidelity. One of the most common examples is permitting male guests to stay overnight in their homes, sometimes sharing the same bed with them. We encountered one woman who could not understand her boyfriend's jealousy. It seems that she told him of her relationship with several men over a period of time. While involved with one man, she allowed another man to pay her air fare to a conference in another city. The man, although married, was a former lover and they slept in the same hotel room without engaging in sex. While at that conference, she invited another man to visit her and stay at her house. By the time of his visit, she was involved with her present boyfriend who objected to the man's visit. The man came anyway and she did not have sexual relations with him. Yet, she had created a low level of trust in her current lover and her continued contact with former lovers did nothing to ameliorate his sexual jealousy.

Coming into contact with former lovers can be a common problem in the black community. Middle class blacks are few in numbers and the places they frequent are the same. Thus, there are numerous cases of black singles dating the friend of a friend. In any social gathering of middle class blacks, an individual's past, present and future lovers may be present. Because this social incest is so pervasive, it may be difficult to maintain a positive image when so much is known about one's sexual affairs. Perforce, indiscreet men may make known their previous sexual affairs with a particular woman, often "passing" her on to their male running partners. Lately, men with lusty sexual appetites have been discussed by their sexual partners and been labeled as "male whores." Women may eschew such a man because "he's been had by everybody." Sleeping around, then, becomes a problem for both sexes. And, it contributes to feelings of sexual jealousy, and social embarrassment, when a mate's previous sexual liaisons are well known.

Women have the greatest cause for sexual jealousy since studies have estimated that as many as 90 percent of American males have had extramarital affairs. While most have no intention of leaving their wives, the "other woman" can be the precipitant force in the termination of a deteriorating marriage.[26] Black women, in particular, face stiff competition for the few available and desirable men. Most of the desirable black males are already married, but some single black women realize that nothing is forever. If unable to find an unattached man, they are not reluctant to seek one who belongs to another woman. As a result, many married black women resign themselves to accepting a man's infidelity, as long as he is not disrespectful. Others adopt the motto, "What's good for the goose is good for the gander." They, too, engage in extramarital affairs although they tend to be more discreet in their sexual liaisons.

The consequences of such a reaction and counter-reaction are predictable. Even in relationships where fidelity is the norm, sexual jealousy may occur. Jealousy may be more a cause of marital disruption than actual infidelity. There is ample evidence that it is a contributory cause to the 130 percent increase in divorces among blacks during the 1970s.[27] Moreover, it has created a low level of trust among blacks engaged in intimate relationships. Single black women are all too aware of the many married men who approach them for dates and sexual favors. Certainly, it is not surprising that many of them see all men as being incapable of having a monogamous marriage. More to the point, they will have a low level of trust in their future husbands, especially if they were married when they embarked on their intimate association.

Sexual jealousy may have always been a reality. But, the current prevalence of infidelity is largely a product of the sexual revolution and the changes in women's roles. In earlier periods, married men were more faithful because there were few women available to them. Women were monogamous because they were economically dependent on men and society punished their sexual transgressions in the harshest manner. A return to the constraints on women is not being argued here. The sexual revolution liberated America from its puritanical and hypocritical moral order and freed the female libido for fuller expression. Still, sexual jealousy is not just a function of negative psychological forces residing in the individual. In many ways it is a realistic reflection of the options people have for sexual variety in their lives and the social arrangements that promote infidelity.

Summary

The problems black men and women have in their relationships often are shaped by external forces. Many have been unable to form a monogamous family due to structural impediments. In a society where money is the measure of the man, many black males are excluded as potential mates because they lack the economic wherewithal to support a family in a reasonable manner. Given the traditional role definitions for women, definitions internalized by many black males, the highly educated black woman finds herself victimized by the fact that she has a higher educational and income level than most of the black men in her pool of eligibles. Both of those factors are products of institutional racism·and black history in America. Hence, the conflict between men and women may be more apparent than real. The real problem may be largely a demographic one with strong class overtones. There simply are not enough black men to go around and the ones available are not regarded as viable mates. As Patrice Rushen, the singer, has stated, "I think it is just a way to divert our attention from the fact that we have things that must be done together to make some headway. We're not dealing in times that afford us the luxury of being able to feel there's a problem with black men that automatically creates a problem for the black woman and vice-versa. We have to look for where these problems come from—and we might find it ain't us."[28]

Regardless of the source of the problem, the high number of unmarried and divorced blacks signals that all is not well between black men and women. The unbalanced ratio of men to women and the greater degree of "power" given to men is a combustible combination that creates a potential problem. In men this power is often manifested as arrogance and insensitivity to women's needs. For women, feelings of insult and injury can add up to outrage. White racism may have been the force which shaped black relationships and its spectre may remain with us for the foreseeable future. However, the future of the black family may rest upon those blacks who resist the notion that racism will determine their personal relationships. Otherwise, it seems clear that racism may have decisively determined the nature of the most intimate association between men and women. Then, their capacity to resist racism itself may be brought into question. A house divided against itself cannot stand.

NOTES

1. U.S. Bureau of the Census, "Marital Status and Living Arrangements: March 1980," Washington, D.C.: U.S. Government Printing Office, 1981.

2. Suzanne Bianchi and Reynolds Farley, "Racial Differences in Family Living Arrangements and Economic Well Being: An Analysis of Recent Trends," *Journal of Marriage and the Family* 41 (August 1979): 537–552.

3. Herbert Gutman, *The Black Family in Slavery and Freedom 1750–1925* (New York: Pantheon, 1976).

4. U.S. Bureau of the Census, "Marital Status and Living Arrangements: March 1973," Washington, D.C., U.S. Government Printing Office, 1974.

5. Paul C. Glick and Karen Mills, *Black Families: Marriage Patterns and Living Arrangements* (Atlanta: Atlanta University, 1974), p. 9.

6. U.S. Bureau of the Census, "Current Population Reports, Series p. 20, No. 314, Washington, D.C., U.S. Government Printing Office, 1978, p. 31. Most of the men in that class, however, are married.

7. Ibid.

8. Graham Spanier and Paul Glick, "Mate Selection Differentials Between Whites and Blacks in the United States," *Social Forces* 58 (August 1980).

9. U.S. Bureau of the Census, "Marital Status and Living Arrangements: March 1980," op. cit.

10. Ibid.

11. Quoted in Dan Dorfman, "Tempest in the Take-Out Game," *San Francisco Examiner*, November 18, 1979, pp. 3–13.

12. Ibid. Some very exclusive restaurants hand the female member of the duo a menu without prices listed, a practice that has drawn the protests of some feminists.

13. C.f. Beth Trier, "Beauty—Is It Only Pocketbook Deep?" *San Francisco Chronicle*, June 12, 1980, p. 43.

14. Bianchi and Farley, op. cit.

15. "Home Buying Needs Working Wife," *The San Francisco Sunday Examiner and Chronicle*, May 18, 1980, p. 34.

16. "S.F. Economist Traces Housing Crisis," *The San Francisco Sunday Examiner and Chronicle*, April 20, 1980.

17. Frederick Engels, *The Origin of the Family, Private Property, and the State* (Chicago: Charles W. Kerr, 1920).

18. Lee Rainwater, *Behind Ghetto Walls* (Chicago: Aldine, 1970), p. 63.

19. Ibid.

20. Robert Bell, "Comparative Attitudes About Marital Sex Among Negro Women in the United States, Great Britain, and Trinidad," *Journal of Comparative Family Studies I.* (Autumn); 71–81.

21. Rainwater, *Behind Ghetto Walls* (Chicago: Aldine, 1970), p. 63.

22. William M. Chavis and Gladys J. Lyles, "Divorce Among Educated Black Women," *Journal of the National Medical Association* 67 (March 1975): 128–134.

23. Bernard Farber, *Kinship and Family Organization* (New York: John Wiley and Sons, 1966).

24. "Sex Lives of Cosmopolitan Readers," *The San Francisco Chronicle*, August 4, 1980, p. 1.

25. Ibid.

26. Lewis Yablonsky, "How Infidelity Can Strengthen Ailing Marriages," *The Detroit Free Press,* February 15, 1979, p. 5-C.

27. Robert Staples, *The World of Black Singles: Changing Patterns of Male-Female Relations* (Westport, Connecticut: Greenwood Press, 1981).

28. Patrice Rushen quoted in *Jet Magazine,* April 10, 1980, p. 30.

Further Questions

1. Would you prefer to marry someone whose education is comparable to yours? If this is not possible, would you prefer to marry someone with more or less education?

2. Does a man's spending a lot of money on a woman justify his becoming sexually aggressive toward her at the end of the evening?

3. Is it rational to demand absolute fidelity from a mate? If so, is infidelity itself a sufficient reason for breaking off the marriage or relationship? Does the answer to this question depend on the gender of the person who has been unfaithful?

4. If persons of your gender who are more attractive than you are available, do you think of the possibility of losing your partner to one of them, either temporarily or permanently?

5. Would you consider becoming involved with someone who has had many sexual affairs? Would whether you expected to meet the previous partners make a difference? Would you give a different answer if you were of the other gender?

VI.5   Implications of the Emerging Family

JOHN SCANZONI

John Scanzoni speaks of a new ideal of marriage, the "progressive family," in which traditional gender roles are ignored and decisions are made in a context of equality. Commitment is not loyalty to conventional norms, but rather to ideals of "solidarity and cohesion." As with any other ideal, participants might fail to live up to the mandate of the "progressive family."

Scanzoni is Professor of Sociology at the University of Florida and has published widely on matters pertaining to the family.

Reading Questions

1. Would you accept the idea that everything in a relationship is negotiable, and that no partner should have more power than the other partner to influence any outcome?

2. If everything is negotiable, responsibilities for work in the home and in the workplace would have to be worked out by each couple. Are you prepared to make a commitment to that kind of arrangement?

3. Are stability and tranquility in a relationship more important than keeping everything in a state where changes through renegotiation are always possible?

Conservative Responses

ASKING WHAT CONSERVATIVE men and women want from marriage highlights the matter of hierarchy (nonequal-partner marriage) and the differential status and power of the sexes. Traditional women, for instance, want nurture (including sexual satisfactions) and emotional support from their husbands; but they also expect husbands to be the ultimate financial mainstay of the household. Likewise, traditional men want nurture and support from wives; in addition, they expect wives to be ultimately responsible for household duties and child care. This fixed difference in responsibilities and opportunities is, in large measure, what locks women into subordinate status within the household and, if they venture forth, within the larger society as well—not only in capitalist but also in communist societies. Moreover (although it may vary somewhat by social class), traditional women and men expect their spouses to subordinate all other friendships to the marital relationship. Friendships in which couples socialize as pairs are deemed most desirable; having same-gender friendships in which the spouse is not central is less desirable but is at least acceptable; extraordinarily suspect are opposite-gender friendships.

A third facet of what conservatives want from marriage (besides economic and household arrangements and companionship patterns) pertains to children. Marriage and family are thought to be inseparable—the anticipated gratifications of children make unthinkable the idea of voluntary childlessness (Polonko and Scanzoni, 1981). Moreover, the woman is the prime parent. . . . What is primarily expected from children is that they should conform to the same basic scripts in the same ways as their parents.

The response of conservatives to the . . . question, regarding what to *give* to marriage/family, is equally apparent. Conservatives are prepared to *conform* to the received scripts and to give *commitment* to their spouses, children, and parents. Commitment is defined in terms of the unswerving loyalty (permanence for its own sake) described by Swidler (1980). . . .

Finally, what do conservatives perceive family doing for the larger whole? Since to them there is only *one* family and *one* society, they see family contributing (through conformity and commitment of both adults and children) to a whole in which their preferences are carried out in its religious, educational, political, and economic realms. . . .

. . . [Marital] order (defined as maintenance of the status quo) is achieved through conformity and (the conservative view of) commitment, obedience, and obligation. Yet, . . . this ideal . . . makes no realistic allowance for several kinds of potentially disruptive elements. One that is becoming increasingly (and painfully) apparent to a great many ordinary citizens is that it constitutes a financial "straight-jacket"—it takes more money to maintain than most people have. Fundamental to this ideal is a husband who earns enough dollars to support his family in all sorts of contingencies—thus freeing the mother from the necessity of paid employment. Intrinsic to this monetary ideal are the following notions: (1) that all husbands are highly motivated achievers who strongly wish to perform occupationally to the full extent of their capacities; (2) that all husbands have access to at least adequate educational and occupational opportunities—a notion quite indefensible in the case of many blacks and some whites; and (3) that husbands and wives will live together for five or six decades, and wives will not need to face the possibility of having to provide for themselves (and their children) through marketplace activity.

Second, and related, the conservative model assumes that contingencies such as mental and physical impairments can somehow always be "managed" by means of the family's own tangible and intangible resources. However, it is clear that, beginning with the Social Security Act and extending through welfare, Medicare, and more recent programs directed toward families with impaired persons, enormous government effort has been expended to assist families lacking necessary levels of those resources.

Third, and also related, this vision of family assumes a two-parent household; it further assumes that both parents place high premiums on the overall development of their children. However, death, divorce, and out-of-wedlock births are producing growing numbers of single-parent households, which subvert this assumption of "intactness"; the growing need for foster care programs and an increasing awareness of parental indifference and neglect, as well as actual child abuse, also subvert the assumption of universal parental solicitude.

To be sure, conservatives are aware of these three kinds of negative elements, but they do not interpret them as casting doubt on the workabil-

ity of their model—their vision. . . . But progressives wonder if these disruptive elements do not instead constitute more evidence of the nonsynchrony of the twentieth-century family with modern Western society. After all, progressives ask, how viable can a model of family possibly be for the late twentieth century that stems primarily from the nineteenth century? Consequently, if we put the . . . critical questions to progressives, we get very different responses . . .

Progressive Responses

. . . Bear in mind that conservatives *expect* certain fixed-role performances from each spouse. Progressives hold no specific expectations of this type. However, what is requisite for each spouse and what each spouse must be prepared to *give* to the arrangement (the second critical issue above) is genuinely wholehearted attention to equitable, fair, and just decision making regarding any and all matters. . . .

. . . [I]n marriage, the context for equitable decision making begins by ignoring fixed role structures and, instead, giving ascendance and prime significance to the two mutually shared and overriding interests of love and work. Once acknowledging the desirability of the equal-partner ideal, the task incumbent on the couple is to participate effectively (that is, equitably, justly) in the necessarily complicated processes of demand and policymaking covering both love and work. . . .

However, conservatives and other critics of the equal-partner model are fearful of its individualistic implications. . . . [H]ow can any sort of bonding take place? Does marriage simply degenerate to the level of spouses selfishly plucking from each other what they can, and then exiting when they have gotten all they want? . . .

. . . [T]his sort of exploitation is, of course, always possible. But exploitation is just as possible within conventional arrangements—perhaps it is even more likely, because women find themselves at a disadvantage to men both in terms of tangible and intangible resources. Indeed, even if no exploitation occurs under the emerging model, . . . permanence for its own sake and stability do not carry the same *overriding* significance in the progressives' vision as they do in the conservatives'. But facing up to the reality of *potential* flux does not assume selfishness and irresponsibility. Quite the contrary is true[:] . . . that the modern intimate relationship requires as much energy, attention, and careful thought as does the modern career means that one ignores, neglects, overlooks, or takes relationship matters for granted at one's own peril if one values continuity. Given that reality, one could say . . . that the emerging model engenders a greater degree of selflessness and responsibility than is often the case under the conservatives' model.

There is considerable literature (Lewis and Pleck, 1979; Pleck and Pleck, 1980) suggesting that many women do not feel that their husbands are making adequate levels of inputs into intimacy and nurture, into child care and household chores, or into appreciation for their autonomy strivings. However, given that these women tend to be in conventional marriages, there is often little they can do to alter what they perceive as male irresponsibility and selfishness. Appeals can be made by women and counselors, and through self-help books, but the fact of greater male status and privilege means that ultimately changes in conventional marriages are largely a matter of male goodwill.[1] Consequently, at least the *potential* for male selfishness is greater under the conservatives' model because women are at an inherent disadvantage.

By way of contrast, no gender disadvantage *inheres* in the progressives' . . . equal-partner model. Ideally and potentially, women and men with comparable levels of tangible and intangible resources form relationships in order that both might pursue the twin goals of optimum love (expressive) and work (instrumental) well-being. Nevertheless, owing to the basic notion that each partner is ultimately resource independent. . . . each is more able to ensure that the other's ir-

responsibility or selfishness is kept in check during those periods of perceived inequity when the mutuality of the preceding ideals is overlooked. Since, in particular, the woman is not ultimately dependent on the male for economic support or identity, he is less likely to be able to "take her for granted." Because he does not "possess" her (he cannot say, "She is mine," in the same sense that his father could speak of his mother), he must be alert to the very real possibility that she may eventually terminate the relationship if he does not continue to contribute inputs that will satisfy her. And, of course, the woman in such a relationship must exercise the same vigilance, since she does not have her mother's security of "belonging" to someone. The realization of the absolute necessity of continuing to make worthwhile inputs is a major distinguishing feature of the progressives' model; it is this realization that tends to militate against (but does not guarantee the absence of) selfishness and irresponsibility in pursuing the four emerging facets of love and intimacy. . . .

. . . To combat atomistic individualism on the one hand and suspicious insecurity on the other, equal-partner couples endeavor to maintain what . . . might . . . be described as a sense of equitable reciprocity. Thus, during demand and policymaking (decision-making) processes pertinent to intimacy issues, for example, couples communicate, discuss, and negotiate with each other in a spirit of mutual cooperation, with the best interests of each party kept in full view (see Scanzoni and Szinovacz, 1980). Neither subordinates his or her interests *merely* on the basis of gender tradition—such as the woman being willing to settle for less than desired sexual pleasure or equitable task sharing, or either partner automatically avoiding close cross-gender friendships. But, at the same time, each partner realizes that compromises and concessions must inevitably occur if the other is to be satisfied and the relationship maintained. Moreover, each realizes that, after all, their relationship is the source of their current gratifications. As long as these types of gratifications are deemed worthwhile, it would be counterproductive to jeopardize the relationship by behaving in a selfish or irresponsible manner. . . .

. . . [W]ithin the conventional model, the assumption was that since the relationship was unquestionably permanent, one could and should invest in it the totality of one's tangible and intangible resources (including energy and effort, and so forth). It was thought that such investments were sure to pay off in the long run. But, if no long run is assured, why make the sorts of investments necessary to establish [reciprocity] and to nurture trust? The fact is, of course, that many conventional marriages have not been permanent; nevertheless, people made great investments in them, based on their faith and trust that they would be permanent. Since conventional marriages (in which permanence is valued for its own sake) do not *guarantee* an atmosphere conducive to the growth of trust, the question becomes, what does? In actuality, there is no guarantee whatsoever that whenever parties make themselves vulnerable to and make investments in each other that the investments will be worthwhile or that the vulnerability will not be exploited.

But the only alternative to trusting is not trusting; the only option aside from investment is the withholding of significant inputs. And clearly, at both the micro and macro levels, it is demonstrably true that the risk involved in vulnerability and trust can be far more satisfying and desirable than not risking.[2] . . . Given that there is no alternative to risk, the fundamental issue becomes, are the risks greater and potentially more damaging when one naively dismisses or overlooks the possibility of risk (as in the conventional model), or are its potentially negative effects minimized when the risks are faced and one takes appropriate steps to manage them as effectively as possible? If we assume that the latter option is relatively less punishing than the former, and thus more desirable, then increasing numbers of persons are likely to favor the emerging *process* model of equal-partner marriage.

Doing so in no way relinquishes the vital notions of trust and commitment. Instead, the possibilities of achieving them appear just as great, if not greater, than was the case under the conventional model. . . .

In short, progressives argue that redefining marriage so as to eliminate the idea of permanence as an end in itself (while simultaneously making people, older as well as younger, aware of the reality of the increasing likelihood of marital impermanence—assuming that mid-1970s divorce rates remain constant, Weed [1980] estimates that within 40 years, virtually half of those mid-1970s marriages will have been legally terminated) would go a long way toward reducing guilt, anxiety, lowered self-esteem, and other forms of painful termination reactions. These individual benefits would be in addition to the prime social consideration that once the high probability of impermanence is grasped, some people may take the sorts of steps described above to guard against it. Progressives wish to guard against it because, although they reject permanence for its own sake, they strongly value "continuity with stimulation." The distinction can be illustrated by contrasting a placid, ripple-free lake with a mountain stream. The lake presents a picture of quiet, orderly, predictable, safe *stability* and tranquility. But the stream, while continuous, is moving, shifting, changing—and, if there are rapids, it can be hazardous to travel. The image it projects is continuity balanced with stimulation and challenge.

Consequently, the fundamental issue is not, as conservatives claim, "responsibility versus irresponsibility," but, instead, which image or vision of marriage/family is preferred. For example, in reflecting on his wife's divorcing him because "she needs freedom, independence, out from under what she felt was a smothering relationship," Martin (1976: 383) observes, "I don't feel this way but I am left with a crumbled view of a marital world which doesn't have much popularity anymore." He goes on to suggest that his wife was irresponsible for behaving as she did and for repudiating a lifestyle in which their four boys played in the woods behind their "large comfortable house in Connecticut. . . . Across the street [is] a lake where the whole family goes swimming and boating" (p. 384). During the winter they play ice hockey on the lake, and "snug" before "the big fireplace in [their] living room." While no one could or would object to these activities in themselves, the whole tenor of Martin's essay is that these activities are the essence or core of marriage and family life. The ideal is to arrive at a pleasant, warm, comforting equilibrium in which "you found someone who was the 'other half' . . . and you put them [complementary qualities] together and marched in lockstep through marital happiness." Martin feels that is a *responsible* lifestyle, in contrast to his wife's repudiation of "notions like commitment [permanence for its own sake], responsibility and an even more discredited concept, suffering" (p. 384).

While those are Martin's preferences and opinions, it is not the case that the progressive perspective is "irresponsible," or that "suffering" is repudiated. Yankelovich (1981b), for instance, argues that mutual sacrifices are often required to achieve the "new ethic of commitment" that he sees developing in contemporary American society. In any case, since the term "divorce" still maintains some opprobrium, it might be well to eventually discard its use in the same ways we seek to avoid the use of such terms as "Negro," "queer," "illegitimate," "broad," and so forth. The increasing popularity of expressions such as "formerly married" suggests that the time is ripe for more concerted efforts to describe marriages as having been "dissolved," "terminated," or merely "ended." . . .

Progressives and Order

. . . Parson's (1965) view of commitment was unswerving loyalty to specific conventional norms. A more dynamic approach is to conceive of commitment as "feelings of solidarity and cohesion" (Scanzoni, 1979: 87), which is analogous to

Yankelovich's (1981b: 250) view of the emerging "ethic of commitment" and its link to self-fulfillment. The sense of solidarity is generated through participation in arrangements that are mutually advantageous. As long as the arrangements continue to be perceived as advantageous, there is a sense of solidarity, or commitment (compare Rogers, 1968). But commitment is not a fixed, static state—solidarity and thus commitment can and do fluctuate—it can grow or decline.

For example, let us assume that at some point a couple manages to achieve the sort of "negotiated [family] order" to which Strauss (1978) and others refer. Having achieved this, however, in no way implies that equal-partner couples inevitably maintain equity, justice, and consensus, or that nonlegitimate power (sometimes including violence) and coercion may not sometimes erupt. If and when they do, these *processes* of coercion, nonlegitimate power, and inequity tend to undermine the couple's sense of cohesion or solidarity, and thus commitment. . . . [E]qual-partner couples (whether legally or informally joined) can and do experience certain levels of separation and dissolution. Proportionately, perhaps, the levels may, currently at least, even be greater than among conventional marriages—especially when one spouse who used to be conventional begins to change and starts seeking negotiated equity, while the other prefers to hold on to script conformity (Bowen, 1981; Martin, 1976).

However, such "breakups" are not a threat to social order, or predictability, in the same way that divorce is perceived to be threatening by the conservative subset of the population. To conservatives, if the conventional patterns are disturbed (such as gender-linked behaviors based on permanency), then aspersions are being cast on the "rightness" of their family norms. What is comparable across thousands of conservative families are those specific patterns. But to progressives, what is comparable across families is not males, females, and children acting rigidly in prearranged or scripted ways. Instead what welds equal-partner marriages/families together as a coherent and discernible subset are identifiable patterns of negotiation and decision making pertaining to both task-oriented and intimacy issues. These are the fundamental similarities of behavior that they share.

Distinctive Moral Norms

Underlying these particular behavior patterns, equal-partner households also share at least four *moral norms* in the sense that "moral" is defined by Ellis (1971: 696)—prescriptions that are beyond and greater than one's own narrow self-interests and that are also beyond the realm of participatory decision making. These four norms sharply distinguish the emerging egalitarian from the conventional model. Supplying structure, shape, form, and uniqueness to the equal-partner model, they also demonstrate how it achieves Yankelovich's notion of "social responsibility." One of these is the norm that "everything should be negotiable except the idea that everything is negotiable." This norm is the ultimate and inviolate principle of every genuine democracy. The absence of this moral norm makes a nation, as well as family, something less than fully democratic. Of course, everything cannot always be negotiated satisfactorily, nor is power necessarily consistently symmetrical. But apart from this norm, parties have little *moral* compulsion to seek either mutually satisfactory negotiations or symmetrical power.

A second moral norm that is shared in common by and thus aids in identifying equal-partner households is that demand and policymaking processes themselves, as well as the arrangements to which they give rise, should be characterized by justice and equity, that is, the absence of exploitation. These notions have been discussed elsewhere in this and the prior chapter, but they deserve reiteration at this juncture because they, like the first moral norm, do indeed help us dis-

tinguish progressive from conventional households. And although I discuss violence later in this chapter, it is well to note here that one of the axioms of this second moral norm is that adults should not physically assault each other. It would seem that a precondition for achieving optimum family justice is a remote probability of violence.

A third moral norm, besides "Thou shalt never place anything above negotiation" and "Thou shalt always strive for equity," . . . [is] behavioral interchangeability: "Thou shalt always be prepared to work either in the home or in the marketplace." . . . [T]his norm in no way imposes a fixed rigidity regarding household chores, child care, or paid employment. Since it is tempered by the first norm, neither partner need feel constrained, for example, to be "locked in" to continuous full-time year-round employment. Either may wish to reduce (or increase) his or her occupational efforts at particular times in response to certain circumstances. Of course, a partner's reduction in effort will probably mean that he or she has fewer economic resources, which could very well influence the symmetry of negotiating power in the relationship (Scanzoni and Szinovacz, 1980). In any case, the same flexibility applies to child care and household duties. The pivotal issue here is *capability* to function effectively in any and all of the three cited spheres, depending on the couple's definition of their maximum joint profit at any particular time.

A fourth moral norm [concerns] children, namely, that the prime objective of child socialization should be to actively involve children in age-specific participatory decision making based on the three preceding norms—a socialization that results in positive self-image and sense of control of one's own destiny. . . .

NOTES

1. In a recent analysis of contemporary housework, Andre (1981: 103–104) suggests that women who want

their husbands to participate more fully in household chores should request it, simply resign from housework, or "design a work-sharing system" among household members. She goes on (pp. 131–140) to discuss family *power* relationships, but fails to make sufficiently explicit and specific the logical connections between the two topics (getting husbands to do housework and family power).

2. In a recent classroom discussion of these matters, one student observed that she would prefer to marry and take the risk of marital dissolution in order to enjoy what she sees as marriage benefits, rather than not marry, thus avoiding the possibility of divorce, and forgo marital gratifications.

REFERENCES

Andre, R. (1981) Homemakers: The Forgotten Workers. Chicago: University of Chicago Press.

Bowen, G. L. (1981) "Sex role preferences and marital quality in the military." Ph.D. dissertation, University of North Carolina—Greensboro.

Ellis, D. P. (1971) "The Hobbesian problem of order: a critical appraisal of the normative solution." American Sociological Review 36 (August): 692–703.

Fisher, R. and W. Ury (1981) Getting to Yes: Negotiating Agreement without Giving in. Boston: Houghton Mifflin.

Lewis, R. A. and J. H. Pleck [eds.] (1979) "Men's roles in the family." Family Coordinator 28 (October): special issue.

Martin, A. (1976) "I am one man, hurt," pp. 382–385 in J. Blankenship (ed.) Scenes from Life: Views of Family, Marriage, Intimacy. Boston: Little, Brown.

Parsons, T. (1965) "The normal American family," pp. 31–50 in S. M. Farber et al. (eds.) Man and Civilization: The Family's Search for Survival. New York: McGraw-Hill.

Pleck, E. H. and J. H. Pleck (1980) The American Man. Englewood Cliffs, NJ: Prentice-Hall.

Polonko, K. and J. Scanzoni (1981) Patterns Compared for the Voluntarily Childless, Postponing Childless, Undecided Childless, and Mothers. Final Report, National Institute for Child Health and Human Development (Contract 1-HD-92805).

Rogers, C. R. (1968) "Man-woman relationships in the year 2000." Journal of Applied Behavioral Science 4, 3: 270–272.

Scanzoni, J. (1979) "Social exchange and behavioral interdependence," pp. 61–98 in T. L. Huston and R. L. Burgess (eds.) Social Exchange and Developing Relationships. New York: Academic.

Scanzoni, J. and M. Szinovacz (1980) Family Decision-Making: A Developmental Sex Role Model. Beverly Hills, CA: Sage.

Strauss, A. (1978) Negotiations: Varieties, Contexts, Processes, and Social Order. San Francisco: Jossey-Bass.

Swidler, A. (1980) "Love and adulthood in American Culture," pp. 120–150 in N. J. Smelser and E. H. Erikson (eds.) Themes of Love and Work in Adulthood. Cambridge, MA: Harvard University Press.

Weed, J. A. (1980) "National estimates of marriage dissolution and survivorship." Vital and Health Statistics 3, 19.

Yankelovich, D. (1981b) New Rules: Searching for Self-Fulfillment in a World Turned Upside Down. New York: Random House.

Further Questions

1. Is there some value in maintaining the traditional structure in your marriage (or relationship) just because it is the traditional structure?

2. Is it a good idea for spouses to discuss the terms of the marital commitment before they make that commitment? Should these terms be subject to renegotiation if either spouse changes her or his mind?

3. In considering whether you want to get married (or stay married, or get married again), are you thinking more of the personal side or of the status marriage would give you?

VI.6   Is "Straight" to "Gay" as "Family" Is to "No Family"?

KATH WESTON

Kath Weston outlines a gay and lesbian understanding of "family." A nonprocreative sexual identity precludes a definition of "family" in terms of sexual intercourse and genealogy. Without implying that gay or lesbian identity is itself chosen, Weston calls the nonheterosexual analog to heterosexual marriage "families we choose."

Weston teaches in the Department of Social and Behavioral Sciences at Arizona State University West. *Families We Choose: Lesbians, Gays, Kinship*, from which this selection was taken, is her first book. Another excerpt appears in Part IV.

Reading Questions

1. Does "family" just have one definition? If so, what is it?
2. Must "family" (past, present, or future) have a biological component? If so, what is it?
3. What do you think of the idea held by the conservative element of society that lesbians and gays are a threat to "the family," and perhaps to "society" as well?

FOR YEARS, and in an amazing variety of contexts, claiming a lesbian or gay identity has been portrayed as a rejection of "the family" and a departure from kinship. In media portrayals of AIDS, Simon Watney (1987:103) observes that "we are invited to imagine some absolute divide between the two domains of 'gay life' and 'the family,' as if gay men grew up, were educated, worked and lived our lives in total isolation from the rest of society." Two presuppositions lend a dubious credence to such imagery: the belief that gay men and lesbians do not have children or establish lasting relationships, and the belief that they invariably alienate adoptive and blood kin once their sexual identities become known. By presenting "the family" as a unitary object, these depictions also imply that everyone participates in identical sorts of kinship relations and subscribes to one universally agreed-upon definition of family.

Representations that exclude lesbians and gay men from "the family" invoke what Blanche Wiesen Cook (1977:48) has called "the assumption that gay people do not love and do not work," the reduction of lesbians and gay men to sexual identity, and sexual identity to sex alone. In the United States, sex apart from heterosexual marriage tends to introduce a wild card into social relations, signifying unbridled lust and the limits of individualism. If heterosexual intercourse can bring people into enduring association via the creation of kinship ties, lesbian and gay sexuality in these depictions isolates individuals from one another rather than weaving them into a social fabric. To assert that straight people "naturally" have access to family, while gay people are destined to move toward a future of solitude and loneliness, is not only to tie kinship closely to procreation, but also to treat gay men and lesbians as members of a nonprocreative species set apart from the rest of humanity (cf. Foucault 1978).

It is but a short step from positioning lesbians and gay men somewhere beyond "the family"—

unencumbered by relations of kinship, responsibility, or affection—to portraying them as a menace to family and society. A person or group must first be outside and other in order to invade, endanger, and threaten. My own impression from fieldwork corroborates Frances FitzGerald's (1986) observation that many heterosexuals believe not only that gay people have gained considerable political power, but also that the absolute number of lesbians and gay men (rather than their visibility) has increased in recent years. Inflammatory rhetoric that plays on fears about the "spread" of gay identity and of AIDS finds a disturbing parallel in the imagery used by fascists to describe syphilis at mid-century, when "the healthy" confronted "the degenerate" while the fate of civilization hung in the balance (Hocquenghem 1978). . . .

At the height of gay liberation, activists had attempted to develop alternatives to "the family," whereas by the 1980s many lesbians and gay men were struggling to legitimate gay families as a form of kinship. When Armistead Maupin spoke at a gathering on Castro Street to welcome home two gay men who had been held hostage in the Middle East, partners who had stood with arms around one another upon their release, he congratulated them not only for their safe return, but also as representatives of a new kind of family. Gay or chosen families might incorporate friends, lovers, or children, in any combination. Organized through ideologies of love, choice, and creation, gay families have been defined through a contrast with what many gay men and lesbians in the Bay Area called "straight," "biological," or "blood" family. If families we choose were the families lesbians and gay men created for themselves, straight family represented the families in which most had grown to adulthood.

What does it mean to say that these two categories of family have been defined through contrast? One thing it emphatically does *not* mean is that heterosexuals share a single coherent form of family (although some of the lesbians and gay men doing the defining believed this to be the case). I am not arguing here for the existence of some central, unified kinship system vis-à-vis which gay people have distinguished their own practice and understanding of family. In the United States, race, class, gender, ethnicity, regional origin, and context all inform differences in household organization, as well as differences in notions of family and what it means to call someone kin.[1] . . .

Kinship and Procreation

Since the time of Lewis Henry Morgan, most scholarly studies of familial relations have enthroned human procreation as kinship's ultimate referent. According to received anthropological wisdom, relations of blood (consanguinity) and marriage (affinity) could be plotted for any culture on a universal genealogical grid. Generations of field-workers set about the task of developing kinship charts for a multitude of "egos," connecting their subjects outward to a network of social others who represented the products (offspring) and agents (genitor/genetrix) of physical procreation. In general, researchers occupied themselves with investigations of differences in the ways cultures arranged and divided up the grid, treating blood ties as a material base underlying an array of crosscultural variations in kinship organization.

More recently, however, anthropologists have begun to reconsider the status of kinship as an analytic concept and a topic for inquiry. What would happen if observers ceased privileging genealogy as a sacrosanct or objective construct, approaching biogenetic ties instead as a characteristically Western way of ordering and granting significance to social relations? After a lengthy exercise in this kind of bracketing, David Schneider (1972, 1984) concluded that significant doubt exists as to whether non-Western cultures recognize kinship as a unified construct or domain. Too often unreflective recourse to the biogenetic symbolism used to prioritize relationships in Anglo-European societies subordinates an understanding of how particular cultures construct social ties to the project of crosscultural comparison. But suppose for a moment that blood is not intrinsically thicker than water. Denaturalizing the genealogical grid would require that procreation no longer be postulated as kinship's base, ground, or centerpiece.

Within Western societies, anthropologists are not the only ones who have implicitly or explicitly subjected the genealogical grid to new scrutiny. By reworking familiar symbolic materials in the context of nonprocreative relationships, lesbians and gay men in the United States have formulated a critique of kinship that contests assumptions about the bearing of biology, genetics, and heterosexual intercourse on the meaning of family in their own culture. nlike Schneider, they have not set out to deconstruct kinship as a privileged domain, or taken issue with cultural representations that portray biology as a material "fact" exclusive of social significance. What gay kinship ideologies challenge is not the concept of procreation that informs kinship in the United States, but the belief that procreation *alone* constitutes kinship, and that "nonbiological" ties must be patterned after a biological model (like adoption) or forfeit any claim to kinship status.

In the United States the notion of biology as an indelible, precultural substratum is so ingrained that people often find it difficult to take an anthropological step backward in order to examine biology as symbol rather than substance. For many in this society, biology is a defining feature of kinship: they believe that blood ties make certain people kin, regardless of whether those individuals display the love and enduring solidarity expected to characterize familial relations. Physical procreation, in turn, produces biological links. Collectively, biogenetic attributes are supposed to demarcate kinship as a cultural domain, offering a yardstick for determining who counts as a "real" relative. Like their heterosexual counterparts, lesbians and gay men tended to naturalize biology in this manner. . . .

Not all cultures grant biology this significance for describing and evaluating relationships. To read biology as symbol is to approach it as a cultural construct and linguistic category, rather than a self-evident matter of "natural fact." At issue here is the cultural valuation given to ties traced through procreation, and the meaning that biological connection confers upon a relationship in a given cultural context. In this sense biology is no less a symbol than choice or creation. Neither is inherently more "real" or valid than the other, culturally speaking.

In the United States, Schneider (1968) argues, "sexual intercourse" is the symbol that brings together relations of marriage and blood, supplying the distinctive features in terms of which kinship relations are defined and differentiated. A relationship mediated by procreation binds a mother to a daughter, a brother to a sister, and so on, in the categories of genitor or genetrix, offspring, or members of a sibling set. Immediately apparent to a gay man or lesbian is that what passes here for sex per se is actually the *hetero*sexual union of two differently gendered persons. While all sexual activity among heterosexuals certainly does not lead to the birth of children, the isolation of heterosexual intercourse as a core symbol orients kinship studies toward a dominantly procreative reading of sexualities. For a society like the United States, Sylvia Yanagisako's and Jane Collier's (1987) call to analyze gender and kinship as mutually implicated constructs must be extended to embrace sexual identity.

The very notion of gay families asserts that people who claim nonprocreative sexual identities and pursue nonprocreative relationships can lay claim to family ties of their own without necessary recourse to marriage, childbearing, or childrearing.[2] By defining these chosen families in opposition to the biological ties believed to constitute a straight family, lesbians and gay men began to renegotiate the meaning and practice of kinship from within the very societies that had nurtured the concept. Theirs has not been a proposal to number gay families among variations in "American kinship," but a more comprehensive attack on the privilege accorded to a biogenetically grounded mode of determining what relationships will *count* as kinship. . . .

From Biology to Choice

Upon first learning the categories that framed gay kinship ideologies, heterosexuals sometimes mentioned adoption as a kind of limiting case that appeared to occupy that borderland between biology and choice. In the United States, adopted children are chosen, in a sense, although biological offspring can be planned or selected as well, given the widespread availability of birth control. Yet adoption in this society "is only understandable as a way of creating the social fiction that an actual link of kinship exists. Without biological kinship as a model, adoption would be meaningless" (Schneider 1984:55). Adoption does not render the attribution of biological descent culturally irrelevant (witness the many adopted children who, later in life, decide to search for their "real" parents). But adoptive relations—unlike gay families—pose no fundamental challenge to either procreative interpretations of kinship or the culturally standardized image of a family assembled around a core of parent(s) plus children.

Mapping biological family and families we choose onto contrasting sexual identities (straight and gay, respectively) places these two types of family in a relation of opposition, but *within* that relation, determinism implicitly differentiates biology from choice and blood from creation. Informed by contrasting notions of free will and the fixedness often attributed to biology in this culture, the opposition between straight and gay families echoes old dichotomies such as nature versus nurture and real versus ideal. In families we choose, the agency conveyed by "we" emphasizes each person's part in constructing gay families, just as the absence of agency in the term "biological family" reinforces the sense of blood as an immutable fact over which individuals exert little control. Likewise, the collective subject of families we choose invokes a collective identity—who are "we" if not gay men and lesbians? In order to identify the "we" associated with the speaker's "I," a listener must first recognize the correspondence between the opposition of blood to choice and the relation of straight to gay.

Significantly, families we choose have not built directly upon beliefs that gay or lesbian identity can be chosen. Among lesbians and gay men themselves, opinions differ as to whether individuals select or inherit their sexual identities. In the aftermath of the gay movement, the trend has been to move away from the obsession of earlier decades with the etiological question of what "causes" homosexuality. After noting that no one subjects heterosexuality to similar scrutiny, many people dropped the question. Some lesbian-feminists presented lesbianism as a political choice that made a statement about sharing their best with other women and refusing to participate in patriarchal relations. In everyday conversations, however, the majority of both men and women portrayed their sexual identities as either inborn or a predisposition developed very early in life. Whether or not to act on feelings already present then became the only matter left to individual discretion. "The choice for me wasn't being with men or being a lesbian," Richie Kaplan explained. "The choice was being asexual or being with women."

In contrast, parents who disapproved of homosexuality could convey a critical attitude by treating gay identity as something elective, especially since people in the United States customarily hold individuals responsible for any negative consequences attendant upon a "free choice." One man described with dismay his father's reaction upon learning of his sexual identity: "I said, 'I'm gay.' And he said, 'Oh. Well, I guess you made your choice.'" According to another, "My father kept saying, 'Well, you're gonna have to live by your choices that you make. It's your responsibility.' What's there to be responsible [about]? I was who I *am*." When Andy Wentworth disclosed his gay identity to his sister,

She asked me, how could I *choose* to do this and to ignore the health risks . . . implying that this was a conscious, 'Oh, I'd like to go to the movies today' type of choice. And I told her, I said, 'Nobody in their right mind would go through this *hell* of being gay just to satisfy a whim.' And I explained to her what it was like growing up. Knowing this other side of yourself that you can't tell anybody about, and if anybody in your family knows they will be upset and mortified.

Another man insisted he would never forget the period after coming out when he realized that he felt good about himself, and that he was not on his way to becoming "the kind of person that they're portraying gay people to be." What kind of person is that, I asked. "Well, you know, wicked, evil people who *decide* that they're going to be evil."

Rather than claiming an elective gay identity as its antecedent, the category "families we choose" incorporates the meaningful *difference* that is the product of choice and biology as two relationally defined terms. If many gay men and lesbians interpreted blood ties as a type of social connectedness organized through procreation, they tended to associate choice and creativity with a total absence of guidelines for ordering relationships within gay families. Although heterosexuals in the Bay Area also had the sense of creating something when they established families of their own, that creativity was often firmly linked to childbearing and childrearing, the "pro-" in procreation. In the absence of a procreative referent, individual discretion regulated who would be counted as kin. For those who had constructed them, gay families could evoke utopian visions of self-determination in the absence of social constraint. . . .

Gone are the days when embracing a lesbian or gay identity seemed to require a renunciation of kinship. The symbolic groundwork for gay families, laid during a period when coming out to relatives witnessed a kind of institutionalization, has made it possible to claim a sexual identity that is not linked to procreation, face the possibility of rejection by blood or adoptive relations, yet still conceive of establishing a family of one's own.

NOTES

1. On the distinction between family and household, see Rapp (1982) and Yanagisako (1979).

2. See Foucault (1978) on the practice of grouping homosexuality together with other nonprocreative sex acts, a historical shift that supplanted the earlier classification of homosexuality with adultery and offenses against marriage. According to Foucault, previous to the late eighteenth century acts "contrary to nature" tended to be understood as an extreme form of acts "against the law," rather than something different in kind. Only later was "the unnatural" set apart in the emerging domain of sexuality, becoming autonomous from adultery or rape. See also Freedman (1982:210): "Although the ideological support for the separation of [erotic] sexuality and reproduction did not appear until the twentieth century, the process itself began much earlier."

REFERENCES

Bourdieu, Pierre. 1977. *Outline of a Theory of Practice*. New York: Cambridge University Press.

Cook, Blanche Wiesen. 1977. "Female Support Networks and Political Activism: Lillian Wald, Crystal Eastman, Emma Goldman." *Chrysalis* 3:44–61.

FitzGerald, Frances. 1986. *Cities on a Hill: A Journey Through Contemporary American Cultures*. New York: Simon & Schuster.

Foucault, Michel. 1978. *The History of Sexuality*. Vol. 1. New York: Vintage.

Freedman, Estelle B. 1982. "Sexuality in Nineteenth-Century America: Behavior, Ideology, and Politics." *Reviews in American History* 10:196–215.

Hocquenghem, Guy. 1978. *Homosexual Desire*. London: Alison & Busby.

Rapp, Rayna. 1982. "Family and Class in Contemporary America: Notes Toward an Understanding of Ideology." In Barrie Thorne with Marilyn Yalom, eds., *Rethinking the Family*, pp. 168–187. New York: Longman.

Schneider, David M. 1968. *American Kinship: A Cultural Account*. Englewood Cliffs, N.J.: Prentice-Hall.

————— 1972. "What Is Kinship All About?" In Priscilla Reining, ed., *Kinship Studies in the Morgan Centennial Year.* Washington, D.C.: Anthropological Society of Washington.

————— 1984. *A Critique of the Study of Kinship.* Ann Arbor: University of Michigan Press.

Silverstein, Charles. 1977. *A Family Matter: A Parents' Guide to Homosexuality.* New York: McGraw-Hill.

Watney, Simon. 1987. *Policing Desire: Pornography, AIDS, and the Media.* Minneapolis: University of Minnesota Press.

Yanagisako, Sylvia Junko and Jane Fishburne Collier. 1987. "Toward a Unified Analysis of Gender and Kinship." In Jane Fishburne Collier and Sylvia Junko Yanagisako, eds., *Gender and Kinship: Essays Toward a Unified Analysis,* pp. 14–50. Stanford: Stanford University Press.

Further Questions

1. Homosexual unions are chosen. Does this mean that heterosexual ones are *not* chosen?

2. Are heterosexual unions established, at least in part, for the purpose of procreation? If so, does this mean childless heterosexual marriages and heterosexual unions lack something?

3. Should your sexual orientation make a difference in your place in the family into which you were born?

Fighting for Same Sex Marriage   VI.7

CRAIG R. DEAN

Pursuing the idea of marriage as a legal concept, Craig R. Dean has filed a lawsuit against the District of Columbia for discriminating against him and his lover. The District is denying them, as a gay couple, the right to enter into that legal relationship. Dean and his partner are both lawyers in Washington, D.C.

Reading Questions

1. Is there any good reason to withhold marital benefits from same-sex couples? In particular, should they be denied the option of next-of-kin status in medical and legal decisions?

2. Is there any reason to believe that same-sex couples cannot attain the level of love and commitment we believe necessary to a good heterosexual marriage?

3. Would allowing same-sex couples to marry debase the institution of marriage in any way?

THE DISTRICT OF COLUMBIA has denied my lover, Patrick Gill, and I the right to marry because we are a same-sex couple. As a result, we filed a lawsuit alleging violation of the district's

Human Rights Act and discrimination by failing to follow the marriage law.

As gay men, we do not believe our love is of any less magnitude or importance than that of any other couples in a long-term committed relationship. For that reason we want the legal recognition of our Holy Union ceremony which would be offered without question if one of us was female.

We demand the same marriage rights and benefits that heterosexual couples have. These rights and benefits protect and reinforce relationships both from without and within. Yet these rights are denied to us for only one reason—that we are a gay couple.

Married couples have many rights that unmarried couples—even domestic partners—do not have. In the District of Columbia alone there are more than 100 automatic marriage-based rights.

Heterosexuals can meet tonight in a bar and have more rights through marriage within five days than Patrick and I are able to obtain after five years together. This is an incredible act of multiple discrimination and we are doing something about it.

A few have chosen to publicly criticize us. One criticism charges that if we win our lawsuit, Congress may intervene and change the D.C. marriage law.

The homophobes would love it if we continue to allow ourselves to be cowed by fear of what a few bigots in Congress may or may not do.

Shall we be modern-day Uncle Toms, or should we stand up and fight for our rights? If we ever get to the point that Congress has to intervene, we will have already achieved a huge legal and perceptual victory.

Another argument states that, if we lose, we set bad legal precedent. Yet, how much worse can it get? Does anyone know of a jurisdiction in the United States where two men can get married? The point is, the only way to go is up.

Furthermore, at this time, we are not making any broad constitutional claims that may end up in the Supreme Court—although we certainly could cite the First Amendment guarantee separating church and state. Instead, we are asking for an interpretation of local laws in D.C. courts.

In light of the strong foundation of our case in favorable case law, statutes and policy, D.C. is the best jurisdiction to bring a case of this type.

As for whether gays and lesbians should seek marriage at all, some critics say that homosexuals should not mimic heterosexual lifestyles. This argument buys into the homophobic idea that gay and lesbian marriage makes a farce of the marital institution.

Whether marriage is good or bad is irrelevant. Just as some heterosexual couples choose not to marry, gay men and lesbians should have the option to marry if they so choose.

Marriage has traditionally been an attractive option for people as it provides stability and societal respectability to the relationship. Same-sex marriage would increase desegregation, tolerance and acceptance of the gay and lesbian community.

A few gay critics have actually attacked us for "not being ideal litigants." Who can honestly claim to sit in judgement of the entire gay and lesbian community and decide who may fight for their rights? What the gay movement needs is more, not fewer, individuals stepping forward and demanding their rights.

We demand full equality—now. Some may call this a shortcut. But the real shortcut would have been to give into homophobia and give up without a fight.

Heterosexual Privilege

Legal marriage offers heterosexual couples many benefits unavailable or widely inaccessible to same-sex couples. These benefits include:

- reducing their tax liability by filing joint income returns;
- Social Security or other retirement funds for surviving spouses and dependents;
- health, life and disability insurance and other spousal benefits from employers;

- automatic inheritance and rights of survivorship;
- social status contributory to professional and political advancement;
- immunity from subpoenas requiring testimony against a spouse;
- automatic spousal coverage in many automobile and property insurance policies;
- the immediate right to U.S. residency for an alien who marries a citizen;

- easy access to joint custody of spouse's children;
- next-of-kin status in medical and legal decisions;
- joint ownership of real and personal property and protection of that property from each other's creditors; and
- eligibility for joint memberships, family and spousal discounts, and joint credit.

Further Questions

1. Should same-sex couples have opportunities to establish joint custody of the children of one of the partners?

2. Is the question of whether marriage is good or bad simply irrelevant to whether same-sex couples should have this option?

3. Do legal benefits of marriage serve, in part, to reinforce the personal side of the relationship?

The Married Woman   VI.8

SIMONE DE BEAUVOIR

Simone de Beauvoir attacks the gender role system in marriage. The system oppresses the woman and, through her, the man as well. She suggests that the remedy is to prohibit marriage as a "career" for women.

Other excerpts from Simone de Beauvoir's *The Second Sex* appear in Parts I, IV, X, and XIII.

Reading Questions

1. In the social world, is the status of a married woman more legitimate than that of a single woman? Does the age of a single woman make any difference to whether she is socially legitimate?

2. Are housework, shopping, and cooking rewarding work, if these are all a person does? Does the amount of satisfaction a person gains from doing only this kind of work depend on the circumstances in which the work is done?

3. Do the parents of a woman (or man) have a right to put pressure upon her (or him) to marry?

MARRIAGE IS THE DESTINY traditionally offered to women by society. It is still true that
most women are married, or have been, or plan
to be, or suffer from not being. The celibate
woman is to be explained and defined with reference to marriage, whether she is frustrated, rebellious, or even indifferent in regard to that
institution. . . .

. . . [F]or both parties marriage is at the same
time a burden and a benefit; but there is no symmetry in the situations of the two sexes; for girls
marriage is the only means of integration in the
community, and if they remain unwanted, they
are, socially viewed, so much wastage. This is why
mothers have always eagerly sought to arrange
marriages for them. In the last century they were
hardly consulted among middle-class people.
They were offered to possible suitors by means of
"interviews" arranged in advance. Zola describes
this custom in *Pot-Bouille*.

"A failure, it's a failure," said Mme Josserand,
falling into her chair. M. Josserand simply said:
"Ah!"

"But," continued Mme Josserand in a shrill
voice, "you don't seem to understand, I'm telling you that there's another marriage gone, and
it's the seventh that has miscarried.

"You hear," she went on, advancing on her
daughter. "How did you spoil this marriage?"

Bertha realized that it was her turn.

"I don't know, Mamma," she murmured.

"An assistant department head," her mother
continued, "not yet thirty, and with a great
future. A man to bring you his pay every
month; substantial, that's all that counts. . . .
You did something stupid, the same as with the
others?"

"No, Mamma, certainly not."

"When you were dancing with him you disappeared into the small parlor."

Bertha said in some confusion: "Yes,
Mamma—and as soon as we were alone he
wanted to act disgracefully, he hugged me and
took hold of me like this. Then I got scared and
pushed him against a piece of furniture."

Her mother interrupted, furious again:
"Pushed him against the furniture! You wretch,
you pushed him!"

"But, Mamma, he was holding on to me."

"So? He was holding on to you, fancy that!
And we send these simpletons to boarding
school! What do they teach you, tell me! Ah,
just for a kiss behind the door! Should you really
tell us about such a thing, your parents? And
you push people against furniture, and you spoil
chances to marry!"

She assumed a didactic air and continued:

"That's the end, I give up, you are just stupid, my dear. Since you have no fortune, understand that you have to catch men some other
way. The idea is to be agreeable, to gaze
tenderly, to forget about your hand, to allow little intimacies without seeming to notice; in a
word, you fish for a husband. . . . What bothers
me is that she is not too bad, when she feels like
it. Come, now, stop crying and look at me as if
I were a gentleman courting you. See, you drop
your fan so that when he picks it up he will
touch your fingers. . . . And don't be stiff, let
your waist bend. Men don't like boards. And
above all don't be a ninny if they go too far. A
man who goes too far is done for, my dear."

Through the long evening of furious talk the
girl was docile and resigned, but her heart was
heavy, oppressed with fear and shame. . . .

In such circumstances the girl seems absolutely
passive; she *is* married, *given* in marriage by her parents. Boys *get* married, they *take* a wife. They look
in marriage for an enlargement, a confirmation of
their existence, but not the mere right to exist; it
is a charge they assume voluntarily. Thus they can
inquire concerning its advantages and disadvantages, as did the Greek and medieval satirists; for
them it is one mode of living, not a preordained
lot. They have a perfect right to prefer celibate solitude; some marry late, or not at all.

In marrying, woman gets some share in the
world as her own; legal guarantees protect her
against capricious action by man; but she becomes his vassal. He is the economic head of the
joint enterprise, and hence he represents it in the

view of society. She takes his name; she belongs to his religion, his class, his circle; she joins his family, she becomes his "half." She follows wherever his work calls him and determines their place of residence; she breaks more or less decisively with her past, becoming attached to her husband's universe; she gives him her person, virginity and a rigorous fidelity being required. She loses some of the rights legally belonging to the unmarried woman. Roman law placed the wife in the husband's hands *loco filiæ*, in the position of a daughter; early in the nineteenth century the conservative writer Bonald pronounced the wife to be to her husband as the child is to its mother; before 1942 French law demanded the wife's obedience to her husband; law and custom still give him great authority, as implied in the conjugal situation itself.

Since the husband is the productive worker, he is the one who goes beyond family interest to that of society, opening up a future for himself through cooperation in the building of the collective future: he incarnates transcendence. Woman is doomed to the continuation of the species and the care of the home—that is to say, to immanence. The fact is that every human existence involves transcendence and immanence at the same time; to go forward, each existence must be maintained, for it to expand toward the future it must integrate the past, and while intercommunicating with others it should find self-confirmation. These two elements—maintenance and progression—are implied in any living activity, and for *man* marriage permits precisely a happy synthesis of the two. In his occupation and his political life he encounters change and progress, he senses his extension through time and the universe; and when he is tired of such roaming, he gets himself a home, a fixed location, and an anchorage in the world. At evening he restores his soul in the home, where his wife takes care of his furnishings and children and guards the things of the past that she keeps in store. But she has no other job than to maintain and pro-

vide for life in pure and unvarying generality; she perpetuates the species without change, she ensures the even rhythm of the days and the continuity of the home, seeing to it that the doors are locked. But she is allowed no direct influence upon the future nor upon the world; she reaches out beyond herself toward the social group only through her husband as intermediary.

Marriage today still retains, for the most part, this traditional form. And, first of all, it is forced much more tyrannically upon the young girl than upon the young man. . . .

. . . A single woman in America, still more than in France, is a socially incomplete being even if she makes her own living; if she is to attain the whole dignity of a person and gain her full rights, she must wear a wedding ring. Maternity in particular is respectable only for a married woman; the unwed mother remains an offense to public opinion, and her child is a severe handicap for her in life.

For all these reasons a great many adolescent girls—in the New World as in the Old—when asked about their plans for the future, reply today as formerly: "I want to get married." But no young man considers marriage as his fundamental project. Economic success is what will bring him adult standing; such success may imply marriage—especially for the peasant—but it can also preclude it. The conditions of modern life—less stable, more uncertain than in the past—make the responsibilities of marriage especially heavy for the young man. Its benefits, on the other hand, have decreased, since it is easily possible for him to obtain board and room and since sexual satisfaction is generally available. No doubt marriage can afford certain material and sexual conveniences: it frees the individual from loneliness, it establishes him securely in space and time by giving him a home and children; it is a definitive fulfillment of his existence. But, for all that, the masculine demand is on the whole less than the feminine supply. A father can be said less to give his daughter than to get rid of her; the girl in search of a husband is not responding to a masculine demand, she is trying to create one. . . .

. . . The male is called upon for action, his vocation is to produce, fight, create, progress, to transcend himself toward the totality of the universe and the infinity of the future; but traditional marriage does not invite woman to transcend herself with him; it confines her in immanence, shuts her up within the circle of herself. She can thus propose to do nothing more than construct a life of stable equilibrium in which the present as a continuance of the past avoids the menaces of tomorrow—that is, construct precisely a life of happiness. In place of love, she will feel a tender and respectful sentiment known as conjugal love, wifely affection; within the walls of the home she is to manage, she will enclose her world; she will see to the continuation of the human species through time to come.

But no existent ever relinquishes his transcendence, even when he stubbornly forswears it. The old-time bourgeois thought that in preserving the established order, in showing its virtues through his own prosperity, he was serving God, his country, a regime, a civilization: to be happy was to fulfill his function as a man. Woman, too, must envisage purposes that transcend the peaceful life of the home; but it is man who will act as intermediary between his wife as an individuality and the universe, he will endue her inconsequential life of contingency with human worth. Obtaining in his association with his wife the strength to undertake things, to act, to struggle, he is her justification: she has only to put her existence in his hands and he will give it meaning. This presupposes a humble renunciation on her part; but she is compensated because, under the guidance and protection of masculine strength, she will escape the effects of the original renunciation; she will once more become essential. Queen in her hive, tranquilly at rest within her domain, but borne by man out into limitless space and time, wife, mother, mistress of the home, woman finds in marriage at once energy for living and meaning for her life. We must now see how this ideal works out in reality. . . .

The ideal of happiness has always taken material form in the house, whether cottage or castle; it stands for permanence and separation from the world. Within its walls the family is established as a discrete cell or a unit group and maintains its identity as generations come and go; the past, preserved in the form of furnishings and ancestral portraits, gives promise of a secure future; in the garden the seasons register their reassuring cycle in the growth of edible vegetables; each year the same springtime with the same flowers foretells the return of immutable summer, of autumn with its fruits no different from the fruits of any other autumn: neither time nor space fly off at a tangent, they recur in their appointed cycles. In every civilization based on landed property an ample literature sings the poetry of hearth and home; in such a work as Henry Bordeaux's *La Maison* it sums up all the middle-class values: fidelity to the past, patience, economy, foresight, love of family and of the native soil, and so on. It often happens that the poets of the home are women, since it is woman's task to assure the happiness of the family group; her part, as in the time when the Roman *domina* sat in the atrium, is to be "lady of the house."

Today the house has lost its patriarchal splendor; for the majority of men it is only a place to live in, no longer freighted with the memory of dead generations, no longer encompassing the centuries to come. But still woman is all for giving her "interior" the meaning and value that the true house and home once had. In *Cannery Row* Steinbeck describes a vagrant woman who was determined to decorate with rugs and curtains the discarded engine boiler in which she lived with her husband; he objected in vain that the curtains were useless—"We got no windows." . . .

In domestic work, with or without the aid of servants, woman makes her home her own, finds social justification, and provides herself with an occupation, an activity, that deals usefully and satisfyingly with material objects—shining stoves, fresh, clean clothes, bright copper, polished furniture—but provides no escape from immanence and little affirmation of individuality. Such work has a negative basis: cleaning is getting rid of dirt, tidying up is eliminating disorder. And under impoverished conditions no satisfaction is possible; the hovel remains a hovel in spite of woman's sweat and tears: "nothing in the world can make it pretty." Legions of women have only this endless struggle without victory over the dirt. And for even the most privileged the victory is never final.

Few tasks are more like the torture of Sisyphus than housework, with its endless repetition: the clean becomes soiled, the soiled is made clean, over and over, day after day. The housewife wears herself out marking time: she makes nothing, simply perpetuates the present. She never senses conquest of a positive Good, but rather indefinite struggle against negative Evil. A young pupil writes in her essay: "I shall never have house-cleaning day"; she thinks of the future as constant progress toward some unknown summit; but one day, as her mother washes the dishes, it comes over her that both of them will be bound to such rites until death. Eating, sleeping, cleaning—the years no longer rise up toward heaven, they lie spread out ahead, gray and identical. The battle against dust and dirt is never won.

Washing, ironing, sweeping, ferreting out rolls of lint from under wardrobes—all this halting of decay is also the denial of life; for time simultaneously creates and destroys, and only its negative aspect concerns the housekeeper. Hers is the position of the Manichæist, regarded philosophically. The essence of Manichæism is not solely to recognize two principles, the one good, the other evil; it is also to hold that the good is attained through the abolition of evil and not by positive action. . . . [W]oman is not called upon to build a better world: her domain is fixed

and she has only to keep up the never ending struggle against the evil principles that creep into it; in her war against dust, stains, mud, and dirt she is fighting sin, wrestling with Satan.

But it is a sad fate to be required without respite to repel an enemy instead of working toward positive ends, and very often the housekeeper submits to it in a kind of madness that may verge on perversion, a kind of sadomasochism. The maniac housekeeper wages her furious war against dirt, blaming life itself for the rubbish all living growth entails. When any living being enters her house, her eye gleams with a wicked light: "Wipe your feet, don't tear the place apart, leave that alone!" She wishes those of her household would hardly breathe; everything means more thankless work for her. Severe, preoccupied, always on the watch, she loses *joie de vivre,* she becomes overprudent and avaricious. She shuts out the sunlight, for along with that come insects, germs, and dust, and besides, the sun ruins silk hangings and fades upholstery; she scatters naphthalene, which scents the air. She becomes bitter and disagreeable and hostile to all that lives: the end is sometimes murder. . . .

The preparation of food, getting meals, is work more positive in nature and often more agreeable than cleaning. First of all it means marketing, often the bright spot of the day. And gossip on doorsteps, while peeling vegetables, is a gay relief for solitude; to go for water is a great adventure for half-cloistered Mohammedan women; women in markets and stores talk about domestic affairs, with a common interest, feeling themselves members of a group that—for an instant—is opposed to the group of men as the essential to the inessential. Buying is a profound pleasure, a discovery, almost an invention. As Gide says in his *Journal,* the Mohammedans, not knowing gambling, have in its place the discovery of hidden treasure; that is the poetry and the adventure of mercantile civilizations. The housewife knows little of winning in games, but a solid cabbage, a ripe Camembert, are treasures that must be cleverly won from the unwilling store-keeper; the game is to get the best for the least money; economy means not so much helping the budget as winning the game. She is pleased with her passing triumph as she contemplates her well-filled larder.

Gas and electricity have killed the magic of fire, but in the country many women still know the joy of kindling live flames from inert wood. With her fire going, woman becomes a sorceress; by a simple movement, as in beating eggs, or through the magic of fire, she effects the transmutation of substances: matter becomes food. There is enchantment in these alchemies, there is poetry in making preserves; the housewife has caught duration in the snare of sugar, she has enclosed life in jars. Cooking is revelation and creation; and a woman can find special satisfaction in a successful cake or a flaky pastry, for not everyone can do it: one must have the gift.

Here again the little girl is naturally fond of imitating her elders, making mud pies and the like, and helping roll real dough in the kitchen. But as with other housework, repetition soon spoils these pleasures. The magic of the oven can hardly appeal to Mexican Indian women who spend half their lives preparing tortillas, identical from day to day, from century to century. And it is impossible to go on day after day making a treasure hunt of the marketing or ecstatically viewing one's highly polished faucets. The male and female writers who lyrically exalt such triumphs are persons who are seldom or never engaged in actual housework. It is tiresome, empty, monotonous, as a career. If, however, the individual who does such work is also a producer, a creative worker, it is as naturally integrated in life as are the organic functions; for this reason housework done by men seems much less dismal; it represents for them merely a negative and inconsequential moment from which they quickly escape. What makes the lot of the wife-servant ungrateful is the division of labor which dooms her completely to the general and the inessential. Dwelling-place and food are useful for life but

give it no significance: the immediate goals of the housekeeper are only means, not true ends. She endeavors, naturally, to give some individuality to her work and to make it seem essential. No one else, she thinks, could do her work as well; she has her rites, superstitions, and ways of doing things. But too often her "personal note" is but a vague and meaningless rearrangement of disorder.

Woman wastes a great deal of time and effort in such striving for originality and unique perfection; this gives her task its meticulous, disorganized, and endless character and makes it difficult to estimate the true load of domestic work. Recent studies show that for married women housework averages about thirty hours per week, or three fourths of a working week in employment. This is enormous if done in addition to a paid occupation, little if the woman has nothing else to do. The care of several children will naturally add a good deal to woman's work: a poor mother is often working all the time. Middle-class women who employ help, on the other hand, are almost idle; and they pay for their leisure with ennui. If they lack outside interests, they often multiply and complicate their domestic duties to excess, just to have something to do.

The worst of it all is that this labor does not even tend toward the creation of anything durable. Woman is tempted—and the more so the greater pains she takes—to regard her work as an end in itself. She sighs as she contemplates the perfect cake just out of the oven: "it's a shame to eat it!" It is really too bad to have husband and children tramping with their muddy feet all over her waxed hardwood floors! When things are used they are soiled or destroyed—we have seen how she is tempted to save them from being used; she keeps preserves until they get moldy; she locks up the parlor. But time passes inexorably; provisions attract rats; they become wormy; moths attack blankets and clothing. The world is not a dream carved in stone, it is made of dubious stuff subject to rot; edible material is as equivocal as Dali's fleshy watches: it seems inert, inorganic, but hidden larvæ may have changed it into a cadaver. The housewife who loses herself in things becomes dependent, like the things, upon the whole world: linen is scorched, the roast burns, chinaware gets broken; these are absolute disasters, for when things are destroyed, they are gone forever. Permanence and security cannot possibly be obtained through them. The pillage and bombs of war threaten one's wardrobes, one's house.

The products of domestic work, then, must necessarily be consumed; a continual renunciation is required of the woman whose operations are completed only in their destruction. For her to acquiesce without regret, these minor holocausts must at least be reflected in someone's joy or pleasure. But since the housekeeper's labor is expended to maintain the *status quo,* the husband, coming into the house, may notice disorder or negligence, but it seems to him that order and neatness come of their own accord. He has a more positive interest in a good meal. The cook's moment of triumph arrives when she puts a successful dish on the table: husband and children receive it with warm approval, not only in words, but by consuming it gleefully. The culinary alchemy then pursues its course, food becomes chyle and blood.

Thus, to maintain living bodies is of more concrete, vital interest than to keep a fine floor in proper condition; the cook's effort is evidently transcended toward the future. If, however, it is better to share in another's free transcendence than to lose oneself in things, it is not less dangerous. The validity of the cook's work is to be found only in the mouths of those around her table; she needs their approbation, demands that they appreciate her dishes and call for second helpings; she is upset if they are not hungry, to the point that one wonders whether the fried potatoes are for her husband or her husband for the fried potatoes. This ambiguity is evident in the general attitude of the housekeeping wife: she takes care of the house for her husband; but she also wants him to spend all he earns for furnishings and an electric refrigerator. She desires to make him happy; but she approves of his activities only in so far as they fall within the frame of happiness she has set up. . . .

Marriage incites man to a capricious imperialism: the temptation to dominate is the most truly universal, the most irresistible one there is; to surrender the child to its mother, the wife to her husband, is to promote tyranny in the world. Very often it is not enough for the husband to be approved of and admired, for him to be counselor and guide; he issues commands, he plays the lord and master. All the resentments accumulated during his childhood and his later life, those accumulated daily among other men whose existence means that he is browbeaten and injured— all this is purged from him at home as he lets loose his authority upon his wife. He enacts violence, power, unyielding resolution; he issues commands in tones of severity; he shouts and pounds the table: this farce is a daily reality for his wife. He is so firm in his rights that the slightest sign of independence on her part seems to him a rebellion; he would fain stop her breathing without his permission. . . .

To "catch" a husband is an art; to "hold" him is a job—and one in which great competence is called for. A wise sister said to a peevish young wife: "Be careful, making scenes with Marcel is going to cost you your *job.*" What is at stake is extremely serious: material and moral security, a home of one's own, the dignity of wifehood, a more or less satisfactory substitute for love and happiness. A wife soon learns that her erotic attractiveness is the weakest of her weapons; it disappears with familiarity; and, alas, there are other desirable women all about. . . .

A human relation has value only in so far as it is directly experienced; the relations of children to parents, for example, take on value only when they are consciously realized; it is not to be wondered at that conjugal relations tend to relapse from the condition of directly experienced emotion, and that the husband and wife lose their liberty of feeling in the process. This complex mixture of affection and resentment, hate, constraint, resignation, dullness, and hypocrisy called conjugal love is supposedly respected only by way of extenuation, whitewash. But the same is true of affection as of physical love: for it to be genuine, authentic, it must first of all be free.

Liberty, however, does not mean fickleness: a tender sentiment is an involvement of feeling which goes beyond the moment; but it is for the individual alone to determine whether his will in general and his behavior in detail are to be such as to maintain or, on the contrary, to break off the relation he has entered upon; sentiment is free when it depends upon no constraint from outside, when it is experienced in fearless sincerity. The constraint of "conjugal love" leads, on the other hand, to all kinds of repressions and lies. And first of all it prevents the couple from really knowing each other. Daily intimacy creates neither understanding nor sympathy. The husband respects his wife too much to take an interest in the phenomena of her psychic life: that would be to recognize in her a secret autonomy that could prove disturbing, dangerous; . . . On the other hand, the wife does not know her husband; she thinks she perceives his true aspect because she sees him in his daily round of inessential circumstances; but man is first of all what he *does* in the world among other men. . . . As a woman has said: "One marries a poet, and when one is his wife the first thing to be noticed is that he forgets to pull the chain in the toilet." . . .

. . . The couple should not be regarded as a unit, a closed cell; rather each individual should be integrated as such in society at large, where each (whether male or female) could flourish without aid; then attachments could be formed in pure generosity with another individual equally adapted to the group, attachments that would be founded upon the acknowledgment that both are free.

This balanced couple is not a utopian fancy: such couples do exist, sometimes even within the frame of marriage, most often outside it. Some mates are united by a strong sexual love that leaves them free in their friendships and in their work; others are held together by a friendship that does not preclude sexual liberty; more rare are those who are at once lovers and friends but do not seek in each other their sole reasons for living. Many nuances are possible in the relations between a man and a woman: in comradeship, pleasure, trust, fondness, cooperation, love, they can be for each other the most abundant source of joy, richness, and power available to human beings. Individuals are not to be blamed for the failure of marriage: it is—counter to the claims of such advocates as Comte and Tolstoy—the institution itself, perverted as it has been from the start. To hold and proclaim that a man and a woman, who may not even have chosen each other, *are in duty bound* to satisfy each other in every way throughout their lives is a monstrosity that necessarily gives rise to hypocrisy, lying, hostility, and unhappiness. . . .

Men are enchained by reason of their very sovereignty; it is because they alone earn money that their wives demand checks, it is because they alone engage in a business or profession that their wives require them to be successful, it is because they alone embody transcendence that their wives wish to rob them of it by taking charge of their projects and successes.

Inversely, the tyranny exercised by woman only goes to show her dependence: she knows that the success of the couple, its future, its happiness, its justification rest in the hands of the other; if she seeks desperately to bend him to her will, it is because she is alienated in him—that is, her interests as an individual lie in him. She makes a weapon of her weakness; but the fact remains that she is weak. Conjugal slavery is chiefly a matter of daily irritation for the husband; but it is something more deep-seated for the woman; a wife who keeps her husband at her side for hours because she is bored certainly bothers him and seems burdensome; but in the last analysis he can get along without her much more easily than she can without him; if he leaves her, she is the one whose life will be ruined. The great difference is that with woman dependency is interiorized: she *is* a slave even when she behaves with apparent freedom; while man is essentially independent and his bondage comes from without. If he seems to be the victim, it is because his burdens are most evident: woman is supported by him like a parasite; but a parasite is not a conquering master. The truth is that just as—biologically—males and females are never victims of one another but both victims of the species, so man and wife together undergo the oppression of an institution they did not create. If it is asserted that *men* oppress *women*, the husband is indignant; he feels that *he* is the one who is oppressed—and he is; but the fact is that it is the masculine code, it is the society developed by the males and in their interest, that has established woman's situation in a form that is at present a source of torment for both sexes.

It is for their common welfare that the situation must be altered by prohibiting marriage as a "career" for woman. Men who declare themselves antifeminists, on the ground that "women are already bad enough as it is," are not too logical; it is precisely because marriage makes women into "praying mantises," "leeches," "poisonous" creatures, and so on, that it is necessary to transform marriage and, in consequence, the condition of women in general. Woman leans heavily upon man because she is not allowed to rely on herself; he will free himself in freeing her—that is to say, in giving her something to *do* in the world.

Further Questions

1. If a wife had sufficient income of her own and a place in the world that did not depend upon her husband's position, would the problems de Beauvoir perceives in the traditional marriage be as likely to occur?

2. Can a woman make a weapon of her weakness? If so, how much is she to blame for doing so?

3. Is conjugal love difficult to maintain because spouses have constraints upon them to remain in the marriage?

The Case for Feminist Revolution   VI.9

SHULAMITH FIRESTONE

Shulamith Firestone is appalled by the amount of effort a woman expends to get herself a husband and enter the oppressive institution of marriage. She suggests three alternative ways of life which, if viable, would allow some flexibility in the choice of whether or not to marry.

Firestone's *The Dialectic of Sex* was one of the leading books in the feminist wave of the early 1970s, and she herself was active in many feminist protest demonstrations.

Reading Questions

    1. Suppose you had a profession you really liked. Would you be able to organize your life, as a single person, around its demands, activities, and benefits?

    2. For a couple, does living together have advantages that are precluded by a commitment like marriage?

    3. Would you feel comfortable living in a "household," a group of people living under one roof, with personal relations among them left up to individual choice?

UNDER INCREASING PRESSURE, with the pragmatic bases of the marriage institution blurred, sex roles relaxed to a degree that would have disgraced a Victorian. *He* had no crippling doubts about his role, nor about the function and value of marriage. To him it was simply an economic arrangement of some selfish benefit, one that would most easily satisfy his physical needs and reproduce his heirs. His wife, too, was clear about her duties and rewards: ownership of herself and of her full sexual, psychological, and housekeeping services for a lifetime, in return for long-term patronage and protection by a member of the ruling class, and—in her turn—limited control over a household and over her children until they reached a certain age. Today this contract based on divided roles has been so disguised by sentiment that it goes completely unrecognized by millions of newlyweds, and even most older married couples.

    But this blurring of the economic contract, and the resulting confusion of sex roles, has not significantly eased woman's oppression. In many cases it has put her in only a more vulnerable position. With the clear-cut arrangement of matches by parents all but abolished, a woman, still part of an underclass, must now, in order to gain the indispensable male patronage and protection, play a desperate game, hunting down bored males while yet appearing cool. And even once she is married, any overlap of roles generally takes place on the wife's side, not on the husband's: the "cherish and protect" clause is the first thing forgotten—while the wife has gained the privilege of going to work to "help out," even of putting her husband through school. More than ever she shoulders the brunt of the marriage, not only emotionally, but now also in its more practical aspects. She has simply added his job to hers.

    A second cultural prop to the outmoded institution is the privatization of the marriage experience: each partner enters marriage convinced that what happened to his parents, what happened to his friends can never happen to him. Though Wrecked Marriage has become a national hobby, a universal obsession—as witnessed by the booming business of guidebooks to marriage and divorce, the women's magazine industry, an affluent class of marriage counselors and shrinks, whole repertoires of Ball-and-Chain jokes and gimmicks, and cultural products such as soap opera, the marriage-and-family genre on TV, e.g., *I Love Lucy* or *Father Knows Best,* films and plays like Cassavetes' *Faces* and Albee's *Who's Afraid of Virginia Woolf?*—still one encounters everywhere a defiant "We're different" brand of optimism in which the one good (outwardly exemplary, anyway) marriage in the community is habitually cited to prove that *it* is possible.

    The privatization process is typified by comments like, "Well, I know I'd make a great mother." It is useless to point out that *everyone* says that, that the very parents or friends now dismissed as "bad" parents and "poor" marital partners all began marriage and parenthood in exactly the same spirit. After all, does anyone *choose* to have a "bad" marriage? Does anyone *choose* to be a "bad" mother? And even if it were a question of "good" vs. "bad" marital partners or parents, there will always be as many of the latter as the former; under the present system of universal marriage and parenthood just as many spouses and children must pull a bad lot as a good one; in fact any classes of "good" and "bad" are bound to recreate themselves in identical proportion.* Thus the privatization process functions to keep people blaming themselves, rather than the institution, for its failure: Though the institution consistently proves itself unsatisfactory, even rotten, it encourages them to believe that somehow their own case will be different.

Warnings can have no effect, because logic has nothing to do with why people get married. Everyone has eyes of his own, parents of his own. If he chooses to block all evidence, it is because he must. In a world out of control, the only institutions that grant him an *illusion* of control, that seem to offer any safety, shelter or warmth, are the "private" institutions: religion, marriage/family, and, most recently, psychoanalytic therapy. . . .

And yet marriage in its very definition will never be able to fulfill the needs of its participants. . . . We need to start talking about new alternatives that will satisfy the emotional and psychological needs that marriage, archaic as it is, still satisfies, but that will satisfy them better. But in any proposal we shall have to do at least one better than marriage on our feminist scale, or despite all warnings people will stay hooked—in the hope that just this once, just for them, marriage will come across.

---

* But what does this dichotomy of good/bad really mean? Perhaps after all, it is only a euphemistic *class* distinction: sensitive and educated, as opposed to uneducated, underprivileged, harassed, and therefore indifferent. But even though a child born to educated or upper-class parents is luckier in every respect, and is apt to receive a fair number of privileges by virtue of his class, name, and the property he is due to inherit, the distribution of children is equal among all classes—if indeed children born to the unfortunate do not outnumber the others—in this way reproducing in identical proportion the original inequality.

IV: Alternatives

The classic trap for any revolutionary is always, "What's your alternative?" But even if you *could* provide the interrogator with a blueprint, this does not mean he would use it: in most cases he is not sincere in wanting to know. In fact this is a common offensive, a technique to deflect revolutionary anger and turn it against itself. Moreover, the oppressed have no job to convince all people. All *they* need know is that the present system is destroying them.

But though any specific direction must arise organically out of the revolutionary action itself, still I feel tempted here to make some "dangerously utopian" concrete proposals—both in sympathy for my own pre-radical days when the Not-Responsible-For-Blueprint Line perplexed me, and also because I am aware of the political dangers in the peculiar failure of imagination concerning alternatives to the family. There are, as we have seen, several good reasons for this failure. First, there are no precedents in history for feminist revolution—there have been women revolutionaries, certainly, but they have been used by male revolutionaries, who seldom gave even lip service to equality for women, let alone to a radical feminist restructuring of society. Moreover, we haven't even a literary image of this future society; there is not even a *utopian* feminist literature in existence. Thirdly, the nature of the family unit is such that it penetrates the individual more deeply than any other social organization we have: it literally gets him "where he lives." I have shown how the family shapes his psyche to its structure—until ultimately, he imagines it absolute, talk of anything else striking him as perverted. Finally, most alternatives suggest a loss of even the little emotional warmth provided by the family, throwing him into a panic. The model that I shall now draw up is subject to the limitations of any plan laid out on paper by a solitary individual. Keep in mind that these are not meant as final answers, that in fact the reader could probably draw up another plan that would satisfy as well or better the four structural imperatives laid out above. The following proposals, then, will be sketchy, meant to stimulate thinking in fresh areas rather than to dictate the action.

* * *

The most important characteristic to be maintained in any revolution is *flexibility*. I will propose, then, a program of multiple options to exist simultaneously, interweaving with each other, some transitional, others far in the future. An individual may choose one "life style" for one decade, and prefer another at another period.

1) *Single Professions*. A single life organized around the demands of a chosen profession, satisfying the individual's social and emotional needs through its own particular occupational structure, might be an appealing solution for many individuals, especially in the transitional period.

Single professions have practically vanished, despite the fact that the encouragement of reproduction is no longer a valid social concern. The old single roles, such as the celibate religious life, court roles—jester, musician, page, knight, and loyal squire—cowboys, sailors, firemen, cross-country truck drivers, detectives, pilots had a prestige all their own: there was no stigma attached to being professionally single. Unfortunately, these roles seldom were open to women. Most single female roles (such as spinster aunt, nun, or courtesan) were still defined by their sexual nature.

Many social scientists are now proposing as a solution to the population problem the encouragement of "deviant life styles" that by definition imply nonfertility. Richard Meier suggests that glamorous single professions previously assigned only to men should now be opened to women as well, for example, "astronaut." He notes that where these occupations exist for women, e.g., stewardess, they are based on the sex appeal of a young woman, and thus can be only limited way stations on the way to a better job or marriage.

And, he adds, "so many limitations are imposed [on women's work outside the home] . . . that one suspects the existence of a culture-wide conspiracy which makes the occupational role sufficiently unpleasant that 90 percent or more would choose homemaking as a superior alternative." With the extension of whatever single roles still exist in our culture to include woman, the creation of more such roles, and a program of incentives to make these professions rewarding, we could, painlessly, reduce the number of people interested in parenthood at all.

2) *"Living Together."* Practiced at first only in Bohemian or intellectual circles and now increasingly in the population at large—especially by metropolitan youth—"living together" is becoming a common social practice. "Living together" is the loose social form in which two or more partners, of whatever sex, enter a nonlegal sex/companionate arrangement the duration of which varies with the internal dynamics of the relationship. Their contract is only with each other; society has no interest, since neither reproduction nor production—dependencies of one party on the other—is involved. This flexible non-form could be expanded to become the standard unit in which most people would live for most of their lives.

At first, in the transitional period, sexual relationships would probably be monogamous (single standard, female-style, this time around), even if the couple chose to live with others. We might even see the continuation of strictly nonsexual group living arrangements ("roommates"). However, after several generations of nonfamily living, our psychosexual structures may become altered so radically that the monogamous couple, or the "aim-inhibited" relationship, would become obsolescent. We can only guess what might replace it—perhaps true "group marriages," transexual group marriages which also involved older children? We don't know.

The two options we have suggested so far—single professions and "living together"—already exist, but only outside the mainstream of our society, or for brief periods in the life of the normal individual. We want to *broaden* these options to include many more people for longer periods of their lives, to transfer here instead all the cultural incentives now supporting marriage—making these alternatives, finally, as common and acceptable as marriage is today.

But what about children? Doesn't everyone want children sometime in their lives? There is no denying that people now feel a genuine desire to have children. But we don't know how much of this is the product of an authentic liking for children, and how much is a displacement of other needs. We have seen that parental satisfaction is obtainable only through crippling the child: The attempted extension of ego through one's children—in the case of the man, the "immortalizing" of name, property, class, and ethnic identification, and in the case of the woman, motherhood as the justification of her existence, the resulting attempt to live through the child, child-as-project—in the end damages or destroys either the child or the parent, or both when neither wins, as the case may be. Perhaps when we strip parenthood of these other functions, we will find a real instinct for parenthood even on the part of men, a simple physical desire to associate with the young. But then we have lost nothing, for a basic demand of our alternative system is some form of intimate interaction with children. If a parenthood instinct does in fact exist, it will be allowed to operate even more freely, having shed the practical burdens of parenthood that now make it such an anguished hell.

But what, on the other hand, if we find that there is no parenthood instinct after all? Perhaps all this time society has persuaded the individual to have children only by imposing on parenthood ego concerns that had no proper outlet. This may have been unavoidable in the past—but perhaps it's now time to start more directly satisfying those ego needs. As long as natural reproduction is still necessary, we can devise less destructive cultural inducements. But it is likely that, once the ego investments in parenthood are removed, artificial reproduction will be developed and widely accepted.

3) *Households*. I shall now outline a system that I believe will satisfy any remaining needs for children after ego concerns are no longer part of our motivations. Suppose a person or a couple at some point in their lives desire to live around children in a family-size unit. While we will no longer have reproduction as the life goal of the normal individual—we have seen how single and group nonreproductive life styles could be enlarged to become satisfactory for many people for their whole lifetimes and for others, for good portions of their lifetime—certain people may still prefer community-style group living permanently, and other people may want to experience it at some time in their lives, especially during early childhood.

Thus at any given time a proportion of the population will want to live in reproductive social structures. Correspondingly, the society in general will still need reproduction, though reduced, if only to create a new generation.

The proportion of the population will be automatically a select group with a predictably higher rate of stability, because they will have had a freedom of choice now generally unavailable. Today those who do not marry and have children by a certain age are penalized: they find themselves alone, excluded, and miserable, on the margins of a society in which everyone else is compartmentalized into lifetime generational families, chauvinism and exclusiveness their chief characteristic. (Only in Manhattan is single living even tolerable, and that can be debated.) Most people are still forced into marriage by family pressure, the "shotgun," economic considerations, and other reasons that have nothing to do with choice of life style. In our new reproductive unit, however, with the limited contract (see below), childrearing so diffused as to be practically eliminated, economic considerations nonexistent, and all participating members having entered only on the basis of personal preference, "unstable" reproductive social structures will have disappeared.

This unit I shall call a *household* rather than an extended family. The distinction is important: The word *family* implies biological reproduction and some degree of division of labor by sex, and thus the traditional dependencies and resulting power relations, extended over generations; though the size of the family—in this case, the larger numbers of the "extended" family—may affect the strength of this hierarchy, it does not change in structural definition. "Household," however, connotes only a large grouping of people living together for an unspecified time, and with no specified set of interpersonal relations. How would a "household" operate?

Limited Contract. If the household replaced marriage perhaps we would at first legalize it in the same way—if this is necessary at all. A group of ten or so consenting adults of varying ages*

---

* An added advantage of the household is that it allows older people past their fertile years to share fully in parenthood when they so desire.

could apply for a license as a group in much the same way as a young couple today applies for a marriage license, perhaps even undergoing some form of ritual ceremony, and then might proceed in the same way to set up house. The household license would, however, apply only for a given period, perhaps seven to ten years, or whatever was decided on as the minimal time in which children needed a stable structure in which to grow up—but probably a much shorter period than we now imagine. If at the end of this period the group decided to stay together, it could always get a renewal. However, no single individual would be contracted to stay after this period, and perhaps some members of the unit might transfer out, or new members come in. Or, the unit could disband altogether.

There are many advantages to short-term households, stable compositional units lasting for only about a decade: the end of family chauvinism, built up over generations, of prejudices passed down from one generation to the next, the inclusion of people of all ages in the childrearing process, the integration of many age groups into one social unit, the breadth of personality that comes from exposure to many rather than to (the idiosyncrasies of) a few, and so on. . . .

Further Questions

1. Is privatization of marriage and parenthood (disbelief that what generally happens will happen in a particular case) a real hazard? Should people who are contemplating marriage and parenthood think about the hazards?

2. Before making a marital commitment, which is intended to be permanent, would it be a good idea for a person to try some of Firestone's alternatives to marriage?

3. Are there advantages, disadvantages, or both to living in a multigenerational unit with, for example, other people's biological children as part of the unit?

Marriage as a Bad Business Deal   VI.10

MICHAEL D. BAYLES

In this selection Michael Bayles argues that many marriages, second and late ones in particular, can be unwise and unfair from a financial point of view. Like "Niccola Machiavelli," Bayles accepts the view that each partner's share of the assets in marriage is what they could expect to receive in the event of a divorce; too often, this share is not in proportion to what the person has contributed to the marriage.

Bayles wrote widely in the areas of ethics and applied ethics.

Reading Questions

1. Should persons with property or high incomes be wary of a marriage lacking safeguards to protect their assets?
2. Does a homemaking spouse make a substantial contribution toward enabling the bread-winning spouse to produce income?
3. Should the division of assets in a divorce enable each ex-spouse to have the same standard of living?

> While reasonableness is rarely the main ingredient in the decision to marry, the law should not make the choice to marry unreasonable *per se.*[1]

ALTHOUGH MANY FACTORS can be involved in the reasonableness of marriage, this paper focuses on only one—the financial settlement in the event of divorce. Recent changes in divorce law and demographic patterns of marriage and divorce are making marriage an unreasonable decision for an increasingly large segment of the population. It is exceedingly difficult to alter demographic patterns intentionally. If marriage is to be an economically reasonable decision for many persons, divorce laws pertaining to financial settlements need to be revised. Ironically, recent changes in divorce law were intended to correct inequities in the past law. While the changes produce more equity in divorces conforming to past patterns of marriage and divorce, they unfortunately tend to produce inequity in significant and growing patterns of marriage and divorce.

The major recent changes in laws about financial settlements on divorce concern what property is to be divided, how that property is divided, and the award of alimony or maintenance. A pervasive trend has been to increase the property to be divided. One aspect of this trend is to classify more property as marital or community and, therefore, less as nonmarital or separate. Another aspect is to expand the category of property, for example, by including unvested pensions and professional licenses. With the demise of fault-based divorce, marital fault has become a less important basis for division of property, although many states still permit it to be considered.[2] While a significant minority of states divide marital property equally, the dominant trend has been toward so-called equitable distribution. Finally, alimony as a lifelong award to a dependent spouse has generally been replaced with short-term "rehabilitative" alimony to enable a dependent spouse to acquire job training and become economically independent.

During the 1970s, partly in response to the drive for equality of the sexes, equal division of property and diminution of alimony were emphasized. An equal division of property supposedly reflects the equality of the sexes. Alimony is often considered demeaning and in practice is usually not fully collected. Recently, however, equal division of property has been viewed less favorably. To provide an equal division of property, the family home must often be sold, sometimes leaving a spouse having custody of the children with inadequate housing. Moreover, one spouse, usually the husband, might have a higher earning capacity. Consequently, post-divorce economic equality and thus sexual equality do not necessarily result.[3]

Recent divorce law changes and even some suggestions for further change are based on the most prevalent past pattern of marriage and divorce. This traditional pattern was of couples marrying at a young age, the wife staying home to raise a family, and divorce after a substantial number of years. The changes and suggestions also fit marriage at a young age with divorce after a few years involving little property and no children. However, two other patterns of marriage and divorce are becoming increasingly significant. One prominent pattern involves second and subsequent marriages.[4] These marriages naturally occur at a later age than first marriages.[5] The financial consequences of divorce are more important for the reasonableness of such marriages than others, because while about half of all marriages end in divorce, the rate is even higher for second and third marriages. Moreover, because one or both parties might have been through a perhaps financially difficult divorce, these people are more apt to consider financial aspects than

people in first marriages. The other growing pattern is simply marriage at an older age than before.[6] As marriages in both these patterns involve older people, often both partners have established jobs or careers in which they expect to continue. In both of these newer patterns, spouses are more likely to bring significant property to the marriage than in the traditional pattern.

This paper focuses on the law governing division of financial assets and contends that the new laws can make marriage unwise and unfair in the newer patterns. The decrease in alimony awards is less significant in these newer patterns, because both partners are likely to have established employment or careers. The classification of property as marital and nonmarital together with the current method of distribution is unreasonable and unfair when applied to these new patterns of marriage and divorce. A significant minority of states classify all property as marital. Even in the majority of states which distinguish between marital and nonmarital property, the classification is likely to be unfair in the newer patterns of marriage. New ways of treating pensions on divorce also contribute to making such marriages financially unwise. The principles of distribution do not correct and may exacerbate the problems resulting from the classification of property.

Marriage as an Economic Partnership

Divorce law's purposes and underlying concept of marriage can significantly affect its contours. Four purposes of divorce law, especially as concerns property distribution, are assumed.[7] (1) The law should provide a sharp and clean break so that the ex-spouses can get on with their lives with minimal personal and financial contact. Of course, where there are children, continued contact should occur as regards them. (2) The law should have predictable results to minimize disputes and to enable spouses to plan for the consequences of divorce. (3) The law should be fair. If it is, it diminishes reasonable disputes, but the public interest in fairness transcends dispute minimization. (4) The law should not discourage marriage.

The traditional concept of marriage underlying the law has both moral and economic aspects. Today, it is best to distinguish moral and economic concepts of marriage. The moral concept involves public recognition and protection of an intimate sharing and loving relationship providing a setting deemed desirable for child rearing. Historically, the law reflected this moral concept in the prohibition of adultery, fault-based divorce, and the distinction between legitimate and illegitimate children. With the trend against legal enforcement of morality itself and the demise of fault-based divorce, the moral concept has become less significant, especially for divorce.

The historical economic concept of marriage was an identity in the husband. That concept has been replaced by one of an (equal?) economic partnership. Three principles underlie the economic partnership concept.[8] First, the principle of all efforts is that each spouse will contribute all time and effort to the marital unit. Second, the enablement principle is that homemaking enables the income producer's activities. Third, the sharing principle is that spouses expect to share in the financial fortunes of the marital unit. The reasonableness and fairness of current laws for second[9] and late marriages that end in divorce depend largely on the appropriateness of these principles.

As the partnership concept is only for the economic relations of a marriage, it omits some considerations relevant to the total well-being of the marital unit and its partners, for example, psychological well-being and expression of love and commitment. Although the principles of all efforts and enablement are meant to include intangible as well as tangible aspects, the concept is of a semi-arm's length relationship and does not represent a full conception of marriage, especially as participants view it. Nonetheless, the law probably cannot adequately handle a full concept of marriage. The following criticisms reveal that the partnership concept is inadequate even for the economic aspects of marriage.

The all efforts principle is both psychologically and economically inappropriate. The once popular notion that couples should share everything has been discredited. To maintain their separate identities and independence, people now expect to have some separate and individual activities. This is especially true of persons marrying for a second time or at a late age. They have significant past lives as separate individuals. Psychological identity and independence often depend on financial independence. Financial independence can rest on individual income or separate property brought to the marriage that one expects to manage and retain. If both spouses are working, they often think of some of their income as separate; not all efforts are devoted to the marital unit.[10]

The enablement principle seems more plausible. Surely homemaking enables the other person to devote more time to producing income.[11] However, this principle assumes that the income producing spouse can devote more time to producing income and that time spent in homemaking would come from time spent producing income. Neither of these assumptions is necessarily true. People in hourly paid jobs cannot unilaterally increase their hours of work, and salaried workers are not directly paid for overtime. Moreover, homemaking activities usually decrease recreational time rather than work time. The enablement principle becomes even less plausible if it is interpreted to mean that the enablement function's value increases in proportion to the income produced.[12] If one simply values homemaking time as the cost of hiring someone to do the work, then of course it does not increase proportional to the income produced. If one thinks of it as saving the income producer time, then it would be proportional. However, this still mistakenly assumes that homemaking time is taken from employment rather than recreation.

The proportionality interpretation is better founded on the sharing principle. Partners do expect to share the financial benefits of a marriage.

A general formula for a share is $S = S_f \times T$, where T is the total of marital assets and S_f is one spouse's fractional share. Thus, if a spouse's activity is homemaking, assuming S_f remains constant, the value of that spouse's share increases in proportion to the total. However, the general formula does not indicate what fraction of the total marital assets belongs to a spouse. That is, the division need not be in proportion to the amount each contributed or produced. People probably have different conceptions about appropriate shares, and the expectations of a particular couple might change over time. These expectations cannot be the sole basis for determining what the law should be, for they are probably partly shaped by the law. Consequently, while a minority of states divide marital property equally, a large majority distribute it equitably, which allows for unequal shares.[13]

Marital and Nonmarital Property

Partners' expectations of the share of assets they will receive on divorce probably depend in part on the amount of property they bring to the marriage. In first marriages at a young age, usually neither partner has many assets. However, that is often not the case in second and late marriages. For such people, marriage can be economically unreasonable. Consider an example of each of these types. Person A, who is considering a second marriage, owns a car, furniture, and a house valued at $85,000 with a remaining mortgage of $50,000. Person B, who is contemplating a first marriage, is thirty years old, has a full-time job at $28,000 a year, owns a car and 135 shares in the employer's company bought under an employees' stock purchase program, and has $5600 in a mutual fund. Suppose that each is contemplating marriage to a person who, though employed, has an income some $5,000 to $10,000 less per year and no significant property other than an automobile.

A and B can both lose a significant amount of their property should the marriage end in divorce in, say, five years. Crucial to this potential loss is the classification of property as marital or nonmarital. In a significant minority of states, no distinction is made between marital and nonmarital property.[14] In these "hotchpot" states, in dividing the assets the judge will presumably consider how much property each person brought to the marriage.[15] However, that is only a presumption, and the judge need not do so. Consequently, both A and B risk losing a portion of the property they bring to marriage should the marriages end in divorce. In this respect, marriage is economically unreasonable and unfair for A and B.[16] . . .

Replies to Objections

The argument thus far has been that persons entering a second or late marriage with significantly more property than their intended spouses are making a bad business deal. All their property on marriage might be considered in the distribution of assets on divorce. Even if it is not, much of it might be transmuted into marital or community property for division. The income from separate property is often marital property, and the appreciation in value of separate property might be considered marital property. Moreover, they lose independent control over their pensions and might well lose part of their value.

At this point, a critic is likely to object that mere classification of property as marital does not imply that one will lose it. In equal division states, one might, but even in them judges often consider the source of funds. In the majority of states property is divided equitably. So, if one has an equitable claim to a larger share of marital assets, that should be recognized. The classification of property is not dispositive. In short, there are two considerations—what property is to be distributed and how it is to be distributed. No matter what property is considered available for distribution, whether marriage is economically unwise depends crucially on how it is divided.

The problem with the critic's point and current laws is the uncertainty of what will be considered an equitable distribution. In effect, equitable distribution is discretionary distribution.[17] In some states, statutes provide courts only general guidance. In other states, statutes require that certain factors be considered. Among the factors that may be specified are the length of the marriage; the age and health of the parties; their occupations; the amount and sources of their income; their vocational skills and employability; and each's contribution to, or dissipation of, the marital assets.[18] No reasonably precise formula exists to determine what distribution will result from the application of these factors. Some of them pull in opposite directions. For example, contribution supports a larger share for a person who brought greater assets to a marriage or has a higher income. But occupation, amount and sources of income, and vocational skills support a greater share for the spouse who probably contributed less to a marriage than the other spouse. In the final analysis, one must marshal a large amount of data to support one's claim and then trust in judicial discretion.

At this point, a critic might have another objection. If preservation of separate property on divorce is uncertain, then one can make an antenuptial agreement to provide for it.[19] However, the validity of a premarital agreement, especially one looking to divorce, is itself uncertain.[20] Indeed, the Uniform Marriage and Divorce Act merely cites an antenuptial agreement as another factor for a judge to consider in the division of property.[21] Thus, the remedy for uncertainty is itself uncertain. Moreover, antenuptial agreements as well as the earlier suggestion of incorporation can involve significant legal expense making it a bad deal. Nonetheless, nothing in life is certain. Perhaps the combination of a premarital agreement, statutory guidelines (where they

exist), and precedent will suffice for many persons. One can marry for love, not money, but in doing so, it is easier to forgo a possible gain than to risk a loss.

Another objection is that even if the marriages are bad business deals for one partner, they are thus beneficial for the other one. As women have historically lost much in marriage, they need a financial incentive to marry. However, it takes two to marry, and if marriage is a bad business deal for one, that person simply might not marry. As Justice Lee remarked in upholding antenuptial agreements, "Undeniably, some marriages would not come about if antenuptial agreements were not available. This may be increasingly true due to the frequency of marriage dissolutions in our society, and the fact that many people marry more than once."[22] . . .

A critic might also object that after divorce the standard of living of most women, especially those with children, declines, while that of most males increases. The changes and suggestions for further reform are to rectify this injustice. A reply to this objection is somewhat complex as the objection rests on a contestable principle of justice, doubtful factual assumptions, and perhaps a misunderstanding of the argument.

Three competing principles are involved in the distribution of property on divorce. One is equality, perhaps as an equal standard of living after divorce.[23] Another is need; an ex-spouse who is ill or has custody of children has greater need. A third is return for contribution.

The objection rests on a principle of equality as an equal standard of living after divorce. The usual argument for equality is that a spouse has become accustomed to and thus to expect the standard of living enjoyed while married. However, that argument will not do. Whether it is legitimate to expect the standard of living to continue after divorce depends, at least in part, on the law. No such principle of equal standard of living applies to children becoming emancipated and leaving home. Moreover, when one considers second and late marriages, people lived at a lower standard of living prior to marriage, so they have benefited during the period of marriage from a higher standard. The principle of an equal standard of living after divorce is simply not compelling for these marriages. It does make more sense for traditional marriages at a young age with no separate property, but it is impossible to achieve. Even an equal division of assets and income will result in each party having a lower standard of living.

Conclusion

Second and late marriages are two growing patterns of marriage and divorce. Persons entering such marriages are more likely to have substantial financial assets than those first marrying earlier in life. Except for child custody, divorce law primarily regards marriage as an economic partnership. The underlying principles of all efforts, enablement, and sharing are especially questionable for second and late marriages.

A party entering marriage with substantially more assets than the other party faces significant risks of not being able to retain those assets should divorce eventuate. In some states, no distinction is made between marital and nonmarital property for purposes of distribution on divorce. Even if a distinction is drawn, separate property can be transmuted into marital by joint title, use by the marital unit, and perhaps mere commingling with marital property. Income from separate property is often marital, and the property's appreciation in value can become mostly marital. In addition, one might lose some of the value of a pension accrued during marriage, and one loses independent control over how one is to receive it and its distribution on death. Consequently, marriage can be an economically unreasonable decision for people with significant property.

In the majority of states, equitable distribution on divorce can provide such a person a greater share of the assets. However, various principles compete, and several support giving a larger share to the person who probably contributed less. The results depend on judicial discretion and are uncertain. Antenuptial agreements might provide protection for assets brought to a marriage, but their validity is sometimes risky and even if valid they are not always decisive.

Consequently, many second and late marriages are bad business deals. Considerable uncertainty exists about how marital property will be distributed should divorce occur. The purposes of marriage law are undermined. The economic reasonableness of marrying decreases and marriage is thus discouraged. The uncertainty undermines predictability of results, thus fostering disputes. The law's fairness is also doubtful, at best depending on the discretion of judges. As one scholar put it, "What person will enter a business or professional partnership or joint venture if the only liquidation rule is that a court will have discretion to make any order it thinks fit in regard to all the money and property?"[24] Moreover, the intertwining of equity in a house, pension, and business often requires payment over time, thus defeating the purpose of a sharp, clean break. Finally, the economic partnership concept is also shown to be misleading.

Financial assets possessed prior to marriage should not so readily be considered a contribution to the marriage. Those assets, and their income and increase in value, should normally remain nonmarital property. They should become marital only if the owner makes an affirmative act to contribute them to the marriage. Mere use of tangible assets such as a house or automobile should not count as such an act. Use of income to purchase assets for joint use would be such a contribution. If such assets are the primary source of income, such as a business, then at least all income should be deemed marital. Unless stronger protection is given to assets brought to a marriage as separate property, many potential second and late marriages will be economically unwise and could be discouraged.[25] The laws governing the division of property on divorce must be revised if the law is to encourage, or at least not discourage, marriage.

NOTES

1. Harry D. Krause, *Family Law in a Nutshell,* 2d ed. (St. Paul, Minn.: West Publishing Co., 1986), p. 365.

2. Doris Jonas Freed and Timothy B. Walker, "Family Law in the Fifty States: An Overview," *Family Law Quarterly* 21 (1988): 467, and 462–463, Table V.

3. "For without equality in economic resources, all other 'equality' is illusory"; Lenore J. Weitzman, *The Divorce Revolution: Unexpected Social and Economic Consequences for Women and Children in America* (New York: The Free Press, 1985), p. 378.

4. In 1970, 31.4% of marriages taking place in the United States involved at least one previously married partner. By 1985, this number had risen to 45.7%. Bureau of Statistics, U.S. Department of Commerce, *Statistical Abstract of the United States,* 109th ed. (Washington, D.C.: Department of Commerce, Bureau of Statistics, 1989), p. 85, Table 129.

5. In 1985, the median age at first marriage was 23.0 years for women and 24.8 years for men. The median age for divorced people remarrying was 32.7 years for women and 36.0 years for men. *Statistical Abstract,* p. 86, Table 130.

6. In 1975, 65.3% of people who got married in the United States were 24 years old or younger. By 1985, people 24 or younger accounted for only 48.3% of people married in the United States. While these numbers were dropping, the percentage of people who got married between the ages of 25 and 34 rose from 21.1% in 1975, to 34.1% in 1985. Likewise, the percentage of people who got married between the ages of 35 and 44 rose from 6.7% in 1975 to 11.1% in 1985. *Statistical Abstract,* p. 85, Table 128.

If, as argued, the divorce law discourages marriage, one might wonder why marriage rates continue to be so high. Four possibilities suggest themselves. First, the rates would be even higher were it not for the divorce laws. Second, the effect is not so much as to discourage marriage but marriage outside one's economic class. Thus, it affects who people marry but not their marrying. Third, economic considerations are not the only factor involved in determining the overall reasonableness of marriage, so when other factors are considered, marriage might still be reasonable everything considered. Fourth, perhaps some decisions to marry are simply not rational or reasonable; whom one loves does not seem to be rationally based. Whatever the case may be, the law need not and should not contribute to marriage being economically unreasonable.

7. Cf. Caleb Foote, Robert J. Levy, and Frank E. A. Sander, *Cases and Materials on Family Law,* 3rd ed. (Boston: Little, Brown and Co., 1985), p. 660.

8. Joan M. Krauskopf, "Classifying Marital and Separate Property—Combinations and Increase in Value of Separate Property," *West Virginia Law Review* 89 (1987): 997–998, 1019.

9. The expression 'second marriage' is used throughout to include any marriage after the first.

10. In roughly one-third of marriages where both spouses work, they view their earnings as individual, not family, income; Mary Ann Glendon, *The New Family and the New Property* (Toronto: Butterworths, 1981), p. 65, n. 55.

11. I have found that I have more time for professional activities when single, even performing household chores myself, than when married. The loss of time when married stems from activities that might be considered their own reward—for both partners. These self-rewarding activities are not considered in the partnership concept, but as each partner benefits, perhaps equally, they do not affect the economic aspects.

12. Krauskopf takes this interpretation and cites other sources, "Marital and Separate Property," p. 998.

13. See Freed and Walker, "Family Law," pp. 453–54, Table IV. See also Unif. Marriage and Divorce Act (UMDA) § 3.07A, 9A U.L.A. 238 (1973); Foote et al., *Family Law,* p. 664 (citing a source claiming at least 12 states use equal division).

14. See the somewhat different lists in Freed and Walker, "Family Law," pp. 453–454, Table IV; and Lawrence J. Golden, *Equitable Distribution of Property* (Colorado Springs, Colo.: Shepard's/McGraw-Hill, 1983), § 2.02.

15. Golden, *Equitable Distribution,* § 2.02; Foote et al., *Family Law,* p. 658.

16. See Glendon, *The New Family,* p. 63.

17. Glendon, *The New Family,* pp. 63–64.

18. See Freed and Walker, "Family Law," pp. 465–466, for a more complete list.

19. Krauskopf, "Marital and Separate Property," p. 1034.

20. Kraus, *Family Law,* pp. 79–81; Foote et al., *Family Law,* p. 713.

21. § 307(A), 9A U.L.A. 238 (1973).

22. Newman v. Newman, 653 P.2d 728 (Colo. 1982).

23. Weitzman, *The Divorce Revolution,* p. 105.

24. Ian Baxter, "Family Law Reform in Ontario," *University of Toronto Law Journal* 25 (1975): 261.

25. One can speculate on why the law has developed against separate property. Three suggestions are as follows: (1) Divorce reformers fail adequately to assess the present and future patterns of marriage and divorce. Thus, feminists pushed for abolition of alimony and equal division of assets, which did substantial injury to the many women of long traditional marriages. Reformers have now recognized the problems such women face under the new laws and want to make changes to protect them, e.g., Weitzman, *The Divorce Revolution.* But this looks to the past. Now most women work, even over half of those with young children, so the long-married housewife is of declining importance. (2) As equitable distribution increases uncertainty and disputes, it is good for lawyers (see also Glendon, *The New Family,* pp. 66–67). Lawyers also benefit by having more assets in the pot for distribution. (3) Impoverished divorced persons can increase a state's welfare costs, so legislators prefer to place the burden on their former spouses (see also Glendon, *The New Family,* p. 64).

Further Questions

1. If a person with children marries, ought she or he be concerned about their material welfare if her or his assets are not secured against the spouse?

2. If a contemplated marriage does not make good financial sense for a person, is this a valid disincentive for him or her not to go through with that particular marriage?

3. Can it be reasonable for spouses to keep some of their assets as separate rather than marital property? If so, does this undermine the idea of marriage as a union?

Suggested Moral of Part VI

Creating permanent bonds of commitment is important to many couples. Structures for doing so should not be limited to the traditional heterosexual marriage, with its specific gender roles. Many couples would benefit, personally and legally, from having options available that do not require specific gender roles and are not limited to heterosexual couples. A couple should think carefully about whether they want the traditional gender role structure, which can be oppressive to women. We should also develop alternate, socially legitimate lifestyles for persons who do not wish to marry.

Further Readings for Part VI: Bonds

Most libraries stock a large collection of books on marriage and the family because these institutions have been the subject of much study. The following is a small selection from the group, which the reader might find of special interest.

Ifi Amadiume. *Male Daughters, Female Husbands: Gender and Sex in an African Society* (Atlantic Highlands, NJ: Zed Books, 1987). Argument that family gender roles are flexible because they are reversed in a particular African society.

Gloria Bird and Michael J. Sporakowski, eds. *Taking Sides: Clashing Views on Controversial Issues in Family and Personal Relationships* (Guilford, CT: The Dushkin Publishing Group, 1992). Short, lively pieces on issues in marriage and parenthood.

Becky Butler. *Ceremonies of the Heart: Celebrating Lesbian Unions* (Seattle, WA: The Seal Press, 1990). Twenty-seven lesbian couples speak of affirming their commitment through wedding ceremonies.

Barbara Ehrenreich. *The Hearts of Men: American Dreams and the Flight from Commitment* (New York, NY: Anchor, Doubleday, 1983). Argues that the feminist movement was set in motion by men walking away from their roles as breadwinners and success machines. This action on men's part also caused the antifeminist backlash.

Betty Friedan. *The Feminine Mystique* (New York, NY: Dell Publishing Co., 1963). "The problem that has no name" is the emptiness of the life of the suburban housewife.

Betty Friedan. *The Second Stage* (New York, NY: Summit Books, Simon and Schuster, 1986). Redesigning the family so as to better meet human needs.

Jean Schaar Gochros. *When Husbands Come Out of the Closet* (Binghamton, NY: The Haworth Press, 1989). How to cope with a gay husband, including strategies for handling the problem of AIDS.

Clyde Hendrick, ed. *Close Relationships: Development, Dynamics and Deterioration* (Newbury Park, CA: Sage Publications, 1989). What happens to relationships in the long run.

Søren Kierkegaard. "The Aesthetic Validity of Marriage" in *Either/Or,* Vol. 2, translated by Walter Lowrie (New York, NY: Anchor, Doubleday, 1959), pp. 3–157. The difference commitment makes in a relationship.

Mirra Komarovsky. *Blue-Collar Marriage* (New York, NY: Vintage Books, 1962). Classic analysis of working class families, including power configurations.

Susan Krieger. *The Mirror Dance: Identity in a Women's Community* (Philadelphia, PA: Temple University Press, 1983). Women's experiences in an all-woman community.

Robert A. Lewis and Marvin B. Sussman, eds. *Men's Changing Roles in the Family* (New York, NY: The Haworth Press, 1986). Are times changing? This is an interesting study focusing on men's roles in the family.

Eleanor D. Macklin and Roger H. Rubin, eds. *Contemporary Families and Alternative Lifestyles: Handbook on Research and Theory* (Beverly Hills, CA: Sage Publications, 1983). Collection of interesting writings on non-traditional families.

David P. McWhirter and Andrew M. Mattison. *The Male Couple: How Relationships Develop* (Englewood Cliffs, N.J.: Prentice-Hall, 1984). 156 gay couples are studied in 6 temporal stages of their relationships.

Robert C. L. Moffat, Joseph Grcic, and Michael D. Bayles, eds. *Perspectives on the Family* (Lewiston, NY: The Edwin Mellen Press, 1990). Philosophers and other thinkers look at family issues.

Ann Oakley. *The Sociology of Housework* (New York, NY: Pantheon Books, Random House, 1974). Analysis and (fairly negative) evaluation of housework.

Susan Moller Okin. *Justice, Gender and the Family* (New York, NY: Basic Books, 1989). How liberal theories of justice, Rawls' in particular, produce injustices for women in families.

Daniel Perlman and Steve Ducks, eds. *Intimate Relationships: Long Term Relationships* (Newbury Park, CA: Sage Publications, 1987).

Bertrand Russell. *Marriage and Morals* (London: George Allen and Unwin, 1929). A protest against tradition, considered shocking in its day.

John Scanzoni. *Shaping Tomorrow's Family: Theory and Policy for the 21st Century* (Newbury Park, CA: Sage Publications, 1983).

John Scanzoni, Karen Polenks, Jay Teachman, and Linda Thompson. *The Sexual Bond: Rethinking Families and Close Relationships* (Newbury Park, CA: Sage Publications, 1989).

Arlene Skolnick and Jerome H. Skolnick, eds. *Family in Transition* (Boston, MA: Little, Brown and Co., 3rd Edition, 1980).

Barrie Thorne, with Marilyn Yalom, eds. *Rethinking the Family: Some Feminist Questions* (New York, NY: Longman, Inc., 1982). Feminists question some traditional ideas about the family.

Kath Weston. *Families We Choose: Lesbians, Gays, Kinship* (New York, NY: Columbia University Press, 1991). Nice analysis of San Francisco Bay area notions of kinship for gays and lesbians. Should be encouragement to gays and lesbians everywhere.

Part VII

Sex and Sexuality

Introduction

RELATIONSHIPS ROOTED IN GENDER—romances and affairs, one-night stands, and marriages—clearly include sexual activity as an important component. Even when a couple decides upon total abstinence, they believe their decision has been made in an important area. The writers of the pieces in this section discuss sexual activity, its nature, and its very real problems.

VII.1   Sexuality

ROBERT NOZICK

Robert Nozick has a well-developed view of sexual activity. Sexual activity with some-one, he says, is the most intense way to relate to another person. Addressing himself to heterosexual sex, Nozick perceives distinct gender roles.

Nozick is Arthur Kingsley Porter Professor of Philosophy at Harvard University and author of *Anarchy, State and Utopia* and *Philosophical Explanations*. "Love's Bond," from *The Examined Life*, contains some of Nozick's thoughts about life and living. Another writing from *The Examined Life* appears in Part IV.

Reading Questions

1. Would you liken the intensity of sexual activity to watching the end of a closely matched athletic contest or a suspense film, as Nozick does? Does this view suggest that an episode of sexual activity can include goals, and a possibility of "winners" and "losers"?

2. Nozick explains one traditional basic sexual script, roughly, penis, vagina, intercourse, orgasm. Is this script, in some way, central to sexual activity?

3. Is your orgasm the kind of event that can tell your partner how pleased you are with him or her, given that orgasms just happen (or, perhaps, just fail to happen)? If you don't have an orgasm, does this give your partner the message that you are *not* pleased with him or her?

THE MOST INTENSE WAY we relate to another person is sexually. Nothing so concentrates the mind, Dr. Johnson noted, as the prospect of being hanged. Nothing, that is, except sexual arousal and excitement: rising tension, uncertainty about what will happen next, occasional reliefs, sudden surprises, dangers and risks, all in a sequence of heightened attention and tension that reaches toward resolution. A similar pattern of excitement also occurs near the end of closely matched athletic contests and in suspense films. I do not say our excitement at these is at base covertly sexual. Yet the sexual is so preeminent an exemplar of the general pattern of excitement that these others also may hold sexual reverberations. However, only in sex is such intense excitement shared with the object and cause of it.

Sex is not simply a matter of frictional force. The excitement comes largely in how we interpret the situation and how we perceive the connection to the other. Even in masturbatory fantasy, people dwell upon their actions with others; they do not get excited by thinking of themselves or of themselves masturbating while thinking of themselves. What is exciting is interpersonal: how the other views you, what attitude the actions evidence. Some uncertainty about this makes it even more exciting. Just as it is difficult to tickle oneself, so too sex is better with an actual partner on the other end. (Is it the other person or the uncertainty that is crucial?)

Sex holds the attention. If any wanderings of the mind from the immediate sexual situation are permissible, it is only to other sexual fantasies. It bespeaks a certain lack of involvement to be ruminating then about one's next choice of automobile. In part, the focus of attention is on how you are touched and what you are feeling, in part on how you are touching the other person and what he or she is feeling.

At times we focus in sex upon the most minute motions, the most delicate brushing of a hair, the slow progress of the fingertips or nails or tongue across the skin, the slightest change or pause at a point. We linger in such moments and await what will come next. Our acuity is sharpest here; no change in pressure or motion or angle is too slight to notice. And it is exciting to know another is attuned to your sensations as keenly as you are. A partner's delicacy of motion and response can show knowledge of your pleasure and care about its details. To have your particular pleasures known and accepted, to linger in them for as long as you will without any rushing to another stage or another excitement, to receive another's permission and invitation to loll there and play together—*is* there such a thing as sex that is too slow?—to be told in this way that you are deserving of pleasure and worthy of it, can bring a profound sigh.

Not only are old pleasures sensitively and delicately awakened and explored, but one becomes willing to follow to somewhere new, in the hands and mouth and tongue and teeth of someone who has cared and caressed knowingly.

It is not surprising that profound emotions are awakened and expressed in sex. The trust involved in showing our own pleasures, the vulnerability in letting another give us these and guide them, including pleasures with infantile or oedipal reverberations, or anal ones, does not come lightly.

Sex is not all delicacy of knowledge and response to nuanced pleasure. The narrative that begins there, and occasionally returns, also moves along to stronger and less calibrated actions, not so much the taking of turns in attentiveness to each other's pleasures as the mutual growth of stronger and broader excitements—the move from the adult (or the infantile) to the animal. The passions and motions become fiercer and less controlled, sharper or more automatically rhythmic, the focus shifts from flesh to bones, sounds shift from moans and sighs to sharper cries, hisses, roars, mouths shift from tongue and lips to teeth and biting, themes of power, domination, and anger emerge to be healed in tenderness and to emerge yet again in ever stronger and more intense cycles.

In the arena of sex, our very strongest emotions are expressed. These emotions are not always tender and loving, though sometimes, perhaps often, they are. Such strong emotions bring equally strong ones, excited and exciting, in response. The partners see their strongest and most primitive emotions expressed and also contained safely. It is not only the other person who is known more deeply in sex. One knows one's own self better in experiencing what it is capable of: passion, love, aggression, vulnerability, domination, playfulness, infantile pleasure, joy. The depth of relaxing afterward is a measure of the fullness and profoundity of the experience together, and a part of it.

The realm of sex is or can be inexhaustible. There is no limit to what can be learned and felt about each other in sex; the only limit is the sensitivity or responsiveness or creativity or daring of the partners. There always are new depths—and new surfaces—to be explored.

The one maxim is to experiment attentively: to notice what excites, to follow the other's pleasure where it is and goes, to lean into it, to play with variations around it, with stronger or more delicate pressures, in related places. Intelligence helps, too, in noticing whether what excites fits into a larger pattern or fantasy, in testing out that hypothesis and then, through congruent actions and words, sometimes ambiguous, in encouraging it. Through fresh experimentation one can bypass routinized or predictable pleasures. How nice that freedom, openness, creativity, daring, and intelligence—traits not always so amply rewarded in the larger world—bear such exceedingly sweet private fruits.

Sex also is a mode of communication, a way of saying or of showing something more tellingly than our words can say. Yet though sexual actions speak more pointedly than words, they also can be enhanced by words, words that name one's pleasure or lead ahead to greater intensity, words that narrate a fantasy or merely hint at exciting ones that cannot comfortably be listened to.

Like musicians in jazz improvisation, sexual partners are engaged in a dialogue, partly scored, partly improvised, where each very attentively responds to the statements in the bodily motions of the other. These statements can be about one's own self and pleasures, or about one's partner's, or about the two of you together, or about what one would like the other to do. Whether or not they do so elsewhere in life, in sex people frequently and unconsciously do unto others as they would have others do unto them. By the placing or intensity or rate or direction of their pressures and motions they are constantly sending signals, often unawares, about what they want to receive. In manifold ways, also, some parts of the body can stand for or represent others, so that what happens, for example, at the mouth or ear (or palm or armpit or fingers or toes or bones) can intricately symbolize corresponding events elsewhere with coordinate excitement.

In verbal conversations, people speak in different voices, with different ideas, on different topics. In sexual conversation, too, everyone has a distinctive voice. And there is no shortage of new things two people can say, or older things that can be said newly or reminisced about. To speak of *conversations* here does not mean that the sole (nonreproductive) purpose of sex is communica-

tion. There is also excitement and bodily pleasure, desired for themselves. Yet these too are also important parts of the conversation, for it is through pleasurable excitement and the opening to it that other powerful emotions are brought into expression and play in the sexual arena.

In this arena, everything personal can be expressed, explored, symbolized, and intensified. In intimacy, we let another within the boundaries we normally maintain around ourselves, boundaries marked by clothing and by full self-control and monitoring. Through the layers of public defenses and faces, another is admitted to see a more vulnerable or a more impassioned you. Nothing is more intimate than showing another your physical pleasure, perhaps because we learned we had to hide it even (or especially) from our parents. Once inside the maintained boundaries, new intimacies are possible, such as the special nature of the conversation new partners can have in bed after sex. (Might they engage in sex partly in order to have such unposed conversations?)

Is there a conflict between the desire for sexual excitement including orgasm and the deepest knowing of one's partner and oneself? A rush to immediately greater excitement, a focus upon everything else merely as a means to orgasm, would get in the way of deeply opening to another and knowing them. Everything in its proper time. The most intense excitement too can be a route to depth; people would not be so shaken by sex, so awed sometimes by what occurs, if their depths had stayed unplumbed.

Exciting for itself, orgasm also tells your partner how very pleased you are with him or her. When it takes a deeper form, when you allow yourself to become and appear totally without control, completely engulfed, you show the other, and show yourself too, the full extent of that other's power over you and of your comfort and trust in being helpless before him or her.

Pleasing another feels best when it is an accomplishment, a surmountable challenge. Consequently, an orgasm is less satisfying to the giving partner when it comes too early or too late. Too early and it is no accomplishment, too late and only after very much effort, it states that the giving partner is not exciting and pleasing enough. The secret of success with orgasm, as with comedy, is timing.

Orgasm is not simply an exciting experience but a statement about the partner, about the connection to the partner; it announces that the partner satisfies you. No wonder partners care that it happen. Here, too, we can understand the unitive force of simultaneous orgasm, of feeling the most intense pleasure with and from the other person at the very moment that you are told and shown you intensely please him or her.

There are other statements, less about the whole person, more about parts. The penis can be made to feel a welcome entrant in the vagina; it can be kissed lovingly and unhurriedly; it can be made to feel nurturative; it can be delighted in and known for itself; in more exalted moments its fantasy is to be worshiped almost. Similarly, the sweetness and power of the vagina can be acknowledged in its own right, by tender kissing, long knowing, dwelling in the tiniest crevices and emitting those sounds this calls forth. Knowing a partner's body, meditating on the special energy of its parts without rushing anywhere else, also makes a statement the partner receives.

Unlike making love, which can be symmetrical, tender, and turn-taking all the way through, what we might (without any denigration) call "fucking" contains at least one stage where the male displays his power and force. This need not be aggressive, vicious, or dominating, although perhaps statistically it frequently slides into that. The male can simply be showing the female his power, strength, ferocity even, for her appreciation. Exhibiting his quality as a beast in the jungle, with a lion or tiger's fierceness, growling, roaring, biting, he shows (in a contained fashion) his protective strength. This display of force need not be asymmetrical, however. The female can answer (and initiate) with her own ferocity, snarls, hissing, scratching, growling, biting, and she shows too her capacity to contain and tame

his ferocity. It is even more difficult to state in quite the right way matters of more delicate nuance, the special way a woman can at some point *give* herself to her partner.

In sexual intimacy, we admit the partner within our boundaries or make these more permeable, showing our own passions, capacities, fantasies, and excitements, and responding to the other's. We might diagram sexual intimacy as two circles overlapping with dotted lines. There *are* boundaries between the partners here, yet these boundaries are permeable, not solid. Hence, we can understand the oceanic feeling, the sense of merging, that sometimes occurs with intense sexual experience. This is not due merely to the excited feelings directed toward the other; it results from not devoting energy to maintaining the usual boundaries. (At climactic moments, are the boundaries dropped or are they made *selectively* permeable, lowered only for that particular person?)

Much that I have said thus far might apply to single sexual encounters, yet a sexual life has its special continuities over time. There is the extended being together over a full day or several, with repeated and varied intimacies and knowings, scarcely emerging or arising from the presence of the other, with fuller knowledge and feelings fresh in memory as a springboard to new explorations. There are the repeated meetings of familiar partners who scarcely can contain their hunger for each other. There are the fuller enduring relationships of intimacy and love, enhancing the excitement, depth, and sweetness of sexual uniting and enhanced by it.

Not only can one explore in sex the full range of emotions, knowing one's partner and oneself deeply, not only can one come to know the two of you together in union, pursuing the urge to unite or merge with the other and finding the physical joy of transcending the self, not only is (heterosexual) sex capable of producing new life which brings further psychological significance to the act itself—perhaps especially saliently for women, who are able to become the carriers of life within them, with all its symbolic significance —but in sex one also can engage in metaphysical exploration, knowing the body and person of another as a map or microcosm of the very deepest reality, a clue to its nature and purpose.

Further Questions

1. If sex is communication, what exactly can be expressed through this form of activity?
2. If your mind wanders from the activity, is your side of it thereby impoverished?
3. Is it productive to think of heterosexual sex as having built-in gender roles? Is it sometimes a good idea to think of sex instead as an exchange, with no particular gender roles?

VII.2A   The Language of Sex: The Heterosexual Questionnaire

M. ROCHLIN

We can learn something about sexual activity and sexual orientation (homosexual and heterosexual) by looking into what we say about it. M. Rochlin applies the convention that we only question what we consider deviant to the issue of sexual orientation.

Reading Questions

1. Is homosexuality deviant, in need of explanation or questionable, in a way in which heterosexuality is not?
2. Answer some of the questions on the heterosexual questionnaire. (If you are not heterosexual, answer the questions on behalf of someone who is.)

1. What do you think caused your heterosexuality?

2. When and how did you decide you were a heterosexual?

3. Is it possible that your heterosexuality is just a phase you may grow out of?

4. Is it possible that your heterosexuality stems from a neurotic fear of others of the same sex?

5. If you have never slept with a person of the same sex, is it possible that all you need is a good Gay lover?

6. Do your parents know that you are straight? Do your friends and/or roommate(s) know? How did they react?

7. Why do you insist on flaunting your heterosexuality? Can't you just be who you are and keep it quiet?

8. Why do heterosexuals place so much emphasis on sex?

9. Why do heterosexuals feel compelled to seduce others into their lifestyle?

10. A disproportionate majority of child molesters are heterosexual. Do you consider it safe to expose children to heterosexual teachers?

11. Just what do men and women *do* in bed together? How can they truly know how to please each other, being so anatomically different?

12. With all the societal support marriage receives, the divorce rate is spiraling. Why are there so few stable relationships among heterosexuals?

13. Statistics show that lesbians have the lowest incidence of sexually transmitted diseases. Is it really safe for a woman to maintain a heterosexual lifestyle and run the risk of disease and pregnancy?

14. How can you become a whole person if you limit yourself to compulsive, exclusive heterosexuality?

15. Considering the menace of overpopulation, how could the human race survive if everyone were heterosexual?

16. Could you trust a heterosexual therapist to be objective? Don't you feel s/he might be inclined to influence you in the direction of her/his own leanings?

17. There seem to be very few happy heterosexuals. Techniques have been developed that might enable you to change if you really want to. Have you considered trying aversion therapy?

18. Would you want your child to be heterosexual, knowing the problems that s/he would face?

The Language of Sex: VII.2B
Our Conception of Sexual Intercourse

ROBERT BAKER

In this excerpt Robert Baker notes the asymmetry of terminology for heterosexual intercourse, reflecting active-passive gender roles. In addition, many terms for the female role in heterosexual intercourse also mean "harmed," suggesting that the man harms the woman in this type of activity.

Reading Questions

1. Is there some reason why so many terms for sexual intercourse can be used also to indicate harm?

2. In descriptions of sexual intercourse, the man is usually the grammatical subject and the woman is the grammatical object. Is there good reason for this?

. . . CONSIDER THE TERMS WE USE TO identify coitus, or more technically, the terms that function synonymously with "had sexual intercourse with" in a sentence of the form "A had sexual intercourse with B." The following is a list of some commonly used synonyms (numerous others that are not as widely used have been omitted, for example, "diddled," "laid pipe with"):

> screwed
> laid
> fucked
> had
> did it with (to)
> banged
> balled
> humped
> slept with
> made love to

Now, for a select group of these verbs, names for males are the subjects of sentences with active constructions (that is, where the subjects are said to be doing the activity); and names for females require passive constructions (that is, they are the recipients of the activity—whatever is done is done to them). Thus, we would not say "Jane did it to Dick," although we would say "Dick did it to Jane." Again, Dick bangs Jane, Jane does not bang Dick; Dick humps Jane, Jane does not hump Dick. In contrast, verbs like "did it with" do not require an active role for the male; thus, "Dick did it with Jane and Jane with Dick." Again, Jane may make love to Dick, just as Dick makes love to Jane; and Jane sleeps with Dick as easily as Dick sleeps with Jane. (My students were undecided about "laid." Most thought that it would be unusual indeed for Jane to lay Dick, unless she played the masculine role of seducer-aggressor.)

The sentences thus form the following pairs. (Those nonconjoined singular noun phrases where a female subject requires a passive construction are marked with a cross. An asterisk indicates that the sentence in question is not a sentence of English if it is taken as synonymous with the italicized sentence heading the column.[1]

Dick had sexual intercourse with Jane
Dick screwed Jane+
Dick laid Jane+
Dick fucked Jane+
Dick had Jane+
Dick did it to Jane+
Dick banged Jane+
Dick humped Jane+
Dick balled Jane(?)
Dick did it with Jane
Dick slept with Jane
Dick made love to Jane

Jane had sexual intercourse with Dick
Jane was banged by Dick
Jane was humped by Dick
*Jane was done by Dick
Jane was screwed by Dick
Jane was laid by Dick
Jane was fucked by Dick
Jane was had by Dick
Jane balled Dick(?)
Jane did it with Dick
Jane slept with Dick
Jane made love to Dick
*Jane screwed Dick
*Jane laid Dick
*Jane fucked Dick
*Jane had Dick
*Jane did it to Dick
*Jane banged Dick
*Jane humped Dick

These lists make clear that within the standard view of sexual intercourse, males, or at least names for males, seem to play a different role than females, since male subjects play an active role in the language of screwing, fucking, having, doing it, and perhaps, laying, while female subjects play a passive role.

The asymmetrical nature of the relationship indicated by the sentences marked with a cross is confirmed by the fact that the form "__ ed with each other" is acceptable for the sentences not marked with a cross, but not for those that require a male subject. Thus:

> *Dick and Jane had sexual intercourse with each other*
> Dick and Jane made love to each other
> Dick and Jane slept with each other
> Dick and Jane did it with each other
> Dick and Jane balled with each other(*?)
> *Dick and Jane banged with each other
> *Dick and Jane did it to each other
> *Dick and Jane had each other
> *Dick and Jane fucked each other
> *Dick and Jane humped each other
> *(?)Dick and Jane laid each other
> *Dick and Jane screwed each other

It should be clear, therefore, that our language reflects a difference between the male and female sexual roles, and hence that we conceive of the male and female roles in different ways. The question that now arises is, "What difference in our conception of the male and female sexual roles requires active constructions for males and passive for females?"

One explanation for the use of the active construction for males and the passive construction for females is that this grammatical asymmetry merely reflects the natural physiological asymmetry between men and women: the asymmetry of "to screw" and "to be screwed," "to insert into" and "to be inserted into." That is, it might be argued that the difference between masculine and feminine grammatical roles merely reflects a difference naturally required by the anatomy of males and females. This explanation is inadequate. Anatomical differences do not determine how we are to conceptualize the relation between penis and vagina during intercourse. Thus one can easily imagine a society in which the female normally played the active role during intercourse, where female subjects required active constructions with verbs indicating copulation, and where the standard metaphors were terms like "engulfing"—that is, instead of saying "he

screwed her," one would say "she engulfed him." It follows that the use of passive constructions for female subjects of verbs indicating copulation does not reflect differences determined by human anatomy but rather reflects those generated by human customs.

What I am going to argue next is that the passive construction of verbs indicating coitus (that is, indicating the female position) can *also* be used to indicate that a person is being harmed. I am then going to argue that the metaphor involved would only make sense if we conceive of the female role in intercourse as that of a person being harmed (or being taken advantage of).

Passive constructions of "fucked," "screwed," and "had" indicate the female role. They also can be used to indicate being harmed. Thus, in all of the following sentences, Marion plays the female role: "Bobbie fucked Marion"; "Bobbie screwed Marion"; "Bobbie had Marion"; "Marion was fucked"; "Marion was screwed"; and "Marion was had." All of the statements are equivocal. They might literally mean that someone had sexual intercourse with Marion (who played the female role); or they might mean, metaphorically, that Marion was deceived, hurt, or taken advantage of. Thus, we say things as "I've been screwed" ("fucked," "had," "taken," and so on) when we have been treated unfairly, been sold shoddy merchandise, or conned out of valuables. Throughout this essay I have been arguing that metaphors are applied to things only if what the term *actually* applies to shares one or more properties with what the term *metaphorically* applies to. Thus, the female sexual role must have something in common with being conned or being sold shoddy merchandise. The only common property is that of being harmed, deceived, or taken advantage of. *Hence we conceive of a person who plays the female sexual role as someone who is being harmed* (that is, "screwed," "fucked," and so on).

It might be objected that this is clearly wrong, since the unsigned terms do not indicate someone's being harmed, and hence we do not conceive of having intercourse as being harmed. The point about the unsignated terms, however, is that they can take both females and males as subjects (in active constructions) and thus *do not pick out the female role*. This demonstrates that we conceive of sexual roles in such a way that only females are thought to be taken advantage of in intercourse.

The best part of solving a puzzle is when all the pieces fall into place. If the subjects of the passive construction are being harmed, presumably the subjects of the active constructions are doing harm, and, indeed, we do conceive of these subjects in precisely this way. Suppose one is angry at someone and wishes to express malevolence as forcefully as possible without actually committing an act of physical violence. If one is inclined to be vulgar one can make the sign of the erect male cock by clenching one's fist while raising one's middle finger, or by clenching one's fist and raising one's arm and shouting such things as "screw you," "up yours," or "fuck you." In other words, one of the strongest possible ways of telling someone that you wish to harm him is to tell him to assume the female sexual role relative to you. Again, to say to someone "go fuck yourself" is to order him to harm himself, while to call someone a "mother fucker" is not so much a play on his Oedipal fears as to accuse him of being so low that he would inflict the greatest imaginable harm (fucking) upon that person who is most dear to him (his mother).

Clearly, we conceive of the male sexual role as that of hurting the person in the female role—but lest the reader have any doubts, let me provide two further bits of confirming evidence: one linguistic, one nonlinguistic. One of the English terms for a person who hurts (and takes advantage of) others is the term "prick." This metaphorical identification would not make sense unless the bastard in question (that is, the person outside the bonds of legitimacy) was thought to share some characteristics attributed to things that are literally pricks. As a verb, "prick" literally means "to hurt," as in "I pricked myself with a needle"; but the usage in question is as a noun. As a noun, "prick" is a colloquial term for "penis." Thus, the question before us is what characteristic is shared by a penis and a person who harms others (or, alternatively, by a penis and by being stuck by a needle). Clearly, no physical characteristic is relevant (physical characteristics might underlie the Yiddish metaphorical attribution "schmuck," but one would have to analyze Yiddish usage to determine this); hence the shared characteristic is nonphysical; the only relevant shared nonphysical characteristic is that both a literal prick and a figurative prick are agents that harm people.

Now for the nonlinguistic evidence. Imagine two doors: in front of each door is a line of people; behind each door is a room; in each room is a bed; on each bed is a person. The line in front of one room consists of beautiful women, and on the bed in that room is a man having intercourse with each of these women in turn. One may think any number of things about this scene. One may say that the man is in heaven, or enjoying himself at a bordello; or perhaps one might only wonder at the oddness of it all. One does not think that the man is being hurt or violated or degraded—or at least the possibility does not immediately suggest itself, although one could conceive of situations where this was what was happening (especially, for example, if the man was impotent). Now, consider the other line. Imagine that the figure on the bed is a woman and that the line consists of handsome, smiling men. The woman is having intercourse with each of these men in turn. It immediately strikes one that the woman is being degraded, violated, and so forth—"that poor woman."

When one man fucks many women he is a playboy and gains status; when a woman is fucked by many men she degrades herself and loses stature.

Our conceptual inventory is now complete enough for us to return to the task of analyzing the slogan that men ought not to think of women as sex objects.

I think that it is now plausible to argue that the appeal of the slogan "men ought not to think of women as sex objects," and the thrust of much of the literature produced by contemporary feminists, turns on something much deeper than a rejection of "scoring" (that is, the utilization of sexual "conquests" to gain esteem) and yet is a call neither for homosexuality nor for puritanism.

The slogan is best understood as a call for a new conception of the male and female sexual roles. If the analysis developed above is correct, our present conception of sexuality is such that to be a man is to be a person capable of brutalizing women (witness the slogans "The marines will make a man out of you!" and "The army builds *men*!" which are widely accepted and which simply state that learning how to kill people will make a person more manly). Such a conception of manhood not only bodes ill for a society led by such men, but also is clearly inimical to the best interests of women. It is only natural for women to reject such a sexual role, and it would seem to be the duty of any moral person

to support their efforts—to redefine our conceptions not only of fucking, but of the fucker (man) and the fucked (woman). . . .

NOTE

1. For further analysis of verbs indicating copulation see "A Note on Conjoined Noun Phrases," *Journal of Philosophical Linguistics,* vol. 1, no. 2, Great Expectations, Evanston, Ill. Reprinted with "English Sentences Without Overt Grammatical Subject," in Zwicky, Salus, Binnick, and Vanek, eds., *Studies Out in Left Field: Defamatory Essays Presented to James D. McCawley* (Edmonton: Linguistic Research, Inc., 1971). The puritanism in our society is such that both of these articles are pseudo-anonymously published under the name of Quang Phuc Dong; Mr. Dong, however, has a fondness of citing and criticizing the articles and theories of Professor James McCawley, Department of Linguistics, University of Chicago. Professor McCawley himself was kind enough to criticize an earlier draft of this essay. I should also like to thank G. E. M. Anscombe for some suggestions concerning this essay.

Further Questions

1. Answer some of the questions on the heterosexual questionnaire.

2. Is the "fact" that, grammatically, Dick can hump Jane but Jane cannot hump Dick due to gender roles in sex, or is this a mere grammatical matter of no importance?

3. "Prick" literally means "hurt." What does this indicate about male sexuality?

4. Did it ever occur to you that a sexual feeling, or response, might not be a positive occurrence in your life?

VII.3   Who's on Top? Heterosexual Practices and Male Dominance During the Sex Act

MERCEDES STEEDMAN

Mercedes Steedman discusses "who's on top" in sexual activity in a patriarchal context. Men and women alike have ambiguous feelings about women taking sexual initiative or doing much of anything, sexually, outside the traditional sex act, intercourse.

Steedman teaches sociology at Laurentian University, Sudbury, Ontario.

Reading Questions

1. Is assertive sexual behavior in some way "unfeminine"?
2. Is it important that a man be more "knowledgeable" about sex than a woman? If he is more "knowledgeable" about sex, what does he know that she doesn't know?
3. Is it important that women have orgasms? So important that it is sometimes a good idea to "fake" an orgasm?

. . . RECENT EVIDENCE from anatomical examination of male and female muscle construction in the genital area seems to indicate that the vasocongestion process (the engorgement of genital muscle tissue with blood) affects analogous muscles in the penile shaft and in the vaginal-labial system. The physiological processes of vasocongestion and myotonia (muscle spasm) are actually more similar for the two sexes than different.

Survey evidence has suggested that assertive sexual behaviour is still perceived as unfeminine by many women. As a result, women sacrifice sexual pleasure for fear of being perceived as "cheap." The good girl/bad girl dichotomy perpetuates the ideal of innocence as a component of femininity. Yet innocence and restraint are not effective behaviour if one is seeking to be orgasmic. Only 30 percent of Hite's sample reported orgasm through intercourse alone (Hite, 1976:229), and Seymour Fisher's study of 300 women (1972) reported a corresponding figure of only 20 percent. (Although other surveys show slightly higher figures for coital orgasm, it continues to be a minority response.) (See Fisher, 1973.)

Sexual Power/Social Power

Both men and women are asked to accept a code of social passivity for women during the act of coitus. Shere Hite comments on the contradictory message that men give here. "Although many men are very angry with women and suffer profound discomfort due to women's passivity regarding sex—possibly because of buried feelings of guilt and defensiveness, knowing that women are being exploited—most men do not overtly connect this with the need for improving women's status. Most men prefer to think that the problem is simply a lingering vestige of 'Victorian morality'—and prefer to believe that somehow women can be sexually 'free' even though they are not also economically and politically free" (Hite, 1981:736). As long as women remain economically dependent on men, it is risky for them to challenge or threaten men's masculinity in the bedroom. So there is collusion between men and women. Rubin encountered this attitude in her interviews with working-class wives: "One thing I know he likes is that he taught me mostly all I know about sex, so that makes him feel good." Rubin commented: "That seems a strange thing to say when you were married for some years before." The woman replied, "Yeah, I guess you'd think so. Well, you know, he likes to feel that way so why shouldn't he, and why shouldn't I let him?" (Rubin, 1976:142).

In addition, men and women alike continue to feel ambiguous about women's sexual aggression. Few studies have observed the man's reaction to a woman's assertiveness in the bedroom. Hunt's 1974 survey suggests that the norms for women's passivity are changing; he found that women did engage in a greater variety of sexual behaviour than they had some 20 years ago, but their comfort level in doing so seemed closely linked to their education, religiosity, urbanism, income, and age.[1] Allgeier and Fogel's 1978 study of coital positions and sex roles suggests that the changes observed by Hunt remain superficial. Their study of middle-class men and women found that "females rated the woman as dirtier, less respectable, less moral, less good, less desirable as a wife and less desirable as a mother when she was on top than when she was beneath the man during intercourse" (Allgeier and Fogel, 1978:589). Women (but not men) discriminated against the woman-on-top position, despite research evidence that suggests that women enjoy a higher orgasmic response rate when they are on top. A study of American university students conducted by Clinton Jessor (1978) found that women believed men would be "turned off" by women's sexual assertiveness, despite evidence that suggested the opposite to be true (Jessor, 1978:118–28). A woman's femininity is still partly perceived as residing in her receptivity, not in her control. Interestingly, this perception seems to influence women more than men. It would seem that the traditional dictates of appropriate, moral

sex behaviour continue to outweigh reason and the dictates of "liberated" sexuality.

The thing is, there is more at stake here than a good orgasm. Men and women alike are caught up in the view that women must remain the standard-bearers for morally correct behaviour in our society, while pornography pushes the opposite view—that women are sexual aggressors and whores. Men and women alike live with these contradictory conceptions of women's sexuality, and the consequences are often confusing for both. One man said to Lillian Rubin: "It isn't that I mind her letting me know when she wants it, but she isn't very subtle about it. I mean, she could let me know in a nice, feminine way" (Rubin, 1976:143). Referring to oral sex, one respondent stated, "No, Alice isn't that kind of girl. Jesus, you shouldn't ask questions like that. She wasn't brought up to go for all that fancy stuff. . . . There's plenty of women out there to do that kind of stuff with. You can meet them in any bar any time you want to. You don't have to marry those kind" (Rubin, 1976:141). The "liberated" sexuality of the eighties remains a cloak for traditional views of sexuality—and control of women. This control of women is maintained by the active suppression of their sexuality, by the ignoring of their sexuality, or by the rationalization of women's inability to reach orgasm in the traditional sex act, and by a medicalized language that labels women's (and men's) behaviour as "dysfunctional." "Sexual liberation" may have brought in some new rules, but the game remains the same.

Language further confuses the issue. The symbols and verbal clues we use ostensibly communicate real experience, yet they serve to maintain a certain image of sex. For example, the word "foreplay" suggests a prelude to a main event—penetration and orgasm. This language reinforces a conception of the sex act as sequential behaviour. A term such as "impotence" conveys a message about male sexual power (or the lack of it), and links men's power to their ability to maintain an erection. The public representation of the sensual intervenes in the intimate relations of the couple. Masculine dominance is reaffirmed in the erotic imagery of advertising and pornography. As the unreal becomes real, our perceptions of the sexes are distorted. The ad in *Penthouse* magazine for a life-size doll (called "Heaven") epitomizes this fantasy view of sexual experience: "Heaven has only one function in life, to please you. . . . and her only passion is your endless pleasure, your total release!" The ad goes on to say, "In her sultry tones, she'll marvel at your body, plead for mercy when you hurt her, purr from the pleasure you give her and moan with ecstasy the instant she takes your manhood into her warm, willing mouth."[2] The image of feminine sexual submission portrayed here may seem extreme and distorted, but it does reinforce the point that male power is legitimized in popular sexual imagery, and that little room is accorded to female sexual expression.

The masculine dominance of sexual imagery continues to influence our conception of sexual arousal. Sexual images of women are usually constructed for and by the ignorant male observer, to serve as stimulants for solitary sex. As a result they portray women in passive and often vulnerable poses. They present an image of sexual arousal in women that is impossible to duplicate in the actual act of coitus. However, when women's sexual behaviour is perceived as assertive, as in the image of engulfment of the penis by the vagina, it is usually portrayed by pornographic imagery as threatening and castrating. The affirmation of female sexual power remains limited to images constructed by feminist cultural workers, and therefore outside the mainstream. The images that "teach" women what their sexual body language should be are the images of a masculine culture. Pornography, recently challenged by feminists, requires our serious examination for, as Roz Coward so succinctly puts it, "Pornography as a representation of the sexual sets up, reinforces and sexualizes certain behaviors and certain images as erotic and sexual" (Coward, 1982:9–21).

Despite the expectation of intimacy during the sex act, the two sexes remain strangers. Many men remain uncertain of women's behaviour during the sex act; they often misinterpret the signals given by the woman. Hite reports men's accounts of how they know their partner has had an orgasm: "all the women I've ever known have uncontrollable erection of their nipples when they climax"; "she rapidly moves her hips, makes a sound deep in her throat, and smiles"; "she will become short-breathed and many times will dig her fingernails into my shoulders" (Hite, 1981:637–38). While these descriptions may accurately portray arousal stages in women, they in no way represent orgasmic behaviour. . . .

The "discovery" of the female orgasmic potential has not served to free women from sexual repression, for this "discovery" has occurred within a climate of masculine dominance. What this has often meant, in effect, is that a woman's orgasm is used as an indicator of her partner's success as a lover. Given this, it is not surprising that 53 percent of Shere Hite's female informants reported "faking" orgasm at least some of the time (Hite, 1976:257). When a partner's manhood is at stake, a woman does not in fact have ownership of her orgasmic response (any more than she has control over her economic life). Working-class women, more vulnerable to the dictates of men's egos, are quick to assess the significance of this. "I rarely have climaxes. But if it didn't bother my husband it wouldn't bother me. I keep trying to tell him that I know it is not his fault, that he's really a good lover. I keep telling him it's something the matter with me, not with him. But it scares me because he doesn't believe it, and I worry he might leave me for a woman who will have climaxes for him" (Rubin, 1976:152). . . .

NOTES

1. Hunt (1974:198); see also Petras (1978), for a review of these findings.

2. This ad often appears in *Penthouse,* under the title "Heaven Can't Wait."

BIBLIOGRAPHY

Allgeier, Elizabeth Rice, and Arthur F. Fogel. 1978. "Coital Positions and Sex Roles: Responses to Cross Sex Behavior in Bed." *Journal of Consulting and Clinical Psychology* 46 (no. 3):589.

Coward, R. 1982. "Sexual Violence and Sexuality." *Feminist Review* II (summer): 9–21.

Fisher, Seymour. 1973. *Understanding the Female Orgasm.* New York: Bantam.

Hite, Shere. 1976. *The Hite Report: A Nationwide Study on Female Sexuality.* New York: Macmillan.

Hite, Shere. 1981. *The Hite Report on Male Sexuality.* New York: Dell.

Hunt, Morton. 1974. *Sexual Behaviour in the 1970's.* Chicago: Playboy Press.

Jessor, Clinton J. 1978. "Male Responses to Direct Verbal Sexual Initiatives of Females." *Journal of Sex Research* 14 (no. 2):118–128.

Petras, J. 1978. *The Social Meaning of Human Sexuality.* Boston: Allyn and Bacon.

Rubin, Lillian Breslow. 1976. *Worlds of Pain.* New York: Basic Books.

Further Questions

1. Does male sexuality that is too much centered on penis performance run the risk of becoming too much oriented toward a goal and too isolated from other areas of human life?

2. Is the ideal human male always "ready" for sexual performance, whether or not he chooses to take the opportunity to perform?

3. Might sexuality be productively used in expressing attitudes and feelings other than male control or in playful or cooperative activity with one's partner?

In Pursuit of the Perfect Penis: VII.4
The Medicalization of Male Sexuality

LEONORE TIEFER

Leonore Tiefer discusses our current conception of masculinity, which centers on penis performance, erection, and orgasm. These connect readily with male power, achievement, and peer bonding—"acting like a man." She suggests better uses to which male sexuality can be put.

Tiefer does clinical and research work on human sexuality, most recently in the Urology Department of Beth Israel Medical Center, New York City.

Reading Questions

1. Why is it that men can bond through jokes and stories about sexual activity?

2. Is inability to achieve an erection or orgasm about the worst kind of humiliation a man can suffer?

3. Is it appropriate for men who cannot achieve erection or orgasm to seek a medical solution to their "problem"?

Male Sexuality

... SEXUAL COMPETENCE is part—some would say the central part—of contemporary masculinity, whether we are discussing the traditional man, the modern man, or even the "new" man.

> What so stokes male sexuality that clinicians are impressed by the force of it? Not libido, but rather the curious phenomenon by which sexuality consolidates and confirms gender. ... An impotent man always feels that his masculinity, and not just his sexuality, is threatened. In men, gender appears to "lean" on sexuality ... the need for sexual performance is so great. ... In women, gender identity and self-worth can be consolidated by other means. (Person, 1980, pp. 619, 626)

Gagnon and Simon (1973) explained how, during adolescent masturbation, genital sexuality (that is, erection and orgasm) acquires nonsexual motives such as the desire for power, achievement, and peer approval that have already become important during preadolescent gender role training. "The capacity for erection is an important sign element of masculinity and control" (Gagnon & Simon, 1973, p. 62) without which a man is not a man. Gross (1978) argues that by adulthood few men can accept other successful aspects of masculinity in lieu of adequate sexual performance.

Masculine sexuality assumes the ability for potent function, but the performances that earn acceptance and status often occur far from the bedroom. Tolson (1977) has described how working-class men engage in an endless performance of sexual stories, jokes, and routines:

> As a topic on which most men could support a conversation and as a source of jokes, sexual talk and gesture were inexhaustible. In the machine noise, a gesture suggestive of masturbation, intercourse or homosexuality was enough to raise a conventional smile and re-establish a bond over distances too great for talking. (Marsden, quoted in Tolson, 1977, p. 60)

Tolson argues that this type of ritualized sexual exchange validates working men's bond of masculinity in a situation that otherwise emasculates them. This is an example of the enduring homosocial function of heterosexuality that develops from the adolescent experience (Gagnon & Simon, 1973).

Psychologically, then, male sexual performances may have as much or more to do with male gender role confirmation and homosocial status as with pleasure, intimacy, or tension release. This may explain why men express so many rules concerning proper sexual performance: Their agenda relates not merely to personal or couple satisfaction but to acting "like a man" in intercourse in order to qualify for the title elsewhere.

We can draw on the writings of several authorities to compile an outline of the 10 sexual beliefs to which many men subscribe (Doyle, 1983; Zilbergeld, 1978; LoPiccolo, 1985): (1) Men's sexual apparatus and needs are simple and straightforward, unlike women's. (2) Most men are ready, willing, and eager for as much sex as they can get. (3) There is suspicion that other men's sexual experiences approximate ecstatic explosiveness more closely and more often than does one's own. (4) It is the responsibility of the man to teach and lead his partner to experience pleasure and orgasm(s). (5) Sexual prowess is a serious, task-oriented business, with no place for experimentation, unpredictability, or play. (6) Women prefer intercourse to other sexual activities, particularly "hard-driving" intercourse. (7) All really good and normal sex must end in intercourse. (8) Any physical contact other than a light touch is meant as an invitation to foreplay and intercourse. (9) It is the responsibility of the man to satisfy both his partner and himself. (10) Sexual prowess is never permanently earned; each time it must be reproven.

Many of these demands directly require—and all of them indirectly require—an erection. Nelson (1985) pointed out that male sexuality is dominated by a genital focus in several ways: Sexuality is isolated from the rest of life as a unique experience with particular technical performance requirements; the subjective meaning for the man arises from genital sensations first practiced and familiar in adolescent masturbation and directly transferred without thought to the interpersonal situation; and the psychological meaning primarily depends on the confirmation of virility that comes from proper erection and ejaculation.

It is no surprise, then, that any difficulty in getting the penis to do what it "ought" can become a source of profound humiliation and despair, both in terms of immediate self-esteem and the destruction of one's masculine reputation, which, it is assumed, will follow.

> Few sexual problems are as devastating to a man as his inability to achieve or sustain an erection long enough for successful sexual intercourse. For many men the idea of not being able to "get it up" is a fate worse than death. (Doyle, 1983, p. 205)
>
> What's the worst thing that can happen?-I ask myself. The worst thing that can happen is that I take one of these hip beautiful liberated women to bed and I can't get it up. I can't get it up! You hear me? She tells a few of her friends. Soon around every corner there's someone laughing at my failure. (Parent, 1977, p. 15) . . .

The Allure of Medicalized Sexuality

Men are drawn to a technological solution such as the penile prosthesis for a variety of personal reasons which ultimately rest on the inflexible central place of sexual potency in the male sexual script. Those who assume that "normal" men must always be interested in sex and who believe male sexuality is a simple system wherein interest leads easily and directly to erection (Zilbergeld, 1978) are baffled by any erectile difficulties. Their belief that "their penis is an instrument immune from everyday problems, anxieties and fears" (Doyle, 1983, p. 207) conditions them to deny the

contribution of psychological or interpersonal factors to male sexual responsiveness. This denial, in turn, results from fundamental male gender role prescriptions for self-reliance and emotional control (Brannon, 1976).

Medicalized discourse offers an explanation of impotence which removes control, and therefore responsibility and blame, for sexual failure from the man and places it on his physiology. Talcott Parsons (1951) originally argued that an organic diagnosis confers a particular social role, the "sick role," which has three aspects: (1) The individual is not held responsible for his or her condition; (2) illnesses are legitimate bases for exemption from normal social responsibilities; and (3) the exemptions are contingent on the sick person recognizing that sickness is undesirable and seeking appropriate (medical) help. A medical explanation for erectile difficulties relieves men of blame and thus permits them to maintain some masculine self-esteem even in the presence of impotence.

> Understandably, for many years the pattern of the human male has been to blame sexual dysfunction on specific physical distresses. Every sexually inadequate male lunges toward any potential physical excuse for sexual malfunction. From point of ego support, would that it could be true. A cast for a leg or a sling for an arm provides socially acceptable evidence of physical dysfunction of these extremities. Unfortunately, the psychosocial causes of perpetual penile flaccidity cannot be explained or excused by devices for mechanical support. (Masters & Johnson, 1970, pp. 187–188)

Perhaps in 1970 "devices for mechanical support" of the penis were not in widespread access, but we now have available, ironically, precisely the type of medical vindication Masters and Johnson suggested would be the most effective deflection of the "blame" men feel for their inability to perform sexually.

Men's willingness to accept a self-protective, self-handicapping (that is, an illness label) attribution for "failure" has been demonstrated in studies of excuse making (Snyder, Ford, & Hunt, 1985). Reduced personal responsibility is most sought in those situations in which performance is related to self-esteem (Snyder & Smith, 1982). It may be that the frequent use of physical excuses for failure in athletic performance provides a model for men to use in sexuality. Medical treatments not only offer tangible evidence of non-blameworthiness, but they allow men to avoid psychological treatments such as marital or sex therapy, which threaten embarrassing self-disclosure and admissions of weakness men find aversive (Peplau & Gordon, 1985).

The final allure of a technological solution such as the penile prosthesis is its promise of permanent freedom from worry. One of Masters and Johnson's (1970) major insights was their description of the self-conscious self-monitoring, which men with erectile difficulties develop in sexual situations. "Performance anxiety" and "spectatoring," their two immediate causes of sexual impotence, generate a self-perpetuating cycle that undermines a man's confidence about the future even as he recovers from individual episodes. Technology seems to offer a simple and permanent solution to the problem of lost or threatened confidence, as doctors from *Vogue* to the *Journal of Urology* have already noted. . . .

The Rising Importance of Sexuality in Personal Life

The expectation that sexuality will provide ever increasing rewards and personal meaning has . . . been a theme of the contemporary women's movement, and women's changing attitudes have affected many men, particularly widowed and divorced men returning to the sexual "market." Within the past decade, sexual advice manuals have changed their tone completely regarding the roles of men and women in sexual relations (Weinberg, Swenson, & Hammersmith, 1983). Women are advised to take more responsibility for their own pleasure, to possess sexual knowl-

edge and self-knowledge, and to expect that improved sexual functioning will pay off in other aspects of life. Removing responsibility from the man for being the sexual teacher and leader reduces the definition of sexual masculinity to having excellent technique and equipment to meet the "new woman" on her "new" level.

Finally, the new importance of sexual performance has no upper age limit.

> The sexual myth most rampant in our culture today is the concept that the aging process per se will in time discourage or deny erective security in the older-age group male. As has been described previously, the aging male may be slower to erect and may even reach the plateau phase without full erective return, but the facility and ability to attain erection, presuming general good health and no psychological block, continues unopposed as a natural sequence well into the 80-year age group. (Masters & Johnson, 1970, p. 326)

Sex is a natural act, Masters and Johnson said over and over again, and there is no "natural" reason for ability to decline or disappear as one ages. Erectile difficulties, then, are "problems" that can be corrected with suitable treatment. Aging provides no escape from the male sexual role. . . .

Preventive Medicine: Changing the Male Sexual Script

Men will remain vulnerable to the expansion of the clinical domain so long as masculinity rests heavily on a particular type of physiological function. As more research uncovers subtle physiological correlates of genital functioning, more men will be "at risk" for impotence. Fluctuations of physical and emotional states will become cues for impending impotence in any man with, for example diabetes, hypertension, or a history of prescription medication usage.

One of the less well understood features of sex therapy is that it "treats" erectile dysfunction by changing the individual men's sexual script.

This approach is primarily educational—you are not curing an illness but learning new and more satisfactory ways of getting on with each other (Greenwood & Bancroft, 1983, p. 305).

Our thesis is that the rules and concepts we learn [about male sexuality] are destructive and a very inadequate preparation for a satisfying and pleasurable sex life. . . . Having a better sex life is in large measure dependent upon your willingness to examine how the male sexual mythology has trapped you (Zilbergeld, 1978, p. 9).

Sexuality can be transformed from a rigid standard for masculine adequacy to a way of being, a way of communicating, a hobby, a way of being in one's body—and being one's body—that does not impose control but rather affirms pleasure, movement, sensation, cooperation, playfulness, relating. Masculine confidence cannot be purchased, because there can never be perfect potency. Chasing its illusion may line a few pockets, but for most men it will only exchange one set of anxieties and limitations for another.

REFERENCES

Bancroft, J. (1983). *Human sexuality and its problems.* Edinburgh: Churchill-Livingstone.

Brannon, R. (1976). The male sex role: Our culture's blueprint of manhood, and what it's done for us lately. In D. David & R. Brannon (Eds.), *The forty-nine percent majority: The male sex role.* Reading, MA: Addison-Wesley.

Doyle, J. A. (1983). *The male experience.* Dubuque, IA: William C. Brown.

Gagnon, J. H., & Simon, W. (1973). *Sexual conduct: The social sources of human sexuality.* Chicago: Aldine.

Gross, A. E. (1978). The male role and heterosexual behavior. *Journal of Social Issues, 34,* 87–107.

LoPiccolo, J. (1985). Diagnosis and treatment of male sexual dysfunction. *Journal of Sex and Marital Therapy, 11,* 215–232.

Masters, W. H., & Johnson, V. E. (1970). *Human sexual inadequacy.* Boston: Little, Brown.

Nelson, J. (1985). Male sexuality and masculine spirituality. *Siecus Report, 13,* 1–4.

Organization helps couples with impotence as problem. (1984, June 24). *New York Times,* Section, 1, Pt. 2, p. 42.

Parent, G. (1977). *David Meyer is a mother.* New York: Bantam.

Parsons, T. (1951). *The social system.* New York: Free Press.

Peplau, L. A., & Gordon, S. L. (1985). Women and men in love: Gender differences in close heterosexual relationships. In V. E. O'Leary, R. K. Unger, & B. S. Wallston (Eds.), *Women, gender and social psychology.* Hillsdale, NJ: Lawrence Erlbaum.

Person, E. S. (1980). Sexuality as the mainstay of identity: Psychoanalytic perspectives. *Signs, 5,* 605–630.

Snyder, C. R., & Smith, T. W. (1982). Symptoms as self-handicapping strategies: The virtues of old wine in a new bottle. In G. Weary & H. L. Mirels (Eds.), *Integration of clinical and social psychology.* New York: Oxford University Press.

Snyder, C. R., Ford, C. E., & Hunt, H. A. (1985, August). *Excuse-making: A look at sex differences.* Paper presented at the annual meeting of the American Psychological Association, Los Angeles.

Tolson, A. (1977). *The limits of masculinity.* New York: Harper & Row.

Weinberg, M. S., Swensson, R. G., & Hammersmith, S. K. (1983). Sexual autonomy and the status of women: Models of female sexuality in U.S. sex manuals from 1950 to 1980. *Social Problems, 30,* 312–324.

Zilbergeld, B. (1978). *Male sexuality.* Boston: Little, Brown.

Further Questions

1. Suppose that men and women were relatively equal in economic and social power. Would heterosexual sex on equal terms then have a better chance of succeeding?

2. Is there a standard blueprint for heterosexual sex? If so, does this inhibit spontaneity?

3. Should certain types of sexual activity or failure to do something in sexual activity be labeled "dysfunctional"? If so, what function is left unfulfilled?

VII.5A   Gay Basics: Some Questions, Facts, and Values

RICHARD MOHR

Richard Mohr addresses some critical questions directed at gay orientation and gay sexual activity: whether gays are "unnatural"; whether gays are gay by choice; and whether the privacy of sexual activity entails that such activity be kept secret.

Mohr teaches philosophy at the University of Illinois (Urbana) and, as an intellectual presence in North America, has been instrumental in bringing gay issues out of the closet.

Reading Questions

1. Is the only natural form of sexual activity procreative in nature and intent? If so, is everything else that is sexual disgusting as well?

2. Do you think that a person's sexual orientation is something he or she chooses? If so, how would he or she go about making this choice?

3. If heterosexuals don't have to keep their orientation or the fact that they practice heterosexual sex a secret, why should we impose these requirements on homosexuals?

But Aren't They Unnatural?

THE MOST NOTEWORTHY FEATURE of the accusation of something being unnatural (where a moral rather than an advertising point is being made) is that the plaint is being made so infrequently. One used to hear the charge leveled against abortion, but it has dropped from public discourse as anti-abortionists have come to lay their chips on the hope that people in general will come to view abortion as murder. Incest used to be considered unnatural but discourse now usually assimilates it to the moral machinery of rape and violated trust. The charge comes up now in ordinary discourse only against homosexuality. This social pattern suggests that the charge is highly idiosyncratic and has little, if any, explanatory force. It fails to put homosexuality in a class with anything else so that one can learn by comparison with clear cases of the class just what exactly it is that is allegedly wrong with it. Nor is homosexuality even a paradigm case for a class of unnatural acts. In popular morality, the charge that homosexuality is immoral because unnatural appeals to a principle so narrow as to be arbitrary.

What the charge of unnaturalness lacks in moral content is compensated for by the emotional thrust with which it is delivered. In ordinary discourse, when the accusation of unnaturalness is applied to homosexuality, it is usually delivered with venom of forethought. It carries a high emotional charge, usually expressing disgust and evincing queasiness.[1] Probably it has no content other than its expression of emotional aversion. For people get equally disgusted and queasy at all sorts of things that are perfectly natural—to be expected in nature apart from artifice—and that could hardly be fit subjects for moral condemnation. Two examples from current American culture are some people's responses to mothers suckling in public and to women who do not shave body hair. When people have strong emotional reactions, as they do in these cases, without being able to give good reasons for the reactions, one thinks of them not as operating morally and certainly not as grounding a morality for others, but rather as being obsessed and manic. So the feelings of disgust that some people have to gays will hardly ground a charge of immorality. People fling the term "unnatural" against gays in the same breath and with the same force as calling gays "sick" and "gross," and when they do this, they give every appearance of being neurotically fearful, while at the same time violating the moral principle that one needs justifying reasons for moral beliefs.

When "nature" is taken in *technical* rather than ordinary usages, it looks like the notion also will not ground a charge of homosexual immorality. When unnatural means "by artifice" or "made by man," one need only point out that virtually everything that is good about life is unnatural in this sense, that one feature that distinguishes people from most other animals is people's ability to make over the world to meet their needs and desires, and that people's well-being depends upon these departures from nature. On this understanding of the natural and people's nature, homosexuality is perfectly unobjectionable.

Another technical sense of natural is that something is natural, and so good, if it fulfills some function in nature. Homosexuality in this view is unnatural because it allegedly violates the function of genitals, which is to produce babies. One problem with this view is that lots of bodily parts have lots of functions and just because some one activity can be fulfilled by only one organ (say, the mouth for eating) this activity does not condemn other functions of the organ to immorality (say, the mouth for talking, licking stamps, blowing bubbles, or having sex). So the possible use of the genitals to produce children does not, without more, condemn the use of the genitals for other purposes, say, achieving ecstasy and intimacy.

The functional view of nature will provide a morally condemnatory sense to the unnatural only if a thing which might have many uses has but one proper function to the exclusion of all other possible functions. But whether this is so cannot be established simply by looking at the thing. For what is seen is all its possible functions: "it's a stamp-licker," "no, its a talker," "no, it's a bubble-blower," "no, it's a sex organ." It was thought that the notion of function might ground moral authority, but instead it turns out that moral authority is needed to define proper function.

Some people try to fill in this moral authority by appeal to the "design" or "order" of an organ, saying, for instance, that the genitals are designed for the purpose of procreation. But these people intellectually cheat if they fail to make explicit *who* the designer and orderer is. If it is God, the discussion is back to square one—they are holding others accountable for religious beliefs.

Further, ordinary moral attitudes about child-rearing will not provide the needed supplement which in conjunction with the natural-function view of bodily parts would produce a positive obligation to use the genitals for procreation. Society's attitude toward a childless couple is that of pity, not censure—even if the couple could have children. The pity may be an unsympathetic one—that is, not registering a course one would choose *for oneself*—but this does not make it a course one would *require* of others. The couple who discovers they cannot have children are viewed not as having thereby had a debt canceled, but rather as having to forgo some of the richness of life, just as a quadriplegic is not viewed as absolved from some moral obligation to hop, skip, and jump, but is viewed as missing some of the richness of life. Consistency requires, then, that, at most, gays who do not or cannot have children are to be pitied rather than condemned. What *is* immoral is the willful preventing of people from achieving the richness of life. Immorality in this regard lies with those social customs, regulations, and statutes that prevent lesbians and gay men from establishing blood or adoptive families, not with gays themselves.

Sometimes people attempt to establish authority for a moral obligation to use certain bodily parts in only one way simply by claiming that moral laws are natural laws and vice versa. On this account, inanimate objects and plants are good in that they follow natural laws by necessity, animals by instinct, and persons by a rational will. People are special in that they must first discover the laws that govern the species. Now, even if one believes the view—dubious in the post-Newtonian, post-Darwinian world—that natural laws in the usual sense ($e=mc^2$, for instance) have some moral content, it is not at all clear how one is to discover the laws in nature that apply to people.

If, on the one hand, one looks to people themselves for a model—and looks hard enough—one finds amazing variety, including homosexual behavior as a social ideal (upper-class fifth-century B.C. Athenians) and even as socially mandatory (Melanesia today). When one looks to people, one is simply unable to strip away the layers of social custom, history, and taboo in order to see what's really there to any degree more specific than that people are the creatures which make over their world and are capable of abstract thought.

Most people, though, do not even try to see *what's there* but instead simply and by default end up projecting the peculiarities of their culture into the universe as cosmic principles. Anthropology has shown that each and every society—however much it may differ from the next—thinks that its own central norms are dictated by and conform with nature writ large.[2] That this is so should raise doubts that neutral principles are to be found in man's nature that will condemn homosexuality.[3] Man may very well be, as Hannah Arendt claimed, the creature whose nature it is to have no nature. It is by virtue of this human condition that people can be creative and make moral progress.

On the other hand, if for models one looks to nature apart from people, the possibilities are staggering. There are fish that change gender over their lifetimes: should people "follow nature" and be operative transsexuals? Orangutans, genetically our next of kin, live completely solitary lives without social organization of any kind: ought people to "follow nature" and be hermits? There are many species where only two members

per generation reproduce: shall we be bees? The search in nature for people's purpose, far from finding sure models for action, is likely to leave people morally rudderless.[4]

But Aren't Gays Willfully the Way They Are?

It is generally conceded that if sexual orientation is something over which an individual—for whatever reason—has virtually no control, then discrimination against gays is deplorable, as it is against racial and ethnic classes, because it holds people accountable without regard for anything they themselves have done. And to hold a person accountable for that over which the person has no control is a central form of prejudice. . . .

On the one hand, the "choice" of the gender of a sexual partner does not seem to express a trivial desire which might as easily be fulfilled by a simple substitution of the desired object: picking the gender of a sex partner is decidedly dissimilar to picking a flavor of ice cream. If an ice-cream parlor is out of one's flavor, one simply picks another. And if people were persecuted, threatened with jail terms, shattered careers, loss of family and housing, exposed to fatal disease and the like for eating, say, rocky road ice cream, no one would ever eat it; everyone would pick another easily available flavor. But gay sex seems not to be like that. If sexual orientation were an easy choice, Kinsey's statistics on the incidence of homosexuality in America, issued as they were when gay sex was everywhere a felony, would not have been shocking—they would simply have been preposterous, utterly unbelievable, virtually self-refuting.

On the other hand, even if establishing a sexual orientation is not like making a relatively trivial choice, perhaps it is like making the central and serious life-choices by which individuals try to establish themselves as being of some type. Again, if one examines gay experience, this seems not to be the case. For one never sees anyone setting out to become a homosexual, in the way one does see people setting out to become doctors, lawyers, and bricklayers. One does not find gays-to-be picking some end—"At some point in the future, I want to become a homosexual"—and then set about planning and acquiring the ways and means to that end, in the way one does see people deciding that they want to become lawyers, and then sees them plan what courses to take and what sort of temperaments, habits, and skills to develop in order to become lawyers.

The gay experience is quite different. Typically, gay persons-to-be simply find themselves having homosexual encounters and yet at least initially resisting quite strongly the identification of being a homosexual. Such a person even very likely resists having such encounters, but ends up having them anyway. Only with time, luck, and great personal effort does the person gradually come, if she does, to accept her orientation, to view it as a given material condition of life, coming as materials do with certain capacities and limitations. The person then begins to act in accordance with her orientation and its capacities, seeing its actualization as a requisite for an integrated personality and as a central component of personal well-being. As a result, the experience of coming out *to oneself* has for gays the basic structure of a discovery, not the structure of a choice. Far from signaling immorality, the coming out process affords one of the few remaining opportunities in ever more bureaucratic, mechanistic, and socialistic societies to manifest courage. . . .

That gays do take responsibility for sexuality and come out—virtually always in isolation and even into conditions of pervasive and imminent oppression—is a sign of the indomitability of the *individual* human spirit and a justification for viewing the individual as the proper locus of value in society. . . .

NOTES

1. I have suggested elsewhere that it is the narrowing of the scope of unnaturalness as an accusation in ordinary morality taken together with people's highly emotional response to homosexuality that explains why the Catholic Church has recently pulled out all the stops in its opposition to gays. Since the thirteenth century, naturalness had been the ethical engine of Catholic doctrine. If strong popular objections to homosexuality were allowed to fade, Catholic doctrine would lose any link with ordinary morality and so would, as a mode of thought, become no more than an intellectual oddity of, at most, historical interest. See Richard Mohr, "Why the Catholic Church Can't Give Up Its Antigay Position," *The Advocate*, January 20, 1987, no. 464, p. 9, criticizing *Doctrinal Congregation's Letter to Bishops: The Pastoral Care of Homosexual Persons* (Rome, October 1, 1986). The Vatican's English translation of its pastoral letter is published in full in *Origins: NC Documentary Service* (1986) 16(22): 377–82.

2. For striking examples of a culture incorporating homosexuality into its cosmology, see Walter L. Williams, *The Spirit and the Flesh: Sexual Diversity in American Indian Culture* (Boston: Beacon, 1986), pp. 18–22.

3. The British philosopher John M. Finnis has offered a somewhat more sophisticated account of unnaturalness as a ground for considering homosexuality immoral, in "Natural Law and Unnatural Acts," *Heythrop Journal* (1970) 11:365–87. He holds that nature contains a fixed constellation of basic values, which are heterogeneous in such ways that a person cannot in his or her actions maximize them. Immorality consists therefore not in failing to maximize instantiations of the values, but in knowingly "turning away" from any one of them. These values are knowledge, beauty, play, friendship, practical reasonableness, religion and life—or its production. Homosexual acts are therefore supposed to be unnatural and immoral as a turning away from the production of life. Even assuming that this is a coherent position, it has two problems.

First, it is not clear that these values, any or all, are in fact what one would legitimately call *moral* values, that is, values which one might legitimately impose upon others (if not through law, at least through private censure). Indeed, at least the bulk of these values look like goods which are not the concern of anyone or any group other than the individual who does or does not act in accordance with them. If I turn from my contemplation of a beautiful sunset or of dynamic recursion theory to watch an unbeautiful, unintelligent television program, it is a personal failing—not one for which others may legitimately chide or shame, let alone, arrest me. Finnis' values do not have enough oomph, enough *Schwung*, to generate a public morality.

If he claims there is no difference between public and private morality, he will simply have revised our understanding of morality beyond recognition.

Second, it cannot convincingly be claimed that homosexual acts are a turning away from (the production of) life. Finnis has to hold that homosexual acts are like the use of contraceptives, where the use of a condom or the pill or a diaphragm is a conscious, planned attempt to interrupt a course of action that would otherwise likely produce human life. But homosexual acts entail no conscious or even unconscious attempt to interrupt what would otherwise produce human life—any more so than does eating a sandwich or reading a book. The argument could go through only if it had a hidden premise that sex can legitimately exist only for the sake of reproduction, so that homosexuality must be at least a subconscious turning away from what sex is for. But this premise simply collapses the theory back into older, unacceptable forms of natural law ethics.

4. For homosexuality among nonhuman animals, see R. H. Denniston, "Ambisexuality in Animals," in Judd Marmor, ed., *Homosexual Behavior: A Modern Reappraisal*, pp. 25–40 (New York: Basic Books, 1980).

VII.5B   Sex and Cultural Privacy

RICHARD MOHR

Sex and Cultural Privacy

THE CONTOURS OF PRIVACY, in some of its forms, are culturally defined. In all societies there are obligations flowing from customs and mores to keep some activities, possessions, thoughts, and things out of the public eye. These obligations vary widely from culture to culture. In some Muslim countries women have an obligation to veil their faces in public, yet among the North African Tuaureg Muslims only men have such an obligation.[1] In some Inuit tribes, one's name, like the third name of Eliot's cats, is private.[2] Now, some of these diverse privacy customs strike Americans as quaint, silly, or impractical. Others produce horror. That Vietnamese villagers defecate virtually anywhere led many American servicemen to rationalize that the Vietnamese are subhuman.[3]

Some privacy obligations vary widely over time within a culture. Customs, for instance, restricting eating in public have radically liberalized within one generation of Americans, while illness, deaths, and perhaps births are becoming increasingly private matters here.[4] And while colleagues would never dare read what one was composing at a typewriter, they consider what appears on one's wordprocessor screen as public as advertisements on billboards.[5]

Some privacy obligations, however, are nearly universal. Sexual privacy falls into this category, though in many societies this privacy is sought out *not* in the home but in the wild: "[T]he sexual act is usually performed outside, so that privacy can be obtained, in bush, field, forest, or [on a] beach."[6] Mandatory privacy holds true of homosexual as well as heterosexual behavior. Among the "Sambia" of Papua New Guinea, compulsory homosexual behavior is integral to the rites of male maturity and is embedded in a corresponding sexual theology and ideological biology. Yet the mandated homosexual acts are carried out strictly in private—indeed in secret from women.[7] It is not surprising that those states of the United States which have decriminalized and socially tolerate homosexual acts nevertheless do not allow them to scare the horses.

Now, across the range of actions for which there is an *obligation* to privacy, that very obligation generates, in turn, a *right* to privacy. For society cannot consistently claim that these activities must be carried out in private (despite their sometimes manifest public consequences, like population growth) and yet retain a claim to investigate such activity and so, to that extent, make it public behavior. Where there is an unconditional requirement to keep some activity out of the public eye, the activity sufficiently fulfills the requirements of privacy when privacy means that nobody may rightfully spy on an activity.[8]

This right not to be spied on holds all the more strongly where the would-be investigator is the police—acting as a representative of the moral will of society as a whole. The investigation of the act by the police violates any obligation to privacy completely, for it exposes the act to the public as a whole, not only through the publicity of arrest and trial but also simply through the police's role as moral representative of society. To cast the point in constitutional terms, the searching out of socially mandated private behavior causes the search to be unreasonable. The search is irrational because it entails a contradiction: that its object be both hidden and public—made hidden by social demand and public by society's agents.

It makes no difference here whether the behavior itself is socially approved or not. The obligation to privacy cuts across both what is socially condemned—most of the seven deadly sins—and what has society's highest commendation—heterosexual intercourse with benefit of clergy for procreation. To say that something ought not to occur at all is not to say that it ought not to be carried out in private when it does occur. In society's judgement, homosexuality is an evil of this sort. Now not all evils ought to be practiced in private if practiced at all. Murders, rapes, and child abuse, if they must occur, would be better to take place in public—to facilitate arrest. But the plaint from conservative quarters that gays objectionably "flaunt" themselves would have no

force if this were the sort of evil involved. So, in general, the argument here does not presuppose tolerance, let alone acceptance of gays, nor does it beg the question by presuming that gay acts are already legal. Disgust will do. So when gay sex does occur in private, it cannot be rightfully spied on—especially by the police.[9]

Some gay activists have opposed appeals to privacy as the mainstay of gay rights strategies: privacy, especially enforced privacy, is the closet. They claim that what is needed is not gay privacy but gay publicity—to break through the silence and taboos surrounding gay issues and to confront people's unsubstantiated fears of gays.[10]

Now admittedly access to the public is necessary if gays are to make any progress toward social acceptance and in the rough-and-tumble of electoral politics.[11] But here is a case where the activist can have her cake and eat it too. Both gay privacy and gay publicity ought to be and can be protected. The two are not mutually exclusive *even* on an analysis that derives privacy rights in part from privacy obligations—for two reasons.

First, even a rough distinction drawn between privacy and secrecy will allow for publicity, since not all that needs to be private needs to be secret. Second, society can be held accountable to act consistently in its requirements for both privacy and secrecy.

At least in the realm of the sexual, the privacy that society can consistently require applies to specific acts and not to patterns of behavior or to the telltale signs of specific acts. Required privacy applies consistently to tokens of action rather than types. It is specific sexual performances that are to be kept from the public eye—no scaring the horses. But no one supposes that a conspicuously pregnant woman out in public has somehow violated the requirement of sexual privacy that society places over sexual performances, though everyone can make the simple inference that she has had sex. One can infer that (rape and artificial insemination aside) she's that type of person who engages in heterosexual behavior. Similarly, no one supposes that heterosexual couples who wear wedding rings or who take their offspring for walks in parks have violated the obligation to privacy surrounding sex acts, even though the rings publicly commit them to having had sex—the consummation of marriage—as do usually the children, and so all collectively suggest a pattern of heterosexual behavior. It's no secret what type of people we have here. Correspondingly, gays should resist any requirement that makes a secret of what type of people they are.

It is completely coherent to be nonsecretive about what is obliged to be private. It is indiscreet among acquaintances who have not developed some level of trust to ask after the other's religion, though either may offer that information in appropriate contexts. Similarly, while it is indiscreet for someone to ask another whether he had sex last night, the latter may proffer this information if it is apposite to the conversation. Secrets are essentially reports rather than sensations.

Thus generally, an obligation to *privacy*, an obligation to shield specific acts from the vision and hearing of nonparticipants, does not entail a requirement of *secrecy* about the acts—and vice versa. For there can be secrets about things that are perfectly public, like the king's new clothes. Keeping a secret means only living by an obligation not to report some information, but does not entail that one is prevented from having the sensation or experience which might be reported or even that the sensation or experience be kept out of sight.

Now, there is in current society a general requirement of secrecy covering gay behavior patterns and sexual types. (That is why there are no gay characters in comic strips and television advertisements and the like.) But once one passes into the realm of information, reportage, and opinion, one is in the realm of protected free speech rights. Both the general utility of the free flow of information in society and the right of people to speak their minds outstrip quickly any merely conventional obligation to secrecy.[12]

In any case, the enforced secrecy and mandated discreetness surrounding many sex-related matters are often themselves perfectly objectionable, when, for instance, they serve as sources of stigma against whole classes of people. Such current taboos surrounding menstruation, for example, bring home to women that, in society's view, what makes them different from men makes them—in the long shadow of Leviticus—dirty, unwholesome, and inferior.[13] For gays, the taboos mark them as unspeakably gross and disgusting—like shit.

Further, the obligation to secrecy is radically inequitable in its application against gays. Sometimes the inequity is blatant, as when only signs of heterosexual behavior are socially or legally allowed, like public kissing. Sometimes it is more subtle, as when seemingly neutral pressures not to talk of *any* sexual matters have a radically disparate impact against gays. Since social institutions are already tooled to promote heterosexuality, any general bar to discussing sexual matters simply further entrenches the dominant culture. Pseudo-liberal school boards that claim they do not want any teachers' sexual orientation—gay or not—to be known to students and so fire openly gay teachers for allegedly flaunting themselves are simply being disingenuous in theory—and inconsistent in practice. At least, history has yet to record a case of wedding rings causing teachers to be fired by such school boards for flaunting heterosexuality. The gay activist then might well adopt as a slogan: "privacy yes, secrecy no."

NOTES

1. See Robert Murphy, "Social Distance and the Veil," in Schoeman, ed., *Philosophical Dimensions of Privacy*, pp. 34–55. (Cambridge: Cambridge University Press, 1984).

2. See Alan Westin, "The Origins of Modern Claims to Privacy," in Schoeman, ed., *Philosophical Dimensions of Privacy*, p. 73 n. 57.

3. See Charles Nelson, *The Boy Who Picked the Bullets Up* (New York: Morrow, 1981); cf. Westin, *ibid.*, p. 62.

4. Westin, "The Origins of Modern Claims to Privacy."

5. For eye-opening examples of cultural variation in privacy customs, see, for example, Ibid., pp. 56–74.

6. *Ibid.*, p. 63.

7. Gilbert Herdt, *Guardians of the Flutes: Idioms of Masculinity* (New York: McGraw-Hill, 1981), pp. 232–39, 284–88. See generally, Gilbert Herdt, ed., *Ritualized Homosexuality in Melanesia* (Berkeley: University of California Press, 1984) and Walter Williams, *The Spirit and the Flesh: Sexual Diversity in American Indian Culture* (Boston: Beacon, 1986), pp. 252–75. Williams provides an eye-opening international survey of historical and anthropological findings of socially endorsed, institutionalized forms of homosexuality.

8. If the obligation to privacy is conditioned by an additional requirement of full disclosure through reports (say, in the form of records, affidavits, or videos), then the obligation does not automatically trigger the right. For, in that case, if one fails to provide the reports, then one may be investigated. But the obligation to keep sexual activity private, especially gay sex, is not so qualified. People don't want to see it and especially don't want to hear about it.

9. Does this analysis of obligation-engendered privacy rights void income taxes, as at first blush it might appear to do? *Knowledge* of personal wealth and income in contemporary American society is considered a private matter in *certain* dimensions. There is a social obligation not *to ask* another person about his wealth and income, but there is no obligation on him to keep such knowledge private, at least not a very strong one. A person is permitted to say what her income is. The search for knowledge about wealth and income for tax purposes, then, is not irrational and contradictory. Society is not saying, "You may not tell us your income and yet you must tell us your income." The case would be different if there were a social obligation to keep one's wealth itself private—as is the case, for instance, among the timocrats of Plato's *Republic,* for whom conspicuous wealth is a source of shame,

not honor. But for here and now, one need, for tax purposes, only overcome the social presumption against *asking* after wealth and income. In this case, state and society will be relevantly different. Here the state is not functioning as the representative of the populace. Rather, it is fulfilling a role which is specific to the state as state and which is not appropriate for individuals to fulfill, just as criminal arrest procedures are not "representative" of vigilantism, but serve a different function—the administration of justice. The state is not simply efficiently pinch-hitting for the populace as a whole; it is fulfilling a uniquely governmental function, as when at trials the state compels testimony —even that touching on (some) private matters. Nevertheless, society has gone out of its way to protect the private knowledge of income, by narrowly drafting tax procedures and indeed largely relying on voluntary compliance. How much greater then ought the presumption of protections for privacy be in cases where there is an actual obligation to it—as in sexual behavior?

10. See, for example, Marilyn Frye, *The Politics of Reality: Essays in Feminist Theory* (Trumansburg, N.Y.: The Crossing Press, 1983), pp. 152–74; Lisa Bloom, "We are all Part of One Another: Sodomy Laws and Morality on Both Sides of the Atlantic," *New York University Review of Law and Social Change* (1986) 14:1011–16. Bloom calls for the abandonment of a "rights-based legal model" which focuses on individuals' privacy in favor of "the feminist morality model of mutual concern and social cohesion." (p. 1015).

11. See chapter 6, section III.

12. *Carey v. Population Services Int'l,* 431 U.S. 678, 700–2 (1977) (offense and embarrassment held illegitimate grounds for banning display and advertisement of contraceptives).

13. Leviticus 15:19–27.

Further Questions

1. Many bodily parts can perform more than one type of action. If you believe that just one action is a part's natural "function," how would you go about showing this?

2. Have you had the experience of discovering that you wanted something very badly or believed something very deeply by noticing a pattern in the kinds of things you chose to do? If so, does it make sense for people to discover their sexual orientations in this way?

3. Is society oppressive to individuals when it forbids them publicly to reveal certain salient facts about themselves?

VII.6   Lesbian "Sex"

MARILYN FRYE

Marilyn Frye gives a candid account of her understanding of lesbian "sex," much of which applies to women's sexuality more generally. Since women's sexual experience has been relatively neglected, they have no vocabulary in which to talk about, or think through, their sexual experiences.

Frye teaches philosophy and feminist theory at Michigan State University. Her writings are based directly on her life as a woman and lesbian. Other selections by Marilyn Frye appear in Parts I and IV.

Reading Questions

1. If you are a woman (and perhaps, a lesbian) how would you count the number of "times" you have had sex?

2. Is it discouraging to learn that each sexual experience of a long-term married heterosexual couple is, on average, about eight minutes long?

3. Would heterosexual women profit by doing what Frye suggests for lesbians: discussing what we like in the area of sex in the context of a more general discussion of our favorite sorts of experience? Would men also learn something from this kind of discussion with each other?

THE REASONS THE WORD "SEX" is in quotation marks in my title are two: one is that the term "sex" is an inappropriate term for what lesbians do, and the other is that whatever it is that lesbians do that (for a lack of a better word) might be called "sex" we apparently do damned little of it. For a great many lesbians, the gap between the high hopes we had some time ago for lesbian sex and the way things have worked out has turned the phrase "lesbian sex" into something of a bitter joke. I don't want to exaggerate this: things aren't so bad for all lesbians, or all of the time.

But in our communities* as a whole, there is much grumbling on the subject. It seems worthwhile to explore some of the meanings of the

* When I speak of "we" and "our communities," I actually don't know exactly who that is. I know only that I and my lover are not the only ones whose concerns I address, and that similar issues are being discussed in friendship circles and communities other than ours (as witness, e.g., discussion in the pages of the *Lesbian Connection*). If what I say here resonates for you, so be it. If not, at least you can know it resonates for some range of lesbians and some of them probably are your friends or acquaintances.

Reprinted from Lesbian Philosophies, *Jeffner Allen, Ed., (Albany, NY: State University of New York Press, 1990).*

relative dearth of what (for lack of a better word) we call lesbian "sex."

Recent discussions of lesbian "sex" frequently cite the finding of a study on couples by Blumstein and Schwartz,[1] which is perceived by most of those who discuss it as having been done well, with a good sample of couples—lesbian, male homosexual, heterosexual non-married and heterosexual married couples. These people apparently found that lesbian couples "have sex" far less frequently than any other type of couple, that lesbian couples are less "sexual" as couples and as individuals than anyone else. In their sample, only about one-third of lesbians in relationships of two years or longer "had sex" once a week or more; 47% of lesbians in long-term relationships "had sex" once a month or less, while among heterosexual married couples only 15% had sex once a month or less. And they report that lesbians seem to be more limited in the range of their "sexual" techniques than are other couples.

When this sort of information first came into my circle of lesbian friends, we tended to see it as conforming to what we know from our own experience. But on reflection, looking again at what has been going on with us in our long-term relationship, the nice fit between this report and our experience seemed not so perfect after all.

It was brought to our attention during our ruminations on this that what 85% of long-term heterosexual married couples do more than once a month takes on the average 8 minutes to do.[2]

Although in my experience lesbians discuss their "sex" lives with each other relatively little (a point to which I will return), I know from my own experience and from the reports of a few other lesbians in long-term relationships, that what we do that, on average, we do considerably less frequently, takes, on average, considerably more than 8 minutes to do. It takes about 30 minutes, at the least. Sometimes maybe an hour. And it is not uncommon that among these relatively uncommon occurrences, an entire afternoon or evening is given over to activities organized around doing it. The suspicion arises that what 85% of heterosexual married couples are doing more than once a month and what 47% of lesbian couples are doing less than once a month is not the same thing.

I remember that one of my first delicious tastes of old gay lesbian culture occurred in a bar where I was getting acquainted with some new friends. One was talking about being busted out of the Marines for being gay. She had been put under suspicion somehow, and was sent off to the base psychiatrist to be questioned, her perverted tendencies to be assessed. He wanted to convince her she had only been engaged in a little youthful experimentation and wasn't really gay. To this end, he questioned her about the extent of her experience. What he asked was, "How many times have you had sex with a woman?" At this, we all laughed and giggled: what an ignorant fool. What does he think he means, "times?" What will we count? What's to *count?*

Another of my friends, years later, discussing the same conundrum, said that she thought maybe every time you got up to go to the bathroom, that marked a "time." The joke about "how many times" is still good for a chuckle from time to time in my life with my lover. I have no memory of any such topic providing any such merriment in my years of sexual encounters and relationships with men. It would have been very rare indeed that we would not have known how to answer the question "How many times did you do it?"

If what heterosexual married couples do that the individuals report under the rubric "sex" or "have sex" or "have sexual relations" is something that in most instances can easily be individuated into countable instances, this is more evidence that it is not what long-term lesbian couples do . . . or, for that matter, what short-term lesbian couples do.

What violence did the lesbians do their experience by answering the same question the heterosexuals answered, as though it had the same meaning for them? How did the lesbians figure out how to answer the questions "How frequently?" or "How many times?" My guess is that different individuals figured it out differently. Some might have counted a two- or three-cycle evening as one "time" they "had sex"; some might have counted it as two or three "times." Some may have counted as "times" only the times both partners had orgasms; some may have counted as "times" occasions on which at least one had an orgasm; those who do not have orgasms or have them far more rarely than they "have sex" may not have figured orgasms into the calculations; perhaps some counted as a "time" every episode in which both touched the other's vulva more than fleetingly and not for something like a health examination. For some, to count every reciprocal touch of the vulva would have made them count as "having sex" more than most people with a job or a work would dream of having time for; how do we suppose those individuals counted "times?" Is there any good reason why they should *not* count all those as "times?" Does it depend on how fulfilling it was? Was anybody else counting by occasions of fulfillment?

We have no idea how the individual lesbians surveyed were counting their "sexual acts." But this also raises the questions of how heterosexuals counted *their* sexual acts. By orgasms? By *whose* orgasms? If the havings of sex by heterosexual married couples did take on the average 8 minutes, my guess is that in a very large number of those cases the women did not experience orgasms. My guess is that neither the women's pleasure nor the women's orgasms were pertinent in most of the individuals' counting and reporting the frequency with which they "had sex."

So, do lesbian couples really "have sex" any less frequently than heterosexual couples? I'd say that lesbian couples "have sex" a great deal less frequently than heterosexual couples: by the criteria that I'm betting most of the heterosexual people used to count "times," lesbians don't have sex at all. No male orgasms, no "times." (I'm willing to draw the conclusion that heterosexual women don't have sex either; that what they report is the frequency with which their partners had sex.)

It has been said before by feminists that the concept of "having sex" is a phallic concept; that it pertains to heterosexual intercourse, in fact, primarily to heterosex*ist* intercourse, i.e., male-dominant-female-subordinate-copulation-whose-completion-and-purpose-is-the-male's-ejaculation. I have thought this was true since the first time the idea was put to me, some 12 years ago.[3] But I have been finding lately that I have to go back over some of the ground I covered a decade ago because some of what I knew then I knew too superficially. For some of us, myself included, the move from heterosexual relating to lesbian relating was occasioned or speeded up or brought to closure by our knowledge that what we had done under the heading "having sex" was indeed male-dominant-female-subordination-copulation-whose-completion . . . etc. and it was not worthy of doing. Yet now, years later, we are willing to answer questionnaires that ask us how frequently we "have sex," and are dissatisfied with ourselves and with our relationships because we don't "have sex" enough. We are so dissatisfied that we keep a small army of therapists in business trying to help us "have sex" more.

We quit having sex years ago, and for excellent and compelling reasons. What exactly is our complaint now?

In all these years I've been doing and writing feminist theory, I have not until very recently written, much less published, a word about sex. I did not write, though it was suggested to me that I do so, anything in the SM debates; I left entirely unanswered an invitation to be the keynote speaker at a feminist conference about women's sexuality (which by all reports turned out to be an excellent conference). I was quite unable to think of anything but vague truisms to say, and very few of those. Feminist theory is grounded in experience; I have always written feminist political and philosophical analysis from the bottom up, starting with my own encounters and adventures, frustrations, pain, anger, delight, etc. Sometimes this has no doubt made it a little provincial; but it has at least had the virtue of firm connection with *someone's* real, live experience (which is more than you can say for a lot of theory). When I put to myself the task of theorizing about sex and sexuality, it was as though I *had* no experience, as though there was no ground on which and from which to generate theory. But (if I understand the terminology rightly), I have in fact been what they call "sexually active" for close to a quarter of a century, about half my life, almost all of what they call one's "adult life," heterosexually, lesbianly and autoerotically. Surely I have experience. But I seem not to have *experiential knowledge* of the sort I need.

Reflecting on all that history, I realize that in many of its passages this experience has been a muddle. Acting, being acted on, choosing, desiring, pleasure and displeasure all akimbo: not coherently determining and connecting with each other. Even in its greatest intensity it has for the most part been somehow rather opaque to me, not fully in my grasp. My "experience" has in general the character more of a buzzing blooming confusion than of *experience*. And it has occurred in the midst of almost total silence on the part of others about their experience. The experience of others has for the most part also been opaque to me; they do not discuss or describe it *in detail* at all.

I recall an hours-long and heated argument among some eight or ten lesbians at a party a couple of years ago about SM, whether it is okay, or not. When Carolyn and I left, we realized that in the whole time not one woman had said one concrete, explicit, physiologically specific thing about what she actually *did*. The one arguing in favor of bondage: did she have her hands tied gently with ribbons or scarves, or harshly with handcuffs or chains? What other parts of her body were or weren't restrained, and by what means? And what parts of her body were touched, and how, while she was bound? And what liberty did she still have to touch in return? And if she had no such liberty, was it part of her experience to want

that liberty and tension or frustration, or was it her experience that she felt pleased or satisfied not to have that liberty . . . ? Who knows? She never said a single word at this level of specificity. Nor did anyone else, pro or con.

I once perused a large and extensively illustrated book on sexual activity by and for homosexual men. It was astounding to me for one thing in particular, namely, that its pages constituted a huge lexicon of *words*: words for acts and activities, their sub-acts, preludes and denouements, their stylistic variation, their sequences. Gay male sex, I realized then, is *articulate*. It is articulate to a degree that, in my world, lesbian "sex" does not remotely approach. Lesbian "sex" as I have known it, most of the time I have known it, is utterly *in*articulate. Most of my lifetime, most of my experience in the realms commonly designated as "sexual" has been prelinguistic, non-cognitive. I have, in effect, no linguistic community, no language, and therefore in one important sense, no knowledge.

In situations of male dominance, women are for the most part excluded from the formulation and validation of meaning and thereby denied the means to express themselves. Men's meanings, and no women's meanings, are encoded in what is presumed to be the whole population's language. (In many cases, both the men and women assume it is everyone's language.) The meanings one's life and experience might generate cannot come fully into operation if they are not woven into language: they are fleeting, or they hover, vague, not fully coalesced, not connected, and hence not *useful* for explaining or grounding interpretations, desires, complaints, theories. In response to our understanding that there is something going on in patriarchy that is more or less well described by saying women's meanings are not encoded in the dominant languages and that this keeps our experience from being fully formed and articulate, we have undertaken quite deliberately to discover, complete, and encode our meanings. Such simple things as naming chivalrous gestures "insulting," naming

Virginia Woolf a great writer, naming ourselves women instead of girls or ladies. Coining terms like "sexism," "sexual harassment," and "incestor." Mary Daly's new book is a whose project of "encoding" meanings, and we can all find examples of our own more local encodings.*

Meanings should arise from our bodily self-knowledge, bodily play, tactile communication, the ebb and flow of intense excitement, arousal, tension, release, comfort, discomfort, pain and pleasure (and I make no distinctions here among bodily, emotional, intellectual, aesthetic). But such potential meanings are more amorphous, less coalesced into discrete elements of a coherent pattern of meanings, of an *experience,* than any other dimensions of our lives. In fact, there are for many of us *virtually no meanings* in this realm because nothing of it is crystallized in a linguistic matrix.†

What we have for generic words to cover this terrain are the words "sex," "sexual," and "sexuality." In our efforts to liberate ourselves from the stifling, women-hating, Victorian denial that women even *have* bodily awareness, arousal, excitement, orgasms and so on, many of us actively took these words for ourselves, and claimed that we *do* "do sex" and we *are* sexual and we *have* sexuality. This has been particularly important to lesbians because the very fact of "sex" being a phallocentric term has made it especially difficult to get across the idea that lesbians are not, for lack of a penis between us, making do with feeble

and partial and pathetic half-satisfactions.‡ But it seems to me that the attempt to encode our lustiness and lustfulness, our passion and our vigorous carnality in the words "sex," "sexual," and "sexuality" has backfired. Instead of losing their phallocentricity, these words have imported the phallocentric meanings into and onto experience which is not in any way phallocentric. A web of meanings which maps emotional intensity, excitement, arousal, bodily play, orgasm, passion and relational adventure back into a semantic center in male-dominant-female-subordinate-copulation-whose-completion-and-purpose-is-the-male's-ejaculation has been so utterly inadequate as to leave us speechless, meaningless, and ironically, according to the Blumstein and Schwartz report, "not as sexual" as couples or as individuals of any other group.

Our lives, the character of our embodiment, *cannot* be mapped back onto that semantic center. When we try to synthesize and articulate it by the rules of that mapping, we end up trying to mold our loving and our passionate carnal intercourse into explosive 8-minute events. That is not the timing and ontology of the lesbian body. When the only things that count as "doing it" are those passages of our interactions which most closely approximate a paradigm that arose from the meanings of the rising and falling penis, no wonder we discover ourselves to "do it" rather less often than do pairs with one or more penises present.

There are many cultural and social-psychological reasons why women (in white Euro-American groups, but also in many other configurations of patriarchy) would generally be somewhat less clear and less assertive about their desires and about getting their satisfactions than men would generally be. And when we pair up two women in a couple, it stands to reason that those reasons would double up and tend to make

---

* I picked up the word "encoding" as it is used here from the novel *Native Tongue,* by Suzette Haden Elgin (NY: Daw Books, Inc., 1984). She envisages women identifying concepts, feelings, types of situations, etc., for which there are no words in English, and giving them intuitively appropriate names in a women-made language called Laadan.

† Carolyn Shafer has theorized that one significant reason why lesbian SM occasioned so much excitement, both positive and negative, is that lesbians have been starved for language—for specific, detailed, literal, particular, bodily talk with clear non-metaphorical references to parts of our bodies and the ways they can be stimulated, to acts, postures, types of touch. Books like *Coming to Power* feed that need, and call forth more words in response.

‡ Asserting the robustness and unladylikeness of our passions and actions, some of us have called some of what we do "fucking."

relationships in which there is a lowish frequency of clearly delineated desires and direct initiations of satisfactions. But for all the help it might be to lesbian bodies to work past the psychological and behavioral habits of femininity that inhibit our passions and pleasures, my suggestion is that what we have never taken seriously enough is the *language* which forecloses our meanings.

My positive recommendation is this: Instead of starting with a point (a point in the life of a body unlike our own) and trying to make meanings along vectors from that point, we would do better to start with a wide field of our passions and bodily pleasures and make meanings that weave a web across it. To begin creating a vocabulary that elaborates and expands our meanings, we should adopt a very wide and general concept of "doing it." Let it be an open, generous, commodious concept encompassing all the acts and activities by which we generate with each other pleasures and thrills, tenderness and ecstasy, passages of passionate carnality of whatever duration or profundity. Everything from vanilla to licorice, from puce to chartreuse, from velvet to ice, from cuddles to cunts, from chortles to tears. Starting from there, we can let our experiences generate a finer-tuned descriptive vocabulary that maps and expresses the differences and distinctions among the things we do, the kinds of pleasures we get, the stages and styles of our acts and activities, the parts of our bodies centrally engaged in the different kinds of "doing it," and so on. I would not, at the outset, assume that all of "doing it" is good or wholesome, nor that everyone would like or even tolerate everything this concept includes; I would not assume that "doing it" either has or should have a particular connection with love, or that it hasn't or shouldn't have

such a connection. As we explain and explore and define our pleasures and our preferences across this expansive and heterogeneous field, teaching each other what the possibilities are and how to navigate them, a vocabulary will arise among us and by our collective creativity.

The vocabulary will arise among us, of course, only if we talk with each other about what we're doing and why, and what it feels like. Language is social. So is "doing it."

I'm hoping it will be a lot easier to talk about what we do, and how and when and why, and in carnal sensual detail, once we've learned to laugh at foolish studies that show that lesbians don't have sex as often as, aren't as sexual as, and use fewer sexual techniques than other folks.

NOTES

This essay first appeared in *Sinister Wisdom,* vol. 35 (Summer/Fall 1988). In its first version, this essay was written for the meeting of the Society for Women in Philosophy, Midwestern Division, November, 1987, at Bloomington, Indiana. It was occasioned by Claudia Card's paper, "Intimacy and Responsibility: What Lesbians Do," (published in the Institute for Legal Studies Working Papers, Series, 2, University of Wisconsin-Madison, Law School, Madison, WI 53706). Carolyn Shafer has contributed a lot to my thinking here, and I am indebted also to conversations with Sue Emmert and Terry Grant.

1. Philip Blumstein and Pepper Schwartz, *American Couples* (NY: William Morrow and Company, 1983).

2. Dotty Calabrese gave this information in her workshop on long-term lesbian relationships at the Michigan Womyn's Music Festival, 1987. (Thanks to Terry for this reference.)

3. By Carolyn Shafer. See pp. 156–7 of my book *The Politics of Reality* (The Crossing Press, 1983).

Further Questions

1. When someone wonders what lesbians "do" in a sexual encounter, is he or she having problems thinking about a sexual situation that contains no penis?

2. Discussions of "having sex" apparently caused a good deal of merriment in Frye's group of lesbians. If you cannot imagine this merriment in an all-male group, is this because men take themselves too seriously in the area of sex?

3. Would men's thinking about sex benefit from hearing about the sexual experiences of women, couched in vocabulary developed by women?

VII.7   Women and AIDS: Too Little, Too Late

NORA KIZER BELL

Nora Kizer Bell discusses the risk of women contracting AIDS through sexual contact. AIDS is, of course, the worst of the sexually transmitted diseases, because it is a virus for which no cure is foreseeable. Of special interest in this writing is the discussion of the pregnant woman infected with AIDS.

Bell is Professor and Chair of the Department of Philosophy, The University of South Carolina (Columbia).

Reading Questions

1. Does someone who has tested positive for HIV virus, or is otherwise in a high risk category (IV drug user, etc.), have an obligation to inform sexual partners about his or her status?

2. Under what circumstances, if any, is condom use not necessary or outweighed by the benefits of *not* using condoms?

3. If a pregnant woman discovers that she is HIV positive, should she have complete freedom of choice about whether to have an abortion?

. . . ALTHOUGH 90 PERCENT of reported AIDS cases continue to occur among homosexual men or intravenous drug users, a 1987 study notes a disproportionate increase in cases of AIDS over the past three years among women who are heterosexual partners of bisexual men (16%) or of intravenous drug users (67%). From 1981 to 1986 reported cases of AIDS in women increased in parallel with cases in men, and although men with AIDS still clearly outnumber women with AIDS, there is one risk category in which women with AIDS outnumber men with AIDS by a significant margin: persons whose *only* risk factor is heterosexual contact with a person at risk (Guinan and Hardy 1987).

The primary mode of transmission of HIV to women discerned by this study was intravenous drug use (52%). However, the second most common route of transmission to women (21%) was heterosexual contact with someone with AIDS. This compares to a mere 1% of nonhomosexual/bisexual men with AIDS who had this risk factor. Of a total of 456 adults with AIDS whose only risk factor was heterosexual contact with someone at risk, 84 percent were women. It is noteworthy that the proportion of women with AIDS in that risk category increased from 12% in 1982 to 26% in 1986 (Guinan and Hardy 1987, 2040).

As Des Jarlais explains, since approximately 75 percent of IV drug users in the United States are males and since fully 95 percent of those males are predominantly heterosexual,

> there simply are not enough female IV drug users for the majority of the group to have their primary sexual relationships with other IV drug users. The number of females who do not inject drugs themselves but are regular sexual partners of IV drug users has been estimated to be at least half as large as the number of IV drug users. These figures indicate that a large number of persons may become infected with the AIDS virus through the IV user without involvement with IV drugs themselves (1988, 3).

Acknowledging the decrease in HIV transmission among homosexual men, and in light of data such as the above, Guinan and Hardy argue that in the United States, at the present time, "a heterosexual woman is at greater risk for acquiring AIDS through sexual intercourse than is a heterosexual man" (1987, 2041). . . .

The increase in the numbers of heterosexually acquired cases of HIV among women is thought to be the result of two factors: (1) because there are more men than women who are infected, women are more likely than men to encounter an infected partner, and (2) it appears that the efficiency of transmission of the virus is greater from man to woman than from woman to man (Guinan and Hardy 1987; Curran and Jaffe 1988). . . .

In spite of the fact that cases of AIDS in women have been documented from the early

stages of the epidemic in this country and elsewhere, their plight and their place in the epidemic received very little attention. Women weren't educated about their risk factors or about the possible risks to the developing fetus; they themselves wanted to avoid the stigma associated with having a "gay" disease (Ledger 1987, 5). Women were, and still are, "omitted from AIDS brochures and media coverage, and eclipsed in medical research" (Murphy 1988, 65). In campaigns promoting safe sex, men weren't reminded of their responsibilities to their *female* sex partners (Patton 1988). Even today few persons are aware that AIDS is now the leading cause of death among women aged 25 to 29 in New York City (Bacon 1987, 6).

Even though anti-gay sentiment generated a response to AIDS that over-shadowed concerns affecting women, attempts to *combat* homophobia have also been disadvantageous to women.[1] Early in the epidemic, it became clear that disclosure of one's seropositivity had devastating psycho-social effects: job and housing discrimination, increased suicide rates, ostracism, termination of women's parental rights, refusal of health care workers to treat, and so on. For that reason, efforts were begun to develop policy that would be responsible to the privacy rights of persons with AIDS. As important as these efforts were, they had the effect of slowing public health efforts to institute partner notification and contact tracing (both public health strategies long acknowledged as effective in combatting the spread of other sexually transmitted diseases).[2] A recognition of the psycho-social effects of a disclosure of one's seropositivity also led (rightfully) to a fear of any form of selective or mandatory testing, thus ruling out premarital or prenatal testing. In truth, it would have made more sense to expend resources on combatting the underlying discrimination that made protections of confidentiality so important. However, even the time required to confront homophobia among policy makers and the public at large has led to an eclipse of the needs of women with AIDS.

Racism, unfortunately, is also implicated in the neglect of issues affecting women. A report from the CDC in October of 1988 indicated that 26 percent of AIDS cases were among blacks and another 15 percent among hispanics (CDC, 1988). In addition, 53 percent of the women with AIDS are black, and approximately 51 percent of them are engaged either in intravenous drug use or prostitution (Murphy 1988, 66; Curran and Jaffe et al, 1988, 611). Researchers report further that while 78 percent of the reported cases of AIDS in children younger than six years old are in children of color, children of color constitute only 21 percent of the nation's population in that age group (Osterholm and MacDonald 1987).

The disparities in the risk for AIDS among blacks and hispanics must be examined within the context of the social fabric in which AIDS infection occurs, and at the core of that fabric one finds the problems of poverty, drug abuse, teen pregnancy, lack of education, inadequate health care and social support services, prostitution, and child and spouse abuse. These social problems are not only deplorable, but as Osterholm and MacDonald point out, they are very complex. For example, while needle-sharing activities continue to be a problem among the urban poor, especially persons of color, the United States continues to lead the industrialized world in rates of teen pregnancy and birth rates. "In particular, the rate of black, never married women aged 15 through 19 years who are sexually active is almost 35% higher than that of white women" (Osterholm and MacDonald 1987, 2737). Because the social and economic realities for women of childbearing age in the inner cities are not easily remedied, the great weight of female and pediatric AIDS will continue to fall on the communities of color, particularly in these urban settings.

The charges of racism and the complexity of class politics cannot be ignored in attempting to understand and combat the effect of AIDS on women, for women with AIDS represent the least advantaged groups in American society. Already disenfranchised, these women lack the means to command the public's attention to their lot. These women are *not* the idealized "victim" woman. They represent yet another segment of society that has traditionally been considered "disposable." As Murphy concludes, "[s]mall wonder, then, that their plight has received so little attention" (1988, 66).

There are, therefore, important ethical issues relating specifically to women with AIDS that remain to be addressed. In the concluding portions of this discussion I propose to enumerate and examine . . . issues related to recommending condom use . . . and issues surrounding birth control and reproduction.

Condom Use and Women

Michael Simpson, in his work on feminist thanatology, has written of the "nearly universal and persistent relationship between women, sex, and danger" (1988, 202). Historically, women have been subject to dangerous sex; "the risks of pregnancy, childbirth, abortion, miscarriage, and the puerperium have limited woman's potential across the centuries" (Simpson 1988, 202). Women have had to be the principal advocates for improved methods of contraception, for male contraception, for legalization of abortion, and so on.

Knowledge of women's social and moral history underlies the anger some women feel about the place given to their role in the AIDS epidemic. It is no wonder that Kaplan argues,

if men and boys find out that women are united in feeling entitled to protection, that *all* women expect men to behave responsibly, and that we *all* insist on making sure that a man is not infected before we will sleep with him; if he knows that he is not going to get the kind of sex he wants unless he proves that he is not infected, then men's behavior will change. When the majority of women insist on safe sex or hold out on sex until they and their partners are ready to commit themselves to an exclusive relationship or marriage, when we stop buying the nonsense that asking him to wear a condom is healthy assertiveness, then men's behavior will change (Kaplan 1988, 82).

Unfortunately, the concepts of "safe sex" and "just say no" (to sex and drugs) portend a blurring of the sex/death boundaries for women. Condom use is touted as a reasonable method for the prevention of HIV transmission during penetrative sex (Freidland and Klein 1987, 1130), and promoting the use of condoms is said to be a "potentially useful" intervention for preventing HIV infection (Quinn, Glasser, et al, 1988, 202). A great deal of the education concerning condom use has been directed at women, and women have been advised to carry their own condoms. Some authors report that women now constitute 70 percent of the condom-buying market (Patton, 1988). Yet researchers discovered in one study that only 3 percent of men and 4 percent of women reported consistent use of condoms.

Unfortunately, many of the recommendations for AIDS education and condom use fail to take the experience of women into account. Male machismo is reported to lead some men to refuse condom use, preferring, in their words, "the greater thrill of unprotected sex" (Zucker, interview, 1988). While the lure and the excitement of the forbidden and the dangerous are familiar themes in literature and in philosophy, sexual intercourse during the AIDS epidemic can be seen to perpetuate the inequality of women's risk in heterosexual relationships.

In some cultural contexts, a woman's acquiescence to sex on demand is both expected and enforced. Hence, for many women, "just saying no" to sex (or to unprotected sex) has turned into a prescription for battering and other forms of abuse (Bacon 1987, 6). Among the women who are most affected by AIDS, the fact that they are still in situations of unequal power has meant that they now face additional obstacles in ensuring their own bodily safety.

Long aware that condom use was *not* recognized as an effective means of birth control,

women are *now* being told that condom use will effectively prevent AIDS transmission. Yet the rate of the condom's failure to protect against pregnancy was measured in a monthly cycle during which most women were fertile only a few days. Women are justifiably concerned that condoms are not a reasonable protection against a disease that can be transmitted every day of the month. Furthermore, many brochures on "safe sex" concentrate on describing ways to make the condom more palatable to the male sexual experience than they do either on ways to ensure the safety of the woman receptor or on sexual practices that are non-penetrative. The many public health messages recommending condom use have conveyed the impression that the male sexual experience is the primary focus. Lisa Bacon notes as well that reliable safe sex information for lesbians is neither widely distributed nor widely known to be available (1987, 6).

The noticeable absence of research efforts to develop better barriers to transmission for women and to publicize alternative methods of expressing one's sexuality is troubling and remains an important issue in the ethics of AIDS. . . .

While many in society express little compassion for the prostitute who acquires AIDS from her customer, few economic alternatives exist for women in prostitution, and even fewer exist for the drug addicted prostitute. A dehumanizing aspect of prostitution is that it is essentially an involuntary form of labor that grows out of the economically disadvantaged position in which women find themselves. Prostitution is a manifestation of a lack of respect for persons, primarily because those who must prostitute themselves have not been accorded the freedom of choice that accompanies being treated fully as a person.[3] In addition, because prostitutes are at the bottom of the heap in all these other ways, they are among those persons who are often least able to organize to protect themselves. It compounds the moral insult to allow women prostitutes to fall prey to HIV infected "johns" and to believe that that is their due. . . .

Birth Control and Reproduction

Women with AIDS pose further complex ethical issues that involve examining both their reproductive options and their obligations in exercising those options. One such issue grows out of the fact that researchers have found that trends in women with AIDS are good predictors of trends in pediatric AIDS cases, especially among mothers in identifiable risk groups (Guinan and Hardy 1987).

In approximately two-thirds (65%) of the pregnancies of women who are infected with the virus, infection is passed on to the infant, and close to 50 percent of those infants will have disease within two years. The outlook for these children is almost certain death (Koop 1987, 4; Ledger 1987, 5; Piot, Plummer, et al. 1988). Furthermore, about two-thirds of pediatric AIDS cases are the result of transmission from infected mother to child[4] (Koop 1987, 4). More importantly, not only women with AIDS, but also women with ARC and women who are asymptomatic carriers of HIV infection have the potential to transmit the virus perinatally.

HIV infection can be passed from mother to infant in three ways: to the fetus *in utero* through fetal-maternal circulation, to the infant during labor and delivery, and to the infant through infected breast milk (Freidland and Klein 1987, 1130; Curran, Jaffe, et al. 1988, 614; Piot, Plummer, et al. 1988, 575).

Further complicating this issue is the fact that AIDS not only adversely affects the child born to an infected mother, it also seems to accelerate the progression of disease in the pregnant woman herself (Murphy 1988, 73). Sadly, for many women, especially those who are culturally and economically deprived, childbearing sometimes provides a sense of self-esteem and is sometimes culturally expected. Hence, many women who have borne an infected child continue to reproduce "despite intensive culturally specific counseling" (Wofsy 1987, 33). A second pregnancy in an HIV infected mother, however, is even more likely to move her into full blown AIDS at the same time that it produces an infected infant (Murphy 1988, 73). A tragic irony of these findings is that oral contraception is also a factor thought to increase a woman's susceptibility to sexually acquired HIV infection (Piot, Plummer, et al. 1988, 575).

In addition to the risk of infection by vaginal intercourse, women undergoing artificial insemination (AI) are in some danger of HIV infection. Although not a widely published fact, there are close to 10,000 AI births per year in the United States (Murphy 1988, 73). This form of transmission is easily eliminable by instituting procedures for testing donor sperm; the ejaculate of first time donors can be frozen and the donor retested for antibody two to three months before the sperm is used (Ledger 1987, 5). Such testing would continue to ensure that AI remains a legitimate reproductive option for women while protecting them and their unborn fetuses from HIV infection. . . .

One option, abortion, is itself a volatile issue that promises to "increase the difficulty of dealing with HIV infection in the population of pregnant women" (Osterholm and MacDonald 1987, 2737). Contrary to what many right-to-life advocates might argue, there are quite compelling moral grounds for advocating that an infected woman is justified in aborting a fetus she might be carrying: a prospective mother might be said to have an obligation to any potential child to spare it a certain and gruesome death, a prospective mother might be said to have an obligation to ensure and protect her own health for as long as she can (both for her own sake as well as for the sake of others, including the unborn fetus), and a prospective mother might be said to have an obligation to society not to bear children for whom society may have to provide.

The flip side of that argument, however, might suggest that, in the Black context, for example, a prospective mother could be said to have a responsibility *to bear* her child, even with only a 35% survival possibility, in order to maintain the integrity of the Black community.

However, while I acknowledge the necessity of understanding the political and cultural implications of testing and of counseling HIV infected women against reproducing, I believe it is equally important to the racial integrity of communities of color that transmission to their offspring be avoided where that is possible.

A real worry underlying both of these arguments is mandatory testing. For many women, mandatory testing carries with it the specter of forced celibacy, prohibitions against procreation (accompanied by the potential of sanctions against violators), and even the threat of forced abortion.

Apart from evidence that suggests that mandatory testing would have the effect of driving underground those most in need of testing and counseling, it is unclear both what gains could be expected from forced testing in this context and whether such testing even has the potential of reaching those it purports to reach. Many of the women in populations identified as "at risk" either don't marry those who have fathered their offspring or can't afford prenatal care. There is the additional question of determining how such options might be enforced or punished. By imprisonment? By steep fines? By terminating parental rights? By the time an accurate diagnosis were made and the appropriate causal link established, those found to be violators (and victims) would likely be dead or dying. Further, given the current state of the art with respect to testing, the test results themselves may give women a false sense of security about their serological status. Under such circumstances, if testing were mandated, the end hoped for still might not be realized.

In short, that there are strong moral reasons for preventing further spread of AIDS to newborns and for preventing pregnancy in infected women does not imply that policy be *mandated* for accomplishing that end. Some authors even express concern over the domino effect such mandated policies would have on the logic for testing other groups (Patton 1988).

There is yet another argument that needs to be examined, one that will be more familiar to those who have a long standing interest in issues affecting women: a woman must be allowed to weigh for herself the risks inherent in continuing a pregnancy if she is found to be seropositive—only she can evaluate the moral validity of her options.

Preserving women's rights to exercise reproductive choice is said to be important for the reason that the HIV status of the fetus of an infected mother, as well as of asymptomatic mothers who have infected partners, is still highly uncertain and often cannot be determined until some time after birth. Hence, this argument goes, while a woman might elect to terminate a pregnancy if she or her partner is discovered to be HIV infected, she might also justifiably choose to continue the pregnancy. If the prospective mother were carrying the child of a beloved and dying spouse, she might legitimately reason that the risk to the unborn is one that is justified in order to have a part of her spouse live on, or in order to give her own life more meaning, or for sociological and cultural reasons noted above (Murphy 1988, 75).

While I do not believe that mandatory testing is either morally appropriate or enforceable, I do believe that it is morally irresponsible to argue in this case for preserving women's rights to exercise reproductive choice. It seems important to come down hard on someone who would choose a 65% risk of spreading AIDS.[5] Sentimentalism and sexism aside, it seems unconscionable for a person knowingly to risk transmitting a lethal disease to another. Imagine our anger if an HIV infected man or woman were to engage intentionally in unprotected sexual relations with an uninfected partner. It seems uncontroversial to claim that we would feel moral outrage at such an act. It seems equally uncontroversial to claim that we would find it morally objectionable for an infected person knowingly to donate blood. The risk of infecting others with a lethal disease is simply too great. It seems even more objectionable when one doesn't consent to exposing oneself to the risk. For that reason, in the case of a prospective mother who risks transmitting HIV to her fetus, electing to continue the pregnancy seems an even greater abuse of one's moral and sexual responsibility.

Some states have already acknowledged the moral force of claims such as the above by enacting legislation that would make it a criminal act for an individual to engage in intercourse with another without informing that partner of his/her seropositivity[6] (Dickens 1988, 583). Of course, apart from the fact that I'm unsure how to evaluate the enforceability of such laws, it is unrealistic to believe that their payoff will be found in dramatic behavior change. Given the social and cultural context in which most of these women find themselves, it is even less clear what would effect behavior change in seropositive women who continue to conceive. Even so, such laws represent important expressions of a public attitude that such behaviors are wrong and that personal accountability is part of an accepted public morality. Such laws will help shape the moral climate of AIDS.[7] . . .

NOTES

An earlier, much shorter statistical version of this paper will appear in *AIDS Education and Prevention*. In this paper I have chosen to address the more philosophical issues surrounding AIDS/HIV in women. I am extremely grateful to Laura Purdy, Becky Holmes, and the reviewers of this paper for their many helpful and provocative comments.

1. It is important to understand here that I do not lay the blame for this at the feet of the gay community. On the contrary, the gay community historically has been supportive of efforts to secure a higher moral and political status for women.

2. I have argued elsewhere that AIDS does not fit the traditional communicable disease model. Hence, I am aware that partner notification and contact tracing have little in the way of treatment (and nothing in the way of a cure) to offer to those traced and notified. What contact tracing does offer is the information that

one may have been exposed to the virus, and that, I would argue, is information essential for both men and women to have.

3. I am aware that there are a number of feminist analyses of prostitution that discuss how racism keeps Black and Latino women on the streets and lets white women work less conspicuously indoors, and a number of discussions of prostitution as a legitimate form of employment. Although there are important similarities between antiprostitute sentiment and homophobic sentiment, I don't have the space in this paper, unfortunately, to do more than note that fact.

4. Other pediatric cases result from sexual abuse, drug abuse, adolescent intercourse, and hemophilia.

5. I am extremely grateful to my colleague Ferdy Schoeman for discussing the difficulties inherent in taking any position other than this. His suggestions throughout this section were most useful and illuminating.

6. Although Dickens notes that Florida and Idaho have introduced such legislation, I am personally aware that South Carolina has enacted such legislation. Dickens also notes that most jurisdictions have chosen to rely on existing criminal statutes to proscribe some behaviors of the HIV infected person.

7. There are seropositive people who knowingly have unprotected sex, however, just as there are cases of persons who know they have serious risk factors for HIV infection and who aren't seeking to learn their HIV status, yet continue to share sexual and drug using behaviors. I consider this to be morally irresponsible behavior.

REFERENCES

Bacon, Lisa. 1987. Lessons of AIDS: Racism, homophobia are the real epidemic. *Listen Real Loud*. 8(2): 5–6.

Curran, J., Jaffe, H., Hardy, A., Morgan, W., Selik, R., & Dondero, T. 1988. Epidemiology of HIV infection and AIDS in the United States. *Science* 239:610–616.

Des Jarlais, D. and Hunt, D. 1988. AIDS and IV drug use. *AIDS Bulletin* Feb. 1988: 3.

Dickens, B. M. 1988. Legal rights and duties in the AIDS epidemic. *Science* 239: 580–585.

Freidland, G. H. and Klein, R. S. 1987. Transmission of human immunodeficiency virus. *New England Journal of Medicine* 317(18): 1125–1135.

Guinan, M. E. and Hardy, A. 1987. Epidemiology of AIDS in women in the United States: 1981–1986. *JAMA* 257(15): 2039–2042.

Kaplan, H. S. 1988. No sex this year. *New Woman* January: 81–82.

Koop, C. E. 1987. *Report of the surgeon general's workshop on children with HIV infection and their families.* (Excerpts from keynote address.) Public Health Service: US Dept. of HHS. HRS-D-MC 87–1.

Ledger, W. A. 1987. AIDS and the obstetrician/gynecologist: commentary. *Information on AIDS for the Practicing Physician* 2: 5–6.

Murphy, J. S. 1988. Women with AIDS: Sexual ethics in an epidemic. In *AIDS: principles, practices, and politics.* I. Corless and M. Pittman-Lindemann, eds. Washington: Hemisphere.

Osterholm, M. and MacDonald, K. L. 1987. Facing the complex issues of pediatric AIDS: A public health perspective. *JAMA* 258(19): 2736–2737.

Patton, C. 1988. Resistance and the erotic: Reclaiming history, setting strategy as we face AIDS. *Radical Teacher* 68–78.

Piot, P., Plummer, F., Mhalu, F., Lamboray, J., Chin, J., & Mann, J. 1988. AIDS: An international perspective. *Science* 239: 573–579.

Quinn, T., Glasser, D., Cannon, R., Matuszak, D., Dunning, R., Kline, R., Campbell, C., Israel, E., Fauci, A., & Hook, E. 1988. Human immunodeficiency virus infection among patients attending clinics for sexually transmitted diseases. *New England Journal of Medicine* 318(4): 197–203.

Simpson, M. 1988. The malignant metaphor: A political thanatology of AIDS. In *AIDS: principles, practices, and politics* I. Corless and M. Pittman-Lindemann, eds. Washington: Hemisphere.

Wofsy, C. 1987. Intravenous drug abuse and women's medical issues. *Report of the surgeon general's workshop on children with HIV infection and their families.* Public Health Service: US Dept. of HHS. HRS-D-MC 87–1.

Zucker, L. 1988. Interview. USC. Columbia, SC.

Further Questions

1. Should IV drug users be counseled, given bleach to sterilize their needles, etc., in the interest of sexual partners to whom they might transmit the AIDS virus?

2. AIDS was first discovered in gays, and is still known by some as "the gay plague." Does this way of thinking discourage us from noticing that other people are at risk?

3. Should sexually active people, e.g., teenagers, be taught barrier methods of birth control, to slow down progression of the AIDS virus?

My Friend: He's Dead   VII.8

BRENDA TIMMINS

Brenda Timmins recounts the AIDS death of a friend and its impact on her as caregiver and on her husband, who could spend only weekends in her company. She argues that mandatory testing and quarantine of persons testing seropositive are not good alternatives to the experience she went through.

Timmins completed her first year at the University of Waterloo in 1991–92 as a mature student. This essay and her selection in Part X are two of her first attempts at essay writing.

Reading Questions

1. If you discovered you had terminal AIDS, what kind of care could you realistically expect to get during your last days?
2. Would you ever contribute to the care of someone who was dying of AIDS?
3. Suppose your spouse wanted to spend long periods of time away from home taking care of a dying AIDS patient. How would you feel about that?

I

IN 1988, JOHN WAS DIAGNOSED with full-blown AIDS. He and I had been childhood play-mates in a small village in Southern Ontario, and I considered him among my oldest friends. As children, we noticed that his father was usually absent. However, we often talked to John's mother. The women in town called her "ner-vous" and seemed to shun her. This meant, I later concluded, that she was well traveled, crea-tive, musical, and energetic. She was interesting. You can imagine how isolated she must have felt, living in a village whose life centered around bingo and hockey. Occasionally she would just disappear for a few days. Sometimes she would sit by herself in the forest and sing opera arias. (She must have had operatic training in England be-fore she came to Canada.)

This unconventional mother had produced an eccentric son and instilled in him a sense of ad-venture. The paradox, however, was that her strict British background had not prepared her for a child different from others his age. His body movements were sometimes effeminate and he seemed to spend all his time reading. He was dis-tant from his only sibling, a sister, partly because of his mother's influence. Thus, it was not sur-prising that his family totally abandoned my friend when he became a teenager and, without bothering with any "closet" procedure, went straight into an openly gay lifestyle. John's mother died the year before John died, without a reconciliation of any kind with her son. This alienation cost John dearly in emotional terms.

My phone call came early in 1988 from the Toronto hospital where John was undergoing tests. It was a difficult call for John to make. He had a few friends and many co-workers who found him entertaining but few close friends like me. John felt I was the only person he could call. In fact, it took him a week to call me after he was admitted to hospital. John didn't know how I would react to his news and had rehearsed what he was going to say to me. Tests confirmed he had full-blown AIDS.

My initial thought, of course, was that I was going to lose my friend. Only on second thought did I realize that my friend was about to lose his life. No one close to me had died before, and I didn't know what would be expected of me or how to react. I didn't know what to do.

When I entered his private isolation room at the hospital, John was asleep. The room was dark and quiet, giving me some opportunity to study his tiny 100-pound sleeping figure. John lived alone, and I slowly realized that no one had hugged him or touched him in any meaningful way in a long time. No one had ever looked so alone to me as my friend did that afternoon.

Upon waking and finding me in his room, John seemed happy and full of the news of improving test results. Eventually I reminded him of underlying realities.

"We need to talk about practical things," I said.

"I know we do," he replied quietly.

We began to talk more seriously. At this point, John accepted my promises. "I will not abandon you, no matter what happens; no matter how you change, I will be here. I will be with you from beginning to end." (I later put this in writing for him to read when he was alone and feeling lonely.)

Then he became more cheerful and relaxed and seemed better able to confront what lay ahead. John understood I had no previous experience with terminal illness. He understood that I was concerned about making an error that he would not live long enough for me to undo. His idea to forgive me for anything I might do wrong in the remaining days of his life showed unexpected foresight. This forgiveness was one of his greatest gifts to me. With that, I felt I had the courage to begin help with his care.

John was sensitive about his illness and asked me not to tell anyone from our home town, especially his family, that he was sick with AIDS. I thought his privacy was important, under the circumstances, and kept his secret. His sister did not know of his illness and death until more than a year later.

We developed a plan for when he would arrive home from hospital in a few weeks. I would live with him in his apartment from Monday to Friday; during that time I would do my best to take care of him. I worked during the day, and so he would be prepared to go for a walk when I arrived home. I would then go home (a distance of 90 miles) on the weekends, to live with my husband, Jason. Only later, on my way back from the hospital, did I realize that I had not discussed this plan at all with my husband. What had I done? I had made arrangements to live with another man 5 days a week without consulting Jason. I realized I had no idea how Jason would react to my spending time away from *him*.

The discussion with my husband was a quiet one. I assured him that this arrangement was necessary, and by necessity, temporary, even though I had no idea that John was less than one year from his death. Initially, Jason could not understand why I should be the one to take care of John. I explained that there seemed to be no one else who had much affinity to John or could tolerate his eccentric personality and growing signs of paranoia. John was part of my past and I felt responsible for him. I convinced Jason that life might not be tolerable for me if I knew that I had not done my best to protect and accompany John to the end of his life. My gut feeling was just that I very much wanted to care for my friend under these circumstances. Also, I had just made promises to John I could not consider breaking.

Jason understood my point of view, fortunately, and I thought I could pick up the pieces of my relationship with him later. I had not fully considered how much my absence would affect Jason. How was I to know how lonesome he would become in that year? Exhaustion from caring for John meant that my weekends had to be devoted to sleeping. It was not lost on me that I was no longer a real companion to my husband that year. John, Jason, and I were all at the center of a horrible storm, not of our doing.

Ironically, the controversy over whether PWAs (People With AIDS) should be quarantined continued to rage around us during that year. Children with the virus were banned from American schools. PWAs referred euphemistically to their "cancer" to avoid discrimination and alienation. Talk of quarantine continued. Health care workers were under scrutiny. Most people were content to think AIDS was a "gay problem" and unlikely to spread into the "normal population." Televangelists were telling people on national television that AIDS was God's way of condemning homosexuals for their sinful lives. (God was, at last, getting rid of gays.)

Under present social circumstances, dying of AIDS ordinarily means that young men, in what was expected to be the prime of life, are forced to return to bewildered parents and alien, even hostile, environments to be nursed through their last months. Their final humiliation is to be treated as small children once again. Small communities act in unison in condemning their native sons who come home to die.

Clearly, mandatory isolation of AIDS victims would please many people. Before I entered this AIDS storm in 1988, I did not believe people could take it seriously. When I realized that powerful people in organized religion and some politicians were actually having dialogue on this issue, I was shocked. Where do we stop? Who will be next? Atheists? What about people with cancer, or flat feet? The handicapped? If all fails, there are always the Jews!

Quarantine of PWAs is a serious mistake. It would endanger the lives of those *un*affected by the AIDS virus—the very people this measure is designed to protect. In reality, quarantine would actually put unaffected people at greater risk because people who had been tested and found HIV positive would find it wise to disappear into the regular population to avoid being detained against their will. Crime would increase as people attempted to evade testing and quarantine. Also, those people who believed themselves at risk and who would normally seek testing would not voluntarily come forward to be tested. They would have too much to lose. However, if they remain ignorant about their HIV status, they might, in their ignorance, infect someone else.

Perhaps we think such actions are selfish. However, we must understand that people are capable of committing extreme acts in order to maintain their freedom, even when they endanger others. Quarantines are often serious limitations of personal freedom. An example of this was the forced incarceration, behind barbed wire, of immigrants to Canada in the late nineteenth century, who were suspected of harboring tuberculosis. The Soviet Union is only one of many countries to have used quarantine and isolation to pressure citizens with different political views

to conform. Quarantine causes fear and hinders potential of perceived commonalities. It has suspended opportunities to attend school, to socialize in the community, to draw comfort and support from others, and to participate in the world as citizens of that world. A dungeon atmosphere surrounded by barbed wire is hardly a good place to end one's life, especially when you are already in considerable psychological and physical discomfort from a terminal disease. It should be obvious that AIDS victims, like those dying of tuberculosis, are sick and need proper care. Although some maintain that quarantine has been used successfully in the past to contain dangerous diseases, they do not mention that such diseases were spread through airborne particles. AIDS is not transmitted through airborne particles. You cannot *catch* AIDS from the air, or toilet seats, or casual contact.

Gradually, it is coming to public attention that AIDS is not a "gay disease." Everyone is at risk, regardless of sexual orientation. Sharing needles or reusing needles is a major method of transmitting the virus from one body to another. Blood-to-blood contact with an infected person is another. In March 1991, the British medical journal *Lancet*[1] reported a case that baffled doctors because the patient had not been exposed to any of the usual causes of transmission of the virus. He had been impotent for 10 years, received no blood transfusions, and used a sterile needle on the one occasion he used intravenous drugs. His wife was not HIV-positive. Ironically, it was discovered that this patient used to go out with friends in New Jersey and New York and beat gay men. The man often had "large amounts" of his victim's blood on his skin and sustained small cuts on his hands.

So even if quarantine were effective on its victims and humane, there is no way of identifying the group to be quarantined. A journalistic investigation discovered that a Florida dentist, Dr. David Acer, transmitted the virus to patient Kimberly Bergalis (who has since died), despite guidelines[2] which have been set for U.S. doctors.

It was later discovered that Dr. Acer transmitted the disease to two other patients, a woman in her sixties and a man in his thirties, even though HIV is an extremely fragile virus and does not survive for long outside the body. A review of Dr. Acer's dental practice revealed he did not always follow the guidelines. Dr. Acer's staff told investigators that dental instruments were not adequately sterilized, disposable items were reused, and latex gloves were not changed for every patient. These breaches in safety procedures might well explain how three of his patients became infected.[3]

The average consumer of medical services simply does not have basic knowledge of the guidelines, let alone the power, in a treatment situation, to ensure that they are enforced. As for AIDS being caused by gay promiscuity; John had been celibate since 1983, when AIDS first came to public attention as a lethal, sexually transmitted disease. John isolated himself partly because he wanted to live and living his life in full was more important than sex.

II

The first thing John did upon being released from hospital was to buy a second set of dishes for me to use. He did this because he felt that if my husband knew we didn't share dishes, he would feel better about my decision to live in the home of an AIDS victim. (This was not an issue for Jason, because he had read extensively about the disease and was comfortable about my personal safety.) John would spend all afternoon preparing for me to arrive at his apartment, and I think the regularity of my visits helped keep him even and balanced for a time.

Spring arrived, and with it came the realization that John's brain cells were deteriorating. What we hoped would be the last symptom of a death from AIDS came earlier than either of us anticipated. Our conversation about this new development began in despair, since John was sure about what was happening. Suddenly, with an unexpected twist the conversation became animated and theatrical as John took on the persona of a crazed transsexual to entertain me. Fortunately, John's astonishing sense of humor stayed with him until the end. Even the day before his death, John made me laugh out loud. For example, in the course of our regular conversations about "what are we going to do with the body?" John, having investigated the cost of caskets, announced that a good secondhand freezer would be "just fine." At a time when I was fighting stress and fatigue, these conversations were tremendously therapeutic. In fact, this may have been what got me through an experience that, as I look back on it, I wonder how I ever survived.

For several months, the task of making a will consumed John as he catalogued his treasures and reminisced about his short life. He had traveled extensively and returned with a unique collection of things. There was even an eloquent apology to Jason and a gift of books to him in John's will. Then John's ability to read began to dwindle. He had centered his life around reading, and the loss devastated him. I tried to read to him but I made mistakes, and John's impatience with me showed for the first time. Our world was so small by this time that I rented a large color television and had cable installed. Books had prevented this intrusion when John could read. Now he watched everything, day and night— trash and culture, game shows and ballet. My friend came alive again—another problem conquered for a brief moment.

John was becoming difficult to visit, and we noticed that former co-workers who had dropped by in the beginning had stopped coming. My husband was uncomfortable with gay men and did not visit. My relatives called often to see how I was. Occasionally they mentioned John as well, but they never visited. My co-workers slowly and discreetly absorbed my responsibilities at work, and they did listen to me as I described the events in my life with John. I considered this assistance critical in my caring for

John as these conversations were the only outside support I had.

John started to lose his memory in rather terrifying ways. Sometimes I would arrive at his home to find this courageous man crying, huddled in a corner, terrified because he had been in the kitchen and found the kettle on. He thought this meant there was someone else in the apartment. To make him feel safer, we put bars on all the doors and windows and installed a burglar alarm. Another complication was John's seizures, typical in cases of advanced AIDS. The medication for seizures is difficult to administer. If there is too much medication, the patient suffers stroke symptoms. Imagine leaving this medication to be self-administered in the hands of someone with John's memory problems.

There were hallucinations, too. Every evening we would sit quietly and have tea. Without warning John would sometimes become alarmed at something he could see behind me. Alarm would turn to panic as he tried to warn me of imminent danger. His hallucinations involved men with weapons about to attack me from behind. At other times he could see the floor moving and then open up as I turned the corner to walk toward him. He became frantic for my safety and his. His new struggle became very complicated as he tried to hold on to reality. The roller coaster we were on was picking up speed. We both understood that the combination of drugs was causing this crisis, but John would not relinquish control of the drugs. To do so would be relinquishing control of his life.

One night, as John stayed up watching movies, he took the seizure medication every hour instead of three times a day. When I awoke the next morning, I found him with severe stroke symptoms. Blood tests at the hospital indicated that he had five times the acceptable level of all five of his medications. John could not remember how this happened. It was the turning point for us. If this could happen while I slept in the next room, then I could no longer leave him alone during the day while I worked. I looked to the commu-

nity for hospice assistance. Casey House had been in operation for only four months and was the only one of its kind in Ontario. John was two months away from death.

I was desperate, exhausted, and almost incoherent when I arrived at the hospice. I was taken to the Quiet Room, a room expertly designed in calming colors to soothe rattled nerves and make it possible to conduct difficult conversations. The director listened to my attempt to communicate with a patience that I had not expected. He was surprised that I had cared for John for so long without help. At Casey House I found compassion and immediate practical solutions. Miraculously, they had a room for John, and the staff even helped move his personal articles from his apartment to make him more comfortable. Counseling was provided for me both before and after John's death.

John did not want to die, even when he was in this condition. He finally died a gentle, civilized death with no medication and no pain less than a year after diagnosis. Caring, experienced staff made it possible for John to die with dignity. We openly discussed the progression of his death and how it would take place. John wanted me to protect him from resuscitation, because he wanted to die only once. He wanted to be as clearminded as possible so that he could make the experience of his death his own. He also wanted me to protect him from pain.

Even though I was involved in the process, John's death hit me hard. What I was unprepared for was the aftermath of numbness and total absence of emotion. I had stopped feeling anything and was surprised that I didn't cry anymore. I was tired, too tired even to commute to my job, so I remained at John's apartment during the week for months. During this time I took advantage of grief therapy offered by Casey House.

When I finally went home, I spent long stretches of time sitting on the steps at the front of my house, surrounded by garden flowers. I had missed that garden and noticed for the first time that someone had been weeding it for me.

Neighbors began asking me questions about John and AIDS. They were thoughtful and caring questions I could answer.

A couple of maintenance workers stopped by to tell me what they had learned in a course imposed by their employer. They seemed proud of their new alliance with an important social and medical issue and wanted to talk. One thoughtful girl asked me if you could get AIDS by "being in the breath" of someone who had the disease. I was asked to speak to eighth grade students about AIDS and compassion. My experience helped people in my community to begin to talk about AIDS.

Months after John's death, my husband confessed how much he resented my absence and missed me. This resentment was something he had graciously hidden from me for the whole year I had been with John. Jason had not pressured me for more companionship and had not suggested that I should reconsider my decision to care for John. I was thankful that he was still glad to have me home again after a year of living alone.

Not only is everyone essentially at risk, but AIDS has the potential to affect not only the person infected, but also those who take care of AIDS victims and people connected to these caregivers. This could be any of us. Our lives were quite normal before John became ill. His illness and death had a great effect on the three of us, and on my co-workers who supported me in peripheral ways. AIDS concerns all of us. If situations like ours could receive more attention, in particular, if people could come forward with AIDS experiences without fear of recrimination, we could all be better off with respect to the AIDS threat.

NOTES

1. "Gay-basher contracts HIV," *The Globe and Mail, Reuters News Agency, London, England,* March 22, 1991, p. A12.

2. Paul Taylor, "New guidelines for U.S. doctors," *The Globe and Mail and Associated Press,* July 16, 1991, p. A5.

3. Paul Taylor, "Dentists debate AIDS contagion" *The Globe and Mail,* April 1, 1991, p. A1.

Further Questions

1. Is mandatory testing of everyone at risk for AIDS a realistic idea? Who would be the persons who were "at risk" for AIDS?

2. Suppose that persons who were discovered to be HIV positive were quarantined by government order. What impact would that have on daily life?

3. Does anyone ever *deserve* to get AIDS? In particular, could this be God's method of avenging himself upon people with sinful lifestyles?

Suggested Moral of Part VII

Sex today is very much in the control of men and centers around male erection and orgasm. Women's sexual preferences have been ignored to the point that women have difficulties determining what they are or expressing them in language.

Thus a popular conception of heterosexual sex is something a man does to a woman for his pleasure alone. Lesbian sex then becomes an impossibility because no penis is present, and gay sex is unnatural because there are too many penises and no legitimate place to insert them. Men are pressured into equating their sexuality and masculinity on the activity of their penises.

This thinking sets the stage for situations where men control women through sexuality. Every legitimate episode of sex is pleasure for the man with no known pleasure for the woman, who functions only as a receptacle.

The female orgasm is not well understood by the lay practitioner of sex, man or woman. Even when it becomes a goal in a sexual episode, it is not thought of as being important to a woman's well being or gender identity as a man's orgasm is to a man. Woman may thus be cast as "sex-objects" in heterosexual sex from the outset, as long as it is thought that "knowledge" of them is limited to their being bodies from which men receive sexual pleasure.

Further Readings for Part VII: Sex and Sexuality

Jeffner Allen, ed. *Lesbian Philosophies and Cultures* (Albany, NY: State University of New York Press, 1990). Lesbians write from a variety of perspectives.

Robert Baker and Frederick Elliston, eds. *Philosophy and Sex* (Buffalo, NY: Prometheus Books, New Revised Edition, 1984). Nice anthology covering many of the topics of *Gender Basics*.

Regina Barreca. *They Used to Call Me Snow White . . . But I Drifted: Women's Strategic Use of Humor* (New York, NY: Viking, Penguin, 1991). Chapter 6 is especially interesting in illustrating women's sexual preferences.

Judith Barrington, ed. *An Intimate Wilderness: Lesbian Writers on Sexuality* (Portland, OR: The Eighth Mountain Press, 1991). Erotic explorations by top lesbian writers.

Howard Buchbinder, Varda Burstyn, Dinah Forbes, and Mercedes Steedman. *Who's on Top? The Politics of Heterosexuality* (Toronto: Garamond Press, 1987). Four excellent essays on contemporary heterosexual sex.

Andrea Dworkin. *Intercourse* (New York: NY: MacMillan, The Free Press, 1987). How intercourse is a patriarchal institution that enslaves women.

Robert T. Francoeur, ed. *Taking Sides: Clashing Views on Controversial Issues in Human Sexuality* (Guilford, CT: The Dushkin Publishing Group, Inc., Third Edition, 1991). Interesting issues tackled in short writings.

Nancy Friday. *Women on Top: How Real Life Has Changed Women's Sexual Fantasies* (New York, NY: Simon and Schuster, 1991). Sexual fantasies of more than 150 women. Is this sample typical of all women?

Diana Fuss, ed. *Lesbian Theories, Gay Theories* (New York, NY: Routledge, 1991). Nice, imaginative collection.

Celia Kitzinger. *The Social Construction of Lesbianism* (Newbury Park, CA: Sage Publications, Inc., 1989). Exploration of oppression of lesbians by traditional liberal thinking.

Christian McEwen and Sue O'Sullivan, eds. *Out the Other Side* (Freedom, CA: The Crossing Press, 1989). Coming directly to the point on a variety of lesbian issues.

Andy Metcalf and Martin Humphries, eds. *The Sexuality of Man* (Concord, MA: Pluto Press, 1985). Gay and straight men write on male desire, defenses against intimacy, and other topics.

Richard D. Mohr, *Gays/Justice: A Study of Ethics, Society and the Law* (New York, NY: Columbia University Press, 1988). Well-documented, encyclopedic account of social injustice to gays.

Trudy Party and Sandee Potter, eds. *Women-Identified Women* (Palo Alto, CA: Mayfield Publishing Co., 1984). Lesbian issues: coming out, motherhood, the workplace, etc.

Julia Penelope. *Call Me Lesbian: Lesbian Lives, Lesbian Theory* (Freedom, CA: The Crossing Press, 1992). Aspects of lesbian life, e.g., role playing, wimmin-only spaces, sado-masochism.

Richard A. Posner. *Sex and Reason* (Cambridge, MA: Harvard University Press, 1992). Explanation of sexual practices according to concepts borrowed from economic theory. A form of sex is a rational response to a particular situation.

John Preston. *The Big Gay Book: A Man's Survival Guide for the 90's* (New York, NY: Penguin Books, 1991). 534 pages intended as a resource for gay men, e.g., how to join a gay band.

Michael Ruse. *Homosexuality: A Philosophical Inquiry* (Cambridge, MA: Basil Blackwell, 1990). Lengthy, somewhat detached treatment of issues surrounding homosexuality.

Roger Scruton. *Sexual Desire: A Moral Philosophy of the Erotic* (London: Free Press, 1986). Emotions are not founded on belief in the way in which attitudes are.

Simon Shepherd and Nick Wallis, eds. *Coming on Strong: Gay Politics and Culture* (Boston, MA: Unwin and Hyman, 1989). Discussions of gay life.

Ann Snitow, Christine Stansell, and Sharon Thompson, eds. *Powers of Desire: The Politics of Sexuality* (New York, NY: Monthly Review Press, 1983). Issues in sexuality, including heterosexism and male domination.

Alan Soble, ed. *Philosophy of Sex: Contemporary Readings* (Totowa, NJ: Rowman and Littlefield, 1980).

Catharine R. Stimpson and Ethel Spector Person. *Women, Sex and Sexuality* (Chicago, IL: University of Chicago Press, 1980). Notion of women as the "mirror image" of the man in sexuality problematized.

John Stoltenberg. *Refusing to Be a Man: Essays on Sex and Justice* (New York, NY: Penguin, 1990). Male sexuality and male mystique leads to rape, homophobia, and other social ills.

Sharon Dale Stone. *Lesbians in Canada* (Toronto: Between the Lines, 1990). Problems and solutions in situations of lesbians.

C. A. Tripp. *The Homosexual Matrix* (New York, NY: McGraw Hill, Second Edition, 1987). Well-written and thoroughly researched by an associate of Dr. Alfred Kinsey.

Mariana Valverde. *Sex, Power and Pleasure* (Toronto: The Woman's Press, 1985). Heterosexuality, lesbianism, bisexuality, and the shaping of female desire.

Russell Vannoy. *Sex Without Love* (Buffalo, NY: Prometheus Books, 1980). An idea someone had to develop: sex is better without love.

John Wilson. *Love, Sex and Feminism: A Philosophical Essay* (New York, NY: Praeger, 1980). Interesting topics like sexual insults.

READINGS ON AIDS

The ACT UP/ New York Women and AIDS Book Group, eds. *Women, AIDS and Activism* (Toronto: Between the Lines, 1990).

Charles Anderson and Patricia Wilkie, eds. *Reflective Helping in HIV and AIDS* (Bristol, PA: Open Court, 1992).

Marie Antoinette Brown and Gail M. Powell-Cope. *Caring for a Loved One with AIDS* (Seattle, WA: University of Washington, School of Nursing, Community Health, 1992).

Frederic G. Reamer, ed. *AIDS and Ethics* (New York, NY: Columbia University Press, 1991).

Diane Richardson. *Women and AIDS* (New York, NY: Methuen, Inc., 1988).

Part VIII

Rape and Sexual Harassment

Introduction

RAPE AND SEXUAL HARASSMENT are, by definition, sexual actions that are perpetrated on a woman against her will. The writers in this part address themselves to why men do these things and why there is not more resistance (including public complaints) by women.

VIII.1   Men on Rape

TIM BENEKE

Tim Beneke explains how the widespread threat of rape affects lives of women. He also mentions some ways in which men try to blame the women they raped for the rape.

Beneke, a writer living in the San Francisco Bay Area, is the author of *Men on Rape*, (New York, NY: St. Martin's Press, 1982).

Reading Questions

1. How would your life be different if rape were suddenly to end? Would your answer be different if you were of the other gender?

2. Do you feel your clothes must be zipped, buttons done up, everything tucked in because of threat of rape? Is this a matter that would be different for the other gender?

3. Could you be friendlier to people, strangers in particular, if you were not afraid of being taken advantage of sexually? Once again, is this different for the other gender?

4. Is the heterosexual situation a power game won by a woman if she engages a man's interest but doesn't have sex with him, won by the man if sex does occur?

RAPE MAY BE America's fastest growing violent crime; no one can be certain because it is not clear whether more rapes are being committed or reported. It *is* clear that violence against women is widespread and fundamentally alters the meaning of life for women; that sexual violence is encouraged in a variety of ways in American culture; and that women are often blamed for rape.

Consider some statistics:

- In a random sample of 930 women, sociologist Diana Russell found that 44 percent had survived either rape or attempted rape. Rape was defined as sexual intercourse physically forced upon the woman, or coerced by threat of bodily harm, or forced upon the woman when she was helpless (asleep, for example). The survey included rape and attempted rape in marriage in its calculations. (Personal communication)

- In a September 1980 survey conducted by *Cosmopolitan* magazine to which over 106,000 women anonymously responded, 24 percent had been raped at least once. Of these, 51 percent had been raped by friends, 37 percent by strangers, 18 percent by relatives, and 3 percent by husbands. 10 percent of the women in the survey had been victims of incest. 75 percent of the women had been "bullied into making love." Writer Linda Wolfe, who reported on the survey, wrote in reference to such bullying: "Though such harassment stops short of rape, readers reported that it was nearly as distressing."

- An estimated 2–3 percent of all men who rape outside of marriage go to prison for their crimes.[1]

- The F.B.I. estimates that if current trends continue, one woman in four will be sexually assaulted in her lifetime.[2]

- An estimated 1.8 million women are battered by their spouses each year.[3] In extensive interviews with 430 battered women, clinical psychologist Lenore Walker, author of *The Battered Woman,* found that 59.9 percent had also been raped (defined as above) by their spouses. Given the difficulties many women had in admitting they had been raped, Walker estimates the figure may well be as high as 80 or 85 percent. (Personal communication.) If 59.9 percent of the 1.8 million women battered each year are also raped, then a million women may be raped in marriage each year. And a significant number are raped in marriage without being battered.

- Between one in two and one in ten of all rapes are reported to the police.[4]
- Between 300,000 and 500,000 women are raped each year outside of marriage.[5]

What is often missed when people contemplate statistics on rape is the effect of the *threat* of sexual violence on women. I have asked women repeatedly, "How would your life be different if rape were suddenly to end?" (Men may learn a lot by asking this question of women to whom they are close.) The threat of rape is an assault upon the meaning of the world; it alters the feel of the human condition. Surely any attempt to comprehend the lives of women that fails to take issues of violence against women into account is misguided.

Through talking to women, I learned: *The threat of rape alters the meaning and feel of the night.* Observe how your body feels, how the night feels, when you're in fear. The constriction in your chest, the vigilance in your eyes, the rubber in your legs. What do the stars look like? How does the moon present itself? What is the difference between walking late at night in the dangerous part of a city and walking late at night in the country, or safe suburbs? When I try to imagine what the threat of rape must do to the night, I think of the stalked, adrenalated feeling I get walking late at night in parts of certain American cities. Only, I remind myself, it is a fear different from any I have known, a fear of being raped.

It is night half the time. If the threat of rape alters the meaning of the night, it must alter the meaning and pace of the day, one's relation to the passing and organization of time itself. For some women, the threat of rape at night turns their cars into armored tanks, their solitude into isolation. And what must the space inside a car or an apartment feel like if the space outside is menacing?

I was running late one night with a close woman friend through a path in the woods on the outskirts of a small university town. We had run several miles and were feeling a warm, energized serenity.

"How would you feel if you were alone?" I asked.

"Terrified!" she said instantly.

"Terrified that there might be a man out there?" I asked, pointing to the surrounding moonlit forest, which had suddenly been transformed into a source of terror.

"Yes."

Another woman said, "I know what I can't do and I've completely internalized what I can't do. I've built a viable life that basically involves never leaving my apartment at night unless I'm directly going some place to meet somebody. It's unconsciously built into what it occurs to women to do." When one is raised without freedom, one may not recognize its absence.

The threat of rape alters the meaning and feel of nature. Everyone has felt the psychic nurturance of nature. Many women are being deprived of that nurturance, especially in wooded areas near cities. They are deprived either because they cannot experience nature in solitude because of threat, or because, when they do choose solitude in nature, they must cope with a certain subtle but nettlesome fear.

Women need more money because of rape and the threat of rape makes it harder for women to earn money. It's simple: if you don't feel safe walking at night, or riding public transportation, you need a car. And it is less practicable to live in cheaper, less secure, and thus more dangerous neighborhoods if the ordinary threat of violence that men experience, being mugged, say, is compounded by the threat of rape. By limiting mobility at night, the threat of rape limits where and when one is able to work, thus making it more difficult to earn money. An obvious bind: women need more money because of rape, and have fewer job opportunities because of it.

The threat of rape makes women more dependent on men (or other women). One woman said: "If there were no rape I wouldn't have to play games with men for their protection." The threat of rape falsifies, mystifies, and confuses relations between men and women. If there were no rape, women would simply not need men as much, wouldn't need them to go places with at night, to feel safe in their homes, for protection in nature.

The threat of rape makes solitude less possible for women. Solitude, drawing strength from being alone, is difficult if being alone means being afraid. To be afraid is to be in need, to experience a lack; the threat of rape creates a lack. Solitude requires relaxation; if you're afraid, you can't relax.

The threat of rape inhibits a woman's expressiveness. "If there were no rape," said one woman, "I could dress the way I wanted and walk the way I wanted and not feel self-conscious about the responses of men. I could be friendly to people. I wouldn't have to wish I was ugly. I wouldn't have to make myself small when I got on the bus. I wouldn't have to respond to verbal abuse from men by remaining silent. I could respond in kind."

If a woman's basic expressiveness is inhibited, her sexuality, creativity, and delight in life must surely be diminished.

The threat of rape inhibits the freedom of the eye. I know a married couple who live in Manhattan. They are both artists, both acutely sensitive and responsive to the visual world. When they walk separately in the city, he has more freedom to look than she does. She must control her eye movements lest they inadvertently meet the glare of some importunate man. What, who, and how she sees are restricted by the threat of rape.

The following exercise is recommended for men.

> Walk down a city street. Pay a lot of attention to your clothing; make sure your pants are zipped, shirt tucked in, buttons done. Look straight ahead. Every time a man walks past you, avert your eyes and make your face expressionless. Most women learn to go through this act each time we leave our houses. It's a way to avoid at least some of the encounters we've all had with strange men who decided we looked available.[6]

To relate aesthetically to the visual world involves a certain playfulness, spirit of spontaneous exploration. The tense vigilance that accompanies fear inhibits that spontaneity. The world is no longer yours to look at when you're afraid.

I am aware that all culture is, in part, restriction, that there are places in America where hardly anyone is safe (though men are safer than women virtually everywhere), that there are many ways to enjoy life, that some women may not be so restricted, that there exist havens, whether psychic, geographical, economic, or class. But they are *havens,* and as such, defined by threat.

Above all, I trust my experience: no woman could have lived the life I've lived the last few years. If suddenly I were restricted by the threat of rape, I would feel a deep, inexorable depression. And it's not just rape; it's harassment, battery, Peeping Toms, anonymous phone calls, exhibitionism, intrusive stares, fondlings—all contributing to an atmosphere of intimidation in women's lives. And I have only scratched the surface; it would take many carefully crafted short stories to begin to express what I have only hinted at in the last few pages. I have not even touched upon what it might mean for a woman to be sexually assaulted. Only women can speak to that. Nor have I suggested how the threat of rape affects marriage.

Rape and the threat of rape pervades the lives of women, as reflected in some popular images of our culture.

"She Asked for It"—Blaming the Victim[7]

Many things may be happening when a man blames a woman for rape.

First, in all cases where a woman is said to have asked for it, her appearance and behavior are taken as a form of speech. "Actions speak louder than words" is a widely held belief; the woman's actions—her appearance may be taken as action—are given greater emphasis than her words; an interpretation alien to the woman's intentions is given to her actions. A logical extension of "she asked for it" is the idea that she wanted what happened to happen; if she wanted it to happen, she *deserved* for it to happen. Therefore, the man is not to be blamed. "She asked for it" can mean either that she was consenting to have sex and was not really raped, or that she was in fact raped but somehow she really deserved it. "If you ask for it, you deserve it," is a widely held notion. If I ask you to beat me up and you beat me up, I still don't deserve to be beaten up. So even if the notion that women asked to be raped had some basis in reality, which it doesn't, on its own terms it makes no sense.

Second, a mentality exists that says: a woman who assumes freedoms normally restricted to a man (like going out alone at night) and is raped is doing the same thing as a woman who goes out in the rain without an umbrella and catches a cold. Both are considered responsible for what happens to them. That men will rape is taken to be a legitimized given, part of nature, like rain or snow. The view reflects a massive abdication of responsibility for rape on the part of men. It is so much easier to think of rape as natural than to acknowledge one's part in it. So long as rape is regarded as natural, women will be blamed for rape.

A third point. The view that it is natural for men to rape is closely connected to the view of women as commodities. If a woman's body is regarded as a valued commodity by men, then of course, if you leave a valued commodity where it can be taken, it's just human nature for men to take it. If you left your stereo out on the sidewalk, you'd be asking for it to get stolen. Someone will just take it. (And how often men speak of rape as "going out and *taking* it.") If a woman walks the streets at night, she's leaving a valued commodity, her body, where it can be taken. So long as women are regarded as commodities, they will be blamed for rape.

Which brings us to a fourth point. "She asked for it" is inseparable from a more general "psychology of the dupe." If I use bad judgment and fail to read the small print in a contract and later get taken advantage of, "screwed" (or "fucked over") then I deserve what I get; bad judgment makes me liable. Analogously, if a woman trusts a man and goes to his apartment, or accepts a ride hitchhiking, or goes out on a date and is raped, she's a dupe and deserves what she gets. "He didn't *really* rape her" goes the mentality—"he merely took advantage of her." And in America it's okay for people to take advantage of each other, even expected and praised. In fact, you're considered dumb and foolish if you don't take advantage of other people's bad judgment. And so, again, by treating them as dupes, rape will be blamed on women.

Fifth, if a woman who is raped is judged attractive by men, and particularly if she dresses to look attractive, then the mentality exists that she attacked him with her weapon so, of course, he counter-attacked with his. The preview to a popular movie states: "She was the victim of her own *provocative beauty.*" Provocation: "There is a line which, if crossed, will *set me off* and I will lose control and no longer be responsible for my behavior. If you punch me in the nose then, of course, I will not be responsible for what happens: you will have provoked a fight. If you dress, talk, move, or act a certain way, you will have provoked me to rape. If your appearance *stuns* me, *strikes* me, *ravishes* me, *knocks me out,* etc., then I will not be held responsible for what happens; you will have asked for it." The notion that sexual feeling makes one helpless is part of a cultural abdication of responsibility for sexuality. So long as a woman's appearance is viewed as a weapon and sexual feeling is believed to make one helpless, women will be blamed for rape.

Sixth, I have suggested that men sometimes become obsessed with images of women, that images become a substitute for sexual feeling, that sexual feeling becomes externalized and out of control and is given an undifferentiated identity in the appearance of women's bodies. It is a process of projection in which one blurs one's own desire with her imagined, projected desire. If a woman's attractiveness is taken to signify one's own lust and a woman's lust, then when an "attractive" woman is raped, some men may think she wanted sex. Since they perceive their own lust in part projected onto the woman, they disbelieve women who've been raped. So long as men project their own sexual desires onto women, they will blame women for rape.

And seventh, what are we to make of the contention that women in dating situations say "no" initially to sexual overtures from men as a kind of pose, only to give in later, thus revealing their true intentions? And that men are thus confused and incredulous when women are raped because in their sexual experience women can't be believed? I doubt that this has much to do with men's perceptions of rape. I don't know to what extent women actually "say no and mean yes"; certainly it is a common theme in male folklore. I have spoken to a couple of women who went through periods when they wanted to be sexual but were afraid to be, and often rebuffed initial sexual advances only to give in later. One point is clear: the ambivalence women may feel about having sex is closely tied to the inability of men to fully accept them as sexual beings. Women have been traditionally punished for being openly and freely sexual; men are praised for it. And if many men think of sex as achievement of possession of a valued commodity, or aggressive degradation, then women have every reason to feel and act ambivalent.

These themes are illustrated in an interview I conducted with a 23-year-old man who grew up in Pittsburgh and works as a file clerk in the financial district of San Francisco. Here's what he said:

"Where I work it's probably no different from any other major city in the U.S. The women dress up in high heels, and they wear a lot of makeup, and they just look really *hot* and really sexy, and how can somebody who has a healthy sex drive not feel lust for them when you see them? I feel lust for them, but I don't think I could find it in me to overpower someone and rape them. But I definitely get the feeling that I'd like to rape a girl. I don't know if the actual act of rape would be satisfying, but the *feeling* is satisfying.

"These women look so good, and they kiss ass of the men in the three-piece suits who are *big* in the corporation, and most of them relate to me like "Who are *you?* Who are *you* to even *look* at?" They're snobby and they condescend to me, and I resent it. It would take me a lot longer to get to first base than it would somebody with a three-piece suit who had money. And to me a lot of the men they go out with are superficial assholes who have no real feelings or substance, and are just trying to get ahead and make a lot of money. Another thing that makes me resent these women is thinking, "How could she want to hang out with somebody like that? What does that make her?"

"I'm a file clerk, which makes me feel like a nebbish, a nurd, like I'm not making it, I'm a failure. But I don't really believe I'm a failure because I know it's just a phase, and I'm just doing it for the money, just to make it through this phase. I catch myself feeling like a failure, but I realize that's ridiculous."

What exactly do you go through when you see these sexy, unavailable women?

"Let's say I see a woman and she looks really pretty and really clean and sexy, and she's giving off very feminine, sexy vibes. I think, 'Wow, I would love to make love to her,' but I know she's not really interested. It's a tease. A lot of times a woman knows that she's looking really good and she'll use that and flaunt it, and it makes me feel like she's laughing at me and I feel *degraded*.

"I also feel dehumanized, because when I'm being teased I just turn off, I cease to be human. Because if I go with my human emotions I'm going to want to put my arms around her and kiss her, and to do that would be unacceptable. I don't like the feeling that I'm supposed to stand there and take it, and not be able to hug her or kiss her; so I just turn off my emotions. It's a feeling of humiliation, because the woman has forced me to turn off my feelings and react in a way that I really don't want to.

"If I were actually desperate enough to rape somebody, it would be from wanting the person, but it would be a very spiteful thing, just being able to say, 'I have power over you and I can do anything I want with you,' because really I feel that *they* have power over *me* just by their presence. Just the fact that they can come up to me and just melt me and make me feel like a dummy makes me want revenge. They have power over me so I want power over them. . . .

"Society says that you have to have a lot of sex with a lot of different women to be a real man. Well, what happens if you don't? Then what are you? Are you half a man? Are you still a boy? It's ridiculous. You see a whiskey ad with a guy and two women on his arm. The implication is that real men don't have any trouble getting women."

How does it make you feel toward women to see all these sexy women in media and advertising using their looks to try to get you to buy something?

"It makes me hate them. As a man you're taught that men are more powerful than women, and that men always have the upper hand, and that it's a man's society; but then you see all these women and it makes you think 'Jesus Christ, if we have all the power how come all the beautiful women are telling us what to buy?' And to be honest, if just makes me hate beautiful women because they're using their power over me. I realize they're being used themselves, and they're doing it for money. In *Playboy* you see all these beautiful women who look so sexy and they'll be giving you all these looks like they want to have sex so bad; but then in reality you know that except for a few nymphomaniacs, they're doing it for the money; so I hate them for being used and using their bodies in that way.

"In this society, if you ever sit down and realize how manipulated you really are it makes you pissed off—it makes you want to take control. And you've been manipulated by women, and they're a very easy target because they're out walking along the streets, so you can just grab one and say, 'Listen, you're going to do what I want you to do,' and it's an act of revenge against the way you've been manipulated.

"I know a girl who was walking down the street by her house, when this guy jumped her and beat her up and raped her, and she was black and blue and had to go to the hospital. That's beyond me. I can't understand how somebody could do that. If I were going to rape a girl, I wouldn't hurt her. I might *restrain* her, but I wouldn't *hurt* her. . . .

"The whole dating game between men and women also makes me feel degraded. I hate being put in the position of having to initiate a relationship. I've been taught that if you're not aggressive with a woman, then you've blown it. She's not going to jump on *you*, so *you've* got to jump on *her*. I've heard all kinds of stories where the woman says, 'No! No! No!' and they end up making great love. I get confused as hell if a woman pushes me away. Does it mean she's trying to be a nice girl and wants to put up a good appearance, or does it mean she doesn't want anything to do with you? You don't know. Probably a lot of men think that women don't feel like real women unless a man tries to force himself on her, unless she brings out the 'real man,' so to speak, and probably too much of it goes on. It goes on in my head that you're complimenting a woman by actually staring at her or by trying to get into her pants. Lately, I'm realizing that when I stare at women lustfully, they often feel more threatened than flattered."

NOTES

1. Such estimates recur in the rape literature. See *Sexual Assault* by Nancy Gager and Cathleen Schurr, Grosset & Dunlap, 1976, or *The Price of Coercive Sexuality* by Clark and Lewis, The Women's Press, 1977.

2. *Uniform Crime Reports,* 1980.

3. See *Behind Closed Doors* by Murray J. Strauss and Richard Gelles, Doubleday, 1979.

4. See Gager and Schurr (above) or virtually any book on the subject.

5. Again, see Gager and Schurr, or Carol V. Horos, *Rape,* Banbury Books, 1981.

6. From "Willamette Bridge" in *Body Politics* by Nancy Henley, Prentice-Hall, 1977, p. 144.

7. I would like to thank George Lakoff for this insight.

Further Questions

1. Do you still think actions speak louder than words, so that a woman can ask to be raped through the way she behaves, no matter what she says?

2. Is going out alone at night, for a woman, defying danger, as you would by going out into the rain without an umbrella?

3. Is walking on a sidewalk at night like leaving your stereo on the sidewalk, asking for it to be taken?

4. Does an overly trustful woman deserve what she gets, sexually?

5. Is a woman's dressing to look attractive a weapon she uses on the man's sexuality, so that he is blameless if he mounts a sexual counterattack?

6. If you, a woman, say "no" to sex, but later say "yes," does that prove that you meant "yes" all along?

VIII.2   I Never Called It Rape

ROBIN WARSHAW

Robin Warshaw addresses date and acquaintance rape. The dating game often mandates that the man put pressure on the woman and the woman keep things in check, sexually. Men often fail to understand that a woman means "no" when she says it; alcohol and drugs do little to help the situation. Warshaw concludes with an account of how men are taught to rape.

Warshaw is a writer specializing in social issues; her work has appeared in *Ms., Women's Day,* and other publications. This writing is from a longer work conducted under the auspices of *Ms.*

Reading Questions

1. Suppose dating involves a game, which the man wins if sexual activity occurs, the woman wins if it doesn't. Does this mean that a game has been set in place with the consent of both genders, or is it instead that men forced this game on women?

2. Is there such a thing as justifiable rape on a date, where the victim's behavior is responsible for triggering the man's action? If so, can a woman negate her rights to what happens to her body by behaving in a sexually provocative manner?

3. Is it surprising to hear that when men are raped, it is a frightening and painful experience for them as well?

Why Date Rape and Acquaintance Rape Are So Widespread

RAPES BETWEEN MEN AND WOMEN who know each other are happening in big cities, small towns, and rural areas. They occur among all ethnic and religious groups, regardless of education or wealth. Many of these rapes are rooted in the social behavior men and women learn. . . .

DATING RITUALS

This interaction comes into sharpest focus in traditional dating behavior where the male initiates the date by asking the woman out, with him paying all of the expenses or buying the liquor, food, or entertainment. When this happens, the man may expect sexual activity or intercourse, with or without a serious attachment between himself and the woman; she, on the other hand, may want intimacy only after a relationship has developed over a period of time. Even when the woman wants sex without a developed relationship, she may put up a protest because she has been trained that only "bad girls" have sex willingly. Her date, on the other hand, has learned from seeing such behavior (or from the advice of other men) that women often say no when they mean yes.

If the male is nonaggressive sexually, there's no problem. But if he is aggressive, the female enters into a contest with him—either because she really

doesn't want to have sex with him or because she feels she must put up some resistance to maintain a good reputation. Dating then becomes a game which each side tries to win. And date rape may be the result. . . .

And so the game is afoot from the outset of many traditional dates, with the man pressing his attempts at seduction and the woman keeping a check on how sexually involved the couple will become. This balance might be maintained for a long time in a way that is satisfactory to both people. But if the man moves from trying to cajole the woman into sexual activity to forcing her to comply by raping her, he may encounter what seems to him little resistance. That's because the woman's socialization has most likely taught her that she must not express her own wishes forcefully, that she should not hurt other people's feelings or reject them, that she should be quiet, polite, and never make a scene. And, as a girl, she has also learned not to be physical. . . .

INTERPERSONAL VIOLENCE

All it takes to solidify the aggressor/victim relationship of the dating couple is the addition of a belief in using violence to deal with personal conflict. Studies show that may not be a great leap.

A Minnesota survey of 202 male and female college students revealed that, in dating relationships:

- nearly 13 percent had either slapped their date or been slapped
- 14 percent were pushed or did the pushing
- 4 percent were punched or did the punching
- 3.5 percent were struck with an object or did the striking
- 1.5 percent were choked or did the choking
- 1 percent were assaulted with a weapon or committed such an assault. . . .

COMMUNICATION

Miscommunication contributes to the factual and perceptual fogs that cloud acquaintance-rape incidents. This miscommunication may occur because men and women often interpret behavior cues and even direct conversation differently. In general, men give a more sexual reading to behavior and conversation than women do. In a 1982 study conducted by Antonia Abbey of Northwestern University in Evanston, Illinois, male and female subjects watched a male and female actor talk to each other, and the males rated the female actor as being more seductive and promiscuous than did the women. Another study, this one with high school students in California, showed that males consistently rated various dating behaviors, types of dress, and dating activities as signals for sex more often than females did.

Male and female subjects in a 1983 research project read scenarios about college students who went on dates, then evaluated whether the date participants wanted sex from each other. Regardless of who had initiated the date, who had paid for it, or where the couple went, the male students were more likely than their female counterparts to think that the woman in the scenario wanted sex from the man she was with. "It seems likely that a man might misinterpret a woman's behavior and think that she is more interested in him than she really is," writes the study's author, Charlene L. Muehlenhard of Texas A&M University, College Station, Texas. Indeed, many

men only ask a woman out after they've decided that they'd like to have sex with her, whereas many women view dates, especially the first few dates, as opportunities to socialize and learn more about the man.

Some people hope that improving the woman's ability to clearly communicate what she wants will naturally lead the man to understand how to proceed. Although the "deafness" of some males involved in acquaintance rapes may, in part, be due to not being told in a decisive way what the woman wants, many men simply discount what a woman is saying or reinterpret it to fit what they want to hear. They have been raised to believe that women will always resist sex to avoid the appearance of being promiscuous (and, indeed, some do), will always say "no" when they really mean "yes," and always want men to dominate them and show that they are in control. Further, many men have been conditioned to simply ignore women—whether those women are responding positively to sexual interactions or pushing, fighting, kicking, crying, or otherwise resisting them.

When it comes to sexual relations, saying "no" is often meaningless when the words are spoken by a female.

BELIEF IN THE "JUSTIFIABLE" RAPE

The result of these conflicts in communication—the socialized "deafness" of men toward women and the likelihood that a man will interpret a situation to have stronger sexual overtones than a woman will—leads to the belief among many men (and some women) in "justifiable rape," somewhat along the lines of "justifiable homicide." In "justifiable rape," the victim's behavior is seen as being responsible for triggering the man's action. Although there is no legal concept as there is in "justifiable homicide," the idea of "justifiable rape" influences the opinions of everyone from the rape victim's own family to the jury who may sit in judgment of her attacker.

Recent studies show that men believe date rape is more justifiable if one of these circumstances occurs:

- the woman invites the man out on the date
- the man pays for the date
- she dresses "suggestively"
- they go to his place rather than to a movie
- she drinks alcohol or does drugs

Men with traditional attitudes toward women rate these situations as justifying rape significantly more often than do men who hold nontraditional attitudes.

The research also shows that many times men will feel "led on" while women will not have the slightest clue that their actions are being interpreted as sexual. In a 1967 study by Purdue's Eugene Kanin, sexually aggressive college men said they believed their aggression was justified if the woman was "a tease." A 1979 survey of California high school boys showed 54 percent thought rape was justifiable if the girl "leads a boy on."

In a study exploring correlations between people who rated rape as justifiable under certain circumstances and people who actually were involved in sexually aggressive incidents, Texas A&M's Muehlenhard found that men were much more likely than women to say that the woman had hinted beforehand that she wanted the man to ask her out. When she looked at just those subjects whose dates involved sexual aggression, Muehlenhard saw this difference in high relief: 60 percent of men reported that the woman had hinted she was interested in dating him; only 16 percent of the women said they had so hinted. Those men clearly felt "led on" by the women who refused them sex, a feeling which many of them may have regarded as justification for committing rape.

THE ROLE OF ALCOHOL AND DRUGS

It's impossible to consider why acquaintance rape is so widespread without mentioning the correlation between drug and alcohol use and sexual assault.

Ms. **SURVEY STAT** About 75 percent of the men and at least 55 percent of the women involved in acquaintance rapes had been drinking or taking drugs just before the attack.

Although it is certainly possible to drink alcohol without becoming intoxicated, in many social settings—particularly those involving teenagers and young adults—getting drunk is the point of drinking. And because there is really no drug-taking corollary to drinking just one glass of beer, using drugs like marijuana, hashish, cocaine, crack, methamphetamines, LSD, angel dust, and heroin almost always means becoming intoxicated or "high," although the depth of that intoxication may vary from drug to drug.

As has been seen in federal highway safety tests, alcohol begins to affect people in negative ways long before they believe they are actually drunk. Alcohol and drugs distort reality, cloud judgment, and slow reactions, causing men and women to expose themselves to dangers or disregard social constraints that might otherwise influence them.

When intoxicated, a woman's perceptions about what is happening around her and to her become blurred. Her ability to resist an attack is lessened as her verbal and physical response mechanisms become sedated. She may rely on other people to take care of her, to see that she gets home safely, and to protect her from harm. Some men purposely "feed" a woman alcohol or drugs before forcing her to have sex to reduce her defenses. . . . Moreover, women who have become obviously drunk or high on their own often become targets for individual men or groups of men scouting for a victim. And the fact that a woman is drinking, even if she's not drunk, is often believed by men to be a justification for rape (since "good girls" aren't supposed to drink). It also makes police and prosecutors less inclined to press charges in acquaintance and date rapes.

An intoxicated man may become more sexually aggressive, more violent and less interested in what the woman wants than when he's sober. And many men who commit acquaintance rape excuse their acts because they were drunk or under the influence of drugs. . . .

Men Who Rape Women They Know

Rape is not natural to men. If it were, most men would be rapists and they are not. Nonetheless, the answers given by the male college students who participated in the *Ms.* study delineate a sobering incidence of sexual aggression and assault in a predominantly middle-class, educated population.

As was done for the women surveyed, the word "rape" was not used in questions asked of men about their sexual behavior; instead, descriptions of specific acts were given (for example, "Have you ever engaged in sexual intercourse with a woman when she didn't want to by threatening or using some degree of physical force?"). The final tally:

Ms. **SURVEY STATS** In the year prior to the survey, 2,971 college men reported that they had committed:

- 187 rapes;
- 157 attempted rapes;
- 327 episodes of sexual coercion;
- 854 incidents of unwanted sexual contact.

HOW MEN ARE TAUGHT TO RAPE

"Rape is not some form of psychopathology that afflicts a very small number of men," says acquaintance-rape educator Py Bateman. "In fact, rape is not that different from what we see as socially acceptable or socially laudable male behavior."

What differentiates men who rape women they know from men who do not is, in part, how much they believe the dogma of what most boys learn it means to be male—"macho" in the worst sense of the word. Some researchers describe this

variable as the "hypermasculinity" factor. Others have dubbed the men who embody this behavior "male zealots."

Nearly all men are exposed to this sexual indoctrination, but fortunately only some truly adhere to it. These beliefs are chiefly promulgated by other men: fathers, uncles, grandfathers, coaches, youth group leaders, friends, fraternity brothers, even pop stars. Boys are taught through verbal and nonverbal cues to be self-centered and single-minded about sex, to view women as objects from whom sex is taken, not as equal partners with wishes and desires of their own. Boys learn that they must initiate sexual activity, that they may meet with reluctance from girls, but if they just persist, cajole, and refuse to let up, that ultimately they will get what they want. They view their relationships with women as adversarial challenges and learn to use both their physical and social power to overcome these smaller, less important people. . . .

This is what most boys—not just future rapists—learn about being sexual. Little or no mention is made of sex as an interaction between two people who are mutually participating and enjoying it. And few boys have the benefit of learning what good sexual relations are by the example of the men around them. . . .

Language not only leads men to objectify women but to objectify—and so dissociate themselves from—their own sexual organs. The man's penis becomes his "tool" and often he might even give it a name. It thus becomes a creature of its own, with a mind of its own, so the man is absolved of responsibility for its actions. This concept meshes with the popular myth of the male sexual imperative: that is, that once he is sexually aroused, a man cannot stop himself from forcing sex on a woman. Such a belief provides a handy rationalization for a man to use to coerce a woman into having sex ("See what you've done to me? Now we've *gotta* do it."). Moreover, the dissociation of the man from his penis and the myth that he can't be held responsible once he has been turned on makes many date rapes the woman's fault, in the man's view, for arousing him and his "friend." (Belief in these myths isn't limited to men. Studies of male and female college students have shown that both groups believe that sex is a biological drive for men but not for women.)

Reinforcing the effect of language on promulgating hypermasculine sexual behavior are the messages transmitted through popular culture such as movies and television. These messages often mix aggression, force, and sex. In the film *Gone With the Wind* (based on a book written by a woman), Rhett Butler and Scarlett O'Hara are seen drinking and fighting, displaying much anger toward each other. Suddenly, he lifts her off her feet, carries her up that dramatic staircase, and (presumably) to bed. "What happens the next morning?" asks rape educator Bateman. "She's got a big smile on her face!" Proof positive that women really want it, especially if you knock them around a little bit and then physically overpower them.

Bateman also likes to cite a scene from the movie *Saturday Night Fever* as reinforcing the belief that women's wishes should be ignored. In that scene, star John Travolta has just offered to walk the woman of his dreams home (and, hopefully, into an intimate encounter), but she refuses. So he starts to walk away, in the direction of his house, as she turns to walk toward hers. She crosses the street, then turns back to him and calls out, "You shouldn't have asked. You should've just done it." The message to men, Bateman says, is, "If you ask, you're gonna lose an opportunity."

Such scenarios are not dated relics. There are dozens and dozens of recent examples. In 1987, the television program *Moonlighting,* supposedly written for a bright and hip audience, focused on the sexual tension between its lead characters, Maddie Hayes and David Addison, played by the very appealing Cybill Shepherd and Bruce Willis. For two years, *Moonlighting* fans had watched as Maddie and David danced around the issue of getting together sexually, even though everyone knew they wanted to. Finally, the much-awaited night of consummation arrived: ABC even ballyhooed it in TV ads for days in advance. "What happened is they had a fight," Bateman says. "She calls him a bastard and slaps him across the face. He calls her a bitch. And then it's onto the floor, breaking furniture, sweeping vases of flowers off. It was scary. My heart was pounding. I was extremely depressed and distressed." The yuppie lovers battled angrily for several minutes before collapsing into sexual ecstasy. And out in TV viewerland, millions of boys and men saw that this is what women—even smart, independent women like Maddie—really want.

Every now and then there are glimmers of change. A 1988 *Cagney and Lacey* episode realistically dealt with date rape as a widespread phenomenon: The rapist was a successful businessman and the victim was a strong, independent, female cop. . . .

MALE VICTIMS

Perhaps the first question that pops up from the audience at workshops on date rape is, "Don't women rape men, too?" Behind that question is the natural defensiveness many men feel about the subject of rape, especially acquaintance rape. (Women often ask this question too, perhaps out of compassion for the discomfort the men in the workshop are feeling.)

The truth is, men *are* rape victims. Some experts estimate that 10 percent of the victims coming to rape-crisis centers are male even though men are far less likely to seek help after being raped than women. *But almost all male rape victims have been raped by other men.*

However, women do rape, as is known from child sexual-abuse cases. And a few women have raped men, as it is possible to stimulate even a terrified man into having an erection or rape him anally with an object. But the number of women who rape men is infinitesimally small.

The frequent asking of the question, though, demonstrates a certain need on the part of men to believe that women do commit rape and that it happens frequently. Indeed, during acquaintance-rape workshops, college men can often be heard chuckling about how much they wish it would happen to them. That's because they enjoy grade-B movie fantasies of what being assaulted would be like: Perhaps a squad of voluptuous cheerleaders might take them to be their sex prisoners.

Nothing could be further from reality. When men are raped, they are raped by other men, regardless of whether the victim or the assailant(s) are heterosexual or homosexual. It is a frightening, painful, emotionally scarring experience—in short, very like what happens to women who are raped. Men are often brutally beaten during the course of their attacks. They are raped by strangers who assault them on the street, break into their homes, or pick them up hitchhiking. Like women, they are also raped by acquaintances and, in the case of homosexual men, by dates. (Of course, also like women, men are raped as children by relatives, baby-sitters, and other adults.) . . .

Further Questions

1. Is miscommunication regarding whether the woman wants sex due mainly to her not being able to communicate her intentions clearly or to her date's giving more of a sexual reading to the situation than she intends?

2. Is it true that "good girls" don't drink or take drugs, hence any woman who drinks or takes drugs on a date is inviting the man to rape her by ceasing to be a "good girl"?

3. Why do some people continue to suggest that, once aroused, a man finds it difficult or impossible to stop himself from forcing sex on a woman?

VIII.3   Sexual Harassment

ROSEMARIE TONG

Rosemarie Tong describes some forms of sexual harassment. This unwanted sexual attention is coercive when it includes an offer or a threat toward the person to whom it is directed. It is noncoercive when the intent is simply to annoy or offend the person. Gender harassment is the more general category into which sexual harassment falls; the intent of gender harassment is to keep women in their place of subordination.

Tong has published books and articles in feminist philosophy and teaches philosophy at Davidson College (Davidson, North Carolina).

Reading Questions

1. If you are offered something in return for sexual favors by someone who has the power to make life very nasty for you if you refuse the offer, are you being coerced?

2. Are you being harassed if someone does something sexual to you just to annoy you?

3. If someone makes nasty remarks to you about your gender, is this a type of gender harassment? If so, why is gender harassment more important than harassment about the size of your feet?

... As [FEMINISTS] SEE IT, there are two types of sexual harassment: coercive and noncoercive. Coercive sexual harassment includes (1) sexual misconduct that offers a benefit or reward to the person to whom it is directed, as well as (2) sexual misconduct that threatens some harm to the person to whom it is directed. An example of the first instance would be offering someone a promotion only if she provides a sexual favor. An example of the second instance would be stating that one will assign a student a failing grade unless she performs a sexual favor. In contrast, noncoercive sexual harassment denotes sexual misconduct that merely annoys or offends the person to whom it is directed. Examples of noncoercive sexual misconduct are repeatedly using a lewd nickname ("Boobs") to refer to an attractive co-worker, or prowling around the women's dormitory after midnight. What coercive and noncoercive modes of sexual harassment have in common, of course, is that they are unsolicited, unwelcome, and generally unwanted by the women to whom they are directed.[1]

Coercive Sexual Harassment

According to feminists, a coercive act is "one where the person coerced is made to feel compelled to do something he or she would not normally do."[2] This compulsion is accomplished by the coercer's "adversely changing the options available for the victim's choosing."[3] The paradigm case of coercion is, of course, the use of physical or psychological restraint, but *threats* of physical or psychological restraint/reprisal are also coercive to a lesser degree. Although it is difficult to determine whether a sexual harasser has in fact narrowed for the worse the options available for a woman's choosing, John Hughes and Larry May provide two tests to facilitate such determinations: would the woman have "freely chosen" to change her situation before the alleged threat was made for her situation after the broaching of the alleged threat; and, would the woman be made "worse off" than she otherwise would be by not complying with the offer?[4]

Relying on Hughes and May's twofold test, feminists maintain that sexual advances/impositions that threaten some harm to the person to whom they are directed are clearly coercive. "If you don't go to bed with me, Suzy, I'll fail you in this course." Assuming that Suzy has not been secretly longing to sleep with her professor or to flunk her course, she would not freely choose to change her situation to one in which the only way she can attain a passing grade is by sleeping with him. Therefore, because Suzy's professor has adversely altered her options, he has coerced her into a very tight corner; and since a coercive sexual advance is by definition an instance of sexual harassment, Suzy's professor is guilty of sexual harassment.

In contrast to sexual advances backed by threats, feminists admit that sexual advances backed by offers do not constitute clear cases of sexual harassment. Nonetheless, like sexual threats, sexual offers are coercive. It is just that the bitter pill of coercion is coated with a sugary promise: "If you go to bed with me, Suzy, I'll give you an 'A' in this course." According to critics, however, feminists confuse seduction with sexual harassment when they conflate sexual offers with sexual threats—when they insist that every time a man pressures a woman for a sexual favor by promising her a reward he coerces her into saying an unwilling yes to his request. In this connection, Michael Bayles asks feminists to ponder the following hypothetical case:

> Assume there is a mediocre woman graduate student who would not receive an assistantship. Suppose the department chairman offers her one if she goes to bed with him, and she does so. In what sense has the graduate student acted against her will? She apparently preferred having the assistantship and sleeping with the chairman to not sleeping with the chairman and not having the assistantship . . . the fact that choice has undesirable consequences does not make it against one's will. One may prefer having clean teeth without having to brush them; nonetheless, one is not acting against one's will when one brushes them.[5]

As Bayles sees it, the department chairman has not coerced the graduate student to sleep with him. Rather he has seduced her to sleep with him. Consequently, whatever the chairman is guilty of, it is not sexual harassment. Bayles's reasons for insisting that the graduate student has not been coerced are two. First, she would have freely chosen to move from the preoffer stage (no chance of an assistantship) to the postoffer stage (a chance of an assistantship). Second, her options after the sexual offer are not worse than before. If she refuses the sexual offer, she will not lose a chance for an assistantship because she was never in the running; and if she accepts the sexual offer, she will have not only a chance for an assistantship, but an assistantship. Despite the su-

perficial plausibility of Bayles's analysis, feminists (once again following Hughes and May) insist that a deeper reading of the graduate student's dilemma indicates that she has in fact been coerced by her department chairman. In the first place, assuming the graduate student has not been dying to go to bed with her chairman, and that she is not a calculating mercenary who has been hoping for a sexual offer to bail her out of a dead-end career trajectory, it is not clear that she would have freely chosen to move from the preoffer stage to the postoffer stage. The best reason for her not wishing to move to the postoffer stage is that it places her in a "damned if you do, damned if you don't" predicament.

On the one hand, if the graduate student refuses to sleep with her chairman, she will of course *not* receive an undeserved assistantship. In addition, she will place herself at considerable risk. Perhaps the chairman is talking sweetly today only because he thinks the graduate student will be in his bed tomorrow. Should she disappoint him, he may turn against her. This is a real possibility, given the unpredictable character of sexual feelings and the history of reprisals against women who turn down sexual offers. On the other hand, if the graduate student agrees to sleep with the chairman—either because she wants an assistantship or because she fears angering him (a possibility that Bayles overlooks)—she increases her vulnerability to other professors as well as to the chairman. Other professors might imitate their chairman's behavior—after all, he got away with it—adding a degree of instability and potential for arbitrary treatment not only to this particular student's future, but to all female graduate students' futures. Once such considerations are factored in, feminists observe that the chairman has in fact boxed his graduate student into a corner from which she cannot emerge unscathed. Consequently, whatever else the chairman is guilty of (such as depriving a worthy candidate of an assistantship), he is also guilty of sexual harassment.

Noncoercive Sexual Harassment

Clear cases of coercive sexual harassment affect a woman's options so adversely that she gives in to her harasser's threats or offers simply because her other options seem much worse. Unlike the sexual seducer who showers a woman with gifts so that she will at long last *willingly* leap into his arms, the coercive sexual harasser waves his stick or carrot in front of a woman, not caring how *unwilling* she is when she jumps into his bed. Significantly, what distinguishes the noncoercive sexual harasser from both the sexual seducer and the coercive sexual harasser is that his primary aim is not to get a woman to perform sexually for him, but simply to annoy or offend her.

Although it is possible to argue that the ogler's, pincher's, or squeezer's sexual misconduct is coercive, it is difficult. Many women fear calling attention not only to the sexual misconduct of their employers and professors, who can cost them their jobs or academic standing, but also to the sexual misconduct of strangers—strangers who have no long-term economic or intellectual power over them, but who nonetheless have the short-term power of physical strength over them. For example, in a recent *New York Times* article, Victoria Balfour reported that although women are frequently sexually harassed at movie theaters, they very rarely complain to theater managers. One highly educated woman who had been afraid to report an incident of sexual harassment to the theater manager commented: "He might think that somehow I had done something that made the man want to bother me, that I had provoked him. To me, harassment has its implications, like rape." [6] Two other women silently endured a harasser for the duration of another film. Although their harasser's behavior was extremely offensive, they did not report the incident: "He was staring heavily, breathing heavily and making strange noises. We didn't move because we were afraid if we got somebody to deal with him, he'd be waiting outside afterward with a knife." [7] All three of these women kept silent because they feared provoking their harassers to some heinous deed.

To claim that these theatergoers were *coerced* into silence is, according to feminists, to accomplish some good at the risk of effecting considerable harm. On the one hand, the public ought to realize that, for women, being bothered at the movies, in the subways, and on the streets by youthful girl-watchers, middle-aged creeps, and dirty old men is a routine occurrence. On the other hand, women ought not to think of themselves as helpless victims who dare not confront their harassers for fear of retaliatory violence. Therefore, on balance, feminists are of the opinion that it is best to reserve the term *coercive* for cases of sexual harassment that involve specific threats or offers, especially if these threats or offers are made in the context of the workplace or academy. This is not to suggest, however, that feminists think that cases of noncoercive sexual harassment are always less serious than cases of coercive sexual harassment. No woman wants to be coerced into a man's bed; but neither does a woman want to be hounded by a man who takes delight in insulting, belittling, or demeaning her, and who may even find satisfaction in driving her to distraction. . . .

Gender harassment is related to sexual harassment as genus is to species: Sexual harassment is a form of gender harassment. Catharine MacKinnon comments, "Gender *is* a power division and sexuality is one sphere of its expression. One thing wrong with sexual harassment . . . is that it eroticizes women's subordination. It acts out and deepens the powerlessness of women as a gender, *as women*." [8] Whereas gender harassment is a relatively abstract way to remind women that their gender role is one of subordination, sexual harassment is an extremely concrete way to remind women that their subordination as a gender is intimately tied to their sexuality, in particular to their reproductive capacities and in general to their bodily contours.

Examples of verbal sexual harassment include those comments (in this case, written comments) to which female coal miners were subjected at the Shoemaker Mine in the late 1970s. Because women had never worked in the mine before, they were, from the moment they appeared on the scene, scrutinized by male eyes. Although the tension between the female and male coal miners was considerable, it was bearable until a rash of graffiti appeared on the mine walls. The graffiti focused on the women's physical characteristics. For example, one woman who had small breasts was called "inverted nipples," and another woman who supposedly had protruding lower vaginal lips was called the "low-lip express."[9] Subjected to such offensive social commentary on this and other occasions, the female miners found it increasingly difficult to maintain their sense of self-respect, and their personal and professional lives began to deteriorate.

In contrast to these examples of verbal sexual harassment stand more sanitized but not necessarily less devastating examples of verbal gender harassment. Unlike instances of verbal sexual harassment that focus on women's bodies, these latter comments, illustrations, and jokes call attention to women's gender traits and roles. It is interesting that a gender harasser may describe female gender traits and roles either in negative terms (women are irrational, hysterical, defective) or in seemingly positive terms (women are nurturing, self-sacrificing, closer to nature). In both cases, however, the gender harasser will add credence to the *"kinder, kirche, kuche"* theory of womanhood, according to which women's biology and psychology naturally suit them for bearing and raising children, praying in church, and cooking. . . .

. . . Women have to learn to say no, and men have to learn to take a *no* at face value. Moreover, women have to stop blaming themselves when men sexually harass them. This may be particularly difficult for a young woman to do. She may not have met enough different types of men to realize that it's not always something about her or her body that turns a man on, but something about his need to assert himself. Arguably, the more secure a man is about his masculinity, the less need he will have to harass women sexually or otherwise. Failing to understand this, a young woman may berate herself for her harasser's conduct. She may punish herself for being sexed by starving or neglecting her body. The epidemic of anorexia on many campuses is not unrelated to young women's fear of their own sexuality; and the unkempt appearance of some young women is often evidence of their attempt to kill the "temptress" in themselves. . . .

NOTES

1. John C. Hughes and Larry May, "Sexual Harassment," *Social Theory and Practice* 6 (Fall 1980): 251.

2. Ibid., p. 252.

3. Ibid.

4. Ibid.

5. Ibid., p. 249; cf. Michael Bayles, "Coercive Offers and Public Benefits," *The Personalist* 55 (Spring 1974): 142–43.

6. Victoria Balfour, "Harassment at Movies: Complaints Rare," *New York Times,* November 17, 1982, p. C24.

7. Ibid.

8. MacKinnon, *Sexual Harassment of Working Women,* pp. 220–221.

9. Raymond M. Lane, "A Man's World: An Update on Sexual Harassment," *The Village Voice,* December 16, 1981, p. 20.

Further Questions

1. Sometimes men complain that they can't flirt at the workplace or ask their coworkers for dates, because their behavior might be interpreted as sexual harassment. Is there a relevant difference between such activity and sexual harassment?

2. Sometimes we hear that human life is naturally sexual, and so the workplace is sexual along with other settings. Women who don't like this should leave. What is your reaction?

3. Should workplaces have enforced policies forbidding sexual harassment?

The Lecherous Professor: Sexual Harassment on Campus

VIII.4

BILLIE WRIGHT DZIECH AND LINDA WEINER

Billie Wright Dziech and Linda Weiner address sexual harassment of students by faculty on campus. Women are especially vulnerable in campus situations and also are victims of considerable mythology. Faculty use harassment as a way of coping with their own problems. They can get away with it because of the mystique associated with the professoriate.

Reading Questions

1. What is it about student life and student–faculty relations that make students especially vulnerable to harassment by faculty?

2. Do you think that if you were a student being sexually harassed by a faculty member, you could make the proper authorities believe you?

3. Are women taken less seriously than men, hence a woman student's desire to be helped academically by a professor is more easily mistaken for sexual desire?

Contemporary College Women: Myths and Realities

* * *

THE CONSENTING ADULT MYTH

OCCASIONALLY THERE ARE WOMEN STU-DENTS who are attracted to faculty. There are husbands and wives who were once teacher and student. These relatively few examples are cited again and again as proof that relationships between professors and students are private matters and that the concept of sexual harassment should give wide berth to such liaisons. The faculty role may be attractive to some, because it combines intellectual attainment and power, but being attracted to an individual's role and consenting to a relationship are vastly different.

If a professor becomes involved with a student, his standard defense is that she is a consenting adult. Few students are ever, in the strictest sense, consenting adults. A student can never be a genuine equal of a professor insofar as his professional position gives him power over her. Access to a student occurs not because she allows it but because the professor ignores professional ethics and chooses to extend the student-faculty relationship. Whether the student consents to the involvement or whether the professor ever intends to use his power against her is not the point. The issue is that the power and the role disparity always exist, making it virtually impossible for the student to act as freely as she would with a male peer.

In a normal romantic situation, both the man and woman make efforts to assess each other's reasons for pursuing the relationship, to understand their true feelings and desires, and to predict their own and the other's future behaviors and attitudes. In a faculty-student relationship, the enormous role (and frequently age) disparity inhibits the woman so that she herself may have trouble understanding and predicting her feelings. . . . People who promote the consenting adult myth seldom mention that true consent demands full equality and full disclosure. Students lack not only power and equality; they are also frequent victims of professors' distortions of truth. A student may understand and agree to limits in her relationship with a professor, but faculty Casanovas usually forget to inform the woman that she is only one in a long procession of "consenters." . . .

VULNERABILITY

College women may suffer because of misconceptions about their behaviors and characters, but do they also somehow permit themselves to be sexually harassed? An important factor in understanding womens' responses to harassment is the education and socialization of females. . . . The education system, from nursery school through college, reinforces women's dependency and reliance on authority. Women are taught submission, not aggression. They learn that being "good" implies not acting but reacting, not trusting oneself but entrusting oneself to the authorities—parents, clergy, teachers—that promise reward. Forced into a choice between a teacher's wishes and their own, some students do what

they have learned to do best—defer, submit, agree. In their own peculiar ways, they once again act out the roles of "good little girls," doing what teacher says is best. . . .

In addition to the burdens imposed by sexual stereotyping, many women confront new and greater pressures upon entering college. College is not a particularly quiescent juncture in anyone's life. Alumni view the experience far differently from those who are living it. For most students, it is a time of uncertainty, pressure, and confusion, a time in which joy is counterbalanced by despair and achievement, by defeat. Students must decide successfully about academic programs, careers, and personal independence and relationships. College is a period of constant trial and judgment by oneself and others, in truth a far more harrowing experience than students care to admit. . . .

It should not surprise anyone that many women feel less self-confidence and control once they reach college. Most academic environments are patterned after male interests and male behaviors. Since the turn of the century, cognitive rationality and the scientific mode of enquiry have dominated higher education. Women, socialized in humanistic and intuitive forms of knowledge, are at a psychological disadvantage in this kind of environment. The institution's emphasis on competition and intellectual aggressiveness runs counter to all that they have been taught.

There may be a link between women's vulnerability to sexual harassment and their diminished confidence and sense of control in academic settings. Because higher education is a male-dominated institution, college women are often treated less seriously. A man who hopes to become a physician is taken at his word. A woman elicits raised eyebrows and questions about her marriage and child-bearing plans. Her intentions meet with skepticism, so she is forced to prove herself and to endure more from faculty.

Nonassertive women are not the only likely victims for sexual harassers. The data is anecdotal, but there are overwhelming similarities in accounts of counselors, ombudsmen, and administrators who deal with the problem daily. Women who are experiencing serious stress are vulnerable, as are women uncertain about academic programs. Women who are loners, without visible friends, seem to be sought out by harassers. One ombudsman commented, "This will sound really crazy, but I think we tend to have more blondes coming to our office. They aren't beautiful or necessarily even pretty and I haven't kept a running count, but I'm almost sure that's the case." Others note that the nontraditional woman student, the individual attending college after some time has elapsed, also seems to be a target for the lecherous professor.

Harassers are influenced by multiple characteristics in women—physical characteristics, economic status, marital status. However, from analysis of stories of sexual harassment collected from college women, two particularly vulnerable groups arise: minority women and females enrolled in traditionally male fields. The reasons they attract harassers are easy to identify.

A racist stereotype of minority women is that they are "easier" and more responsive to sexual advances. For some males, the sexuality of women of a different race reportedly appears mysterious. Either of these conditions could account for what one counselor describes as some harassers' "quick-target" attitude toward minority women. An even more insidious possibility is that the lecherous professor may sense the unease experienced by some minority women entering the academic environment. If the self-esteem of women students in general is on trial during college, then that of minority females is sorely threatened as they seek to establish credibility in institutions that are not only traditionally male but also white-dominated.

Women in nontraditional fields exhibit some of the uncertainty and vulnerability of minority women. Male-dominated disciplines are governed by a fraternity of men with strong credentials who until very recently were unaccustomed to the presence of women in their classrooms. Women entering these fields tend to be high achievers, often academically superior to their male counterparts. Disconcerted by this new situation, some male faculty are openly hostile to such women; others ignore them. At any rate, female students in engineering, architecture, accounting, medicine, law, and a variety of other historically male disciplines report discomfort in their environments.

The sense of being an intruder can have consequences beyond the classroom. Women who feel themselves "outsiders" are especially vulnerable to displays of interest or kindness from their instructors. Some faculty prey on the distress of such students for their own ends. One administrator observed, "These women feel like such pariahs that they'll hang onto any shred of human kindness, and a lot of faculty are not beyond taking advantage of that fact."

A story told by a black woman professor of accounting reflects the environmental stress. She recalled her own freshman collegiate days when she was singled out by a faculty member who was very arrogant about his five degrees and his predominantly male profession. She was the only one in class whom he did not address by first name; he preferred calling her, "Miss ____." At the end of the quarter he asked to speak with her after class. She was 17 at the time, and he was a middle-aged married man. She described her shock when he asked her to attend a dance with him: "I just looked him in the face and said, 'You're the wrong age, the wrong color; and if you want to take someone to a dance, it ought to be your wife.'"

ATTEMPTS AT COPING

Whatever her age, appearance, race, or field of study, there is vulnerability in the student's status that makes sexual harassment by teachers a most intimate betrayal of trust. In case after case, students report their initial reactions as disbelief and doubt about the most blatant acts.

College is a time when students question their sexual identities and relationships and evaluate their values and self-images. Most see faculty on the other side of the threshold called maturity, part of the adult world, more parents than peers. Sexual harassment by faculty, even in its most impersonal, generalized forms, injects a note of unexpected, incestuous sexuality that shocks the average woman student.

After shock comes the feeling of powerlessness. College professors are older, more adept verbally, more sophisticated socially, and certainly more knowledgeable about the workings of the college or university. A student at a Midwestern university asked, "Who was going to believe me? I was an undergraduate student and he was a famous professor. It was an unreal situation." A graduate student complained to her college counselor:

> What was it that I did that led him to believe I was interested in him in anything but a professional sense? I am quite outgoing and talkative; could that be interpreted wrongly? I realized how utterly vulnerable I was in a situation like this . . . Everything that happened would be interpreted in his favor, if it ever became public. It would be said that I got my signals wrong, that he was just truly interested in helping me in my career.[1]

Closely related to women's feelings of powerlessness are those of guilt. Student victims report feeling responsible, feeling at fault somehow. Some have an almost childlike fear of having broken some rule they did not know. They wonder what they should have known or done to prevent the harassment. "I keep asking myself what I did to get him started. There were twenty-two other girls in the class. Why did he pick on me?" Michelle Y., a student at a southern university, asked.

Women recognize early that power and sexuality are equated by society. Some students are un-sophisticated and fearful about the possibilities suggested by their sexuality; they may develop conflict about it and, correspondingly, guilt about their intentions and behaviors. They know that in cases of sexual harassment and rape someone always asks, "Did she encourage it?" and "Did she enjoy it?" The questions linger in the minds of even the most innocent and make them impotent to confront the harassment. Too many members of both sexes assume that women say "no" when they really mean "yes," that they secretly savor squeezing, patting, and pinching.

Men are not misunderstood or vulnerable to the same degree. An average woman of fifty would never be expected to whet the sexual appetite of a twenty-year-old male, and he would not be accused of seducing her. But people believe a twenty-year-old female can easily be transported to rapture by the attentions of a fifty-year-old male. After a while, the culturally induced confusion makes some women actually begin to doubt their own motivations. They then discover that their abusers prey on their uncertainties.

Paramount in the minds of many student victims is fear of what will happen if they resist or report the professor's behaviors. Victims often believe that the authority of the professor equals power over their futures—in a sense, their lives. Ambivalent about her academic capabilities, the typical student may be devastated when a professor, the symbol of intellect, treats her as if she has only a body and no mind. Even the best students worry about reprisals by the harasser and his associates. They fear that grades, jobs, careers, and sometimes even their physical safety will be threatened. Kelly H., a pre-med student, observed:

> It's easy for someone else to say I should do something about Dr. _____, but how can I? He was the first person at _____ to take my work seriously. At least I think it's my work that made him notice me. He's the one who's pushing for me to get into med school. If I refuse him, then I ruin my whole life.

Another repeated reaction of women victims is their ambivalence about and sometimes sympathy for the harasser. Women students, especially if they are considering making a formal complaint, worry about the professor's career, marriage, and future. Over and over, they comment, "I don't want anything bad to happen to him." A major source of this guilt is the harasser himself; when confronted by a student, harassers often distract them with discussions of personal and professional costs professors pay. Students may also feel guilty because they are flattered by the professor's interest in them. They may find him physically and socially unattractive, but being the object of attention from an older man can be a heady experience. A student may worry that she is stepping out of her proper place by affecting a faculty life, or she may have a certain amount of gratitude for the interest he has in her. This, as much as compassion, may lead to students' frequent pleas that deans or counselors "make sure he doesn't get in a lot of trouble." . . .

Often women who do acknowledge the seriousness of harassment try to cope through avoidance. They invent appointments, enlist the presence of friends, cut class, or even hide to prevent encounters. Another tactic is "dressing down," trying to appear asexual and unattractive to avoid notice. Each of these maneuvers is a passive-aggressive strategy; the student attempts to control external factors in the environment because she realizes she cannot control the professor.

Avoidance strategies indicate that students are sensitive to the power imbalance. They take friends to meetings with harassers because another person can provide reinforcement. They avoid meetings with harassers by claiming obligations equally important to those imposed by faculty. In both cases, students are trying to convince themselves and to communicate to their professors that powers can be offset.

Dressing down is a form of avoidance that demonstrates women's use of clothing to symbolize self-perceptions. A woman may make herself unattractive to escape the attention of an undesirable male, but dressing down may also be a way of declaring feelings of inferiority and victimization. It can express self-doubt as well as desire to deal with a threatening situation. Making oneself unattractive can be a way of declaring, "I don't feel good about myself. I feel inadequate and incompetent to cope with this problem." . . . "Staying away" is not as simple as it sounds. Staying away means that women are forced to drop courses, to alter schedules, sometimes to change majors or colleges because they feel they have no other recourse. Frequently they transfer to other institutions without admitting their reasons. Worst of all, there are students so unable to withstand harassment and so estranged from the institution that the only solution they discover is leaving school. There is no way to determine the number who eventually adopt this drastic measure. Few colleges have adequate exit interviews of graduates, dropouts, or transfers, so information about sexual harassment is not likely to be collected and assessed by proper authorities. Nevertheless, counselors in a variety of schools state emphatically that the number of women who leave college because of harassment is substantial. . . .

Much is heard from educators concerned about the reputations and livelihoods of those accused of harassment, but there is little discussion of the long-term effects it has on the women abused. Sexual harassment obviously has the power to damage careers; women leave colleges every day because they cannot deal with it. It alters their attitudes toward institutions and may have longlasting effects on their perceptions of men and sex. Perhaps most insidious are its influences upon the self-images of those forced to endure it. Higher education has been able to ignore consequences of sexual harassment because the victims' damage and pain are often felt years later, long after women have left the institutional environment and forfeited their claims to its protection.

The Lecherous Professor:
A Portrait of the Artist

* * *

Although there is limited evidence of the number of harassers who may be "loose" on the nation's campuses, one point is clear. They are tolerated because society doubts that men are capable of sexual restraint. Sexual harassers are often defended with the shrugged observation, "After all, they're only human." A middle-aged professor, notorious for pursuing sexual relations with female students, offered a variation on this view: "If you put me at a table with food [with coeds], I eat."

The appeal to "human nature" is a reminder that even in an era of ostensible sexual liberalism and freedom, both men and women suffer and stereotypes die hard. Even in the 1980s, society has not freed itself of the Victorian notion that men are creatures barely capable of controlling their bestial appetites and aggressions. All the contemporary rhetoric about liberating the sexes from stereotypes has done little to change the popular view of the male as a kind of eternal tumescence, forever searching and forever unsatisfied.

Such an attitude demeans the notion of "human." To be human does not mean that a man is at the mercy of his genitalia. Whatever it is that constitutes "humanness" is located in the mind and heart, not the libido. "Human" implies reason, compassion, control—all the qualities that distinguish college professors from their cats and dogs. Without these, they are "only animal," a defense few find appealing. Sexual harassment unquestionably harms females, but men are equally debased when it is allowed to flourish. On the college campus, a very small number of men damage the reputations of colleagues who perform difficult tasks for relatively low wages without "succumbing" to the "irresistible" temptations of women students. . . .

Regardless of the role he assumes or the type of harassment in which he engages, the lecherous professor always controls the circumstances surrounding the student victim. Sexual harassment is a power issue, and the power of the professoriate is enormous. . . . Sexual harassers are people who misuse the power of their positions to abuse members of the opposite sex. Higher education tends to discuss their behavior in the abstract—as if it were unrelated to real-life human beings. But sexual harassment cannot be understood or curtailed until professors are subjected to the same scrutiny as students. What motivates a man with so much education and power over others to act abusively toward women? . . .

It is difficult to determine how the media developed the image of the sexy college professor with the corduroy jacket and the ever-present pipe. He may be alive and well on the silver screen and in the pages of best-sellers, but he is not in abundance at the faculty club or meetings of the American Association of University Professors. The typical professor does not resemble Fred MacMurray, Elliot Gould, Donald Sutherland, or any other of the Hollywood types who have portrayed him over the years. If there is a star who most resembles the typical accounting, art history, or seventeenth-century literature professor, it would have to be Woody Allen. . . .

. . . In popular myth and movies, college professors live in Victorian houses with wood-burning fireplaces, oak staircases, and paneled, book-lined studies. In reality, many drive secondhand cars, consider themselves fortunate to afford tract housing, and wonder how they will accumulate enough money to send their own children to college. A party of professors often means moving the department or college meeting to someone's basement family room to nibble cheddar cheese and drink wine from Styrofoam cups. This scenario is not all that bleak unless one considers the discrepancy between the ideal and actual worlds of academics. College professors are the people who teach others to appreciate expensive and sophisticated equipment, books, art, theater, and music—all that society recognizes as manifestations of "the good life"—and who cannot really afford them for themselves or their families.

In *The Male Mid-Life Crisis,* Nancy Mayer pointed out that "in America success has always meant making money and translating it into status or fame,"[2] and the relationship between financial success, power, and sexuality is a frequent topic of psychologists and organization specialists. In their article "The Executive Man and Women: The Issue of Sexuality," Bradford, Sargent, and Sprague observed:

> An important aspect of the sense of self-identity for both males and females is their masculinity and femininity . . . How do males assert their sexuality? Teenagers resort to fistfighting . . . playing football, and competing against one another to see who can consume more beer or have more dates. While this may do for youth, an educated adult must find more discreet and indirect proofs . . . For many men, work serves as the major vehicle defining their identity, including sexual identity . . . Status and pay of the job also bear an element of sexuality . . . [Men] strive to advance, build up their programs, and compete in meetings partially to obtain status and financial records that connote masculine success, but also to affirm their masculinity more directly.[3]

A professor who sees himself in a static or unsuccessful professional and financial position may choose to exert his masculinity in negative ways. Feelings of frustration and defeat can be displaced onto the women students under his control. He can affirm his authority by being openly abusive to them, or he can turn to them for solace and ego-gratification. The dean of students at a very selective liberal arts college considered such displacement significant in some sexual harassment:

> I guess you might say that many men consider access to females one of the perks of the profession. If you don't make a lot of money, if you can't go to Europe without scrimping and sacrificing, if publication of your dream book seems less and less a reality and even promotion becomes a vain hope, life looks fairly dim. It's also not hard to see why some of these men turn to students for comfort or excitement or what-

ever it is their egos need. Sometimes they're abusive to students because that's a way to deal with their own anger and despair. It's not right, but it's one of the realities we have to live with.

MIDLIFE CRISIS

The frustration and confusion inherent in professional crisis are similar to and sometimes synonymous with those of midlife crisis. Not surprisingly, midlife crisis is the most frequently —if not the only—explanation offered for sexually harassing behavior. Peter A., professor at a large Massachusetts university, voiced this common defense:

> Another problem, and one not easily dismissed, is the fact that many of us are in our thirties and forties and are watching our youth slip away at the very time we're in extremely close contact with women who are just coming into bloom. Let me tell you, it's not easy to hit the beginning of a midlife crisis when you're surrounded by nubile twenty-year-olds.[4]

If a man is going to follow the traditional pattern for male midlife crisis, academe is the best of all possible worlds in which to be. Mayer described this period in the male's life:

> In response to wrenching change, a man at this stage of life is struggling to revise his own self-image and find dignity in the face of undeniable limitations. More than ever, he needs the confirmation of being seen as a powerful and desirable man—a need that the nubile girl is uniquely suited to satisfy. Our culture's most obvious symbol of hot-blooded sexuality, she can meet the aging male's intensified need for reassurance both in public and in private . . .
>
> Seeking refuge from the harsh assaults of this midlife period and release from heightened anxieties that haunt and perplex them, [some men in middle age] confirm their manhood through the worshipful gaze of a nubile girl—who mirrors back an image of their most potent self. Contrary to popular wisdom, men in their middle years are generally drawn to younger women not because they want to recapture their youth,

but because they need to reconfirm their maturity . . .

This, then, is the single most seductive reason for the appeal of the nubile girl: A yielding innocent on whom a man can project whatever fantasy he craves, she makes him feel not merely potent, but also omnipotent. A soothing balm indeed. Where else, after all, can the aging male find a sexual partner who will offer applause and adulation without demanding reciprocal attentions? Who will satisfy his emotional needs without requiring him to cater to hers? Only the young can afford to be so selfless.[5]

The enormous advantage that college professors have over men in similar situations is that for them, the stage is already set. Not only are there more than enough "nubile girls" from whom to choose, but they are women who have already been conditioned to regard the teacher as intellectually omnipotent. As individual desires and needs change over time, a wife who is a peer may become intellectually, professionally, or emotionally menacing; the attraction to a younger woman may lie in her lack of competition or threat. A person with whom the professor has no shared history is cleaner, less complicated. If she is also a student, she exhibits all of the deference that comes with discrepancies in roles, experience, and sophistication. A male confused about responding to an older woman's demands may find those of female students more manageable and less intense.

The middle-aged professor suffering from sexual insecurity may find college women especially appealing sexually. Older women may pose not only intellectual and professional threats but also—and perhaps more important—very real sexual pressure. Their sexual demands are greater, and they increase the anxiety of the male in crisis. One man explained to Mayer:

One thing that's true, though, I think you can get a younger woman to respond to you very strongly. She's going to be less appraising than an older woman. She's had less experience.

There are fewer men in her life to which she can compare you. You can dominate her more, sort of impose your myth on her. And you can feel you're initiating her into all sorts of things and blowing her mind and enslaving her—or whatever the hell it is that you want to do with a woman.[6]

The professor whose sexual insecurity contributes to his harassment of students can easily delude himself. He has heard that women students today are freer and engage in intercourse earlier, so taboos about despoiling or deflowering the innocent can be rationalized. At the same time, women students are, by and large, young and lacking the sexual experience of older, more demanding women. Thus the student seems "safe," a novice flattered by the attentions of the professor who can introduce her to the mysterious pleasures of adult sexuality. And the harasser can delude himself into believing that he has done no harm and that the student is responding to his sexuality rather than his position.

Even when sexual activity with the student is the end of harassment, it is not the only motivation. Mayer noted that contemporary social scientists, " . . . in contrast to Freud, who said all human actions were shaped by sexual needs . . . now suggest the opposite: that sexual activity is often motivated by other needs. Non-sexual needs."[7] At any point in a man's life cycle, but especially during midlife, one such need may be competition with other males. The college professor at forty is in an unusual position: he is surrounded by physically desirable young women, as well as by young men in their physical prime. If he has been reared in traditional fashion, he knows that beyond all the myths about male friendships, the truth is that males are taught to relate to one another in one way—competition. Fasteau was clear on this point:

Competition is the principal mode by which men relate to each other—at one level because they don't know how else to make contact, but more basically because it is the way to demonstrate, to themselves, and others, the key masculine qualities of unwavering toughness and the ability to dominate and control. The result is that they inject competition into situations which don't call for it.[8]

The classroom may be one such situation. Male students represent youth, virility, vigor, uncircumscribed futures—everything the man in midlife crisis may feel himself lacking. Added to this may be the professor's doubts about the masculinity of his profession. The males he teaches in the 1980s are interested in careers in high technology, business, engineering, law, and medicine. His own profession is not especially popular—not only because it does not pay well but also because many men do not view it as particularly masculine. A study by David F. Aberle and Kaspar Naegele found, for instance, that middle-class fathers rejected academic careers for their sons because they did "not consider the academic role to exemplify appropriate masculine behavior."[9] The exception was a father who replied that such a role would be appropriate for his son who was shy, bookish, and needed women to care for him. . . .

The harasser lives by an outlaw code. Relying upon colleagues' reluctance to intervene in student-faculty relationships and the romantic notion that eccentricity is tolerable in academe, he has failed to read the signs of change. Higher education may accept idiosyncratic dress, manners, speech, and interests, but sexual harassment is different from these—less superficial and more threatening to the profession. Once professors realize that their own reputations suffer with that of the harasser, male college professors are likely to find the "eccentricity" of the lecherous professor less tolerable and less deserving of defense.

NOTES

1. Eileen Shapiro, "Some Thoughts on Counseling Women Who Perceive Themselves to Be Victims of Non-Actionable Sex Discrimination: A Survival Guide," in "Sexual Harassment: A Hidden Issue," *On Campus with Women*, Project on the Status and Education of Women (Washington, D.C.: American Association of Colleges, 1978), p. 3.

2. Nancy Mayer, *The Male Mid-Life Crisis* (New York: New American Library, 1978), p. 164.

3. David Bradford, Alice Sargent, and Melinda Sprague, "The Executive Man and Woman: The Issue of Sexuality," *Bringing Women Into Management*, eds. Francine Gordon and Myra Strober (New York: McGraw-Hill, 1975), pp. 18–19.

4. Harry Zehner, "Love and Lust on Faculty Row," *Cosmopolitan*, April 1982, p. 273.

5. Mayer, pp. 107, 111–13.

6. Mayer, p. 108.

7. Mayer, p. 107.

8. Mark Feigen Fasteau, *The Male Machine* (New York: McGraw-Hill, 1974), p. 11.

9. David F. Aberle and Kaspar Naegele, "Middle-Class Fathers' Occupational Role and Attitudes Toward Children," *American Journal of Orthopsychiatry* 22 (1952): 366.

Further Questions

1. Do we have reason to feel sorry for faculty who harass? Sorry enough to overlook the harassment?

2. Middle-aged male professors sometimes think of themselves as sexually irresistible to young students, while this thought rarely occurs in the mind of a middle-aged female professor. Any explanations?

3. Could part of an older professor's interest in a younger student be that he is trying to prove himself as desirable as younger male students?

Suggested Moral of Part VIII

If sex (at least as it is understood by men) is in the control of men, as the writings in part VII suggest, it is a small step to men's using such sex, or threats of same, as weapons against women to keep them in a position of subordination. Rape is an action motivated mainly by power, not sexuality. Sex can also be used as a way of harassing women, either explicitly by threats or less explicitly by suggestions and innuendos, on a sustained basis, of sexual activity.

Further Readings for Part VIII: Rape and Sexual Harassment

Constance Backhouse and Leah Cohen. *Sexual Harassment on the Job* (Englewood Cliffs, NJ: Prentice-Hall, 1981).

Helen Benedict. *Recovery: How to Survive Sexual Assault for Women, Men, Teenagers and Their Friends* (New York, NY: Doubleday, 1985).

Timothy Beneke. *Men on Rape* (New York, NY: St. Martin's Press, 1982). Interviews with men on sexual violence.

Susan Brownmiller. *Against Our Will: Men, Women, and Rape* (New York, NY: Simon and Schuster, 1975). Well-written classic: sustained argument that rape threatens all women and is a crime of violence and power.

Lorenne M. G. Clark and Debra J. Lewis. *Rape: The Price of Coercive Sexuality* (Toronto: Women's Educational Press, 1977). Conflict between two social attitudes toward rape: moral outrage and "wink-wink."

Billie Wright Dziech and Linda Weiner. *The Lecherous Professor: Sexual Harassment on Campus* (Boston, MA: Beacon Press, 1984). Intended to break the silence about this problem.

Lin Farley. *Sexual Shakedown: The Sexual Harassment of Women on the Job* (New York, NY: McGraw-Hill, 1978). Mechanisms of sexual harassment of white women, black women, older women, waitresses, etc.

Nicholas Groth with Jean Birnbaum. *Men Who Rape: The Psychology of the Offender* (New York, NY: Plenum Press, 1979).

Linda E. Ledray. *Recovery from Rape* (New York, NY: Henry Holt and Co., 1986). Handbook for rape survivors.

Silvia Levine and Joseph Koenig, ed. *Why Men Rape: Interviews with Convicted Rapists* (Toronto: MacMillan Canada, 1980). Based on National Film Board of Canada's "Why Men Rape." Rather terrifying.

Catharine A. MacKinnon. *Sexual Harassment of Working Women: A Case of Sex Discrimination* (New Haven, CT: Yale University Press, 1979).

Diana E. H. Russell. *The Politics of Rape: The Victim's Perspective* (New York, NY: Stein and Day, 1975).

Diana E. H. Russell. *Sexual Exploitations* (Beverly Hills: Sage Publications, 1984).

Diana E. H. Russell. *Rape in Marriage* (Bloomington, IN: Indiana University Press, Expanded Edition, 1990). One out of 7 married women is raped by her husband. Why?

Amber Coverdale Sumrall and Dena Taylor, eds. *Sexual Harassment: Women Speak Out* (Freedom, CA: The Crossing Press, 1992). Women's experiences in their own voices. Dedicated to Anita Hill.

Robin Warshaw. *I Never Called It Rape: The Ms. Report on Recognizing, Fighting and Surviving Date and Acquaintance Rape* (New York, NY: Harper and Row, 1988).

Part IX

Sex for Sale

Introduction

Part VIII discussed men using sex, as they understand it, to subordinate and control women. One question of this present section is whether paying a woman for sex she otherwise would not want changes the coercive elements in the sexual situation. Prostitution and pornography are the two chief ways of exchanging sex for money.

IX.1   I'm a Hooker: Every Woman's Profession

TERRI-LEE D'AARON

Terri-Lee d'Aaron describes the twelve years she spent as a prostitute. She argues that being paid gives a woman some control in a sexual situation. She claims, however, that she will always be a hooker, because she is a woman living in a world controlled by men.

D'Aaron now lives in Waterloo, Ontario, speaking to groups about her life as a prostitute and working for feminist causes.

Reading Questions

1. Can receiving money for work enhance the value of the work? Can it enhance the value perceived in the work?

2. Can participating in bargaining over pay for work give a worker more control over her working conditions?

3. Is a client of a prostitute deceiving his wife? Would it be better if he told his wife he was having sex with a prostitute?

LIFE ON THE STREET is as hard as the concrete on which the prostitute walks. With every client, she has fears of being robbed, beaten, raped, or even murdered. With these elements of danger constantly surrounding her, why would a woman choose this way of life? Why was I a hooker for almost 12 years?

I

Receiving money for sex in which she has no other interest gives a prostitute an opportunity to take some control, not only of the act itself, but of her body and her life. Men have placed themselves in a situation of power in all aspects of human life, including sex. They see women as performers of services, e.g., housekeepers and caregivers of men and children. Prostitutes are bodies, available to perform sexual services on an occasional basis. The prostitute gains some control of the situation by only agreeing to have sex for a set price, paid in advance, in a place she knows to be safe for her. Receiving money also lessens her feeling of being "cheap" and "easy." If a client (or "date") has paid the correct price, he is not getting anything cheap, and since handing over money puts him to some trouble and expense, the hooker's services have not been easy to acquire. Special difficulties can arise for him when the price that will suit both of them must be arrived at through bargaining. The hooker is in a better position during such bargaining processes because she can walk away if things get too rough or too difficult. He, on the other hand, has some investment in seeing that a bargain is struck, because he has taken the initiative. His male pride is on the line, even when other options are available nearby. Some men like to brag to other men about having been with a hooker, which indicates that striking an agreement with a hooker raises a man's status with other men.

A hooker is, ordinarily, nothing more to her date than an outlet for his sexuality. He has no other feelings for her, nor does he care about her in particular. She just happens to be available, willing, and convenient. In most cases the two will never see each other again. His lack of feeling is no secret to the hooker, even though there is an unspoken understanding that this will not be mentioned. By turning the event into a commercial transaction, the prostitute shields herself from the impact of sex without caring.

The prostitute also has a moral advantage over her date. She can be completely honest about herself with him, as well as with most other people about her profession. Her date knows he is not the first and that there will be others after him, perhaps within half an hour, depending on circumstances. He, on the other hand, always seems to have something to hide, if not from her, from his wife and family. He can hardly go home and talk about his recent sexual activity with a prostitute.

Moreover, while a hooker has taken no vows of fidelity to anyone, the date must consider his marital vows to his wife. Did he not promise to "forsake all others"? He is not being completely honest, even with himself, in refusing to admit the full implications of the double standard he maintains. Should his wife have sex with someone else, this would make her a bitch, a slut, just plain trash. His infidelities, by contrast, are continuing proof of his manhood, his attractiveness to women, and his ability to have anyone he wants. Also, he is not admitting his lack of concern for his wife. If he really still cares about his wife, what is he doing with a prostitute while his wife waits for him at home? What about the money he has spent on the prostitute, which could have gone to his wife instead? (Some men, in fact, take a cut from their pay checks before they are sent to the bank to conceal such expenditures from their wives.) The man's only defense

is that it is "his" money to spend any way he wants. Often he claims he has done more than enough for his wife in keeping a roof over her head and paying the family bills. In his convoluted reasoning, he may even fly into a rage with his wife if she as much as asks him whether he's been with another woman.

Not all clients of prostitutes are formally married, but most are in relationships in which there is expectation of fidelity, caring, and exclusivity.

II

It is a mistake to think of a hooker as selling her body to a client. If she had done so, he would have bought her outright and would then have to take her home, sell her to someone else, or dispose of her in the nearest trashcan. None of this was part of the bargain struck between hooker and client, and usually this is not something he wants, anyway. This leaves the prostitute with full ownership of her body before, during, and after the activity contracted for. At most, she rents out her body, in exchange for cash, prepaid, according to the terms of the agreement struck. However, since hookers have so little personal involvement in their work (although, as mentioned, they do not discuss this with clients), it might be better to think of them as performing sexual services in exchange for an agreed-upon fee.

Dates are usually physically stronger than hookers. And so, it often happens that they will take by force more than was agreed upon and paid for. This is "rape," according to my understanding of the term. Rape is any form of sex forced on a woman against her will; the reasons why a woman is or is not willing are not relevant. If a prostitute is willing to do something in the area of sex in exchange for money, then she is not being raped. If, however, she is forced to do something that she is not willing to do, or is only willing to do if paid, and payment has not taken place, she has been raped. That sex is her profession makes no difference, since rape is not about sex anyway. It is, as we know, about male power and continued control of women. The only difference between rape and other uses of male power (beatings, threats, etc.) is that in rape male power is exercised by violating a woman's sexuality. I have never forced a man into sex against his will and cannot understand why it is so important to men that they do this, not only to me, but to many other women as well.

III

The constant presence of male power and control in the life of every woman is what leads me to say that all women are, like me, hookers. A woman in a bank or restaurant is working for an agreed-upon payment. However, the bank or restaurant is no different from the streets in male control of payment for work done. On the streets, pimps set the prices for all hookers for a particular service. Regardless of whether a hooker works for a pimp, she is in trouble if she overcharges or undercharges, relative to this fee schedule. Only men can be pimps. It is not possible for a woman to break through the "ceiling" that separates pimps from hookers. How is this situation different from that in a bank or restaurant?

I rented out my body for sexual services while other women rent out their talents of counting money or clearing tables. Or women may be wives at home or wives who go home after work to work again under male-controlled conditions. I did sex work, but then, so does a woman in an office who is required to be pleasing to men in appearance and who is subject to sexual harassment. And so, I maintain, all women are hookers.

A hooker can get off the streets, but it is a decision she must make by herself in the absence of any counseling. I was fortunate, in a way. A year after I left the streets, my best friend died. I was put into counseling because it was noticed that not only was I suffering from grief but also a lot of unresolved anger. I have stayed in counseling, gone back to school for retraining, have my own apartment, a part-time job with a moving company, and a family of three cats. I miss the excitement of the streets, but not enough to go back to the dangers and uncertainties I know I would find there. I hope other prostitutes who want to get out will meet with my luck. However, I still think of myself as a hooker, because I will always be a woman.

Further Questions

1. This writer argues that there is no difference between doing sex work under conditions controlled by men and any other sort of work. Do you agree with her?

2. Is rape *any* form of sex without consent, and does it matter *why* the other person does not consent to sex?

3. Ought conditions be made better for prostitutes? For example, ought there to be established safe places where they can take their clients?

Charges Against Prostitution: IX.2A
An Attempt at a Philosophical Assessment

LARS O. ERICSSON

Lars O. Ericsson and Carole Pateman, the author of selection IX.2B, have fundamental disagreements about what prostitution is and whether the prostitute is oppressed in her work. The debate centers on the nature of the transaction between prostitute and client.

Ericsson teaches at the Filosofiska Institionen, Stockholms Universitet, Stockholm.

Reading Questions

The following questions apply to selections IX.2A and IX.2B.

1. What exactly does a prostitute sell in selling sexual services: her labor, her body, her submission, or something else?
2. Is sexual desire a basic need (like that of food and shelter) so that as long as this need is unfulfilled by consenting partners, it is necessary to have prostitution available as an alternative?
3. Is a prostitute oppressed mainly because of her oppressive working conditions or by her relations with her clients?

PERSONALLY, I MUST CONFESS that I, upon reflection, am no more able to see that coition for a fee is intrinsically wrong than I am able to see that drunkenness is. There is something fanatic about both of these views which I find utterly repelling. If two adults voluntarily consent to an economic arrangement concerning sexual activity and this activity takes place in private, it seems plainly absurd to maintain that there is something intrinsically wrong with it. In fact, I very much doubt that it is wrong at all. To say that prostitution is intrinsically immoral is in a way to refuse to give any arguments. The moralist simply "senses" or "sees" its immorality. And this terminates rational discussion at the point where it should begin. . . .

[Also], the comparison between sex love and mercenary lovemaking is both pointless and naive. That lovers have very little need for the services of hustlers is at best a silly argument against prostitution. Most couples are not lovers. A great number of persons do not even have a sexual partner. And not so few individuals will, in any society, always have great difficulties in finding one. What is the point of comparing the ideal sex life of the sentimentalist with the sexual services of prostitutes in the case of someone whose only alternative to the latter is masturbation? Is there any reason to think that mercenary sex must be impersonal, cold, and impoverished compared with autosex?

By this I do not wish to contend that the typical customer is either unattractive, physically or mentally handicapped, or extremely shy. There is abundant empirical evidence showing that the prostitute's customers represent all walks of life and many different types of personalities.[1] That the typical "John" is a male who for some reason cannot find a sexual partner other than a prostitute is just one of the many popular myths about harlotry which empirical studies seem unable to kill. Approximately 75 percent of the customers are married men,[2] most of whom are "respectable" taxpaying citizens.

This brings us to another aspect of the sentimentalist charge. It is not seldom a tacit and insiduous presupposition of the sentimentalist's reasoning that good sex equals intramarital sex, and that bad sex equals extramarital—especially prostitutional—sex. This is just another stereotype, which deserves to be destroyed. Concerning this aspect, Benjamin and Masters make the following comment: "The experience with a prostitute is probably ethically, and may be esthetically, on a higher level than an affectionless intercourse between husband and wife, such as is all too common in our present society."[3] The demarcation line between marital and mercenary sex is not quality but the contrasting nature of the respective legal arrangements. Furthermore, we must not think that the quality—in terms of physical pleasure—of the sex services of prostitutes varies any less than the quality of "regular" sex. The best prostitutional sex available is probably much better from the customer's point of view than average marital sex.

[Finally], I would like to counter the charge that the prostitute-customer relationship is bad on the ground that it involves the selling of something that is too basic and too elementary in human life to be sold. This is perhaps not a sentimentalist charge proper, but since it seems to be related to it I shall deal with it here.

Common parlance notwithstanding, what the hustler sells is of course not her body or vagina, but sexual *services*. If she actually did sell herself, she would no longer be a prostitute but a sexual slave. I wish to emphasize this simple fact, because the popular misnomer certainly contributes to and maintains our distorted views about prostitution.

But is it not bad enough to sell sexual services? To go to bed with someone just for the sake of money? To perform fellatio on a guy you neither love nor care for? In view of the fact that sex is a fundamental need, is it not wrong that anyone should have to pay to have it satisfied and that anyone should profit from its satisfaction? Is it not a deplorable fact that in the prostitute-customer relationship sexuality is completely alienated from the rest of the personality and reduced to a piece of merchandise?

In reply to these serious charges I would, first, like to confess that I have the greatest sympathy for the idea that the means necessary for the satisfaction of our most basic needs should be free, or at least not beyond the economic means of anyone. We all need food, so food should be available to us. We all need clothes and a roof over our heads, so these things should also be available to us. And since our sexual desires are just as basic, natural, and compelling as our appetite for food, this also holds for them. But I try not to forget that this is, and probably for a long time will remain, an *ideal* state of affairs.

Although we live in a society in which we have to pay (often dearly) for the satisfaction of our appetites, including the most basic and natural ones, I still do not regard food vendors and the like with contempt. They fulfill an important function in the imperfect world in which we are destined to live. That we have to pay for the satisfaction of our most basic appetites is no reason for socially stigmatizing those individuals whose profession it is to cater to those appetites. With this, I take it, at least the nonfanatical sentimentalist agrees. But if so, it seems to me inconsistent to hold that prostitution is undesirable on the ground that it involves the selling of something that, ideally, should not be sold but freely given away. Emotional prejudice aside, there is on *this* ground no more reason to despise the sex market and those engaged in it than there is to despise the food market and those engaged in it.

But still, is there not an abyss between selling meat and selling "flesh"? Is there not something private, personal, and intimate about sex that makes it unfit for commercial purposes? Of course, I do not wish to deny that there are great differences between what the butcher does and what the whore does, but at the same time it seems to me clear that the conventional labeling of the former as "respectable" and the latter as "indecent" is not so much the result of these differences as of the influence of cultural, especially religious and sexual, taboos. That the naked human body is "obscene," that genitalia are "offending," that menstrual blood is "unclean," etc., are expressions of taboos which strongly contribute to the often neurotic way in which sex is surrounded with mysteriousness and secrecy. Once we have been able to liberate ourselves from these taboos we will come to realize that we are no more justified in devaluating the prostitute, who, for example, masturbates her customers, than we are in devaluating the assistant nurse, whose job it is to take care of the intimate hygiene of disabled patients. Both help to satisfy important human needs, and both get paid for doing so. That the harlot, in distinction to the nurse, intentionally gives her client pleasure is of course nothing that should be held against her!

As for the charge that in the prostitute-customer relationship sexuality is completely alienated from the rest of the personality—this is no doubt largely true. I fail to see, however, that it constitutes a very serious charge. My reason for this is, once again, that the all-embracing sex act represents an ideal with which it is unfair to compare the prostitute-customer relationship, especially if, as is often the case, such an all-embracing sex act does not constitute a realizable alternative. Moreover, there is no empirical evidence showing that sex between two complete strangers must be of poor quality. . . .

. . . Is harlotry an unequal practice? And if so, in what precisely does its inequality consist? . . . [One] way of interpreting this allegation is to say that prostitution constitutes exploitation of the female sex, since harlots are being exploited by, inter alia, sex capitalists and customers, and a majority of harlots are women. This interpretation of the allegation merits careful study, and I shall therefore in the first instance limit my discussion to the capitalist exploitation of prostitutes.

It is of course true that not all prostitutes can be described as workers in the sex industry. Some are in point of fact more adequately described as small-scale private entrepreneurs. Others are being exploited without being exploited by sex capitalists. Those who can be regarded as workers in the sex industry—the growing number of girls working in sex clubs and similar establishments for instance—are, of course, according to Marxist theory, being exploited in the same sense as any wage worker is exploited. But exploitation in this Marxist sense, although perhaps effective as an argument against wage labor in general, is hardly effective as an argument against prostitution.

There is no doubt, however, that practically all harlots—irrespective of whether they are high-class call girls, cheap streetwalkers, or sex-club performers—are being exploited, economically, in a much more crude sense than that in which an automobile worker at General Motors is being exploited. I am thinking here of the fact that all of them—there are very few exceptions to this—have to pay usury rents in order to be able to operate. Many are literally being plundered by their landlords—sex capitalists who often specialize in letting out rooms, flats, or apartments to people in the racket. Not a few prostitutes also have to pay for "protection" to mafiosi with close connections to organized crime.

What makes all this possible? And what are the implications of the existence of conditions such as these for the question of the alleged undesirability of prostitution? With respect to the first of these questions the answer, it seems to me, is that the major culprit is society's hypocritical attitude toward harlotry and harlots. It is this hypocrisy which creates the prerequisites for the sex-capitalist exploitation of the prostitutes. Let me exemplify what I mean by society's hypocritical—

and, I might add, totally inconsistent—attitude here. On the one hand, most societies, at least in the West (one deplorable exception is the United States), have followed the UN declaration which recommends that prostitution in itself should not be made illegal.[4] One would therefore expect that someone who pursues a legal activity would have the right to rent the necessary premises to advertise her services, and so on. But not so! The penal code persecutes those who rent out rooms, apartments, and other premises to prostitutes. And an editor of a Swedish newspaper was recently convicted for having accepted ads from "models" and "masseuses." In what other legal field or branch would contradictions such as these be considered tolerable? None, of course! One of the first to point out this double morality of society was Alexandra Kollontay, who as early as 1909 wrote: "But if the state tolerates the prostitutes and thereby supports their profession, then it must also accept housing for them and even—in the interest of social health and order—institute houses where they could pursue their occupation."[5] And the most incredible of all is that the official motivation for outlawing persons prepared to provide harlots with the premises necessary for their legal activity is a paternalistic one: so doing is in the best interest of the hustlers themselves, who would otherwise be at the mercy of unscrupulous landlords! In practice, the risk of being thrown in jail of course scares away all but the unscrupulous individuals, who can charge sky-high rents (after all they take a certain risk) and who often are associated with the criminal world. How can anyone, therefore, be surprised at the fact that not so few hustlers display "antisocial tendencies"?

The conclusion I draw from this is that the crude economic exploitation of the prostitutes is not an argument against prostitution. It rather constitutes an accusation against the laws, regulations, and attitudes which create the preconditions for that exploitation. Society cannot both allow harlotry and deprive harlots of reasonable working conditions (as a concession to "common decency") and still expect that all will be well.

[Another] way of interpreting the charge that prostitution is unequal in the sense that it places a burden on women that it does not place on men is to say that whores are being oppressed, reified, and reduced to a piece of merchandise by their male customers. To begin with the last version of this charge first, I have already pointed out the obvious, namely, that whores do not sell themselves. The individual hooker is not for sale, but her sexual services are. One could therefore, with equal lack of propriety, say of any person whose job it is to sell a certain service that he, as a result thereof, is reduced to a piece of merchandise. I cannot help suspecting that behind this talk of reduction to a piece of merchandise lies a good portion of contempt for prostitutes and the kind of services they offer for sale.

As for the version according to which the whore is reified—turned into an object, a thing—it can be understood in a similar way as the one just dealt with. But it can also be understood as the view that the customer does not look upon the prostitute as a human being but as "a piece of ass." He is not interested in her as a person. He is exclusively interested in her sexual performance. . . . [However], since when does the fact that we, when visiting a professional, are not interested in him or her as a person, but only in his or her professional performance, constitute a ground for saying that the professional is dehumanized, turned into an object? . . .

Both men and women need to be liberated from the harness of their respective sex roles. But in order to be able to do this, we must liberate ourselves from those mental fossils which prevent us from looking upon sex and sexuality with the same naturalness as upon our cravings for food and drink. And, contrary to popular belief, we may have something to learn from prostitution in this respect, namely, that coition resembles nourishment in that if it can not be obtained in any other way it can always be bought. And bought meals are not always the worst. . . .

NOTES

1. See Harry Benjamin and R. E. L. Masters, *Prostitution and Morality* (New York: Julian Press, 1964), chap. 6.

2. Ibid.

3. Ibid., p. 208.

4. United Nations, *Study on Traffic in Persons and Prostitution* (New York, 1959).

5. A. Kollontai, *Brak i semeinaja problema* [Marriage and the family problem] (1909); author's translation, p. 46.

Defending Prostitution: Charges Against Ericsson   IX.2B

CAROLE PATEMAN

Pateman has written extensively on philosophy and feminism and teaches political science at the University of California, Los Angeles. Here she disagrees with what Ericsson says in selection IX.2A.

. . . SERVICES AND LABOR POWER are inseparably connected to the body and the body is, in turn, inseparably connected to the sense of self. Ericsson[1] writes of the prostitute as a kind of social worker, but the services of the prostitute are related in a more intimate manner to her body than those of other professionals. Sexual services, that is to say, sex and sexuality, are constitutive of the body in a way in which the counseling skills of the social worker are not (a point illustrated in a backhanded way by the ubiquitous use by men of vulgar terms for female sexual organs to refer to women themselves). Sexuality and the body are, further, integrally connected to conceptions of femininity and masculinity, and all these are constitutive of our individuality, our sense of self-identity. When sex becomes a commodity in the capitalist market so, necessarily, do bodies and selves. The prostitute cannot sell sexual services alone; what she sells is her body. To supply services contracted for, professionals must act in certain ways, or use their bodies; to use the labor power he has bought the employer has command over the worker's capacities and body; to use the prostitute's "services," her purchaser must buy her body and use her body. In prostitution, because of the relation between the commodity being marketed and the body, it is the body that is up for sale. . . .

. . . Certainly, sexual impulses are part of our natural constitution as humans, but the sale of "sexual services" as a commodity in the capitalist market cannot be reduced to an expression of our natural biology and physiology. To compare the fulfillment of sexual urges through prostitution to other natural necessities of human survival, to argue from the fact that we need food, so it should be available, to the claim that "our sexual desires are just as basic, natural, and compelling as our appetite for food, [so] this also holds for them" . . . is, to say the least, disingenuous. What counts as "food" varies widely, of course, in different cultures, but, at the most fundamental level of survival there is one obvious difference between sex and other human needs. Without a certain minimum of food, drink, and shelter, people die; but, to my knowledge, no one has yet died from want of sexual release. Moreover, sometimes food and drink are impossible to obtain no matter what people do, but every person has the means to find sexual release at hand.

To treat prostitution as a natural way of satisfying a basic human need, to state that "bought meals are not always the worst" . . . neatly, if vulgarly, obscures the real, social character of contemporary sexual relations. Prostitution is not, as Ericsson claims, the same as "sex without love or mutual affection" . . .

The latter is morally acceptable *if* it is the result of mutual physical attraction that is freely expressed by both individuals. The difference between sex without love and prostitution is not the difference between cooking at home and buying food in restaurants; the difference is that between the reciprocal expression of desire and unilateral subjection to sexual acts with the consolation of payment: it is the difference for women between freedom and subjection.

To understand why men (not women) demand prostitutes, and what is demanded, prostitution has to be rescued from Ericsson's abstract contractarianism and placed in the social context of the structure of sexual relations between women and men. Since the revival of the organized feminist movement, moral and political philosophers have begun to turn their attention to sexual life, but their discussions are usually divided into a set of discrete compartments which take for granted that a clear distinction can be drawn between consensual and coercive sexual relationships. However, as an examination of consent and rape makes graphically clear,[2] throughout the whole of sexual life domination, subjection, and enforced submission are confused with consent, free association, and the reciprocal fulfillment of mutual desire. The assertion that prostitution is no more than an example of a free contract between equal individuals in the market is another illustration of the presentation of submission as freedom. Feminists have often argued that what is fundamentally at issue in relations between women and men is not sex but power. But, in the present circumstances of our sexual lives, it is not possible to separate power from sex. The expression of sexuality and what it means to be feminine and a woman, or masculine and a man, is developed within, and intricately bound up with, relations of domination and subordination.

Ericsson remarks that "the best prostitutional sex available is probably much better from the customer's point of view than average marital sex". . . . It is far from obvious that it is either "quality" or the "need" for sex, in the common-sense view of "quality" and "sex," that explains why three-quarters of these customers are husbands. In the "permissive society" there are numerous ways in which men can find sex without payment, in addition to the access that husbands have to wives. But, except in the case of the most brutal husbands, most spouses work out a modus vivendi about all aspects of their lives, including the wife's bodily integrity. Not all husbands exercise to the full their socially and legally recognized right—which is the right of a master. There is, however, another institution which enables all men to affirm themselves as masters. To be able to purchase a body in the market presupposes the existence of masters. Prostitution is the public recognition of men as sexual masters; it puts submission on sale as a commodity in the market. . . .

NOTES

1. L. O. Ericsson, "Charges against Prostitution: An Attempt at a Philosophical Assessment," *Ethics* 90, no. 3 (1980): 335–366.

2. C. Pateman, "Women and Consent," *Political Theory* 8 (1980): 149–168.

Further Questions

1. Prostitution exists and most prostitutes of heterosexual clients are women. What does this indicate about gender relations in the area of sex?

2. Are sex and sexual activity more closely connected with our ideas of our bodies than are the things we do with other parts of our bodies?

3. Do you agree with Ericsson that "bought meals [that is, bought sexual encounters] are not always the worst"?

Pornography in Capitalism: Powerlessness   IX.3

ALAN SOBLE

Alan Soble argues that pornography consumption is a response to powerlessness, allowing users to fantasize sexual encounters any way they wish, thus giving them a sense of control of the sexual situation.

Soble teaches philosophy at the University of New Orleans and has produced books on love, sex, and pornography.

Reading Questions

1. If pornography is used to relieve boredom and powerlessness through fantasy, does this suggest a happy situation regarding sexual relations between (or within) genders?

2. Soble claims that pornography does not wholly determine the content of sexual fantasy; instead, it is a foundation on which the consumer builds his own fantasy. To what extent is this true?

3. Is control of one's sexual partner or of the sexual situation an important element in today's sex? Would sex be better off without it?

MY EXPLANATION for the vast consumption of pornography appeals to both the boredom and the powerlessness yielded by capitalist work relations, the nature of labor, and the centralization of economics and politics. Pornography is a diversion, an escape from the dull, predictable world of work. Continued boredom also partially explains the quantity of pornography consumed. The sexual experience that involves visual stimuli, fantasies, and masturbation is intense (because of the hypersensitized penis), but it is short-lived and requires repetition. Visual stimuli arouse quickly but they need to be replaced with new stimuli, hence the quantity of pornography consumed and the attendant "throwaway" commodification of women's bodies. Powerlessness, however, is the more important factor. Being bored with one's wife or lover, or with life in general, is only a small part of the story. And the boredom is just a form of powerlessness or derived from it. . . .

. . . The consumer of pornography uses the material not so much to learn of sexual variations but to obtain the visual and descriptive foundation upon which to build a fantasy. The brute facts provided by the photograph are transformed into a fantastic scenario, and the consumer creates a drama in which he is director, participant, or member of the audience at will. Pornography appeals to the user in virtue of this dramatic scenario; indeed, its partially undefined content, waiting to be expanded into a full script, explains why men consume it in vast quantities.

Pornography allows men to gain a sense of control. In his fantasy world the consumer of pornography is the boss: Mr. X shall screw Ms. Y in position P and at time t while she wears/disrobes/reveals/lubricates/laughs/exclaims/resists/seduces/pouts/farts in exactly the way the consumer wants. (This explanation also illuminates the appeal of prostitution: with a woman he has hired, a man can experience what he wants when he wants it.) Pornographic fantasies provide sexual experiences without the entanglements, mistakes, imperfections, hassles, and misunderstandings that interfere with pleasure and that accompany sex with a wife, lover, girlfriend, or stranger. Or, if there are to be complications, pornographic fantasy allows men to imagine the particular complications that they find arousing. Of course, no mode of sexual activity is ideal; all forms—masturbation with pornography, paying a prostitute, getting married, having sex with strange women—have their advantages and disadvantages. The vast consumption of pornography over the last twenty-five years implies that men perceive the relative benefits of masturbation with pornography as increasingly significant, enough to make that mode of sexuality a contender equal with the others.[1] And the pleasure of fantasized sexuality is not limited to the pleasure of wanting the fantasized activity to actually occur.[2] The pornographic sexual experience is not always a mere substitute for "real" sexual ac-

tivity; it is often "an authentic, autonomous sexual activity."[3]

In a sense, the grab at control through fantasized arrangements is literally infantile,[4] especially if we understand maturity as a willingness to work out problems with the people one associates with. But the male user of pornography has decided, at least implicitly and for certain times or places, that maturity in this sense is not worth the loss of pleasure.[5] Men want these particular pleasures here and now, and in fantasy they have things exactly the way they want them.[6] We would be expecting far too much of people raised in an infantilizing society were we to complain about such regressions; we would be blaming the victims. The use of pornography is an attempt to recoup in the domain of sexual fantasy what is denied to men in production and politics; in this sense the use of pornography in capitalism provides substitute gratification. Pornographic fantasy gives men the opportunity, which they otherwise rarely have, to order the world and conduct its events according to their individual tastes. In the fantasy world permitted by pornography men can be safely selfish and totalitarian. The illusion of omnipotence is a relief from the estranged conditions of their lives and, with a little rationalization, can make existence in that real world, in which they have substantially less power, bearable. Men use pornography as compensation for their dire lack of power; pornography is therefore not so much an expression of male power as it is an expression of their lack of power. . . .

NOTES

1. Leslie Farber's reading of Masters and Johnson concludes that the perfect orgasm is "wholly subject to its owner's will, wholly indifferent to human contingency or context. Clearly, this perfect orgasm is the orgasm achieved on one's own," through masturbation (*Lying, Despair, Jealousy, Envy, Sex, Suicide, Drugs, and the Good Life*, p. 140). If the perfect orgasm is the one achieved in masturbation, then the important question is not "why do men consume so much pornogra-

phy?" but rather "why do men ever bother with sex with prostitutes, wives, girlfriends, and strangers?" Davis remarks, "Considering the obstacles, one wonders how two people ever manage to copulate at all" (*Smut,* p. 20), and he answers: "Plainly, human beings must possess something sexually arousing that animal species, natural phenomena, and technological products lack. That something else is a social self" (p. 106). But one need not wax so metaphysical to explain why masturbation with pornography does not replace other modes of sexuality altogether. Pornography cannot reproduce certain sexual sensations that can be experienced only with another person. Indeed, the ability of pornography to provide satisfaction is reduced if a person cannot use the material to conjure up fantasies based on memories of "real" sexual activity.

2. See Feagin, "Some Pleasures of Imagination," p. 51.

3. Barrowclough, Review of "Not a Love Story," p. 33.

4. Ann Snitow discusses pornography as satisfying the desire to reexperience the omnipotence of childhood, in "Mass Market Romance," pp. 153–154.

5. Nancy Hartsock argues that men enjoy pornography because it allows them to avoid the dangers of intimacy with women, that men's "fear" of intimacy drives them to reassert control through pornography (*Money, Sex, and Power,* pp. 169–170, 176, 252). But this thesis rules out altogether that for some men masturbation with pornography is a sexual activity in its own right with its own advantages. Hartsock also magnifies men's perceptions of relationships when she says they "fear" intimacy. We should not forget that "a woman without a man is like a fish without a bicycle" works both ways.

6. Molly Haskell makes the same point about women's fantasies ("Rape Fantasy," p. 85).

BIBLIOGRAPHY

Barrowclough, Susan. Review of "Not a Love Story," *Screen* 23, 5 (1982): 26–36.

Davis, Murray. *Smut: Erotic Reality/Obscene Ideology* (Chicago: University of Chicago Press, 1983).

Farber, Leslie. *Lying, Despair, Jealousy, Envy, Sex, Suicide, Drugs, and the Good Life* (New York: Basic Books, 1976).

Feagin, Susan L. "Some Pleasures of Imagination." *Journal of Aesthetics and Art Criticism* 43, 1 (1984): 41–55.

Hartsock, Nancy C. M. *Money, Sex, and Power* (New York: Longman, 1983).

Haskell, Molly. "Rape Fantasy." *Ms.,* November 1976.

Snitow, Ann B. "Mass Market Romance: Pornography for Women is Different." *Radical History Review* 20 (1979): 141–61.

Francis Biddle's Sister: IX.4
Pornography, Civil Rights, and Speech

CATHARINE MACKINNON

Catharine MacKinnon maintains that pornography sexualizes and thereby promotes some of the worst elements of human life: rape, abuse, battery, etc. In other words, pornography eroticizes men's control of women.

MacKinnon is presently on the faculty of the School of Law, University of Michigan, and has published extensively on feminist issues from a legal perspective.

Reading Questions

1. Does pornography promote bad gender relations, and control of women by men in particular, by making these seem "sexy"?

2. Does pornography depict forms of sex, or particular sexual practices, that contain disturbing, demeaning, or harmful elements?

3. Does pornography set out a script for men to follow in sexual relations with women and, by implication, a message that a woman should comply with various male-initiated sexual practices, whether she wants to or not?

. . . PORNOGRAPHY SEXUALIZES RAPE, battery, sexual harassment, prostitution, and child sexual abuse; it thereby celebrates, promotes, authorizes, and legitimizes them. More generally, it eroticizes the dominance and submission that is the dynamic common to them all. It makes hierarchy sexy and calls that "the truth about sex"[1] or just a mirror of reality. Through this process pornography constructs what a woman is as what men want from sex. This is what the pornography means.

Pornography constructs what a woman is in terms of its view of what men want sexually, such that acts of rape, battery, sexual harassment, prostitution, and sexual abuse of children become acts of sexual equality. Pornography's world of equality is a harmonious and balanced place.[2] Men and women are perfectly complementary and perfectly bipolar. Women's desire to be fucked by men is equal to men's desire to fuck women. All the ways men love to take and violate women, women love to be taken and violated. The women who most love this are most men's equals, the most liberated; the most participatory child is the most grown-up, the most equal to an adult. Their consent merely expresses or ratifies these preexisting facts.

The content of pornography is one thing. There, women substantively desire dispossession and cruelty. We desperately want to be bound, battered, tortured, humiliated, and killed. Or, to be fair to the soft core, merely taken and used. This is erotic to the male point of view. Subjection itself, with self-determination ecstatically

relinquished, is the content of women's sexual desire and desirability. Women are there to be violated and possessed, men to violate and possess us, either on screen or by camera or pen on behalf of the consumer. On a simple descriptive level, the inequality of hierarchy, of which gender is the primary one, seems necessary for sexual arousal to work. Other added inequalities identify various pornographic genres or subthemes, although they are always added through gender: age, disability, homosexuality, animals, objects, race (including anti-Semitism), and so on. Gender is never irrelevant.

What pornography *does* goes beyond its content: it eroticizes hierarchy, it sexualizes inequality. It makes dominance and submission into sex. Inequality is its central dynamic; the illusion of freedom coming together with the reality of force is central to its working. Perhaps because this is a bourgeois culture, the victim must look free, appear to be freely acting. Choice is how she got there. Willing is what she is when she is being equal. It seems equally important that then and there she actually be forced and that forcing be communicated on some level, even if only through still photos of her in postures of receptivity and access, available for penetration. Pornography in this view is a form of forced sex, a practice of sexual politics, an institution of gender inequality.

From this perspective, pornography is neither harmless fantasy nor a corrupt and confused misrepresentation of an otherwise natural and healthy sexual situation. It institutionalizes the sexuality of male supremacy, fusing the erotization of dominance and submission with the social construction of male and female. To the extent that gender is sexual, pornography is part of constituting the meaning of that sexuality. Men treat women as who they see women as being. Pornography constructs who that is. Men's power over women means that the way men see women defines who women can be. Pornography is that way. Pornography is not imagery in some relation to a reality elsewhere constructed. It is not a distortion, reflection, projection, expression, fantasy, representation, or symbol either. It is a sexual reality. . . .

In this approach, the experience of the (overwhelmingly) male audiences who consume pornography is therefore not fantasy or simulation or catharsis but sexual reality, the level of reality on which sex itself largely operates. Understanding this dimension of the problem does not require noticing that pornography models are real women to whom, in most cases, something real is being done; not does it even require inquiring into the systematic infliction of pornography and its sexuality upon women, although it helps. What matters is the way in which the pornography itself provides what those who consume it want. Pornography *participates* in its audience's eroticism through creating an accessible sexual object, the possession and consumption of which *is* male sexuality, as socially constructed; to be consumed and possessed as which, *is* female sexuality, as socially constructed; pornography is a process that constructs it that way.

The object world is constructed according to how it looks with respect to its possible uses. Pornography defines women by how we look according to how we can be sexually used. Pornography codes how to look at women, so you know what you can do with one when you see one. Gender is an assignment made visually, both originally and in everyday life. A sex object is defined on the basis of its looks, in terms of its usability for sexual pleasure, such that both the looking—the quality of the gaze, including its

point of view—and the definition according to use become eroticized as part of the sex itself. This is what the feminist concept "sex object" means. In this sense, sex in life is no less mediated than it is in art. Men have sex with their image of a woman. It is not that life and art imitate each other; in this sexuality, they *are* each other.

To give a set of rough epistemological translations, to defend pornography as consistent with the equality of the sexes is to defend the subordination of women to men as sexual equality. What in the pornographic view is love and romance looks a great deal like hatred and torture to the feminist. Pleasure and eroticism become violation. Desire appears as lust for dominance and submission. The vulnerability of women's projected sexual availability, that acting we are allowed (that is, asking to be acted upon), is victimization. Play conforms to scripted roles. Fantasy expresses ideology, is not exempt from it. Admiration of natural physical beauty becomes objectification. Harmlessness becomes harm. Pornography is a harm of male supremacy made difficult to see because of its pervasiveness, potency, and principally, because of its success in making the world a pornographic place. Specifically, its harm cannot be discerned, and will not be addressed, if viewed and approached neutrally, because it *is* so much of "what is." In other words, to the extent pornography succeeds in constructing social reality, it becomes invisible as harm. If we live in a world that pornography creates through the power of men in a male-dominated situation, the issue is not what the harm of pornography is, but how that harm is to become visible. . . .

We define pornography as the graphic sexually explicit subordination of women through pictures or words that also includes women dehumanized as sexual objects, things, or commodities; enjoying pain or humiliation or rape; being tied up, cut up, mutilated, bruised, or physically hurt; in postures of sexual submission or servility or display; reduced to body parts, penetrated by objects or animals, or presented in scenarios of degradation, injury, torture; shown as filthy or inferior; bleeding, bruised, or hurt in a context that makes these conditions sexual. Erotica, defined by distinction as not this, might be sexually explicit materials premised on equality.[3] We also provide that the use of men, children, or transsexuals in the place of women is pornography.[4] The definition is substantive in that it is sex-specific, but it covers everyone in a sex-specific way, so is gender neutral in overall design.

There is a buried issue within sex discrimination law about what sex, meaning gender, is. If sex is a *difference,* social or biological, one looks to see if a challenged practice occurs along the same lines; if it does, or if it is done to both sexes, the practice is not discrimination, not inequality. If, by contrast, sex has been a matter of *dominance,* the issue is not the gender difference but the difference gender makes. In this more substantive, less abstract approach, the concern with inequality is whether a practice *subordinates* on the basis of sex. The first approach implies that marginal correction is needed; the second requires social change. Equality, in the first view, centers on abstract symmetry between equivalent categories; the asymmetry that occurs when categories are not equivalent is not inequality, it is treating unlikes differently. In the second approach, inequality centers on the substantive, cumulative disadvantagement of social hierarchy. Equality for the first is nondifferentiation; for the second, nonsubordination.[5] Although it is consonant with both approaches, our antipornography statute emerges largely from an analysis of the problem under the second approach.

To define pornography as a practice of sex discrimination combines a mode of portrayal that has a legal history—the sexually explicit—with an active term that is central to the inequality of the sexes—subordination. Among other things, subordination means to be in a position of inferiority or loss of power, or to be demeaned or denigrated.[6] To be someone's subordinate is the opposite of being their equal. The definition does not include all sexually explicit depictions *of* the subordination of women. That is not what it says. It says, this which *does* that: the sexually explicit that subordinates women. . . .

The harm of pornography, broadly speaking, is the harm of the civil inequality of the sexes made invisible as harm because it has become accepted as the sex difference. Consider this analogy with race: if you see Black people as different, there is no harm to segregation; it is merely a recognition of that difference. To neutral principles, separate but equal was equal. The injury of racial separation to blacks arises "solely because [they] choose to put that construction upon it."[7] Epistemologically translated: how you see it is not the way it is. Similarly, if you see women as just different, even or especially if you don't know that you do, subordination will not look like subordination at all, much less like harm. It will merely look like an appropriate recognition of the sex difference.

Pornography does treat the sexes differently, so the case for sex differentiation can be made here. But men as a group do not tend to be (although some individuals may be) treated the way women are treated in pornography. As a social group, men are not hurt by pornography the way women as a social group are. Their social status is not defined as *less* by it. So the major argument does not turn on mistaken differentiation, particularly since the treatment of women according to pornography's dictates makes it all too often accurate. The salient quality of a distinction between the top and the bottom in a hierarchy is not difference, although top is certainly different from bottom; it is power. So the major argument is: subordinate but equal is not equal. . . .

The first victims of pornography are the ones in it. To date, it has only been with children, and male children at that, that the Supreme Court has understood that before the pornography became the pornographer's speech, it was somebody's life.[8] This is particularly true in visual media, where it takes a real person doing each act to make what you see. This is the double meaning in a statement one ex-prostitute made at our hearing: "[E]very single thing you see in pornography is happening to a real woman right now."[9] Linda Marchiano, in her book *Ordeal*,[10] recounts being coerced as "Linda Lovelace" into performing for *Deep Throat*, a fabulously profitable film,[11] by being abducted, systematically beaten, kept prisoner, watched every minute, threatened with her life and the lives of her family if she left, tortured, and kept under constant psychological intimidation and duress. . . .

What would justice look like for these women?[12] Linda Marchiano said, "Virtually every time someone watches that film, they are watching me being raped . . . "[13]

NOTES

1. Michel Foucault, "The West and the Truth of Sex," 20 *Sub-Stance* 5 (1978).

2. This became a lot clearer to me after reading Margaret Baldwin, "The Sexuality of Inequality: The Minneapolis Pornography Ordinance," 2 *Law and Inequality: Journal of Theory and Practice* 629 (1984). This paragraph is directly indebted to her insight and language there.

3. *See, e.g.,* Gloria Steinem, "Erotica v. Pornography," in *Outrageous Acts and Everyday Rebellions* 219 (1983).

4. . . . No definition can convey the meaning of a word as well as its use in context can. However, what Andrea Dworkin and I mean by pornography is rather well captured in our legal definition: "Pornography is the graphic sexually explicit subordination of women, whether in pictures or in words, that also includes one or more of the following: (i) women are presented dehumanized as sexual objects, things or commodities; or (ii) women are presented as sexual objects who enjoy pain or humiliation; or (iii) women are presented as sexual objects who experience sexual pleasure in being raped; or (iv) women are presented as sexual objects tied up or cut up or mutilated or bruised or physically hurt; or (v) women are presented in postures of sexual submission, servility or display; or (vi) women's body parts—including but not limited to vaginas, breasts, and buttocks—are exhibited, such that women are reduced to those parts; or (vii) women are presented as whores by nature; or (viii) women are presented being penetrated by objects or animals; or (ix) women are presented in scenarios of degradation, injury, torture, shown as filthy or inferior, bleeding,

bruised, or hurt in a context that makes these conditions sexual." Pornography also includes "the use of men, children or transsexuals in the place of women." Pornography, thus defined, is discrimination on the basis of sex and, as such, a civil rights violation. This definition is a slightly modified version of the one passed by the Minneapolis City Council on December 30, 1983. Minneapolis, Minn., Ordinance amending tit. 7, chs. 139 and 141, Minneapolis Code of Ordinances Relating to Civil Rights (Dec. 30, 1983). The ordinance was vetoed by the mayor, reintroduced, passed again, and vetoed again in 1984. . . . The Indianapolis City and County Council passed a version of it eliminating subsections (i), (v), (vi), and (vii), and substituting instead as (vi) "women are presented as sexual objects for domination, conquest, violation, exploitation, possession, or use, or through postures or positions of servility or submission or display." Indianapolis, Ind., City-County General Ordinance No. 35 (June 11, 1984) (adding inter alia, ch. 16, § 16-3(q)(6) to the Code of Indianapolis and Marion County) . . .

5. *See* Catharine A. MacKinnon, *Sexual Harassment of Working Women* 101–41 (1979).

6. For a lucid discussion of subordination, *see* Andrea Dworkin, "Against the Male Flood: Censorship, Pornography, and Equality," 8 *Harvard Women's Law Journal* 1 (1985).

7. *See* Plessy v. Ferguson, 163 U.S. at 551; Herbert Wechsler, "Toward Neutral Principles of Constitutional Law," 73 *Harvard Law Review* 1 (1959) at 33.

8. *Ferber*, 458 U.S. 747 (1982).

9. *Public Hearings on Ordinances to Add Pornography as Discrimination Against Women,* Committee on Government Operations, City Council, Minneapolis, Minn. (Dec. 12–13, 1983) [hereinafter cited as *Hearings*]. All those who testified in these hearings were fully identified to the City Council. II *Hearings* 75 (testimony of a named former prostitute).

10. Linda Lovelace and Michael McGrady, *Ordeal* (1980).

11. As of September, 1978, *Deep Throat* had grossed a known $50 million worldwide. . . . Many of its profits are untraceable. The film has also recently been made into a home video cassette.

12. This question . . . draw[s] directly on [a s]peech by Andrea Dworkin, in Toronto, Feb. 1984 (account told to Dworkin), reprinted in *Healthsharing*, Summer 1984, at 25.

13. I *Hearings* 56.

IX.5   The Roots of Pornography

DAVID STEINBERG

David Steinberg notes that pornography is not about our real selves but about our fantasies and unfulfilled desires. Because of social conditioning, women's sexual desire is truncated. Pornography fulfills men's fantasy of women possessed with desire for sex with them.

Steinberg is author, editor, and publisher of sex-positive, erotic photography and writing. He has been active in the California and national feminist men's movements for the past fifteen years.

Reading Questions

1. Is the expectation that men be sexual initiators burdensome for men? Who, exactly, expects this of men?

2. Does pornography, which portrays sex between people but very little else, alienate people from their sexual selves?

3. Does pornography, at the same time, validate sex and sexual feeling in a somewhat puritanical society?

IT IS STRIKING THAT in the midst of so much vehement debate on the subject of pornography, there is so little discussion of, or attempt to understand, the nature of the pornographic phenomenon itself. The *Hite Report on Male Sexuality* notes that eighty-nine percent of its respondents report some involvement with pornography. Something basic is going on here.

What is it that makes pornography so popular among American men and, increasingly, among American women? Why does it sell? What does pornography accomplish, or seem to accomplish, for the tens of millions of people who are its market?

For myself, and for virtually all the men I have talked to, pornography is essentially a tool for masturbation, a fantasy enhancer. This is important to remember. Pornography is not about partner sex, not about sexual reality, not about our real lovers and mates, not about our real selves. Though women I have talked to consistently fear that their male lovers expect them to look and act like *Playboy* models or porn stars, I believe that the vast majority of men who use pornography are clear about the difference between images and real people, between archetypes and human beings, between the jet-setters and the rest of us.

To be effective, then, pornography must be good masturbation material. It must address our longings, our unfulfilled desires, the sexual feelings that have power in fantasy precisely because they are unsatisfied in our real lives. So what are some of these unresolved sexual issues addressed by men through pornography?

From my point of view, the most important single issue that welds men so forcefully to pornography is that of sexual scarcity. Although attitudes are changing, most heterosexual men still experience sex from the perspective of scarcity.

Men seem to want sex more than women. Men try to get women to have sex with them. Or, more subtly: Men seem to respect sexual desire more than women do. Men feel resistance to sexual desire from women, expressed as fear, reluctance, disinterest, even revulsion.

Women, sadly, have been handed (and have generally accepted) the cultural role of being the final defenders of puritan antisex. Sexual desire is evil, they are told, or at least low. Men desire. Women—higher, more spiritual beings than men—are to distrust and defend themselves against male desire and will be severely punished if they do not. Women are not to enjoy being the focus for male desire and certainly ought not desire sex for its own sake.

Women are taught to experience sexual desire only in the context of emotional commitment or expression of affection, not as simple bodily hunger. Lust is, by definition, unwomanly. To be a lustful woman—especially a lustful young woman—still carries slutty connotations that few women want to engage.

Let me be clear that I am in no way blaming women for this situation. Nor am I trying to invalidate the many reasons women are protective of themselves sexually—ranging from fear of pregnancy, to fear of rape, to fear of mother, to fear of losing the respect of other women or of men. I am simply noting that we live in a sex economy that produces an ongoing pool of surplus male desire, a culture that fears even the best of male desire, a world that gives men precious little opportunity to be desired, feel desirable, feel attractive and appreciated for our sexual natures.

A closely related issue, one that is perhaps even more significant emotionally, is that of rejection. Even in progressive, "liberated," "enlightened" circles, and certainly in the dominant culture, men still carry the burden for being the sexual initiators, the desirers, and thus, inevitably, the rejected ones. A difficult, dangerous, and painful job but, as they say, somebody has to do it.

I believe that we are only beginning to appreciate the significance of the emotional work men must do to be able to repeatedly express sexual interest and initiative to those who are being taught to reject us. Warren Farrell, author of *Why Men Are the Way They Are,* suggests that men's attempts to deal psychologically with rejection have a lot to do with our need to objectify women—that it is less painful to be rejected by an object than by a thinking, feeling human being. I think he's right.

In any case, fear of rejection, and the resulting negative feelings about ourselves as sexual beings and about our sexual desirability, are difficult aspects of sexual manhood all men grapple with, usually with only partial success. The residue is part of the emotional material we take to pornography.

I believe that these issues—sexual scarcity, desire for appreciation and reciprocation of desire, and fear of being sexually undesirable—are the central forces that draw men to pornography. While violent imagery, by various estimates, accounts for only three to eight percent of all pornography, images that address scarcity, female lust, and female expression of male desirability account for at least seventy-five percent of porn imagery.

Pornography is a vehicle men use to help us fantasize sexual situations that soothe these wounds. The central themes are available, lusty sex, focused on *our* desirability, involving archetypal images of the very women who must represent our felt undesirability in real life. When we buy pornographic magazines, take them to the safety and privacy of our bedrooms, and masturbate to their images (or when we masturbate to the images of these same women on screen), we vent the frustrations born of scarcity, the sexual fears born of rejection, and the sexual insecurity born of being so seldom appreciated by women for our specifically sexual existence.

And which images most effectively accomplish this for us? Images of women who are openly desirous of sex, who look out at us from the page with all the yearning we know so well yet so rarely receive from our partners. Images of women hungry for sex *with us,* possessed by desire *for us.* Women hungry to get their hands on our bodies or get our hands on theirs. Receptive women who greet our sexual desire not with fear and loathing but with appreciation, even gratitude. And glamorous women whose mere bestowal of sexual attention mythically proves our sexual worth.

Is it any wonder that such a sexual world is attractive to so many men? The problem, however, is that although the pornographic fantasies may be soothing in the moment, they often contribute to bad feelings about ourselves over time. This depends on the specific images, what we do with them, and how we feel about ourselves to begin with. But in general, the more the imagery of pornography confirms who we are as sexual people, the better we will probably feel about our sexual energies afterward. Conversely, the more we are told that to be sexually desirable we need to be other than who we really are, the worse we will feel.

From this point of view, much of pornography is likely to affect us negatively (although, again, not all—and we *do* get to pick and choose among the offerings). Michael Castleman, in his book *Sexual Solutions,* notes how seldom pornography includes "any kissing, handholding, caressing, massages, reciprocal undressing, tenderness or discussion of lovemaking preferences." It is sad that pornography speaks so little about softness, vulnerability, uncertainty, intimacy—all of which we know to be important parts of our sexual reality.

But the likelihood that pornography may alienate us from our sexual selves, or the fact that it fails to offer more than temporary relief from our sexual wounds, should not blind us to the very real and valid feelings that attract us to the medium in the first place.

Besides, not all of our attraction to pornography is rooted in pain and fear, and not all of pornography's effects are negative. Pornography is still the medium that most vociferously advocates free and diverse sexual expressiveness, a radical stance in our culture, which is still essentially puritanical and sex-negative. Pornography still serves as an arena for adolescents to get validation and approval for their emerging sexual feelings, whose power far exceeds what society is willing to endorse as proper. Pornography is still an ally for those of us who choose to fight for the full recognition and admiration of our sexual natures in the face of the growing forces of sexual repression.

Pornography is the one arena that is not afraid of the penis, even when erect, that does not find sperm disgusting, that shows pictures of men ejaculating in slow motion, even as other films emphasize the beauty of birds flying or dolphins leaping. And it is in the world of pornography where much of traditional male hatred and fear of vaginas has been redirected toward vaginal appreciation, through what writer Michael Hill calls "graphic and realistic depictions of the cunt as beautiful, tasty, wonderful to smell and touch."

In addition, pornography, for all its *mis*information, is still an important source of real and useful sexual information as well. The "G" spot and the normalcy of female ejaculation have been introduced to mass culture not by sex therapists but by the porn network. Dozens of magazines, and now a feature-length film, have taught men these important aspects of *female* pleasure. Mass acceptance of oral and anal sex as normal sexual practices has been accelerated by the repeated, indeed casual, depiction of these acts in hundreds of porn films.

Porn films in general offer real learn-by-watching information (the information we should all receive as emerging adults, but don't) on all kinds of sexual practices—as long as we bring a critical eye to tell the fake from the real (there's plenty of both), and the friendly from the nasty (also both well-represented). And if we want to encourage our sexual imagination, going to see a variety of sex loops will give us plenty of food for thought, and plenty of support for what we may feel to be our unique infatuations.

Finally, I think it is important to acknowledge that pornography provides a victimless outlet for the basic sexual rage that seems to sit within so many men, whether we like it or not. This is the rage that sadly gets vented at specific women through rape and other forms of sexual assault. It will not go away from the social psyche, pornography or no pornography.

For all the terrible pain this rage has brought to women, we must understand that at the core of this feeling there is a righteous anger: the anger at having our naturally exuberant, lively, pleasurable sexual feelings twisted, stunted, denied, and used against us. This anger needs to be acknowledged, respected, and redirected away from women, toward its appropriate targets: antisexual religious teachings, sex-phobics in general, the complex of societal institutions intent on denying us all the natural exploration of one of life's greatest miracles.

Respecting the roots of male sexual anger may be as uncomfortable for us as respecting the roots of our attraction to pornography. But both are important to own and affirm. If we can respect the core of what attracts us to pornography, we can begin to find ways to have that core more effectively addressed by the sexual materials we use. On the other hand, if we think that every time we're drawn to pornography we only express the worst of ourselves as men, we will both hate ourselves and become trapped in repeating and self-defeating cycles of guilt and rebellion.

What is needed, in my opinion, is not an attempt to drive pornography underground, socially or psychically. If pornography becomes outlawed (again), it, like prostitution, will only come to represent the notion that sex is dirty, even more strongly than it does today. What is needed instead is the development of sexual materials that take the *best* of the pornographic tradition— sexual openness, exploration, and celebration— and add to these egalitarian values, imagination,

artfulness, respect of ourselves, and respect for the power and beauty of sex itself.

We need sexual materials that more fully address our real sexual needs and feelings, materials that help us feel better about ourselves, materials that enable us to resist the antisexual insanity that assaults us every day. We need material with which we can identify without contradicting our best sexual intuitions—photographs and stories whose beauty affirms our own sexual power and worth.

Happily, we can now point to the beginning of such materials. In the past few years, a group of us have developed an erotic theater show, *Celebration of Eros,* a dramatic presentation of poetry and prose with four slide shows set to music, to celebrate the best of our erotic natures. I have also recently edited an extensive hardcover collection of high-quality erotic photography, writing, and drawing, *Erotic by Nature* (Shakti Press/Red Alder Books). Excellent collections of erotic writing by women have recently been edited by Susie Bright (*Herotica,* Down There Press), Laura Chester (*Deep Down,* Faber & Faber), and Lonnie Barbach (*Pleasures: Erotic Interludes,* Doubleday). *Yellow Silk,* a journal of erotic arts whose motto is "all persuasions, no brutality," is in its seventh year of publication. *On Our Backs,* a San Francisco magazine of "entertainment for the adventurous lesbian," is to my knowledge the first explicitly feminist sex magazine anywhere.

We need more. We need what Paula Webster calls "a truly radical feminist pornography-erotica." Recent thinking and writing among the sex radicals of the feminist movement are an encouraging start toward understanding what such a feminist pornography might look like. Hopefully, before too long, when we and our sons and daughters go out to buy some sexual stimulation, we'll all be able to feel good about what we bring home.

Further Questions

1. Is it natural, in some sense, to want a lot of sex, so that lack of sexual desire must be due to social inhibition?

2. In introducing novel forms of sex, does pornography teach people things they should become aware of as possibilities?

3. Would it make sense for a man who wanted to vent his rage on women by rape or other forms of sexual assault to use pornography as an outlet instead?

IX.6   Gays and the Pornography Movement: Having the Hots for Sex Discrimination

JOHN STOLTENBERG

John Stoltenberg draws some interesting connections between gay pornography, homophobia, and woman hating. The typical gay male sex film detaches sex from other relations between people, promotes maleness, degrades the feminine, and makes subordination sexy.

John Stoltenberg is author of *Refusing to Be a Man* (Penguin US/Meridian).

Reading Questions

1. In (hard core) pornography, gay and straight, is there too much emphasis on the genitalia, the penis in particular, to the exclusion of almost everything else?

2. Do people get "soft and awful feelings" about the feminine aspects of themselves, perhaps centering on the fact that one of their parents was female?

3. Does it make sense to resolve such feelings by "being the man" with someone else in a sexual situation?

The World of Gay Male Sex Films

THE TYPICAL GAY MALE SEX FILM is comprised of explicit sex scenes, frequently between strangers, often with a sound track consisting solely of music and dubbed-in groans. During these sex scenes there is almost always an erect penis filling the screen. If the camera cuts away from the penis, the camera will be back within seconds. Scenes are set up so that closeups of penises and what they are doing and what is happening to them show off to best advantage. Most of the closeups of penises are of penises fucking in and out of asses and mouths, being blown, or being jacked off. A penis that is not erect, not being pumped up, not in action, just there feeling pretty good, is rarely to be seen: You wouldn't know it was feeling if it wasn't in action; and in the world of gay male sex films, penises do not otherwise feel anything.

Curiously, there is a great deal of repression of affect in gay male sex films—a studied impassivity that goes beyond amateur acting. The blankness of the faces in what is ostensibly the fever pitch of passion suggests an unrelatedness not only between partners but also within each partner's own body. This is sex labor that is alienated, these dead faces seem to say.

The film edits go by quickly. A few seconds at one angle. Then a few seconds over there. The camera on the cock. Almost always on the cock. The cock almost always hard and pumping. No moments in between anything. How did they get from that to this? Quick cut to the cock. Wait, in between there, wasn't there a moment between them when they just briefly—? Cut. Cut. The rhythms of the sex film are the staccatos of sexual disconnecting; they are not the rhythms of any credible sequence of sexual communion —those moments of changing pace, touching base, remembering who you're with, expressing, responding. All of that is cut out. All of that doesn't show. All that shows is "the action": the progress of the cock, the status of the cock.

Most of the sex acts are acts of detaching. They give the illusion of forging a connection, in the sense of hooking up plumbing; but they seem to be experienced as acts of abstracting apart, of getting off by going away someplace, of not *being there* with anybody. Sucking shots are classics of this sort: There the two men are, a blow job going on between them, and they might as well be at a glory hole.

The sex that is had in gay male sex films is the sex that is showable. And what is shown about it is the fetishized penis. When the obligatory cum shot comes, you see it in slow motion, perhaps photographed from several angles simultaneously, the penis pulled out of its orifice just for the occasion, being pumped away at, squirting, maybe someone trying to catch it in his mouth. There's no way to show how orgasm feels, and the difference between the reality and the representation is nowhere more striking than in the cum shot—a disembodied spurt of fluid to certify the sex is "real." Even leaving aside the rough stuff of gay male pornography—the scenes of forced fellatio, assault and molestation, humiliation and exploitation, chaining and bondage, the violence interlarded among the allegedly noncoercive sucking and fucking, as if to tip us off that in all this sex there is an undercurrent of force and domination—even leaving aside all of that, what exactly is there in the merely explicit sex scenes that recommends itself as good sex? What are we being told that sex can mean *between* people, if anything? What are we being told about what men must become in order to have what looks like blockbuster sex? What are we being told to do with the rest of ourselves?—what are we being told to lop off from ourselves and the history of our relationships with one another and our responsibilities to one another in order to feel at liberty to have sex at all?

The values in the sex that is depicted in gay male sex films are very much the values in the sex that gay men tend to have. They are also, not incidentally, very much the values in the sex that straight men tend to have—because they are very much the values that male supremacists tend to have: taking, using, estranging, dominating— essentially, sexual power-mongering.

I wonder sometimes: Has the saturation of the gay male subculture by these values created a population completely numb to the consequences of pornography for women? Can gay men who are sexually hooked on these values ever perceive the harm that pornography does to women? Or has the world of the gay male sex film become the only world they want to know?

Homophobia and Woman-Hating

. . . Homophobia is not just in the social system, it's not just in the structure, it's not just in the laws. You can feel it in the muscle power of cops when they're cracking gay heads, and you can feel it in the taunts of teenage boys who are on a rampage of gay-baiting and queer-bashing. It's a kind of sexualized contempt for someone whose mere existence—because he is smeared with female status—threatens to melt down the code of armor by which men protect themselves from other men.

And you can also feel homophobia inside yourself. When you're living in an erotic hierarchy, where to be demeaned in sex is to be feminized, and to have power over someone else is to be male—when that's the sexual structure you're supposed to fit into—it leaves you hanging, as if clinging by your fingernails to a cliff, scrambling for the top, terrified to fall. It leaves you eroticizing masculinity as power over other people. And it leaves you enamored of male supremacy as an erotic ideal.

To have internalized homophobia as a gay man means you too dread the degraded status of anything feminine about yourself; it means you too dread that anything about your body might remind you of females in general, or perhaps your mother in particular; it means that in your own queer way, you're in a constant quest "to be the man there." One of the commonest ways to do that is by seizing on the masculinity of someone else whom you perceive as more of a real man than you—because you want to be like him, you want to acquire and assimilate his maleness in order to recharge your gender batteries, which seem to keep running down; because you need the jolt of some juice from a positive pole—and so you try things to interest him or you ingest him or you submit to his aggression sexually or you let him leave some violence on you, on your body, so you'll feel it in the morning. And it works; you get a heavy load of his manhood and it makes you feel as if it's in you too, purging your body of those soft and awful feelings you get from having had one of your parents be female. The patterns of subordination that go on between men help resolve internalized homophobia, momentarily, while you're having sex. Power-game, dominance-and-submission sex works because it lets someone "be the man there"; in fact it can let *two* males be the man there if they're courteous about it, if they follow the rules. The trouble is, this kind of sexuality can escalate;

and often as not it must, completely crossing the line of what is physically and emotionally safe for one partner or the other. Thoroughgoing subordination in sex is not victimless; there *must* be victims, and there are—nobody really knows how many. Coroners know when someone gets killed from something that looks a lot like extreme S/M; there are boys who have been molested, gay men who have been battered and raped in sexual relationships. Nevertheless, there is a sexiness in subordination, and its sexiness for gay men in particular has a lot to do with the fact that subordination in sex helps resolve a misogynist struggle to cling to male supremacy. For a gay man who wants to have that kind of identity—a femiphobic sexual connection with other men—subordinating someone helps reinforce during the time of sex his tenuous connection to an idea of manhood that only exists because it exists over and against women. It works—until it doesn't work. It tends to leave you rather addicted to forms of passion that exclude compassion, and it can lead very easily to forms of restraint and bondage, control-and-power head trips, and physical abuse that can leave someone in the relationship feeling very much unsafe, very unwhole, very unequal, and very ripped off.

Consider in this context the current political strategy to achieve social acceptability for queers loving queers. We cannot chip away at this thing called homophobia—through laws and litigation and luncheons and so on—without going to the root of the sex-class system, without dismantling the power structure of men over women, which is an *eroticized* power structure. So long as that structure stays in place, homophobia will stay put too, because homophobia is necessary to the maintenance of men's power over women. The system of male supremacy can't tolerate queerness; it will never tolerate queerness. It needs the hatred of women and of queerness in order to prevail, in order to keep men doing to women what men are supposed to do to women.

The system of gender polarity requires that people with penises treat people without as objects, as things, as empty gaping vessels waiting to be filled with turgid maleness, if necessary by force. Homophobia is, in part, how the system punishes those whose object choice is deviant. Homophobia keeps women the targets. Homophobia assures a level of safety, selfhood, self-respect, and social power to men who sexually objectify correctly. Those of us who are queer cannot fully appreciate our precarious situation without understanding precisely where we stand in male supremacy. And our situation will not change until the system of male supremacy ends. A political movement trying to erode homophobia while leaving male supremacy and misogyny in place won't work. Gay liberation without sexual justice can't possibly happen. Gay rights without women's rights is a male-supremacist reform.

The Eroticization of Sex Discrimination

Sex discrimination has been culturally eroticized —made sexy—and those of us who are stigmatized for being queer are not immune.

It may be difficult to realize how completely sex discrimination has constructed the homosexuality that many of us feel. Though some of us perhaps think we know something about how male supremacy constructs the heterosexuality we have observed, or participated in, we're probably less aware of how sex discrimination has affected the way our personal homoeroticism has taken shape in our lives. But try to imagine, if you can, the difference between making love with someone when gender is not important, when gender is totally irrelevant, and having some kind of sexual release with a partner when what is paramount is your urgency to feel your or your partner's sexedness. If I were to put into words something that would help jog your memory of these two different experiences (assuming you've had at least one of each), I would say it's the difference between, on the one hand, a kind of overwhelming blending or a deeply mutual and vigorous erotic melding, and on the other hand a kind of tactile combat or tension in which

various hierarchy dramas have an erotic impact. The difference is the difference between eroticized empathy and eroticized power disparity— or between eroticized equality and eroticized subordination.

Being a male supremacist in relation to another body is a quite commonplace mode of sexual behaving. Sometimes, though not always, the urgency to "be the man there" gets expressed in ass-fucking—while one guy is fucking, for instance, he slaps the other guy's butt around and calls him contemptuous names, swats and insults that are sexually stimulating, which may progress to physically very brutal and estranging domination. Many gay men seem to think that there is no woman-hating in the sex that they have. Sexualized woman-hating, they believe, is the straight man's burden. So why do gay men sometimes find themselves all bent out of shape after a relationship between two lovers goes on the rocks— and it was a relationship in which one man was always objectified, or always pressured into sex, or forced, or battered, or perhaps always dominatingly ass-fucked, and in his growing unease over this arrangement of power and submission he found himself feeling "feminized" and resenting it, meanwhile his partner just kept fucking him over, both in and out of bed? No woman-hating in gay sex? Clap your hands if you believe. Sexualized woman-hating does not have a race or a class or a sexual orientation.[1] It does not even have a gender, as lesbian devotees of sadomasochism have shown.[2] Gay men play at treating each other "like a woman" all the time. Sometimes in jest. Sometimes in grim earnest.

The personal classified ads in certain gay periodicals bear concise witness to the way in which the male-supremacist sex-class system has constructed many men's homoeroticism:

Hot blond model 30's hot buns & face loves to be degraded by sexy kinky guys . . .

Submissive WM [white male] 40 sks strict dad 35–50 for discipline sessions. Can be spanked with strap or whip. Can be tied up . . .

Wanted: Yng hot jocks to play pussy! Scene: I drop by your apt. U greet me in black lace panties, stockings, and bra. In my sweats is a 9″ red hot tool. The fun begins . . .

Very dominant/aggressive master 29, 6′2″, 170 lbs. hung 8″ seeks slaves for verbal abuse, slapping, & handcuffing. You must be 6′ in height, weigh over 180 lbs. and work out. Hairy chest and beard a plus . . .

White master & son need houseboy for lifetime ownership . . .

I am looking for slaves to fill an opening in my selective stable . . .

I'm seeking a dominant master in full leather who is willing to train a real novice. Age and looks are unimportant, but you must be a masculine, serious, demanding, health-conscious top . . .

[Gay white male] slave 35 6′ 170 clnshvn broad shoulders big chest gdlkng wishes to serve tall slim master 28–42. Training may include [verbal abuse, bondage, bootlicking, discipline] . . .

And finally, here's one headlined simply "Punishment":

Ass strapping, bend over paddling, abrasion, [deep fist-fucking, cock-and-ball torture, tit torture, bondage and discipline, humiliation] . . . [3]

The political reality of the gender hierarchy in male supremacy requires that we make it resonate through our nerves, flesh, and vascular system just as often as we can. We are *supposed* to respond orgasmically to power and powerlessness, to violence and violation; our sexuality is *supposed* to be inhabited by a reverence for supremacy, for unjust power over and against other human life. We are not supposed to experience any other erotic possibility; we are not supposed to glimpse eroticized justice. Our bodies are not supposed to abandon their sensory imprint of what male dominance and female subordination are sup-

posed to be to each other—even if we are the same sex. Perhaps *especially* if we are the same sex. Because if you and your sex partners are not genitally different but you are emotionally and erotically attached to gender hierarchy, then you come to the point where you have to impose hierarchy on every sex act you attempt—otherwise it doesn't feel like sex.

Erotically and politically, those of us who are queer live inside a bizarre double bind. Sex discrimination and sex inequality require homophobia in order to continue. The homophobia that results is what stigmatizes our eroticism, makes us hateful for how we would love. Yet living inside this system of sex discrimination and sex inequality, we too have sexualized it, we have become sexually addicted to gender polarity, we have learned how hate and hostility can become sexual stimulants, we have learned sexualized antagonism toward the other in order to seem to be able to stand ourselves—and in order to get off. Sex discrimination has ritualized a homosexuality that dares not deviate from allegiance to gender polarity and gender hierarchy; sex discrimination has constructed a homosexuality that must stay erotically attached to the very male-supremacist social structures that produce homophobia. It's a little like having a crush on one's own worst enemy—and then moving in for life.

If indeed male supremacy simultaneously produces both a homophobia that is erotically committed to the hatred of homosexuality *and* a homosexuality that is erotically committed to sex discrimination, then it becomes easier to understand why the gay community, taken as a whole, has become almost hysterically hostile to radical-feminist antipornography activism. One might have thought that gay people—who are harassed, stigmatized, and jeopardized on account of prejudice against their preference for same-sex sex—would want to make common cause with any radical challenge to systematized sex discrimination. One might have thought that gay people, realizing that their self-interest lies in the obliteration of homophobia, would be among the first to endorse a political movement attempting to root out sex inequality. One might have thought that gay people would be among the first to recognize that so long as society tolerates and actually celebrates the "pornographizing" of women—so long as there is an enormous economic incentive to traffic in the sexualized subordination of women—then the same terrorism that enforces the sex-class system will surely continue to bludgeon faggots as well. One might have thought, for that matter, that gay men would not require the sexualized inequality of women in order to get a charge out of sex—or that a gay man walking through a porn store, perhaps on his way to a private booth in a back room, would stop and take a look at the racks and racks of pictures of women gagged and splayed and trussed up and ask himself exactly why this particular context of woman-hate is so damned important to his blow job. . . .

Why Pornography Matters

The political function of pornography is analogous to the centrality of segregation in creating and maintaining race discrimination. Segregation was speech in the sense that it expressed the idea that blacks are different and inferior. But it was speech embodied in action—wherever there was segregation, there was something done to a class of victims: There was discrimination created, perpetuated, and institutionalized; there was damage to hearts and minds. Similarly, pornography contains and expresses many ideas about the "natural" servility and sluttishness of women, about how much women want to be ravished and abused, but in the real world, pornography

functions as speech embodied in a practice—a thing actually done to an individual victim, the woman in it, and a thing actually done to women as a class.

Mere sexual explicitness does not create sex discrimination. And no damage to anyone's civil rights is done by so-called erotica, which may be defined as sexually explicit materials premised on equality, mutuality, reciprocity, and so forth. Pornography is something else. Pornography, which creates and maintains sex discrimination, is that sexually explicit material which actively *subordinates* people on account of their sexual anatomy; it puts them down, makes them inferior. Subordination is something that is done *to* someone; and it is often invisible, because the values in pornography link it to what many people think of as sex: a social hierarchy between men and women; objectification, which robs a person of his or her human status; submission, as if it's a person's "nature" to be a slave, to be servile; and violence, viewed as "normal" when it comes to sex. Pornography is what does that; pornography is that which produces sex discrimination by making subordination sexy. . . .

NOTES

1. For a discussion of woman-hating in gay male pornography, see Andrea Dworkin, *Pornography: Men Possessing Women* (New York: Perigee, 1981), pp. 36–45.

2. See Robin Ruth Linden et al., eds. *Against Sadomasochism: A Radical Feminist Analysis* (East Palo Alto, Calif.: Frog in the Well, 1983).

3. Typical personal-ad excerpts culled from the *New York Native,* 24 February 1986, pp. 55–56. Portions in brackets spell out coded abbreviations in the original.

Further Questions

1. Does pornography convey a bad message when it portrays "good" sex as just the genital action filmed by the camera, to the exclusion of other interpersonal aspects of the episode?

2. Does neglect of the whole interpersonal situation in pornography allow for the possibility of eroticized subordination?

3. Can pornography, as sexually explicit material, be produced in such a way that no one is subordinated because of her or his anatomy?

Suggested Moral of Part IX

Women exchange sex for money, either as prostitutes or as subjects depicted in pornography. Although there is some reason to believe that what is sold is sexuality, most of these writers agree that subordination, or at least the appearance of it, is what men are really after. A thriving market in female subordination, of course, does little to put an end to it. We do have the idea that if there is a high demand for something in the market, there must be something valuable about it.

Further Readings for Part IX: Sex for Sale

Laurie Bell, ed. *Good Girls, Bad Girls: Sex Trade Workers and Feminists Face to Face* (Toronto: The Women's Press, 1987). Feminists and prostitutes speak on sex work, together and separately.

Susan G. Cole, *Pornography and the Sex Crisis* (Toronto: Amanita Enterprises, 1989). Pornography is sexuality socially constructed to maintain male power.

David Copp and Susan Wendell, eds. *Pornography and Censorship* (Buffalo, NY: Prometheus Books, 1983). Spectrum of perspectives on pornography, leaning toward the conservative end.

Frederique Delacoste and Priscilla Alexander, eds. *Sex Work: Writings by Women in the Sex Industry* (Pittsburgh, PA: Cleis Press, 1987). Women in sex work speak for themselves, their experiences, and their attitudes toward what they do.

Edward Donnerstein, Daniel Linz, and Steven Penrod, eds. *The Question of Pornography* (New York, NY: Macmillan, The Free Press, 1987). Studies of degradation and violence in pornography.

Andrea Dworkin. *Pornography: Men Possessing Women* (New York, NY: Penguin, 1979). An all-bad view of pornography.

Barbara Meil Hobson. *Uneasy Virtue: The Politics of Prostitution and the American Reform Tradition* (New York, NY: Basic Books, 1987). Researched in cell blocks, dusty corners of courthouses, etc.

Laura Lederer, ed. *Take Back the Night: Women on Pornography* (New York, NY: Bantam Books, 1980).

Linda Lovelace. *Ordeal* (Secaucus, NJ: Citadel Press, 1980). Linda Marchiano writes of her coercion into "Linda Lovelace," the porn star.

Catharine A. MacKinnon. *Feminism Unmodified: Discourses on Life and Law* (Cambridge, MA: Harvard University Press, 1987). Pornography, rape, sexual harassment, and other issues discussed with all the stops let out.

Richard B. Milner and Christina Andrea Milner. *Black Players: The Secret World of Black Pimps* (Boston, MA: Little, Brown and Co., 1972).

Gail Pheterson, ed. *A Vindication of the Rights of Whores* (Seattle, WA: Seal Press, 1989). Voices of prostitutes from around the world.

Helen Reynolds. *The Economics of Prostitution* (Springfield, IL: Charles C. Thomas, Publisher, 1986). Good discussion of incentives for prostitution.

Carolyn See. *Blue Money* (New York, NY: David MacKay Co, Inc., 1974). Notes on porn stars and others in the porn trade.

D. Kelly Weisberg. *Children of the Night: A Study of Adolescent Prostitution* (Lexington, MA: Lexington Books, 1985).

Linda Williams. *Hard Core: Power, Pleasure and the Frenzy of the Visible* (Berkeley, CA: University of California Press, 1989). Diverse perspectives. What porn does, including what it does to women. Argues against censorship.

Part X

Fertility Control: Contraception and Abortion

Introduction

THE WRITINGS IN THIS PART discuss whether there is a right to fertility control: contraception or abortion. Abortion is clearly the more serious matter, because the issue then is whether to terminate a form of human life that is developing into an infant; and an infant is expected to have a definite place in the human community.

X.1   The Purpose of Sex

ST. THOMAS AQUINAS

St. Thomas Aquinas articulates a creed we have come to associate with Roman Catholicism. Contraception is wrong because it frustrates the natural end of sexuality which is continuation of the human species. Hence no one has a right to use contraceptives.

Aquinas (c. 1224–1274) has been given a special position of respect in Roman Catholic scholarship. He was heavily influenced by Aristotle in his child-oriented approach to marriage.

Reading Questions

1. Do you think of semen as having a purpose, so that it would be a bad thing if semen were emitted under conditions where this purpose could not be fulfilled?

2. Suppose there is a tendency for men to remain with women after the sexual act. Would the explantion be that a woman could not, by herself, care for any offspring generated?

3. Does it then follow that marriage is the only appropriate context for sexual activity, and that contraceptives have no rightful place in human life?

The Reason Why Simple Fornication Is a Sin According to Divine Law, and that Matrimony is Natural

1. WE CAN SEE the futility of the argument of certain people who say that simple fornication is not a sin. For they say: Suppose there is a woman who is not married, or under the control of any man, either her father or another man. Now, if a man performs the sexual act with her, and she is willing, he does not injure her, because she favors the action and she has control over her own body. Nor does he injure any other person, because she is understood to be under no other person's control. So, this does not seem to be a sin.

2. Now, to say that he injures God would not seem to be an adequate answer. For we do not offend God except by doing something contrary to our own good, as has been said. But this does not appear contrary to man's good. Hence, on this basis, no injury seems to be done to God.

3. Likewise, it also would seem an inadequate answer to say that some injury is done to one's neighbor by this action, inasmuch as he may be scandalized. Indeed, it is possible for him to be scandalized by something which is not in itself a sin. In this event, the act would be accidentally sinful. But our problem is not whether simple fornication is accidentally a sin, but whether it is so essentially.

4. Hence, we must look for a solution in our earlier considerations. We have said that God exercises care over every person on the basis of what is good for him. Now, it is good for each person to attain his end, whereas it is bad for him to swerve away from his proper end. Now, this should be considered applicable

to the parts, just as it is to the whole being; for instance, each and every part of man, and every one of his acts, should attain the proper end. Now, though the male semen is superfluous in regard to the preservation of the individual, it is nevertheless necessary in regard to the propagation of the species. Other superfluous things, such as excrement, urine, sweat, and such things, are not at all necessary; hence, their emission contributes to man's good. Now, this is not what is sought in the case of semen, but, rather, to emit it for the purpose of generation, to which purpose the sexual act is directed. But man's generative process would be frustrated unless it were followed by proper nutrition, because the offspring would not survive if proper nutrition were withheld. Therefore, the emission of semen ought to be so ordered that it will result in both the production of the proper offspring and in the upbringing of this offspring.

5. It is evident from this that every emission of semen, in such a way that generation cannot follow, is contrary to the good for man. And if this be done deliberately, it must be a sin. Now, I am speaking of a way from which, *in itself,* generation could not result: such would be any emission of semen apart from the natural union of male and female. For which reason, sins of this type are called *contrary to nature.* But, if by accident generation cannot result from the emission of semen, then this is not a reason for it being against nature, or a sin; as for instance, if the woman happens to be sterile.

6. Likewise, it must also be contrary to the good for man if the semen be emitted under conditions such that generation could result but the proper upbringing would be prevented. We should take into consideration the fact that, among some animals where the female is able to take care of the upbringing of offspring, male and female do not remain together for any time after the act of generation. This is obviously the case with dogs. But in the case of animals of which the female is not able to provide for the upbringing of offspring, the male and female do

stay together after the act of generation as long as is necessary for the upbringing and instruction of the offspring. Examples are found among certain species of birds whose young are not able to seek out food for themselves immediately after hatching. In fact, since a bird does not nourish its young with milk, made available by nature as it were, as occurs in the case of quadrupeds, but the bird must look elsewhere for food for its young, and since besides this it must protect them by sitting on them, the female is not able to do this by herself. So, as a result of divine providence, there is naturally implanted in the male of these animals a tendency to remain with the female in order to bring up the young. Now, it is abundantly evident that the female in the human species is not at all able to take care of the upbringing of offspring by herself, since the needs of human life demand many things which cannot be provided by one person alone. Therefore, it is appropriate to human nature that a man remain together with a woman after the generative act, and not leave her immediately to have such relations with another woman, as is the practice with fornicators.

7. Nor, indeed, is the fact that a woman may be able by means of her own wealth to care for the child by herself an obstacle to this argument. For natural rectitude in human acts is not dependent on things accidentally possible in the case of one individual, but, rather, on those conditions which accompany the entire species.

8. Again, we must consider that in the human species offspring require not only nourishment for the body, as in the case of other animals, but also education for the soul. . . . children must be instructed by parents who are already experienced people. Nor are they able to receive such instruction as soon as they are born, but after a long time, and especially after they have reached the age of discretion. Moreover, a long time is needed for this instruction. Then, too, because of the impulsion

of the passions, through which prudent judgment is vitiated, they require not merely instruction but correction. Now, a woman alone is not adequate to this task; rather, this demands the work of a husband, in whom reason is more developed for giving instruction and strength is more available for giving punishment. Therefore, in the human species, it is not enough, as in the case of birds, to devote a small amount of time to bringing up offspring, for a long period of life is required. Hence, since among all animals it is necessary for male and female to remain together as long as the work of the father is needed by the offspring, it is natural to the human being for the man to establish a lasting association with a designated woman, over no short period of time. Now, we call this society *matrimony*. Therefore, matrimony is natural for man, and promiscuous performance of the sexual act, outside matrimony, is contrary to man's good. For this reason, it must be a sin.

9. Nor, in fact should it be deemed a slight sin for a man to arrange for the emission of semen apart from the proper purpose of generating and bringing up children, on the argument that it is either a slight sin, or none at all, for a person to use a part of the body for a different use than that to which it is directed by nature (say, for instance, one chose to walk on his hands, or to use his feet for something usually done with the hands) because man's good is not much opposed by such inordinate use. However, the inordinate emission of semen is incompatible with the natural good; namely, the preservation of the species. Hence, after the sin of homicide whereby a human nature already in existence is destroyed, this type of sin appears to take next place, for by it the generation of human nature is precluded.

10. Moreover, these views which have just been given have a solid basis in divine authority. That the emission of semen under conditions in which offspring cannot follow is illicit is quite clear. There is the text of Leviticus (18:22–23): "thou shalt not lie with mankind as with womankind . . . and thou shalt not copulate with any beast." And in I Corinthians (6:10): "Nor the effeminate, nor liers with mankind . . . shall possess the kingdom of God."

11. Also, that fornication and every performance of the act of reproduction with a person other than one's wife are illicit is evident. For it is said: "There shall be no whore among the daughters of Israel, nor whoremonger among the sons of Israel" (Deut. 23:17); and in Tobias (4:13): "Take heed to keep thyself from all fornication, and beside thy wife never endure to know a crime"; and in I Corinthians (6:18): "Fly fornication."

12. By this conclusion we refute the error of those who say that there is no more sin in the emission of semen than in the emission of any other superfluous matter, and also of those who state that fornication is not a sin. . . .

Further Questions

1. Is continuation of the human race so important that anything that intervenes with this is so bad that only homicide is worse?

2. In times of underpopulation, producing many offspring betters a species' chances of survival. Is the same true in situations where the problem is overpopulation?

3. Aquinas thinks that, in the human species, a single parent cannot normally care adequately for her offspring. Are conditions that encourage or preclude success as a single parent so complex and so variable that Aquinas should not speak of a single array of such conditions as being "normal?"

Society and the Fertile Woman: Contraception   X.2A

JANET RADCLIFFE-RICHARDS

Janet Radcliffe-Richards supports the right of any woman who wishes to separate sex and pregnancy to use contraception. In a situation of overpopulation, moreover, the taxpayers' dollars could scarcely be put to better use than providing free contraceptives to those who would not otherwise use them.

Another selection by Radcliffe-Richards appears in Part II.

Reading Questions

1. A husband wants (more) children; his wife does not. What's the best solution to this problem?

2. A state wants to increase its population. Should it be entitled to restrict access to contraception on these grounds? Which group would fare the worst under such restriction, and is it fair for the state to impose this kind of hardship on them?

3. I am a taxpayer. I do not want to subsidize people who want sex without children, by providing them with free contraceptives. Am I being reasonable? Would it be more reasonable if I were asked instead to help support children whose parents could not provide for them?

The Freedom to Use Contraception

THE PROPOSITION that there should be no law preventing free access to contraceptives is a relatively uncontroversial one in nearly all civilized countries these days. At least, the main opposition to it usually comes from religious groups, and there is no space to discuss their views in a book like this one, because a challenge to their tenets calls for an analysis of the foundations of the religion itself, which has nothing to do with feminism.[1] However, even though the controversy about contraception has now receded a good deal it is still worth discussing the issues, because they do appear from time to time and it is as well to have properly thought-out arguments in readiness for their revival.

Roughly speaking, apart from the objections of religious groups, there seem to be three possible reasons for forbidding or controlling access to contraceptives. One is the fear that readily available birth control will encourage unsanctioned sex; one is the wish of some men to prevent their wives from using contraceptives (there are some who actually succeed); and one is the wish of a state to increase its population. The first two of these do not seem to be worth much discussion, given even the most basic principles about the rights of women. If a woman wants sex that is her own concern, and if it is possible to separate sex and pregnancy she should be allowed to. (It is, incidentally, rather ironic to see some people now wanting to preserve the threat of unwanted pregnancy to make women afraid of indulging in sex, when presumably the original reason for the sanctions on sex was the likelihood of its resulting in pregnancy.) The case of a husband who wants children can be equally briefly dismissed. Any man whose wife wants no more children (or none at all) is no doubt entitled to find another woman to bear his children if he can, but at no point is he entitled to regard his wife as his property, to do as he likes with. The only situation worth discussing in any detail, therefore, is the third: the case of a state which wants to increase its population.

The desire to increase population happens from time to time. Nationalism is a thing which has always encouraged a high birth rate, from Sparta to Nazi Germany and beyond. As Kate Millett said, "population growth [is closely linked] with the ambitions of a military state; more children must be born to die for the country."[2] Expanding and developing countries also often want to increase their populations, so that there is more labour at hand for mines, factories and agriculture. Racial minority groups may want to increase their numbers, so that they are not swamped by the majority. And in some places now, a new phenomenon, people are becoming so worried about the future age structure of the population that governments are beginning to think that if they do not encourage the birth of more children there will be no one to look after the present generation when it is old. Countries with such attitudes might perhaps try to prevent contraception, as Nazi Germany did.[3]

We may well object to nationalism, and given the general rate of increase of the world's population we may well object to any encouragement to increase populations at all. However, those issues are not feminist ones. The feminist question is whether, *if* it were legitimate to want to increase a population, it would be acceptable to do so by means of forbidding or limiting contraception. It is not enough to answer, as though it were obvious, that every woman has the right to whatever number of children she wants: that is the question at issue, and if we want to maintain that it ought to be so, arguments must be found. . . .

However, this can be done without difficulty. If a state wants more children what it should do is put its resources into making sure that all the women who want children can have them, because in that way the state gets what it wants by means of making sure that individuals get more of what they want. What it should certainly not do is forbid access to contraception, because that way *the people who get children are not the ones who want them most, but the ones who can least do without sex*. This sort of method of population increase lowers the level of well-being in society, because it forces parenthood on unwilling people, and gives children the severe handicap of being unwanted. It also means that people who are absolutely determined to do without children are therefore forced to do without sex, which does them a great deal of harm and benefits nobody. And furthermore, if state money is going into customs inspectors and police and law courts to control people who do try to get contraceptives, it means that less is available for fertility clinics, childminders and other things which could help women who did want children to bear as many as possible. They too are therefore deprived of possible happiness.

In other words, a state which wants to increase its population has two alternative ways of going about it: it can get what it wants by means of making individuals happier, or by means of making them unhappy. To forbid contraception is to take the second of these options, and is therefore quite unacceptable. It may also be added as a corollary that since freedom to control reproduction is to the benefit of all, no child should be able to reach puberty without knowing that contraception is available, and how to get it.

Free Contraceptives

That argument establishes that a state ought to allow free access to contraceptives, but it by no means justifies the feminist demand that contraceptives ought to be state-supplied from easily accessible clinics, and above all that they should be free. Perhaps it seems superfluous to argue that case now that in Britain we actually have a free state-supplied contraceptive service, but there are still people who oppose it, just as there are people who still oppose full sex education in schools, so it is as well to complete the battery of arguments on the feminist side. It is not at all obvious that contraception ought always to be free, especially in any country which did want to increase its population. It is no good just stating that the ability to separate sex and pregnancy is a basic human right, and presuming it is obviously true. It is very easy for people to draw up lists of things they would like and call them rights, but if other people are to be asked to work to supply the money to pay for them, they have to be justified with care.

The fact is that the people who say that they object to paying for other people's pleasures, tiresome as they usually are, have at least a *prima facie* case. For most people, certainly, it is an extremely good thing to be able to separate sex and procreation, because sex is such a good thing and being burdened with unwanted children such a very bad one, but not everyone needs to do it. Some people are not interested in sex, or are homosexual, or are sterile, or want children. Some people want more sex than others. But the way a free service is provided is more or less to collect taxes from *everyone* to provide contraceptives for the benefit only of the people who want them. If we are concerned with freedom, would it not be fairer to leave the people who do not want contraceptives to spend their money on something they themselves would like, rather than make them subsidize the indulgers in non-procreative sex? Should we not reduce taxes, and let people buy their own contraceptives? That is what an argument about *freedom* would suggest. (It is, of course, true that all kinds of other things are already paid for by all for the benefit of some, but each case of this should be justified; no *general* argument from freedom can provide it.)

Nevertheless it is possible to justify free contraception, not on any general grounds of fundamental rights and freedom, but on specific grounds arising out of times and circumstances.

In the first place, nearly everybody now is worried by the fact that our population is at present too *large,* both in the world as a whole and in our own country. *Obviously* the first thing to do about that is to make sure that, as the slogans say, every child is a wanted child. It is, therefore, well worth our while to make it easy for people to avoid having children, and not to force them to choose between contraceptives and other things like cigarettes or clothes, or food for the other children there are already. When the population needs reducing nobody should have to trust to luck or the safe period and hope for the best. This is one case where we can very easily achieve what is good for everyone by giving individuals more of what they want.

In the second place, however unfashionable it is to say such things, it is a simple fact that there is a pretty high correlation between the groups of people who, for whatever reason, cannot be bothered with contraception, and those most likely to produce children who are going to be very expensive to the state in one way and another. Whatever uncharitable and imperceptive remarks people may make about leaving feckless parents to the consequences of their folly, no one can reasonably blame the children, or think that we ought to allow them to suffer. There are thousands or millions of women who can hardly be persuaded to take care even now that the service is free, and are only too delighted to find obstacles between themselves and the clinic (which is not surprising, given the usual nature of clinics, but that is another matter). If contraceptives had to be paid for there would be no chance of these women's going anywhere near one.

It is beyond question that at present free contraception is one of the best investments of taxpayers' money there is, and people who are obsessed with the idea that they are paying for other people's pleasures should spend more time considering the other things they would have to pay for if they stopped paying for the pleasures. Or rather, they should realize that since people will have their pleasures anyway, paid for or not, what they are really paying for is lessening the bad consequences of those pleasures for *everyone*.

In conclusion, then, feminists have the best possible case for their insistence that contraception should be free and on demand. Its general *availability* is defensible on general moral grounds, and there are overwhelming practical arguments, in the present state of things, for making it free as well.

NOTES

1. If, for instance, someone says that abortion is out of the question because the Bible says so, the first question to be asked is why one should take any notice of the Bible. That is obviously not a question to be tackled in a book on feminism. Since I can see no good reason to accept any claims of people to have direct knowledge of the will of God, any such arguments must be left out of the discussion.

2. Millett, *Sexual Politics,* p. 224.

3. Ibid., pp. 226–7.

Further Questions

1. My religious convictions are that contraception is wrong and I never use birth control. Do I have a right to force my views on others by making contraceptives unavailable to them? If I do so force others, what reason can I give them?

2. Is it primarily the responsibility of the woman to ensure that a pregnancy does not result from heterosexual intercourse? If it is her responsibility, is this because she is responsible for the fact that sexual activity occurred? Is it because she is the one who needs to be protected from pregnancy?

3. Does anyone ever have the right to ask anyone else not to use contraceptives because contraceptives would "spoil the moment" of sexual activity? If so, explain the circumstances which would make "the moment" more important than contraceptive protection.

X.2B   Society and the Fertile Woman: Abortion

JANET RADCLIFFE-RICHARDS

Janet Radcliffe-Richards also addresses the issue of prohibiting abortion. Her idea is that if abortion is permitted to anyone, despite the case for rights of the unborn child, it should be universally permitted, because the circumstances under which a fetus is conceived would not make substantial changes in any rights it might have.

Reading Questions

1. Is abortion ordinarily not permissible, except in cases of rape? If rape is so excepted, does this mean that the fetus' right to life can be diminished by the manner in which it was conceived? If so, why?

2. Should an exception to the idea that abortion is impermissible be made if the fetus has a substantial chance of being abnormal? Why or why not?

3. Should abortion be permitted when a pregnancy or birth will endanger the physical or mental health of the mother? If so, does this mean that the mother's health is more important than the fetus' life? Who should make this decision?

The Moral Issue of Permitting Abortion

. . . THE PROHIBITION OF ABORTION, if it is unjust, is not obviously so. The innocuous sound of the claim that women want nothing more than the control of their own bodies is misleading. Even if that claim is accepted, any such rights must always be limited by the consequences for other people, and you cannot have the undisputed right to live if the price of your life is someone else's, or the right to be happy at the cost of someone else's misery. Whatever conclusion we come to about the rights and wrongs of abortion, it is quite wrong to ignore the fact that the anti-abortionists have an undoubted *case* when they point out that the mother is not the only person involved in an abortion. . . .

. . . [F]eminists cannot ignore the *prima facie* case that the unborn child has rights. You cannot just assert "It is clear that the foetus is not a human being, plain and simple. The woman *is* a human being,"[1] and think that settles the matter. Yet again, if feminists want abortion at the mother's desire, a case has to be made out, and not just asserted. . . .

. . . It is no good saying that people ought all to be allowed to follow their own principles, because that as a matter of fact presupposes *another* moral principle (that people ought all to be allowed to follow their own moral principles in peace), and there is nothing sacrosanct about that one either. Most of us certainly do not accept it. So what is to be done? Are we left with no alternative but to try to force our will on the opposition?

In the last analysis that would probably be true. The question is of whether we have actually got to the last analysis yet.

A Feminist Challenge

. . . [T]he subject of consistency in attitudes to killing in general and abortion in particular is an enormous one, and I want to concentrate here on one small area which is of particular interest. It concerns the view that abortion is acceptable in some special cases, but that it is not generally acceptable; a view which is of interest because it is so very commonly held, and is even enshrined in the law of most countries. The arguments to be brought against the consistency of this position will of course leave unscathed the people who are opposed to abortion altogether (which is not to suggest that other arguments of a similar kind might not scathe many of them), but they are important because if they are successful they force people into one extreme position or the other: they show that people must in consistency either object to abortion altogether, or allow it on demand. (Actually they do not entail quite the second extreme, but something so like it as to make little difference in practice. That will be explained soon.) And what they also seem to show is that *where the law allows any abortions at present, it ought in consistency to allow (nearly) all.*

There seem to be three sorts of case in which people who disapprove of abortion in general would accept that it was reasonable to perform abortions, and where the law also finds them acceptable. They are abortion in the case of rape, in the case of a deformed or possibly deformed child, and in the case of damage to the mental or physical health of the mother. In each of these cases arguments will be produced to try to show that the present state of law and public opinion *cannot be accounted for by any considerations based on a concern for the rights of the foetus, but can be accounted for by attitudes to the mother,* which shows that the issues are of genuine feminist concern.[2] They also try to show that *any* acceptable principle which allowed some abortions should also allow nearly all. That is of course, as said earlier, essentially a challenge to people who want to keep something like the present state of things, to produce an acceptable principle which will allow them to do it or to change their attitudes.

Abortion in the Case of Rape

This case is probably the most interesting and the most decisive from the feminist point of view, because there seems to be no possible acceptable reason for allowing abortion to victims of rape while withholding it from other unwilling mothers.

There is of course no difficulty at all in understanding why people think that abortion should be allowed to a rape victim. It certainly does seem most unfair that a woman who has conceived unwillingly, as a result of rape, should be forced to bear her child. That presents no problem, on its own. What is difficult is to reconcile that attitude with maintaining at the same time that other women should not be given abortions if they want them. This can be seen by comparing the cases of a raped and an unraped woman who are seeking abortions, and seeing what the differences in the two cases are.

The first thing which is absolutely clear is that *there is no difference at all in the status of the two unborn children*. This is important, because the usual reason people give for objecting to abortions is something to do with the sanctity of human life, but it is quite clear that if you think abortion is all right in the case of rape you *cannot* think of that foetus as being a full human being, with full human rights. It would be quite unthinkable to take the life of an adult human being to save a different human being from undeserved unhappiness. Imagine, for instance, what would be said if anyone tried to kill someone in order to give vital organs to someone else (perhaps a relative) who had been the innocent victim of a criminal attack. If you really thought that the child of the raped mother was fully human you might do what you could to compensate her in other ways, but would not offer to kill her child. But since the child of the other mother must therefore not be fully human either, you cannot explain reluctance to allow abortion to her by arguments about the sanctity of human life. Since the children are the same, and since neither (apparently) is being counted as of full human status, what is the reason for taking different attitudes to abortion in the two cases?

It is quite obvious that since there is no difference in the children the relevant difference must lie in the mothers, and it is clear what that differ-

ence must be. It must be that the raped mother cannot be held responsible for her unwelcome position, whereas the other one can. And this does indeed seem to account for many people's being willing to allow abortion in the case of rape but not abortion in general. . . .

. . . We are willing to help people to avoid the consequences of misfortune, but only of misfortune: in general people must be made to bear the consequences of their actions, and this is why women who could have avoided their pregnancies must be made to bring them to term.

The idea that people should have to take the consequences of their actions is fair enough, up to a point. If, for instance, you were careless about your electric wiring, and did nothing about it in spite of constant warnings from other people, you could hardly blame them if they refused to help you when your house burned down. Your family and friends and insurance company would be quite justified in saying that it was all your fault, so you must bear the consequences alone. However, although that is true, it is not a proper analogy with the abortion case. At the moment we are only considering whether unraped women should be *allowed* to have abortions, not whether they should be given *assistance* in getting them. We are here separating the questions of whether abortion should be allowed and whether it should be state-assisted. The fire analogy suggests that we should perhaps *help* the victims of rape and not others, but it does not show that we should not allow the others to seek their own abortions. The analogy with preventing the others from seeking abortion is not the insurance company's refusing to help with rebuilding a house which had burnt down through your own fault; it is rather as though they said 'It's all your own fault, you must take the consequences, so now we will forcibly prevent your getting a new house even by your own efforts, and make sure you live in a tent for the rest of your life.'

There are in the nature of things no natural, inevitable consequences of most actions. People make mistakes and suffer setbacks as a result, but what happens in the long run depends not only on the nature of the mistake, but also on the action they take to put matters right afterwards. Or rather (and this is the point), the only time when we insist that a particular consequence must follow a particular action, and do not allow people to try to escape the consequence by their own unaided activity, is *when the consequence is intended as a punishment.* Unless we are trying to punish people, we do not actually try to prevent their putting right the bad consequences they have brought on themselves, even though we may refuse to help them.

It looks, then, as though we have here a theory which fits the facts. Since abortions are allowed in the case of rape, the foetus cannot be regarded as a full human being. If, then, pregnancy is forced on other unwilling mothers, it is not because the child is a human being whose life is sacrosanct. Why then are such mothers not automatically allowed to have abortions? One plausible explanation is that the child is being used as an instrument of punishment to the mother, and that talk of the sanctity of life is just being used to disguise that fact.

If that is right, what is the mother being punished for? It cannot be for conceiving, since that is not generally regarded as a crime. The willing mother is not regarded as worthy of punishment, any more than is the unwilling woman who is the victim of rape. It looks as though the only thing which the woman who conceives accidentally has done to differentiate herself from these others is to have indulged willingly in sex without being willing to bear a child. Can that be what is really thought to deserve punishment? Can it be that you are morally all right if you put up with sex if you see it as a means to an acceptable end (having a child) or if it is forced on you against your will, but not if you actually *want* it? It may sound incredible, but there seems to be nothing else which fits the facts. (It is also, incidentally, a theory which would apparently account for a good many of the appalling stories about the practice of abortion.[3] Much of what actually goes on in abortions suggests that if women are to escape the suffering of actually bearing the child, they must

be made to suffer in the abortion. It would be very interesting to find out how much correlation there was between people who were generally hostile to sex and those who objected to abortion.)

We seem to have reached the conclusion, therefore, that the readiest explanation of a willingness to allow abortions to rape victims but not otherwise is a wish to punish sex in women who could have prevented their conceptions. This may not be the only explanation which is consistent with the facts, but the onus is now on the many people who will hotly repudiate this account of their motives to provide a more acceptable alternative explanation which also meets the case. . . .

Abortion of Abnormal Foetuses

We come now to the question of the position of people who are willing to allow the mother of an abnormal or possibly abnormal child to have an abortion at her desire, but not to allow abortion on demand to women in general. Here the arguments which can be brought on the feminist side are less strong. They do not show that there is no principle which *could* account for some such attitude, only that *current practice* does not seem to be supported by any consistent and acceptable principle. Once again it looks as though it is impossible to explain the attitudes people have by reference to the rights of the children, which is the usual ground people give for their objecting to abortion, but that they may be explainable by reference to attitudes to mothers.

Why is the abortion of abnormal foetuses allowed? One possible reason is the suffering of the mother and other members of the family. However, that is not at issue at the moment because that principle might equally well allow the abortion of a perfectly normal child in, say, an overcrowded family, and therefore really comes into the next section, which is about whether abortion should be allowed on the grounds of the mother's health. When people say that abnormal foetuses can be aborted, but that there should not be abortion on demand in general, their position seems to be based on the idea of there being an intrinsic difference between the children in the two cases, rather than anything specifically to do with the mother.

One possible, and likely, reason is perhaps a wish to spare an abnormal child a life of suffering. That does well enough for many kinds of abnormality, but it still does not account for all. One of the commonest grounds for allowing abortion is mongolism, and a mongol child is not by nature unhappy. If it is unhappy it is only because its environment makes it so, and therefore from any argument that mongol children should be aborted on the grounds that they are likely to be unhappy because they are unwanted, it seems to follow that any unwanted child should be aborted because it is unlikely to be happy in its home environment. Since this is not generally accepted we need a different ground for allowing abortion in cases like that. But perhaps it is not too difficult to find. Perhaps the idea is that since the most essential characteristic of human beings is mental ability and level of awareness, anyone who is seriously defective is not really human, and can be sacrificed for that reason. So perhaps we can account for a willingness to abort abnormal foetuses by a combination of two principles: first, that a mentally abnormal one does not count as fully human, and second, that a physically abnormal one is to be spared a life of suffering.

This way of looking at things is not without its problems. One of the most serious is to reconcile this idea with most people's total opposition to infanticide. If a mentally abnormal *foetus* is not fully human and can be sacrificed for that reason, why do the same considerations not apply to a mentally abnormal *infant*? And if the point of abortion in the case of the physically handicapped is to prevent future suffering, why does that not allow for killing physically handicapped infants? It seems rather hard that you should be eligible to be spared a life of misery if you are lucky enough to be discovered in time, but not if you have the misfortune to have your disabilities undetected until birth. These principles for allowing abortions certainly entail allowing infanticide for the same reasons.

Another problem for anyone who wants to take this line but also forbid abortion in general is to justify abortion of the physically abnormal foetus. If all mentally normal foetuses have a full human right to life, why may foetuses who are only *physically* handicapped be aborted? If they are fully human, surely they ought to be born and then left to decide themselves later whether the quality of their lives was so bad that they would prefer to be without life.

However, leaving aside those tricky problems (which is not to imply that they are unimportant), the most serious difficulty for people who want to uphold present abortion practices is that these allow abortion not only in the case of abnormal foetuses, but also in the case of *possibly* abnormal ones. This is one aspect of present policy which seems absolutely impossible to reconcile with any idea of forbidding abortion in general on the grounds of the rights of the unborn child.

The point is this. In general when people want to forbid abortion they concentrate on the rights of the child, and when they say that it is all right to abort abnormal foetuses they are implying that *because of the difference between these children and normal ones* the whole case is changed; the abnormal foetus is not entitled to the same kind of consideration as the normal one, whose rights are inviolable. But this way of looking at things, even if it had no problems in itself, cannot account for the fact that as things are, many *normal* children are aborted under the policies which prevent abnormal births. A woman is entitled to abortion, for instance, if she develops German measles during the early part of pregnancy. There is a likelihood that the child may be defective in cases of this sort, but it is by no means certain. The situation is even more curious in the case of chromosomally linked diseases like haemophilia. This is a disease which a boy in a carrier family has a fifty-fifty chance of inheriting, while a girl will be either only a carrier or completely free.[4] There are at present no ante-natal means of diagnosing the disease, but it is possible to find out the sex of unborn children, and the procedure at present is to offer carrier women amniocentesis to find out the sex of an unborn child, and abortion if it turns out to be male. This means not only that there is a fifty-fifty chance of aborting a normal child, but also a fifty-fifty chance of allowing an abnormal one (a carrier girl, through whom the misery of the condition will be transmitted) to be born.

The reason why this kind of policy cannot be reconciled with a general prohibition of abortion on the grounds of the inviolable rights of the foetus is that *it does itself* concede that a normal unborn child can be aborted. The case might hold if only children *known* to be abnormal were aborted, but the fact that possibly normal ones can be sacrificed too shows that a normal child is not, in fact, thought automatically to have a full human right to live. If it had such a right there would be no question of killing it. It would be quite out of the question to kill a full human being on the fifty-fifty chance that you might be killing someone else you wanted to kill. (If there are two people in a building, one of whom is a notorious murderer, you do not shoot dead the first one to come out. People do not lose their rights through accidentally being in situations where it is difficult to distinguish them from other people who have not the same rights.) In any such case it would be better to wait until after birth and then kill any child that did turn out to be defective. Even if defective foetuses somehow miraculously acquired full human status at birth in spite of having been without it before, it would still be no worse to kill one then than to abort a normal infant before birth, if that normal child had full human rights all along.

If a normal foetus has rights of its own, those rights surely cannot be rendered null by the fact that we do not *know* whether the foetus in question is of a sort to have those rights or not.[5] Of course we might be excused if we made a mistake, and aborted a normal child we had good reason to think was abnormal, but that does not account for our being willing to sacrifice one which may be abnormal but equally well may be normal. If it may be normal and a normal child has those rights, we must respect them until we find out. And since we do not do this, it must follow

that we do *not* regard a normal foetus as fully human, *do* think it can be sacrificed, and therefore are left with the problem of explaining why, in spite of this, we want to prevent the mothers of children who are believed to be normal from seeking abortion.

Obviously it is not going to be an easy matter, and while people who still think that present practice can indeed be explained by reference to the rights of unborn children are working out what principles could justify their position, we are entitled to look for alternative explanations. Once again, we can make sense of everything if we concentrate not on the rights of the child, but on social attitudes to mothers. It can all be explained in terms of two principles. The first is that (however inexplicable it may be) although abortion may sometimes be condoned, infanticide can never be. The second is that a woman who wants a child but by misfortune is carrying (or even may be carrying) one of the wrong sort, which will bring her unhappiness through no fault of her own, is to be pitied and allowed to have an abortion. (As mentioned before, the practice in the case of haemophilia does not stop the transmission of the disease. What it does is give the mother the satisfaction of having a child whose childhood is normal, even though her daughter may have the unhappiness herself of going through amniocentesis and abortions, and may give birth to boys who actually suffer from the disease.) Once again, it looks as though the real purpose behind the practice is to protect "innocent" women who would suffer if their children were born, while not providing an all-purpose escape route for the "guilty"; and once again it seems impossible to explain the innocence and guilt except in terms of whether sex was indulged in with the intention of producing children or not. This does seem to account for what actually goes on, and until another more plausible explanation is produced feminists do seem justified in saying that anyone who is willing to allow abortion to a mother with a possibly abnormal child should be willing to allow abortion to any woman at all.

Abortion for the Mother's Health

Finally there is the matter of abortion on the grounds of danger to the physical or mental health of the mother. People who think this is acceptable presumably take the view that the unborn child has some value, and may not be killed except for very serious reasons. This view certainly goes further towards the feminist position than the other two, because it does by implication concede that the child is expendable for the well-being of the mother, but even so the present state of practice shows a confusion which is unfair to women.

The question is considerably complicated by the complexity of the question of what it is to be in poor health. If the issue really is one of *health* of the mother (that is, trouble inherent to the mother) rather than general distress (that is, trouble which may result from the environment rather than something intrinsic), then the present state of things is certainly a ground for feminist complaint. Since the degree of suffering may be the same in either case, we may wonder why one kind may be prevented by abortion while the other may not, and may think that the readiest explanation is once again in terms of rescuing the innocent (the people who through no fault of their own find their health endangered by pregnancy) while not letting off the improvident, who should have realized that unwanted children would interfere with their lives in one way or another, and therefore should have taken care accordingly.

Still, that may be hair splitting. In practice the whole thing seems to be much vaguer than that, and "social" arguments are allowed to enter the question (though it is noteworthy that women are referred for decision to *doctors,* who are presumably supposed to be judges of health rather than of happiness). But even so, even bringing the mother's general well-being and that of her family into the question, what are the doctors supposed to be deciding? Presumably whether or not the suffering caused by the child's birth would be great enough to justify an abortion.

But why should a doctor decide that? Suppose we agree that it is within the range of medical competence to assess how much suffering a woman will endure as a result of going through with her pregnancy, that still does not account for a doctor's deciding whether she *should* go through with it or not. The question of how much suffering is acceptable as a ground for the sacrifice of the child has *nothing at all to do with a doctor's professional expertise:* it is a matter which a doctor is no more competent to decide than anyone else. If the law really intended that an abortion should be performed on the grounds of a certain level of suffering, but not less, it should stipulate that abortion cases were to be decided by courts, using doctors only as expert witnesses. But nothing like this happens. It is well known that doctors differ radically in the amount of sympathy they have with women seeking abortions, and that the women who eventually get them are not the ones who will suffer most through not having them, but the ones who are lucky enough to have a sympathetic doctor, or who are rich and knowledgeable enough to look around and find one. The real sufferers, as usual, are the least competent and most oppressed.

The conclusion is that as things stand at the moment there is no real concern to estimate the value of the unborn child, or for the degree of suffering which would justify an abortion. All the law does, in effect, is make sure that a woman may not decide for herself whether to have an abortion, and send her to someone else in the position of a suppliant for favours, or even a culprit.[6] It does nothing else. It certainly does not attempt anything in the way of a systematic assessment of the value of unborn children or a safeguarding of their rights, and as the law now stands there is no reason whatever for stopping where we are, and not going forward to a state where all women who want abortions can have them. This would not mean that children were sacrificed any more "frivolously" than they are at present, given that some doctors allow abortions very freely. . . .

Abortion on Demand

. . . The[se] arguments . . . have been aimed at one particular group of people: those who hold that abortion is morally defensible in some situations but not others. The conclusions have been these. First, that there appears to be *no* acceptable principle which would allow abortion in the case of rape, but not automatically to other women who wanted abortions. Second, that in the case of abortion for abnormal or possibly abnormal infants, and abortion in the case of the endangered health of the mother, current attitudes and practice do not seem to be explicable in terms of any acceptable set of principles; certainly not in any about the value of the life of the unborn child. To the arguments of each of the foregoing sections it should be added that of course anyone who wants to accept *all* the usual reasons for allowing abortion, but still not allow it on demand, has an even greater problem in finding a single principle to cover all three kinds of case than arises for each one separately. In all these cases it does, however, seem possible to explain all that goes on in terms of attitudes to the mother and a wish to punish sex. Apart from that, there seems no other explanation than (perhaps well-intentioned) confusion. People who approve of abortion in the case of rape, therefore, or of the amount of abortion which is allowed by present-day therapeutic practice, seem to have no legitimate reason for opposing abortion on demand.

One question which does arise out of this, however, is whether it follows that an all-or-nothing attitude ought to be taken to abortion, or whether it is possible to find a consistent set of acceptable principles which would allow some abortions but not all. If abortion is allowed at all, must it be allowed on demand?

The question is too large to go into fully here, but something can be said about it. . . .

I suspect that the only kind of principle which could possibly succeed in allowing some abortions but not all, and which was also consonant with other attitudes to life and death, would be one which took the view that the value of any life was proportional to its degree of complexity and autonomy. This would make the value of the unborn child very slight at conception, but constantly increasing to reach full human rights some time in infancy. As its value increased the reasons for which it could be sacrificed would have to be more serious, and it would not, for instance, be acceptable to have an abortion in advanced pregnancy to avoid some relatively minor inconvenience. As far as I can see, however, any such principle as this would have the effect that no more than the mother's wishes would be needed to justify a *very early* abortion. Since if abortion were readily available all abortions would be early, this sort of principle would in effect allow abortion on demand. I can think of no principle which would allow some abortions but not others and which would not have this consequence.[7]

NOTES

1. Betsy Stone, "Women and Political Power," in *Feminism and Socialism,* ed. Linda Jenness (New York) 1973, p. 35.

2. Most arguments about abortion concern such matters as whether the unborn child is a person, and whether abortion is therefore murder. Questions like these have nothing to do with justice for women, and are therefore not feminist questions.

3. Simone de Beauvoir (*The Second Sex,* trans. H. M. Parshley (London) 1960, p. 226) comments on the deliberate withholding of anaesthetics during abortions, for which there could be no other reason than a wish to punish. This may no longer be official policy, but it still seems to happen. One of the contributors to Marion Meade's *Bitching* (London) 1973 (p. 96) describes an abortion where she was told, with no reason given, that she could not have an anaesthetic, and then told when she was screaming with pain 'You're getting just what you deserve' and 'Remember this next time you fuck.'

4. Haemophilia is connected with the X chromosome, and the disease exists when the individual has no unaffected X chromosome. Since a male has only one X chromosome, if that is affected he has

haemophilia. The female, however, has two, and if only one of them is affected she will not have the disease, though she will be a carrier unless both are clear. It is almost impossible for both the female's X chromosomes to be affected.

5. This argument would probably be rejected by people who accept what is known as the doctrine of Double Effect. An account of this, and objections to it, can be found in Jonathan Glover, *Causing Death and Saving Lives* (Harmondsworth) 1975.

6. This all reinforces the empirical evidence to suggest that much of the present restriction on abortion has its real origins in the wish of the medical profession to have as much power as possible in its hands.

7. The acceptability of such a view can best be estimated by looking at some of its consequences for abortion and infanticide. These things seem to follow:

1. Infanticide of normal infants is not acceptable; the mother's main suffering has passed after the time of birth, and if she does not want the child it should be adopted.

2. A mentally subnormal child is (on the autonomy and complexity view) consistently less valuable than a normal one of the same age, and therefore can be sacrificed later to prevent a comparable degree of suffering. Given that a mentally abnormal person may cause suffering to others, as well as being of lesser intrinsic value than normal people, this could allow for infanticide in cases of mental abnormality.

3. A physically, but not mentally, deformed child would have the same intrinsic value as a normal one, but could be sacrificed at a later stage because the potential suffering its life would be likely to cause would be greater; suffering to the child as well as others.

The principles underlying this, by the way, are unaffected by arguments that the degree of suffering and so on has been miscalculated here. If, for instance, someone argues that mentally abnormal children do not cause suffering, then that alters the practical judgment about the circumstances in which it should be sacrificed, but not the principles (of value and suffering) which underlie that judgment.

Further Questions

1. We believe that people should be responsible for the consequences of their actions. How does this bear on the question of whether abortion is permissible?

2. In the case of a pregnancy with twins, do you think it is all right to abort the healthy twin if this is the only way to abort the one that will be abnormal? How, if at all, is aborting a healthy twin in order to abort the abnormal one different from aborting a single fetus?

3. Should doctors or other medical personnel be judges of whether a pregnancy or birth endangers the mother's health? If not, how should this decision be made?

X.3   The Mother

SIMONE DE BEAUVOIR

Simone de Beauvoir explores some of the high feelings surrounding the idea of the permissibility of abortion. A woman has internalized the social stigma of abortion and realizes its seriousness. She also, however, realizes the seriousness of not "getting rid of it."

Other selections by de Beauvoir appear in Parts I, IV, VI, and XIII.

Reading Questions

1. Is there a paradox in the scorn some segments of society have for abortion, while simultaneously having little concern for the welfare of children, once they are born? If so, what is the paradox?

2. Would it help a woman trying to make a well-reasoned decision about abortion if those around her were not sanctimonious about the virtue of motherhood? What comments, if any, would be more helpful to her?

3. Is it understandable that women find obtaining and going through an abortion a humiliating experience? If this is due to circumstances that can be changed, what are these circumstances?

IT IS IN MATERNITY that woman fulfills her physiological destiny; it is her natural "calling," since her whole organic structure is adapted for the perpetuation of the species. But we have seen already that human society is never abandoned wholly to nature. And for about a century the reproductive function in particular has no longer been at the mercy solely of biological chance; it has come under the voluntary control of human beings. Certain countries have officially adopted scientific methods of contraception; in nations under Catholic influence it is practiced in a clandestine manner: either the man uses *coitus interruptus* or the woman rids her body of the sperm after intercourse. These forms of contraception are frequently a source of conflict and resentment between lovers or married couples; the man dislikes having to be on his guard at the moment of enjoyment; the woman detests the disagreeable task of douching; he is resentful of the woman's too fertile body; she dreads the germs of life that he risks placing within her. And both are appalled when in spite of all precautions she finds herself "caught." This happens frequently in countries where contraceptive methods are primitive. Then resort is had to an especially desperate remedy: that is, abortion. No less illegal in countries that permit contraception, it is far less often needed. But in France it is an operation to which many women are forced to resort and which haunts the lovelife of most of them.

There are few subjects on which bourgeois society displays greater hypocrisy; abortion is considered a revolting crime to which it is indecent even to refer. For an author to describe the joy and the suffering of a woman in childbirth is quite all right; but if he depicts a case of abortion, he is accused of wallowing in filth and presenting humanity in a sordid light. Now, there are in France as many abortions per year as there are births. It is thus a phenomenon so widespread that it must in fact be regarded as one of the risks normally implied in woman's situation. The law persists, however, in making it a misdemeanor and so requires that this delicate operation be performed in secret. Nothing could be more absurd than the arguments brought forward against the legalization of abortion. It is maintained that the operation is a dangerous one. But honest physicians recognize . . . that "abortion performed by a competent specialist in a hospital, and with proper precautions, does not involve the grave dangers asserted by the penal code."[1] On the contrary, what makes it a serious risk for women is the way in which it is actually done under present conditions. The lack of skill on the part of abortionists and the bad conditions under which they operate cause many accidents, some of them fatal.

Enforced maternity brings into the world wretched infants, whom their parents will be unable to support and who will become the victims of public care or "child martyrs." It must be pointed out that our society, so concerned to defend the rights of the embryo, shows no interest in the children once they are born; it prosecutes the abortionists instead of undertaking to reform that scandalous institution known as "public assistance"; those responsible for entrusting the children to their torturers are allowed to go free; society closes its eyes to the frightful tyranny of brutes in children's asylums and private foster homes. And if it is not admitted that the fetus belongs to the woman who carries it, it is on the other hand agreed that the child is a thing belonging to its parents and at their mercy. Within a single week we have lately seen a surgeon commit suicide because he was convicted of practicing abortion, and a father who had beaten his son almost to death given three months in prison, with sentence suspended. Recently a father let his son die of croup, for lack of care; a mother refused to call a doctor for her daughter, because of her complete submission to God's will: at the cemetery children had thrown stones at her; but when certain journalists expressed their indignation, a number of worthy people protested that children belong to their parents, that no interference by outsiders is allowable. Published reports indicate that as a result of this attitude a million French children are in physical and moral danger. Arab women in North Africa cannot resort to abortion, and seven or eight out of ten children born to them die; yet no one is disturbed because this pitiable and absurd excess of maternities kills their maternal feeling. If all this favors morality, what is to be the thought of such a morality? It must be said in addition that the men with the most scrupulous respect for embryonic life are also those who are most eagerly officious when it comes to condemning adults to death in war. . . .

Sometimes abortion is referred to as a "class crime," and there is much truth in this. Contraceptive knowledge is widespread in the middle class, and the existence of the bathroom makes practical application easier than in the homes of workers and peasants without running water; middle-class young women are more prudent than others; and among people in easy circumstances the infant is not so heavy a charge. Poverty, crowded quarters, and the need for women to work outside the home are among the most frequent causes of abortion. It would seem that most often the couple decides to limit births after two maternities; and so it is that the repulsive aborted woman is also the splendid mother cradling two blond angels in her arms: one and the same person. But in lower-income groups miscarriage and abortion, however desperately needed, usually mean the resignation of despair and much suffering for each woman concerned.

The severity of this ordeal varies greatly according to circumstances. The woman conventionally married or comfortably "kept," sure of a man's support, having money and relatives, enjoys great advantages. In the first place, she finds it easier than do others to obtain recommendation for a "therapeutic abortion"; if necessary she can afford a trip to some place where the attitude toward abortion is one of liberal toleration, such as Switzerland. In the present state of gynecological knowledge the operation involved is not dangerous when performed by a specialist with all the advantages of sterile technique and, if needed, the resources of anesthesia; in the absence of official collusion, she can find unofficial help that is equally safe: she knows good addresses, she has enough money to pay for conscientious care, and she need not wait until her pregnancy is advanced; she will be treated with consideration. Some of these privileged persons assert that the little accident is good for the health and improves the complexion.

But, on the other hand, few distressful situations are more pitiable than that of an isolated young girl, without money, who finds herself driven to a "criminal" act in order to undo a "mistake" that her group considers unpardonable. Just this is the case each year in France with about 300,000 employees, secretaries, students, workers, and peasant women; illegitimate motherhood is still so frightful a fault that many prefer suicide or infanticide to the status of unmarried mother: which means that no penalty could prevent them from "getting rid" of the unborn baby. The common story is one of seduction, in which a more or less ignorant girl is led on by her irresponsible lover until the almost inevitable happens, with concealment from family, friends, and employer a necessity, and an abortion the dreaded but only conceivable means of escape.

It is often the seducer himself who convinces the woman that she must rid herself of the child. Or he may have already abandoned her when she finds herself pregnant, or she may generously wish to hide her disgrace from him, or she may find him incapable of helping her. Sometimes she declines to bear the infant not without regret; for some reason—it may be because she does not decide immediately to do away with it, or because she knows no good address, or because she does not have ready money and has lost time in trying useless drugs—she has reached the third, fourth, or fifth month of her pregnancy when she undertakes to get rid of it; the abortion will then be far more dangerous, painful, and compromising than in earlier months. The woman is aware of this; she attempts her deliverance in anguish and despair. . . .

. . . Crudely begun and poorly cared for, the abortion is often more painful than normal childbirth, it may be accompanied by nervous upsets that can verge on an epileptic fit, it is capable of giving rise to serious internal disorders, and it can induce a fatal hemorrhage. . . .

. . . The fact that the operation they have undergone is clandestine and criminal multiplies its dangers and gives it an abject and agonizing character. Pain, illness, and death take on the appearance of a chastisement: we know how great is the difference between suffering and torture, accident and punishment; through all the risks she takes, the woman feels herself to be blameworthy, and this interpretation of anguish and transgression is peculiarly painful.

This moral aspect of the drama is more or less intensely felt according to circumstances. It hardly comes in question for women who are highly "emancipated," thanks to their means, their social position, and the liberal circles to which they belong, or for those schooled by poverty and misery to disdain bourgeois morality.

There is a more or less disagreeable moment to live through, and it must be lived through, that is all. But many women are intimidated by a morality that for them retains its prestige even though they are unable to conform to it in their behavior; they inwardly respect the law they transgress, and they suffer from this transgression; they suffer still more from having to find accomplices.

First of all they undergo the humiliation of begging and cringing: they beg for an address, they beg a doctor and a midwife to take care of them; they risk being haughtily turned down, or they expose themselves to a degrading complicity. The deliberate invitation of another to commit an illegal act is an experience unknown to most men, and one that a woman undergoes in a confusion of fear and shame. In her heart she often repudiates the interruption of pregnancy which she is seeking to obtain. She is divided against herself. Her natural tendency can well be to have the baby whose birth she is undertaking to prevent; even if she has no positive desire for maternity, she still feels uneasy about the dubious act she is engaged in. For if it is not true that abortion is murder, it still cannot be considered in the same light as a mere contraceptive technique; an event has taken place that is a definite beginning, the progress of which is to be stopped. . . .

Men tend to take abortion lightly; they regard it as one of the numerous hazards imposed on women by malignant nature, but fail to realize fully the values involved. The woman who has recourse to abortion is disowning feminine values, her values, and at the same time is in most radical fashion running counter to the ethics established by men. Her whole moral universe is being disrupted. From infancy woman is told over and over that she is made for childbearing, and the splendors of maternity are forever being sung to her. The drawbacks of her situation—menstruation, illnesses, and the like—and the boredom of household drudgery are all justified by this marvelous privilege she has of bringing children into the world. And now here is man asking woman to relinquish her triumph as female in order to preserve his liberty, so as not to handicap his future, for the benefit of his profession!

The child is no longer a priceless treasure at all, to give birth is no longer a sacred function; this proliferation of cells becomes adventitious and troublesome; it is one more feminine defect. In comparison, the monthly bother seems a blessing: now the return of the red flow is anxiously watched for, that flow which had seemed horrifying to the young girl and for which she was consoled by the promised joys of motherhood. Even when she consents to abortion, even desires it, woman feels it as a sacrifice of her femininity: she is compelled to see in her sex a curse, a kind of infirmity, and a danger. Carrying this denial to one extreme, some women become homosexual after the trauma of abortion.

Furthermore, when man, the better to succeed in fulfilling his destiny as man, asks woman to sacrifice her reproductive possibilities, he is exposing the hypocrisy of the masculine moral code. Men universally forbid abortion, but individually they accept it as a convenient solution of a problem; they are able to contradict themselves with careless cynicism. But woman feels these contradictions in her wounded flesh; she is as a rule too timid for open revolt against masculine bad faith; she regards herself as the victim of an injustice that makes her a criminal against her will, and at the same time she feels soiled and humiliated. She embodies in concrete and imme-diate form, in herself, man's fault; he commits the fault, but he gets rid of it by putting it off on her; he merely says some words in a suppliant, threatening, sensible, or furious tone: he soon forgets them; it is for her to interpret these words in pain and blood. Sometimes he says nothing, he just fades away; but his silence and his flight constitute a still more evident breach of the whole moral code established by males.

The "immorality" of women, favorite theme of misogynists, is not to be wondered at; how could they fail to feel an inner mistrust of the presumptuous principles that men publicly proclaim and secretly disregard? They learn to believe no longer in what men say when they exalt woman or when they exalt man: the one thing they are sure of is this rifled and bleeding womb, these shreds of crimson life, this child that is not there. It is at her first abortion that woman begins to "know." For many women the world will never be the same. . . . As Stekel very justly says: "The law forbidding abortion is unmoral, since it is necessarily bound to be violated every day, every hour. . . ."

NOTE

1. Magnus Hirshfeld, late director of the Institute for Sexual Research in Berlin. Some of his work is presented in *Sexual Anomalies and Perversions* (Emerson Books, 1944) – Tr.

Further Questions

1. Is there hypocrisy in a state's putting heavy restrictions on availability of abortion, but at the same time eagerly sending adults to war and almost certain death? What difference is there, if any, between abortion and killing in war?

2. Is it an argument in favor of legalizing all abortions that some women will otherwise have illegal abortions under stressful and dangerous conditions? If legalized abortion is worse, even if it puts an end to dangerous illegal abortions, why is it worse?

3. Would men take unwanted pregnancy and abortion more seriously if it were something that happened in their bodies? What changes do you think would be made in men's thinking, were this to happen?

Why Abortion Is Immoral   X.4

DON MARQUIS

Don Marquis argues that what makes abortion wrong is that it constitutes loss of the fetus' future, one expected to be very much like our own. This makes most cases of contemplated abortion morally wrong, for the same reason that most killings are wrong.

Marquis works in applied ethics and teaches philosophy at the University of Kansas.

Reading Questions

1. What makes killing a person wrong? Do the same considerations make destroying a fetus wrong as well?

2. Under what circumstances is dying a bad thing? Is an aborted fetus a death that takes place under the same circumstances that make death of an adult a bad thing?

3. If it could be shown that a fetus, in its early stages, could not feel or think, would that make abortion permissible when the fetus was in those early stages?

II.

... WHAT PRIMARILY MAKES KILLING WRONG is neither its effect on the murderer nor its effect on the victim's friends and relatives, but its effect on the victim. The loss of one's life is one of the greatest losses one can suffer. The loss of one's life deprives one of all the experiences, activities, projects, and enjoyments that would otherwise have constituted one's future. Therefore, killing someone is wrong, primarily because the killing inflicts (one of) the greatest possible losses on the victim. To describe this as the loss of life can be misleading, however. The change in my biological state does not by itself make killing me wrong. The effect of the loss of my biological life is the loss to me of all those activities, projects, experiences, and enjoyments which would otherwise have constituted my future personal life. These activities, projects, experiences, and enjoyments are either valuable for their own sakes or are means to something else that is valu-

able for its own sake. Some parts of my future are not valued by me now, but will come to be valued by me as I grow older and as my values and capacities change. When I am killed, I am deprived both of what I now value which would have been part of my future personal life, but also what I would come to value. Therefore, when I die, I am deprived of all of the value of my future. Inflicting this loss on me is ultimately what makes killing me wrong. This being the case, it would seem that what makes killing *any* adult human being prima facie seriously wrong is the loss of his or her future. . . .[1]

The claim that what makes killing wrong is the loss of the victim's future is directly supported by two considerations. In the first place, this theory explains why we regard killing as one of the worst of crimes. Killing is especially wrong, because it deprives the victim of more than perhaps any other crime. In the second place, people with AIDS or cancer who know they are dying believe, of course, that dying is a very bad thing for them.

They believe that the loss of a future to them that they would otherwise have experienced is what makes their premature death a very bad thing for them. A better theory of the wrongness of killing would require a different natural property associated with killing which better fits with the attitudes of the dying. What could it be?

The view that what makes killing wrong is the loss to the victim of the value of the victim's future gains additional support when some of its implications are examined. In the first place, it is incompatible with the view that it is wrong to kill only beings who are biologically human. It is possible that there exists a different species from another planet whose members have a future like ours. Since having a future like that is what makes killing someone wrong, this theory entails that it would be wrong to kill members of such a species. Hence, this theory is opposed to the claim that only life that is biologically human has great moral worth, a claim which many antiabortionists have seemed to adopt. This opposition, which this theory has in common with personhood theories, seems to be a merit of the theory.

In the second place, the claim that the loss of one's future is the wrong-making feature of one's being killed entails the possibility that the futures of some actual nonhuman mammals on our own planet are sufficiently like ours that it is seriously wrong to kill them also. Whether some animals do have the same right to life as human beings depends on adding to the account of the wrongness of killing some additional account of just what it is about my future or the futures of other adult human beings which makes it wrong to kill us. No such additional account will be offered in this essay. Undoubtedly, the provision of such an account would be a very difficult matter. Undoubtedly, any such account would be quite controversial. Hence, it surely should not reflect badly on this sketch of an elementary theory of the wrongness of killing that it is indeterminate with respect to some very difficult issues regarding animal rights.

In the third place, the claim that the loss of one's future is the wrong-making feature of one's being killed does not entail, as sanctity of human life theories do, that active euthanasia is wrong. Persons who are severely and incurably ill, who face a future of pain and despair, and who wish to die will not have suffered a loss if they are killed. It is, strictly speaking, the value of a human's future which makes killing wrong in this theory. This being so, killing does not necessarily wrong some persons who are sick and dying. Of course, there may be other reasons for a prohibition of active euthanasia, but that is another matter. Sanctity-of-human-life theories seem to hold that active euthanasia is seriously wrong even in an individual case where there seems to be good reason for it independently of public policy considerations. This consequence is most implausible, and it is a plus for the claim that the loss of a future of value is what makes killing wrong that it does not share this consequence.

In the fourth place, the account of the wrongness of killing defended in this essay does straightforwardly entail that it is prima facie seriously wrong to kill children and infants, for we do presume that they have futures of value. Since we do believe that it is wrong to kill defenseless little babies, it is important that a theory of the wrongness of killing easily account for this. Personhood theories of the wrongness of killing, on the other hand, cannot straightforwardly account for the wrongness of killing infants and young children. Hence, such theories must add special ad hoc accounts of the wrongness of killing the young. The plausibility of such ad hoc theories seems to be a function of how desperately one wants such theories to work. The claim that the primary wrong-making feature of a killing is the loss to the victim of the value of its future accounts for the wrongness of killing young children and infants directly; it makes the wrongness of such acts as obvious as we actually think it is. This is a further merit of this theory. Accordingly, it seems that this value of a future-like-ours theory of the wrongness of killing shares strengths of both sanctity-of-life and personhood accounts while avoiding weaknesses of both. In addition, it meshes with a central intuition concerning what makes killing wrong.

The claim that the primary wrong-making feature of a killing is the loss to the victim of the value of its future has obvious consequences for the ethics of abortion. The future of a standard fetus includes a set of experiences, projects, activities, and such which are identical with the futures of adult human beings and are identical with the futures of young children. Since the reason that is sufficient to explain why it is wrong to kill human beings after the time of birth is a reason that also applies to fetuses, it follows that abortion is prima facie seriously morally wrong. . . .

Of course, this value of a future-like-ours argument, if sound, shows only that abortion is prima facie wrong, not that it is wrong in any and all circumstances. Since the loss of the future to a standard fetus, if killed, is, however, at least as great a loss as the loss of the future to a standard adult human being who is killed, abortion, like ordinary killing, could be justified only by the most compelling reasons. The loss of one's life is almost the greatest misfortune that can happen to one. Presumably abortion could be justified in some circumstances, only if the loss consequent on failing to abort would be at least as great. Accordingly, morally permissible abortions will be rare indeed unless, perhaps, they occur so early in pregnancy that a fetus is not yet definitely an individual. Hence, this argument should be taken as showing that abortion is presumptively very seriously wrong, where the presumption is very strong—as strong as the presumption that killing another adult human being is wrong.

III.

How complete an account of the wrongness of killing does the value of a future-like-ours account have to be in order that the wrongness of abortion is a consequence? This account does not have to be an account of the necessary conditions for the wrongness of killing. Some persons in nursing homes may lack valuable human futures, yet it may be wrong to kill them for other reasons. Furthermore, this account does not obviously have to be the sole reason killing is wrong where the victim did have a valuable future. This analysis claims only that, for any killing where the victim did have a valuable future like ours, having that future by itself is sufficient to create the strong presumption that the killing is seriously wrong. . . .

IV.

. . . Paul Bassen[2] has argued that, even though the prospects of an embryo might seem to be a basis for the wrongness of abortion, an embryo cannot be a victim and therefore cannot be wronged. An embryo cannot be a victim, he says, because it lacks sentience. His central argument for this seems to be that, even though plants and the permanently unconscious are alive, they clearly cannot be victims. What is the explanation of this? Bassen claims that the explanation is that their lives consist of mere metabolism and mere metabolism is not enough to ground victimizability. Mentation is required.

The problem with this attempt to establish the absence of victimizability is that both plants and the permanently unconscious clearly lack what Bassen calls "prospects" or what I have called "a future life like ours." Hence, it is surely open to one to argue that the real reasons we believe plants and the permanently unconscious cannot be victims is that killing them cannot deprive them of a future life like ours; the real reason is not their absence of present mentation. . . .

. . . Suppose a severe accident renders me totally unconscious for a month, after which I recover. Surely killing me while I am unconscious victimizes me, even though I am incapable of mentation during that time. It follows that Bassen's thesis fails. Apparently, attempts to restrict the value of a future-like-ours argument so that fetuses do not fall within its scope do not succeed. . . .

VI.

The purpose of this essay has been to set out an argument for the serious presumptive wrongness of abortion subject to the assumption that the moral permissibility of abortion stands or falls on the moral status of the fetus. Since a fetus possesses a property, the possession of which in adult human beings is sufficient to make killing an adult human being wrong, abortion is wrong. . . .

. . . [T]his analysis can be viewed as resolving a standard problem—indeed, *the* standard problem —concerning the ethics of abortion. Clearly, it is wrong to kill adult human beings. Clearly, it is not wrong to end the life of some arbitrarily chosen single human cell. Fetuses seem to be like arbitrarily chosen human cells in some respects and like adult humans in other respects. The problem of the ethics of abortion is the problem of determining the fetal property that settles this moral controversy. The thesis of this essay is that the problem of the ethics of abortion, so understood, is solvable.

NOTES

1. I have been most influenced on this matter by Jonathan Glover, *Causing Death and Saving Lives* (New York: Penguin, 1977), ch. 3; and Robert Young, "What Is So Wrong with Killing People?" *Philosophy*, I.IV, 210 (1979): 515–528.

2. "Present Sakes and Future Prospects: The Status of Early Abortion," *Philosophy and Public Affairs*, XI, 4 (1982): 322–326.

Further Questions

1. Suppose a dog, or some extraterrestrial life form, turns out to have expectations of a future of the same quality as members of our own species. Would it then be wrong to kill it? What features must nonhuman life forms possess in order to make killing them wrong?

2. If a pregnant woman knows that bringing her fetus to term will seriously compromise her future, as well as the futures of her other children, should she take this into account in deciding whether to have an abortion, or does only the fetus's future matter?

3. If a victim's future is what matters, do those with greater life expectancy (e.g., fetuses) matter more than older people, who can expect to live only a few more years? If quality of a person's future matters, how bad must this future be expected to be before it is permissible to kill them, or let them die?

X.5   What about Us?

BRENDA TIMMINS

Brenda Timmins argues that women should have unrestricted access to abortion as well as to contraception because parents have serious problems accepting and caring for children with handicaps. She writes a compelling, first-hand description of what life is like for such children.

Another selection by Timmins appears in Part VII.

Reading Questions

1. If you thought you might be expecting a child with a fetal defect, would you try to get a prenatal diagnosis? What role would the results play in your decision about whether to have an abortion?

2. If a prenatal diagnosis revealed that the fetus was seriously handicapped, would you choose to have an abortion? How would you justify your decision to someone else?

3. What role should the other parent play in making decisions about prenatal testing or abortion? Which parent should have the final say in case the two cannot reach agreement?

As long as women do not have unrestricted access to contraception and abortion, they will not have the same freedoms as men in matters of sexuality. It is a basic injustice for one gender to have less freedom than the other in this area, especially in light of the possibility that sexual activity may result in a defective fetus.

In the National Film Board's "Prenatal Diagnosis: To Be or Not To Be",[1] a film about prenatal testing for fetal defects and subsequent choice of abortion, only parents and doctors were interviewed. Most of these parents were happy to care for their children in spite of their children's handicaps and were able to express themselves in positive ways. This was also true in other documentary films on this subject I have seen in the past. However, films with this orientation give the impression that this is the whole story, furnishing material for comfortable journalism supported by the medical community.

I have considerable evidence that a group that should be included is left out of this process. I would like to see handicapped children who have reached adulthood interviewed on film about the effects their conditions had on their families. As a member of this group, I will present in writing my own experiences and what they meant to me.

I spent the year 1967 as a patient on the Serious Surgical Ward at the Hospital for Sick Children in Toronto. During that year I had the opportunity to speak at some length with other seriously handicapped children. These conversations developed spontaneously in response to surrounding events.

On my third day on the floor, one of the children died. The standard procedure on the floor required the children to stay wherever they were, with the door closed, until after the body was removed. I was startled to realize that children as young as four were quite familiar with this procedure. This happened frequently. Naturally it left the children in a sombre mood. One eight-year-old boy said quietly, "His family will be okay now." Every single one of us knew the meaning of this statement.

During that year, I saw that children very quickly became accustomed to being institutionalized as long as the routines were reliable and there were playmates, fun, and mischief. On our ward there were no rules. I was familiar with the numerous rules elsewhere in the hospital and soon realized that we had both more staff and no rules for a reason. Sometimes at night, the staff would move our strykers and stretchers into the hallway, side by side, and the patients would hold hands and try to sleep. "Trying to save electricity," the staff told us. "Trying to save lives," we thought. During my stay, not one parent stayed through the night.

Most of the children on that ward were surprisingly happy. Aside from the pain of surgery and treatments, there were few problems. The entire environment was designed to fill the needs of the handicapped children. There were no bullies because bullies were removed by the gigantic, authoritarian head nurse. There was lots of food, TV, and books. Regular patterns emerged that were beneficial to all. We became family by necessity.

During that year, I witnessed enormous acts of compassion among the children on this otherwise all-boys' ward. (I was the only girl.) I have not seen such acts of compassion since. Sunday School was a dry affair and, in order to escape these weekly meetings, the children would bring their pillows, braces, and IV stands to my room and sit on the floor while I read to them. At fifteen, I was the oldest patient on the floor. As I read, they would turn the pages, and we would talk.

Most of the boys were happier to be in hospital than at home. Sundays brought episodes of unusual behaviour from almost everyone because that was visiting day for parents. My reading became crucial to the children's well-being on Sundays. They would come to and go from my room all during the day, beginning at 6:00 A.M., to report to the others on whether I was well enough to read that particular Sunday. The children's relationships with their parents were not healthy. The amount of conflict in their families was enormous, and the children were quite aware of the fact that their inabilities and deformities were at the core of the conflict. Handicapped children are a terrible inconvenience to everyone concerned.

"Fake a seizure. They'll put you in isolation. Then your parents won't stay!" advised one very experienced nine-year-old to another. The boys' visits with unhappy parents were stiff and formal because communication was so difficult. Those children whose parents did not visit were just as anxious as those who had Sunday parental visits. One ten-year-old girl from another ward was in hospital for six months; in that time her parents did not visit her once. Her parents lived only a few kilometres away in Oakville. Some of the children wandered off the floor on Sundays, hoping to get lost elsewhere in the hospital to avoid their parents. The children were protecting themselves and each other as best they could.

My own parents would visit once a month and would find the floor of my room covered with horribly deformed children who would not leave the room until I read their entire stack of books. Along with most of the other fathers, my own father had difficulty relating to deformed children (me included, of course) and would soon leave. After my parents left, the smallest children would start to giggle. My parents' departure was perceived as another success in our community!

One delightful ten-year-old was second-generation Italo-Canadian, who referred to his family as "the mourners." The women in the family would dress in black and come to the hospital every day to cry over this first-born son. (The men in the family did not come to the hospital.) This boy was relegated to a wheelchair. Unfortunately, the visitors from his extended family could see only the wheelchair. This exceptional boy was funny, musical, spoke three languages, and possessed unusual peacemaking skills, demonstrated by his mediating conflicts on the ward. He was painfully aware of the controversy his disability caused his family, and he was far happier in his institutional setting.

One boy, who had survived many operations to enable him to walk, refused to try to walk after a final successful operation. This refusal caused quite a stir in the ward. He would not take a step and said he preferred to remain in his chair. This controversy (survivor vs. medical staff) went on for weeks, until finally the boy would not speak to anyone about walking. The adults involved were puzzled by his silence. In particular, his parents were angry with him for his "attitude." The truth of the matter was that he did not want to go home. His parents were fighting all the time over what to do about him. Because of long periods of hospitalization, he didn't know his siblings very well and was happier where he was.

In this type of setting, nonfunctioning bodies quickly became a commonality. We were instant comrades. We helped each other, as best we could, to get through surgery, which was quite often worse than anyone on the outside would be able to imagine. There were many deaths, and everyone understood that we were only temporary companions.

Most of the children on this life-and-death ward were happy to be alive. However, they were all painfully aware of the struggles their families were going through concerning them. The problem affected not only anguished parents but also siblings, grandparents, aunts, and uncles. Deformities can cast a dark shadow on families and can seriously damage even the strongest of family bonds. Marriages broke down. There was widespread neglect and alcoholism as well as battering of the handicapped children themselves.

Handicapped children do cost money. At that time, average medical insurance covered 80% of hospital stays. In my own case, experimental surgery cost $100,000 (in 1967 dollars) for use of staff and the largest operating theatre. In conjunction with operating room costs, there were the cost of drugs and a room at $500 a day. My parents refused to give their consent for my surgery because they did not want to pay the remaining 20%. Although they had real estate holdings that could have been liquidated, this was too high a cost for the surgery that would extend my life. Finally, the threat of court order and police arriving at the door made it possible for me to have reconstructive surgery. Mine was not the only family falling apart for financial reasons connected with the costs of rehabilitating a handicapped child.

Suppose now that, before I was born, prenatal tests like amniocentesis were available to assess problematic pregnancies. Suppose also that abortion was readily available as an option. Should such tests reveal a serious difficulty in the developing fetus, then the parents of children like me would have had some choice as to whether to let us make an unwelcome appearance in the family. My parents' lives would have been much happier had I emerged in another family. My sister and brother would not have had to live through years of unending violence, conflict, and emotional neglect while my parents waged an enormous battle against me and the medical authorities, only to lose this battle in the end.

Parents in families like mine don't want to talk about responsibilities like me. Their inability to cope and continuing intolerance are not key subjects for average parents like mine. As well, both the handicapped children and their siblings do not want to discuss these matters. The doctors do not want to talk to these parents any more than is absolutely necessary. This could be why there are no interviews on film recording this type of situation. So why should anyone be expected to see the importance of prenatal testing and making abortion available as an option? It would be advantageous for parents at risk of producing handicapped children to talk to the children's adult counterparts to help them with such difficult decisions. If parents made an informed decision to bring a deformed fetus to term, they would very likely have an easier time coping afterwards. There would also be an opportunity to prepare other members of the family for the postnatal situation.

Although parenthood is not an issue for me, if I were faced with the decision to abort a severely handicapped child, I would not hesitate to do so.

I would like to close with a positive anecdote. One quiet day in the ward, an eight-year-old boy and I were playing checkers. Now this was quite a feat because I was on a stryker frame and he was in a wheelchair. Another boy was making the moves for me because I couldn't reach the board. These games took hours and required enormous cooperation. The eight-year-old had never walked. After eighteen hip ball/socket operations, the doctors had finally found a material that his body did *not* reject. The boy had never really considered walking and thought the doctors were "pretty stupid" not to get him straightened out in eighteen tries. Finally, the doctors got it right!

I was with this boy when he took his first steps, and watched his life suddenly turn around. We spent the afternoon talking about what this meant. He knew I had been mobile in the past, and he wanted to talk about running and what you were supposed to do with your arms when you ran. We talked about walking in mud, sand, and water. He wanted to know what to do if you "just fall over" sometime. We covered running shoes, flip flop sandals, grass, sand castles, etc. Before leaving the hospital, he walked into my room to say goodbye and left surrounded by a loving, joyful family.

NOTE

1. "Prenatal Diagnosis: To Be or Not To Be" National Film Board, 1981, Canada.

Further Questions

1. Are we being unrealistic about the possibilities of fetal defects, believing that every child born will be a healthy child? If so, how should our lack of realism be corrected?

2. Are we realistic in our expectations regarding whether we are prepared to accept and care for a handicapped child? If we do decide to institutionalize a handicapped child after it is born, how would we justify such a decision?

3. What can be done for handicapped children, who are not accepted by their parents, other than keeping them in hospitals and other institutions on a long-term basis?

X.6   Abortion and Bad Reasoning

ALIX NALEZINSKI

Alix Nalezinski discusses some mistakes he has heard people make in abortion discussions. Nalezinski is a graduate student in philosophy at the University of Waterloo (Waterloo, Ontario).

Reading Questions

1. Does the issue of whether abortion is right or wrong reduce to personal opinion, to majority opinion, or to whatever is the law? Is this true of other moral issues as well, and if so, which ones?

2. Should we show more tolerance in matters of abortion than in other issues that directly affect personal lives? In particular, should we let the pregnant woman make the final decision about whether an abortion would be morally permissable in her circumstances?

THE ISSUE OF WHETHER OR NOT to allow abortions for those who want them has two sides. The pro-choice side argues either that a fetus is not a person with any "right to life" or

that even if it is a person, a woman's right to decide what to do with her body supersedes the rights of a fetus. The right-to-life or anti-choice side argues that the fetus is a person with a claim on the woman's body. There are those in the middle who favour abortion in some cases and not in others, but their position is essentially based on the reasons given by one or the other of the two sides.

While the two sides try to give the strongest arguments they can for their positions, weak arguments are often put forth. This commentary discusses these weak arguments. My purpose is not to argue for one side or the other but to demonstrate *why* some of the arguments are weak. This is not to say that one must give up one's position. Not at all. Notice that I am talking about errors in *reasoning*. I hope the result will be a shift from the weak arguments to a discussion of the strong and relevant views because people will have learned about the pitfalls and errors that lead either to dead ends or to views that people did not mean in the first place.

This commentary has three sections. The first one discusses the weak arguments shared by both sides of the abortion debate. The second and third sections discuss the weak arguments given by pro-choice and right-to-life advocates, respectively.

I: Shared Common Errors

1. BASING THE MATTER ON PERSONAL VIEWS

Some people make comments like, "It's only your personal opinion anyway." Or, "Whatever position you take, it's only what you feel is right and people have different feelings."

Comment: Many people on both sides of the abortion issue often state that it's only what one thinks that is somehow relevant. What do these people mean? The comments are a bit obscure. Do the people mean that it is one's own opinion that counts in deciding whether or not to have an abortion, as some who are pro-choice contend? If so, this comment assumes that there is a right to an abortion rather than being an argument for it. Lest people be guilty of begging the question, they need to give an argument as to whether or

not choosing an abortion should be left to personal choice—to a person's own opinion.

Alternately, some who are right-to-life advocates may intend their comments to mean that they do not have a strong enough reason for opposing abortion, so to avoid having their view criticized they claim that what one thinks is one's own opinion and should not be criticized.

I agree that everyone is entitled to his or her own opinion; no one should be denied his or her own opinion on the abortion issue. But that is not in dispute here. No one is saying that freedom of thought should be interfered with. Rather, what is being said, and what is important, is that in discussing whether or not abortion should be allowed, one's views are open to critical evaluation. Perhaps in the end one's views will be right, or perhaps they will be without foundation, but one will not know until one discusses them and discovers the reasons for them.

Relativism Perhaps the people who claim that it is one's opinion that counts have some sort of relativism in mind. They may think that there is no truth or relevant matter that can be made sense of in this abortion debate, and so in the end truth is simply what one thinks.

Comment: Relativism is not a tenable view. It contains too many problems. To begin with, if truth is simply what one thinks, then consider the following situation. Suppose that *A* wants to steal from *B*. Does his thinking that he should do this now make it right? On the relativism view it should. And now the plot thickens. Suppose that *B* does not want to be stolen from. Since what *B* thinks is to be true, then it is also wrong for there to be a theft of *B*'s property. But now there are two completely contradictory views being held as true: *A* is to be allowed to steal from *B* because he wants to *and B* is not to be stolen from because this is what he wants. The result is that one knows only what people think, but not why. One needs reasons to determine which view is correct.

Tolerance Are those who put forth a view like relativism simply calling for tolerance on the issue? Perhaps, but this does not help. A plea for tolerance is useful to prevent people from doing such things as shooting at each other when they disagree on an issue. A plea for tolerance does not, however, help decide which view is correct; only reasoned discussion can do that. Each person going to his own corner only prevents fisticuffs; it does not determine who has the better argument, and if there is a relevant argument stronger than any objection to it, then the side with the weaker argument is wrong.

2 . APPEALS TO THE MAJORITY

Some people argue that a majority of people either support or oppose abortion. Therefore, abortion should or should not be allowed based on which side the majority favour.

Comment: This appeal to "what the majority think" is not relevant because morality is not based on what the majority happen to think at a given time. It is quite possible, after all, for the majority to think one day (or at one time) that X is the morally correct thing to do and then to change their mind the next and think that X is wrong and that Y is correct. Yet this will not do as a basis for morality for two reasons:

1. Morality is something that holds true independent of what people think at the time. For example, theft is wrong whether many people want to steal on a Monday or whenever.
2. Even if the majority do not change their mind, the majority are not some sort of special entity such that we can know the truth by merely taking a poll. The majority are simply people. Because they are simply people, what they think cannot be automatically correct. One needs to examine the reasons for their position.

3 . APPEAL TO LEGALITIES

Some people claim that a position either pro or con can be developed from the law. They may point either to a particular law that allows/forbids abortion or to a specific clause in the constitution that can be interpreted as allowing/forbidding abortion.

Comment: An appeal to the law to resolve the issue is not helpful because there is no guarantee that the law is just. One needs an argument about the justice of the law on abortion. But then one is simply discussing whether or not abortion should be allowed.

4 . ON BEING RIGHT

One often hears comments like, "People opposed-to/in-favor-of abortion are egocentrics. They see only their views as right. They are unable to see other people's points of view."

Comment: What do comments like this mean? They mean that people have views and that the people think that their views are correct. This is a given. The point is that we should discuss the value of their arguments. Thus the arguments, not the level of their commitment, should be discussed.

5 . IF YOU CAN'T BEAT 'EM, SLANDER 'EM

During arguments about abortion, one often hears the people on one side yelling something like, "People who support abortion are baby-killers," and those on the other side yelling something like, "Those opposed to abortion only want to keep women at home."

Comment: The use of emotionally laden terms gets us nowhere. Name-calling solves and proves nothing because one can use emotional appeals to justify almost anything. Indeed, history is replete with such examples. The point, then, is to discuss the reasons given by the opponent.

II: Errors in Pro-Choice Arguments

1 . IF ONLY THEY GOT PREGNANT . . .

If those who oppose abortion found themselves with an unwanted pregnancy, then they would have an abortion.

Comment: Some people might change their minds, but this only shows that people change their minds; this does not in itself make abortion right.

Sometimes, however, those who argue the preceding point think that the person has changed her mind for important reasons. If so, then one should discuss *why* those reasons are good ones. For example, does the person now think that a woman has the final say over her body? Or is there some other reason?

2. BUT THEY'LL STILL GET AN ABORTION

Would those who oppose abortion rather have women seek back-street abortions in unsafe conditions? In such cases, women are at a terrible risk of getting an infection and having their lives threatened by the unsafe conditions. Thus pro-choice advocates conclude that it is better to make abortion legal because then abortions will take place in safe clinics and hospitals.

Comment: The lack of safety of illegal abortions does not make them right, nor does it mean that abortions should be legalized so that they will be safer or easier to obtain. For example, stealing is difficult to do. Should we legalize it so that thieves, burglars, and muggers will have an easier time, such as by having the victims brought to them so the thieves will not have to stalk the victims or worry about the police? I think not.

One can argue, though, that making abortion illegal is wrong, by arguing either that a woman has the right to do with her body as she chooses or that the allegedly bad consequences which the law is designed to prevent simply aren't as bad as the consequences of making abortion illegal; surely the fact that illegal abortions jeopardize a person's health and safety is important.

3. ABORTION HAS BEEN HERE AWHILE

Abortion has been around for a long time, and making it illegal will not make it go away.

Comment: Simply because people do something, even for a long time, does not make it right. People have been doing things such as stealing for a long time, but that does not mean that attempts should not be made to prevent them from stealing. Of course, this does not mean that abortion is immoral. It means only that if one favours allowing abortion, one needs a separate argument to that effect.

4. EACH SITUATION IS DIFFERENT

Each situation is different, and no one can understand the factors that lead a woman to decide to have an abortion.

Comment: On a weak interpretation, this means that each situation is so different that no one can understand anyone, and the result is that there is no reason to even talk to each other about abortion or about how each person feels. But people talk to each other all the time about their situations. And people can imagine themselves in other people's shoes, at least well enough to enable them to understand each other.

On a strong interpretation, one can argue that each situation produces various reasons why a woman could make the decision to have an abortion. Some of the reasons may be relevant to one situation, some to another. The fact that one situation calls for one set of reasons whereas another situation calls for another set need not necessarily present a problem for the pro-choice position. But the important point is to discuss those reasons.

5. ON CONTRACEPTIVE FAILURE

At present, there is no contraceptive that is 100% safe and effective. So pro-choice advocates conclude that safe and legal abortion is needed as a backup for contraceptive failure.

Comment: There is a confusion of terms here. Abortion is not contraception because contraception is designed to *prevent* conception from taking place—to prevent a fetus from coming into being. But abortion is the ending of a pregnancy being. But abortion is the ending of a pregnancy *after* conception has taken place. It is quite possible for someone to favour allowing contraception but to be opposed to abortion because the reasons for allowing contraception may have nothing to do with the opposition to abortion. If one wants to allow abortion, then one must argue that the fetus has no right to life strong enough to outweigh the mother's right to abort.

6. ANTI-CHOICE COERCES MOTHERHOOD

If abortion is not allowed, then the woman is being forced into motherhood against her will.

Comment: Those opposed to choice cannot be held to be trying to force women into motherhood. They are not permitted (nor are they even trying) to go out and kidnap women and have them impregnated against their will, nor are they necessarily saying that women must be pregnant in the first place, though some might think this. Rather, those opposed to choice think that they are protecting the rights of the unborn for what they think are important reasons. The focus now must be on the strength of these reasons. If they are weak, then to stop a pregnant woman from getting an abortion when she wants one is to force her to be a mother when she does not want to be one.

7. ANTI-CHOICE PUNISHES THE MOTHER

Not allowing the mother a choice in the matter of abortion punishes the mother by requiring her to carry the child.

Comment: Not allowing a mother a choice of abortion is not punishing the mother. Those opposed to choice think that they are protecting the rights of the fetus. And if so, then requiring a pregnant woman to carry the fetus to term is an unfortunate side effect of protecting the rights of the fetus.

III: Errors in Anti-Choice Arguments

1. GOD FORBIDS ABORTION

Some people think that abortions are forbidden by God.

Comment: Simply because someone thinks that God commands something does not necessarily make it right. It would not be thought right if God commanded people to rape, torture, and steal.

Some people think, though, that the God who does the commanding is a loving God who would not order us to do such terrible things. Instead, His commands are based on his love for us. In issuing commands, God takes into account our interests, concerns, and limitations. Perhaps a loving God would permit abortion if a woman were not able to or did not want to carry on with a pregnancy due to some important reasons and factors. If so, then, the focus of the discussion is now on what is important for humans and not on what God simply commands.

Some may reply that even though there may appear to us to be good reasons to allow abortions, a loving God may have reasons to forbid abortions—reasons that we simply cannot understand—much as children are not capable of understanding why their parents forbid some actions. But if He is a loving God then, like a loving parent, He should be able to offer some consolation we can understand as to why He would forbid us to do something. None seems to be forthcoming.

2. EVERYTHING HAS A PURPOSE

Some people think that everything, including pregnancy (accidental or otherwise), has a purpose with which abortion would interfere.

Comment: It does not follow that if things have a purpose, then abortion is not to be allowed. If we are to let nature take its course, then we should let natural things such as diseases take their course. There is nothing wrong with removing an inflamed appendix that would cause death. If one thinks that interfering with some natural things (e.g., curing the sick) is permissible but interfering with others (e.g., not letting someone choose an abortion) is not, then one needs an argument for that. The reasons for such an argument will involve something other than an appeal to nature.

3. ABORTION AS PUNISHING THE CHILD

Some think abortion is punishing the child.

Comment: Women who have abortions are not punishing the child because they do not think that the fetus has done anything wrong. Those who support choice think that a woman has the right to remove a fetus from her body. Whether or not she has the right to do so is what must be addressed.

4. ABORTIONS GALORE

It has been argued that if abortion is allowed, then women will get them all the time rather than using contraceptives as a means of preventing birth.

Comment: There are two problems with this argument. To begin with, if there is a right to abortion, then when and how many times a woman has an abortion is irrelevant; she is simply doing what she has a right to do—just as if she were doing something like reading, praying, or studying.

Second, it should be noted that the argument may also be empirically false. For example, in Canada, where a law that regulated abortion was struck down as unconstitutional by the Supreme Court a few years ago, thus legally permitting abortions, there has not been an increase in the number of abortions.

Such things as knowledge of contraception increase the use of contraception. Women do not take having an abortion lightly, even when they have a right to it. Women know that it can be a difficult decision and procedure; they prefer contraception.

5. THE ADOPTION OPTION

Some people are opposed to abortion because they think that the child can always be given up for adoption if it is not wanted by the birth mother. In this way, a woman need not be required to be a mother by having to keep the child, and those who cannot have their own children, but still want children, can have them.

Comment: Suppose that no one wants to adopt the child. Does this mean that abortion is permissible if the only reason for forbidding abortion is on the ground that some person is willing to adopt? It would seem so on this view. But those opposed to abortion are opposed to it whether or not someone is willing to adopt because they think that there is something wrong with allowing abortion itself. It is those reasons that need to be discussed; the adoption option is not an issue to the debate.

Further Questions

1. Is the fact that women will get abortions whether or not abortion is legal a good reason to legalize abortion?

2. Are the circumstances under which women seek abortion so different from one another that no blanket rule will cover which abortions would be permissible and which not permissible?

3. Does not allowing an abortion sometimes force women to be mothers against their will? Is protecting the fetus from being destroyed more important under these circumstances?

Suggested Moral of Part X

Even if contraception and abortion can be classified together as "fertility control," abortion is much more controversial, because it destroys a form of life that is developing into a human baby.

What is known now as the right-to-life, or pro-life, position holds that abortion is morally wrong for this reason. Pro-life advocates, in fact, hold that abortion is so seriously wrong that the state must protect the fetus from being destroyed by abortion for much the same reasons as it must protect the life of any innocent person who is incapable of protecting it himself.

The other position on abortion calls itself pro-choice because its central contention is that the pregnant woman herself, not the state, should have the final choice on whether she is allowed to have an abortion. Believers in pro-choice may or may not believe that abortion is morally wrong. (Usually they believe that earlier abortions are morally better than later abortions and that, under ideal circumstances, only those who wanted children would conceive them.) Their reason for being pro-choice is that, however wrong an abortion may be, it is morally worse to deprive a woman of the choice of having one. The basis of a woman's right to make the choice is, first, that the abortion or pregnancy is something that will happen in her body; and, second, that she has only two alternatives after the child is born: giving the child to some unknown person to raise, perhaps never seeing it again, or taking the main responsibility of raising it herself (since, as the writers of Part XII argue, raising a child is still very much a responsibility of the mother). It must also be added that state "protection" of the life of the fetus can often result in illegal abortion with death of the fetus and high likelihood of substantial damage to, or death of, the mother as well.

The main question regarding abortion, then, is whether the state can force a pregnant woman to become a mother, in the name of protecting the life of something that is not yet a baby, but will develop into one if an abortion does not take place. This is not an easy question to answer, as the writings in Part X show.

Most feminists, however, place a higher value on the quality of life for the pregnant woman than on protection of the process of bringing a fetus to term as a baby. Only through assurance that women are not burdened with unwanted pregnancies and unwanted children to raise can women and men have equal access to what human life has to offer, including the option of heterosexual intercourse. The pro-choice position, then, must be the suggested moral of Part X.

Further Readings for Part X: Fertility Control

BOOKS

Lynn S. Baker, MD. *The Fertility Fallacy: Sexuality in the Post Pill Age* (New York, NY: Holt, Rinehart and Winston, 1981). The fallacy is believing that fertility can be controlled by social policy. With the advent of "the pill," biological fertility control is here to stay, the only question being how we will use it.

Daniel Callahan. *Abortion: Law, Choice and Morality* (New York, NY: The Macmillan Co., 1970). Callahan calls abortion a "nasty problem" and attacks it from a multitude of perspectives.

Anne Collins. *The Big Evasion: Abortion, The Issue That Won't Go Away* (Toronto: Lester and Orpen Dennys, 1985).

John Connery, S.J. *Abortion: The Development of the Roman Catholic Perspective* (Chicago, IL: Loyola University Press, 1970).

Gary Crum and Thelma McCormack. *Abortion: Pro-Choice or Pro-Life* (Washington, DC: The American University Press, 1992). Each author takes a side in heated debate.

David M. Feldman. *Birth Control in Jewish Law: Marital Relations, Contraception, and Abortion as Set Forth in the Classic Texts of Jewish Law* (New York, NY: New York University Press, 1968).

Jay L. Garfield and Patricia Hennessey, ed. *Abortion: Moral and Legal Perspectives* (Amherst, MA: University of Massachusetts Press, 1984).

Beverly Wildung Harrison. *Our Right to Choose: Toward a New Ethic of Abortion* (Boston, MA: Beacon Press, 1983). Develops a new theology to mesh with the new ethic.

Thomas W. Hilger, Dennis J. Horan, and David Mall, eds. *New Perspectives on Abortion* (Frederick, MD: University Publications of America, Inc., 1981).

Jane E. Hodgson, ed. *Abortion and Sterilization: Medical and Social Aspects* (New York, NY: Academic Press, 1981).

Helen B. Holmes, Betty B. Hoskins, and Michael Gross, eds. *Birth Control and Controlling Birth: Women-Centered Perspectives* (Clifton, NJ: Humana Press, 1980).

Stanley Johnson. *Life Without Birth* (Boston, MA: Little, Brown and Co., 1970). Voluntary family planning as a solution to world population explosion.

Hans Lotstra. *Abortion: The Catholic Debate in America* (New York, NY: Irving Publishers, 1985). Balanced, critical approach.

Henry Morgantaler, MD. *Abortion and Contraception* (Don Mills, ON: General Publishing Co., 1982). Canada's prime mover in establishing abortion clinics speaks to the medical and ethical issues.

Bernard N. Nathanson, MD. with Richard Ostling. *Aborting America* (New York, NY: Doubleday Inc., 1979). Director of the largest abortion clinic in the world explains some years later to the public his experiences, his doubts, his final conclusions.

Rosaline Pollack Petchesky. *Abortion and Women's Choice: The State, Sexuality and Reproductive Freedom* (New York, NY: Longman, 1984).

Margaret Sanger, *Motherhood in Bondage* (New York, NY: Brentano's Publishers, 1928). Early activist for contraception publishes some of her correspondence, e.g., "I was married when I was fifteen, have been married only four years and have three children already. . . ."

_____*The New Motherhood* (London: Jonathan Cape, 1922).

_____*Women and the New Race* (New York: NY: Blue Ribbon Books, 1920).

Janet E. Smith, *Humanae Vita: A Generation Later* (Washington, DC: The Catholic University of America Press, 1991). Discussion and defense of Pope Paul VI's encyclical condemning contraception.

L. W. Sumner, *Abortion and Moral Theory* (Princeton: NJ: Princeton University Press, 1981). A philosopher tries to strike a moderate position.

Edward D. Tyler, ed. *Birth Control: A Continuing Controversy* (Springfield, IL: Charles C. Thomas, Publisher, 1967). Doctors and other professionals discuss issues.

Martha C. Ward. *Poor Women, Powerful Men: America's Great Experiment in Family Planning* (Boulder, CO: Westview Press, 1986). Is family planning the answer to such problems as poor women with dead babies?

Robert G. Weisbord. *Genocide: Birth Control and the Black American* (Westport, CT: Greenwood Press, 1975).

J. Philip Wogaman, ed. *The Population Crisis and Moral Responsibility* (Washington, DC: The Public Affairs Press, 1973). Issues addressed by ethicists, theologians, and population experts.

ARTICLES AND ANTHOLOGIES ON ABORTION BY PHILOSOPHERS

Marshall Cohen, *et al.*, eds. *The Rights and Wrongs of Abortion* (Princeton: Princeton University Press, 1974). Reprints of articles from *Philosophy and Public Affairs* by John Finnis, Judith Jarvis Thompson, Michael Tooley, and Roger Wertheimer.

Joel Feinberg, ed. *The Problem of Abortion* (Belmont, CA: Wadsworth Publishing Co., 1973). More articles by noted philosophers.

Joel Feinberg. "Abortion" in *Matters of Life and Death: New Introductory Essays in Moral Philosophy,* Tom Regan, ed. (New York, NY: Random House, 1981).

Steven Ross. "Abortion and the Death of the Fetus" in *Philosophy and Public Affairs* 11 (1982), pp. 232–245.

Mary Anne Warren, "On the Moral and Legal Status of Abortion" *The Monist* 51 (January 1973), pp. 43–61.

Part XI

Reproduction: Hi Tech/Low Tech

Introduction

EVEN THOUGH THERE HAS BEEN SOME TALK of male gestation and laboratory gestation of human infants, pregnancy and delivery are still activities only of women. Writers in this section react in various ways to this situation.

XI.1   If Men Could Menstruate

GLORIA STEINEM

Gloria Steinem speaks to the possibility of men menstruating. She argues that this would put menstruation in an entirely different light from the somewhat shameful cast it has at present.

Other selections by Steinem appear in Parts I and XIII.

Reading Questions

1. If menstruation, in the ordinary course of events, happens once a month to every woman, and if other forms of bleeding do not call for concealment, why are efforts made to conceal menstrual blood from the public eye?

2. Should premenstrual syndrome be taken seriously enough so that any woman who suffers from it has access to medical relief, or even time off from work if she needs it? Is menstruation taken too seriously if women are automatically thought to be incapacitated while menstruating?

3. Menstruation has traditionally been taken to mark the onset and cessation of womanhood. Does it make much sense to treat only that part of a woman's life when she menstruates as her era of being a *real* woman? In what respects, if any, is a nonmenstruating woman lacking full properties of womanhood?

LIVING IN INDIA made me understand that a white minority of the world has spent centuries conning us into thinking a white skin makes people superior, even though the only thing it really does is make them more subject to ultraviolet rays and wrinkles.

Reading Freud made me just as skeptical about penis envy. The power of giving birth makes "womb envy" more logical, and an organ as external and unprotected as the penis makes men very vulnerable indeed.

But listening recently to a woman describe the unexpected arrival of her menstrual period (a red stain had spread on her dress as she argued heatedly on the public stage) still made me cringe with embarrassment. That is, until she explained that, when finally informed in whispers of the obvious event, she had said to the all-male audience, "and you should be *proud* to have a menstruating woman on your stage. It's probably the first real thing that's happened to this group in years!"

Laughter. Relief. She had turned a negative into a positive. Somehow her story merged with India and Freud to make me finally understand the power of positive thinking. Whatever a "superior" group has will be used to justify its superiority, and whatever an "inferior" group has will be used to justify its plight. Black men were given poorly paid jobs because they were said to be "stronger" than white men, while all women were relegated to poorly paid jobs because they were said to be "weaker." As the little boy said when asked if he wanted to be a lawyer like his mother, "Oh, no, that's women's work." Logic has nothing to do with oppression.

So what would happen if suddenly, magically, men could menstruate and women could not?

Clearly, menstruation would become an enviable, boastworthy, masculine event:

Men would brag about how long and how much.

Young boys would talk about it as the envied beginning of manhood. Gifts, religious ceremonies, family dinners, and stag parties would mark the day.

To prevent monthly work loss among the powerful, Congress would fund a National Institute of Dysmenorrhea. Doctors would research little about heart attacks, from which men were hormonally protected, but everything about cramps.

Sanitary supplies would be federally funded and free. Of course, some men would still pay for the prestige of such commercial brands as Paul Newman Tampons, Muhammad Ali's Rope-a-Dope Pads, John Wayne Maxi Pads, and Joe Namath Jock Shields—"For Those Light Bachelor Days."

Statistical surveys would show that men did better in sports and won more Olympic medals during their periods.

Generals, right-wing politicians, and religious fundamentalists would cite menstruation ("*menstruation*") as proof that only men could serve God and country in combat ("You have to give blood to take blood"), occupy high political office ("Can women be properly fierce without a monthly cycle governed by the planet Mars?"), be priests, ministers, God Himself ("He gave this blood for our sins"), or rabbis ("Without a monthly purge of impurities, women are unclean").

Male liberals or radicals, however, would insist that women are equal, just different; and that any woman could join their ranks if only she were willing to recognize the primacy of menstrual rights ("Everything else is a single issue") or self-inflict a major wound every month ("You *must* give blood for the revolution").

Street guys would invent slang ("He's a three-pad man") and "give fives" on the corner with some exchange like, "Man, you lookin' *good!*"

"Yeah, man, I'm on the rag!"

TV shows would treat the subject openly. (*Happy Days:* Richie and Potsie try to convince Fonzie that he is still "The Fonz," though he has missed two periods in a row. *Hill Street Blues:* The whole precinct hits the same cycle.) So would newspapers. (SUMMER SHARK SCARE THREATENS MENSTRUATING MEN. JUDGE CITES MONTHLIES IN PARDONING RAPIST.) And so would movies. (Newman and Redford in *Blood Brothers!*)

Men would convince women that sex was *more* pleasurable at "that time of the month." Lesbians would be said to fear blood and therefore life itself, though all they needed was a good menstruating man.

Medical schools would limit women's entry ("they might faint at the sight of blood").

Of course, intellectuals would offer the most moral and logical arguments. Without that biological gift for measuring the cycles of the moon and planets, how could a woman master any discipline that demanded a sense of time, space, mathematics—or the ability to measure anything at all? In philosophy and religion, how could women compensate for being disconnected from the rhythm of the universe? Or for their lack of symbolic death and resurrection every month?

Menopause would be celebrated as a positive event, the symbol that men had accumulated enough years of cyclical wisdom to need no more.

Liberal males in every field would try to be kind. The fact that "these people" have no gift for measuring life, the liberals would explain, should be punishment enough.

And how would women be trained to react? One can imagine right-wing women agreeing to all these arguments with a staunch and smiling masochism. ("The ERA would force housewives to wound themselves every month": Phyllis Schlafly. "Your husband's blood is as sacred as that of Jesus—and so sexy, too!": Marabel Morgan.) Reformers and Queen Bees would adjust their lives to the cycles of the men around them. Feminists would explain endlessly that men, too, needed to be liberated from the false idea of

Martian aggressiveness, just as women needed to escape the bonds of "menses-envy." Radical feminists would add that the oppression of the nonmenstrual was the pattern for all other oppressions. ("Vampires were our first freedom fighters!") Cultural feminists would exalt a female bloodless imagery in art and literature. Socialist feminists would insist that, once capitalism and imperialism were overthrown, women would menstruate, too. ("If women aren't yet menstruating in Russia," they would explain, "it's only because true socialism can't exist within capitalist encirclement.")

In short, we would discover, as we should already guess, that logic is in the eye of the logician. (For instance, here's an idea for theorists and logicians: If women are supposed to be less rational and more emotional at the beginning of our menstrual cycle when the female hormone is at its lowest level, then why isn't it logical to say that, in those few days, women behave the most like the way men behave all month long? I leave further improvisations up to you.)[1]

The truth is that, if men could menstruate, the power justifications would go on and on.

If we let them.

NOTE

1. With thanks to Stan Pottinger for many of the improvisations already here.

Further Questions

1. If men were the only ones who menstruated, would they take it as a status symbol and brag about it, as Steinem suggests? (If so, think of some possible examples of this in addition to the ones given by Steinem.)

2. Menstrual blood is traditionally thought of as unclean. Do you think Steinem is correct in saying that if men menstruated, menstruation would be treated as a necessity to purge impurities? What do "unclean" and "impurities" mean in the preceding question?

3. Would hypothetical menstruating men look down on hypothetical nonmenstruating women because the latter are not synchronized with the universe and hence lacking in understanding of much of anything, as Steinem suggests? How might synchronization with the universe contribute to understanding it?

XI.2   Childbirth

CHRISTINE OVERALL

Christine Overall believes that a pregnant woman should be the one who makes the final decisions about the birth of her baby. She claims that putting medical personnel in charge of decisions is of dubious benefit to the baby and can negate the value of the birthing experience as a meaningful, self-affirming event for the woman.

Overall teaches philosophy at Queen's University, Kingston, Ontario. *Ethics and Human Reproduction* was her first book.

Reading Questions

1. Do you see childbirth as a situation in which the baby's needs, as perceived by medical personnel, ought to take precedence over the pregnant woman's wishes? If some of the pregnant woman's wishes should take precedence, which wishes are they?

2. Quoting Bayles, Overall speaks of an "ethically ideal childbirth," as being a vaginal delivery with healthy mother and child. Does this mean that someone has done something wrong (and, if so, who?) if either the mother or child is damaged in delivery, or if the delivery is by caesarean section?

3. Do you think that childbirth can be one of the high points of a woman's life, especially if she gives birth with very little intervention on the part of medical personnel? If so, exactly what makes this a high point? Are women who don't give birth, or don't give birth in this way, missing something important in life?

Conflict between Pregnant Woman and Fetus

... ACCORDING TO "the medical belief in an adversary relationship between the mother and the baby,"

> the baby must be stopped from ripping its mother apart, and the surgical scissors [performing an episiotomy, that is, a cut in the mother's perineum] are considered to be more gentle than the baby's head. At the same time, the mother must be stopped from crushing her baby, and the obstetrical forceps are seen as being more gentle than the mother's vagina.[1]

Thus in a 1984 discussion paper of the Ontario Medical Association (OMA) entitled "Issues Relating to Childbirth,"[2] the pregnant woman and her fetus (and, later, the baby) are seen as adversaries competing to get their needs filled. The pregnant woman is primarily a container or environment for the fetus; her interests are often different from—even in conflict with—those of her fetus. The paper states,

> We are ... beginning to see claims for dual medical-legal rights and new responsibilities, one set for the mother and an increasingly well-defined set for the fetus. There is a growing need to discuss how we are going to resolve social conflicts between the rights of the mother and the rights of the fetus and newborn. Quite separately, appropriate and useful medical care for the fetus will require the mother to assume some risks without any benefit to herself since for some procedures she is the only route to the fetus.[3]

There are a number of problems with this type of approach to the pregnant woman/fetus relationship. First, seeing the pregnant woman as the "route to the fetus" has the effect of literally depersonalizing her, reducing her to a mere environment in which the fetus grows. It obscures the fact that she is, or ought to be, an independent and autonomous adult, with full decision-making powers and legal rights to determine what occurs to and within her own body. The discussion paper's approach appears to demote the pregnant woman to a derivative ontological and moral status, making questions of her safety and well-being secondary to questions about the safety and well-being of the fetus. . . .

. . . [T]he antifeminist perspective on childbirth sees the alleged conflict between pregnant woman and fetus as an unequal struggle: the pregnant woman is the potential oppressor of her fetus. During birth she must therefore voluntarily abdicate her power over it, and if she will not, the resolution of this unequal conflict requires the oppression of the pregnant woman by medical and legal authorities.

What sorts of sacrifice are expected of pregnant women in the process of birth? First, parturient women are ordinarily expected to abandon any preference they may have for birthing at home. In most of the Western world, and particularly in North America, women are supposed to give birth in a hospital. Moreover, they are not permitted much choice in their attendants at birth; in particular, they are often prevented (and again, this is a special problem in North America) from having the services of midwives, and even close friends and relatives (other than her husband, if she has one) are not allowed to be present.

Giving birth in the hospital requires further sacrifices of the parturient women. She must often accept extensive technological intervention in her labor, sometimes at the expense of lack of personal attention from birth "attendants." For example, she may be left *unattended* except for the presence of a fetal heart monitor, which gives the misleading impression that she is being watched. External monitors require straps around the woman's abdomen and impose limitations on her movements during labor. Internal monitors require electrodes that are passed through the woman's vagina and are clipped or screwed into the fetus's scalp.[4]

Additional medical interventions in the course of a hospital birth include the following:[5]

- Shaving of the perineal area
- Enemas
- Intravenous feeding
- Artificial induction of labor, which may, in some cases, be done for the sake of the physician's convenience[6]
- Withholding of food and liquids during labor
- Stimulation of labor by means of oxytocin
- Analgesia and anesthesia
- Artificial rupture of membranes (amniotomy)
- Use of the lithotomy (horizontal supine) position and stirrups for delivery
- Episiotomy, which does not seem to reduce the incidence of tears,[7] and may even be associated with a greater incidence of lacerations

- Use of forceps
- Cesareans
- Postnatal separation of mother and infant.

For the laboring woman a hospital birth can be an extraordinarily alienating experience:

> Her clothes are sent away and she wears a standard gown. Her name is appended a hospital number. She is cleansed (shaved, washed and given an enema). Communication with her family and friends is monitored by the staff and severely curtailed. Instruments are attached to her to monitor the child's heart beat. Drugs are given to partially anesthetize her. She is physically inspected mainly in the area of her genitals. She is expected to remain lying down and, at inspections, near delivery and afterwards, her legs are in straps which retain them in a raised and apart position.[8]

Thus the sacrifices inherent in many hospital births also include such psychological costs as loss of autonomy and self-esteem.[9]

Although these sacrifices are presented as being mainly for the sake of the fetus's welfare, in fact it is not entirely clear that the infant always, or even usually, benefits from them. Fetal heart monitors, to take just one example, are inaccurate; they can create the impression of fetal distress, resulting in unnecessary procedures such as cesarean sections. The necessary immobilization may be uncomfortable for the woman and even detrimental to her and the fetus.[10] In general, it seems likely that the twentieth-century drop in infant mortality rates owes little to the procedures of hospital births and much to improved maternal diet, clean water, and adequate sanitation, housing, and working conditions.[11] There is no evidence of a causal relationship (in addition to a mere correlation) between the gradual drop in neonatal mortality rates in the last century and the rise in rates of hospital births.

Hence there is nothing self-evident about the value orientation exemplified in standard hospital birth practices. If some physicians regard the pregnant woman as a "route to the fetus" who during childbirth must sacrifice her interests to those of the fetus, they ought to *defend* that approach and not merely assume that it is legitimate. And so even if it is assumed, for the sake of argument, that on some occasions and in some circumstances (though certainly not all) the pregnant woman's interests and those of her fetus are not compatible, then the predominant question must be: To what degree, if at all, should the pregnant woman sacrifice her interests or permit them to be sacrificed? It is certainly not obvious that decisions about care for pregnant woman and fetus should necessarily subordinate the woman's freedom, interests, and well-being to those of her fetus. . . .

Beyond its unquestioning emphasis upon the priority of fetal rights, a further problem with the assumption that there is a conflict between maternal and fetal rights and needs is that it is not at all obvious that fetus and pregnant women *should* in fact always be viewed as adversaries, competing to get their needs filled. . . . [O]rdinarily during the course of pregnancy activities and resources—for example, mild exercise, nourishing food, and unpolluted air—that are beneficial for the mother are also beneficial for the fetus. Conversely, activities and environments—such as smoking, dangerous work environments, and exposure to disease—that are harmful for the fetus are also harmful for the pregnant woman. This relationship of shared benefit and vulnerability does not cease during the activity of childbirth.

Furthermore, it is unlikely that a pregnant woman sees herself as being in competition with her fetus; on the contrary, women ordinarily want the best for their future baby and are willing to go to considerable lengths to secure it.[12] Although it is undoubtedly true that some women may be unhappy during pregnancy, or may fear (perhaps with very good reason) the process of giving birth, those women who are involved in preparing and planning for the circumstances of their child's birth certainly perceive themselves as acting on behalf of, and in the best interests of, their fetus. . . .

However, insofar as there is ever a necessity to override the pregnant woman's decisions—whether because of her lack of knowledge or lack of competence—this necessity would have to be demonstrated, and not simply assumed to hold in all cases. Surely in no other human relationship does an unrelated person believe he has grounds unilaterally to appoint himself another's advocate without prior invitation. Certainly such a belief runs counter to the general practice in most other aspects of parent/child relationships.

This general practice is ably described by Paul Thompson in a discussion of the "*prima facie* prerogative [of parents] to choose on behalf of their children."[13] Thompson points out that there is a great range of activities in which it is justifiably assumed that parents have a legitimate right to determine their children's participation.[14] There is no general reason to suppose that childbirth is different; there are no compelling grounds (such as the expectation of great harm) to justify overriding the parent's prerogative. Hence insofar as the fetus needs an advocate, there is no reason to regard the physician rather than the pregnant woman as the appropriate advocate.

Conflict between Safety and Other Values

In his discussion of childbirth, Michael Bayles also criticizes the belief that the physician should be the advocate of the fetus. He describes it as follows:

Many physicians claim that they best represent the interests of the fetus. They do not deny that almost all women are interested in the well-being of their baby, but the woman's interests can conflict with those of the baby. For example, the woman's interests in the psychological and social aspects of birth are probably greater than those of the child, and women might sacrifice the physical safety of the fetus for their own psychological fulfillment. Even if maternal-infant bonding is beneficial for the baby, it is not as important as its physical well-being. Moreover, it is precisely in the area of physical safety that physicians have expertise. Consequently, it is claimed, they should make the decisions about childbirth.[15]

Interestingly, although Bayles rejects the notion that the physician is the appropriate advocate for the fetus, he nevertheless accepts, along with many antifeminist theorists, the assumption that there may be a conflict between the psychological needs of the pregnant woman and the requirements of safety for her and the fetus. . . .

Values and Goals in Childbearing

The emphasis by nonfeminist and antifeminist writers on an alleged conflict between safety and psychosocial needs appears to be connected with two other basic beliefs. The first concerns the nature of risk-taking in childbirth, and the second concerns the significance of childbearing. To examine both of these requires some thought about the values and goals of childbirth.

A recurrent ideal cited in nonfeminist and antifeminist literature on birth is the health of the baby and the mother. From this point of view, "a 'successful' pregnancy is one which results in a physically healthy baby and mother as assessed in the period immediately following birth."[16] Bayles, for example, describes "the ethically ideal childbirth" as involving "a vaginal delivery with a healthy mother and infant."[17] The OMA Discussion Paper says that in the traditional system of provision of reproductive care by physicians, the physician's goal was "to facilitate the birth of a healthy baby"; hospitals attempted to "ensure efficient functioning of the hospital and safety of patients."[18] (This in itself is an interesting priority of values!)

As Bayles himself readily acknowledges, this quest for a healthy baby and mother is translated, in practice, into an all-out attempt to "make the best of the worst possible outcome, no matter what the likelihood of its occurring."[19] For example, while claiming that "the chances for a suc-

cessful labor and delivery are certainly 98 out of 100 or greater,"[20] one physician states that if one is "interested in taking that 2% chance [of an unsuccessful birth outcome], then fetal monitoring is unnecessary. [But] if one is interested in optimizing the chances for *every* fetus, fetal monitoring is *essential.*"[21] The quest is most clearly exemplified in the medical establishment's insistence that home birth is dangerous and that all births should take place in a hospital. The Ontario Medical Association asserts categorically that "planned home births involve increased and avoidable risks to the health of the mother, foetus and newborn infant"; it therefore opposes without reservation all planned home births.[22] The American College of Obstetricians and Gynecologists has a similar position.[23]

Planned home births, however, have an impressive safety record,[24] comparing very favorably with hospital births in terms of both mortality and morbidity rates. Hence the fact that there is a low rate of unforeseeable risk in any birth (for instance, as a result of cord prolapse or postpartum hemorrhage[25]) does not morally justify approaching all births as if they involved the highest degree of risk.

> Probably 20 per cent of births are to mothers with no high-risk factor identifiable before delivery, yet about 10 per cent of perinatal deaths are to such mothers. To ensure that these unpredictable dangerous births take place in consultant hospitals, obstetricians recommend that all births should take place there, for they claim that the chances of a successful outcome are then improved. However valid the claim may be in individual cases, the available statistical evidence does not support it in general. It does not show that an increased rate of hospitalization promotes the objective of reducing overall mortality.[26]

Similarly, the low rate of unforeseeable risk to pregnant women and their fetuses of riding in automobiles does not justify enforced banishment from cars![27] It is impossible to eliminate all risks completely from human activities; an attempt must be made to make a realistic assessment of and preparation for possible dangers and, where possible, to reduce or compensate for them.

The fact that there may be an unforeseen negative outcome of one particular woman's birth choice—for example, in favor of home birth—does not by itself demonstrate that *all* similar choices are therefore unjustified. More important still, the occurrence of an unforeseen negative outcome is not even sufficient to show that the specific choice itself was unjustified. To see this, imagine the following analogous case. An individual decides to take her family for a car ride. The weather is fine, road conditions are good, the woman drives carefully and defensively. Nevertheless an accident occurs and an occupant of the car is injured. The fact that an injury occurred does not show that the decision to take the car ride in the first place was unjustified. Given all of the foreseeable information at the time, and given the appropriate precautions the driver took, the car ride was an entirely justified activity. Similarly, if a low-risk mother chooses home birth and takes all appropriate precautions for the circumstances of the birth, then the fact that an unforeseen injury occurs is not sufficient to show that her choice was unjustified.

No studies exist to support the justification of universal hospitalization, and existing studies of the safety of home versus hospital are often misused by the medical profession.[28] Furthermore, as Paul Thompson points out,

> hospital birth, while reducing a number of risks which are present in home birth, introduces new risks and increases remaining risks. And . . . it is not immediately obvious that the negative outcomes of the new risks introduced by hospital birth are more desirable than those of the risks of home birth which have been eliminated or reduced.[29]

Assessments both of what constitutes a benefit and of what constitutes a benefit substantial enough to warrant taking a risk to achieve it are value judgments.[30] Moreover, there is good evidence to suggest that contemporary medical practice creates what is regarded as a risk by defining certain conditions—such as having had three previous births—as high risk.[31] Hence the error in positions such as that of the OMA is that they fail to recognize that the mere acknowledgment of the possible existence of a risk does not by itself entail a particular course of action; a further evaluation of the significance of the risk is necessary, and such an evaluation is a moral, not a medical, judgment. Moreover, in light of the implausibility of assuming that pregnant woman and fetus are in conflict, it is not even very obvious that risks and benefits can or should be assessed separately for each of them.[32] . . .

Who ought to make decisions about the evaluation of risk in childbirth, and how should those decisions be made? I suggest that they should be made by the pregnant woman herself, through a process that places the childbirth event within the more general context of her life. Childbearing is not something that merely happens to women, but is a process in which women are (or can be) actively engaged. "Birth cannot simply be a matter of techniques for getting a baby out of one's body,"[33] and childbirth is not just a type of production.[34] Although hospitals do not reward, encourage, or even recognize competence in giving birth,[35] there is a very important conceptual and experiential difference between giving birth and being delivered. "When the *mother* is seen as delivering, then the attendant is assisting—aiding, literally attending. But when the *doctor* is delivering the baby, the mother is in the passive position of *being delivered*."[36]

It therefore seems unduly pessimistic to claim, as does Bayles, that "there does not appear to be any way to justify one attitude toward risk rather than another."[37] Evaluation of possible risk in childbirth, and of the importance of achieving a healthy baby and mother, requires situating the birth event within the wider circumstances of the mother's life. This is not to say that the familiar antifeminist belief in a conflict between safety and psychosocial needs must be reinstated. Instead it is necessary to reconstruct, from the point of view of the laboring woman, the very nature of what have been called "psycho-social needs" and "psycho-social interests."[38] Is it correct to say that the pregnant woman seeks to "personally grow and experience to the fullest a basic aspect of [her] femininity"? Or that "childbirth is an opportunity for personal development and growth"?[39] Or, as Bayles remarks, that "women generally want childbirth to be a rewarding personal experience"?[40] . . .

> The suggestion that the childbearing experience is central to a woman's life[41] need not be at all incompatible with a feminist perspective on birth. It is of course necessary to avoid prescribing, as so many writers have in the past,[42] what childbirth *must* be like, or how it *must* be experienced,[43] and to avoid describing it romantically as a necessarily transcendent, quasi-mystical experience. The point being made is not that a woman is incomplete without experiencing birth, nor that childbearing is women's natural work, nor even that childbirth is always a happy event.

Instead what is being pointed to is the simple fact that childbirth is, or can be, if not skewed in its meaning by a medical reconstruction, a powerful, self-affirming, and memorable event whose meaning is not isolated but resonates throughout all of the woman's subsequent experiences as a woman and as a mother.[44] Since women now tend to have fewer children and have few, if any, opportunities to participate in other women's births, childbirth is for most of those who undertake it a journey into the unknown. Giving birth is a chance to come to know oneself and one's strengths, and to weave that knowledge into a more general understanding of the significance of one's life. Insofar as a "rewarding personal experience" (to use Bayles's phrase) is sought by pregnant women, that experience arises not just from the relatively brief events surrounding birth but from the mother-baby relationship and from the integration of motherhood into the woman's life pattern.[45]

Hence the conclusion must be that, in general, decisions about the birth of her baby belong primarily to the pregnant woman herself, for whom the process is not some isolated medical emergency but a vital part of the living of her life. And although it is impossible to specify uniformly what all births ought to be like, it can at least be said that they should not be founded upon the belief that the pregnant woman's interests conflict with those of her fetus, or that safety requirements must conflict with psychological needs. Ordinarily childbearing need not and should not require sacrifices of the pregnant woman.

NOTES

1. Barbara Katz Rothman, *Giving Birth: Alternatives in Childbirth* (Harmondsworth, England: Penguin Books, 1984), p. 277.

2. OMA Committee on Perinatal Care, "Ontario Medical Association Discussion Paper on Directions in Health Care Issues Relating to Childbirth" (Toronto, 1984). Although the paper is said not to represent present OMA policy (p. 1), it can be taken as representative of standard medical views on childbearing and on the relationship of the pregnant woman to her fetus.

3. *Ibid.,* p. 12.

4. Sheila Kitzinger, "The Social Context of Birth: Some Comparisons between Childbirth in Jamaica and Britain," in *Ethnography of Fertility and Birth,* ed. Carol P. MacCormack (London: Academic Press, 1982), p. 183.

5. For a complete discussion, see Yvonne Brackbill, June Rice, and Diony Young, *Birth Trap: The Legal Low-Down on High-Tech Obstetrics* (St. Louis: C. V. Mosby, 1984) pp. 1–38 and Doris Haire, "The Cultural Warping of Childbirth" (Seattle, Wash.: International Childbirth Education Association, 1972).

6. Ronald R. Rindfuss, Judith L. Ladinsky, Elizabeth Coppock, Victor W. Marshall, and A. S. Macpherson, "Convenience and the Occurrence of Births: Induction of Labor in the United States and Canada," in *Women and Health: The Politics of Sex in Medicine,* ed. Elizabeth Fee (Farmingdale, N. Y.: Baywood, 1982), pp. 37–58.

7. Janice Armstrong, "The Risks and Benefits of Home Birth" (unpublished paper, 1982), p. 10.

8. A. D. Jones and C. Dougherty, "Childbirth in a Scientific and Industrial Society," in MacCormack, *Ethnography of Fertility and Birth,* p. 280.

9. Brackbill et al., *Birth Trap,* pp. 3–4.

10. Armstrong, "Risks and Benefits of Home Birth," p. 2.

11. C. P. MacCormack, "Biological, Cultural and Social Adaptation in Human Fertility and Birth: A Synthesis," in *Ethnography of Fertility and Birth,* pp. 18–19.

12. David Stewart and Lewis E. Mehl, "A Rebuttal to Negative Home Birth Statistics Cited by ACOG," in *21st Century Obstetrics Now!* I, 2nd ed., ed. Lee Stewart and David Stewart (Chapel Hill, N.C.: NAPSAC, 1977), p. 29.

13. Paul Thompson, "Home Birth: Consumer Choice and Restrictions of Physician Autonomy," *Journal of Business Ethics* 6 (1987): 76.

14. But, as will be argued in chapter 8 [of *Ethics and Human Reproduction,* Christine Overall, Boston: Unwin Hyman, 1987] those rights are not unlimited.

15. Michael D. Bayles, *Reproductive Ethics* (Englewood Cliffs, N.J.: Prentice-Hall, 1984), p. 80.

16. Hilary Graham and Ann Oakley, "Competing Ideologies of Reproduction: Medical and Maternal Perspectives on Pregnancy," in *Women, Health and Reproduction,* ed. Helen Roberts (London: Routledge & Kegan Paul, 1981), p. 54.

17. Bayles, *Reproductive Ethics,* p. 83.

18. "OMA Discussion Paper," p. 9.

19. Bayles, *Reproductive Ethics,* p. 80.

20. Henry Klapholz, "The Electronic Fetal Monitor in Perinatology," in Holmes et al., *Birth Control and Controlling Birth,* p. 167.

21. *Ibid.,* p. 173, my emphasis.

22. "OMA Discussion Paper," p. 30.

23. Richard H. Aubry, "The American College of Obstetricians and Gynecologists: Standards for Safe Childbearing," in Stewart and Stewart, *21st Century Obstetrics Now!,* p. 20.

24. Brackbill et al., *Birth Trap,* pp. 59–61; Gerard Alan Hoff and Lawrence J. Schneiderman, "Having Babies at Home: Is It Safe? Is It Ethical?" *Hastings Center Report* 15 (December 1985): 21.

25. Armstrong, "Risks and Benefits of Home Births," p. 4.

26. Marjorie Tew, "The Case against Hospital Deliveries: The Statistical Evidence," in *The Place of Birth,* ed. Sheila Kitzinger and J. A. Davis (Oxford: Oxford University Press, 1978), p. 65.

27. Compare Thompson, "Home Birth: Consumer Choice," pp. 75–78.

28. Stewart, "The Case for Home Birth," pp. 221–223.

29. Paul Thompson, "Childbirth in North America: Parental Autonomy and the Welfare of the Fetus," unpublished paper, Toronto, Ontario (1984): 5.

30. *Ibid.,* p. 10.

31. Barbara Katz Rothman, "Awake and Aware, or False Consciousness," in Romalis, *Childbirth: Alternatives to Medical Control,* p. 177.

32. As some recommend: e.g., Hoff and Schneiderman, "Having Babies at Home," p. 24.

33. Sheila Kitzinger, *The Experience of Childbirth* 3rd ed., (Harmondsworth, England: Penguin Books, 1972), p. 21; compare Kitzinger, *Women as Mothers,* p. 24.

34. Adrienne Rich, "The Theft of Childbirth," in *Seizing Our Bodies: The Politics of Women's Health,* ed. Claudia Dreifus (New York: Vintage Books, 1977), p. 162.

35. Germaine Greer, *Sex and Destiny: The Politics of Human Fertility* (London: Secker & Warburg, 1984), p. 17.

36. Rothman, *Giving Birth,* p. 174, her emphasis.

37. Bayles, *Reproductive Ethics,* p. 81.

38. "OMA Discussion Paper," p. 33.

39. *Ibid.,* pp. 22, 24.

40. Bayles, *Reproductive Ethics,* p. 83.

41. As Adrienne Rich points out ("*The Theft of Childbirth*", p. 152), at times Kitzinger takes this claim too far—when, for example, she refers to births as "perhaps the most important moments of their [women's] lives" (Kitzinger, *The Experience of Childbirth,* p. 20).

42. Richard W. Wertz and Dorothy C. Wertz, *Lying-In: A History of Childbirth in America* (New York: Schocken Books, 1977), pp. 188–189.

43. Lester Dessez Hazell's moving "Truths about Birth" remind us that each birth is unique (Lester Dessez Hazell, "Spiritual and Ethical Aspects of Birth: Who Bears the Ultimate Responsibility?" in Stewart and Stewart *21st Century Obstetrics Now!,* p. 259).

44. Kitzinger, *Giving Birth,* p. 31; Graham and Oakley, "Competing Ideologies of Reproduction," p. 54.

45. Graham and Oakley, p. 54; Rich, "The Theft of Childbirth," pp. 161–162. If, for example, she returns to work after she has ostensibly recovered from the birth, "she is not the same worker who left to bear a child. Asking her to continue as if nothing had happened is absurd" (Greer, *Sex and Destiny,* p. 13).

1. Are hospital procedures in birthing (e.g., as described by Overall) humiliating experiences? If so, which procedures, and why are they humiliating?

2. If your baby were delivered by caesarean section, or if forceps were used on your baby's head during delivery, would you feel that you had somehow failed as a woman? What exactly does being a success as a woman have to do with delivering a baby in a certain way?

3. Since it is impossible to eliminate risk from all human activity (e.g., riding in automobiles), is it silly to try to maximize safety for the infant during delivery by "making the best of the worst possible outcome" (Bayles)? If this idea is silly, what is a better idea?

XI.3   Children by Donor Insemination: A New Choice for Lesbians

FRANCIE HORNSTEIN

Francie Hornstein describes her conception of a child by donor insemination. This possibility gives lesbians and heterosexual women without partners a new option in reproductive choice. In addition, self-insemination clinics offer women more control over the process of reproduction.

Hornstein has worked for reproductive choices for women and for lowering infant death rates among poor and minority communities since the late 1960s.

Reading Questions

1. Does the element of control a woman has in self-insemination (in selecting the donor and doing the insemination herself) make this an attractive option for women? For example, if you are (or were) a woman, would this be attractive for you?

2. What would you tell a child who was so conceived?

3. If you were in a permanent partnership with someone who would not be your child's biological parent, would the birth of your child pose potential problems in your relationship? If so, what kinds of problems?

IN SPITE OF THE MANY DIFFICULTIES involved in making any kind of far-reaching change, donor insemination has been an enormously exciting step in breaking through the constraints placed on women by sexist prohibitions. It has opened the door for allowing women to arrange their lives in a way that best suits their needs. For lesbians and some heterosexual women, donor insemination represents a new reproductive choice—and one which can remain in our control.

My decision to conceive a child by donor insemination was a long time coming. It was nearly seven years between the time I first considered the possibility and when I began trying to get pregnant. The one recurring reservation in what had become a passionate desire to have children was my fear for how the children would cope with being from a different kind of family.

I knew I would be sorry if I never had children; sorry not only for giving up a part of life I really wanted, but for not making a decision that I believed was right. I felt I was as worthy of having children as any other person. To not have children simply because I was a lesbian would have been giving up on a goal that was very dear to me.

I had always wanted to have children. I can remember when I was very young, as far back as elementary school, being afraid that I would never have children because I didn't think I would ever get married. Of course when I was eight years old I didn't realize that I was lesbian—I just could never imagine myself married to a man. Marrying a woman might have been more appealing, but that option was never presented to me.

No one has yet written a chronicle of feminist-controlled donor insemination, though some of us are beginning to collect information. It seems that small groups of women in different parts of the country began discussing and actually doing donor insemination beginning in the middle to late 1970s. For the most part, we were unaware of one another's existence. It wasn't until after several of us had children and either heard about each other through the grapevine or met at conferences that we began comparing notes.

I first tried donor insemination in 1973, while I was working at the Feminist Women's Health Center in Los Angeles. I was unable to use the services of the sperm bank because they would only accept married women as candidates for insemination. It was difficult finding donors and I was absorbed in long hours of work in the women's health movement, so the work involved in my getting pregnant was shelved for a few years. With the help of my co-workers and the encouragement of my lover, I finally began trying to get pregnant in 1977.

I think it was significant that I was working at the Feminist Women's Health Center at the time I got pregnant. It seemed particularly fitting that the same women who developed the practice of menstrual extraction, a procedure which could be used for early abortion, also were among the pioneers in the practice of self-help donor insemination. We figured if we could safely help a woman end her pregnancy without the help of physicians and patriarchal laws, we could certainly help women get pregnant.

My co-workers at the FWHC and I learned how to do the insemination in the same self-help way we learned about other aspects of women's health. We read medical journals and textbook articles, talked with physicians who did the procedure and combined that information with plain, down-to-earth common sense.

Finding donors was the most difficult part of the whole process for me. At the time I got pregnant, there was only one sperm bank in the city. It was owned and operated by a physician who had a private infertility practice and who was very conservative in selecting his clientele. He declined to make his services available to women who were not married, not to mention lesbians.

The only option open to us at the time was to find donors through our friends. I wanted to be able to give the children the option of knowing their father, so we preferred a situation in which the donor was known either to us or to a friend. Eventually, we were able to find donors.

The insemination itself was simple. All we had to do was have the donor ejaculate into a clean container, draw up the semen into a clean syringe (with the needle removed) and inject it into the vagina. We already knew how to do vaginal self-examination with a speculum, so we were familiar with the anatomy of the cervix, the opening of the uterus where the sperm needs to be put. Other women we later spoke with who didn't have access to medical supplies, such as syringes, improvised with common household items. A turkey baster, now synonymous with self-help insemination, works just fine. One innovative woman had her donor ejaculate into a condom, then she simply turned the condom inside-out in her vagina. Some women either insert a diaphragm or cervical cap to hold the semen near the cervix or they lie down for a half-hour or so after inserting the semen.

After our son was born, in the fall of 1978, my lover and I were asked to talk about our experiences at a variety of feminist conferences and programs. It was then that we began meeting other women who either had children or wanted to have children by donor insemination. Since that time, we have personally met women from several states and Canada and have heard about women from England and throughout Europe who are also having children by donor insemination, without the assistance of physicians. We have met two women who had children before 1978, but are sure there must be others. We had also heard that women in England had been using donor insemination for a number of years before women in the US. A friend visited a woman in England who has a 12-year-old son conceived by donor insemination.

The majority of women we have met who have had children by donor insemination are lesbians, though there is now a growing number of single, heterosexual women who are choosing donor insemination as a way of getting pregnant. Some of these women prefer being single, but want to have children; others haven't yet met men they want to live with or have children with, but because of their age or other reasons, don't want to wait for marriage before having children.

Several feminist health groups have begun making donor insemination available to women who ordinarily would not be able to use the services of sperm banks. In 1978, the Feminist Women's Health Center in Los Angeles began a donor insemination program. A commercial sperm bank had just opened up in the city and the only requirement for obtaining sperm from

them was a physician's order. The FWHC used their staff physicians to order sperm for women requesting insemination. The Vermont Women's Health Center and the Chelsea Health Center in New York City also assisted women in getting pregnant by donor insemination. In 1982, the Oakland Feminist Women's Health Center began their own sperm bank, the Sperm Bank of Northern California, tailor-making the health services to conform to their own feminist values and expectations rather than the medical model of the traditional sperm banks.[1]

The Oakland FWHC program varies from other sperm banks in a number of important ways. The aspects that distinguish their services are their willingness to provide sperm to any woman, regardless of her marital status, sexual preference, or physical disability; their provision of extensive, but non-identifying social and health background information of donors; a policy which permits women to examine a catalogue of donor information and to select their own donor; and possibly most important, a donor "release-of-information contract" which donors have the option of signing which gives their consent to provide their name to any children conceived from their sperm, when the child reaches the age of majority.

One thing the feminist health services have in common with one another is their attempt to de-medicalize the procedure of donor insemination. In most instances, physicians do not perform the insemination. Although the feminist health workers are willing to assist their clients who ask for their help, they prefer to provide the information so that women can do the insemination themselves, most often with the help of lovers or friends.

The intention on the part of feminist health services who provide donor insemination is less a desire to branch out into additional services but rather a strong political statement in support of a woman's right to make her own reproductive decisions. The feminist clinics find themselves in the unique position of having physicians on staff who have access to commercial sperm banks and want to make the resource available to the community. But they are adamant about their belief that physicians should not make decisions for women about whether or not they will have children. Because of the services provided by the Oakland Feminist Women's Health Center and the other clinics, and the work of women who have done self-help donor insemination and who are talking publicly about their experiences, a great many women, particularly lesbians, are now able to have children by donor insemination.

In discussing women's rights to make reproductive decisions, the positive impact of self-help donor insemination cannot be underestimated. But the practice does not exist in isolation and carries its fair share of potential problems and unanswered questions.

A woman deciding to having children on her own terms and without the inclusion of an on-site father is seen as attacking the traditional notion of a proper family. In spite of the fact that a large proportion of children end up living with their mothers only, it remains more threatening to patriarchy for a woman to *choose* to set up such an arrangement than to merely end up that way as a result of divorce, desertion or death.

While feminists are trying to make room for a variety of acceptable models for families, a number of patriarchal institutions are objecting to donor insemination as a means for creating a different kind of social unit. One incident is particularly illustrative of the reaction of the medical establishment and the state and local government to a woman's choosing to become pregnant by donor insemination.

In 1981, a woman in Milwaukee, Wisconsin, was inseminated by a physician and became pregnant. The woman was single and employed in a part-time job which did not provide health insurance coverage. She subsequently applied for medical assistance from the county social service agency for help in paying her maternity care bills. She was told that she would also qualify for Aid to Families with Dependent Children (AFDC) after her baby was born. The incident began the first public skirmish in the country about the rights of a single woman to have children by donor insemination.

The medical community was divided on the issue, with a number of outspoken physicians calling for a ban on the insemination of single women who could not prove financial stability. Although the physician who inseminated the woman held firm to his belief that a woman has the right to decide to bear children, the situation incensed other physicians and politicians who thought a single woman, especially a low-income single woman, had no right to intentionally have children.

Conservative politicians in the city and state governments called for actions ranging from a resolution for the county to file a paternity suit against the woman's physician to an amendment to a bill introduced into the state legislature which would have considered it unprofessional conduct for a physician to inseminate a woman under similar circumstances. The bill was vetoed by the governor.[2]

For the most part, women who are having children by donor insemination are not in such a public spotlight. Yet there are still a number of difficult issues we must face—even under the best of circumstances. We must all decide what to tell our children about their fathers. Our families, who may not share our feminist perspectives yet whose attachments we don't want to lose, often find it difficult to accept our lesbian families and our decisions to have children. Our children may well want to have contact or relationships with their fathers (in the event that they are known and can be located). We need to establish and protect the rights of partners of lesbians who may not be biological parents of the child, but who may be parents in every other sense of the word. And what do we do when a known donor who, after the baby is born, has a change of heart and wants more of a relationship with the child than was his original intention? These are all real issues that have and will continue to come up.

In addition to creating a new option for lesbians and other women who find that donor insemination is, for them, the best way to have children, it has been reassuring and exciting that a variety of support systems have grown right along with the numbers of women who have children by this method. Several feminist attorneys around the country have acquired considerable information about legal implications of donor insemination and have provided invaluable assistance to those of us having children. In many cities, women who have children or want to have children by donor insemination have started information and support groups. The groups provide as much benefit for the children as for the mothers. Even though the children are all still fairly young, they are growing up knowing that there are other children whose families are like theirs.

I think it is unwise and dishonest to gloss over many of the complex issues involved in donor insemination. Serious consideration and care must be taken for our children as they grow. Our children are not subjects in a social experiment but human beings with feelings whom we deeply love. There needs to be continuous support for mothers and for the rights of non-biological mothers who are part of the children's lives. We need to recognize the interests of the donors. But in the midst of trying to carve out new ways of doing things in an ethical way, we should also take joy in the fact that we have broken new ground. We have created new and important life choices for many people. We have taken back a little more of what is rightly ours—the chance to make decisions about how we will live our lives.

NOTES

1. Information about the Sperm Bank of Northern California was obtained in a personal communication with Laura Brown, Director of the Oakland Feminist Women's Health Center. The services of the Sperm Bank can be made available to interested people living outside the Northern California area. For more information write: Sperm Bank of Northern California, 2930 McClure Street, Oakland, CA. 94609.

2. Facts about the Milwaukee, Wisconsin, donor insemination case were provided in a personal communication with Dan Wikler, Program in Medical Ethics, Center for Health Sciences, University of Wisconsin.

Further Questions

1. Donor insemination produces a separation between sex and reproduction, because the former is not necessary for the latter. Do you think perceiving them as separate processes, each with its own worth, a good idea? Does it impair anything in the idea of sex with the aim of procreation that is worth preserving?

2. Does donor insemination undermine the ideal of the traditional family where children are conceived in marriage through sexual intercourse? Would it cause problems not found in a traditional family structure? If so, what problems would it cause?

3. Should children conceived by donor insemination qualify, along with their mothers, for full public assistance benefits? As a taxpayer, would you mind supporting these children and mothers through public assistance?

Selling Babies and Selling Bodies   XI.4

SARA ANN KETCHUM

Sara Ann Ketchum discusses contracted motherhood (CM), a situation where a woman contracts with a couple to bear a child for them. Usually, the child is conceived by artificial insemination with the man's sperm. The practice could perhaps be subsumed under selling babies, thus commodifying children. There is also the possibility that what is commodified is the woman's body, through her sale of her reproductive services.

Ketchum has taught philosophy, written articles on feminist philosophy, and now works as an attorney for the US government.

Reading Questions

1. Is contracted motherhood just like sperm donation except for the fact that more time and energy are required for a pregnancy than for an ejaculation?

2. If the birth mother is paid for gestating and delivering the baby, should this be regarded as selling the baby? Is it better classified as putting the baby up for adoption?

3. Is a woman's reproductive capacity the kind of thing that should not be bought and sold? Is reproductive capacity like sexuality in this respect; that is, is contracted motherhood like prostitution?

ONE OBJECTION to what is usually called "surrogate motherhood" and which I will call "contracted motherhood" (CM) or "baby contracts"[1] is that it commercializes reproduction and turns human beings (the mother and/or the baby) into objects of sale. If this is a compelling objection, there is a good argument for prohibiting (and/or not enforcing contracts for) commercial CM. Such a prohibition would be similar to laws on black market adoptions and would have two parts, at least: (1) a prohibition of commercial companies who make the arrangements and/or (2) a prohibition on the transfer of money to the birth mother for the transfer of custody (beyond expenses incurred). I will also argue that CM law should follow adoption law in making clear that pre-birth agreements to relinquish parental rights are not binding and will not be enforced by the courts

(the birth mother should not be forced to give up her child for adoption).

CM and AID: The Real Difference Problem

CM is usually presented as a new reproductive technology and, moreover, as the female equivalent of AID (artificial insemination by donor) and, therefore, as an extension of the right to privacy or the right to make medical decisions about one's own life. There are two problems with this description: (1) CM uses the same technology as AID—the biological arrangements are exactly the same—but intends an opposite assignment of custody. (2) No technology is necessary for CM as is evidenced by the biblical story of Abraham and Sarah who used a "handmaid" as a birth mother. Since artificial insemination is virtually uncontroversial it seems clear that what makes CM controversial is not the technology, but the social arrangements—that is, the custody assignment. CM has been defended on the ground that such arrangements enable fertile men who are married to infertile women to reproduce and, thus, are parallel to AID which enables fertile women whose husbands are infertile to have children. It is difficult not to regard these arguments as somewhat disingenuous. The role of the sperm donor and the role of the egg donor/mother are distinguished by pregnancy, and pregnancy is, if anything is, a "real difference" which would justify us in treating women and men differently. To treat donating sperm as equivalent to biological motherhood would be as unfair as treating the unwed father who has not contributed to his children's welfare the same as the father who has devoted his time to taking care of them. At most, donating sperm is comparable to donating ova; however, even that comparison fails because donating ova is a medically risky procedure, donating sperm is not.

Therefore, the essential morally controversial features of CM have to do with its nature as a social and economic institution and its assignment of family relationships rather than with any technological features. Moreover, the institution of CM requires of contracting birth mothers much more time commitment, medical risk, and social disruption than AID does of sperm donors. It also requires substantial male control over women's bodies and time, while AID neither requires nor provides any female control over men's bodies. Christine Overall notes that when a woman seeks AID, she not only does not usually have a choice of donor, but she also may be required to get her husband's consent if she is married. The position of the man seeking CM is the opposite; he chooses a birth mother and his wife does not have to consent to the procedure (although the mother's husband does). [One such contract] contains a number of provisions regulating [the birth mother's] behavior, including: extensive medical examinations, an agreement about when she may or may not abort, an agreement to follow doctors' orders, and agreements not to take even prescription drugs without the doctor's permission. Some of these social and contractual provisions are eliminable. But the fact that CM requires a contract and AID does not reflects the differences between pregnancy and ejaculation. If the sperm donor wants a healthy child (a good product), he needs to control the woman's behavior. In contrast, any damage the sperm-donor's behavior will have on the child will be present in the sperm and could, in principle, be tested for before the woman enters the AID procedure. There is no serious moral problem with discarding defective sperm; discarding defective children is a quite different matter.

Commodification

SELLING BABIES

The most straightforward argument for prohibiting baby-selling is that it is selling a human being and that any selling of a human being should be prohibited because it devalues human life and human individuals. This argument gains moral force from its analogy with slavery. Defenders of baby contracts argue that baby selling is unlike selling slaves in that it is a transfer of parental rights rather than of ownership of the child—the adoptive parents cannot turn around and sell the baby to another couple for a profit. What the defenders of CM fail to do is provide an account of the wrongness of slavery such that baby-selling (or baby contracts) do not fall under the argument. . . .

Those who defend CM while supporting laws against baby-selling distinguish CM from paid adoptions in that in CM the person to whom custody is being transferred is the biological (genetic) father. This suggests a parallel to custody disputes, which are not obviously any more appropriately ruled by money than is adoption. We could argue against the commercialization of either on the grounds that child-regarding concerns should decide child custody and that using market criteria or contract considerations would violate that principle by substituting another, unrelated, and possibly conflicting, one. In particular, both market and contract are about relations between the adults involved rather than about the children or about the relationship between the child and the adult.

Another disanalogy cited between preadoption contracts and CM is that, in preadoption contracts the baby is already there (that is, the preadoption contract is offered to a woman who is already pregnant, and, presumably, planning to have the child), while the mother contract is a contract to create a child who does not yet exist, even as an embryo. If our concern is the commodification of children, this strikes me as an odd point for the *defenders* of CM to emphasize. Producing a child to order for money is a paradigm case of commodifying children. The fact that the child is not being put up for sale to the highest bidder, but is only for sale to the genetic father, may reduce some of the harmful effects of an open market in babies but does not quiet concerns about personhood.

Arguments for allowing CM are remarkably similar to the arguments for legalizing black-market adoptions in the way they both define the problem. CM, like a market for babies, is seen as increasing the satisfaction and freedom of infertile individuals or couples by increasing the quantity of the desired product (there will be more babies available for adoption) and the quality of the product (not only more white healthy babies, but white healthy babies who are genetically related to one of the purchasers). These arguments tend to be based on the interests of infertile couples and obscure the relevance of the interests of the birth mothers (who will be giving the children up for adoption) and their families, the children who are produced by the demands of the market, and (the most invisible and most troubling group) needy children who are without

homes because they are not "high-quality" products and because we are not, as a society, investing the time and money needed to place the hard to adopt children. . . .

. . . Not only does the baby become an object of commerce, but the custody relationship of the parent becomes a property relationship. If we see parental custody rights as correlates of parental responsibility or as a right to maintain a relationship, it will be less tempting to think of them as something one can sell. We have good reasons for allowing birth-mothers to relinquish their children because otherwise we would be forcing children into the care of people who either do not want them or feel themselves unable to care for them. However, the fact that custody may be waived in this way does not entail that it may be sold or transferred. If children are not property, they cannot be gifts either. If a mother's right is a right to maintain a relationship, it is implausible to treat it as transferrable; having the option of terminating a relationship with A does not entail having the option of deciding who A will relate to next—the right to a divorce does not entail the right to transfer one's connection to one's spouse to someone else. Indeed, normally, the termination of a relationship with A ends any right I have to make moral claims on A's relationships. Although in giving up responsibilities I may have a responsibility to see to it that someone will shoulder them when I go, I do not have a right to choose that person.

SELLING WOMEN'S BODIES

Suppose we do regard mother contracts as contracts for the sale or rental of reproductive capacities. Is there good reason for including reproductive capacities among those things or activities that ought not to be bought and sold? We might distinguish between selling reproductive capacities and selling work on a number of grounds. A conservative might argue against commercializing reproduction on the grounds that it disturbs family relationships, or on the grounds that there are some categories of human activities that should not be for sale . . . that there are some activities that are close to our personhood and that a commercial traffic in these activities constitutes treating the person as less than an end (or less than a person).

One interpretation of the laws prohibiting baby selling is that they are an attempt to reduce or eliminate coercion in the adoption process, and are thus based on a concern for the birth mother rather than (or as well as) the child. All commercial transactions are at least potentially coercive in that the parties to them are likely to come from unequal bargaining positions and in that, whatever we have a market in, there will be some people who will be in a position such that they have to sell it in order to survive. Such concerns are important to arguments against an open market in human organs or in the sexual use of people's bodies as well as arguments against baby contracts of either kind.

As Margaret Radin (Market-Inalienability. *Harvard Law Review* 100: 1849–1937, 1987) suggests, the weakness of arguments of this sort—that relationships or contracts are exploitative on the grounds that people are forced into them by poverty—is that the real problem is not in the possibility of commercial transactions, but in the situation that makes these arrangements attractive by comparison. We do not end the feminization of poverty by forbidding prostitution or CM. Indeed, if we are successful in eliminating these practices, we may be reducing the income of some women (by removing ways of making money) and, if we are unsuccessful, we are removing these people from state protection by making their activities illegal. Labor legislation which is comparably motivated by concern for unequal bargaining position (such as, for example, minimum wage and maximum hours laws, and health and safety regulations) regulates rather than prevents that activity and is thus less vulnerable to this charge. Radin's criticism shows that the argument from the coerciveness of poverty is insufficient as a support for laws rejecting commercial transactions in personal services. This does not show that the concern is

irrelevant. The argument from coercion is still an appropriate response to simple voluntarist arguments—those that assume that these activities are purely and freely chosen by all those who participate in them. Given the coerciveness of the situation, we cannot assume that the presumed or formal voluntariness of the contract makes it nonexploitative.

If the relationship of CM is, by its nature, disrespectful of personhood, it can be exploitative despite short-term financial benefits to some women. The disrespect for women as persons that is fundamental to the relationship lies in the concept of the woman's body (and of the child and mother-child relationship) implicit in the contract. I have argued elsewhere that claiming a welfare right to another person's body is to treat that person as an object:

> An identity or intimate relation between persons and their bodies may or may not be essential to our metaphysical understanding of a person, but it is essential to a minimal moral conceptual scheme. Without a concession to persons' legitimate interests and concerns for their physical selves, most of our standard and paradigm moral rules would not make sense; murder might become the mere destruction of the body; assault, a mere interference with the body . . . and so on. We cannot make sense out of the concept of assault unless an assault on S's body is ipso facto an assault on S. By the same token, treating another person's body as part of my domain—as among the things that I have a rightful claim to—is, if anything is, a denial that there is a person there.[2]

This argument is, in turn, built on the analysis of the wrongness of rape developed by Marilyn Frye and Carolyn Shafer in "Rape and Respect":

> The use of a person in the advancement of interests contrary to its own is a limiting case of disrespect. It reveals the perception of the person simply as an object which can serve some purpose, a tool or a bit of material, and one which furthermore is dispensable or replaceable and thus of little value even as an object with a function.[3]

We can extend this argument to the sale of persons. To make a person or a person's body an object of commerce is to treat the person as part of another person's domain, particularly if the sale of A to B gives B rights to A or to A's body. What is objectionable is a claim—whether based on welfare or on contract—to a right to another person such that that person is part of my domain. The assertion of such a right is morally objectionable even without the use of force. For example, a man who claims to have a *right* to sexual intercourse with his wife, on the grounds of the marriage relationship, betrays a conception of her body, and thus her person, as being properly within his domain, and thus a conception of her as an object rather than a person.

Susan Brownmiller, in *Against Our Will,* suggests that prostitution is connected to rape in that prostitution makes women's bodies into consumer goods that might—if not justifiably, at least understandably—be forcibly taken by those men who see themselves as unjustly deprived.

> When young men learn that females may be bought for a price, and that acts of sex command set prices, then how should they not also conclude that that which may be bought may also be taken without the civility of a monetary exchange? . . . legalized prostitution institutionalizes the concept that it is a man's monetary right, if not his divine right, to gain access to the female body, and that sex is a female service that should not be denied the civilized male.[4]

The same can be said for legalized sale of women's reproductive services. The more hegemonic this commodification of women's bodies is, the more the woman's lack of consent to sex or to having children can present itself as unfair to the man because it is arbitrary.

A market in women's bodies—whether sexual prostitution or reproductive prostitution—reveals a social ontology in which women are among the things in the world that can be appropriately commodified—bought and sold and, by extension, stolen. The purported freedom that such institutions would give women to enter into the market by selling their bodies is paradoxical. Sexual or reproductive prostitutes enter the market not so much as *agents* or subjects, but as commodities or objects. This is evidenced by the fact that the pimps and their counterparts, the arrangers of baby contracts, make the bulk of the profits. Moreover, once there is a market for women's bodies, all women's bodies will have a price, and the woman who does not sell her body becomes a hoarder of something that is useful to other people and is financially valuable. The market is a hegemonic institution; it determines the meanings of actions of people who choose not to participate as well as of those who choose to participate.

CONTRACT

The immediate objection to treating [a CM dispute] as a contract dispute is that the practical problem facing the court is a child custody problem and to treat it as a contract case is to deal with it on grounds other than the best interests of the child. That the best interests of the child count need not entail that contract does not count, although it helps explain one of the reasons we should be suspicious of this particular contract. There is still the question of whether the best interests of the child will trump contract considerations (making the contract nonbinding) or merely enter into a balancing argument in which contract is one of the issues to be balanced. However, allowing contract to count at all raises some of the same . . . objections as the commodification problem. As a legal issue, the contract problem is more acute because the state action (enforcing the contract) is more explicit.

Any binding mother contract will put the state in the position of enforcing the rights of a man to a woman's body or to his genetic offspring. But this is to treat the child or the mother's body as objects of the sperm donor's rights, which, I argued above, is inconsistent with treating them as persons. This will be clearest if the courts enforce specific performance and require the mother to go through with the pregnancy (or to abort) if she chooses not to or requires the transfer of custody to the contracting sperm-donor on grounds other than the best interests of the child. In those cases, I find it hard to avoid the description that what is being awarded is a person and what is being affirmed is a right to a person. I think the . . . argument still applies if the court refuses specific performance but awards damages. Damages compensate for the loss of something to which one has a right. A judge who awards damages to the contracting sperm donor for having been deprived of use of the contracting woman's reproductive capacities or for being deprived of custody of the child gives legal weight to the idea that the contracting sperm donor had a legally enforceable *right* to them (or, to put it more bluntly, to those commodities or goods).

The free contract argument assumes that [a birth mother's] claims to her daughter are rights (rather than, for example, obligations or a more complex relationship), and, moreover, that they are alienable, as are property rights. If the baby is not something she has an alienable right to, then custody of the baby is not something she can transfer by contract. In cases where the state is taking children away from their biological parents and in custody disputes, we do want to appeal to some rights of the parents. However, I think it would be unfortunate to regard these rights as rights to the child, because that would be to treat the child as the object of the parents' rights and violate the principles that persons and persons' bodies cannot be the objects of other people's rights. The parents' rights in these cases should be to consideration, to nonarbitrariness and to respect for the relationship between the parent and the child.

Concluding Remarks

. . . There is increasing concern that women cannot predict in advance whether or not they and their family[5] will form an attachment to the child they will bear nor can they promise not to develop such feelings (as some of the contracts ask them to do). There is also increasing concern for the birth-family and for the children produced by the arrangement (particularly where there is a custody dispute). A utilitarian might respond that the problems are outweighed by the joys of the adopting/sperm donor families, but, if so, we must ask: are we simply shifting the misery from wealthy (or wealthier) infertile couples to poorer fertile families and to the "imperfect" children waiting for adoption?

These considerations provide good reason for prohibiting commercialization of CM. In order to do that we could adopt new laws prohibiting the transfer of money in such arrangements or simply extend existing adoption laws, making the contracts non-binding as are prebirth adoption contracts and limiting the money that can be transferred. There are some conceptual problems remaining about what would count as prohibiting commodification. I find the English approach very attractive. This approach has the following elements (1) it strictly prohibits third parties from arranging mother contracts; (2) if people arrange them privately, they are allowed, (3) the contracts are not binding. If the birth-mother decides to keep the baby, her decision is final[6] (*and* the father may be required to pay child-support; that may be too much for Americans). (4) Although, in theory, CM is covered by limitations on money for adoption, courts have approved payments for contracted motherhood, and there is never criminal penalty on the parents for money payments.

NOTES

1. Terms such as "surrogate mother" and "renting a womb" are distortions—the surrogate mother *is* the mother, and she is giving up her child for adoption just as is the birth mother who gives up her child for adoption by an unrelated person. This language allows the defenders of paternal rights, to argue for the importance of biological (genetic) connection when it comes to the *father's* rights, but bury the greater physical con-

nection between the mother and the child in talk that suggests that mothers are mere receptacles (shades of Aristotle's biology) or that the mother has a more artificial relationship to the child than does the father or the potential adoptive mother. But, at the time of birth, the natural relationship is between the mother and child. (I discuss this issue further in "New Reproductive Technologies and the Definition of Parenthood: A Feminist Perspective." [Presented at Feminism and legal theory: Women and intimacy, a conference sponsored by the Institute for Legal Studies at the University of Wisconsin–Madison, 1987.]) A relationship created by contract is the paradigm of artificiality, of socially created relationship, and the most plausible candidate for a natural social relationship is the mother-child bond. I will be using "contracted motherhood" and "baby contracts" (a term offered by Elizabeth Bartholet) rather than "surrogate motherhood" and "surrogacy." I will use "baby contracts" as the more general term, covering paid adoption contracts as well as so called "surrogate mother" arrangements. I have not yet found a term that is either neutral between or inclusive of the motherhood aspects and the baby-regarding aspects.

2. Ketchum, Sara Ann, "The Moral Status of the Bodies of Persons, *Social Theory and Practice* (1984), 25–38.

3. Frye, Marilyn and Carolyn Shafer "Rape and Respect" in *Feminism and Philosophy*. Mary Vetterling-Braggin et al. Totowa, NJ, Littlefield and Adams, 1977.

4. Brownmiller, Susan *Against Our Will,* New York: Simon and Schuster, 1975.

5. One former surrogate reports that her daughter (11 at the time of the birth and now 17) is still having problems:

> Nobody told me that a child could bond with a baby while you're still pregnant. I didn't realize then that all the times she listened to his heartbeat and felt his legs kick that she was becoming attached to him.

Another quotes her son as having asked, "You're not going to give them me, are you?"

6. This presupposes a presumption in favor of the birth-mother as custodial or deciding parent. I have argued for that position on the grounds that, at the time of birth, the gestational mother has a concrete relationship to the child that the genetic father (and the genetic mother, if she is not the gestational mother) does not have. Without that presumption and without a presumption of sale or contract, each case would be subject to long custody disputes.

Further Questions

1. Is it appropriate to regard children as beings that parents have rights to, in particular, the sorts of rights that can be transferred or sold to someone else? If parents have such rights, does this mean children are not fully human?

2. Ought CM contracts be revocable, so that the birth mother can keep the baby and return the money if she wishes? If the birth mother does keep the baby, does she owe the adopting couple anything more than the money they paid her to gestate the baby?

3. Would CM contracts be less objectionable if they were arranged privately, without a third party acting as intermediary between the birth mother and the adopting couple? In absence of a third party, could the adopting couple victimize the birth mother? Could she victimize them?

XI.5A   The Ethics of Surrogacy

JONATHAN GLOVER ET AL., THE GLOVER REPORT TO THE EUROPEAN COMMISSION

This chapter of the report discusses some moral questions that arise if any form of surrogate motherhood is permitted.

Reading Questions

1. Suppose you wanted a child but, for some reason, could not gestate one biologically. Under what circumstances would you think it morally permissible to have a surrogate mother gestate one for you?

2. Do you think a child is wronged in any way if he is gestated by a surrogate mother? If he is harmed in some way, is he better or worse off than if he had been adopted in a traditional manner?

3. Should potential surrogate mothers be screened? Should potential adoptive couples be screened? If so, in whose interest should such screening take place?

THE TWO CENTRAL QUESTIONS are whether surrogate motherhood is morally acceptable and whether it should be legally permitted. These questions are not identical, but they are related.

If any policy short of a total ban is adopted, the main further questions are these:

Should there be surrogacy contracts? Should they be legally enforceable either when the surrogate breaks the restrictions imposed on her during pregnancy, or when she changes her mind about handing over the child?

Should the contents of contracts be regulated, either to protect the surrogate from exploitation, or to protect the interests of the child?

Should there be screening of surrogate mothers? Possible problem cases include heavy smokers and people with severe psychological problems. They also include the sister or other close relation of the potential parent, who may be particularly likely to volunteer, but whose role might create family problems later.

What is the role of intermediaries, such as doctors, clinics and agencies? Should there be profit-making agencies?

1. The Case for Surrogacy

Part of the case is straightforward. Surrogacy relieves childlessness. For women who have had repeated miscarriages, or who suffer from conditions making pregnancy dangerous, surrogacy may be the only hope of having a child.

Another, more problematic, argument appeals to the interests of the child who would not have existed without surrogacy.

Another argument appeals to liberty. Some strong justification is needed for preventing people from bearing children to help their sisters or friends. And a similar strong justification is needed for preventing people freely contracting to do this for someone for money. This argument relates to the legality of surrogacy, but does nothing to show that surrogacy is a good thing in itself. The central case for that has to rest on relieving the burden of childlessness.

2. The Case against Surrogacy

(a) The children: One line of thought appeals to the rights of the child. It appears in the Catholic document issued by the Congregation for the Doctrine of the Faith, which says that surrogacy "offends the dignity and the right of the child to be conceived, carried in the womb, brought into the world and brought up by his own parents."

This case seems to us not overwhelming. Even if the child has a strong interest in being created sexually, to call this a *right* is to claim that it trumps *any* interests of the childless couple. This requires that being the child of a surrogate is such an indignity that, by comparison, relieving *any* degree of the potential parents' misery is to count for nothing. We have not found the powerful supporting argument this would need.

The objection is made even weaker by a further problem. For the potential child, the alternative to surrogacy may be nonexistence. It seems unlikely that the child will see surrogacy as so bad as to wish he or she had not been born at all. The "right" looks like one the child will later be glad was not respected. It is hard to see the case for giving this supposed interest any weight at all, let alone for saying that it justifies leaving people unwillingly childless.

Another argument appeals to the psychological effects of surrogacy on the child. If the surrogacy is paid for there is a danger that the child will think he or she has been bought. Also, it is sometimes suggested that surrogacy breaks a bond formed by the time of birth. Dr John Marks, the chairman of the British Medical Association, has said: "By the time a baby is born there is a bond between the mother and the child. With surrogacy you break that bond. You are depriving the child of one natural parent. We think that is wrong" (The *Guardian*, May 8, 1987). It is reported that the General Medical

Council may ban doctors from involvement in surrogacy. This step has already been taken in West Germany.

The surrogate mother may well feel a bond between herself and the child. But is there reason to believe in any bond in the other direction before birth? Or could this be an illusion created by projecting the mother's feelings on to the foetus? If the child's feelings are a reason against surrogacy, the baby has to have, by the time of birth, highly specific feelings towards the particular woman who bears him. The evidence for this can charitably be described as slight.

Suppose, for the sake of argument, that there is such a bond. It is then undesirable to break it. But, where it is broken, is the child so harmed that it would have been better if he or she had not been born? For this is what banning surrogacy on these grounds seems to imply. We do not have such drastic thoughts about people who are adopted. The British Medical Association's Board of Science is quoted as saying that while adoption may be "the next best thing" for a child facing an uncertain future, any arrangement where a surrogate mother hands over the child "dooms it to second best from the start" (*The Independent*, May 8, 1987). But is it obvious here that no life at all is preferable to "second best"?

(b) Conflicts: The conflicts sometimes arising between the potential parents and the surrogate mother may harm the child, and this is part of the case against surrogacy.

(c) Effects on the family: Perhaps introducing a third party so intimately into the process of having children may weaken the institution of the family. (In West Germany, the report of the Benda Commission considers a legal ban on surrogacy with the exception of surrogacy by relatives.)

(d) The surrogate mother: The position of the surrogate mother varies, according to whether she is bearing a child to help a sister or friend, or has made a commercial arrangement. There is the criticism that surrogacy is an invasion of her bodily integrity. This criticism may be weaker if she willingly agreed than if she was forced into it

by money problems. Sometimes she may bitterly regret having agreed to give away the baby.

. . . [T]here is [also] a danger of her being exploited. Financial pressures may put her in a weak position to resist contractual conditions which give little weight to her interests.

Another important motive for volunteering to act as a surrogate seems to be the desire for friendship with the parents-to-be. As this is usually exactly what the parents-to-be do *not* want, it is an illusory objective. She wants friendship: she is treated as a provider of a service, and afterwards dismissed.

3. Policy

Is surrogacy something to encourage or not? The Warnock Committee said, "The question of surrogacy presented us with some of the most difficult problems we encountered." We found this too. The central issue is the conflict between the interests of the childless couple and those of the surrogate mother.

Some members of the committee are opposed to surrogacy in principle, because of what the practice does to the surrogate mother. The invasion of her bodily integrity, the disappointment of any hopes for friendship with the family who receive the child, the psychological trauma of giving up the baby, and the possibility of regrets for the rest of her life, add up to a very strong case against surrogacy. There is also the possibility of ill effects on the surrogate's own family, particularly on her own children.

Other members of the committee share these anxieties, but are sufficiently impressed by the needs of infertile couples to think that some cases of surrogacy are beneficial. Whichever view we take, we agree both that surrogacy should not be illegal, and also that, if it *does* take place, it should be subject to certain restrictions.

A general legal ban would be unenforceable. Moreover there is a powerful consideration which also influenced the Warnock Committee: the birth of a child should not have a taint of criminality. We recommend that surrogacy should not itself be illegal.

The surrogate mother is notably vulnerable, and any acceptable arrangements for surrogacy must give her a lot of protection. The child should be protected against prolonged battles between the surrogate and the potential parents. These two considerations support restrictions which may in practice greatly reduce the frequency of surrogacy. While this will leave some infertile couples childless, we think this is a lesser evil than the ones such restrictions would be designed to avert.

4. Agencies and Regulation

Sometimes surrogates will be relations or friends helping people they know well. But there is a case for the option of making arrangements through a clinic or other agency. They will have more experience of the problems than the couple or the surrogate mother. They will know what should go into a contract. And they will be able to carry out any necessary screening either of couples or of surrogate mothers.

Where these agencies are public, they should operate on guidelines open to public inspection. If there are private agencies, they should be publicly inspected and licensed.

5. Making Contracts Unenforceable against the Surrogate Mother

We think that the surrogate mother should remain free to decide for herself whether or not to have an abortion. And we think she should not be forced to hand over the child against her will. In these respects at least, any contract should not be enforceable against her.

This is mainly to protect the surrogate mother. But there are other reasons. If the contract were enforceable, a pregnant surrogate who started to change her mind might become depressed. This could be bad for the child. If a contract were enforced against a reluctant surrogate the couple might feel guilty, which could interfere with their relationship with the child. If the child found out (as would be likely in a system not based on anonymity), the relationship might again be disturbed.

6. The Claims of the Biological Father

This policy of unenforceability supports the claims of the surrogate mother against those of the biological father. In cases of dispute over the baby, some think that the father's right to his child should not be overridden. There are two main arguments for this: he has a right arising out of a contract freely entered into by the surrogate, and he *is* the biological father.

(a) The contract: This is partly a claim about a legal right. In many countries, such contracts are unenforceable, and so this legal right does not exist. The issue is whether they *should* be enforceable, and this cannot be settled by citing what the law happens to be.

Most legal systems refuse to recognize some kinds of contract, such as those in which people sell themselves into slavery. This refusal is a restriction of liberty: it excludes people's freedom to bind themselves in certain ways. It is a protection against people doing themselves great harm or giving away vital liberties. It is a form of "paternalism": restricting people's freedom in their own interests.

Some are opposed to all paternalism. Too much paternalism can be a danger to liberty. But the case of contracting to become a slave illustrates the difficulty of excluding all paternalism. Stopping people making enforceable slavery contracts protects one of their vital interests. It also protects far more freedom than it takes away. We think that these reasons (as well as the other non-paternalist ones) apply to making surrogacy contracts unenforceable.

(b) The biological link: The other basis for the father's claim to take the child from the reluctant surrogate mother is that he *is* the biological father. This case also seems to us not decisive. The father is genetically linked to the child. But so, in one form of surrogacy, is the surrogate mother.

And even in the other form, "womb leasing," she has still carried and given birth to the child. This too is a biological link, and often creates, on her side at least, an emotional link as well.

The father's interests are not negligible here. Because of the genetic link, he is likely to care a lot about the child. And, if the surrogate changes her mind, he and his partner will have the anguish of childlessness compounded by disappointed expectations.

But it is not obvious that, of the biological bonds, the genetic one should trump the others to give the father a right to the child. And, severe as the couple's disappointment is, we do not think it justifies forcing a woman to endure the anguish of being made to give up the child she has given birth to.

The possibility of the surrogate mother changing her mind should be accepted by the couple as one of the risks of this way of trying to overcome childlessness when embarking on it.

7. Protecting the Child

If there is to be surrogate motherhood, the child needs protection from emotional damage. In every way things should be as normal for the child as possible. This is one reason why surrogacy should not be illegal. It cannot be good for children to know that their social parents or surrogate mother committed a crime through having them.

It is also surely bad for children if there are long legal battles over them. And even if the battles lasted only for a few months, the insecurity in the (social or surrogate) mother looking after the child could interfere with bonding, as would any transfer which then took place. These are further reasons for making the contract unenforceable in this respect against the surrogate mother. Her decision to keep the baby should be final.

But they are equally reasons for making her decision *not* to keep the baby final. Once the baby has been voluntarily handed over to the social parents, further upheavals around the child should be avoided. The social parents should be recognized as the legal parents beyond further challenge, even if the surrogate later changes her mind.

The surrogate mother should normally be regarded as having no right to a further relationship with the child who has been handed over. Visits or other contact could undermine the child's security about who his or her parents are. There are special cases, as when a relation or close friend acts as a surrogate. But, in other cases, we think that the child's interests require severance of the relationship to be the norm. (Though there is a case for the child having the right to be told on reaching maturity the identity of the surrogate mother. The case is like that for non-anonymity of donors already discussed.)

8. Screening Potential Social Parents

No individual should be put in the position of breaking the law by becoming a surrogate or by contracting with one. But agencies could adopt a policy of screening potential surrogates or potential parents, and it would be possible for *them* to be legally required to do so.

We think there should be a background presumption that reproductive help should be available to those who request it, subject to competing claims for resources, and with certain exceptions where special reasons apply. But, because of the special problems of surrogacy, particularly for the surrogate mother, we think that agencies should only help those who cannot have children in other ways, or where serious medical risks are involved. The desire not to interrupt a career does not seem sufficient reason for imposing the risks and traumas of surrogacy on another woman, even if she is prepared to accept them.

9. Screening Potential Surrogate Mothers

There is now little screening of surrogate mothers. They are not easily found, and screening may seem just a way of reducing their number still further. But some screening, or at least counselling, would be in the interests of everyone. It is possible, for instance, that women who have been very promiscuous, or who have had a long series of unstable relationships, or who have been abandoned in childhood, are more likely to resist giving up the baby, or else to suffer from extreme depression over it.

Some screening would be on behalf of the potential surrogate herself. Apart from the psychological aspects, she may want to know that pregnancy will not carry any special health risks for her. The screening period might give her time to think about her decision, and about its implications for herself and for her family. The agency should provide her with counselling help during this period.

Some screening should be on behalf of the child. Heavy smokers, alcoholics and other addicts may harm the child and these conditions should be grounds for exclusion. (*Grounds* for exclusion: where surrogates are very hard to obtain, these grounds may *perhaps* be overridden. From the later perspective of the child, it may be better to have run those risks, or even to have suffered some harm, than not to have been born at all.)

Some screening should be on behalf of the potential parents. The kind of history linked with the surrogate changing her mind about handing over the baby seems a reasonable ground for exclusion. There are other grounds. In one case, a surrogate repeatedly extracted more money from the potential parents, threatening to kill herself unless they paid (Noel Keane and Denis Breo: *The Surrogate Mother*, New York, 1981, quoted in Peter Singer and Deane Wells: *The Reproduction Revolution*, Oxford, 1984, pages 116–117). No doubt it is hard to pick up this sort of thing in advance. But, where there is reason to suspect it, the potential parents would have reason to complain if the agency accepted the woman as a surrogate.

There are obviously difficulties in predicting who will be a good surrogate mother. Those rejected by agencies would be free to be surrogates by private arrangement. These comments about screening are intended as general guidance. Good agencies will revise their criteria in the light of their experience, and in the light of evidence collected in studies of other cases.

Further Questions

1. Suppose there were a legal ban on surrogacy and suppose, realistically, that it was not completely enforceable. Would children then illegally born of surrogates bear too much taint of criminality?

2. Is there ever sufficient reason for a biological father's claim to a child to take precedence over that of the surrogate mother in case both want the child after it is born?

3. Should you resort to surrogacy only if there is no other way you can have a child? Should you be required to have a partner if you are going to raise a child gestated by someone else?

Having Children and the Market Economy   XI.5B

JONATHAN GLOVER ET AL., THE GLOVER REPORT TO THE EUROPEAN COMMISSION

This 7th chapter of the report discusses payment of surrogate mothers and semen donors and also whether there should be commercial agencies ("third parties") for surrogacy.

Reading Questions

1. If you were (or are) a man, would you consider donating semen to a sperm bank? Would whether you were paid influence your decision? If you were (or are) a woman, are there circumstances under which you would become an egg donor?

2. Suppose surrogate mothers were paid at an hourly rate better than that of a secretary. Would such payment make surrogates more or less exploited than if they were unpaid?

3. Would you consider a ban on sperm donation or surrogate motherhood a restriction on someone's liberty of earning a living in the way he or she chooses? If so, do you think these practices should be banned anyway because they exploit those who choose to engage in them?

WITH BOTH SURROGATE MOTHERS and semen donors, the question of payment comes up. We discuss these issues briefly, and then turn to the more important issue of whether there should be commercial agencies for surrogacy.

These may be straightforward questions about efficiency, to be answered by seeing what works best. In part, they are questions of that sort. But, entangled with those pragmatic problems are some deeper issues about what sort of society we want.

1. Semen Donors

. . . [S]ome hospitals and sperm banks pay semen donors, while egg donors are rarely paid. Is it better when semen donors are also unpaid?

The case for payment is mainly that it brings in more donors, as the Necker Hospital found when it stopped paying. Payment also gives some recognition to the donor. And it is a way of ending the donor's involvement.

On the other hand, as with blood donation, payment may lead unsuitable people to apply, lying about their medical history (perhaps one of AIDS) in order to be paid (Richard Titmuss: *The Gift Relationship, From Human Blood to Social Policy,* London, 1970, chapter eight). And, although Necker Hospital found that unpaid donors were fewer, they were more diverse in their socio-economic background.

There are further arguments against payment. By giving donors a "reason" to account for their donation, it may incline them to think less about the implications of what they are doing. Is our aim to obtain the maximum number of donors, no matter how, or do we want men to think about what they are going to do before they do it? Semen donation may mean nothing to the traditional anonymous medical student, but he can be motivated by payment. On the other hand, a man who has himself either experienced difficulty in having children or who has had an infertile couple in his family or among his friends, may be someone to whom donation makes very good sense. He may find reasons for giving semen without having to be motivated by money.

Payment also deprives donors of the chance of doing something purely for others. Blood donors sometimes say that paying for blood would debase the value of the act, and make it feel less worth doing. Payment and non-payment seem to lead to two different conceptions of donation.

Our inclinations are strongly towards a non-commercial ethos for donation, and we are impressed by the ethos of some of the systems developed in France. An economic case is always easy to understand, as is a case based on a quantifiable change, such as a larger or smaller number of donors. But policies adopted for such reasons can have more subtle side-effects, often of a kind not easily measurable. The issues we are concerned with are not only about easily measurable effects, such as how many infertile couples are enabled to have children. What matters most is how these techniques can be used to enrich people and their relationships, rather than diminish them. The *central* focus of this report is not technology but people. And so we think it right to stress the way payment affects the psychology of donation, turning what could be an enriching act of altruism into an act more like selling an old motorbike. Every time we institutionalize the commercial solution rather than the altruistic one, we take a small step further towards a society where more relationships are permeated by the motive of economic gain.

Our preference for a non-commercial ethos is strong, both for semen donation and for egg donation. But we do not think the case against commercialism is powerful enough to justify a legal ban, which would anyway probably be unenforceable. We would like to see strong public campaigns for altruistic donation, bringing the plight of the infertile to the front of public attention. Only after such a policy has been tried should the market be thought of as a last resort policy to fill any remaining gap.

2. Should Surrogate Mothers Be Paid?

Surrogate mothers do something really important for the potential parents. Unlike semen donation, surrogacy involves a lot of inconvenience and some risk. Apart from women helping sisters or friends, unpaid surrogates are hard to find.

If surrogacy is to be available to childless people without altruistic sisters, payment may be hard to escape. There is again the question of whether we want to encourage the spread of the market into this area. Payment brings the danger of poor women being exploited. They may be pressured into surrogacy by their need of money. One way of making it less exploitative (apart from making the contract unenforceable, and excluding people who have health risks) would be to make the payment substantial. But, on the other hand, high pay may make it even harder for a woman needing money to resist.

In one way, the higher the pay the less the exploitation. But commercialism, with its pressure on poor women to embark on surrogacy they may later regret, seems a greater evil. It is better for fees to surrogates to be nonexistent or kept to a minimum. This may reduce drastically the number of surrogate mothers. That seems to us more acceptable than the commercial alternative. The payment of surrogates should not be illegal, as such a law would be unenforceable, and because of the need to avoid a child's birth being tainted with criminality.

3. Commercial Agencies

The payment of sperm donors or of surrogate mothers at all lets market forces into childbearing. But it does so in a small way. Commercial agencies create much more of the ethos of the market.

Some of the arguments against market forces appeal to the public interest. For instance monetary incentives may encourage medically unsuitable people to sell blood or semen. And, in the present context, where would-be parents have paid a surrogacy agency, they may be more willing to engage in lengthy legal battles, even at considerable psychological cost to the child.

There is a case against banning commercial surrogacy agencies. A ban restricts people's freedom to earn their living in the way they choose. It also restricts the freedom of others by making surrogacy less available. If the agencies meet a demand, making them illegal will frustrate it. If there is no demand, making them illegal may be said to be unnecessary, on the grounds that they will go out of business anyway.

The suggestion that, if there is no demand for their services, the agencies will go out of business is naive. Commercial organizations can often create a demand for previously unwanted products. (An issue then arises as to whether such supplier-induced demands should be taken less seriously

than others.) But the central argument is the appeal to liberty. It is true that banning commercial agencies is a restriction of liberty. But so is any law. And any law is either unnecessary or else stops some people doing what they want to do. There is a presumption against restricting liberty. Are there reasons powerful enough to justify doing so in this case?

A major argument for banning commercial agencies is to protect surrogate mothers from being exploited. But, desirable as this is, it might be done by regulating how agencies operate. Regulation is still an interference with the market, but one easy to justify on principles similar to those used to prevent companies operating factories that are unhealthy or unsafe to work in.

Many who oppose the extension of the market into this area would not be satisfied with commercial agencies being subject to controls to prevent exploitation. The opposition is not based only on worries about exploitation, but also stems from the idea that childbearing is simply not something to which buying and selling are appropriate.

There are two main arguments for limiting the market. One is based on equal access to certain basic goods. The other is linked to a preference for a society not dominated by money values.

(a) Equal access to basic goods: It is widely accepted that the services of the police should not depend on the citizen's ability to pay. Some of the arguments for non-commercial health systems have the same basis. Basic medical care and protection against crime are held to be such fundamental interests that they should be equally available to rich and poor. One argument against commercializing the new reproductive techniques would place help necessary for having children in this category of fundamental interests.

(b) Limiting the dominance of money values: Money is only a means of exchange for goods and services. But the dominance of money transactions can affect the values of a society, by making people less inclined to unpaid acts of altruism. And a society can be dominated by money in a

different way: wealth or income can increasingly colour people's relationships.

4. The Exclusion of Commercial Agencies

The case for equal access to basic goods carries some weight against commercial surrogacy agencies. But it could be questioned whether this kind of help with having children qualifies as one of the basic goods where money should be irrelevant. It would be perfectly consistent to think that essential medical treatment should be available equally, but to deny that this held for surrogacy.

The stronger argument seems to be that based on resisting the encroachments of commerce on the intimate relationships of parenthood. Even here the case can be questioned. If commercial agencies are banned, surrogacy will often be arranged through a non-commercial agency. And the intimate relationships to be protected are between man and woman, parents and children, not those with the non-commercial agency. So why should a commercial agency make any difference?

The difference is a matter of the way commercialism changes the way we see the things that are bought and sold. Almost inevitably they come to be seen as commodities. And some aspects of life seem particularly inappropriate to the market. Having children may be seen in this way because it is such a central part of our lives, and because it is bound up with such deep and intimate experiences. Comparisons with prostitution are made when surrogacy is commercialized.

Intimate and commercial relationships do not fit together easily. In relationships between friends or lovers, or in families (at least as they should be), we confront each other without calculating commercial gain, and do not assess each other mainly in terms of wealth. In families and between friends, gifts are more common than sales. This antagonism between intimacy and commerce is part of the reason why prostitution does not seem the ideal model of sexual partnership, and why other forms of commercialization of sex are tolerated rather than admired.

No doubt it is impossible to prevent individuals paying others for sex; but, if a large company set up as an agency for prostitution, this might seem an unacceptable further step towards turning sex into a commodity. In a similar way, commercial surrogacy agencies can be seen as contributing to a society in which parenthood is seen as another commodity. And, because relationships are partly constituted by how they are seen, this threatens an unwelcome change in the relationship itself.

Because the commercialization of intimate relationships seems something to resist, and because restricting the liberty of commercial organizations seems less intrusive than restricting the liberty of individuals, we do not favour permitting commercial agencies for surrogacy.

The question of commercial agencies may be one of the few we have considered where there is room for a distinctively Western European approach. In the United States, there is a strong presumption in favour of the free market, while the countries of Eastern Europe operate with a strong presumption against it. Generalizations about people living in large geographical regions are obviously suspect, but in Western Europe there does seem to be a strong current of opinion favouring a society between these extremes. We think that the policy of discouraging payment to surrogates without imposing a legal ban, and of banning commercial agencies, fits this approach.

Further Questions

1. Is producing a child a basic human necessity, like the need for basic health care and protection against crime, so that new forms of reproduction, such as surrogate motherhood, should be available to as many persons as possible?

2. If a large company set up an agency for prostitution, would this be a step toward turning sex into a commodity? Do the same considerations apply to setting up large surrogacy agencies; i.e., would they tend to turn reproduction into a commodity?

3. If commercial surrogacy (agencies and exchange of money) is prohibited, would unpaid, private surrogacy arrangements be morally permissible?

Suggested Moral of Part XI

There are several ways of thinking about a woman's biological function in reproduction. One is that gestation and delivery are a source of esteem and self-worth. Therefore a woman should retain control over these processes. Allowing others (men, lawyers, doctors, etc.) to make decisions instead may cause self-alienation. However, there are other persons to consider in such decisions besides the woman herself. An undamaged baby, even if elaborate technology is required, is essential to a successful delivery. Moreover, new techniques that make surrogacy possible, with or without commercialization, raise new questions about a woman's using her reproductive capacity in the service of others, infertile couples in particular. Is putting the welfare of others ahead of her own in the area of reproduction yet another way in which a woman can suffer from oppression? If women are viewed as so much reproductive plumbing, this perspective and its consequences would be a form of oppression. However, it is not clear that new reproductive technology, or consideration of persons other than the woman herself, oppresses women in all cases. No clear moral emerges from Part XI. Perhaps in the area of reproduction technology has progressed faster than has our thinking about its proper use.

Further Readings for Part XI: Reproduction: Hi Tech/Low Tech

James Aiman. *Infertility: Diagnosis and Management* (New York, NY: Springer Verlag, 1984).

Rita Arditti, Renate Duelli Klein and Shelley Minden, eds. *Test-Tube Women: What Future for Motherhood?* (Boston, MA: Pandora Press, Routledge & Kegan Paul, 1984).

Michael D. Bayles. *Reproductive Ethics* (Englewood Cliffs, NJ: Prentice-Hall, 1984).

David R. Bomham, Maureen E. Dalton, and Jennifer C. Jackson, eds. *Philosophical Ethics in Reproductive Medicine* (New York, NY: Manchester University Press, 1990).

Thomas Buckley and Alma Gottlieb, ed. *Blood Magic: The Anthropology of Menstruation* (Berkeley, CA: The University of California Press, 1988).

C. O. Carter, ed. *Developments in Human Reproduction and Their Eugenic Ethical Implications* (New York, NY: Academic Press, 1983).

Ruth Chadwick, ed. *Ethics, Reproduction and Genetic Control* (New York, NY: Routledge, 1987).

Gena Corea. *The Mother Machine: Reproductive Technologies from Artificial Insemination to Artificial Womb* (New York, NY: Harper & Row, 1985).

Claudia Dreifus, ed. *Seizing Our Bodies: The Politics of Women's Health* (New York, NY: Vintage, Random House, 1977).

Anthony Dyson and John Harris, eds. *Experiments on Embryos* (New York, NY: Routledge, 1990).

Barbara Ehrenreich and Deidre English. *For Her Own Good:* 150 *Years of the Experts' Advice to Women* (Garden City, NY: Anchor Books, 1978).

Ellen Frankfort. *Vaginal Politics* (New York, NY: Quadrangle Books, 1972). Who controls women's reproductive systems?

Jonathan Glover et al. *Ethics of New Reproductive Technologies: The Glover Report to the European Commission* (DeKalb, IL: Northern Illinois Press, 1989). Especially recommended for its multifaceted, lucid approach to these issues.

Germaine Greer. *Sex and Destiny: The Politics of Human Fertility* (London: Secker and Warburg, 1984).

Helen B. Holmes. *The Custom-Made Child? Women-Centered Perspectives* (Clifton, NJ: Humana Press, 1981).

Barbara Katz Rothman. *Giving Birth: Alternatives in Childbirth* (Harmondsworth, England: Penguin, 1984).

Sheila Kitzinger. *The Experience of Childbirth* (Harmondsworth, England: Penguin, 1974).

Sheila Kitzinger. *The Complete Book of Pregnancy and Childbirth* (New York, NY: Alfred A. Knopf, 1980).

Miriam D. Mazor and Harriet F. Simons, eds. *Infertility: Medical, Emotional and Social Considerations* (New York, NY: Human Sciences Press, 1984).

Mary O'Brien. *The Politics of Reproduction* (London, Routledge & Kegan Paul, 1981).

Oliver O'Donovan. *Begotten or Made?* (New York, NY: Oxford: The Clarendon Press, 1984). Includes a discussion of transsexual surgery.

Christine Overall. *Ethics and Human Reproduction: A Feminist Analysis* (Boston, MA: Unwin Hyman, 1987).

Helen Roberts, ed. *Women, Health and Reproduction* (New York, NY: Routledge & Kegan Paul, 1981).

Shelly Romalis, ed. *Childbirth: Alternatives to Medical Control* (Austin, TX: University of Texas Press, 1981).

Barbara Katz Rothman. *Giving Birth: Alternatives in Childbirth* (Harmandsworth, England: Penguin, 1984).

Joan Rothschild, ed. *Machine Ex Dea: Feminist Perspectives on Technology* (New York, NY: Pergamon Press, 1983).

Jocelynne A. Scutt, ed. *The Baby Machine: Reproductive Technology and the Commercialization of Motherhood* (London: The Merlin Press, 1990). Are women better or worse off with new reproductive technology?

William Walters and Peter Singer, eds. *Test Tube Babies: A Guide to Moral Questions, Present Techniques and Future Possibilities* (New York, NY: Oxford University Press, 1982).

Mary Warnock. *A Question of Life: The Warnock Report on Human Fertilization and Embryology* (New York, NY: Basil Blackwell, 1984).

Mary Anne Warren, *Gendercide: The Implications of Sex Selection* (Totawa, NJ: Rowman and Allenheld, 1985). Will female fetuses be selected out?

Don P. Wolf and Martin M. Quigley. *Human In Vitro Fertilization and Embryo Transfer* (New York, NY: Plenum Press, 1984).

Joan Offerman Zuckerberg, ed. *Gender in Transition: A New Frontier* (New York, NY: Plenum Medical Book Co., 1989). New reproductive technologies strike at the heart of gender.

Part XII

Raising Children: Mothers and Fathers

Introduction

B EARING CHILDREN (GESTATION AND DELIVERY) and raising them (accompanying them from the delivery room to adulthood) are two separate domains, as contracted motherhood (surrogate motherhood), discussed in Part XI, illustrated. Part XI discussed the circumstances under which women should bear children. The writers in this part focus on the raising of children and the division of labor between the mother and father.

XII.1   Ambition

SUSAN BROWNMILLER

Susan Brownmiller discusses the strong connection between femininity and bearing and raising children. Such "nurturance" travels quickly from child care and family care to care of almost anyone who needs it.

Another selection from Brownmiller's *Femininity* appears in Part II.

Reading Questions

1. Is there a natural transition from gestation to nursing to an obligation of continuing care for a child? If so, what is the basis of this transition? Is it possible to change it so that these functions can be performed by different people?

2. Can it be a symbol of the successful man to have an economically dependent wife at home? Is having an economically successful wife in the workplace an even better emblem of success for her husband?

3. Are the physical signs of trying hard (sweating, grunting, and other indications of strain) considered unfeminine? Think of some examples where these signs either enhance or detract from a woman's femininity. How do they affect a man's masculinity?

IF PRETTINESS AND GRACE were the extent of it, femininity would not be a puzzle, nor would excellence in feminine values be so completely at odds with other forms of ambition. In a sense this entire inquiry has been haunted by the question of ambition, for every adjustment a woman makes to prove her feminine difference adds another fine stitch to the pattern: an inhibition on speech and behavior, a usurpation of time, and a preoccupation with appearance that deflects the mind and depletes the storehouse of energy and purpose. If time and energy are not a problem, if purpose is not a concern, if the underlying submissiveness is not examined too closely, then the feminine esthetic may not be a handicap at all. On the contrary, high among its known satisfactions, femininity offers a welcome retreat from the demands of ambition, just as its strategic use is often good camouflage for those wishing to hide their ambition from public view. But there is

no getting around the fact that ambition is not a feminine trait. More strongly expressed, a lack of ambition—or a professed lack of ambition, or a sacrificial willingness to set personal ambition aside—is virtuous proof of the nurturant feminine nature which, if absent, strikes at the guilty heart of femaleness itself.

When applied to women, nurturance embraces a love of children, a desire to bear them and rear them, and a disposition that leans toward a set of traits that are not gender-specific: warmth, tenderness, compassion, sustained emotional involvement in the welfare of others, and a weak or nonexistent competitive drive. Nurturant labor includes child care, spouse care, cooking and feeding, soothing and patching, straightening out disorder and cleaning up dirt, little considerations like sewing a button on a grown man's raincoat, major considerations like nursing relationships and mending rifts, putting the demands of family and others before one's own, and dropping one's work to minister to the sick, the troubled and the lonely in their time of need.

When nurturance is given out of love, disposition or a sense of responsible duty, the assumption exists that whatever form it takes—changing a diaper or baking a tray of raisin-nut cookies—the behavior expresses a woman's biological nature. When nurturing acts are performed by men, they are interpreted as extraordinary or possibly suspect. When nurturance is provided by maids, housekeepers, kindergarten teachers or practical nurses, its value in the marketplace is low.

Are women the nurturing sex by anatomical design? In the original sense of nurture, what the body can do to support new life, of course the answer is yes. Femaleness in humans and other mammals is defined by the manner of reproduction: gestation and nourishment inside the womb followed by nursing the dependent young upon birth. Few would deny that the nurturant responsibilities of motherhood begin as a biological process, and that suckling connects the labor of birth to the social obligation of continuing care. Or so the rhythms of nature undisturbed by human civilization suggest.

In the depths of the forest or on the grassy plains of the savanna, wherever groupings of mammals exist in the wild, milk is the crucial lifeline from mother to infant. Cleaning, carrying and protecting from danger are closely related acts, although the indifferent mother is not unknown. Active maternal nurturance is the stable core of the social order for animals that live in groups, marked by strong bonds of kinship and positions of high rank and power (for some) that frequently pass to the next generation. Behavior that appears more pronounced in the male of some species—fighting, displays of dominance, defense against predators, grabbing the best and largest portion—does not compare in social cohesion to the bond of maternal relation. In hunting and gathering bands, the earliest form of human society that was once universal, the dual purpose of female work was central to group survival. Responsible for bearing and rearing the next generation, as well as for collecting and preparing the basic foods for everyday needs, woman the mother and gatherer matched the productive labor and communal importance, at least, of man the hunter, as she does today in the Kalahari desert where remnant foraging groups, the !Kung San, continue their traditional ways.

It was no fault of women or men, or even of their ambitious yearnings, that as civilization advanced, the unchanging nature of biologically determined work became increasingly tangential to societal progress. To gain dominion over nature and bend it to human will, the restless intelligence of the Homo sapiens brain required a carefree reproductive system and physical strength, attributes that were characteristically male. With the cultivation of land and permanent towns, with the unleashing of competitive drives and personal ambitions that led to the accumulation of property and the rise of stratified classes, the necessary tasks of reproduction and nurture were no longer at the vital center of human endeavor. Inexorably and conclusively, the logic of femaleness with its inherent capacity for two kinds of purposeful labor, reproductive and "other," became a less powerful force in the social order than the single-minded capabilities of males. . . .

Refinement of one's feminine nature by staying at home in love and devotion was not meant for women of the working poor who labored side by side with their men on the land, or those who came to the city with their families to put in twelve hours a day at the mills. Neither did women at the upper levels of society need instruction in the feminine impropriety of labor. Born to a fashionable life of esthetic indulgence and a continual round of social engagements, they showed the usual eagerness of their privileged station to hand over all practical work, including the rearing of children, to the care of servants. It took the scrambling ambitions of a powerful new middle class—hardworking, ingenious, acquisitive and insecure—to impose the ideal of the aristocratic, leisured lady on women of its own kind as a hallmark of upward direction. It took a bourgeois value system propelled by industrious struggle and material gain to pridefully create a woman of total economic dependency in a home in which she now ranked as an ornamental possession, and to see her as a reward of free enterprise, a tribute to the virile success of men. . . .

When it comes to her own success, it has never been becoming for a woman to try hard. Sweat under the arms, a clenched jaw, an unladylike grunt—these are, after all, the unavoidable signs of straining effort. A man may keep his nose to the grindstone, but a woman had better stop now and again to powder hers. Appearance, we are told, is more feminine than result. Unremarkably, the tiny handful of ambitious careers with certified feminine allure remain those glamorous big dreams with a slim chance of realization (actress, singer, model, interviewer on television) in which looking attractive is a part of performance, so the desire to be noticed can be partly excused. . . .

Motherhood and ambition have been seen as opposing forces for thousands of years. Largely because of the new feminist movement, the internalized conflict as well as the external reality recently have become a subject of renewed attention. For many women, perhaps most, motherhood versus personal ambition represents the heart of the feminine dilemma. In the work of psychologist Carol Gilligan, ambivalence in making and sticking to some hard decisions (abortion, career choice), long considered a feminine weakness, has been shown to stem from the ethics and responsibilities of motherhood—the importance of "caring relationships"—as women perceive their role.

But if ambition and motherhood have been in conflict, femininity and motherhood have not had a happy conjunction either. The swollen belly, edema in legs and feet, the heaving flood tide of birth, the breast as a lactating organ, and the fatiguing chores of child care are not glamor-ous, sexy, delicate, romantic, refined or passive, as these words are usually defined.

The desire to be a mother can be a powerful ambition, too, especially when the opportunity is slow in coming. Responsive to the ticking of the biological clock, the motivation to produce and raise a child of one's own (for whatever reason, and the reasons are legion) and the gratifications that a child may bring are spurred by an urgency that is as unique to femaleness as motherhood itself. On the other hand, motherhood is so universally perceived as the ultimate proof of the feminine nature and the intended purpose of female existence that few women have the courage to admit that they do not have the gift for it, or that given a choice, they would rather marshal their energies, their sensitivities and their gratifications in other directions.

Duality of purpose is built into female biology in ways that are hard to resist (and without the freedom of contraceptive choice, in ways that are hard to avoid). The single-mindedness with which a man may pursue his nonreproductive goals is foreign not only to the female procreational ability, it is alien to the feminine values and emotional traits that women are expected to show. The human sentiments of motherhood (goodness, self-sacrifice and a specialty in taking care of the wants of others) are without question desirable characteristics for the raising of children, but I would argue strenuously that women do not possess these traits to a greater degree by biological tendency than men.

Without a radical restructuring of a social order that works well enough in its present form for those extremely ambitious, competitive men whose prototypical ancestors arranged it, and who have little objective reason, just yet, to change the rules, what hope is there for a real accommodation of dual-purpose ambition? The corporate hierarchy has no compelling motivation to modify what it demands of its career employees, and the prizes at the top of the heap go to those who pursue them with single-minded devotion. Pursuit of achievement in literature, science and the arts is a single-minded ambition that will never be restructured, for the competition, understandably, is fierce. Whatever form it takes, satisfying work that earns a decent income is always in short supply, and men are right when they say that the required expenditure of time and effort leaves little room for life's other rewards. Yet a man, if he wishes, may acquire a woman, or a succession of women, to provide him with the rewards of emotional support, practical nurturance, a home and a family. A woman responding to the same needs and desires must split in two and become the traditional reward herself, at least that part which is firmly rooted in biological fact.

Is it unfair for a woman to expect that her desire to be a full-time mother should be accommodated for an unspecified number of years? Should another woman avoid motherhood entirely in order to secure the full chance that any man might have for economic autonomy and satisfying work? Does a society that understands the need for successive generations have a moral obligation to ease the way for a third woman intent on fulfilling both aspects of her dual-purpose ambition? Should one set of expectations be viewed as a predictable retreat into a feminine tradition of dependence, another as a singular expression of unfeminine aspirations, and the third as an admirable solution possible only for the extremely ambitious, extremely energetic few, or for those who are lucky to live with more mildly ambitious, nurturing partners?

There are no easy answers to these questions.

Further Questions

1. Is a display of ambition in the workplace considered unfeminine? Give some examples (hypothetical or real) where a woman is either applauded or criticized for indicating that she is ambitious.

2. Do you think a mother's physical signs of pregnancy, delivery, lactation, and childcare are fairly unglamorous and unromantic? If so, does this indicate a certain tension between society's idea that a woman be glamorous and its idea that she be a mother?

3. Is there any way to "change the rules" for survival and achievement in the workplace so that the workplace can accommodate women who want to be mothers? What kinds of changes would you propose? Would these changes accommodate fathers who want to take care of their children?

Marianismo: XII.2
The Other Face of *Machismo* in Latin America

EVELYN P. STEVENS

Evelyn P. Stevens reports on *marianismo*, the feminine counterpart of *machismo* in Hispanic cultures, especially in Latin America. This secular set of beliefs and practices portrays the ideal woman as a mother, morally superior, patient, and with an infinite capacity for humility and self-sacrifice. The ideal of *marianismo* fits nicely with the ideal of *machismo* (aggressiveness, intransigence, and arrogance) in men and gives women some practical advantages which many are loathe to give up.

Stevens lived much of her life in Latin America. Her 1965 article on "machismo" in the *Western Political Quarterly* was the first scholarly treatment of this subject in US social science literature.

Reading Questions

1. Is there a prevailing belief (even outside of Hispanic cultures) that women are expected to be patient, humble, and self-sacrificing with men, much as a mother would be with little boys? Is this expectation advantageous or disadvantageous to particular women? Illustrate your answer with some examples.

2. Is *marianismo* a beneficial force in keeping women out of the work place in times of high unemployment, and in giving a woman who does enter the work place a chance to tend a sick child and an opportunity to get low-cost care from her extended family? Are there disadvantages for a woman in being perceived primarily as a mother?

. . . IN THE INTEREST OF CLARITY in the following discussion, the term *machismo* will be used to designate a way of orientation which can be most succinctly described as the cult of virility. The chief characteristics of this cult are exaggerated aggressiveness and intransigence in male-to-male interpersonal relationships and arrogance and sexual aggression in male-to-female relationships.[1]

It has only been in the quite recent past that any attention has been focused on the other face of the problem. Women generally have maintained a discreet reserve with respect to the subject of *marianismo,* possibly because a very large segment of that group fears that publicity would endanger their prerogatives. A short time ago, however, a handful of male writers began to focus on this heretofore neglected pattern of attitudes and behavior. In this way, the term *hembrismo* ("femaleism") has been introduced by one observer, while *feminismo* has been used by another.[2]

Marianismo is just as prevalent as *machismo* but it is less understood by Latin Americans themselves and almost unknown to foreigners. It is the cult of feminine spiritual superiority, which teaches that women are semidivine, morally superior to and spiritually stronger than men. It is this pattern of attitudes and behavior that will be the principal focus of attention in the present paper, but it will often be necessary to refer to the dynamic interplay between the two phenomena.

Both *marianismo* and *machismo* are New World phenomena with ancient roots in Old World cultures. Many of the contributing elements can be found even today in Italy and Spain, but the fully developed syndrome occurs only in Latin America.[3] . . .

Although all mestizo social classes are permeated with *machismo* and *marianismo* characteristics, the same statement does not hold true with respect to other ethnic groupings. Indigenous communities, while patriarchal in structure and value orientations, do not seem to share the *machismo-marianismo* attitudes as long as they retain their cultural "purity."

Marianismo is not a religious practice, although the word *marianism* is sometimes used to describe a movement within the Roman Catholic church which has as its object the special veneration of the figure of the Virgin Mary. That cult, as it is practiced throughout the world, is rooted in very ancient religious observances that have evolved within the church itself, at times with the enthusiastic endorsement of ecclesiastical authorities and at other times with at least the tolerance of those authorities.

Marianism, or *Mariology,* as most theologians prefer to call the religious movement, has provided a central figure and a convenient set of assumptions around which the practitioners of *marianismo* have erected a secular edifice of beliefs and practices related to the position of women in society. It is that edifice, rather than the religious phenomenon, which is the object of this study.

The roots of *marianismo* are both deep and widespread, springing apparently from primitive awe at woman's ability to produce a live human creature from inside her own body. This is the aspect of femininity which attracted the attention of the early artists who fashioned the Gravettian "venuses" of the upper Paleolithic era. In those small crude sculptures, the figures have enormous breasts and protruding bellies, as though they were pregnant. To the early men and women who posed the ontological question in its simplest terms—"Where did I come from?"—the answer must also have seemed simple, and on the basis of circumstantial evidence, woman was celebrated as being the sole source of life.

Archeological research points to southern Russia, to the region around the Caspian Sea, as the source of inspiration for the cult of the mother goddess as we know it in the Western world, but not long afterward traces began to appear in the Fertile Crescent and the Indus Valley, as well as in Crete and the area around the Aegean Sea. During these early stages the female figure appeared alone, unaccompanied by any male figure, and for this reason she is sometimes described as the "unmarried mother."[4] . . .

Just how the excessive veneration of women became a distinguishing feature of Latin Ameri-

can secular society is difficult to determine. Two points are clear, however: this veneration parallels that which is rendered to the religious figure of the Virgin Mary, and the secular aspect is different both qualitatively and quantitatively from the attitude toward women which prevails in those very European nations where the religious cult is most prevalent.

Latin American mestizo cultures—from the Rio Grande to the Tierra del Fuego—exhibit a well-defined pattern of beliefs and behavior centered on popular acceptance of a stereotype of the ideal woman. This stereotype, like its *macho* counterpart, is ubiquitous in every social class. There is near universal agreement on what a "real woman" is like and how she should act. Among the characteristics of this ideal are semidivinity, moral superiority, and spiritual strength. This spiritual strength engenders abnegation, that is, an infinite capacity for humility and sacrifice. No self-denial is too great for the Latin American woman, no limit can be divined to her vast store of patience with the men of her world.[5] Although she may be sharp with her daughters—and even cruel to her daughters-in-law—she is and must be complaisant toward her own mother and her mother-in-law for they, too, are reincarnations of the great mother. She is also submissive to the demands of the men: husbands, sons, fathers, brothers.[6]

Beneath the submissiveness, however, lies the strength of her conviction—shared by the entire society—that men must be humored, for after all, everyone knows that they are *como niños* (like little boys) whose intemperance, foolishness, and obstinacy must be forgiven because "they can't help the way they are." These attitudes are expressed with admirable clarity by the editor of a fashionable women's magazine in Chile. When asked, "Is there any Chilean woman whom you particularly admire?" she answered, "Sincerely, I would mention a humble woman from the slums who did our laundry. She had ten children, and her husband spent his time drunk and out of work. She took in washing and ironing, and gave her children a good start in life. She is the typical Chilean woman of a [certain] sector of our society. She struggles valiantly until the end."[7]

But to the unalterable imperfection of men is attributable another characteristic of Latin American women: their sadness. They know that male sinfulness dooms the entire sex to a prolonged stay in purgatory after death, and even the most diligent prayerfulness of loving female relatives can succeed in sparing them only a few millennia of torture.

The sadness is evidenced in another highly visible characteristic of women. Custom dictates that upon the death of a member of her family, a woman shall adopt a distinctive mourning habit. The periods of mourning and the types of habit are rigidly prescribed. The death of a parent or husband requires lifetime full mourning: inner and outer clothing of solid black, unrelieved by even a white handkerchief. Deaths of brothers, sisters, aunts, and uncles require full mourning for three years, and those of more distant relatives require periods varying from three months to a year. After each period of full mourning ensues a prescribed period of "half-mourning" during which the grieving woman may at first wear touches of white with her black clothes, graduating with the passage of time to gray and lavender dresses.

Mourning is not simply a matter of dress. The affected person must also "show respect" for the deceased by refraining from any outward manifestation of happiness or joviality and to deny herself the company of others who may legitimately indulge in levity. This means abstention from attending parties, going to the cinema, or even watching television. Purists insist that cultural events such as concerts and lectures also fall under the ban.

Of course, these rules are supposed also to apply to men, but as "everybody knows" that they do not possess the spiritual stamina to endure such rigors, they usually render only token compliance with custom, often reduced to the wearing of a black armband for a short period. Although during mourning periods their women-ruled households are gloomy places, their escape to more joyful surroundings is condoned and often encouraged. Mistresses and other female companions "by the left" are not required to mourn.[8]

By the age of thirty-five, there are few women who have escaped the experience of at least a short period of mourning and by forty-five, a large majority of women are destined to wear black for the rest of their lives. It is thus in the woman of middle age that we finally see all of the characteristics of full-blown *marianismo* coming into majestic flower. The author is familiar with the rather extreme case of a reputedly saintly Puerto Rican woman who had been widowed in her early twenties and who boasted that she had not attended the cinema since then, had never seen a television program, and had refused to pass the house in which her husband had died. Such exemplary devotion made the woman an object of general admiration, an example held up to the younger generation of more frivolous females.

As a result of this usage, the image of the Latin American woman is almost indistinguishable from the classic religious figure of the *mater dolorosa,* the tear-drenched mother who mourns for her lost son. The precursor of that figure can be found in the myths of many pre-Christian Mediterranean cultures: the earth goddess who laments the seasonal disappearance of her son and who sorrowfully searches for him until the return of spring restores him to her.[9]

Does this mean that all Latin American women conform to the stereotype prescribed by *Marianismo?* Obviously not; as in most human societies, individual behavior often deviates widely from the ideal. But the image of the black-clad mantilla-draped figure, kneeling before the altar, rosary in hand, praying for the souls of her sinful menfolk, dominates the television and cinema screens, the radio programs, and the popular literature, as well as the oral tradition of the whole culture area. This is Latin America's chief export product, according to one native wit.[10]

The same culture provides an alternate model in the image of the "bad woman" who flaunts custom and persists in enjoying herself. Interestingly enough, this kind of individual is thought not to be a "real woman." By publicly deviating from the prescribed norm, she has divested herself of precisely those attributes considered most characteristically feminine and in the process has become somewhat masculine.

This brings us to the question of sexual behavior and here, too, as might be expected, practice frequently deviates from prescription. The ideal dictates not only premarital chastity for all women, but postnuptial frigidity. "Good" women do not enjoy coitus; they endure it when the duties of matrimony require it. A rich lexicon of circumlocutions is available to "real" women who find it necessary to refer to sexual intercourse in speaking with their priest, their physician, or other trusted confidant. *"Le hice el servicio,"* they may say ("I did him [my husband] the service").[11]

The norm of premarital chastity is confined principally to the urban and provincial middle class, as consensual unions predominate among peasants and urban slum dwellers. Nubility and sexual activity are frequently almost simultaneous events, although the latter occasionally precedes the former.[12]

Even in middle- and upper-class society, norms of sexual behavior are often disregarded in practice. Premarital chastity is still highly prized, and many Latin American men take an unconscionable interest in the integrity of their fiancées' hymens. But the popular refrain, *el que hizo la ley hizo la trampa,* is particularly applicable in this context. A Peruvian woman writes with convincing authority that a large number of socially prominent young women in that country engage in coitus and then have surgical repair of the hymen performed in private hospitals—a practice that goes back at least to fifteenth-century Spain, when the operation was performed by midwives who often acted in the dual capacity of procuresses and mistresses of houses of assignation (see for example the *Tragicomedia de Calixto y Melibea,* the literary classic known popularly as *La Celestina*).[13]

An undetermined number of upper-middle and upper-class young women practice other varieties of sexual activity, calculated to keep the hymen intact. But a girl will usually engage in these variations only with her fiancé, and then largely as a stratagem for maintaining his interest in her until they are married. As long as he feels reasonably certain that his fiancée has not previously engaged in this kind of behavior with another man, a Latin American male may encourage or even insist on her "obliging" him in this way. But he must reassure himself that she is not enjoying it. A Peruvian journalist reveals the male insistence on the fiction of the frigidity of "good" women in such reported remarks as: "So-and-so is a bad woman; once she even made love with her husband in the bathtub," and "American women [*gringas*] are all prostitutes; I know one who *even takes the initiative*" (italics in original).[14]

At first glance, it may seem that these norms are imposed on women by tyrannical men—"male chauvinists," as contemporary English-speaking feminists would call them. But this assumption requires careful scrutiny, especially when it is remembered that during the preschool years the socialization of boys takes place almost entirely through the medium of women: mother, sisters, widowed or spinster aunts who live under one roof as part of the extended family, and female servants. From the women in the family a boy absorbs the attitudinal norms appropriate for his social class and from the servants, when he reaches adolescence—or often even before—he picks up the principal store of behavioral expertise which will suffice him in adult life. It is common practice for a prudent middle-class mestizo mother of a pubescent boy to hire a young female servant for general housework "and other duties," the latter expression being a euphemism for initiating the boy into adult heterosexual experience. "On such creatures," comments the writer previously cited, "a man lavishes his store of honorable semen and his Christian contempt."[15]

At this juncture it may be useful to ask ourselves a question suggested by the apparent contradiction posed by the foregoing material. On the one hand, our Latin American informants paint us a picture of the ideal woman which would inspire pity in the most sanguine observer. Woman's lot seems to be compounded of sexual frustration, intellectual stagnation, and political futility in a "repressive and *machista* society."[16] On the other hand, it is quite apparent that many women contribute to the perpetuation of the myths which sustain the patterns described. Why would they work against their own interests—if, indeed, they do? Might it not be possible that while employing a distinctive repertory of attitudes, they are as "liberated" as most of them really wish to be?

Alternative Models

If we picture the options available to women, we can see that they cover a wide range including the ideal prescribed by myth and religion as well as an earthy and hedonistic life-style, and even occasionally a third variant characterized by an achievement-oriented puritan ethic. Some women choose to pattern their behavior after the mythical and religious ideal symbolized by the figure of the Virgin Mary. Others deviate from this ideal to a greater or lesser degree in order to obtain the satisfaction of their individual desires or aspirations. The ideal itself is a security blanket which covers all women, giving them a strong sense of identity and historical continuity.

As culture-bound foreigners, we are not qualified to define the interests of Latin American women. We cannot decide what is good for them or prescribe how they might achieve that good. If we were to ask whether, on the whole, Latin American women are happier and better "adjusted" (adjusted to what?) than, say, North American women, we would be forced to admit that the measurable data on which to base an answer are not available and probably never will be. It would appear then that the only meaningful question is whether the restrictions on individual action are so ironclad as to preclude any possibility of free choice.

Undeniably, the pattern of attitudes and behavior which we have described puts a distinctive stamp on Latin American society; certainly there are enormous pressures on individual women to conform to the prescriptions. Sometimes the results are tragic, both for the individual and for the society which is deprived of the full benefit of the individual's potential contribution. A notable example of this kind of tragedy is provided by the life and death of Sor Juana Inés de la Cruz of Mexico, whose genius was denied and finally crushed by her ecclesiastical superiors.

But what of Manuela, the mistress of Simón Bolívar? Sublimely unconcerned with the stereotype of saintliness, she made her own decisions. The collective judgment of Latin American society accords her a measure of esteem not often associated with women who conform to the *marianismo* ideal.

The question of personal identity is much less troublesome to Latin American women than to their North American sisters. The Latin American always knows who she is; even after marriage she retains her individuality and usually keeps her family name, tacking on her husband's name and passing both names on to her children. The fiction of unassailable purity conferred by the myth on saint and sinner alike makes divorce on any grounds a rather unlikely possibility, which means that married women are not often faced with the necessity of "making a new life" for themselves during middle age. When her husband indulges in infidelity, as the *machismo* norm expects and requires him to do, the prejudice in favor of the wife's saintliness guarantees her the support of the community.

In developing societies plagued by massive unemployment and widespread underemployment, economists might question the value of throwing larger numbers of women into the already overcrowded labor market. It is hard to assess the extent to which *marianismo* contributes to the present low participation of women in economically productive endeavors.[17] To assume that all or nearly all women would work outside the home if they were given the opportunity to do so is an example of the kind of thinking that sometimes vitiates the conclusions of militant feminists. My inquiries among a very small sample of women from several Latin American countries indicate that when a woman acquires expertise of a kind that is socially useful, she is quite likely to find a remunerative post in conditions far more favorable than her counterpart in, say, the United States or Western Europe. Expertise in Latin America is at such a premium that she will find little competition for a suitable post.

A Latin American mother is seldom faced with the dilemma, so publicized in the United States, of having to choose between her children or her paid job. When women work outside of their home, *marianismo* makes it plain that no employer, whether he or she be a corporation president, a university dean, or a government official, has the right to ask a mother to neglect a sick child in order to keep a perfect attendance record at the office, classroom, or factory. The granting of sick leave to the mother of a sick child is not so much a matter of women's rights as a matter of the employer's duty to respect the sacredness of motherhood which the individual woman shares with the Virgin Mary and with the great mother goddesses of pre-Christian times.

Middle-class women who have marketable skills also have fewer role conflicts because other female members of the extended family, and an abundant supply of low-cost domestic servants, are available for day-to-day care of dependent children. Nonworking married middle-class women are far more fortunate than their North American counterparts; the Latin American women are free to shop or visit with friends as often as they like, without worrying about their children. The point is that as we simply do not know why only a small proportion of women work outside of the home in Latin America, we must leave open the possibility that a considerable number may have freely chosen to have their *marianismo* cake and eat it too.

Conclusion

This excursion into the realm of Latin American culture has revealed a major variant on the universal theme of male-female relationships. We have traced the major characteristics of these relationships as they have developed over thousands of years and as they are observed today. Our historical perspective enables us to see that far from being an oppressive norm dictated by tyrannical males, *marianismo* has received considerable impetus from women themselves. This fact makes it possible to regard *marianismo* as part of a reciprocal arrangement, the other half of which is *machismo.*

The arrangement is not demonstrably more "unjust" than major variants on the same theme in other parts of the world. While some individuals of both sexes have been "victimized" by the strictures, it appears that many others have been able to shape their own life-styles and derive a measure of satisfaction, sometimes because of and sometimes in spite of the requirements of the system.

It seems unlikely that this pattern of male-female relationships can persist indefinitely without undergoing important modification. The mestizos—precisely that part of Latin American society which is characterized by *machismo-marianismo*—are not a traditional group, in the sense of that word used by anthropologists. All observable facets of Latin American mestizo society are experiencing the effects of rapid and far-reaching changes, from which the phenomenon we have described could hardly be exempt. In fact, some signs are already apparent that the current generation of middle-class university students hold somewhat different values with regard to relationships between the sexes than those of their parents. This was particularly evident during the 1968 student strike in Mexico, with reference to male-female role perceptions.

In my opinion, however, *marianismo* is not for some time yet destined to disappear as a cultural pattern in Latin America. In general, women will not use their vote as a bloc to make divorce more accessible, to abolish sex discrimination (especially preferential treatment for women), or to impose upon themselves some of the onerous tasks traditionally reserved for men. They are not yet ready to relinquish their female chauvinism.

NOTES

1. For a discussion of this term and its social and political implications, see Evelyn P. Stevens, "Mexican Machismo: Politics and Value Orientations," *Western Political Quarterly,* 18, no. 4 (December 1965), pp. 848–57.

2. *Mundo Nuevo,* no. 46 (April 1970), pp. 14–50, devotes an entire section to the topic of "Machismo y feminismo," in which several authors use the term *hembrismo.* Neither *feminismo* nor *hembrismo* seem to me as satisfactory as my own term *marianismo,* for reasons made plain by the text.

3. See for example Julian Pitt-Rivers, ed., *Mediterranean Countrymen, Essays in the Social Anthropology of the Mediterranean* (Paris and La Haye: Mouton, 1963).

4. See Edwin Oliver James, *The Cult of the Mother Goddess* (London: Thames and Hudson, 1959), and Erich Neumann, *The Great Mother: An Analysis of the Archetype* (New York: Pantheon Books, 1955).

5. Carl E. Batt, "Mexican Character: An Adlerian Interpretation," *Journal of Individual Psychology,* 5, no. 2 (November 1969), pp. 183–201. This author refers to the "martyr complex."

6. See Rogelio Díaz-Guerrero, "Neurosis and the Mexican Family Structure," *American Journal of Psychiatry,* 112, no. 6 (December 1955), pp. 411–17, and by the same author, "Adolescence in Mexico: Some Cultural, Psychological, and Psychiatric Aspects," *International Mental Health Research Newsletter,* 12, no. 4 (Winter 1970), pp. 1, 10–13.

7. Rosa Cruchaga de Walker and Lillian Calm, "¿Quién es la mujer chilena?" *Mundo Nuevo,* no. 46 (April 1970), pp. 33–38. The woman quoted in the interview is the wife of an engineer and the mother of two children. Although she professes to admire the laundress, she obviously does not emulate her life-style.

8. *Por la izquierda:* illicit.

9. James, *Cult of the Mother Goddess,* pp. 49 ff.

10. Salvador Reyes Nevares, "El machismo en Mexico," *Mundo Nuevo,* no. 46 (April 1970), pp. 14–19.

11. J. Mayone Stycos, *Family and Fertility in Puerto Rico* (New York: Columbia University Press, 1955). See also Theodore B. Brameld, *The Remaking of a Culture* (New York: Harper and Brothers, 1959).

12. Lloyd H. Rogler and August B. Hollingshead, *Trapped* (New York: John Wiley and Sons, 1965), pp. 133–47. See also the publications of Oscar Lewis on Mexico and Puerto Rico.

13. Ana María Portugal, "La peruana ¿'Tapada' sin manto?" *Mundo Nuevo,* no. 46 (April 1970), pp. 20–27.

14. José B. Adolph, "La emancipación masculina en Lima," *Mundo Nuevo,* no. 46 (April 1970), pp. 39–41.

15. Ibid., p. 39.

16. Portugal, "La peruana ¿'Tapada' sin manto?" p. 22.

17. Some representative figures for Mexico and other Latin American countries are given in Ifigenia de Navarrete's *La mujer y los derechos sociales* (Mexico: Ediciones Oasis, 1969).

Further Questions

1. Is it paradoxical that Latin *marianismo* comes into full flower only in the middle-aged woman whose children have reached adulthood? In particular, would a mother be better typified by a younger woman, since her (presumably) younger children require more care and attention?

2. Is a woman (Latin American or not) who is frivolous or exuberant and gets a lot of enjoyment out of life somewhat suspect? For example, if a woman enjoys sex or a large wardrobe of clothing, should we think she has overstepped the bounds of propriety?

3. If a woman (Latin American or not) has not borne and raised children of her own, should we think of her as irresponsible and not due full respect as a woman?

When Women and Men Mother   XII.3

DIANE EHRENSAFT

Diane Ehrensaft speaks to the issue of shared parenting; the heterosexual couple shifts a substantial amount of day-to-day childcare away from the mother to the father. This kind of arrangement has both advantages and drawbacks for each parent, relative to the traditional arrangement where the mother takes most of the responsibilities.

Ehrensaft is a developmental and clinical psychologist, a faculty member of the Wright Institute in Berkeley.

Reading Questions

1. Is it fair to ask the mother to take most of the childcare responsibilities if both she and the father have full-time employment in the workplace? If not, what is a good alternative that will ensure that the children are well taken care of?

2. Does shared parenting challenge the traditional division of work by gender where it can really be felt, at home, as universal childcare, or wages for motherhood, do not? Explain your thinking.

3. Would shared parenting cut into a source of power, control, and esteem for women which centers around the idea of a "good mother"? Do women who think of themselves primarily as "good mothers" always have alternative sources of power, control, and esteem?

Shared Parenting in a Capitalist Context

. . . WHO IS ENGAGED in shared parenting? Any two individuals both of whom see themselves as primary caretakers to a child or children. As defined by Nancy Press Hawley, elements of shared parenting include: (a) intimacy, both between sharing adults and between adults and children; (b) care of the child in a regular, daily way; (c) awareness of being a primary caretaker or parent to the children; (d) ongoing commitment; and (e) attention paid to the adult relationship.[1] In addition to daily caretaking functions, we are talking about two individuals who fully share responsibility for the ongoing intellectual, emotional, and social development of the child.* . . .

* This framework differentiates shared *parenting* from shared *custody,* in which two parents, separated or divorced, share the children back and forth.

The traditional socialist belief is that entry into the sphere of production is the ultimate road to women's liberation: Only through entering the socialized arena of paid work can women establish the collective political leverage to free themselves from their shackles of oppression. Instead, we find the reverse to be true. Women now have a double workload—as paid worker and as housewife and primary parent. While many fathers have come forward to help out with kids and housework, doing more work in the family than in our parents' time, the full sharing of parenting between women and men remains a rare phenomenon. When we hear about mothers and fathers away all day at work, and dad coming home to plop in front of the TV while mom puts in her extra day's work as housewife and mother, we feel compelled to demand shared parenting as a mass phenomenon rather than the rare experience it is now. At the same time we recognize the ideological and power dynamics that maintain the status quo. Mom will be reluctant to shoo dad away from the TV if the consequence is that he and his larger paycheck walk out the door, leaving her to support three kids on her own. . . .

It is true that much of feminist writing and politics in the last ten years, with the exception of sex-role socialization and childcare projects, has been focused specifically on *woman* and her oppression, and only tangentially on men and the needed changes in their gender-related experience ("leave it to the men to figure that out"). Radical and socialist feminists, in particular, identified the nuclear family as a patriarchal underpinning of women's oppression and therefore often shied away from solutions, such as shared parenting, that might ostensibly reinforce this abhorrent social institution. Some radical feminists have taken the extreme "matriarchal" position that men ought not to be involved in the rearing of children at all. It has been liberal feminists who have spoken most directly to the issues of fathers who parent. While socialist feminists have remained abstract (dealing with the larger issues of sex, race, and class), and radical feminists have tended to avoid male-female parenting issues, liberal feminists have tackled the structural reforms that speak most directly to the actual experiences of daily parenting life. Liberal feminism also claims among its ranks more mothers than any other feminist tendency. Nevertheless, as more left feminists have children in an atmosphere where it is no longer politically incorrect and recognize that, to be effective, socialist feminism too must connect more directly to people's daily lives, we, too, begin looking for analyses of parenting and male-female relationships. . . .

. . . [S]hared parenting among heterosexual couples demands that men enter the feminine sphere of baby powder and diapers. Their doing so is the practical embodiment of the socialist-feminist demand that women's traditional work be socially recognized and shared. But rather than turning to the state or to the public sphere —as in the demand for wages for housework/ mothering or for universal childcare—shared parenting challenges the mystique of motherhood and the sexual division of labor at another critical point of reproduction: the home. As stated by a sharing father, "For me, the equal sharing of child care has meant bringing the feminist 'war' home—from the abstraction it would have remained in my mind, to those concrete day-to-day realities that transform us as few other situations I can think of."[2] It is a demand that accepts the viability of heterosexuality as one, though not the only, structure for personal life, but insists on a radical transformation in male-female relationships.

At this moment, shared parenting has several social and political dimensions. We have already pinpointed the pressing need to relieve growing numbers of women from the dual oppression of paid worker and primary parent. Also, in theory shared parenting (1) liberates women from full-time mothering; (2) affords opportunities for more equal relationships between women and men; (3) allows men more access to children; (4) allows children to be parented by two nurturing figures and frees them from the confines of an "overinvolved" parent who has no other outside identity; (5) provides new socialization experiences and possibly a breakdown in gender-differentiated character structures in children; (6) challenges the myth buttressed by sociobiology that women are better equipped biologically for parenting and that women *are* while men *do*; and (7) puts pressure on political, economic, and social structures for changes such as paternity and maternity leaves, job sharing, and freely available childcare facilities.

What, though, do we know about the actual implementation of shared parenting today? We have few models from the past, and few reports of present experiences. A woman writing about "Motherhood and the Liberated Woman" urges that "if women's liberation is to mean anything for people who have children or want to have them it must mean that fathers are in this, too. But in what ways it must change, my husband

and I don't exactly know."[3] What can we conclude about the viability and political significance of shared parenting from the experience of those men and women who are trying to share "mothering"?

The Dialectics of Pampers and Paychecks: The Sexual Division of Labor in Shared Parenting

CAN MEN MOTHER?

In this argument, the word "mothering" is used specifically to refer to the day-to-day *primary* care of a child, to the consciousness of being *directly* in charge of the child's upbringing. It is to be differentiated from the once-a-week baseball games or daily 25 minutes of play that characterize the direct parenting in which men have typically been involved. One mother aptly characterizes shared parenting thus: "To a child Mommy is the person who takes care of me, who tends my daily needs, who nurtures me in an unconditional and present way. Manda has two mothers; one is a male, Mommy David, and the other a female, Mommy Alice."[4]

According to recent psychological studies, anyone can "mother an infant who can do the following: provide frequent and sustained physical contact, soothe the child when distressed, be sensitive to the baby's signals, and respond promptly to a baby's crying. Beyond these immediate behavioral indices, psychoanalysts argue that anyone who has personally experienced a positive parent-child relationship that allowed the development of both trust and individuation in his or her own childhood has the emotional capabilities to parent. Although sociobiologists would take issue, there is no conclusive animal or human research indicating that female genitals, breasts, or hormonal structure provide women with any better equipment than men for parenting.[5] On the other hand, years in female-dominated parenting situations and in gender differentiated cultural institutions can and do differentially prepare boys and girls for the task of "mothering."[6] And in adulthood, social forces in the labor market, schools, media, etc. buttress these differential abilities. To understand what happens when two such differentially prepared individuals come together to parent, two issues have to be addressed: parenting and power, and the psychic division of labor in parenting.

POWER AND PARENTING

Numerous items in the popular press have acclaimed a shifting in family structure: women have become more and more interested in and committed to extra-familial lives, while men have fled from the heartless world to the haven of the family. Knowing that theirs is not the only paycheck coming in, more men walk off the job, come late to work, rebel against the work ethic. The articles speak optimistically of a new generation of "family men" and "career women" and a greater sharing among men and women in both family and work life.[7] But we who know the behind-the-scenes story take a moment of pause. We women who have shared parenting with men know the tremendous support and comfort (and luxury) of not being the only one there for our children. We see the opportunities to develop the many facets of ourselves that were not as easily afforded to our mothers, or to other women who have carried the primary load of parenting. We watch our children benefit from the full access to two rather than to one primary nurturing figure, providing them with intimacy with both women and men, with a richer, more complex emotional milieu, and with role models that challenge gender stereotypes. We see men able to develop more fully the nurturant parts of themselves as fathers, an opportunity often historically denied to them. And we develop close, open, and more equal relationships between men and women as we grapple with the daily ups and downs of parenting together. The quality of our lives no doubt has been improved immensely by the equalization of parenting responsibilities between men and women.

Yet we also know another side of the experience, that shared parenting is easier said than done. Because it has remained so unspoken, it is this latter reality I wish to speak to here, while urging the reader to keep in mind the larger context of the successes, the improvements in daily life, and the political import that accompany the shared parenting project.

> Men and women are brought up for a different position in the labor force: the man for the world of work, the woman for the family. This difference in the sexual division of labor in society means that the relationship of men as a group to production is different from that of women. For a man the social relations and values of commodity production predominate and home is a retreat into intimacy. For the woman the public world of work belongs to and is owned by men.[8]

While men hold fast to the domination of the "public sphere," it has been the world of home and family that is woman's domain. Particularly in the rearing of children, it is often her primary (or only) sphere of power. For all the oppressive and debilitating effects of the institution of motherhood, a woman *does* get social credit for being a "good" mother. She also accrues for herself some sense of control and authority in the growth and development of her children. As a mother she is afforded the opportunity for genuine human interaction, in contrast to the alienation and depersonalization of the workplace:

> A woman's desire to experience power and control is mixed with the desire to obtain joy in child-rearing and cannot be separated from it. It is the position of women in society as a whole, their dependent position in the family, the cultural expectation that the maternal role should be the most important role for all women, that make the exaggerated wish to possess one's child an entirely reasonable reaction. Deprived and oppressed, women see in motherhood their only source of pleasure, reward, and fulfillment.[9]

It is this power and control that she must partially give up in sharing parenting equally with a father.

What she gains in exchange is twofold: a freedom from the confines of 24-hour-a-day motherhood, and the same opportunity as her male partner to enter the public world of work and politics, with the additional power in the family that her paycheck brings with it. But that public world, as Rowbotham points out, is controlled and dominated by men and does not easily make a place for women within it. The alteration in gender relations within the shared parent family is not met by a simultaneous gender reorganization outside the home. A certain loosening of societal gender hierarchies (e.g., the opening of new job opportunities for women) no doubt has prefigured and created the structural conditions that have allowed a small number of men and women to share parenting at this historical moment. But those structural changes are minor in contrast to the drastic alteration of gender relations and power necessary for shared parenting to succeed. So the world the sharing mother enters as she walks out her door will be far less "fifty-fifty" than the newly created world within those doors.

For a man taking on parenting responsibilities, the gain is also twofold: he gains access to his children and is able to experience the pleasures and joys of childrearing. His life is not totally dominated by the alienated relations of commodity production. He is able to nurture, to discover the child in himself. But he, too, loses something in the process. First, in a culture that dictates that a man "make something of himself," he will be hard pressed to compete in terms of time and energy with his male counterparts who have minimal or no parenting responsibility. In short, parenting will cut into his opportunities for "transcendence." Second, the sharing father is now burdened with the daily headaches and hassles of childcare which can (and do) drive many a woman to distraction—the indelible scribble on the walls, the search for a nonexistent good child-care center, the two-hour tantrums, and so on. He has now committed himself to a sphere of work that brings little social recognition—I'm *just* a housewife and a mother.

In *shared* parenting, the gains and losses are not equal for men and women. Mom gives up some of her power only to find societally induced guilt feelings for not being a "real" mother, and maybe even for being a "bad" mother. (Remember: for years she may have grown up believing she should and would be a full-time mommy when she was big.) The myth of motherhood remains ideologically entrenched far beyond the point when its structural underpinnings have begun to crumble. She gives up power in the domestic sphere, historically her domain, with little compensation from increased power in the public sphere. Discrimination against women in the labor force is still rampant. She will likely have less earning power, less job opportunity, less creative work, and less social recognition than her male partner. When push comes to shove, she is only a "working mother." (There is as yet no parallel term "working father.")

The power dynamic for a sharing father is quite different and more complicated. On one level he gains quite a bit of authority in the daily domestic sphere of childrearing, a heretofore female domain. But by dirtying his hands with diapers he also removes himself from his patriarchal pedestal as the breadwinning but distant father, a position crucial to men's power in the traditional family. He now does the same "debasing" work as mama, and she now has at least some control of the purse strings. Nonetheless, as the second "mother" the father has encroached on an arena of power that traditionally belongs to women, while at the same time he most likely retains more economic and social power vis-à-vis mom in the public world of work and politics.

The societal reaction is also double-edged for the sharing father. Given the subculture that most current sharing parents come from, in his immediate circles dad often receives praise for being the "exceptional" father so devoted to his children or so committed to denying his male privileges. In challenging a myth as deeply embedded as motherhood, the man who marches with baby bottle and infant in arm can become quite an anti-sexist hero. But in the larger culture reactions are often adverse. A man who stays home to care for children is assumed by many to be either disabled, deranged, or demasculinized. One father, pushing his child in a stroller past a school on a weekday afternoon, was bemused by a preadolescent leaning out the school window yelling, "Faggot, Faggot." Some time ago my grandmother, in response to my mother's praise of my husband's involvement with our children, snapped, "Well, of course, he doesn't work." But as pressures of shifting family structures increase, popular response is rapidly swinging in the sharing father's favor, at least among the middle classes; and the response to his fathering from his most immediate and intimate circles is most likely a positive or even laudatory one.

When the results are tabulated, the gains and losses for men and women are not comparable: women come out behind. Where does this newly experienced power imbalance leave mothers and fathers vis-à-vis their commitment to shared parenting? Women can feel deprived of status both at home and at work. The experienced sexual inequalities in the world outside the family can create a tension in the "sharing" mother to reclaim dominance as primary parent and establish control and autonomy *somewhere:**

> I was angry and I was jealous. I was jealous because he not only had the rewards of parenthood, he was into work he could relate to. I think one reason I nursed as long as I did was to keep myself as Amanda's most special person. It

---

* In the public sphere of work, this is paralleled by the resistance of female childcare workers to allowing men in their field, as it is one area of paid work where women do have control (and can get jobs).

was also difficult to share one area of competence I felt I had. . . . After all, if she prefers David, what else do I have. I am woman therefore mother. I held on to my ambivalent identity as student in order to have something of my own.[10]

Structural forces dictate that she'll be much more successful in claiming control in the family sphere than in the public sphere. For some women, particularly those who start as primary parents and then move to shared parenting, it is not a question of reclaiming, but of giving up control for parenting to men in the first place.

> Neither of us could find a satisfactory way to increase his involvement. The children would have nothing to do with him. This situation probably came about because he was home less often and also because for many years the children were my own arena and thus my main base of power. At some level I probably did not want Ernie to be equally important in the lives of the children.*[11]

The reclaiming or unwillingness to give up a more primary role in parenting is not easy. It often culminates in frustration or anger (self- or other-directed) when a woman sees herself as doing more or too much parenting in comparison to her male partner.

The man, on his part, can feel a number of things when his female partner claims more parenting responsibility for herself: resistant to being shut out by mom, inadequate in his own seeming lack of parenting skills, relieved to relinquish 50 percent of control in a sphere that he was never meant or prepared to participate in anyway. This is not to say that father merely reacts to mother's power tactics. As we will discuss more fully in the next section, he is often quite active in "granting" women increased power in the

---

* This desire to maintain parenting within woman's sphere as a source of power might have some influence, conscious or unconscious, on the feminist movement's tendency to avoid demands for fathers' involvement in parenting.

sphere of parenting to give him the time he wants, needs, or has been conditioned to devote to extra-familial activities.

The underlying point is this: powerful tensions arise when the sexual divisions of labor and power in the family are altered without simultaneous sweeping restructuring of gender-related power relations outside the family. Women under advanced capitalism spend too much time feeling powerless to relish a situation where, under the auspices of liberation, they find themselves with less power. I have watched many a sharing mother—undervalued, sexually harassed, or discriminated against at the workplace—waffle on her outside work identity and refocus on the pleasure, reward, and fulfillment that one can find in identity as a mother. This is not to say that she relinquishes her paid work, but that, indeed, she becomes a *working mother*. Fathers, for their part, are not often prepared for the arduous, but undervalued task they're taking on in becoming the other mommy:

> I get an empty feeling when people ask me what I'm doing. Most of my energy in the last six months has focused on Dylan, on taking care of him and getting used to his being here. But I still have enough man-work expectations in me that I feel uncomfortable just saying that.[12]

Even if he, too, balks at the alienation of the workplace, the flight into parenthood is not a likely one.

The tension between men and women over this issue was illustrated by the marked female-male differences in response to the first draft of this essay. Women, whether mothers or non-mothers, urged me to emphasize how *rare* it is for men to involve themselves in parenting or for shared parenting actually to work. Men, on the other hand, wanted me to put more emphasis on the growing involvement of men in family life and the actual fathering that men have done historically *and continue to do*. Both are true, and both reflect the unresolved dialectic between women and men regarding responsibility.

PHYSICAL VERSUS PSYCHIC DIVISION OF LABOR IN PARENTING

The tensions in shared parenting cannot, however, be reduced to power politics in personal relationships. External expectations, attitudes, and ideology collide with deeply internalized self-concepts, skills, and personality structures to make the breakdown of the sexual division of labor in parenting an exciting but difficult project. Often the sharing of *physical* tasks between mothers and fathers is easily implemented —you feed the baby in the morning, I'll do it in the afternoon; you give the kids a bath on Mondays, I'll do it on Thursdays. What is left at least partially intact is the sexual division of the *psychological* labor in parenting. There is the question, "Who carries around in their head knowledge of diapers needing to be laundered, fingernails needing to be cut, new clothes needing to be bought?" Answer: mother, because of years of socialization to do so. Vis-à-vis fathers, sharing mothers often find themselves in the position of cataloguer and taskmaster—we really should change the kids' sheets today; I think its time for the kids' teeth to be checked. It is probable that men carry less of the mental load of parenting, regardless of mutual agreements to share the responsibility of parenting; this leaves the women more caught up in parenting's psychic aspects.

The more significant division of psychological labor, however, is the different intrapsychic conflict men and women experience in integrating their parent and non-parent identities. We already looked at the power imbalance that pulls mothers back into the home and fathers away from it. Women often feel tremendous ambivalence or guilt in relinquishing full-time mothering responsibilities. This is common among all women who depart from full-time mothering, either by working outside the home or sharing parenting responsibility with other(s):

The myth of motherhood takes its toll. Employed mothers often feel guilty. They feel inadequate, and they worry about whether they are doing the best for their children. They have internalized the myth that there is something their children need that only they can give them.[13]

To have children but turn over their rearing to someone else—even their father—brings social disapproval: a mother who does this must be "hard," "unloving," and of course, "unfeminine."[14]

Numerous studies denying any ill effects to children who are not totally mother-raised tend to be overlooked in favor of sensationalist reports of the delinquency, psychopathology, and emotional deficiencies that supposedly will befall our children if they are not provided with the proper "mother-love." And this love is "naturally" *woman's* duty and domain. Raised in this culture, even the most committed feminist "sharing" mother will experience doubt. Doubts and fears are profound because the stakes are so high. By sharing parenting, we are experimenting with the growth and development of our children; we are adopting new childrearing structures in the face of reports from psychologists, pediatricians, and politicians that we will bring ruin to our young.

These fears are fueled by pressures from individuals in the sharing mother's immediate life. Her mother is often appalled or threatened by her daughter's deviation from her own parenting model. Relatives are often resistant to the notion that a man should hang around the house taking care of a kid. People will inadvertently (or deliberately) turn to mother rather than father in asking information about the children. Letters from school come addressed to "Dear Mother." From the point of view of the outside world, even though men are being given more and more attention for their participation in family life, father remains an invisible or minimal figure in the daily rearing of children. A feeling so deeply internalized as "mother guilt," constantly rekindled by these external pressures and messages, creates in the sharing mother a strong ambivalence. Our intellectual selves lash out at Alice Rossi's telling us that we as women are the best-made parents, but our emotional selves struggle hard to calm the fear that our feminist views on motherhood may be ill-founded.

If mother guilt were not enough, women are confronted with two additional conflicts. First, the traditional structures of childrearing have produced in a woman a psychological capacity to mother. With personal observations and experience to back her up, she may have a hard time believing that a father, with no parallel long-term preparation, is really capable of fulfilling "mothering" responsibilities. As she watches her male partner stick the baby with a diaper pin (even though she as a new parent may have done the same thing the day before) or try unsuccessfully to calm a screaming child, her suspicions are confirmed. Thus, internal forces pressure the mother to reclaim control over parenting, so she can be assured her children survive intact. Men are often accomplices in this process: "Some men act out unconscious resistance to shared parenting by accentuating their ignorance, asking a lot of questions they could figure out themselves."[15] Sometimes women are not willing to be teachers. In the short run, they find it easier to do it themselves.

The second conflict arises from a woman's establishment of an "extra-mother" identity. We've already mentioned that women do not accrue much social recognition at the workplace, that they are seen as mothers first and workers second, and that when attempting shared parenting, women sometimes retreat from the world of paid work back into the female sphere of family life. Within her own psyche the sharing mother has a hard time integrating a work identity with being a mother: "When you go out to work, the job is something you *do*. But the work of a housewife and mother is not just something you do, it's something you *are*."[16]

For men, however, the experience is quite different. Historically, since the advent of industrialization, fathers' daily involvement with the kids in the nuclear family has been peripheral—usually concentrated on evening, weekend, and holiday play or instructional activities. Fathers have always been important figures in their children's lives and socialization experiences, even if as a result of their absence. The traditional father is actively involved in his child's life as breadwinner, as role model, as disciplinarian, but not in the day-to-day nurturant fashion that shared parenting dictates. The challenge for the man in shared parenting is to move from being a "father" to a "mother."

Today the growing participation of men in the birth experience of their children often stops at the delivery room doors. Contrasted to mothers, the sharing father more likely enters the parenting experience with a notion that parenting is something you *do* rather than someone you are. In early preparation for this consciousness, preschool boys in a recent study not once reported "Daddy" as something they would be when they grew up, while a majority of girls named "Mommy" as a projected adult identity.[17] In popular writing today, involved fathering is often presented as a *choice*, "only if the man wants to." . . .

Even when a man repudiates the work or public success ethic, which has occurred in our generation, he seldom turns to parenting as the locus of fulfillment and positive identity. This is well illustrated in the *San Francisco Chronicle* account of a financial wizard on Wall Street, a father of three, who took a year off to find himself. He spent his time lying on the couch, talking on the phone, collecting tropical fish, setting himself a "schedule bristling with physical, intellectual, and cultural self-improvement projects," and "marveling" at his wife's frantic schedule as homemaker and mother. His only parenting activity during this year was watching his son from behind a tree when his class had sports in the park.[18] Does this represent, at least in part, the actual content of "Men's growing involvement in the family" which is making such a media splash?

Coming home to a haven where one's own psychological needs can be nurtured is a far cry from taking on new responsibilities for the nurturance of others. . . .

NOTES

1. Nancy Press Hawley, "Shared Parenthood," in Boston Women's Health Collective, *Ourselves and Our Children* (New York: Random House, 1978).

2. Kenneth Pitchford, "The Manly Art of Child Care," *Ms.*, October 1978, p. 98.

3. D. Baldwin, "Motherhood and the Liberated Woman," *San Francisco Chronicle*, 12 October 1978.

4. Alice Abarbenal, "Redefining Motherhood," in *The Future of the Family*, edited by Louise Kapp Howe (New York: Simon & Schuster, 1972), p. 366.

5. Cf. Ann Oakley, *Woman's Work*, ch. 8: "Myths of Woman's Place, 2: Motherhood" (New York: Vintage, 1974); Wini Breines, Margaret Cerullo, and Judith Stacey, "Social Biology, Family Studies, and Antifeminist Backlash," *Feminist Studies*, February 1978, pp. 43–68.

6. Nancy Chodorow, *The Reproduction of Mothering: Psychoanalysis and the Sociology of Gender* (Berkeley: University of California Press, 1978).

7. See, for example, Betty Friedan, "Feminism Takes a New Turn," *New York Times Magazine*, 16 November 1979; Caroline Bird, *The Two-Paycheck Marriage* (New York: Rawson, Wade, 1979); Jane Geniesse, "On Wall Street: The Man Who Gave Up Working," *San Francisco Chronicle*, 11 November 1979; Lindsy Van Gelder, "An Unmarried Man," *Ms.*, November 1979.

8. Sheila Rowbotham, *Woman's Consciousness, Man's World* (Baltimore: Penguin, 1973), p. 61.

9. Oakley, *Woman's Work*, p. 220.

10. Abarbenal, "Redefining Motherhood," p. 360.

11. Quoted interview in Hawley, "Shared Parenthood," p. 134.

12. David Steinberg, *Fatherjournal: Five Years of Awakening to Fatherhood* (Albion, Calif.: Times Change Press, 1977), p. 37.

13. Oakley, *Woman's Work*, p. 211.

14. *Ibid.*, p. 189.

15. Hawley, "Shared Parenthood," p. 139.

16. Rowbotham, *Woman's Consciousness*, p. 76.

17. Barbara Chasen, "Sex Role Stereotyping and Pre-Kindergarten Teachers," *Elementary School Journal*, 1974, pp. 74, 225–35.

18. Jane Geniesse, "On Wall Street: The Man Who Gave Up Working," *San Francisco Chronicle*, 11 November 1979.

Further Questions

1. Do you think shared parenting furthers a situation of equality between men and women? If so, what particular gender equalities would shared parenting promote?

2. Would there be a real gain for fathers in shared parenting, since they would have a greater experience in childrearing? Are there losses to the father as well? What special gains or losses for fathers are in question here?

3. Does parenting have psychological aspects (responsibilities for seeing to it that things are done, as opposed to doing them) that are more difficult to transfer from one parent to the other? Are the most difficult aspects of parenting also the most difficult ones for one parent to transfer to the other?

XII.4   Why Men Don't Rear Children

M. RIVKA POLATNICK

M. Rivka Polatnick examines the reasons why men don't rear children. She perceives a feedback situation where women's responsibility for childrearing contributes to women's powerlessness, which then, in turn, leaves women the less desirable of the breadwinner/childraiser parental roles.

Polatnick: "My given name honors my great-grandmother Rivka, a Czechoslovakian Jew who was known as a wise woman and lived until the Nazis came."

Reading Questions

1. Is achievement in the workplace the major source of prestige and power in North American society today? If not, what is an even greater source of prestige and power, and is this source equally open to both genders?

2. Is it true that under ideal circumstances, most people would want to have children but would not want childcare responsibilities to interfere with workplace activities? If so, what would such ideal circumstances be like?

3. Does unpaid work tend to be underrated? Along with that, does the worker tend to be underrated as well? Does paid work buy more free time? Discuss, in connection with some examples.

. . . IF, AS I WILL ARGUE, the current allocation of childrearing responsibility to women must be understood in the context of their subordinate position in society, then two different causal relationships suggest themselves:

1. Because women are the rearers of children, they are a powerless group vis-à-vis men.
2. Because women are a powerless group vis-à-vis men, they are the rearers of children. . . .

Women's responsibility for childrearing certainly contributes to their societal powerlessness, but this is only one component of the total "power picture." It will be my contention in the rest of this paper that the second causal relationship is operative as well. Thus, the causal model that will inform my discussion can be represented best by a feedback arrangement:

$$\left(\begin{array}{c} \text{Women are a powerless group vis-à-vis men.} \\ \text{Women are the rearers of children.} \end{array} \right)$$

My task will be to explain, elaborate, and justify this "power analysis." . . .

I will discuss the undesirability of the childrearing job under two general categories: (a) the advantages of avoiding childrearing responsibility (which are, primarily, the advantages of breadwinning responsibility), and (b) the disadvantages attached to childrearing responsibility.

Breadwinning Beats Childrearing

Full-time childrearing responsibility limits one's capacity to engage in most other activities. However, the most important thing, in power terms that childrearers can't do is to be the family breadwinner.[1] This is the job that men prefer as their primary family responsibility. If offers important power advantages over the home-based childrearing job.

MONEY, STATUS, POWER

First, and of signal importance, breadwinners earn money. "Money is a source of power that supports male dominance in the family. . . . Money belongs to him who earns it, not to her who spends it, since he who earns it may withhold it."[2]

Second, occupational achievement is probably the major source of social status in American society.

In a certain sense the fundamental basis of the family's status is the occupational status of the husband and father. [The wife/mother] is excluded from the struggle for power and prestige in the occupational sphere [while the man's breadwinner role] carries with it . . . the primary prestige of achievement, responsibility, and authority.[3]

Even if one's occupation ranks very low in prestige and power, other tangible and intangible benefits accrue to wage earners, such as organizational experience, social contacts, "knowledge of the world," and feelings of independence and competence. Moreover, the resources that breadwinners garner in the outside world do not remain on the front porch; breadwinning power translates significantly into power within the family. This is in direct contradiction to the notion of "separate spheres": the man reigning supreme in extrafamilial affairs, the woman running the home-front show. . . .

The correlation between earning power and family power has been substantiated concretely in a number of studies of family decision-making.[4] These studies show that the more a man earns, the more family power he wields; and the greater the discrepancy between the status of the husband's and wife's work, the greater the husband's power. When the wife works too, there is a shift toward a more egalitarian balance of power and more sharing of household burdens.*

Lois Hoffman has proposed four explanations for the increased family power of working wives, which convey again some of the power resources connected with breadwinning:

1. [Women who work have more control over money] and this control can be used, implicitly or explicitly, to wield power in the family.

2. Society attaches greater value to the role of wage earner than to that of housewife and thus legitimizes for both parents the notion that the former should have more power.

3. An independent supply of money enables the working woman to exert her influence to a greater extent because she is less dependent on her husband and could, if necessary, support herself in the event of the dissolution of the marriage.

4. Working outside the home provides more social interaction than being a housewife. This interaction has been seen as leading to an increase in the wife's power because of: (a) the development of social skills which are useful in influencing her husband; (b) the development of self-confidence; (c) the greater knowledge of alternative situations that exist in other families; and (d) the more frequent interaction with men, which may result in the feeling that remarriage is feasible.[5]

Not only does the woman's working modify the power relation between husband and wife, it also affects the gender power distribution in the whole family: when the mother works, daughters

---

* This should not imply, however, that women who earn more than their husbands necessarily have superior power, since the subordinate position of women stems from multiple causes.

are likely to become more independent, and sons more dependent and obedient.[6] . . .

MEN WANT TO BE THE BREADWINNERS

Men have good reason, then, to try to monopolize the job of principal family breadwinner (much as they may appreciate a second income). Husbands' objections to wives working "stem from feelings that their dominance is undermined when they are not the sole or primary breadwinners."[7] There is also

> the feeling of being threatened by women in industry, who are seen as limiting opportunities for men, diminishing the prestige of jobs formerly held only by men, and casting a cold eye on masculine pretensions to vocational superiority.[8]

These feelings are quite justified; as Benson so neatly understates it, "The male fear of competition from women is not based solely on myth."[9]

Where outright forbidding of the wife to work is no longer effective, the continued allocation of childrearing responsibility to women accomplishes the same end: assuring male domination of the occupational world. Should all other barriers to economic power for women suddenly vanish, childrearing responsibility would still handicap them hopelessly in economic competition with men.

Of course, children are not just a handy excuse to keep women out of the job market. Most people—male and female—want to have them, and somebody has to rear them. Men naturally prefer that women do it, so that having children need not interfere with their own occupational pursuits.

> Since housewife and mother roles are preferred for women, it is considered distasteful and perhaps dangerous to upgrade their occupational status. Apparently there is a fear of mass defections from maternal responsibility. Perhaps

there is also a hidden suspicion that the woman's employment is symptomatic of a subversive attitude toward motherhood.[10]

Both these motives, therefore—the desire to limit females' occupational activities, and the desire to have children without limiting their own occupational activities—contribute to a male interest in defining childrearing as exclusively woman's domain. Thus,

> there has been consistent social effort as a norm with the woman whose vocational proclivities are completely and "naturally" satisfied by childbearing and childrearing, with the related domestic activities.[11] . . .

MEN WANT WOMEN TO BE THE CHILDREARERS

By propagating the belief that women are the ones who really desire children, men can then invoke a "principle of least interest": that is, because women are "most interested" in children, they must make most of the accommodations and sacrifices required to rear them. Benson says that "fatherhood . . . is less important to men than motherhood is to women, in spite of the fact that maternity causes severe limitations on women's activities."[12] My own version would be that fatherhood is less important to men than motherhood is to women *because* childrearing causes severe limitations on the childrearer's activities. . . .

Women too imbibe the ideology of motherhood, but men seem to be its strongest supporters. By insuring that the weight of childrearing responsibility falls on women's shoulders, they win for themselves the right of "paternal neglect." As Benson observes, "The man can throw himself into his work and still fulfill male obligations at home, mainly because the latter are minimal. [Men have] the luxury of more familial disengagement than women."[13]

Of course, men as family breadwinners must shoulder the *financial* burden involved in raising children: they may have to work harder, longer hours, and at jobs they dislike. But even factory workers enjoy set hours, scheduled breaks, vacation days, sick leave, and other union benefits. To the extent that men *can* select work suited to their interests, abilities, and ambitions, they are in a better position than women arbitrarily assigned to childrearing. And to the extent that breadwinning gains one the resources discussed earlier (money, status, family power, etc.), financial responsibility is clearly preferable, in power terms, to "mothering" responsibility.

CHILDREARING RESPONSIBILITY HANDICAPS WOMEN

From the perspective of women—the more affluent women faced with "mother/career conflict," the poorer women faced with "mother/any job at all conflict"—men possess the enviable option to "have their cake and eat it too," that is, to have children without sacrificing their activities outside the home. A woman knows that becoming a parent will adversely affect her occupational prospects. "For a period, at least, parenthood means that . . . whatever vocational or professional skills she may possess may become atrophied.[14] During this period of retirement the woman

> becomes isolated and almost totally socially, economically, and emotionally dependent upon her husband. . . . She loses her position, cannot keep up with developments in her field, does not build up seniority. . . . If she returns to work, and most women do, she must begin again at a low-status job and she stays there— underemployed and underpaid.[15]

Not only during the period of childrearing do women become economically or professionally disadvantaged vis-à-vis men; most women's lives have already been constructed in anticipation of that period. "Helpful advice" from family, friends, and guidance counselors, and discriminatory practices in the schools and in the job

market steer women toward jobs and interests compatible with a future in childrearing.

With the assistance of relatives, babysitters, or the few day-care centers that exist, women can hold certain kinds of jobs while they're raising children (often part-time, generally low-status). Women without husbands, women with pressing financial needs, women who can afford hired help, may work fulltime despite the demands of "mothering."[16] But to an important extent, occupational achievement and childrearing responsibility are mutually exclusive. A 40-hour work-week permits more family involvement than did a 72-hour work-week, but it's still difficult to combine with primary responsibility for children (given the lack of institutional assistance). Furthermore, the higher-status professional jobs frequently demand a work week commitment closer to the 72-hour figure. Men can hold these jobs and also father families only because they can count on a "helpmeet" to take care of children and home. Thus it is said that the wages of a man buy the labor of two people. Without this back-up team of wife/mothers, something would have to give.

Alice Rossi has suggested that the period of women's lives spent at home rearing children is potentially the peak period for professional accomplishment:

> If we judge from the dozens of researches Harvey Lehman has conducted on the relationship between age and achievement, . . . the most creative work women and men have done in science was completed during the very years contemporary women are urged to remain at home rearing their families. . . . Older women who return to the labor force are an important reservoir for assistants and technicians and the less demanding professions, but only rarely for creative and original contributors to the more demanding professional fields.[17]

The woman who tries to work at home while raising children finds that this is not too practicable a solution. Writer/critic Marya Mannes noted with regard to her own profession: "The creative woman has no wife to protect her from intrusion. A man at his desk in a room with closed door is a man at work. A woman at a desk in any room is available."[18]

MAINTAINING THE STATUS QUO

If working hours and career patterns were more flexible, if childcare centers were more widely available, and if "retired mothers" reentering the workforce received special preference rather than unfavorable treatment,* childrearing would exact a less heavy toll on women's occupational achievement. Because men benefit from the status quo, they ignore, discourage, or actively resist such reform proposals. Alternative arrangements for rearing children, for balancing work commitment with family commitment, are not pressing concerns for men; the structural relegation of women to domestic service suits their interests very well.

Women's responsibility for children in the context of the nuclear family is an important buttress for a male-dominated society. It helps keep women out of the running for economic and political power. As Talcott Parsons states:

> It is, of course, possible for the adult woman to follow the masculine pattern and seek a career in fields of occupational achievement in direct competition with men of her own class. It is, however, notable that in spite of the very great progress of the emancipation of women from the traditional domestic pattern only a very small fraction have gone very far in this direction.† It is also clear that its generalization would only be possible with profound alterations in the structure of the family.[19]

I have chosen to focus upon breadwinning (economic activity) as the most important thing, from a power perspective, that childrearers can't do. Moreover, other activities—educational, political, cultural, social, recreational—suffer when one's life becomes centered around children and home.‡ The "on call" nature of "mothering" responsibility militates against any kind of sustained, serious commitment to other endeavors. A full-time mother loses

> the growth of competence and resources in the outside world, the community positions which contribute to power in the marriage. The boundaries of her world contract, the possibilities of growth diminish.[20]

While women are occupied with domestic duties, men consolidate their resources in the outside world and their position of command in the family. By the time most women complete their childrearing tenure, they can no longer recoup their power losses.

Childrearing: Not an Equal Sphere

By my explicit and implicit comparisons of breadwinning with childrearing, I have already asserted that the former is the more desirable "sphere" of action. Now I will discuss more directly the disadvantages of the childrearing job.

MONEY, STATUS, POWER

Once again, let's begin with the simple but significant matter of money. Money is a prime source of power in American society, and tending one's own children on a full-time basis is not a salaried activity.

> In sheer quantity, household labor, including child care, constitutes a huge amount of socially necessary production. Nevertheless, in a society based on commodity production, it is not usually considered "real work" since it is outside of trade and the market place. . . . In a society in which money determines value, women are a group who work outside the money economy.

---

* Consider how the reentry of veterans into the workforce is eased by special benefits and preferential treatment.

† One might well inquire what this "very great progress" is, if "only a small fraction" of women are actually involved.

‡ Here again, there's been little effort, for the sake of *female* childrearers, to develop more flexible programs of higher education and professional training.

Their work is not worth money, is therefore valueless, is therefore not even real work. And women themselves, who do this valueless work, can hardly be expected to be worth as much as men, who work for money.[21]

Performing well at the job of childrearer may be a source of feminine credentials, but it is not a source of social power or status. Of all the possible adult roles for females, "the pattern of domesticity must be ranked lowest in terms of prestige," although "it offers perhaps the highest level of a certain kind of security."[22] When a woman bears and raises children, therefore, she is fulfilling social expectations and avoiding negative sanctions, but she "is not esteemed, in the culture or in the small society of her family, in proportion to her exercise of her 'glory,' childbearing."[23]

The rewards for rearing children are not as tangible as a raise or a promotion, and ready censure awaits any evidence of failure: "if the child goes wrong, mother is usually blamed."[24] Thus the male preference for the breadwinner role may reflect (among other things) an awareness that "it's easier to make money than it is to be a good father. . . . The family is a risky proposition in terms of rewards and self-enhancement."[25] . . .

CHILDREARING:
NOT A SEPARATE SPHERE

Despite the empirical evidence that women lose family power when they become mothers, one is still tempted to believe that by leaving childrearing to women, men have surrendered a significant area of control. This belief is based on the erroneous notion that women preside over childrearing as a separate sovereign domain. On the contrary, men's authority as family provider/family "head" carries right over into childrearing matters. Men may have surrendered the regular responsibility and routine decision-making, but they retain power where important decisions are concerned (including what the routine will be).

In a sample of adolescents studied by Charles Bowerman and Glen Elder (1964), the father was reported to be the dominant parent in childrearing matters as often as the mother, in spite of the fact that mother does most of the actual work; apparently she often finds herself responsible for doing the menial chores without having the stronger voice in "childrearing policy."[26]

Constantina Safilios-Rothschild found that American men delegate to their wives many of the minor decisions related to rearing children and running a home—"those decisions, the enactment of which involves time-consuming tasks." This suggests to her that

> American husbands do not wish to take on "bothersome" decisions which are not crucial . . . and take too much of the time and energy that they prefer to dedicate to their work or leisure-time activities.[27] . . .

Taking care of children, therefore, does not provide women with any real power base. Men can afford to leave childrearing *responsibility* to women because, given their superior power resources, they are still assured of substantial childrearing *authority*.

THE NATURE OF THE JOB

Childrearing, I have argued, is not a source of money, status, power in the society, or power in the family. The childrearing job is disadvantageous in terms of these major assets, but there are also drawbacks inherent in the nature of the work itself. The rearing of children "involves long years of exacting labor and self-sacrifice," but

> the drudgery, the monotonous labor, and other disagreeable features of childrearing are minimized by "the social guardians." On the other hand, the joys and compensations of motherhood are magnified and presented to consciousness on every hand. Thus the tendency is to create an illusion whereby motherhood will appear to consist of compensations only, and thus come to be desired by those for whom the illusion is intended.[28]

The responsibilities of a childrearer/homemaker are not confined to a 40-hour work-week.

Margaret Benston estimates that for a married woman with small children (excluding the very rich), "the irreducible minimum of work . . . is probably 70 or 80 hours a week."[29] In addition to the actual hours of work, there is the constant strain of being "on call." Thus, another consideration in why the husband's power is greatest when the children are young "may be the well-described chronic fatigue which affects young mothers with preschoolers."[30]

Furthermore, women are adults (assertions that they have "childlike" natures notwithstanding), and they need adequate adult company to stimulate their mental faculties.

> A lot of women become disheartened because babies and children are not only not interesting to talk to (not everyone thrills at the wonders of da-da-ma-ma- talk) but they are generally not empathic, considerate people.[31]

Although interaction with young children is certainly rewarding in many ways, childrearers can lose touch with the world outside their domestic circle. In addition, American society segregates the worlds of childhood and adulthood; adults who keep close company with children are *déclassé*. . . .

From the perspective of an ambitious person, taking full-time care of your own children is rather like baking your own bread: it might be nice if one had the time, but there are more important things to be done. Thus you pay for the service of having someone else do it, increasing your financial burden but freeing yourself of a time-consuming task.

Fathers, with full social support, can buy a significant degree of freedom from direct family responsibility. They have a category of people at hand—women—constrained by social forces to accept that responsibility. Women have no such convenient group to whom they can pass the childrearing buck. For mothers, the price of escape from childrearing—financial, social, psychological—is usually too high.

"MOTHERLY SELFLESSNESS"

A final relevant feature of the childrearing job itself is that mothers are obliged to subordinate their personal objectives and practice "selflessness"—putting the needs of others first, devoting themselves to the day-to-day well-being of other family members, loving and giving "unconditionally." Such domestic service may be deemed virtuous, but it isn't a path to power and success. Males primed for competitive achievement show no eagerness to suppress their personal ambitions and sacrifice their own interests to attend to others' immediate wants.

Furthermore, men desire from women the same services and support, the same ministration to everyday needs, that mothers are supposed to provide for children. ("I want a wife to keep track of the children's doctor and dentist appointments. And to keep track of mine too. . . . a wife who will pick up after my children, a wife who will pick up after me.")[32] "Mothering" behavior is not very different from "feminine" behavior. By grooming females for "nurturance," men provide a selfless rearer for their children and an accommodating marriage partner for themselves. . . .

NOTES

1. Many women work during some of the childrearing years, but if they have husbands, they are very rarely the principal breadwinner. In 1978, working wives contributed about 26% to family income (U.S. Dept. of Labor, *Monthly Labor Review*, April 1980, p. 48).

2. Reuben Hill and Howard Becker, eds., *Family, Marriage, and Parenthood* (Boston: D. C. Heath, 1955), p. 790.

3. Talcott Parsons, "Age and Sex in the Social Structure" in *The Family: Its Structure and Functions*, edited by Rose Laub Coser (New York: St. Martin's Press, 1964), pp. 258, 261–62.

4. For a full report, see Leonard Benson, *Fatherhood: A Sociological Perspective* (New York: Random House, 1968).

5. Lois Wladis Hoffman, "Effects of the Employment of Mothers on Parental Power Relations and the Division of Household Tasks," *Marriage and Family Living* 22 (February 1960): 33.

6. Benson, *Fatherhood*, pp. 302–3.

7. Phyllis Hallenbeck, "An Analysis of Power Dynamics in Marriage," *Journal of Marriage and the Family* 28 (May 1966): 201.

8. Helen Mayer Hacker, "The New Burdens of Masculinity," *Marriage and Family Living* 19 (August 1957): 232.

9. Benson, *Fatherhood*, p. 293.

10. *Ibid*.

11. Leta S. Hollingworth, "Social Devices for Impelling Women to Bear and Rear Children," *The American Journal of Sociology* 22 (July 1916): 20.

12. Benson, *Fatherhood*, p. 292.

13. Benson, *Fatherhood*, pp. 132, 134.

14. Robert F. Winch, *The Modern Family*, rev. ed. (New York: Holt, Rinehart and Winston, 1964), p. 434.

15. Dair L. Gillespie, "Who Has the Power? The Marital Struggle," *Journal of Marriage and the Family* 33 (August 1971): 456.

16. In 1960, 18.6 percent of mothers with children under the age of six were in the labor force in some capacity; 11.4 percent were working 35 hours or more per week. By 1970, the proportion of these mothers in the paid labor force at least part time or looking for paid jobs reached 32 percent, and in March 1979, 45 percent. The percentage actually working full time, year-round, remains low, however (U.S. Department of Labor, *Monthly Labor Review*, April 1980, p. 49). The increase in those working at least part time can probably be explained by the economy's need for more service and clerical workers, families' needs for more income because of recession and inflation, the increase in the percentage of mothers who are single, and the effects of the Women's Liberation Movement. Ongoing research will reveal to what extent men have taken on more childrearing work (U.S. Bureau of the Census, *Statistical Abstract of the U.S.: 1971* [Washington, D.C.: U.S.G.P.O., 1971], Table 332; and *A U.S. Census of Population: 1960, Subject Reports: Families* [Washington, D.C.: U.S.G.P.O., 1963], Final Report PC(2)-44, Table 11).

17. Alice S. Rossi, "Barriers to the Career Choice of Engineering, Medicine, or Science Among American Women" in *Women and the Scientific Professions*, edited by Jacquelyn A. Mattfeld and Carol G. Van Aken (Westport, Conn.: Greenwood Press, 1965), pp. 102–3, 107.

18. Quoted in Betty Rollin, "Motherhood: Who Needs It?" in *Family in Transition*, edited by Arlene S. Skolnick and Jerome H. Skolnick (Boston: Little, Brown, 1971), p. 352.

19. Parsons, "Age and Sex in the Social Structure," pp. 258–59.

20. Gillespie, "Who Has the Power?" p. 456.

21. Margaret Benston, "The Political Economy of Women's Liberation" in Garskof, *Roles Women Play*, p. 196.

22. Parsons, "Age and Sex in the Social Structure," p. 261.

23. Judith Long Laws, "A Feminist Review of Marital Adjustment Literature," *Journal of Marriage and the Family* 33 (August 1971): 493.

24. Benson, *Fatherhood*, p. 12.

25. Myron Brenton, *The American Male* (New York: Coward-McCann, 1966), p. 133.

26. Benson, *ibid.*, p. 157.

27. Constantina Safilios-Rothschild, "Family Sociology or Wives' Family Sociology?" in *Journal of Marriage and the Family* 31 (May 1969): 297.

28. Hollingsworth, "Social Devices," pp. 20–21, 27.

29. Benston, "Political Economy," p. 199.

30. Hallenbeck, "An Analysis of Power Dynamics in Marriage," p. 201.

31. Rollin, "Motherhood," p. 353.

32. Judy Syfers, "Why I Want a Wife," in *Notes From the Third Year* (New York, 1971), p. 13.

Further Questions

1. Can men afford to leave the responsibilities for rearing children to women because these responsibilities are not a source of much real power, and because men can retain *authority*, even without the responsibilities? Explain your answer.

2. If you are a young woman, planning to have children, is it a wise idea to enter the job market with the idea of finding something compatible with a future of childrearing? If so, what kind of position would you look for? If not, how can you justify your plans to have children combined with a career that possibly precludes your rearing these children?

3. Should "retired mothers" re-entering the workforce get special benefits and preferential treatment comparable to that of war veterans re-entering the workforce? What similarities or dissimilarities between "retired mothers" and war veterans justify your answer?

XII.5A   Anna Karenina, Scarlett O'Hara, and Gail Bezaire: Child Custody and Family Law Reform

SUSAN CREAN

Susan Crean reveals some hypocrisy behind the claim that mothers are "natural child-raisers." Should the parents separate, the father will often attempt to take custody of the child. This is exactly what happened to Anna Karenina, Scarlett O'Hara, and Gail Bezaire. (Gail Bezaire lost custody of her children because she was a lesbian, and after she abducted them from their father, who was abusing them, she was tried and sentenced for the abduction.)

Crean lives in Toronto and travels widely. *In the Name of the Fathers* is her fourth book.

Reading Questions

1. In a custody dispute, the parent with more money often has more influence over the outcome. Is this fair? If not, what would be a fair way of settling a custody dispute?

2. If the child's best interests should be considered in a custody dispute, by what standards should these "best interests" be judged?

3. Should a parent's sexual conduct affect whether the parent wins custody of the child? Should it affect whether she or he has access to the child? Explain your answer.

* * *

UNLIKE MOTHERHOOD, custody is not a natural phenomenon. That is, it is a human invention —which is to say a patriarchal invention that apparently must have followed upon the discovery of biological paternity. As I imagine the evolu-

tion, it was marked by transition from an ideology of belonging—to clan, tribe, or family—which is essentially an expression of collective identity, to an ideology of ownership or the expression of possession by individuals. In other words, it developed out of the notion of practical responsibility (for that which one carries and cares for) into the power to control and to dispose of the lives of others. In that sense, custody is definitely related to the practice of slavery. To those people who did not invent the idea but were forced to submit to it, child custody must at first have seemed as absurd as the idea of owning the land. . . .

. . . Motherhood may have been the most hallowed of female occupations, ordained by God and all his earthly bishops, but until the nineteenth century women had no legal rights whatsoever to their offspring. They lived with them and cared for them at the pleasure of their husbands, who could, and occasionally did, disown their wives, divorce them, or have them committed to institutions to separate them from their children permanently and against their will. In the rare instances where marriage breakdown led to divorce, every woman faced the real possibility of losing her children forever. If she "deserted" the matrimonial home she instantly became legally childless and propertyless. Similarly, if she committed adultery she lost her dower rights and might well never see her children again. If she did, it was only because of her husband's generosity. . . .

From the 19th century we have the unforgettable story of Anna Karenina. In Tolstoy's novel the child loss at least is not hidden, even though it is subordinated to the larger theme of Anna's annihilation by the exploding forces of passion and social opprobrium. Anna commits the unpardonable sin of adultery. Her husband refuses to permit a divorce, so she cannot marry her lover Vronsky and is thereby sentenced to life in social limbo, a sentence which carries no parole and over which she has absolutely no control. The love-child she has with Vronsky is Karenin's according to law, and Vronsky himself has no paternal rights to his daughter or to any children he might have with Anna, an injustice he angrily laments. "Think of the bitterness and horror of such a position. Conceive the feelings of a man who knows that his children, the children of the woman he loves, will not be his, but will belong to someone who hates them, and will have nothing to do with them!"

Meanwhile Karenin forbids any contact between Anna and her son, Seriozha, and the boy is cruelly informed that his mother is dead. As well she might be described—for society refused to acknowledge the existence of women who strayed beyond the protection of husband; they were disqualified, defrocked, as wives and mothers. What else was there for Anna to be? Vronsky could go on being Vronsky, but Anna was branded a Scarlet Woman; she was conspicuous, tainted, and therefore ostracized. Like Niobe she tempted the fates by committing an act of love, in her case the unsanctioned love of another man. In nineteenth-century Russia she might as well have died. In the end, of course, she does die—by her own hand. Like Niobe she is turned to stone.

In another immensely popular epic about love and loss (and a child caught in between), the plot includes a parental kidnapping which is so downplayed both in the novel and in its Hollywood rendition that few people even remember it. Margaret Mitchell's *Gone with the Wind* is a Harlequinesque romance about the stormy love affair between Scarlett O'Hara, stubborn southern belle, and Rhett Butler, professional rake and racketeer. However, it could just as accurately be described as the chronicle of a marriage coming apart at the seams—having never been made really, except in bed. Although the marital discord is in the league of *Who's Afraid of Virginia Woolf*, it is cushioned by genteel nostalgia and the magnificence of the antebellum American South. The relationship between Rhett and Scarlett is abusive, even violent, nonetheless. There is a scene of marital rape, lots of miscommunication and bridled anger, and eventually Rhett takes off for England with their young daughter, Bonnie Blue, who had been living with Scarlett since her parents separated. In London, the child is inconsolable; she screams for her mother in her sleep, and Rhett is finally forced to take her home, whereupon she has an accident on her pony and is killed.

The earlier scenes of big, burly Rhett playing sensitive, loving father are now supplanted by the picture of a broken, despairing man, pushed to the edge of sanity by grief. Scarlett, however, gets next to no attention as the mother of the little girl, and even less sympathy. Throughout the film and the book, she is depicted as selfish and silly, albeit Irish and determined. A childish woman, she seems incapable of unconditionally loving anything but herself (and possibly the family estate, Tara). It is Rhett who gets the kudos for mothering, not Scarlett. Rhett is, naturally, the proverbial diamond in the rough, a thoroughly macho man who nevertheless displays uncommon tolerance and great forbearance. In a 180 degree reversal of stereotypes he ultimately commands sympathy as the aggrieved husband, and it is Scarlett who gets blamed for being flighty, insincere and exhausting everyone's patience. And for failing to live up to the minimum standards of wife- and motherhood. Whatever disasters befall her—her daughter's death, Rhett's desertion—are, it is broadly hinted, thoroughly deserved. So when Rhett gets around to uttering those frameable words, "Frankly, my dear, I don't give a damn," Scarlett is left to weep alone.

*   *   *

Ostensibly focusing on the needs of the children, custody disputes today typically focus on parents trying to "prove" each other unfit or incompetent. Such disputes provoke mudslinging matches in court and, as many family law lawyers will admit, the contest is far from fair or objective. Jeffrey Wilson, a Toronto lawyer who has championed the cause of children's rights for years, comments with chagrin: "This is a huge grey area—the child's best interests. For a long time it was thought to be custody by the father, then it was the mother, and today it is whoever bonds. Bonding is the in-thing with psychiatrists now and as sure as I am sitting here, it will be something else in ten years. I can still remember a case in the U.S. in the sixties in which a judge declared that 'mulatto kids' should go with their black parent rather than their white. The interpretations can be that ridic-

ulous because 'best interests' can mean whatever you want it to mean. Like beauty, it is in the eye of the beholder." Wilson is not the only lawyer who frankly agrees that winning a custody suit has become a matter of money. Money won't guarantee a successful outcome, but lack of it has certainly lost many a case. "Basically," he says, "you can win a custody suit if you have enough money. And in my experience men enjoy doing battle in court more than women do and are better equipped to hire lawyers and to talk lawyers' language."

*   *   *

There are other ways money talks in custody court. Judges routinely consider such things as a spouse's employment prospects, current income, and capital assets, which obviously relate to economics. Questions about who can provide the more stable home and who is the more stable parent can involve money as well. What happens when disaster strikes or adversity befalls? As one judge said in a 1980 decision, "financially the father's proposal offers greater security, and although such financial security could, should the mother have custody, be compensated for by an award of maintenance, in any unexpected adversity the wife's proposal would lack this depth of security." In this case the child was awarded to the father. Similarly, a situation where the mother in fulfilling a traditional homemaker's role has not worked outside the home or has done part-time work, and where she now has to "retrain" and move into the work force full-time, can be a major upheaval in the domestic routine and could no doubt be interpreted as a destabilizing event. Some judges have seen it that way, awarding custody of children to a father because he has a second wife who can stay at home with the children, something their mothers can no longer afford to do.

*   *   *

Even though there was a time when marriage was supposed to be indissoluble and forever (as well as made in heaven), adultery by men was not in itself considered to be an attack or a betrayal. It was thought to be normal (though not necessarily nice) behaviour, thoroughly acceptable and forgiveable. The law simply enshrined what men have been telling women for centuries: "But it didn't mean anything; it was like shaking hands." For long decades women were thus required by law to be more faithful and more forgiving than men, to believe in and dedicate their lives to the very idea of marriage. Even when her husband was long gone, the infamous "dum casta" clauses stipulated that her marital rights, such as they were, only obtained so long as she remained chaste. It sounds positively medieval to us now, but there are still vestiges of these "while chaste" provisions in many laws, and although they are no longer directed to a particular gender they still do relate rights to a person's conduct. (Ontario's family law, for example, empowers the court to take the conduct of a spouse into account when deciding on the amount of maintenance to be ordered, if such conduct is deemed to have been "so unconscionable as to constitute a gross repudiation of the relationship." The Divorce Act also states that a person's past conduct shall not be a consideration for a court deciding custody "unless the conduct is relevant to the ability of that person to act as a parent of the child.")

To this day, people assume when a couple separates that the event puts the woman in such a precarious and vulnerable social position that she must watch herself and carefully guard her reputation. Free advice pours in unsolicited, with reminders about not allowing "other" men to visit overnight and not being seen with too many different male friends. Antique ideas and double standards hang about the culture like dustballs long after they have been cleared off the law books, which exasperates family law experts like Malcolm Kronby. In his handbook, *Canadian Family Law,** Kronby writes: "I'd like to have a

* Kronby, Malcolm C. *Canadian Family Law.* Toronto: Stoddart, 1986.

nickel for every woman who has been terrified by a threat from her husband that he'll take the children away, and she'll never see them again because she has been unfaithful. Even where the husband and wife have been separated for years, the threat still arises." It does happen, however, that women lose custody of their children because of circumstances which have little to do with their talents as parents or their track record as mothers. Conduct, as it is interpreted in Canadian courts, is very often a matter of appearances and sexual stereotypes. What is considered relevant behaviour in one parent may not be in the other. The law may have eliminated gender bias in its letter, but it cannot eliminate it in judges; and some rights are to this day dependent on a person's conduct.

* * *

The major change in the last decade has been the emergence of joint custody, a concept virtually unheard of before 1975 and a category which the Central Divorce Registry did not even include on its statistics-gathering forms until recently. Although it looks straightforward, the term joint custody can be misleading, for it refers only to legal guardianship, the right to make decisions about a child's upbringing, education, religion, language, and so forth. It does not require or necessarily entail shared physical custody or imply any regular involvement with the child by both parents. It should not therefore be mistaken for a co-parenting arrangement, although it can and sometimes does involve that. Joint custody can exist with one parent having no physical contact with the children or it can involve a man and woman co-operating in a fully-fledged shared parenting program where both individuals are equally involved and develop a new way of being parents together. Such an arrangement, however, does not actually need legal joint custody order to exist. A father does not have to have legal rights to his child to share in parenting. It does seem, though, that many men feel alienated by the label "non-custodial parent" and want a titular connection to their children, and the authority that goes with it, free and clear of their ex-wives' control. . . .

In the circumstances, it seems strange that fathers' rights groups are springing up just now, in the late eighties, claiming that the courts are biased in favour of mothers and against them as custodians. Mothers once more are obviously losing favour, and rather rapidly at that. Whatever "favour" they have had, in any case, came very late in history and has always been limited and provisional. Even during the recent heyday of the maternal presumption, there were legal principles at work in the justice system which favoured fathers —less well known perhaps, but there all the same—paternal presumption for older children and sons, for instance. A so-called bias against fathers could just as easily be interpreted as a fair reflection of the reality that women generally do have a more substantial and ongoing experience tending children than their husbands do and are, on the whole, more keenly interested in child-rearing. The fathers' rights phenomenon begs for some answers and some questions: why is joint custody being championed? Is their cause or their claim about children?

*   *   *

The outcome of divorce can be crushing for many women, especially for those coming out of a long marriage or those who consciously chose to be full-time mothers and now find that their jobs have been eliminated without appeal, and that they must find work outside the home, delegate mothering to someone else and see the children in the spaces between work and housework. If, in the middle of the emotional turmoil surrounding separation and the complex reorganization of family and financial life, a woman is faced with the possibility of her husband suing for custody, it is easy to understand how she might give ground financially in order to stave off that threat of losing her children—to the point of accepting an unjust property settlement and or maintenance levels that are plainly inadequate. Indeed, family law practitioners report that custody

is being dragged into financial negotiations more frequently, often enough that lawyers can no longer counsel their female clients that custody of their children is assured. It no longer is; and it never was absolutely guaranteed. With increasing regularity women go into the separation process telling their lawyers that "no, he'll never fight me for the children; he has no interest in custody," only to eat their words bitterly when he does precisely that a few months later. When things get sticky in settlement negotiations, given the poker-game mentality of these proceedings, custody is too valuable a chip to be kept out of play. The threat of a custody challenge is becoming a routine tactic, as in: "If that's the kind of money you expect, I can do it cheaper. I'll take the children," or "If you are going to demand this large a settlement, I'll sue you for custody."

I am not saying that all men who express interest in retaining custody are disingenuous or out for revenge. The tremendous change in family life over the past two decades in the wake of the sexual and feminist revolutions has affected men as well as women and children. As women questioned traditional marriage and motherhood, notions of fatherhood began to change too. As some men began to participate in the births of their children (their presence in hospital delivery rooms at one time being strictly prohibited, the very idea considered peculiar) and became more actively involved with childcare, naturally they would want to continue their close relationships with their children after separation. Indeed, hundreds, maybe thousands, of couples have organized such an arrangement for themselves privately and have simply worked out their own way of sharing the parenting by mutual agreement and co-operation. With or without help from lawyers, therapists, and friends, they have found ways to parent together while living apart, and formed a new type of relationship as parents. But then, these are not the people who are counted in custody statistics, and no one really knows how they have settled their affairs.

*   *   *

Further Questions

1. A father leaves all child care responsibilities to the mother until they separate, and then he insists that she cannot simultaneously earn a living and take care of the children. Why does he think he is able to?

2. What does "joint custody" of children mean if the divorcing couple are getting along so badly that they cannot make any joint decisions regarding the children's future?

The Anti-Feminist Backlash: XII.5B
Or Why Custody Is a Fatherhood Issue

SUSAN CREAN

Susan Crean claims that "fathers' rights" advocates are not trying for nonsexist settlements of custody, visiting rights, and support payments. Instead, they are trying to make a case against mothers, claiming that it is women—not sexism in the family, work force, and judicial system—who are the cause of family problems, both before and after divorce.

Reading Questions

1. Is the role of supermom (wife, mother, and work force participant) so demanding that a woman can be relieved to shed the first component of the role, that of being a wife? What do you think should be done about the predicament (overwork) of supermoms?

2. In a custody dispute, should the heterosexual nuclear family be perceived as the ideal situation in which to place a child? Which parent would most likely be awarded custody if this were the basis of the decision?

ADVOCATES FOR MEN'S RIGHTS have always been with us in one guise or another, and "fathers' rights" advocates have been on the scene for the better part of a decade. Recently they have been attracting mainstream attention, gathering strength and visibility by taking on a broader (and softer) political agenda. Since Manitoba started the trend in provincial support payment enforcement schemes, their lobbying efforts have intensified and they have been successfully get-ting stories into the papers which paint a picture of men as hard done by, misunderstood, patient fathers-in-exile. Increasingly we are hearing about men who are the innocent victims of malicious women and young girls who make false accusations of sexual abuse against them. By pressing for perfectly reasonable things like paid paternity leave and tax deductions for unmarried fathers who do not live with their children and contribute their upkeep without court orders, moreover, they are able to curry the favour of public opinion and right-thinking liberals who haven't yet glimpsed their real agenda.

* * *

Despite the established facts that men are the main perpetrators of violence and sexual abuse in families and rarely participate in housework or childcare, men's rights advocates would have us believe that the only thing preventing them from turning into kind and skilled parents after they leave the marriage is their ex-wives. And it is only the vindictiveness of their ex-wives that is responsible for their children's problems after separation. Tellingly, the target of men's rights advocates' ire is not the male superstructure and the discriminatory judicial system, but women.

* * *

The case for fathers' rights is a case against mothers; it is not a positive one attempting to deal with sexism from a male perspective; it denies that sexism even exists and blames the gross excesses of male behaviour (rape, abuse, and violence) on women. Instead of admitting the systemic discrimination which debilitates their ex-wives and families after divorce, they claim that the reverse is true, that women are the privileged ones in divorce. And always, whenever the men's rights movement speaks, there comes the sound of whining voices, accusations and stories with villains and victims, no compassion or regret—only the hard, grim face of denial.

* * *

As many writers have reported, the division of labour in the home and the organization of the work force create a disincentive for men and career women to engage in child-rearing. As more women have entered the work force the social expectations for motherhood have simply expanded to include that work, effectively landing modern women with two full-time jobs without the support services obviously required. It means struggling to be Supermom, and it is no wonder that some women find it a relief to shed the third role (that of wife), if only because of the time and energy it requires. But in court, women who stray so much as a jot or a tittle from the straight and narrow ideal of motherhood are likely to find themselves in trouble.

* * *

If she is working-class and poor, a mother's chances of getting good legal advice are as slim as her chances of getting adequately paying work. If she lives in a rural community her isolation and distance from support services work against her. If she is lesbian, although Canadian courts are not supposed to deny custody on the grounds of sexual orientation, chances are her life will be scrutinized and a judge will declare her way of life prejudicial to her children.

Because custody decisionmakers have a picture of the ideal family (which is to say the heterosexual nuclear family) in the back of their minds, it is not surprising that many custody decisions give the children to the parent who can offer the family set-up which most closely resembles it. Boyd* cites several cases where mothers who had to leave the home to work lost out to fathers who were also working full-time, but who could offer substitute female childcare. In one case the father was awarded custody on condition that his mother care for the child, which prompted Boyd's wry comment: "One wonders whether the grandmother herself should not have been competing with the mother for custody of the child." And she further notes, "Paternal grandparents are exhorted to assist fathers in parenting much more frequently than are maternal grandmothers, hinting that the courts view fathers as needing more help in performing childcare than do mothers." In another case, a young doctor who proposed to hire a housekeeper to care for his daughter was given custody, the rationale being that the mother would have to make a

---

* Boyd, Susan B. "Child Custody, Ideology and Female Employment," Unpublished paper, 1986.

similar arrangement because she too was working, despite the fact that the child had been living with the mother for two years, and custody was only claimed by the father when she made a request for increased child support.

Boyd also found a marked tendency for the courts to overplay the contribution of fathers to childcare, often taking the least demonstration of interest as grounds for declaring him an excellent parent. Just as often, his actual contribution to childcare is never even investigated. While mothers are assumed to have difficulty in combining work and mothering, judges "fall over backwards so as not to give the impression they think employed fathers neglected their parenting." In one case Boyd cites, a father was given sole custody of his two young children although their mother was described as warm and demonstrative and he as highly controlled, disciplined, intellectual, and a solitary person. The judge noted, furthermore, that: "It is true that before the separation he did not devote as much time and attention to the children as [his wife] would have liked and that he was preoccupied with his work and with achieving success. It is equally true, however, that he made a significant contribution to the care of the children and to the household even though with respect to the children, his undemonstrative nature may have made it appear that he was not as loving as he might have been." Asks Boyd: "Would a mother have been rewarded for similarly prioritizing her work over the needs of the children?" What about the children? Were they happy to be placed in the custody of their father? Have they found solace and security in the judge's assurance that he is really a much more loving man than he appears to them to be?

* * *

Of course, what this shows is that courts and their various professional attendants are very far removed from the everyday experience of most women and oblivious to the changes taking place in the practice and even the conceptualization of mothering by women. For instance, the idea of lesbian co-parenting is no longer an idea; it exists and by its existence reinvents the very idea of the family. The lesbian family is still based on a two-parent model, two adults connected by an emotional and sexual bond, although the child is the biological offspring of only one. It defies both the language and the conventions of heterosexual family life, and challenges the very definition of "mother." What does the word *mother* mean in such a context, (or, for that matter, the term *father* in a male homosexual family)?

For one thing, the lesbian family demonstrates how terribly narrow the term *mother* is; lesbian couples complain that when the impending birth is announced, people invariably ask who "the mother" is, meaning the biological mother. And what does it do for the verb "to mother"? Of course, fathering has also been undergoing change, attracting the attention of mental health professionals, researchers, and policymakers. As a social phenomenon it has acquired a certain cachet among some men who, for instance, no longer think it sissy work to change the kid's diaper or take her to daycare. Writer and broadcaster David Suzuki reports that one of the biggest responses he has ever had from the public was to a magazine piece he wrote about his experience taking primary care of his two small daughters. In many ways, fatherhood is an idea whose time has come, even though the public fascination with it is superficial—as superficial as is the statistical commitment of men to childcare and housework. It is, just the same, something the women's movement has always seen as valuable and necessary; but it arrived just as the divorce rate was exploding and as fathers were leaving their families in unprecedented numbers.

There is nothing to indicate that men as a group are any more interested in, or capable of delivering, sound twenty-four-hour parenting than they ever were. The joys of fatherhood and the number of men engaging in it are being grossly exaggerated; and, while we all pay lip-service to the idea, we may be missing the point, which is that fatherhood is in crisis. The only people speaking up for it at the moment are fatherhood's greatest enemies: the men's rights activists who are only interested in post-marriage fatherhood as it reflects their personal power. Yet the men's rights phenomenon is having an insidi-ous influence on the ideology and actions of the mainstream of which few people, including pro-gressive men, are aware—an influence which threatens to make fatherhood just another word for patriarchy.

Further Questions

1. Suppose a child has been in the care of one parent for the duration of the child's life. Should custody of the child be transferred to the other parent because this other parent is now in a position to offer the child a better family set-up? If so, what features of the set-up would be relevant to transferring custody?

2. Should the sexual orientation of a parent make any difference to whether he or she becomes the custodial parent? Explain how, if at all, parental sexual orientation makes a differ-ence in matters of custody.

3. If you are a man, do you plan to become actively engaged in care of your children (provided that you have children)? If so, what sorts of things do you plan to do in this area? Would your contributions to childcare be a sufficient basis for your claiming custody of the children if you and your wife should separate?

Suggested Moral of Part XII

One strand of tradition links womanhood strongly with motherhood. Through becoming mothers, bearing and raising children, some women gain a place in the world as well as esteem and respect from others. There are, however, disadvantages to child raising responsibilities, especially when a woman also wants a career in the workplace. One solution, which is meeting with resistance, especially from men, is for the mother and father to share these responsibilities. A common view is that children are better off when raised by their mother; however, this idea explodes in the legal system when the couple separates and the father attempts to take custody of the children, claiming that he would be a better parent. Should a woman become a mother with all these potential hazards in the path of motherhood?

Many women, quite understandably, have difficulties making decisions about whether to have children. But suppose the patriarchal elements infusing parenthood (discussed by the authors in this section) were eliminated and parents could make arrangements for the care of their children in the absence of such influences. Then a woman could choose to be a parent with the same freedom as a man. Under these cir-cumstances, childcare might be more welcome by those choosing to undertake it and not perceived by the individual responsible for it as an unwanted interference with whatever else she wanted to do with her life.

Further Readings for Part XII: Raising Children: Mothers and Fathers

William R. Beer. *Househusbands: Men and Housework in American Families* (South Hadley, MA: J. F. Bergin Publishers, 1983). Housework: why men do it, how they like it, and why more men do not do it.

Jessie Bernard. *The Future of Motherhood* (New York, NY: The Dial Press, 1974). Thorough critique of traditional attitudes toward maternity and a hopeful look toward its future.

Bruno Bettelheim. *The Children of the Dream* (New York, NY: Avon Books, 1969). Somewhat idealized description of communal childrearing on an Israeli kibbutz.

Graham B. Blaine, Jr. *Are Parents Bad for Children?* (New York, NY: Coward, McCann and Geoghegan, 1973).

Jeffrey Blustein. *Parents and Children* (New York, NY: Oxford University Press, 1982). Duties, responsibilities and problems between parents and children.

John Bowlby. *Child Care and the Growth of Love* (Baltimore, MD: Penguin Books, 1973).

Paula J. Caplan. *Don't Blame Mother: Mending the Mother-Daughter Relationship* (New York, NY: Harper & Row, 1989). A psychologist takes a hard broom to Freudian cobwebs.

Nancy Chodorow. *The Reproduction of Mothering* (Berkeley, CA: University of California Press, 1978). Influential book arguing that mothering is doomed to repeat itself in daughters.

Brenda O. Daly and Maureen T. Reddy, eds. *Narrating Mothers: Theorizing Maternal Subjectivities* (Knoxville, TN: The University of Tennessee Press, 1991). What the experience of mothering is like under varying conditions.

Frederick Engels. *The Origin of the Family, Private Property and the State* (New York, NY: International, 1975). The patriarchal family is founded on private property. Women can be freed only through socialism.

Marilyn Fabe and Norma Wikler. *Up Against the Clock: Career Women Speak on the Choice to Have Children* (New York, NY: Random House, 1979).

Janet Finch. *Married to the Job: Wives' Incorporation in Men's Work* (Boston, MA: George Allen and Unwin, 1983). Taking on your husband's job and its impact on your life.

Sigmund Freud. "Femininity" (1933) in Jean Strouse, ed. *Women and Analysis* (New York, NY: Grossman, 1974). Girls' childhoods are so bad that their only hope of normality lies in becoming mothers.

Nancy Friday. *My Mother/My Self* (New York, NY: Delacorte, 1977). Popular book, so it must have struck a responsive chord in many women.

Barbara Furneaux. *Special Parents* (Children with Special Needs Series) (Philadelphia, PA: Open University Press, 1988). The impact of handicapped children on their parents.

Tuula Gordon. *Feminist Mothers* (New York, NY: New York University Press, 1990). Patriarchal construction of motherhood can be combatted by an alternative ideology, feminism.

Geoffrey L. Greif. *Single Fathers* (Lexington, MA: Lexington Books, 1985). What happens when fathers have custody of their children.

Michael Hardy and Graham Crow, eds. *Lone Parenthood* (New York, NY: Harvestor Wheatsheaf, 1991). Coping with the constraints of single parenthood and creating opportunities within it.

Hilary Homans. *The Sexual Politics of Reproduction* (Brookfield, VT: Gower Publishing Co., 1985). Reproduction in a social context of male control.

Dwight J. Ingle. *Who Should Have Children?* (New York, NY: Bobbs-Merrill, 1973). Justification of selective population control.

Miriam M. Johnson. *Strong Mothers, Weak Wives: The Search for Gender Equality* (Berkeley, CA: University of California Press, 1988). Critique of popular ideas on motherhood.

Sheila B. Kamerman and Alfred J. Kahn. *Mothers Alone: Strategies for a Time of Change* (Dover, MA: Auburn House Publishing Co., 1988). Questions of going back to work, public support, personal life, etc.

Charlie Lewis and Margaret O'Brien, eds. *Reassessing Fatherhood: New Observations on Fathers and the Modern Family* (Newbury Park, CA: Sage Publications, 1987). How changes in the fatherhood role affect fathers' experiences.

Robert A. Lewis and Robert E. Salt, eds. *Men in Families* (Newbury Park, CA: Sage Publications, 1986). Response to Barbara Ehrenreich's *The Hearts of Men* (see Further Readings for Part VI), attempting to explain why men want to be involved in marriage and parenthood.

Elizabeth A. Mulroy, ed. *Women as Single Parents: Confronting Institutional Barriers in the Courts, the Workplace and the Housing Market* (Dover, MA: Auburn House Publishing Co., 1988).

Onora O'Neill and William Ruddick, eds. *Having Children: Philosophical and Legal Reflections on Parenthood* (New York, NY: Oxford University Press, 1979).

Adrienne Rich. *Of Women Born: Motherhood as Experience and Institution* (New York, NY: W. W. Norton, 1976). Discussion of motherhood in patriarchy, beginning with personal experience.

Bryan E. Robinson and Robert L. Barret. *The Developing Father: Emerging Roles in Contemporary Society* (New York, NY: The Guilford Press, 1986). Includes single fathers, stepfathers, gay fathers, and teenage fathers.

Barbara Katz Rothman. *Recreating Motherhood: Ideology and Technology in a Patriarchal Society* (New York, NY: W. W. Norton and Co., 1989). Woman-centered vision of reshaping technology to serve our purposes; includes more "fathering" on the part of men.

Sara Ruddick. *Maternal Thinking* (Boston, MA: Beacon Press, 1989). Maternal thinking can be done by women or men and can be directed at more situations than child raising.

Anna and Arnold Silverman. *The Case Against Having Children* (New York, NY: David MacKay Co., 1971). Don't have children for the wrong reasons. There are alternatives.

Joyce Trebilcot, ed. *Mothering: Essays in Feminist Theory* (Totowa, NJ: Rowman and Allenheld, 1984). Excellent collection of feminist writings on mothering.

Estela V. Welldon. *Mother, Madonna and Whore* (London: Free Association Books, 1988). Motherhood is sometimes chosen for unconscious, perverse reasons.

Part XIII

Youngsters and Oldsters

Introduction

AGEISM, OPPRESSION OF OLDER PEOPLE, has only recently come to public attention, even within feminism and movements of other oppressed groups. Relatively little
has been written on this subject, despite the fact that aging affects everyone. The writings in this section address some of the problems of aging and focus on the oppression
of older women by younger women as an offshoot of patriarchy.

XIII.1   Why Young Women Are More Conservative

GLORIA STEINEM

Gloria Steinem describes the typical mentality of younger women, the women on a college or university campus in particular. Their optimistic perspective, due partly to the value placed on them by patriarchal society, tends to make them lean toward conservatism. Many of them can be expected to develop a more realistic outlook on women's situations as they grow older.

Other selections by Steinem appear in Parts I and XI.

Reading Questions

1. As a young woman on a campus, do you feel that you are in the position of a consumer of services, paid for by you, your family, the government, or your institution's endowment? If so, do you think you have certain privileges as a consumer, relative to those who provide these services?

2. Is it true that male-dominated cultures place the most value on younger women because they have full potential for work, sex, and childbearing? If male dominance is not the source of value in younger women, what is? Or is youth not particularly valuable in a woman?

3. Do campus women sometimes participate in a female guilt trip in which they feel that if they are not studying hard and having a wonderful personal life at the same time, it is primarily their own fault? Give some examples of such guilt trips. Do men participate in these to the same extent as do women?

IF YOU HAD ASKED ME a decade or more ago, I certainly would have said the campus was the first place to look for the feminist or any other revolution. I also would have assumed that student-age women, like student-age men, were much more likely to be activist and open to change than their parents. After all, campus revolts have a long and well-publicized tradition, from the students of medieval France, whose "heresy" was suggesting that the university be separate from the church, through the anticolonial student riots of British India; from students who led the cultural revolution of the People's Republic of China, to campus demonstrations against the Shah of Iran. Even in this country, with far less tradition of student activism, the populist movement to end the war in Vietnam was symbolized by campus protests and mistrust of anyone over thirty.

It has taken me many years of traveling as a feminist speaker and organizer to understand that I was wrong about women; at least, about women acting on their own behalf. In activism, as in so many other things, I had been educated to assume that men's cultural pattern was the natural or the only one. If student years were the peak time of rebellion and openness to change for men, then the same must be true for women. In fact, a decade of listening to every kind of women's group—from brown-bag lunchtime lectures organized by office workers to all-night rap sessions at campus women's centers; from housewives' self-help groups to campus rallies—has convinced me that the reverse is more often true. Women may be the one group that grows more radical with age. Though some students are big exceptions to this rule, women in general don't begin to challenge the politics of our own lives until later.

Looking back, I realize that this pattern has been true for my life, too. My college years were full of uncertainties and the personal conservatism that comes from trying to win approval and fit into the proper grown-up and womanly role, whether that means finding a well-to-do man to be supported by or a male radical to support. Nonetheless, I went right on assuming that brave exploring youth and cowardly conservative old age were the norms for everybody, and that I must be just an isolated and guilty accident. Though every generalization based on female culture has many exceptions, and should never be used as a crutch or excuse, I think we might be less hard on ourselves and each other as students, feel better about our potential for change as we grow older—and educate reporters who announce feminism's demise because its red-hot center is not on campus—if we figured out that for most of us as women, the traditional college period is an unrealistic and cautious time. Consider a few of the reasons.

As students, women are probably treated with more equality than we ever will be again. For one thing, we're consumers. The school is only too glad to get the tuitions we pay, or that our families or government grants pay on our behalf. With population rates declining because of women's increased power over childbearing, that money is even more vital to a school's existence. Yet more than most consumers, we're too transient to have much power as a group. If our families are paying our tuition, we may have even less power.

As young women, whether students or not, we're still in the stage most valued by male-dominant cultures: we have our full potential as workers, wives, sex partners, and childbearers.

That means we haven't yet experienced the life events that are most radicalizing for women: en-

tering the paid-labor force and discovering how women are treated there; marrying and finding out that it is not yet an equal partnership; having children and discovering who is responsible for them and who is not; and aging, still a greater penalty for women than for men.

Furthermore, new ambitions nourished by the rebirth of feminism may make young women feel and behave a little like a classical immigrant group. We are determined to prove ourselves, to achieve academic excellence, and to prepare for interesting and successful careers. More noses are kept to more grindstones in an effort to demonstrate newfound abilities, and perhaps to allay suspicions that women still have to have more and better credentials than men. This doesn't leave much time for activism. Indeed, we may not yet know that it is necessary.

In addition, the very progress into previously all-male careers that may be revolutionary for women is seen as conservative and conformist by outside critics. Assuming male radicalism to be the measure of change, they interpret any concern with careers as evidence of "campus conservatism." In fact, "dropping out" may be a departure for men, but "dropping in" is a new thing for women. Progress lies in the direction we have not been.

Like most groups of the newly arrived or awakened, our faith in education and paper degrees also has yet to be shaken. For instance, the percentage of women enrolled in colleges and universities has been increasing at the same time that the percentage of men has been decreasing. Among students entering college in 1978, women *outnumbered* men for the first time. This hope of excelling at the existing game is probably reinforced by the greater cultural pressure on females to be "good girls" and observe somebody else's rules.

Though we may know intellectually that we need to have new games with new rules, we probably haven't quite absorbed such facts as the high unemployment rate among female Ph.D.s; the lower average salary among women college graduates of all races than among counterpart males who graduated from high school or less; the middle-management ceiling against which even those eagerly hired new business-school graduates seem to bump their heads after five or ten years; and the barrier-breaking women in nontraditional fields who become the first fired when recession hits. Sadly enough, we may have to personally experience some of these reality checks before we accept the idea that lawsuits, activism, and group pressure will have to accompany our individual excellence and crisp new degrees.

Then there is the female guilt trip, student edition. If we're not sailing along as planned, it must be *our* fault. If our mothers didn't "do anything" with their educations, it must have been *their* fault. If we can't study as hard as we think we must (because women still have to be better prepared than men), and have a substantial personal and sexual life at the same time (because women are supposed to care more about relationships than men do), then we feel inadequate, as if each of us were individually at fault for a problem that is actually culture-wide.

I've yet to be on a campus where most women weren't worrying about some aspect of combining marriage, children, and a career. I've yet to find one where many men were worrying about the same thing. Yet women will go right on suffering from the double-role problem and terminal guilt until men are encouraged, pressured, or otherwise forced, individually and collectively, to integrate themselves into the "women's work" of raising children and homemaking. Until then, and until there are changed job patterns to allow equal parenthood, children will go right on growing up with the belief that only women can be loving and nurturing, and only men can be intellectual or active outside the home. Each half of the world will go on limiting the full range of its human talent.

Finally, there is the intimate political training that hits women in the teens and early twenties: the countless ways we are still brainwashed into assuming that women are dependent on men for our basic identities, both in our work and our personal lives, much more than vice versa. After all, if we're going to enter a marriage system that's still legally designed for a person and a half, submit to an economy in which women still average about fifty-nine cents on the dollar earned by men, and work mainly as support staff and assistants, or *co*-directors and *vice*-presidents at best, then we have to be convinced that we are not whole people on our own.

In order to make sure that we will see ourselves as half-people, and thus be addicted to getting our identity from serving others, society tries hard to convert us as young women into "man-junkies"; that is, into people who are addicted to regular shots of male-approval and presence, both professionally and personally. We need a man standing next to us, actually and figuratively, whether it's at work, on Saturday night, or throughout life. (If only men realized how little it matters *which* man is standing there, they would understand that this addiction depersonalizes them, too.) Given the danger to a male-dominant system if young women stop internalizing this political message of derived identity, it's no wonder that those who try to kick the addiction—and, worse yet, to help other women do the same—are likely to be regarded as odd or dangerous by everyone from parents to peers.

With all that pressure combined with little experience, it's no wonder that younger women are often less able to support each other. Even young women who espouse feminist goals as individuals may refrain from identifying themselves as "feminist": it's okay to want equal pay for yourself (just one small reform) but it's not okay to want equal pay for women as a group (an economic revolution). Some retreat into individualized career obsessions as a way of avoiding this dangerous discovery of shared experience with women as a group. Others retreat into the safe middle ground of "I'm not a feminist but. . . ." Still others become politically active, but only on issues that are taken seriously by their male counterparts. . . .

This cultural pattern of youthful conservatism makes the growing number of older women going back to school very important. They are life examples and pragmatic activists who radicalize women young enough to be their daughters. Now that the median female undergraduate age in this country is twenty-seven because so many older women have returned, the campus is becoming a major place for cross-generational connections.

None of this should denigrate the courageous efforts of young women, especially women on campus, and the many changes they've pioneered. On the contrary, they should be seen as even more remarkable for surviving the conservative pressures, recognizing societal problems they haven't yet fully experienced, and organizing successfully in the midst of a transient student population. Every women's history course, rape hot line, or campus newspaper that is finally covering *all* the news; every feminist professor whose job has been created or tenure saved by student pressure, or male administrator whose consciousness has been permanently changed; every counselor who's stopped guiding women one way and men another; every lawsuit that's been fueled by student energies against unequal athletic funds or graduate school requirements: all those accomplishments are even more impressive when seen against the backdrop of the female pattern of activism. . . .

. . . [T]he definition of "political," on campus as elsewhere, tends to be limited to who's running for president, who's demonstrating against corporate investments in South Africa, or which is the "moral" side of some conventional revolution, preferably one that is thousands of miles away.

As important as such activities are, they are also the most comfortable ones when we're young. They provide a sense of virtue without much disruption in the power structure of our daily lives. Even when the most consistent energies on campus are actually concentrated around feminist issues, they may be treated as apolitical and invisible. Asked "What's happening on campus?" a student may reply, "The antinuke movement," even though that resulted in one demonstration of two hours, while student antirape squads have been patrolling the campus every night for two years and women's studies have begun to transform the very textbooks we read.

No wonder reporters and sociologists looking for revolution on campus often miss the depth of feminist change and activity that is really there. Women students themselves may dismiss it as not political and not serious. Certainly, it rarely comes in the masculine sixties style of bombing buildings or burning draft cards. In fact, it goes much deeper than protesting a temporary symptom—say, the draft—and challenges the right of one group to dominate another, which is the disease itself.

Young women have a big task of resisting pressures and challenging definitions. Their increasing success is a miracle of foresight and courage that should make us all proud. But they should know that they, too, may grow more radical with age.

One day, an army of gray-haired women may quietly take over the earth.

Further Questions

1. As a young woman student, do you feel your main focus should be on proving yourself and preparing for an interesting, successful career, especially if the presence of women is relatively new in your field? Are young men experiencing the same types of difficulty and, if so, to a greater or lesser extent than young women?

2. What, if anything, can be done for women who are "man-junkies," addicted to regular shots of male approval and presence to get on well in life? Are there men who are "woman-junkies" and, if so, what can be done to help them?

3. Do you find it difficult to call yourself "feminist" even though you share many goals with feminism? Is it more or less difficult to do this if you are a man?

XIII.2   Age, Race, Class, and Sex: Women Redefining Difference

AUDRE LORDE

Audre Lorde believes that it too often happens that differences among people cause fear, loathing, rejection, and oppression. Ageism is a belief in the inherent superiority of one group of people over another, conjoined with a belief in the right to dominate the group thought inferior.

Another selection by Lorde appears in Part I.

Reading Questions

1. Do you think that ideas of young people are more suited to today's world than those of older people? Are young people more aware of social realities because they bring fresh ideas to what they find, or are older people better at assessing social realities because they have had more experience?

2. Suppose an older person sometimes despairs at young people's making the same mistakes her generation did, not having learned anything from past mistakes. Is she justified in doing so? Should young people pay more attention to what older people say, or are they better off making their own mistakes and learning from them?

3. If one group of people is oppressing another, is it the responsibility of the oppressed to speak up and make their voices heard by the oppressors? Does the oppressor group have any responsibilities to the oppressed to learn of their situation, such as asking the oppressed to speak and listening to them when they do?

MUCH OF WESTERN EUROPEAN HISTORY conditions us to see human differences in simplistic opposition to each other: dominant/subordinate, good/bad, up/down, superior/inferior. In a society where the good is defined in terms of profit rather than in terms of human need, there must always be some group of people who, through systematized oppression, can be made to feel surplus, to occupy the place of the dehumanized inferior. Within this society, that group is made up of Black and Third World people, working-class people, older people, and women.

As a forty-nine-year-old Black lesbian feminist socialist mother of two, including one boy, and a member of an inter-racial couple, I usually find myself a part of some group defined as other, deviant, inferior, or just plain wrong. Traditionally, in american society, it is the members of oppressed, objectified groups who are expected to stretch out and bridge the gap between the actualities of our lives and the consciousness of our oppressor. For in order to survive, those of us for whom oppression is as american as apple pie have always had to be watchers, to become familiar with the language and manners of the oppressor, even sometimes adopting them for some illusion of protection. Whenever the need for some pretense of communication arises, those who profit from our oppression call upon us to share our knowledge with them. In other words, it is the responsibility of the oppressed to teach the oppressors their mistakes. I am responsible for educating teachers who dismiss my children's culture in school. Black and Third World people are expected to educate white people as to our humanity. Women are expected to educate men. Lesbians and gay men are expected to educate the heterosexual world. The oppressors maintain their position and evade responsibility for their own actions. There is a constant drain of energy which might be better used in redefining ourselves and devising realistic scenarios for altering the present and constructing the future.

Institutionalized rejection of difference is an absolute necessity in a profit economy which needs outsiders as surplus people. As members of such an economy, we have all been programmed to respond to the human differences between us with fear and loathing and to handle that difference in one of three ways: ignore it, and if that is not possible, copy it if we think it is dominant, or destroy it if we think it is subordinate. But we have no patterns for relating across our human differences as equals. As a result, those differences have been misnamed and misused in the service of separation and confusion.

Certainly there are very real differences between us of race, age, and sex. But it is not those differences between us that are separating us. It is rather our refusal to recognize those differences, and to examine the distortions which result from our misnaming them and their effects upon human behavior and expectation.

Racism, the belief in the inherent superiority of one race over all others and thereby the right to dominance. Sexism, the belief in the inherent superiority of one sex over the other and thereby the right to dominance. Ageism. Heterosexism. Elitism. Classism.

It is a lifetime pursuit for each one of us to extract these distortions from our living at the same time as we recognize, reclaim, and define those differences upon which they are imposed. For we have all been raised in a society where those distortions were endemic within our living. Too often, we pour the energy needed for recognizing and exploring difference into pretending those differences are insurmountable barriers, or that they do not exist at all. This results in a voluntary isolation, or false and treacherous connections. Either way, we do not develop tools for using human difference as a springboard for creative change within our lives. We speak not of human difference, but of human deviance.

Somewhere, on the edge of consciousness, there is what I call a *mythical norm*, which each one of us within our hearts knows "that is not me." In america, this norm is usually defined as white, thin, male, young, heterosexual, christian, and financially secure. It is within this mythical norm that the trappings of power reside within this society. Those of us who stand outside that power often identify one way in which we are different, and we assume that to be the primary cause of all oppression, forgetting other distortions around difference, some of which we ourselves may be practising. By and large within the women's movement today, white women focus upon their oppression as women and ignore differences of race, sexual preference, class, and age. There is a pretense to a homogeneity of experience covered by the word *sisterhood* that does not in fact exist.

Unacknowledged class differences rob women of each other's energy and creative insight. Recently a women's magazine collective made the decision for one issue to print only prose, saying poetry was a less "rigorous" or "serious" art form. Yet even the form our creativity takes is often a class issue. Of all the art forms, poetry is the most economical. It is the one which is the most secret, which requires the least physical labor, the least material, and the one which can be done between shifts, in the hospital pantry, on the subway, and on scraps of surplus paper. Over the last few years, writing a novel on tight finances, I came to appreciate the enormous differences in the material demands between poetry and prose. As we reclaim our literature, poetry has been the major voice of poor, working class, and Colored women. A room of one's own may be a necessity for writing prose, but so are reams of paper, a typewriter, and plenty of time. The actual requirements to produce the visual arts also help determine, along class lines, whose art is whose. In this day of inflated prices for material, who are our sculptors, our painters, our photographers?

When we speak of a broadly based women's culture, we need to be aware of the effect of class and economic differences on the supplies available for producing art.

As we move toward creating a society within which we can each flourish, ageism is another distortion of relationship which interferes with our vision. By ignoring the past, we are encouraged to repeat its mistakes. The "generation gap" is an important social tool for any repressive society. If the younger members of a community view the older members as contemptible or suspect or excess, they will never be able to join hands and examine the living memories of the community, nor ask the all important question, 'Why?' This gives rise to a historical amnesia that keeps us working to invent the wheel every time we have to go to the store for bread.

We find ourselves having to repeat and relearn the same old lessons over and over that our mothers did because we do not pass on what we have learned, or because we are unable to listen. For instance, how many times has this all been said before? For another, who would have believed that once again our daughters are allowing their bodies to be hampered and purgatoried by girdles and high heels and hobble skirts? . . .

Further Questions

1. Is a normal person (a paradigm by which others are judged) white, thin, male, young, heterosexual, and financially secure? Is it disturbing when we don't meet one or more of these criteria? What is it that makes these criteria so important?

2. Within an oppressed group, how good are we at recognizing yet further forms of oppression that happen to those in the group other than ourselves? How can we increase our awareness of others' problems?

3. If we do not listen to older people and take them seriously, will we miss out on the "living memories" of our community? Are these "living memories" important for us to know about? Discuss, in connection with some examples.

From Maturity to Old Age   XIII.3

SIMONE DE BEAUVOIR

Simone de Beauvoir describes the plight of the aging woman who has completed what tradition has expected of her. She married and raised children who are now able to do without her. Now, it seems, with half of her adult life before her, she has nothing left to do.

Other selections from de Beauvoir's *The Second Sex* appear in parts I, IV, VI, and X.

Reading Questions

1. To what extent is a woman's social value dependent on her fertility and the erotic attractiveness only the relatively young possess? To what extent is this true of men as well?

2. Is growing old a horrible and depressing idea for most people? If so, why? Is there anything about growing old that we can look forward to?

3. As a woman, if you anticipate that you will have to spend part of the end of your life without a man, do you wonder what will become of you? Would you be less worried about being alone if you were a man? Do you think you will be able to look to other women for companionship?

THE INDIVIDUAL LIFE HISTORY of woman—because she is still bound up in her female functions—depends in much greater degree than that of man upon her physiological destiny; and the curve of this destiny is much more uneven, more discontinuous, than the masculine curve. Each period in the life of woman is uniform and monotonous; but the transitions from one stage to another are dangerously abrupt; they are manifested in crises—puberty, sexual initiation, the menopause—which are much more decisive than in the male. Whereas man grows old gradually, woman is suddenly deprived of her femininity; she is still relatively young when she loses the erotic attractiveness and the fertility which, in the view of society and in her own, provide the justification of her existence and her opportunity for happiness. With no future, she still has about one half of her adult life to live.

"The dangerous age" is marked by certain organic disturbances, but what lends them importance is their symbolic significance. The crisis of the "change of life" is felt much less keenly by women who have not staked everything on their femininity; those who engage in heavy work—in the household or outside—greet the disappearance of the monthly burden with relief; the peasant woman, the workman's wife, constantly under the threat of new pregnancies, are happy when, at long last, they no longer run this risk. At this juncture, as at many others, woman's discomforts come less from her body than from the anxious concerns she feels regarding it. The moral drama commonly begins before the physiological phenomena have appeared, and it comes to an end only after they have long since been done away with.

Long before the eventual mutilation, woman is haunted by the horror of growing old. The mature man is involved in enterprises more important than those of love; his erotic ardor is less keen than in the days of his youth; and since in him the passive qualities of an object are not called for, the changes in his face and body do not destroy his attractiveness. In woman, on the contrary, it is usually toward thirty-five, when all inhibitions have been finally overcome, that full erotic development is attained. Then it is that her sexual desires are strongest and she most keenly wishes to have them satisfied; she has gambled much more heavily than man on the sexual values she possesses; to hold her husband and to assure herself of his protection, and to keep most of her jobs, it is necessary for her to be attractive, to please; she is allowed no hold on the world save through the mediation of some man. What is to become of her when she no longer has any hold on him? This is what she anxiously asks herself while she helplessly looks on at the degeneration of this fleshly object which she identifies with herself. She puts up a battle. But hair-dye, skin treatments, plastic surgery, will never do more than prolong her dying youth. Perhaps she can at least deceive her mirror. But when the first hints come of that fated and irreversible process which is to destroy the whole edifice built up during puberty, she feels the fatal touch of death itself.

One might think that the woman most ardently enraptured with her youth and beauty would be the one to be most disturbed; but not at all: the narcissist is too concerned with her person not to have foreseen its inevitable decline and made her preparations for retreat. She will suffer, to be sure, from her mutilation, but at least she will not be taken by surprise, and she will become adapted soon enough. The woman who has been forgetful of self, devoted, self-sacrificing, will be much more upset by the sudden revelation: "I had only one life to live; think what my lot has been, and look at me now!" To the astonishment of everyone, a radical change occurs in her: what has happened is that, dislodged from her sheltering occupations, her plans disrupted, she finds herself suddenly, without recourse, put face-to-face with herself. Beyond that milestone against which she has unexpectedly stumbled, it seems to her that there will be nothing more for her to do than merely survive her better days; her body will promise nothing; the dreams, the longings she has not made good, will remain forever unfulfilled. In this perspective she reviews the past; the moment has come to draw a line across the page, to make up her accounts; she balances her books. And she is appalled at the narrow limitations life has imposed upon her. . . .

. . . Sometimes she gives herself up to a dreamy and passive gloominess. But more often she suddenly undertakes to save her lost existence. She makes a show of this personality which she has just discovered in contrasting it with the meanness of her fate; she proclaims its merits, she imperiously demands that justice be done it. Matured by experience, she feels that at last she is capable of making her mark; she would like to get into action again. And first of all, she tries with pathetic urgency to turn back the flight of time. A woman of maternal type will assert that she can still have a child: she tries passionately to create life once again. A sensual woman will endeavor to ensnare one more lover. The coquette is more than ever anxious to please. One and all, they declare that they never felt so young. They want to persuade others that the passage of time has never really touched them; they begin to "dress young," they assume childish airs. The aging woman well knows that if she ceases to be an erotic object, it is not only because her flesh no longer has fresh bounties for men; it is also because her past, her experience, make her, willy-nilly, a person; she has struggled, loved, willed, suffered, enjoyed, on her own account. This independence is intimidating; she tries to disown it; she exaggerates her femininity, she adorns herself, she uses perfume, she makes herself all charm, all grace, pure immanence. She babbles to men in a childish voice and with naïve glances of admiration, and she chatters on about when she was a little girl; she chirps instead of talking, she claps her hands, she bursts out laughing. And she enacts this comedy with a certain sincerity. For her new interests, her desire to get out of the old routine and begin anew, make her feel that she is starting life again.

But in fact there is no question of a real start; she sees in the world no objectives toward which she might reach out in a free and effective manner. Her activity takes an eccentric, incoherent, and fruitless form, because she can compensate only in a symbolic way for the mistakes and failures of the past. For one thing, the woman of the age we are considering will try to realize all her wishes of childhood and adolescence before it is too late: she may go back to her piano, take up sculpture, writing, travel, she may learn skiing or study foreign languages. She now welcomes with open arms—still before it is too late—everything she has previously denied herself. . . .

But the world has not been changed; the peaks remain inaccessible; the messages received —however brilliantly manifest—are hard to decipher; the inner illuminations fade; before the glass stands a woman who in spite of everything has grown one day older since yesterday. The moments of exaltation are succeeded by sad hours of depression. The organism manifests this rhythm because the decline of the female sex hormones is compensated for by an overactivity of the pituitary gland; but above all it is the psychological state that governs this alternation of mood. For the woman's restlessness, her illusions, her fevor, are only a defense reaction against the overruling fatality of what has been. Once more anguish is at the throat of the woman whose life is already done before death has taken her. . . .

It is in the autumn and winter of life that woman is freed from her chains; she takes advantage of her age to escape the burdens that weigh on her; she knows her husband too well to let him intimidate her any longer, she eludes his embraces, at his side she organizes a life of her own—in friendship, indifference, or hostility. If his decline is faster than hers, she assumes control of the couple's affairs. She can also permit herself defiance of fashion and of "what people will say"; she is freed from social obligations, dieting, and the care of her beauty. As for her children, they are old enough to get along without her, they are getting married, they are leaving home. Rid of

her duties, she finds freedom at last. Unfortunately, in every woman's story recurs the fact we have verified throughout the history of woman: she finds this freedom at the very time when she can make no use of it. This recurrence is in no wise due to chance: patriarchal society gave all the feminine functions the aspect of a service, and woman escapes slavery only at times when she loses all effectiveness. Toward fifty she is in full possession of her powers; she feels she is rich in experience; that is the age at which men attain the highest positions, the most important posts; as for her, she is put into retirement. She has been taught only to devote herself to someone, and nobody wants her devotion any more. Useless, unjustified, she looks forward to the long, unpromising years she has yet to live, and she mutters: "No one needs me!" . . .

The actress, the dancer, the singer become teachers: they mold pupils; the intellectual—like Mme de Charrière in her Colombier retreat—indoctrinates disciples; the devotee gathers spiritual daughters about her; the woman of gallantry becomes a madam. If they bring an ardent zeal to their proselyting, it is never through pure interest in the field of effort; what they are passionately seeking is reincarnation in their protégées. Their tyrannical generosity gives rise to almost the same conflicts as those between mothers and daughters united by ties of blood. It is also possible to adopt grandchildren; and grandaunts and godmothers readily play a role like that of the grandmother. But in any case it is very rare for a woman to find in her posterity—natural or adopted—a justification for her declining years: she fails to make the career of a single one of these young existences truly hers. Either she persists in the effort to take it over and is consumed in struggles and scenes that leave her disappointed and exhausted; or she resigns herself to no more than a modest participation, as usually happens. The older mother and the grandmother repress their ideas of domination, they conceal their resentments; they content themselves with whatever their children finally give them. But in that case they get little help from them. They are left to face the desert of the future without occupation, a prey to loneliness, regret, and boredom.

Here we come upon the sorry tragedy of the aged woman: she realizes she is useless; all her life long the middle-class woman has often had to solve the ridiculous problem of how to kill time. But when the children are grown, the husband a made man or at least settled down, the time must still be killed somehow. Fancywork was invented to mask their horrible idleness; hands embroider, they knit, they are in motion. This is no real work, for the object produced is not the end in view; its importance is trifling, and to know what to do with it is often a problem—one can get rid of it, perhaps, by giving it to a friend or to a charitable organization, or by cluttering the mantelpiece or center table. This is no longer a game that in its uselessness expresses the pure joy of living; and it is hardly an escape, since the mind remains vacant. It is the "absurd amusement" described by Pascal; with the needle or the crochet-hook, woman sadly weaves the very nothingness of her days. Water-colors, music, reading serve in much the same way; the unoccupied woman, in applying herself to such matters, is not trying to extend her grasp on the world, but only to relieve her boredom. An activity that does not open the future falls back into vain immanence; the idle woman opens a book and throws it aside, opens the piano only to close it, resumes her embroidering, yawns, and finally takes up the telephone. . . .

But it does happen that, in spite of everything, certain of the women we are considering are entirely committed to some enterprise and become truly effective; these women are no longer seeking merely to occupy their time, they have goals in view; producers in their own right, they are outside the parasitic category we are considering here. But this about-face is rare. The majority of these women, in their private or public activities, do not have in mind a result to be achieved, but merely some way of occupying themselves—and no occupation is worth while when it is only a means of killing time. Many of them are adversely affected

by this; having behind them a life already finished, they are confused in much the same way as adolescents before whom life is not yet open; they feel no pull, around them in both cases is the wasteland; contemplating any action, they mutter: "What's the use?" But the adolescent male is drawn willy-nilly into a masculine way of life that discloses responsibilities, aims, values; he is thrown out into the world, he makes decisions, he commits himself to some enterprise. If it is suggested to the older woman that she should start out toward a new future, she will sadly reply that it is too late. Not that henceforth her time is limited, for a woman goes into retirement very early; but she lacks the spirit, the confidence, the hope, the anger, that would enable her to look around and find new goals.[1] She takes refuge in the routine that has always been her lot; repetition becomes her pattern. . . .

Old women take pride in their independence; they begin at last to view the world through their own eyes; they note that they have been duped and deceived all their lives; sane and mistrustful, they often develop a pungent cynicism. In particular, the woman who "has lived" knows men as no man does, for she has seen in man not the image on public view but the contingent individual, the creature of circumstance, that each man in the absence of his peers shows himself to be. She knows women also, for they show themselves without reserve only to other women: she has been behind the scenes. But if her experience enables her to unmask deceits and lies, it is not sufficient to show her the truth. Amused or bitter, the wisdom of the old woman still remains wholly negative: it is in the nature of opposition, indictment, denial; it is sterile. In her thinking as in her acts, the highest form of liberty available to the woman parasite is stoical defiance or skeptical irony. At no time of life does she succeed in being at once effective and independent.

NOTE

1. Few indeed are those, like Grandma Moses, the celebrated American painter, who take to new and fruitful work in their old age.—TR.

Further Questions

1. Do you look forward to an age when you will be retired from your tasks in life (children, job, etc.)? At the same time do you fear that there will be nothing much to do (within your means) after all this is over? Does your answer to this question depend on your gender?

2. Will it be good or bad for you to reach a time in life when you can say "No one needs me!"? Would it be better or worse if you were of the other gender?

3. Do you believe that, at the end of life, the truth will be revealed, or that you will have learned falsehoods? Exactly what truth are you expecting to be revealed? What kinds of falsehoods do you expect to have learned?

It Hurts to Be Alive and Obsolete   XIII.4

ZOE MOSS

Zoe Moss (a pseudonym she used for fear of losing her job for publishing this writing) speaks of the aging (43-year-old) woman, alive and obsolete. The world, she says, has no further use for her at that age.

Reading Questions

1. According to the media, is growing old one of the worst things that can happen to a woman? Give some examples. Does the media send the same message—or a different one—to men regarding aging?

2. Would a woman look out of place if she attended an important event wearing clothes that were five or six years out of date? Can a younger woman defy fashion more easily than an older woman? Is it easier for men to keep wearing out-dated clothes than it is for women?

3. Is it more difficult for a woman to find companionship of any sort when she is over forty? If so, is this because she rejects other people or because they reject her? Would finding companionship be easier if she were a man?

WHAT, FAT, FORTY-THREE, and I dare to think I'm still a person? No, I am an invisible lump. I belong in a category labelled *a priori* without interest to anyone. I am not even expected to interest myself. A middle-aged woman is comic by definition.

In this commodity culture, we are urged and coerced into defining ourselves by buying objects that demonstrate that we are, or which tell us that they will make us feel, young, affluent, fashionable. Imagine a coffee table with the best-sellers of five years ago carefully displayed. You giggle. A magazine that is old enough—say, a *New Yorker* from 1944 with the models looking healthy and almost buxom in their padded jackets—or a dress that is far enough gone not to

give the impression that perhaps you had not noticed fashions had changed, can become campy
and delightful. But an out-of-date woman is only
embarrassing.

The mass media tell us all day and all evening
long that we are inadequate, mindless, ugly, disgusting in ourselves. We must try to resemble
perfect plastic objects, so that no one will notice
what we really are. In ourselves we smell bad,
shed dandruff, our breath has an odor, our hair
stands up or falls out, we sag or stick out where
we shouldn't. We can only fool people into liking
us by using magic products that make us products, too.

Women, especially, are commodities. There is
always a perfect plastic woman. Girls are always
curling their hair or ironing it, binding their
breasts or padding them. Think of the girls with
straight hips and long legs skulking through the
1890's with its women defined as having breasts
the size of pillows and hips like divans. Think of
the Rubens woman today forever starving and
dieting and crawling into rubber compression
chambers that mark her flesh with livid lines and
squeeze her organs into knots.

If a girl were to walk into a party in the clothes
of just five or six years past, in the make-up and
hairstyle of just that slight gap of time, no one
would want to talk to her, no man would want to
dance with her. Yet what has all that to do with
even a man and a woman in bed? This is not only
the middle class I am talking about. I have seen
hippies react the same way to somebody wearing
old straight clothes.

It is a joke, but a morbid one. My daughter
has a girlfriend who always laughs with her hand
up to her mouth because she is persuaded her
teeth are yellow, and that yellow teeth are hideous. She seems somber and never will she enjoy a
natural belly laugh. Most young girls walk
around with the conviction that some small part
of their anatomy (nose, breasts, knees, chin) is so
large or so small or so misshapen that their whole
body appears to be built around that part, and all
of their activities must camouflage it.

My daughter is a senior in college. She already
talks about her "youth" with a sad nostalgia. She
is worried because she is not married. That she
has not met anyone that she wants to live that
close to, does not seem to figure in her anxiety.
Everything confirms in her a sense of time passing, that she will be left behind, unsold on the
shelf. She already peers into the mirror for wrinkles and buys creams and jellies to rub into her
skin. Her fear angers me but leaves me helpless.
She is alienated from her body because her
breasts are big and do not stand out like the
breasts of store mannequins. She looks twenty-
one. I look forty-three.

I want to beg her not to begin worrying, not
to let in the dreadful daily gnawing already.
Everyone born grows up, grows older, and ages
every day until he dies. But every day in seventy
thousand ways this society tells a woman that it is
her sin and her guilt that she has a real living
body. How can a woman respect herself when
every day she stands before her mirror and accuses her face of betraying her, because every day
she is, indeed, a day older.

Everything she reads, every comic strip, every
song, every cartoon, every advertisement, every
book and movie tells her that a woman over
thirty is ugly and disgusting. She is a bag. She is
to be escaped from. She is no longer an object of
prestige consumption. For her to have real living
sexual desires is obscene. Her touch is thought to
contaminate. No man "seduces" a woman older
than him: there is no conquest. It is understood
she would be "glad for a touch of it." Since she
would be glad, there can be no pleasure in the
act. Either this society is mad or I am mad. It is
considered incredible that a woman might have
had experiences that are valuable or interesting
and that have enriched her as a person. No, men
may mature, but women just obsolesce.

All right, says the woman, don't punish me! I
won't do wrong! I won't get older! Now, if a
woman has at least an upper-middle-class income, no strong commitments such as a real career or a real interest in religion or art or politics;

if she has a small family and hired help; if she has certain minimal genetic luck; if she has the ability to be infinitely fascinated by her own features and body, she may continue to present a youthful image. She can prolong her career as sexual object, lying about her age, rewriting her past to keep the chronology updated, and devoting herself to the cultivation of her image. Society will reward her greatly. Women in the entertainment industry are allowed to remain sexual objects (objects that are prestigeful to use or own—like Cadillacs) for much of their lives.

To be told when you have half your years still to wade through and when you don't feel inside much different than you did at twenty (you are still you!—you know that!), to be told then that you are cut off from expressing yourself sexually and often even in friendship, drives many women crazy—often literally so.

Don't tell me that it is human nature for women to cease to be attractive early. In primitive society a woman who is still useful—in that by all means far more humane definition than ours—will find a mate, whom she may share as she shares the work with his other wives. Black women are more oppressed on the job and in almost every other way in this society than white women, but at least in the ghetto men go on assuming a woman is sexual as long as she thinks so too.

Earlier, mythology in which "the widow" is a big sex figure, French novels in which the first mistress is always an older woman, the Wife of Bath, all reinforce my sense that there is nothing natural about women's obsolescence.

I was divorced five years ago. Don't tell me I should have "held on to my husband." We let go with great relief. Recently he has married a woman in her late twenties. It is not surprising he should marry someone younger: most people in this society are younger than my ex-husband. In my job, most of the people I meet are younger than I am, and the same is true of people who share my interests, from skiing to resistance to the war against Vietnam.

When my daughter was little I stayed home, but luckily for me I returned to work when she entered school. I say luckily, because while I believe my ex-husband has an obligation to help our daughter, I would never accept alimony. I can get quite cold and frightened imagining what would have happened if I had stayed home until my divorce, and then, at thirty-eight, tried to find work. I used to eat sometimes at a lunchroom where the rushed and overworked waitress was in her late forties. She had to cover the whole room, and I used to leave her larger tips than I would give someone else because to watch her made me conscious of women's economic vulnerability. She was gone one day and I asked the manager at the cash register about her. "Oh, the customers didn't like her. Men come in here, they want to see a pretty face."

I have insisted on using a pseudonym in writing this article, because the cost of insisting I am not a cipher would be fatal. If I lost my job, I would have an incredible time finding another. I know I will never "get ahead." Women don't move up through the shelves of a business automatically or by keeping their mouths shut. I could be mocked into an agony of shame for writing this—but beyond that, I could so easily be let go.

I am gregarious, interested in others, and I think, intelligent. All I ask is to get to know people and to have them interested in knowing me. I doubt whether I would marry again and live that close to another individual. But I remain invisible. I think stripped down I look more attractive on some abstract scale (a bisexual Martian judging) than my ex-husband, but I am sexually and socially obsolete, and he is not. Like most healthy women my face has aged more rapidly than my body, and I look better with my clothes off. When I was young, my anxiety about myself and what was to become of me colored all my relationships with men, and I was about as sensual as a clotheshanger. I have a capacity now for taking people as they are, which I lacked at twenty; I reach orgasm in half the time and I know how to please. Yet I do not even dare show a man that I find him attractive. If I do so, he may react as if I had insulted him: with shock, with disgust. I am not even allowed to be affectionate. I am supposed to fulfill my small functions and vanish.

Often when men are attracted to me, they feel ashamed and conceal it. They act as if it were ridiculous. If they do become involved, they are still ashamed and may refuse to appear publicly with me. Their fear of mockery is enormous. There is no prestige attached to having sex with me.

Since we are all far more various sexually than we are supposed to be, often, in fact, younger men become aware of me sexually. Their response is similar to what it is when they find themselves feeling attracted to a homosexual: they turn those feelings into hostility and put me down.

Listen to me! Think what it is like to have most of your life ahead and be told you are obsolete! Think what it is like to feel attraction, desire, affection toward others, to want to tell them about yourself, to feel that assumption on which self-respect is based, that you are worth something, and that if you like someone, surely he will be pleased to know that. To be, in other words, still a living woman, and to be told every day that you are not a woman but a tired object that should disappear. That you are not a person but a joke. Well, I am a bitter joke. I am bitter and frustrated and wasted, but don't you pretend for a minute as you look at me, forty-three, fat, and looking exactly my age, that I am not as alive as you are and that I do not suffer from the category into which you are forcing me.

Further Questions

1. Is growing older something that someone should be ashamed of, so that the symptoms should be hidden as much as possible? If there is shame about aging, what is its source? What, if anything, can be done about it?

2. Does society punish people, and women in particular, for getting older? If so, what forms does such punishment take? Is there anything we can do about it?

3. Is it worthwhile hanging onto a marriage that has become empty of content in order not to be alone in one's old age? If your answer depends on the circumstances, specify the circumstances under which it is or is not worthwhile. Is the answer the same for both genders?

XIII.5   Look Me in the Eye

BARBARA MACDONALD

Barbara Macdonald and her partner, Cynthia Rich, went to a march to Take Back the Night. The monitor, a younger woman, took Barbara aside to ask her if she could keep up, but she could not look Barbara in the eye. After examining her own shame and anger, Barbara reflects on the history that led to this encounter.

Macdonald (b. 1913) is a lesbian feminist activist, writer, and lecturer who now lives in San Diego, CA. *Look Me in the Eye* has been widely influential in feminist theory on aging.

Reading Questions

1. Does the role of the mother in today's society in any way influence the way younger people view older women? Explain your answer with some examples.

2. Do some people find it difficult to look certain sorts of people in the eye (e.g., old people, battered women, disabled people)? If so, what do you think the source of the difficulty is, and what do you propose as a solution?

3. Give some examples in which people, as individuals, personally neglect an older person. What do you think are the reasons for this type of attitude?

... WHERE ARE THE Susan B. Anthonys, the Carrie Nations, the Pankhursts today? These post-menopausal women were marching all over the place a hundred years ago, and no one was asking them if they could keep up. It was then I realized that this is probably the first time in history that the mass of rebelling angry women are so young. In the first wave in this country and in England, angry women in mid-life and older were marching and visible. In the photographs in Emmeline Pankhurst's *My Own Story,* I see older women marching with younger women, and older women were smashing windows and setting fires all over London, and women in mid-life and older were going to prison and going on hunger strikes and being force fed. . . .

It is probably evidence of our growth and increasing strength that for the first time younger women make up the mass of the second wave. Made possible for the first time because young women are more knowledgeable than they were a hundred years ago, better read and with more literature to read than ever before. And freer, because the younger woman of today is not caught in enforced heterosexual coupling until much later in her life and may, in fact, not choose heterosexuality. A hundred years ago, much of the radical feminist political action was probably not

visible to most young women, who were in domestic servitude or were already burdened with unwanted pregnancies and small children, unable to read and with no way out. This increased visibility of young women is certainly due, in part, to the efforts of the older women of the first wave.

But the primary reason that the second wave is made up of young women is that the second wave rose out of a different time in patriarchal history—it rose out of a time of a patriarchally supported white middle class youth culture. This important difference in the two waves is not one that I can dismiss lightly with the popular observation that emphasis on youth neglects an older population. That is to trivialize what has been taking place since the first wave and the development of the youth culture. It does not make clear to me what happened to me in the Boston march. It does not explain to me why I do not have eye to eye contact with younger women as I enter my mid sixties, and it does not explain to me what happened to the older feminist activists who were such an important part of our earlier history.

In the first wave, when the angry older women were marching, most women were slaves to their husbands; as were his children whom he could put to work in factories, mines, or into domestic servitude as soon as they were strong enough. The mother had no real power over her life and no real power over the lives of her children. But it was profitable for the father to give the mother seeming authority over the children. In his absence, she represented his authority and kept the children in subjection. Frequently she was beaten by her husband for her children's insubordination, and she in turn beat the children to keep them in line.

But with the advent of child labor laws and children's rights, the father lost power over his children. Out from under the father's tyranny, the children were a burden and an expense instead of a source of income, and they became solely the woman's problem. The mother still had the care of the children, but now she had to try to control them without the father's power. Once the father had said to the mother, "I want them fed; feed them. I want them clothed for the workplace; clothe them. I want them God-fearing and industrious; teach them. I want them obedient; beat them." But now it was not in the father's interest to control the children, and he did not transfer his power to the mother. Instead, she was left powerless to protect herself from their battering demands. The children, out from under the tyranny of the father's rule, were free in their own way to tyrannize the powerless mother. Now it was the children who borrowed power from the father, who were saying to her, "Feed me, clothe me. Buy me everything. The fathers say you must." And indeed the fathers are saying clearly, "The children must have everything. If you are a good mother, your children's laundry will be Downy soft and perfumed. You will tempt your children's appetites and feel pride to hear them demand, 'More sausages, Mom.' You will send them out in white clothes to play in the mud to prove that you know how to wash their clothes cleaner than the woman next door. You will make sure the environment your children live in is scrubbed, polished, sanitized and odorless. You will wipe their noses and bottoms

with the softest tissue in the world, all the time rubbing your hands in lotion so your callouses and red cracks won't feel rough on your children's soft skin."

It seems to me that never in such a few years has the patriarchy been able to develop a new elite leisure class of consumers and a slave class to serve them—an elite class that stays out of the job market and does not threaten the father's job, but consumes endlessly to ensure his job.

A hundred years ago, the mother's value to the Fathers was that she raised God-fearing industrious children who could bring income into the family until they left home. Now the mother's value to the Fathers is that she raises children to expect the best, to be good consumers, to remain as children as long as possible and out of the job market and she hopes that society will value her for how well she serves them. The elitism of the children is still exploitation of the children. Now, instead of the exploitation by the single father, it is the exploitation by the collective Fathers. But the woman is still slave, and now she has two masters to serve.

Today, the evidence is all around us that youth is bonded with the patriarchy in the enslavement of the older woman. There would, in fact, be no youth culture without the powerless older woman. There can be no leisure elite consuming class unless it is off the back of someone. The older woman is who the younger women are better than—who they are more powerful than and who is compelled to serve them. This is not true of men; older men still have power, power to be president, power to be Walter Cronkhite, and power to marry younger women. Men are not the servants of youth; older women are.

The lines between the powerful and the powerless have always had to be very clearly drawn, and nowhere is this more evident than in the clothes of men, the young, and women. The clothes of the young woman are designed to, at least, give the illusion of power and freedom, and the clothes of the older woman are designed to make her look sexless, dowdy, and separated from the rest of society. Little boys and young men for high occasions dress fashionably like older men, in suit and vest, but no young woman dresses fashionably by imitating the dress of older women.

It becomes more clear that the present attitude of women in their twenties and thirties has been shaped since childhood by patriarchy to view the older woman as powerless, less important than the fathers and the children, and there to serve them both; and like all who serve, the older woman soon becomes invisible. . . .

I watched the 80 "Women to Watch in the '80s" go by in *Ms.* magazine last month, and I learned that there are only six women in their fifties worth watching and only one woman in her sixties worth watching. That's invisibility.

I find the whole line-up of women to watch in the '80s very patriarchal and I would prefer not to see it at all. But worse, *Ms.* magazine asked older women to make the selection, a selection that excluded them. That's one way to get permission to oppress—ask the older woman, not to be co-equal, but to step aside for the younger woman. Sheila Tobias stepped aside by saying, "established women have the responsibility to boost others. One reason the first wave of feminism died out is that it failed to create new leaders."

To me something in her statement smacks of maternal self-sacrifice and invisibility: the young women asked Tobias to make herself invisible and she made herself invisible. Nor do I think that the first wave of feminism died because the women failed to create new leadership. I think it died because the women decided to put their own needs aside to help the good old boys win a war; and when they got ready to take up the struggle again, they discovered they were slave to two masters.

Given the nature of the question put to Tobias, it is not surprising that she responded in patriarchal language: the word *boost* suggests help on "the way up," someone on the bottom boosting another to a higher level. Such an image conjures up the possibility that the one being boosted may well have her foot on the booster. Such a word seems a long way from the beginnings of this second wave that consciously avoided hierarchical structure.

I hurt that the committee who selected the eighty women to watch tells me that I am invisible, that no sixty-five-year-old woman is still in process and worth watching; but they give no better message to the women who are pictured there in their forties, as it must be plain to them that they will be invisible in ten years, in their fifties and sixties.

Several months have gone by since Cynthia and I went to the Boston march, and I only begin to see how I came to be there at sixty-five in this particular time in our history and how the monitor came to be there. I only begin to see who we both are and how men are still defining our feelings about ourselves and each other.

—1979

Further Questions

1. Macdonald claims "youth is bonded with patriarchy in the enslavement of the older woman." What does this mean? If it is true, what are some examples of it in television ads, wording in media reports, and words and actions in daily life?

2. Is there an attitude that an older woman must serve others, or step aside for them, which is founded in expectations of this sort of deference from mothers? If so, is it paradoxical that a woman's status is lessened when she is perceived as a mother?

3. Are older persons avoided because aging is thought to be contagious? If so, is the avoidance of older women explained by the fact that their aging is perceived as more contagious than men's aging?

XIII.6   The View from over the Hill

BABA COPPER

Baba Copper describes the perspective of older women, which she calls "the view from over the hill." She has special concerns about ageism in lesbian communities.

Copper was an old lesbian artist, writer, and mother who lived in Fort Bragg, CA until her death in August 1988.

Reading Questions

1. Is an older person entitled to live in the present instead of being treated like a museum piece? Does anyone like being asked systematically about only her past, with no questions asked about her present life?

2. Are older women supposed to listen to other people's troubles while not mentioning any of their own? That is, is there something special about an older person, or an older woman, that relegates her to the role of listener when anyone's troubles come up for discussion?

3. Is "daughterism"—stereotyping older women as mothers by younger women—a dangerous phenomenon for older women? If it is dangerous, what does this indicate about the status of a mother from the perspective of someone younger?

YOUTH SEES ITSELF as immune to the threat of aging. I can remember the day when I used the phrase "over the hill" to describe an old woman. The implications of the phrase and my complicity in those implications never crossed my mind. Now from experience I understand that someone over the hill is metaphorically out of sight. In my youthful complacency, by using that phrase I was banishing old age from my awareness. Now that I am old, I have become increasingly curious about why I needed to reassure myself in this way.

Every woman gets older from the day she is born, but there are great variations in the impact of this fact upon different lives and upon different times in those lives. There are endless unexamined contradictions in the prejudice which women feel toward the old women they themselves are or are becoming. Lesbian ageism is probably the ultimate extension of these self-defeating contradictions. It is this that I need to examine, since the greater part of my experience of ageism has been with lesbians. As the years beyond fifty-eight have accumulated, I have found it increasingly difficult to participate in the social and political life of the lesbian community. This difficulty has reflected a change in my status as ascribed by other women, not in my capacity for effective or enjoyable involvement. A subtle transition has taken place in which I have slipped from the category of "tolerated" (passing for middle aged) to a new and shunned identity which has no name but "old."

The old woman finds herself captured by stereotypes which drain her initiative and shatter her self-respect. The mythical prototypes of the Wicked Old Witch with unnatural powers, the Old Bad Mother with neurotic power needs, and the Little Old Lady, ludicrously powerless, cloud the individuality of every woman past sixty. Since childhood all of us have been bombarded by systematic distortions of female aging in fairy tales, legends, books, movies, plays and TV. Age prejudice encourages substitution of these manufactured realities for the real human being with real personal powers whom we encounter. Ageism rationalizes the discarding of old women—as workers, friends, lovers, relatives.

Feminism has taught me to scrutinize closely male reversals of women's truths. The blatant reversal of old women's reality, not only in our culture, but cross-culturally and down through patriarchal history, tells me something about the psychological and political needs which stereotypes such as the Wicked Old Witch fulfill. *One of the primary definitions of patriarchy is the absence of old women of power.* Simmering in the psyche of the Father are his ancient fears of the old matriarch and her potential use of power; preferential treatment of her daughters over her sons; matrilineal inheritance; incitement to resistance against the institution of marriage; or support for the insubordination of a daughter to a husband. The accumulated experience of old women has always been a part of what Adrienne Rich called "the enormous potential counterforce (to patriarchy) that is having to be restrained."[1]

I believe that there is an important reservoir of lesbian energy denied by this false consciousness, this "othering" of the old lesbian. Access to that reservoir of energy is guarded by women acting upon unexamined traditions, attitudes rooted in the commonplace. They are rewarded by increased power within our limited world. But in carrying the double-edged sword of ageism, they wound themselves. Ultimately, they serve the interests of male dominance.

One of the pledges I made when I found myself going "over the hill" was that I would learn to articulate the great complexity of the experience of ageism as it takes place between women. Detailing the particulars, especially the startling erosion of the relative safety of middle age, will not satisfy me. Rather, I need to explore the root sources of my dilemma, speculating about the conscious and unconscious motivations of the

women who seek to diminish me. I recognize that my present and future pain is identical to that which I have caused others. It is time that we stop this inter-generational warfare. I would like to believe that I am not the only one dissatisfied with the low priority which lesbian feminism has assigned to these divisions between us.

Inventing Lesbian Identity— Who We Are, or Could Be

If lesbianism ever becomes a mass phenomenon, it will be because it offers women the opportunity to explore a fundamentally new social identity. No longer subject to male sexual choice, we learn not only to choose, but to decide for ourselves on what ethical and erotic basis to make choices of all kinds. Without being particularly conscious of what we are doing, lesbians are collectively forging an unprecedented female identity through the living of our lives.

Choices are often made on the basis of assumptions. The assumptions which we make automatically and unconsciously in default of rational decisions are the vast ground of all human relations. They are as necessary to action as being able to breathe without awareness. But default assumptions are often intimately tied to nuances of hierarchy, which in turn falsely inform our identity or sense of self. It is here that lesbian choices need politically guided attention. Patriarchal standards of taste—rules of esthetic and erotic choices—perpetuate male structures of power. If we allow male defined standards of choice to be our default standards, we maintain female powerlessness. We waste the opportunity which our lesbianism provides: to choose how to choose.

This is particularly true in relation to age prejudice, since so many of the default assumptions which diminish a woman as she ages are derived from sexism. Male contempt for the older woman as unfit for the reproducer/sex object roles filled by younger women (still the primary source of female power in the patriarchy) is the foundation of the old woman's powerless position. Being largely barred from the working world further diminishes our status. If we are not sex objects or breeders or caretakers or wage workers, we are loathsome since it is these *roles* which make females legitimate in male judgment. As Susan Sontag, in her deeply ageist and heterosexist article, "The Double Standard of Aging,"[2] pointed out: "That old women are repulsive is one of the most profound esthetic and erotic feelings in our culture."

Lesbians, the group within women's culture most self-conscious about patriarchal values, cultivate the illusion that we waltz to our own tunes. Yet lesbians, like everyone else, are all getting older. Our community is so ill-prepared for this that old lesbians find themselves disappearing right off the edge of reality. The ageism we encounter teaches us that we are obsolete; that we should not be able to imagine ourselves powerful, either physically or socially. It is a standard default assumption of the lesbian political community that old lesbians are conservative (or at least politically incorrect) and inflexible. Above all else we are expected to be submissive to women younger than ourselves who are the "right" age to exert power within the lesbian world. We are asked to be walking contradictions to the cliches of lesbian identity which all of us are in the process of inventing. Unless old lesbians are re/membered as sexual, attractive, useful, integral parts of the woman-loving world, current lesbian identity is a temporary mirage, not a new social statement of female empowerment. . . .

Is This What Young Lesbians Really Want?

I am confined within my category—an old woman, potential scapegoat. I do not mean to say that all my experience is negative all the time. But the fear, contempt and rage which many women unconsciously carry for old women are latent. The discharge of these irrational feelings is postponed only to the moment when I do not please. *I feel like a walking lightning rod.*

Over and over, I have had the same experience, both with lesbians near my age and younger. When I exert my powers on "their side," in agreement or in service to them, all is well. The mirror they hold up to me reflects "capable, intuitive, likable, creative, interesting." But when I exert myself in my own interests or defense, I find that I am punished. What they want—no, demand—from me is unconditional love, support and service. Their effort to control my behavior takes many forms, but is often distinguished by explosive intensity or irrational anger. Suddenly I get lots of negativity and trashing, not the "I feel" kind but the accusatory "You are" kind. I have become the Bad Mother or the Wicked Witch. Then their mirror says "self-centered, overpowering, coercive, withholding."

I, in turn, must process this feedback through the filter of my years. Have I suddenly gone through some startling personality change which makes me radically different from the woman I was ten, twenty, thirty years before? What about the lesbian identity I am struggling to perfect—assertive, un-self-sacrificing, honest? How can I gauge whether or not these women are being ageist? Maybe this is the way they always act. But why, then, am I having so many of these experiences in the last few years? Why do other women refuse to negotiate differences with me? What about our feminist determination to work things through, to refuse to treat each other as men have treated us? The self-doubt built into these questions is bottomless. Always I ask myself, "Are you too sensitive? Is this awkwardness perhaps *your* fault?"

I do not have answers. All I can do is list some of the ways in which old lesbians may find ourselves used within the lesbian community. Some are from personal experience, some from watching the experience of other old women. (Obviously not all women participate in these offenses, nor do all old women experience them, nor are they limited to interactions between lesbians.)

The old woman is one whose labor/energy can be assimilated by everyone. We are someone to listen to others' troubles without telling ours. We are the dump where others are free to unload. It is considered politically correct to extract money or favors from us without a fair exchange of goods, labor or services. We are subject to a different code of honor than other women. For instance, an old woman who owns her own home, who is near retirement from a good paying job, or who has a little capital from a divorce settlement, may be branded as a rich woman. The age barrier to further income from wages—a barrier which radically changes old women's relationship to capital—is ignored with youthful chauvinism. We are a Class Enemy. We can be envied with impunity, ripped off with righteous indignation. Any resistance we muster in our own defense is punished severely. *Self-defense is absolutely unallowable in a mother figure.*

There is a look of wary readiness in the eyes of many old women. Our bodies often unconsciously reflect our humiliation. We have demonstrated a remarkable ability to internalize our own coercion. The body language of many old women speaks of our position at the age/sex nadir—the ones no one wants to be. We are seen as the cause of many frustrations, disappointments and failures. The emphasis is laid upon our differences, our faults, our style, our mistakes, the general *difficulty* in dealing with us. Although our experience, perhaps our expertise, is needed, others avoid ceding to us either leadership or credit. In typical patterns of rationalization, almost everyone agrees that we *ourselves* are the ones who caused the offenses committed against us. Once we are found guilty, judgment is passed from mouth to mouth, with everyone else hearing about it but us. Often we are unsure of what the real accusation is. We are usually short of allies, social power, and self-love. It is through interactions like these that women carry out the horizontal violence against ourselves, using our energies to do the essential work of preserving "woman's place."

I try to be the kind of person everyone likes. I listen well, I nurture, I create goodies, and I give comfort. I touch others even though I am seldom touched. I don't complain a lot. I suppress my needs, ignore the contempt or sexual invisibility I experience. (I bite my tongue and walk around as if on eggs!) I find myself metamorphosed into the stereotypical granny, even though I judge the role intolerably demeaning. This violation of Self is unhealthy, as feminists have been quick to testify in relation to male definitions of appropriate heterosexual female behavior or femininity. The personality I feel I am being asked to assume as an old woman is even more docile/submissive than that asked of me as a young woman throughout my life with men. It is the polar opposite of the independent assertive dyke that I smashed my traditional world into bits to become.

Whose Mother Are We Defeating and Why?

There is no way to talk about ageism between women without focusing on mother/daughter relations. Sometimes I feel as if ageism is misnamed; that the problem should be called Daughterism. One of the ways that a young woman can get a taste of her future is to be turned into a mother-figure by a peer, who may or may not be older. At the lesbian summer camp of Califia, where all are invited to generate workshops, I spontaneously wrote *Daughterism* on the schedule, interested to see how other women would respond. Forty young women showed up, eager to describe their confusion over being used as a mother by friends, fellow workers, or lovers. Thematic to their testimony was self-blaming speculation as to why their *looks* evoked this manipulative behavior in others. ("I just know that it is because I have big breasts!") None had any theoretical framework with which to view her misery. From *my* vantage point, at that time nearly over the hill, all these women were potential daughters, capable of using me as they had been used.

I have often wondered if it wouldn't be possible to make a fortune by manufacturing a T-shirt which, in large letters across the breasts, said: I AM NOT YOUR MOTHER. Most older women find themselves stereotyped as mothers by younger women. This erasure of our individuality is unfair, but the psychological underside is downright ugly. If the older woman triggers childhood angst in the younger, the older may find herself bearing a burden of projected hostility without the slightest clue as to what is going on. (Psychologists seem to agree that many people need to recreate unresolved childhood experience.) All women have been taught to see mothers as fair prey, to be used as the giver-who-does-not-get.

The other side of the mother/daughter coin is the legitimate rage of the daughter for being raised by her mother to fulfill goals that are largely in violation of her own self-realization, especially when seen through lesbian eyes. With few exceptions, lesbians have in common the experience of growing up mothered by a woman who abided by traditional patriarchal motherhood. It is the mother's *job* to prepare the daughter for the use of men. She must teach her, by example, how to assume the terrible responsibility for maintaining the center—the stabilizing core of family and the private world. She must instruct her in the self-defeating standards of taste which will govern the daughter's attitudes toward her own body and face, her personality, and her choices of life adventures. Successful mothering is still measured in terms of the daughter's attractiveness to men, her success in a male-controlled work world, and her reproductive capacity. These successes depend to a large degree upon the daughter's ability to assimilate into male culture. She must learn to conform to the aesthetic rules which deify female youth and teach allegiance to a hierarchy which will forever divide her from other women. I do not believe that true reconciliation between women is possible until daughter-rearing goals are radically modified. The betrayal of the Daughter by her loving Mother poisons the relationships between all women, but most clearly those between young women and old women. . . .

Do Lesbians Really Need Old Victims?

Youth provides women with a temporary illusion of opportunity in the work world. As youth is the primary requirement for the role of phallus stiffener, there are a great number of jobs for which only young women qualify. There is a chasm of identity which comfortably separates young women from women who they perceive as not passing. Old women are segregated and desexualized by both men and younger women. This attitude tends to make legitimate the assumption that all women not in that category are sexually accessible to men. "The woman who too decisively resists sexual overtures in the work place is accused of being 'dried-up' and sexless or lesbian."[3] A young woman's fear that these descriptions will be applied to *her* may reduce her will to resist unwanted sexual advances. Fear of being seen as too old to harass may lead young women to participate in the displacement of older women workers. In the competition between women for work, younger women have played scab to the struggle of older women for recognized seniority and reasonable pay.

There is a limited period of time in a woman's life when she is allowed to exert the power which masculinist values bestow upon sexual energy. My personal experience of street hassling illustrates this. As an adolescent, my need for recognition accepted any offering, even though I wondered constantly whether the whistle was for *me*—for my specialness. By seventeen, this question had found its answer. I began the long period of developing techniques of rebuff. As my body thickened and my hair grayed, there was a time when I simply forgot about harassment. Then suddenly I became aware that not only was unwanted attention absent, but my personal space—the ground ceded to me by those who passed me on the street—had shrunk. No man or woman met my eye. Through the absence of harassment, I discovered the invisibility of age. Invisibility needs to be described in all its subjective horror. It takes many forms, the most searing being its sexual form. One scarcely recovers from the ambivalence which sexual objectification evokes when one is plunged into the emotional vacuum which its withdrawal triggers.

Lesbian youth worship differs little from heterosexual youth worship. But the deprivation of sexual recognition between women which takes place after middle age (or the point when a woman no longer passes for young) includes withdrawal of the emotional work which women do to keep the flow of social interactions going: compliments, questions, teasing, touching, bantering, remembering details, checking back, supporting.

These are ethical issues which younger lesbians need to consider in their relations with older women. What do lesbians want to do about those human connections which do not directly enhance the primary goals of career or personal gratification? Are we so captive to the cultural fear of female obsolescence that we let time and indifference gradually strip women of power, work, visibility, and finally human contacts? We need to negotiate a feminist code of honor between young and old, designed for our ultimate and mutual benefit. The call for this must come from young lesbians, as well as old. . . .

The way to respond to *all* accusations of ageism is identical to how we must respond to accusations of racist, classist, physicalist, or sexist behavior. This is not necessarily to say that the action or absence of action has been correctly named. Nevertheless, we must do a lot of listening, both inwardly and outwardly. Resistance, excuses or rationalizations only compound our problems. There are basic questions which fifteen years of feminism have taught us to ask: Who profits? What are the hidden assumptions? Why have we ignored it? How many of the culturally mandated attitudes have we internalized? When an old woman raises the issue of ageism, do not explain to her what you *really* meant. Listen.

Since there are so few from my side of the hill making demands or even expressing dissatisfaction, there are many who challenge me by demanding concrete examples of ageism. If I am not pressed for a story about my past, I am asked for an example which will illustrate the charges I have made. Both demands annoy me. Like most people, I am focused on my present life, not my past. I am not some walking museum of memorabilia, either camp or quaint, to be mined by others' curiosity. . . .

The Politics of Female Age

In a man, longevity seems to produce one of two results: either an extinction of his only identity through retirement, or the expansive power of the old judge or chairman or academic or mogul who dies with his boots on. The latter is the modern equivalent of attainment of godhood when finally he can do no wrong. During the scramble up the ladder, doubts and compromises may sometimes have softened his developing omnipotence. But being at the top and being old is a poisonous combination. Once there, he may never know the face of candor. He is *yes*ed without respite.

Few old women suffer personally from this syndrome, but we may be forced to observe it in the old men we know, or to absorb the great-hero-Patrimyth of the soap operas, the movies and party politics. Often we must choose between such men for high office; to them we must entrust our financial well-being; our lives rest in their bellicose hands as they manipulate military "security." If we have had a husband or a male boss, we know why they are the way they are. We have watched power erode their judgment in small significant steps as we served the male-on-the-way-up.

Yet women as a class resist the leadership or the experience of old women—almost as if they were patriarchs upon whom there were no curbs, who had secret power they could not limit. The old woman must not be listened to, must not be trusted, must not wield power, must not influence our lives, must not gain our attention.

This deeply ingrained reversal of our own self-interest is ancient conditioning. Thus it is that the patriarchs have taught us to contain and defang the potential revolt which the experienced woman might ferment against him.

NOTES

1. Adrienne Rich, "Compulsory Heterosexuality and Lesbian Existence," *Signs,* vol. 5, no. 4. (Summer 1980).

2. Susan Sontag, "The Double Standard of Aging," *Saturday Review of the Society* (September, 1977).

3. Rich, "Compulsory Heterosexuality and Lesbian Existence."

Further Questions

1. Is the absence of powerful older women and the simultaneous presence of powerful older men inevitable in patriarchy? If so, explain the inevitability.

2. Do younger people tend to see themselves as immune from processes of aging? If so, what effect does this have on their attitudes toward old people?

3. Does being debarred from the workplace constitute a factor that diminishes one's status? If this is one reason why older people—older women in particular—have diminished status, is there any way this problem can be remedied?

Suggested Moral of Part XIII

Aging is feared, not only because of possible physical debilitation, but also because an older person, especially if she is a woman, is often socially oppressed. Patriarchy causes younger women to be oppressors of older women. Such oppression takes the form of excluding older women from an important part in family life, the workplace, and the community. An older woman is either invisible, a thing of the past, or a mother, rather than an integral part of the community. The role of "mother" seems particularly bad to younger women because these younger women often (correctly) believe that their own mothers betrayed them by preparing them to be used by men. Patriarchy is the root cause of silencing older women and excluding them from positions of power.

Further Readings for Part XIII: Youngsters and Oldsters

With people living longer, gerontology is expanding both in practice and as an area of study. There are, however, disappointingly few works that take the perspective of the aged person as a starting point. There are even fewer which take gender into account in aging, or which could be appropriately tagged as feminist in approach. The following selections are some works that attempt to orient themselves in these directions.

Sara Arber and Jay Ginn. *Gender and Later Life: A Sociological Analysis of Resources and Constraints* (Newbury Park, CA: Sage Publications, 1991). These authors claim that feminist sociologists neglect the elderly because they cannot relate them to their own experiences.

Leah Cohen. *Small Expectations: Society's Betrayal of Older Women* (Toronto: McClelland and Steward, Ltd, 1984). Society rejects the old and is particularly disdainful of older women.

Baba Copper. *Over the Hill: Reflections on Ageism Between Women* (Freedom, CA: The Crossing Press, 1988). Should be required reading for all feminists.

Simone de Beauvoir. *The Coming of Age,* Patrick O'Brian, tr. (New York, NY: G. P. Putnam's Sons, 1972). Old age, both as experienced and as a social phenomenon.

Joseph L. Esposito. *The Obsolete Self: Philosophical Dimensions of Aging* (Berkeley, CA: The University of California Press, 1987). Experiences of aging and an explanation of how social forces shape perceptions of aging.

Janet Ford and Ruth Sinclair. *Sixty Years On: Women Talk About Old Age* (London: The Women's Press, Ltd., 1987). Old women in Britain speak of their experiences.

Jaber F. Gubrium, ed. *Time, Roles and Self in Old Age* (New York, NY: Human Sciences Press, 1976). Disengagement and retirement of older persons and the "generation gap" with younger persons.

Jon Hendricks and C. Davis Hendricks, eds. *Dimensions of Aging: Readings* (Cambridge, MA: Winthrop Publishers, 1979). Interdisciplinary problems approach to aging.

Margot Jeffreys, ed. *Growing Old in the Twentieth Century* (New York, NY: Routledge, 1989). Discusses issues like income, retirement, support networks, and racism.

Gari Lesnoff-Caravalglia, ed. *Aging and the Human Condition* (New York, NY: Human Sciences Press, 1982). Interesting aspects of experiences of the elderly, e.g., time is perceived as a continuous present.

Barbara Macdonald with Cynthia Rich. *Look Me in the Eye: Old Women, Aging, and Ageism* (San Francisco, CA: Spinsters Book Co., expanded edition, 1991). Both writers combine ground-breaking feminist theory on ageism with direct personal experience.

B. F. Skinner and M. F. Vaughan. *Enjoy Old Age: A Program of Self-Management* (New York, NY: W. W. Norton and Co., 1983). Fairly cheerless advice, much of which is denial of age, e.g., "Old people are boring when they talk about their illnesses."

Susan Sontag. "The Double Standard of Aging" in *Saturday Review of the Society,* September 1977. Baba Copper calls this a "deeply ageist and heterosexist article."

Ruth Raymond Thorne. *Women and Aging: Celebrating Ourselves* (Binghampton, NY: Haworth Press, 1992). Better advice than Skinner/Vaughan on taking charge of your aging.

James E. Thornton and Earl R. Winkler, eds. *Ethics and Aging: The Right to Live, The Right to Die* (Vancouver: The University of British Columbia Press, 1988). Coming to terms with some problems of aging.